FRENCH
LEARNER'S DICTIONARY

FRENCH-ENGLISH / ENGLISH-FRENCH
Revised and updated

LIVING LANGUAGE®

FRENCH
LEARNER'S
DICTIONARY
FRENCH-ENGLISH / ENGLISH-FRENCH
Revised and updated

Revised by Liliane Lazar, Ph.D.

Adjunct Associate Professor of French Hofstra University

French teacher
Great Neck Public Schools

Based on the original by Ralph Weiman

This work was previously published under the title *Living Language*™
Common Usage Dictionary: French by Ralph Weiman, Mary Finocchiaro,
and Remunda Cadoux.

Published by Living Language, A Random House Company, New York,
New York.

Living Language is a member of the Random House Information Group.

www.livinglanguage.com

LIVING LANGUAGE and colophon are registered trademarks of Random
House, Inc.

If you're traveling, we recommend **Fodor's Guides.**

This book is available for special discounts for bulk purchases for sales
promotions or premiums. Special editions, including personalized covers,
excerpts of existing books, and corporate imprints, can be created in large
quantities for special needs. For more information, write to Special Markets/
Premium Sales, 1745 Broadway, MD 6-2, New York, NY, 10019 or e-mail
specialmarkets@randomhouse.com.

Printed in the United States of America

978-1-4000-2444-5

10   9   8   7   6   5   4   3   2   1

CONTENTS

INTRODUCTION

The *Living Language® French Dictionary* lists more than 20,000 of the most frequently used French words, gives their most important meanings and illustrates their use. This revised edition contains updated phrases and expressions, as well as many new entries related to business, technology and the media.

1. More than 1,000 of the most essential words are capitalized to make them easy to find.

2. Numerous definitions are illustrated with phrases, sentences and idiomatic expressions. Where there is no close English equivalent for a French word or where the English equivalent has several meanings, the context of the illustrative sentences helps to clarify the meanings.

3. Because of these useful phrases, the *Living Language® French Dictionary* also serves as a phrase book and conversation guide. The dictionary is helpful both to beginners who are building their vocabulary and to advanced students who want to perfect their command of colloquial French.

4. The French expressions (particularly the idiomatic and colloquial ones) have been translated into their English equivalents. However, literal translations have been added to help the beginner. For example, under the entry

MAIN, *hand,* you will find: Ils vont la main dans la main. *They always agree with each other. ("They always go hand in hand.")* This dual feature also makes the dictionary useful for translation work.

EXPLANATORY NOTES

Literal translations are in quotation marks.

Very colloquial words, phrases and sentences are marked *fam.* (*expression familière* "colloquial expression, colloquialism").

Certain adjectives that end in *-al* in the masculine singular and the *-ale* in the feminine singular take *-aux* in the masculine plural. This plural ending is indicated in dictionary entries. However, since the feminine plural maintains, in all cases, the regular ending *-ales,* it has not been expressly indicated in the dictionary entries.

		masculine	feminine
EXAMPLES:	sing.	*cordial*	*cordiale*
	plu.	*cordiaux*	*cordiales*
	sing.	*égal*	*égale*
	plu.	*égaux*	*égales*

Other adjectives of this type include:

amical	*intégral*	*médical*	*principal*
central	*international*	*mental*	*sentimental*
commercial	*latéral*	*national*	*social*
horizontal	*loyal*	*oriental*	*spécial*
idéal	*marital*	*original*	*triomphal*
immoral			

In written French, capital letters do not generally show an accent. However, for precision's sake, we have included all appropriate accent marks on every word entry. In the sample sentences we have followed the normal French practice of omitting accents on capital letters.

The dictionary uses the following abbreviations:

m. = masculine
f. = feminine
pl. = plural
adj. = adjective
fam. = familiar
pron. = pronoun

French-English

A

À, au (*contraction of* à + le), **aux** (*pl.*
contraction of à + les) *to, at.*
Je vais à Paris. *I'm going to Paris.*
Traduisez-moi ça mot à mot. *Translate this
for me word for word.*
Attendez-donc à plus tard. *Wait until later.*
Retrouvons-nous à la gare. *Let's meet at the
station.*
A tout à l'heure. *See you in a little while.*
A demain. *See you tomorrow.* ("*Until
tomorrow.*")
C'est la première rue à droite. *It's the first
street to your (the) right.*
Il est au jardin. *He's in the garden.*
Au mois de mai. *In the month of May.*
Au revoir. *Good-bye.*

abaisser *to lower; reduce.*
s'abaisser *to stoop, lower oneself.*
abandon *m. abandonment, desertion,
surrender.*
abandonner *to abandon, desert, leave.*
J'abandonne la course. *I'm out of the race.*
abat-jour *m. lampshade.*
abattre *to pull down; kill; get depressed.*
On a abattu les arbres de l'allée. *They pulled
down the trees in the lane.*
On a abattu le cheval. *They killed the horse.*
Elle se laisse abattre. *She lets herself get
discouraged (depressed).*
abattu *adj. discouraged, depressed, downcast.*
Je l'ai trouvée très abattue. *I found her very
much depressed.*
abdomen *m. abdomen*
abeille *f. bee.*
abîmer *to damage, spoil.*
s'abîmer *to get spoiled, decay; ruin.*
S'abîmer la santé. *To ruin one's health.*
abolir *to abolish.*
abominable *adj. abominable.*
abondamment *abundantly.*
Nous en avons abondamment. *We have
plenty of it.*
abondance *f. abundance.*
Il y en a en abondance. *There's plenty of it.
It's very plentiful.*
Il parle avec abondance. *He speaks fluently.*
Abondance de biens ne nuit pas. *You can't
have too much of a good thing.
("Abundance of good things doesn't
hurt.")*
abondant *adj. abundant.*
La main-d'oeuvre est abondante dans cette
région. *Manpower (labor) is plentiful
in this region. There is an abundant
labor supply in this region.*
abonder *to be plentiful.*

Le gibier abonde dans ce pays. *Game is
plentiful in this region (part of the
country).*
J'abonde parfaitement dans votre sens. *I
share your opinion completely. I'm in
complete agreement with you.*
abonné *m. subscriber.*
Les abonnés au téléphone, au gaz, à
l'électricité, etc. *Telephone
subscribers; consumers of gas,
electricity, etc.*
Pour tout changement d'adresse les abonnés
doivent joindre 10 francs. *For any
change of address, subscribers must
send ("attach") 10 francs. (Newspaper,
magazine, etc.)*
abonnement *m. subscription.*
Prendre un abonnement à un journal. *To
subscribe to a newspaper.*
Une carte d'abonnement. *A season ticket.*
abonner *to subscribe.*
Etes-vous abonné à cette revue? *Do you
subscribe to this magazine? Are you a
subscriber to this magazine?*
s'abonner *to subscribe.*
Je m'y abonnerai. *I'm going to subscribe
to it.*
ABORD *m. access, approach; outskirt.*
D'abord je n'avais pas compris; mais
maintenant, j'y suis. *At first, I didn't
understand, but now I get it (now I've
caught on).*
De prime abord. *At first sight.*
Il est d'un abord difficile. *It's difficult to get
to see him. He's hard to reach.*
Les abords de la ville sont charmants. *The
outskirts of the town are very nice
("charming").*
abordable *adj. accessible.*
La côte est abordable. *The coast is easy to
approach.*
Leurs prix sont abordables. *Their prices are
reasonable (within one's means).*
abordage *m. collision (of ships).*
Le brouillard était la cause de l'abordage.
*The fog was responsible for ("was the
cause of") the collision.*
aborder *to land; accost, address, go up to.*
Ils abordent dans une île. *They landed on an
island.*
Le bateau a abordé à quai. *The boat docked.
The boat came alongside the dock.*
Il l'a abordé pour lui demander son chemin.
He went up to him to ask him the way.
aboutir *to lead to; succeed.*
Cela n'aboutira à rien. *That won't come
(lead) to anything.*
Où aboutit cette route? *Where does this
road lead to?*

Il paraissait très anxieux d'aboutir. *He seemed very anxious to succeed.*

aboyer *to bark.*

abrégé *m. outline, summary.*

abréger *to abbreviate.*
Pour abréger. *In short. To be brief.*
Comment abrégez-vous ce mot? *How do you abbreviate this word?*
Il faut que j'abrège mon séjour. *I'll have to cut my stay short.*

abréviation *f. abbreviation.*
Quelques abréviations françaises (*Some French abbreviations*):
D. or d. Ditto. *Ditto.*
Et Cie. Et Compagnie. *And Co.*
F. Franco. *Postage prepaid. Delivery free.*
M. Monsieur. *Mr.*
Mgr Monseigneur. *Mgr.*
Mlle Mademoiselle. *Miss.*
Mlles Mesdemoiselles. *Misses (Miss pl.).*
MM Messieurs. *Messrs.*
Mme Madame. *Mrs.*
Mmes Mesdames. *Madames.*
N.B. Nota bene. *N.B.*
P.S. Post-Scriptum. *P.S. Postscript.*
P. et T. Postes et Télécommunications. *Post and Telegraph Office.*
R.S.V.P. Répondez s'il vous plaît. *Please answer.*
S.V.P. S'il vous plaît. *Please.*
T.S.F. Télégraphie sans fil. *Radio.*
T.S.V.P. Tournez s'il vous plaît. *Turn (the knob). Turn over (a page).*

abri *m. shelter.*
Mettez-vous à l'abri. *Take shelter.*

abricot *m. apricot.*

abriter *to shelter, protect.*

s'abriter *to take shelter.*

abrupt *adj. abrupt.*

ABSENCE *f. absence.*
En son absence. *In his absence.*
Mon absence a-t-elle été remarquée? *Did anyone notice my absence?*

absent *m. absent.*
Les absents ont toujours tort. *The absent are always in the wrong.*

ABSENT *adj. absent.*
Sont-ils absents? *Are they absent?*
Il est absent de Paris. *He's away from Paris. He's not in Paris now.*

s'absenter *to be absent.*
Il faut que je m'absente pour quelques instants. *I'll have to be away for a few minutes. I have to leave for a few minutes.*
S'absenter pour affaires. *To go away on business.*
S'absenter de l'école. *To stay away from school.*

absolu *adj. absolute.*

ABSOLUMENT *absolutely.*
Absolument rien. *Absolutely nothing.*
Il me le faut absolument. *I need it badly. I must have it without fail (at all costs).*

absorber *to absorb.*

s'absorber *to be absorbed.*

s'abstenir *to abstain, refrain from.*

abstrait *m. abstract.*
Il discute toujours dans l'abstrait. *He's always arguing in the abstract.*

abstrait *adj. abstract.*

absurde *adj. absurd.*
C'est absurde! *It's absurd! It's ridiculous!*

absurdité *f. absurdity.*
Vous dites des absurdités. *You're talking nonsense.*

abus *m. abuse.*

abuser *to abuse; take advantage of.*
Il a abusé de son autorité. *He abused his authority.*
Vous abusez de sa patience. *You're trying his patience. You're taking advantage of his patience.*

s'abuser *to be mistaken.*
Vous vous abusez. *You're mistaken.*

abusif (abusive *f.*) *adj. abusive.*

académie *f. academy.*

accablant *adj. oppressive, crushing.*
Il fait une chaleur accablante. *The heat is oppressive.*

accabler *to weight down, overcome, overwhelm.*
Cette chaleur vous accable. *This heat overcomes you (gets you down).*

accéder *to accede to, comply with.*

accélérateur *m. accelerator.*
Appuyer sur l'accélérateur. *To step on the gas.*

accélération *f. acceleration.*

accélérer *to quicken.*
Accélérons le pas. *Let's walk faster. Let's quicken our pace.*

accent *m. accent.*
Parler anglais avec un accent. *To speak English with an accent.*
Où se trouve l'accent tonique dans ce mot? *Where is the accent in this word?*
Accent aigu. *Acute accent.*
Accent circonflexe. *Circumflex accent.*
Accent grave. *Grave accent.*

accentuer *to accent; accentuate.*

acceptable *adj. acceptable.*

acceptation *f. acceptance.*

ACCEPTER *to accept.*

acception *f. meaning.*
Ce mot a plusieurs acceptions. *This word has several meanings.*

Dans toute l'acception du mot. *In every
  sense of the word.*
accès *m. access.*
J'ai accès à leurs dossiers. *I have access to
  their files.*
Leur propriété est d'accès difficile. *Their
  estate is difficult to reach.*
Accès interdit. *No admittance.*
Il a souvent des accès de mauvaise humeur.
  He often has fits of bad temper.
accessible *adj. accessible.*
accessoire *m. accessory.*
ACCIDENT *m. accident.*
Il a eu un accident d'automobile. *He had
  (met with) an automobile accident.*
Nous nous sommes rencontrés par accident.
  We met by accident (by chance).
accidentel (accidentelle *f.*) *adj. accidental.*
accidentellement accidentally.
acclamer *to acclaim, hail, cheer.*
s'acclimater *to become acclimatized or
  adapted.*
accommodant *adj. accommodating.*
Ce marchand est très accommodant. *This
  storekeeper is very accommodating.*
accommoder *to accommodate, suit.*
L'hôtel peut accommoder quatre-vingt-dix
  personnes. *The hotel can accommodate
  ninety people.*
Cela m'accommode à merveille. *That suits
  me fine (to a T).*
s'accommoder *to put up with, be satisfied
  with.*
Il s'accommode de tout. *He's satisfied with
  anything. He's easy to suit (please).*
accompagner *to accompany.*
Ils l'ont accompagné(e) à la gare. *They took
  him (her) to the station.*
accompli *adj. accomplished.*
Un fait accompli. *An accomplished fact. A
  fait accompli.*
accomplir *to complete, finish.*
s'accomplir *to happen; be fulfilled.*
Sa prédiction s'est accomplie. *His
  prediction came true.*
accomplissement *m. achievement, fulfillment.*
ACCORD *m. accord, agreement.*
Parvenir à un accord. *To reach an
  agreement.*
D'un commun accord. *By common consent.*
Je suis d'accord. *I agree.*
D'accord, soit. *All right, agreed. ("Agreed,
  let it be that way.")*
D'accord, allez-y. *All right, do it (go
  ahead).*
accorder *to grant.*
s'accorder *to agree.*
Son récit ne s'accorde pas avec le vôtre. *His
  story doesn't agree with yours.*

Votre cravate ne s'accorde pas avec votre
  costume. *Your tie doesn't match your
  suit.*
accoster *to accost, address, speak to.*
accoucher *to give birth to; lie in.*
accouchement *m. childbirth.*
accourir *to rush up, run up.*
Ils ont accouru à son secours. *They ran to
  his (her) help.*
accoutumer *to accustom.*
J'y suis accoutumé maintenant. *I'm used to
  it now.*
s'accoutumer *to accustom oneself to, get used
  to.*
On s'accoutume à tout. *One gets used to
  everything.*
accrocher *to hang up, hook.*
Accrochez votre pardessus et votre chapeau
  au porte-manteau. *Hang your coat
  and hat on the coatrack (clothes-
  stand).*
accroître *to increase, augment, enlarge.*
s'accroître *to increase.*
s'accroupir *to squat.*
accueil *m. reception.*
On lui fit bon accueil. *They welcomed him
  warmly. They gave him a warm
  reception.*
Sa proposition n'a pas reçu un très bon
  accueil. *His (her) suggestion
  (proposition) was not very well
  received.*
accueillir *to receive, welcome.*
On accueillera favorablement votre requête.
  Your request will be favorably received.
On m'accueillit très cordialement. *They
  received me very cordially.*
accu(mulateur) *m. storage battery.*
accumulation *f. accumulation.*
accumuler *to accumulate.*
accusation *f. accusation, charge.*
accuser *to accuse; acknowledge.*
N'accusez jamais sans preuve. *Never accuse
  without proof.*
Nous vous accusons réception de votre
  dernière lettre. *We acknowledge receipt
  of your last letter.*
s'acharner *to set about (a thing) furiously,
  pursue relentlessly.*
La malchance s'acharne contre lui. *Ill luck
  pursues him relentlessly.*
ACHAT *m. purchase.*
Allez-vous faire des achats? *Are you going
  shopping?*
ACHETER *to buy.*
J'ai acheté cette auto bon marché. *I bought
  this car cheaply.*
acheteur *m. buyer, purchaser.*
ACHEVER *to complete, end, finish.*

Achevez toujours ce que vous commencez.
Always finish what you begin.
Ne l'interrompez pas. Laissez-le achever.
Don't interrupt him. Let him finish.
acide *noun (m.) and adj. acid.*
ACIER *m. steel.*
acompte *m. partial payment in advance,
installment.*
Un acompte de dix francs. *Ten francs on
account.*
ACQUÉRIR *to acquire, purchase.*
acquisition *f. acquisition, purchase.*
acquit *m. discharge, receipt, acquittal.*
Par manière d'acquit. *For form's sake.*
Par acquit de conscience. *For conscience's
sake. To salve one's conscience.*
acquitter *to acquit; receipt.*
Il a été acquitté. *He was acquitted.*
Il a acquitté la facture. *He receipted the bill.*
s'acquitter *to perform; pay a debt.*
Il s'est bien acquitté de sa mission. *He
carried out his mission successfully.*
Il s'est acquitté de ses dettes. *He paid off his
debts.*
ACTE *m. act, action, deed.*
Ses actes ont été désavoués par son chef.
*His actions were repudiated by his
chief.*
Une comédie en trois actes. *A comedy in
three acts. A three-act play.*
Faire acte de présence. *To put in an
appearance.*
L'acte est en bonne et due forme. *The deed
is in proper form.*
acteur *m. (actrice f.) actor.*
actif *m. assets, credit.*
ACTIF *(active f.) adj. active.*
C'est un homme très actif. *He's a very
active man.*
Il mène une vie active. *He leads an active
life.*
ACTION *f. action; stock.*
C'est un homme d'action. *He's a man of
action.*
L'action se passe en 1830. *The action takes
place in 1830.*
Ces actions sont cotées à la Bourse. *These
stocks are quoted on the stock
exchange.*
activer *to quicken, accelerate.*
activité *f. activity.*
L'usine est en activité. *The factory is in
operation.*
actualité *f. actuality.*
Les actualités au cinéma. *The newsreel.*
C'est tout à fait d'actualité. *It's the topic of
the day.*
ACTUEL *(actuelle f.) adj. of the present time,
current.*

Le gouvernement actuel. *The present
government.*
Dans l'état actuel des choses. *In the present
state of affairs. The way things
(conditions) are now.*
actuellement *now, nowadays, at the present
time.*
adaptation *f. adaptation.*
adapter *to adapt.*
s'adapter *to adapt oneself to; fit, suit.*
ADDITION *f. addition; restaurant check.*
Il y a une erreur dans l'addition. *There's a
mistake in the addition.*
J'ai demandé l'addition au serveur. *I asked
the waiter for the check.*
ADDITIONNEL *(additionnelle f.) adj.
additional.*
ADDITIONNER *to add up.*
ADIEU *good-bye (In southern France,* Adieu
*is an everyday word for good-bye. In
other parts of France,* Adieu *is used
only when one doesn't expect to see
someone for a long time.)*
adjacent *adj. adjacent.*
adjectif *m. adjective.*
adjoindre *to add.*
Ils lui ont adjoint un assistant. *They gave
him an assistant.*
s'adjoindre *to take as an assistant, associate
with.*
Il s'est adjoint un associé. *He took a
partner.*
adjoint *(adjointe f.) noun and adj. assistant.*
Il est adjoint au directeur. *He's (the, an)
assistant director.*
ADMETTRE *to admit.*
Il est généralement admis que . . . *It's
generally admitted that . . .*
Les enfants ne sont pas admis. *Adults only.
("Children not admitted.")*
Etre admis à un examen. *To pass an
examination.*
Sa requête n'a pas été admise. *His (her)
request was not (has not been) granted.*
Cette affaire n'admet aucun retard. *The
(this) matter admits of no delay.*
administrateur *n. (administratrice f.)
administrator, director.*
administration *f. administration.*
administrer *to administer; manage.*
admirable *adj. admirable.*
Quel temps admirable! *What glorious
weather!*
admiration *f. admiration.*
admirer *to admire.*
admission *f. admission.*
adopter *to adopt.*
Le projet de loi fut adopté à l'unanimité.
The bill was adopted unanimously.

adoption *f. adoption.*

adorer *to adore.*

adoucir *to soften; smooth; sweeten.*

ADRESSE *f. address.*
Voilà mon adresse. *Here's my address.*
Le maire a lu une adresse au président. *The mayor read an address to the President.*

ADRESSER *to address.*
Cette lettre vous est adressée. *This letter is addressed to you.*
Adressez le paquet par la poste. *Send the parcel by mail.*
C'est lui qui m'a adressé à vous. *He referred me to you.*

S'ADRESSER *to apply to.*
S'adresser ici. *Apply here.*
Addressez-vous à ce monsieur là-bas. *Ask that gentleman over there.*
C'est à vous que cela s'adresse. *This it meant for you.*

ADULTE *m. adult.*

ADVENIR *to happen, occur.*
Il est advenu une chose inattendue. *Something unexpected occurred.*
Qu'en est-il advenu? *What became of it? What happened to it?*
Advienne que pourra. *Come what may.*
Je le ferai quoi qu'il advienne. *I'll do it, come what may. I'll do it, no matter what happens.*

adverbe *m. adverb.*

adversaire *m. adversary, opponent, rival.*

adversité *f. adversity.*

affable *adj. affable.*

affaiblir *to weaken.*

AFFAIRE *f. affair, business, matter.*
Il est dans les affaires. *He's in business. He's a businessman.*
Il est à ses affaires. *He's at his office.*
Comment vont les affaires? *How's business?*
Les affaires sont les affaires. *Business is business.*
Où en est l'affaire? *How does that matter stand?*
Voilà mon affaire. *That's just what I want (need).*
Il fait mon affaire. *He's the man I need.*
Faire l'affaire de. *To meet the needs of.*
J'ai votre affaire. *I have just the thing for you.*
Quelle affaire! *What a mess! What a bother (trouble)!*
Il a égaré ses affaires. *He's mislaid his things.*
Ce n'est pas votre affaire. *That's not your concern. That's no business of yours.*
Se tirer d'affaire. *To get out of a difficulty.*

C'est une affaire de goût. *It's a matter of taste.*
J'en fais mon affaire. *Leave it to me. I'll see to it. I'll take charge of it. I'll make it my business to see about it.*

affairé *adj. busy.*
Il a toujours l'air affairé. *He always looks busy.*

affairement *m. bustle.*
Quel affairement! *What a hustle and bustle!*

s'affaler *to fall, drop.*

affamé *adj. hungry, famished.*

affecté *adj. moved, affected.*

affecter *to affect, influence.*

affection *f. affection.*
Prendre quelqu'un en affection. *To take a liking to someone. To grow attached to someone.*

affectueux (affectueuse *f.*) *adj. affectionate.*

affermir *to strengthen.*

affiche *f. poster.*

afficher *to post a bill.*

affirmatif (affirmative *f.*) *adj. affirmative.*

affirmative *f. affirmative.*
Il a répondu par l'affirmative. *He (has) replied in the affirmative.*

affirmer *to affirm, assert, maintain.*
Certaines personnes affirment . . . *Some (certain people) maintain . . .*
Il l'a affirmé sous serment. *He asserted it under oath.*

affliction *f. affliction.*

affliger *to afflict, pain, grieve.*

affluence *f. flow, affluence, crowd.*
L'heure d'affluence. *Rush hour.*

s'affoler *to fall into a panic.*
Ne vous affolez pas. *Don't get excited.*

affranchir *to free.*

affranchissement *m. postage.*

affreux (affreuse *f.*) *adj. horrible, dreadful, frightful.*
Il fait un temps affreux. *The weather's awful.*
J'ai un mal de tête affreux. *I have an awful headache.*

affront *m. insult.*

affût *m. hiding-place.*
Etre à l'affût. *To be on the watch.*

AFIN DE *so that, in order to.*
Il se dépêche afin de partir plus tôt. *He's hurrying so he can leave earlier.*

afin que *so that, in order that.*

africain *noun and adj. African.*

agaçant *adj. annoying, irritating.*
C'est agaçant. *It's irritating (upsetting). It gets on your nerves.*

agacer *to irritate, get on one's nerves.*
Ce bruit m'agace. *This noise gets on my nerves.*

ÂGE *m. age, period, era.*
    Quel âge avez-vous? *How old are you?*
    Il est entre deux âges. *He's middle-aged.*
    Elle est d'un certain âge. *She's middle aged.*
    Il a pris de l'âge ces derniers temps. *He's aged a lot recently.*
    On apprend à tout âge. *It's never too late to learn. One is never too old to learn.*
    Le Moyen-Age. *The Middle Ages.*
âgé *adj. aged.*
    Il est âgé de douze ans. *He's twelve years old.*
    Elle est beaucoup plus âgée que son mari. *She's much older than her husband.*
agence *f. agency.*
    J'ai l'agence de leur maison pour la région. *I have the agency (branch office) of their firm for this region.*
    Une agence télégraphique. *A news agency.*
    L'agence de voyage. *Travel agency.*
agenda *m. notebook, diary.*
agent *m. agent.*
    Je suis l'agent de cette firme. *I'm the agent (representative) of this firm.*
    Agents de police. *Police officers.*
aggraver *to aggravate, increase the gravity of.*
s'aggraver *to aggravate, get worse.*
    La situation s'aggrave. *The situation is growing (getting) worse.*
agile *adj. agile.*
AGIR *to act.*
    Il agit toujours de cette façon. *He always acts that way.*
    Réfléchissez avant d'agir. *Think before you act. Look before you leap.*
S'AGIR DE *to be a question of, a matter of.*
    De quoi s'agit-il? *What's the matter? What's it a question of?*
    Je ne sais pas de quoi il s'agit. *I don't know what it's all about. I don't know what the problem (question) is.*
    Voici ce dont il s'agit. *The thing is this. This is the question (problem).*
    Il s'agit d'une forte somme. *A lot of money is involved.*
agitation *f. agitation.*
agiter *to stir, shake.*
s'agiter *to be agitated, restless; fret.*
agneau *m. lamb.*
agonie *f. agony.*
agrafe *f. hook; clip.*
agrandir *to enlarge.*
agrandissement *m. enlargement.*
agréable *adj. agreeable, pleasant.*
    Une soirée agréable. *A pleasant evening.*
agréer *to accept.*
    Veuillez agréer mes salutations empressées. *Very truly yours.*
agrément *m. consent; pleasure; favor.*

agriculteur *m. farmer.*
agriculture *f. farming.*
aguets *m. pl. used in the following expression:*
    Se tenir aux aguets. *To be on the watch. To be on one's guard.*
ah! *ah! oh!*
ahuri *adj. flurried, confused.*
AIDE *f. aid, help.*
    Il est venu à notre aide. *He came to our aid. He helped us.*
aide *m. aide, assistant.*
AIDER *to help.*
    Aidez-moi à porter les bagages. *Help me carry the bags.*
aie! *ouch!*
aieux *m. pl. ancestors.*
aigle *m. eagle.*
aigre *adj. sour; bitter.*
aigu (aiguë *f.*) *adj. sharp, acute.*
    L'accent aigu. *Acute accent.*
    Elle poussa un cri aigu. *She let out a shrill cry.*
aiguille *f. needle.*
    Aiguille à tricoter. *Knitting needle.*
aiguiser *to sharpen.*
aile *f. wing.*
AILLEURS *elsewhere, somewhere else.*
    C'est moins cher ailleurs. *It's less expensive elsewhere.*
    Par ailleurs. *Besides. Otherwise.*
    D'ailleurs, il est parti. *Besides, he's gone (he's left).*
    Nulle part ailleurs. *Nowhere else.*
    Partout ailleurs. *Everywhere else.*
AIMABLE *adj. amiable, kind, pleasant, likeable.*
    Vous êtes bien aimable. *That's very kind (nice) of you. ("You are very kind.")*
    C'est très aimable à vous. *That's very kind of you.*
    Voulez-vous être assez aimable de me passer le sel? *Will you please pass me the salt?*
    Elle a l'air aimable. *She looks (seems to be) pleasant.*
AIMER *to love, like.*
    Aimer bien. *To like very much.*
    J'aimerais. *I'd like.*
    J'aime le café. *I like coffee.*
    J'aime mieux l'autre. *I like the other one better. I prefer the other.*
    Je n'aime pas ça. *I don't like that.*
aîné *noun and adj. eldest, elder, senior..*
AINSI *so, thus, in this way.*
    Ainsi soit-il. *So be it; amen.*
    Et ainsi de suite. *And so on. And so forth.*
    Pour ainsi dire. *So to speak.*
    C'est ainsi qu'on l'appelle. *That's his name.*
    S'il en est ainsi. *If that's the case.*
    Est-ce bien ainsi? *Is it all right this way?*

AIR m. air.

Vous êtes dans un courant d'air. *You're in a draft.*

Prendre l'air. *To get some air.*

En plein air. *Out of doors, in the open air.*

Il a cinquante ans, mais il n'en a pas l'air. *He's fifty but he doesn't look it.*

Cela en a tout l'air. *It looks very much like it.*

Elle a l'air jeune. *She looks young. She has a youthful appearance.*

La maison était tout en l'air. *The house was in disorder.*

Ce sont des paroles en l'air. *It's just idle (empty) talk.*

Je connais cet air-là. *I know that tune (melody).*

aise f. ease, comfort, convenience.

Il était assis bien à son aise. *He was seated very comfortably.*

Mettez-vous à l'aise. *Make yourself comfortable.*

Je ne suis pas à mon aise. *I don't feel comfortable (at ease).*

J'en suis bien aise. *I'm glad of that.*

aisé adj. easy, comfortable, well off.

Ce n'est pas chose aisée. *It's not an easy matter.*

Une famille aisée. *A well-to-do family.*

aisément easily.

Cela se croit aisément. *That's easy to believe.*

ajourner to adjourn, postpone.

AJOUTER to add.

ajuster to adjust, adapt.

alarmant adj. alarming.

alarme f. alarm.

alarmer to alarm.

album m. album.

alcool m. alcohol.

alcoolique adj. alcoholic.

Une boisson alcoolique. *An alcoholic beverage.*

alentour around.

alentours m. pl. surroundings.

Aux alentours de. *In the vicinity of.*

alerte noun f. and adj. alert; alarm.

alibi m. alibi.

aligner to arrange in a line, line up.

aliment m. food.

alimentation f. nutrition.

allemand noun and adj. German.

Pouvez-vous traduire ceci en allemand? *Can you translate this into German?*

C'est un Allemand. *He's a German.*

aller m. going.

Au pis aller. *At the worst.*

Un billet d'aller. *A one-way ticket.*

Un billet d'aller retour. *A round-trip ticket.*

ALLER to go; to feel; to suit, fit, become; to be all right.

Où allez-vous? *Where are you going?*

Aller à pied. *To walk.*

Comment puis-je y aller? *How can I go (get) there?*

Allons chez moi. *Let's go to my house.*

Allez lentement. *Go slow.*

Etes-vous jamais allé en Amérique? *Have you ever been to America?*

Ce chemin va à Paris. *This road leads to Paris.*

Cela va sans dire. *That goes without saying.*

Allez! *Go! Go on!*

Allez-y! *Go on ahead! Go ahead! Go on!*

Allons-y! *Let's go there. Let's go! Let's get started (going)!*

Allons donc! *Nonsense! You don't really mean that! You can't really be serious!*

Allons, décidez-vous. *Come on, make up your mind.*

Cela me va. *That suits me. That's fine as far as I'm concerned.*

Ce climat ne me va pas. *This climate doesn't agree with me.*

Sa robe lui va bien. *Her dress is very becoming.*

Il va pleuvoir. *It's going to rain.*

Qu'est-ce que vous allez manger? *What are you going to (have to) eat?*

Comment ça va?—Tout va bien. *How are things?—Everything's fine.*

Comment va la santé?—*How's your health?*

Comment allez-vous? *How are you?*

Je vais très bien. *I'm very well.*

Est-ce que votre pendule va bien? *Does your clock keep good time?*

Midi va sonner. *It's almost noon.*

En allant à la Côte d'Azur. *On the way to the Riviera.*

Il va y avoir une mêlée. *There's going to be a fight.*

Va pour soixante-cinq francs! *Sold for sixty-five francs!*

Vas-y! *Go there! Go ahead! Go to it!*

S'EN ALLER to go away, leave.

Il est temps de s'en aller. *It's time to leave.*

Allez-vous-en. *Go away.*

alliance f. alliance; wedding ring.

allô hello (on telephone).

allonger to lengthen.

allumage m. ignition.

allumer to light.

ALLUMETTE f. match.

Avez-vous une allumette? *Do you have a match?*

allure f. gait; appearance, looks.

Cela a beaucoup d'allure. *That looks smart.*

allusion f. allusion, hint.

Faire allusion à. *To allude to. To refer to. To hint at.*

ALORS *then.*

C'était la coutume alors. *It was the custom then (in those days).*

Et alors, qu'est-ce qui est arrivé? *And what happened then?*

Alors c'est dit? *Well then, it's agreed?*

Oh! Chic alors *(fam.) Oh! that's good! That's swell!*

Ah non, alors! *I should think not! Certainly not!*

Alors là. *As for that. Well then.*

alpaga *n. alpaca.*

En alpaga. *In (of) alpaca.*

ALPHABET *m. alphabet.*

alpinisme *m. mountain climbing.*

Faire de l'alpinisme. *To go mountain climbing.*

altérer *to alter.*

alternative *f. alternative, choice.*

alterner *to alternate.*

altitude *f. altitude.*

amabilité *f. kindness.*

amateur *m. amateur; connoisseur.*

ambassadeur (ambassadrice *f.) ambassador.*

ambiance *f. atmosphere.*

ambitieux (ambitieuse *f.) adj. ambitious.*

ambition *f. ambition.*

ambulance *f. ambulance.*

ÂME *f. soul.*

Etat d'âme. *Mood.*

C'est une âme sensible. *He (she) is a sensitive person.*

améliorer *to ameliorate, improve.*

amende *f. fine.*

AMENER *to bring.*

Il prit un autobus qui l'amena juste devant l'immeuble. *He took a bus which brought him right in front of the building.*

Vous pouvez amener votre ami. *You can bring your friend along.*

amer (amère *f.) adj. bitter.*

AMÉRICAIN *noun and adj. American.*

Amérique *f. America.*

Amérique du Nord (Sud). *North (South) America.*

ameublement *m. furniture.*

ameuter *to stir up.*

AMI *m. friend.*

C'est un de mes meilleurs amis. *He's one of my best friends.*

Ce sont des amis intimes. *They're close friends.*

amical (amicaux *pl.) adj. friendly.*

amidon *m. starch.*

amiral *m.* (amiraux *pl.) admiral.*

AMITIÉ *f. friendship; pl. regards.*

Une amitié solide. *A strong friendship.*

Mes amitiés chez vous. *My best regards to your family.*

Si vous lui écrivez, faites-lui mes amitiés. *If you write him, give him my regards.*

AMOUR *m. love.*

amoureux (amoureuse *f.) adj. in love.*

Il est tombé amoureux d'elle. *He fell in love with her.*

ample *adj. ample, spacious.*

amplement *amply.*

ampleur *f. ampleness; breadth.*

ampoule *f. electric bulb; blister.*

amusant *adj. amusing.*

amusement *m. amusement.*

amuser *to amuse.*

Ça m'amuse. *It amuses me. I find it amusing.*

S'AMUSER *to have a good time.*

Au revoir, amusez-vous bien. *Good-bye, have a good time (have fun).*

Nous nous sommes bien amusés hier. *We enjoyed ourselves yesterday. We had a good time yesterday.*

AN *m. year.*

Il y a un an. *A year ago.*

J'y habite depuis vingt ans. *I've lived there for twenty years.*

Une fois par an. *Once a year.*

analyse *f. analysis.*

analyser *to analyze.*

ancêtre *m. ancestor.*

ANCIEN (ancienne *f.) adj. ancient; former.*

Cela évoque d'anciens souvenirs. *That brings back old memories.*

Mon ancien professeur se trouvait là par hasard. *My former teacher happened to be there.*

ancre *f. anchor.*

âne *m. donkey; jackass.*

anéantir *to annihilate, destroy.*

anesthésique *m. anesthetic.*

ange *m. angel.*

ANGLAIS *noun and adj. English.*

Parlez-vous anglais? *Do you speak English?*

Comment appelez-vous ceci en anglais? *What do you call this in English? What's the English word for this?*

Il a filé à l'anglaise. *He took French leave.*

angle *m. angle.*

Angleterre *f. England.*

angoisse *f. anguish.*

Angoisses de conscience. *Qualms of conscience.*

animal (animaux *pl.) noun (m.) and adj. animal.*

animé *adj. animated, spirited, lively.*

Le dessin animé. *The cartoon (animated).*
animer *to animate, enliven.*
anneau *m. ring.*
ANNÉE *f. year.*
  Bonne année! *Happy New Year!*
  L'année qui vient. *The coming year. Next year.*
anniversaire *m. birthday; anniversary.*
ANNONCE *f. announcement; advertisement.*
  Il vont mettre une petite annonce dans le journal. *They're going to put an ad in the paper.*
annoncer *to announce.*
annuaire *m. directory, telephone book.*
  L'annuaire de téléphone. *Telephone directory.*
annuel (annuelle *f.*) *adj. annual, yearly.*
annuler *to annul, make void.*
anonyme *adj. anonymous.*
  Société anonyme. *Joint-stock company.*
anormal (anormaux *pl.*) *adj. abnormal.*
antécédent *noun (m.) and adj. antecedent.*
antenne f. *aerial; antenna.*
  Hors d'antenne. *Off the air.*
  Passer à/avoir l'antenne. *To go/be on the air.*
  Sur l'antenne. *On the air.*
  Antenne parabolique *f. Satellite dish.*
antérieur *adj. anterior, previous.*
anticiper *to anticipate.*
  Avec mes remerciements anticipés. *Thanking you in advance (in a letter).*
antiquaire *m. antiquary; antique dealer.*
antique *adj. antique; ancient.*
antiquité *f. antiquity.*
  Il est marchand d'antiquités. *He's an antique dealer.*
antiseptique *adj. antiseptic.*
anxiété *f. anxiety.*
  J'éprouvais de l'anxiété avant son retour. *I was very worried before he got back. ("I experienced some anxiety before his return.")*
ANXIEUX (anxieuse *f.*) *adj. anxious.*
  Il paraissait très anxieux d'aboutir. *He seemed very anxious to succeed.*
AOÛT *m. August.*
apaiser *to appease, pacify.*
(en) aparté *aside, in a stage whisper.*
apathie *f. apathy.*
APERCEVOIR *to perceive, observe.*
  Je vous ai aperçu dans la foule. *I got a glimpse of you in the crowd.*
  Je l'aperçois. *I see him.*
S'APERCEVOIR *to perceive, notice.*
  Il ne s'aperçoit de rien. *He doesn't notice anything.*
  Il est parti sans qu'on s'en aperçoive. *He left without anyone seeing him.*
  Il s'est aperçu à temps de son erreur. *He*

caught his mistake (noticed his error) in time.
aperçu *m. glimpse; brief account.*
  Il m'a donné un aperçu de la situation. *He gave me a brief account of the situation.*
apitoyer *to move to pity.*
s'apitoyer *to pity.*
aplatir *to flatten.*
aplomb *m. self-assurance; impudence.*
  Quel aplomb! *What impudence!*
apostrophe *f. apostrophe; reproach.*
APPARAÎTRE *to appear.*
  Soudainement il est apparu. *Suddenly he appeared.*
APPAREIL *m. apparatus; equipment.*
  Ne quittez pas l'appareil, s'il vous plaît. *Please hold the wire a minute. ("Don't leave the telephone . . .")*
  Appareil photo(graphique). *Camera.*
  Appareil cinématographique. *Movie camera.*
apparence *f. appearance.*
  Sauver les apparences. *To keep up appearances.*
apparent *adj. apparent.*
apparition *f. appearance; brief visit.*
  Faire son apparition. *To make one's appearance.*
appartement *m. apartment.*
APPARTENIR *to belong to.*
  A qui appartient cet objet? *Whom does this (thing, object) belong to?*
appel *m. call.*
  Faire l'appel. *To call the roll.*
APPELER *to call.*
  Appelez-moi quand vous serez prêt. *Call me when you're ready.*
  Appelez le médecin. *Call the doctor.*
  Comment vous appelez-vous? *What's your name?*
  Comment l'appelle-t-on? *What's his (her) name?*
  Je m'appelle. *My name is.*
APPÉTIT *m. appetite.*
  Ça m'a coupé l'appétit. *That took away (spoiled) my appetite.*
  Aiguiser l'appétit. *To whet the appetite.*
  Bon appétit! *Hearty appetite!*
applaudir *to applaud, cheer.*
applaudissement *m. applause.*
appliquer *to apply.*
appointements *m. pl. salary.*
APPORTER *to bring.*
  Apportez-moi une tasse de thé. *Bring me a cup of tea.*
  Il apporta du soin à le faire. *He exercised care in doing it.*
appréciation *f. appreciation; estimation.*
apprécier *to value, appreciate.*

appréhender *to seize; fear, dread.*
J'appréhende de la voir. *I dread seeing her.*
J'appréhende qu'il ne soit trop tard. *I'm afraid it will (may) be too late.*
appréhension *f. apprehension, dread.*
APPRENDRE *to learn.*
Il n'est pas difficile d'apprendre une langue étrangère. *It's not hard to learn a foreign language.*
Elle apprend à conduire. *She's learning how to drive.*
apprenti *noun and adj. apprentice.*
apprentissage *m. apprenticeship.*
apprêt *m. preparation.*
apprêter *to prepare.*
s'apprêter *to prepare oneself, get ready.*
Elle s'apprête à sortir. *She's getting ready to go out.*
apprivoiser *to tame.*
approbation *f. approbation, approval.*
approchant *adj. similar, approximate.*
Si vous n'avez pas ce que je veux, donnez-moi quelque chose d'approchant. *If you don't have what I want, give me something like it.*
approche *f. approach, advance.*
APPROCHER *to approach, come near.*
N'approchez pas, il y a du danger. *Don't go (come) near. It's dangerous.*
L'heure approche. *The hour is drawing near. It's almost time.*
Approchez la lampe. *Bring the lamp closer.*
S'APPROCHER *to approach, come near.*
Je me suis approché de lui. *I came near him.*
Ne vous approchez pas. *Don't come any closer.*
approfondir *to investigate, fathom.*
Approfondir une question. *To get to the root (bottom) of a matter.*
s'approprier *to appropriate, usurp.*
approuver *to approve.*
Approuvez-vous ce que j'ai dit? *Do you approve of what I said?*
approximatif (approximative *f.*) *adj. approximate.*
approximativement *approximately.*
appui *m. support.*
C'est grâce à leur appui que j'ai pu y parvenir. *I was able to succeed thanks to their help.*
Voici un exemple à l'appui de ma thèse. *Here's an example which supports my argument.*
appuyer *to support; to press, to push.*
Il m'a dit qu'il appuierait ma demande. *He told me he would support my request.*
Elle a appuyé sur le bouton. *She pressed the button.*
s'appuyer *to lean upon, use as support.*

Appuyez-vous sur mon bras. *Lean on my arm.*
Appuyez-vous à la rampe pour monter l'escalier. *Hold on to the banister going up the stairs.*
âpre *adj. hard, rough.*
APRÈS *after.*
Après vous! *After you!*
Vous avez eu raison après tout. *You were right after all.*
Eh bien! Après? *Well, what next?*
APRÈS-DEMAIN *m. the day after tomorrow.*
J'espère vous donner sa réponse après-demain. *I hope to give you his answer the day after tomorrow.*
APRÈS-MIDI *m (sometimes f.) afternoon.*
Il est toujours là l'après-midi. *He's always there in the afternoon.*
La représentation commence à trois heures de l'après-midi. *The performance begins at three p.m.*
Il a passé tout l'après-midi chez moi. *He spent all afternoon at my place.*
apte *adj. apt, fit.*
aptitude *f. aptitude, ability.*
aquarelle *f. water color (painting).*
araignée *f. spider.*
arbitraire *adj. arbitrary.*
arbitre *m. arbitrator, umpire, referee.*
arbre *m. tree.*
arc *m. bow; arc.*
arche *f. arch.*
architecte *m. architect.*
architecture *f. architecture.*
archive *f. file, menu (computer).*
ardent *adj. ardent.*
ardeur *f. ardor, fervor.*
ardu *adj. steep; arduous.*
arête *f. fish-bone.*
ARGENT *m. silver; money.*
Cette cuillère est en argent. *This spoon is made of silver.*
Il gagne beaucoup d'argent. *He's making (makes) a great deal (a lot) of money.*
Argent comptant. *Ready money. Cash.*
Il n'en a pas pour son argent. *He didn't get his money's worth.*
Le temps c'est de l'argent. *Time is money.*
Assez (suffisamment) d'argent. *Enough money.*
argenterie *f. silverware.*
argument *m. proof, evidence.*
arithmétique *f. arithmetic.*
arme *f. arm, weapon.*
armée *f. army.*
armement *m. armament.*
armer *to arm.*
armistice *m. armistice.*
armoire *f. wardrobe.*

arracher *to pull out.*
Le dentiste m'a arraché une dent. *The dentist pulled my tooth out.*
Impossible de lui arracher une parole. *You can't get a word out of him.*
arrangement *m. arrangement.*
ARRANGER *to arrange, put in order.*
Arrangez toutes ces choses. *Put all these things in order.*
Soyez tranquille, je vais arranger tout ça. *Don't worry, I'll straighten everything ("all this") out.*
s'arranger *to prepare oneself; put up with.*
Arrangez-vous. *Manage as best you can. Do the best you can.*
Laissez-moi faire et tout s'arrangera. *Leave that to me ("Let me do it") and everything will come out all right.*
Cela s'arrangera. *It will come out all right in the end.*
ARRÊT *m. stop, halt; arrest; sentence.*
Où se trouve l'arrêt de l'autobus? *Where does the bus stop? Where's the bus stop?*
Quel est le prochain arrêt? *What's the next stop?*
Il y a un mandat d'arrêt lancé contre lui. *A warrant has been issued for his arrest.*
ARRÊTER *to stop; arrest.*
Attendez que les voitures soient arrêtées. *Wait until the traffic stops.*
Ma montre est arrêtée. *My watch (has) stopped.*
Arrêtez-le! *Arrest him!*
S'ARRÊTER *to stop.*
Arrêtons-nous ici. *Let's stop here.*
Quand le prochain train arrive-t-il, et combien de temps s'arrête-t-il? *When does the next train arrive and how long does it stop?*
La pendule s'est arrêtée. *The clock stopped.*
ARRIÈRE *m. back.*
Vous trouverez ce paquet à l'arrière de ma voiture. *You'll find that package in the back of my car.*
ARRIÈRE *behind, backwards.*
Faites deux pas en arrière. *Take two steps backwards.*
Il est toujours en arrière pour ses paiements. *He's always behind in his payments.*
Pourquoi restez-vous toujours en arrière? *Why do you always remain behind?*
arrière-grand-mère *f. great-grandmother.*
arrière-grand-père *m. great-grandfather.*
arrière-petit-fille *f. great-granddaughter.*
arrière-petit-fils *m. great-grandson.*
arrivée *f. arrival.*
Nous étions là à l'arrivée du train. *We were there when the train arrived ("at the arrival of the train").*

ARRIVER *to arrive, happen.*
Ils sont arrivés trop tard. *They arrived too late.*
Le train doit arriver à midi. *The train is due at noon.*
Tâchez d'arriver de bonne heure. *Try to come early.*
Les voilà qui arrivent. *Here they come.*
Arriver à ses fins. *To attain one's ends.*
Que vous est-il arrivé? *What happened to you?*
C'est arrivé trois jours de suite. *That's happened three days in a row.*
Quoi qu'il arrive. *Come what may.*
arrogance *f. arrogance, haughtiness.*
arrondir *to round out.*
arrondissement *m. district, borough, ward (Paris).*
arroser *to water, irrigate.*
ART *m. art.*
Les beaux-arts. *The fine arts.*
ARTICLE *m. article.*
L'importation de cet article est prohibée. *The importation of this article is prohibited.*
Avez-vous lu l'article de fond du journal de ce soir? *Did you read the editorial in this evening's paper?*
Faire l'article d'un produit. *To boost a product.*
artificiel (artificielle f.). *adj. artificial.*
artisan *m. or f. artisan, craftsperson.*
artisanat *m. arts and crafts.*
Les produits de l'artisanat. *Handicrafts.*
artiste *m. artist.*
as *m. ace.*
As de pique. *Ace of spades.*
C'est un as au tennis. *He's a tennis ace.*
ASCENSEUR *m. elevator.*
Est-ce que cet ascenseur descend? *Is this elevator going down?*
aspect *m. aspect.*
asperge *f. asparagus.*
aspirateur *m. vacuum cleaner.*
aspirer *to inhale; aspire to.*
assaillir *to assault.*
assemblée *f. assembly, meeting.*
assembler *to assemble.*
ASSEOIR *to seat.*
Faites-donc asseoir monsieur. *Give the gentleman a seat.*
Nous sommes assis dans la quatrième rangée. *We have seats in the fourth row.*
Je suis assis dans un courant d'air. *I'm sitting in a draft.*
Il faut asseoir cette affaire sur une base solide. *We have to establish this business on a solid basis.*

S'ASSEOIR *to sit down ("to seat oneself").*
Asseyez-vous. *Sit down.*

ASSEZ *enough, quite, rather.*
Est-ce assez comme cela? *Is that enough?*
Ça va?—Assez bien, merci. *How are you?*
("How are things?")—Quite well,
thank you.
En voilà assez! *That's enough!*
J'en ai assez! 1. *I have enough of it.* 2. *I'm*
fed up (with it).

assidu *adj. assiduous*

assiette *f. plate.*
Vous avez une assiette plate et une assiette
creuse. *You have a dinner plate and a*
soup plate.

assigner *to assign.*

assimiler *to assimilate.*

assis *seated, sitting.*
Une place assise. *Seat (bus, etc.).*

ASSISTANCE *f. assistance; attendance;*
audience.
Assistance publique. *Government agency*
for social welfare.
Une assistance nombreuse. *A large*
audience.

assistant *m. assistant.*

ASSISTER *to assist; attend.*
Assistons ces pauvres gens. *Let's help these*
poor people.
N'oubliez pas d'assister à la séance
d'ouverture de la société. *Don't forget*
to attend the opening meeting of the
society.

association *f. association; partnership.*
L'association a été dissoute. *The partnership*
was (has been) dissolved.
Association de football. *A soccer club.*

associer *to associate.*

assortiment *m. assortment.*

assortir *to match; assort.*

assurance *f. assurance, insurance.*
Agréez l'assurance de mes sentiments
distingués. *Yours very truly (in a*
letter).
L'assurance sur la vie. *Life insurance.*
Faire assurer. *To have (something) insured.*

assurer *to assure; insure; ascertain.*
Assurer contre l'incendie. *To insure against*
fire.

astronaute *m., f. astronaut.*

atelier *m. workshop, studio.*

atmosphère *f. atmosphere.*

atome *m. atom.*

atroce *adj. atrocious.*

ATTACHER *to attach, fasten.*
Attachez cela avec une épingle. *Fasten that*
with a pin.
Attachez-le avec la corde. *Tie it with the*
string (cord, rope).

Attachez tous ces paquets ensemble. *Tie all*
these parcels together.
Ils sont attachés l'un à l'autre. *They're very*
attached to each other.
Je n'y attache aucune importance. *I don't*
attach any importance to it.

attaque *f. attack.*

attaquer *to attack.*

ATTEINDRE *to attain, reach.*
J'ai couru mais je n'ai pu l'atteindre. *I ran*
but I couldn't catch up with him (her).
Les prix ont atteint un nouveau maximum.
Prices have reached a new high.
J'ai atteint mon but. *I've reached my goal.*

ATTENDRE *to wait.*
Attendez ici. *Wait here.*
Attendez un moment. *Wait a minute.*
Il attend depuis deux heures. *He's been*
waiting for two hours.
Attendez-vous une lettre? *Do you expect a*
letter? Are you expecting a letter?
Le train était attendu à onze heures
cinquante. *The train was expected at*
eleven-fifty.
Nous attendons du monde. *We're expecting*
company.
Attendre que (+ subjunctive). *To wait until.*
En attendant. *In the meantime.*
Faire attendre. *To keep (someone) waiting.*

S'ATTENDRE *to expect.*
Je ne m'attendais pas à cela. *I didn't expect*
that.

attendrir *to soften, make tender.*

s'attendrir *to be moved.*
Elle s'attendrit facilement. *She's easily*
moved.

attente *f. waiting.*
Dans l'attente de vous lire. *Awaiting your*
reply (in a letter).
Ils sont dans l'attente de nouvelles de leur
fils. *They're waiting for news from*
their son.

attentif (attentive *f.*) *adj. attentive.*

ATTENTION *f. attention.*
Faites attention à ce qui se passe. *Pay*
attention to what's going on.
Attention! Pay attention! *Look out! Watch*
out!
Attention à la marche! *Watch the step!*
Attention! Peinture fraîche! *Be careful. Wet*
paint.
Faites attention, vous lui faites mal. *Be*
careful, you're hurting him (her).

attentivement *carefully.*
Voulez-vous relire cela attentivement? *Will*
you reread this carefully?

atterrir *to land (airplane).*

attirer *to attract, draw.*
Elle attire tous les regards. *She attracts*

everyone's attention ("all the glances").

Vous avez attiré sa colère. *You've made him angry.*

attitude *f. attitude.*

ATTRACTION *f. attraction.*

Paris exerce une grande attraction sur les étrangers. *Paris has a great attraction for foreigners.*

C'est l'attraction principale du spectacle. *It's the main feature of the show.*

attrait *m. attraction, charm.*

Dépourvu d'attrait. *Unattractive.*

ATTRAPER *to catch.*

Attrape! *Catch!*

Il a attrapé un rhume. *He caught a cold.*

Le peintre a attrapé la ressemblance. *The painter caught the likeness.*

Vous êtes bien attrapé. *You've been fooled (taken in).*

attrayant *adj. attractive.*

Elle est très attrayante. *She's very attractive.*

attribuer *to attribute.*

attrister *to sadden.*

AU (aux *pl.*) *See À.*

aube *f. dawn.*

AUCUN *adj. no, no one, not any.*

Je n'y ai aucun intérêt. *I haven't any interest in it.*

Aucun de ceux-ci ne me dit. *I don't care for any of these.*

Cela ne fait aucun doute. *There isn't any doubt about it. There's no doubt about it.*

Laissez-le dire, cela n'a aucune importance. *Let him say what he wants. It doesn't matter at all.*

Je n'ai de vouvelles d'aucun d'eux. *I haven't had any news from any of them.*

Cette mesure n'a plus aucune raison d'être. *There is no longer any justification for this measure.*

Aucun étudiant n'a réussi à l'examen. *Not one (not a single) student passed the examination.*

audace *f. audacity.*

audacieux (audacieuse *f.*) *adj. audacious.*

AU-DELA *beyond.*

L'au-delà. *The hereafter.*

AU-DESSOUS *below.*

Dix degrés au-dessous de zéro. *Ten degrees below zero.*

Au-dessous de la moyenne. *Below average.*

AU-DESSUS *above.*

Au-dessus de la porte. *Above the door.*

Au-dessus de tout éloge. *Beyond all praise.*

AU-DEVANT *toward.*

Aller au-devant de quelqu'un. *To go to meet someone.*

Aller au-devant du danger. *To anticipate a danger.*

Aller au-devant des désirs de quelqu'un. *To anticipate someone's wishes.*

augmentation *f. increase; raise.*

augmenter *to increase.*

s'augmenter *to increase.*

AUJOURD'HUI *today; nowadays.*

Je n'ai rien à faire aujourd'hui. *I have nothing to do today.*

Je pars (d')aujourd'hui en huit. *I'm leaving a week from today.*

Je reviendrai (d')aujourd'hui en quinze. *I'll be back (in) two weeks from today.*

Quel jour du mois est-ce aujourd'hui? *What's today's date?*

C'est aujourd'hui le cinq. *Today is the fifth.*

Aujourd'hui même. *Today, this very day.*

aumône *f. alms, charity.*

auparavant *formerly, earlier; first.*

Auparavant c'était tout différent. *Formerly (previously) it was completely different.*

Auparavant passez à la banque. *Go to the bank first.*

auprès *near by, close by.*

Il est toujours auprès de lui. *He's always near him.*

Agir auprès de quelqu'un. *To use one's influence with someone.*

auquel (à laquelle *f.*, auxquels *m. pl.*, auxquelles *f. pl.*) *to which, to whom.*

Auquel de ces hommes voulez-vous parler? *To which of these men do you wish to speak?*

aurore *f. dawn.*

AUSSI *also.*

Lui aussi viendra avec nous. *He will also come with us. He, too, will come with us.*

Aussi peu que possible. *As little as possible.*

Il était tard, aussi nous ne sommes pas sortis. *It was late, so we didn't go out.*

Il est aussi grand que vous. *He's as tall as you are.*

Aussi loin que le regard peut s'étendre. *As far as the eye can reach.*

AUSSITÔT *at once, immediately.*

Aussitôt couché, je m'endors. *As soon as I get into bed, I fall asleep. I no sooner get into bed than I go off to sleep.*

Aussitôt dit, aussitôt fait. *No sooner said than done.*

Je suis désireux de partir aussitôt que possible. *I'm anxious (eager) to leave as soon as possible.*

Je m'en occuperai aussitôt que j'aurai un moment de libre. *I'll take care of it as soon as I have a free moment.*

AUTANT *as much, as many.*

S'il gagne autant que vous le dites. *If he earns as much as you say.*

Répétez votre leçon autant que vous le pouvez. *Repeat your lesson as many times as you can.*

Pour autant qu'il est en mon pouvoir. *In so far as I can. In so far as it lies within my power.*

D'autant plus. *All the more.*

AUTEUR *m. author.*

C'est le dernier livre paru de cet auteur. *This is the latest (most recent) book by this author.*

Les droits d'auteur. *Royalties.*

authentique *adj. authentic.*

AUTO *f. See also* automobile.

Savez-vous conduire une auto? *Can you drive a car?*

Voyager en auto. *To travel by car.*

autobus *m. bus.*

Quel autobus dois-je prendre pour y aller? *What bus do I (should I) take to get there?*

Un arrêt d'autobus. *A bus stop.*

autocar *m. bus, coach (outside of city).*

automatique *adj. automatic.*

AUTOMNE *m. autumn, fall.*

AUTOMOBILE *f. automobile.*

Il fut presque écrasé par une automobile. *He was almost run over by an automobile.*

autonome *adj. autonomous.*

autonomie *f. autonomy, self-government.*

autorisation *f. authorization.*

Vous avez mon autorisation. *You have my permission.*

autoriser *to authorize.*

Il m'a autorisé à le faire. *He authorized me to do it.*

autorité *f. authority.*

Il fait autorité en la matière. *He's an authority on the subject.*

Les autorités locales. *The local authorities.*

Il l'a fait de sa propre autorité. *He did it on his own initiative.*

AUTOUR *around.*

Les planètes gravitent autour du soleil. *The planets revolve ("gravitate") around the sun.*

Il y a une grande cour de récréation autour de l'école. *There's a large yard (playground) around the school.*

Ils se sont rangés autour de la table. *They gathered around the table.*

Regardez autour de vous, vous le trouverez. *Look around you. You'll find it.*

AUTRE *adj. other.*

Ceux-ci sont moins bons que les autres. *These aren't as good as the others.*

Faites-lui une autre offre. *Make him another offer.*

Traversons de l'autre côté. *Let's cross over to the other side.*

Donnez-moi autre chose. *Give me something else.*

Et avec ça, vous faut-il autre chose? *Will you need anything else (in addition to this)?*

C'est un tout autre cas. *That's an entirely different case. It's another thing entirely.*

Vous trouverez cela autre part. *You'll find that somewhere else.*

Je l'ai vu l'autre jour. *I saw him the other day.*

A une autre fois. *Until another time.*

Il passe d'une extrémité à l'autre. *He goes from one extreme to another.*

Ni l'un ni l'autre ne vaut rien. *Neither one is any good.*

Il va arriver d'un jour à l'autre. *He'll arrive any day now.*

D'autre part. *On the other hand.*

En d'autres termes. *In other words.*

Rien d'autre. *Nothing else (more).*

AUTREFOIS *formerly, in former times.*

J'en ai entendu parler autrefois. *I formerly (earlier, a long time ago) heard people speak about it.*

Les beaux jours d'autrefois. *The good old days.*

AUTREMENT *otherwise.*

Autrement nous y serions allés. *Otherwise we would have gone there.*

autrui *others, other people.*

Ne faites pas à autrui ce que vous ne voudriez pas qu'on vous fît. *Do unto others as you would have others do unto you. ("Don't do to others what you would not have others do to you.")*

avalanche *f. avalanche.*

avaler *to swallow.*

avance *f. advance.*

Il est toujours en avance. *He's always ahead of time.*

Il faudra réserver vos chambres bien à l'avance. *You'll have to reserve your rooms well in advance.*

AVANCER *to advance.*

Nous avancions à peine, tant la foule était dense. *The crowd was so thick that we couldn't move ahead (advance).*

Cela ne vous avancera guère. *That won't get you very far.*

Ma montre avance de trois minutes. *My watch is three minutes fast.*

Ne lui avancez pas d'argent. *Don't advance him any money.*

Avancer une théorie. *To advance a theory.*

AVANT *before.*

Il faut que nous le voyions avant qu'il parte. *We must see him before he leaves.*

Avant tout, faites ça. *First of all, do this.*

Elle ne rentre pas de l'école avant cinq heures. *She doesn't come home from school until five.*

Ils sont partis en avant. *They've gone on ahead.*

Avant mardi. *Before Tuesday.*

Avant de manger. *Before eating.*

Avant peu. *Before long.*

Deux cents ans avant J.C. *200 B.C.*

Le pneu avant. *The front tire.*

AVANTAGE m. *advantage.*

C'est à votre avantage. *It's to your advantage.*

Vous avez l'avantage sur moi. *You have the advantage over me.*

Vous auriez avantage à. *It would be to your advantage to.*

avantageux (avantageuse f.) *adj. advantageous.*

AVANT-HIER m. *the day before yesterday.*

Je l'ai rencontré avant-hier. *I met him the day before yesterday.*

avare m. and f. *noun and adj. miser; avaricious, miserly.*

avarice f. *avarice.*

avarié adj. *damaged.*

AVEC *with.*

Venez avec moi. *Come with me.*

Etes-vous d'accord avec moi? *Do you agree with me?*

Avec plaisir. *With pleasure. Gladly.*

Avec grand plaisir. *With great pleasure. Very gladly.*

Avec succès. *Successfully.*

AVENIR m. *future.*

Ne recommencez pas à l'avenir. *Don't do it again in the future.*

C'est un homme d'avenir. *He's a man with a bright future.*

aventure f. *adventure.*

Je vais vous raconter ma récente aventure. *I'll tell you about an experience I had recently.*

Il racontait une de ses aventures en Amérique. *He was relating an experience of his in America.*

Elle dit la bonne aventure. *She tells fortunes.*

AVENUE f. *avenue.*

averse f. *short sudden shower.*

aversion f. *aversion, dislike.*

Il l'a en aversion. *He dislikes him (her).*

avertir *to inform; warn.*

Je vous en avertirai. *I'll let you know.*

avertissement m. *information, notification; warning.*

aveu m. *admission, avowal, confession.*

Faire l'aveu de. *To admit. To confess.*

aveugle m. and f. *noun and adj. blind; blind person.*

aviateur m. *aviator.*

aviation f. *aviation.*

avide adj. *greedy, eager.*

avion m. *airplane.*

Voyager en avion. *To travel by plane.*

Envoyer par avion. *To send by air(mail).*

AVIS m. *opinion; advice; notice.*

A mon avis. *In my opinion.*

Référez-vous-en à son avis. *Be guided by his advice.*

Sauf avis contraire, j'y serai. *Unless you hear to the contrary, I'll be there.*

Avis au lecteur. *Note to the reader (in a book).*

AVISER *to inform; consider.*

Je vous en aviserai. *I'll inform you by letter.*

Avisez-moi de votre venue. *Let me know in advance if you come.*

Il y avisera. *He'll study (consider) the matter.*

Nous aviserons. *We'll think the matter over.*

avocat m. *lawyer.*

avoir m. *possessions, property.*

Voilà tout son avoir. *That's all he has.*

AVOIR *to have.*

Est-ce que vous avez des cigarettes sur vous? *Do you have any cigarettes ("on you")?*

Il était un temps où il avait beaucoup d'argent mais maintenant il n'en a plus. *There was a time when he had a lot of money but he no longer has any.*

Il a vingt ans. *He's twenty years old.*

Il y a beaucoup de monde. *There are many people. There's a crowd.*

Qu'est-ce qu'il a? *What's the matter with him?*

Vous avez tort. *You're wrong.*

J'avais raison. *I was right.*

J'ai faim. *I'm hungry.*

Il a soif. *He's thirsty.*

Elle a peur. *She's frightened. She's afraid.*

J'ai chaud. *I'm warm.*

Avez-vous froid? *Are you cold?*

Pourquoi avoir honte? *Why be ashamed?*

Contre qui en a-t-il? *Whom does he have a grudge against?*

Merci beaucoup.—Il n'y a pas de quoi. *Thank you very much.—Don't mention it.*

J'aurais dû y aller. *I should have gone there.*

Vous aurez besoin de cela. *You'll need that.*

Il y avait beaucoup de monde dans le magasin. *There were a lot of people in the store.*

Il n'y avait rien à faire, il y est allé quand même. *There was nothing we could do about it; he went there just the same.*

Après avoir reçu le chèque. *After receiving the check.*

Auriez-vous? *Would you have?*

J'ai à écrire une lettre. *I have to write a letter.*

J'ai une lettre à écrire. *I have a letter to write.*

Avoir besoin de. *To need.*

Avoir de la chance. *To be lucky.*

Avoir confiance en. *To trust.*

Avoir de la peine. *To grieve, be in sorrow.*

Avoir envie de. *To want to, feel like.*

Avoir hâte de. *To be looking forward.*

Avoir l'air riche. *To look, seem, appear rich.*

Avoir l'habitude de. *To be in the habit of, be used to.*

Avoir l'intention de. *To intend.*

Avoir les cheveux noirs. *To have black hair.*

Avoir lieu. *To take place, occur.*

Avoir l'occasion de. *To have the opportunity to.*

Avoir mal à la gorge. *To have a sore throat.*

Avoir mauvaise mine. *To look bad.*

Avoir sommeil. *To be sleepy.*

En avoir assez de. *To have enough, be sick of something.*

En avoir pour: Vous en aurez pour longtemps. *It will take you a long time, you'll have a long wait.*

N'avoir qu'à. *To have only to.*

Vous n'avez qu'à demander. *You need only ask.*

avortement *m. abortion.*

avouer *to confess.*

Il a tout avoué. *He confessed everything.*

Avouez donc tout! *Come on, make a clean breast of it!*

J'ai honte d'avouer que j'ai oublié votre adresse. *I'm ashamed to confess I've forgotten your address.*

AVRIL *m. April.*

axe *m. axis.*

azur *adj. azure, blue.*

B

BA (-bonne action) *f. Good deed.*

baby-foot *m. table-football.*

baby-sitter *m., f. baby-sitter.*

Baby-sitting. *Baby-sitting.*

bac; baccalauréat. *High-school diploma; GCE A-levels.*

Bachelier *m.,* bachelière *f. Holder of the bac.*

Bachot *m. same as* bac; baccalauréat.

Bachoter. *To cram for an exam.*

bactérie *f. bacterium.*

badaud *m. loiterer, idler.*

BAGAGE *m. luggage, baggage.*

Vos bagages sont-ils enregistrés? *Is your baggage checked?*

Faites descendre mes bagages. *Have my bags brought down.*

Fourgon à bagages. *Baggage car.*

Bagages à main. *Hand luggage.*

Défaire les bagages. *To unpack the bags.*

bagatelle *f. trifle.*

Pour lui ce n'est qu'une bagatelle. *It's a mere trifle for him.*

bague *f. ring.*

baguette *f. stick.*

baie *f. bay.*

baigner *to bathe, wash.*

se baigner *to bathe.*

Défense de se baigner dans le lac. *No swimming in the lake.*

baignoire *f. bathtub.*

bail *m.* (baux *pl.*) *lease.*

bâillement *m. yawning.*

bâiller *to yawn.*

bain(s) *m. bath.*

Salle de bain. *Bathroom.*

baiser *m. kiss.*

baisse *f. fall, decline.*

baisser *to lower, let down.*

Baisser les yeux. *To look down. To lower one's eyes.*

Donner tête baissée dans un piège. *To rush headlong into a trap.*

se baisser *to stoop.*

Il s'est baissé pour le ramasser. *He stooped to pick it up.*

bal *m. ball.*

balai *m. broom.*

balance *f. balance, scales.*

Faire pencher la balance. *To turn the scales.*

balancer *to balance; swing, sway, rock; hesitate.*

balayer *to sweep.*

balcon *m. balcony.*

balle *f. ball (golf, tennis), bullet.*

ballet *m. ballet.*

ballon *m. ball (football, soccer).*

banal *adj. banal, commonplace.*

banc *m. bench.*

bandage *m. bandage.*

bande *f. band.*

Bande de cuir. *Leather strap.*

Faire bande à part. *To keep aloof.*

Bande dessinée. *Comic strip, cartoon.*

La bande magnétique. *Tape (recording); videotape.*

banlieue *f. suburbs.*

bannir *to banish.*
BANQUE *f. bank.*
  Des billets de banque. *Bank notes.*
banquet *m. banquet.*
banquette *f. bench.*
banquier *m. banker.*
baptiser *to baptize.*
baraque *f. booth, hut.*
barbare *adj. barbarous, cruel.*
barbe *f. beard.*
  Je dois me faire faire la barbe. *I have to get a shave.*
  J'ai la barbe dure. *I have a tough beard.*
  Quelle barbe (fam.)! *What a drag!*
barre *f. bar.*
barrer *to bar.*
barrière *f. barrier, gate.*
bas *m. stocking, lower part.*
  Le bas du pantalon retroussé. *The cuffs on the trousers.*
BAS (basse *f.*) *adj. low.*
  Je l'ai acheté à bas prix. *I bought it cheap(ly).*
  Mes fonds sont bas. *My funds are low. I'm running short of money.*
BAS *adv. low.*
  Chercher quelque chose de haut en bas. *To look (search) high and low for something.*
  A bas . . . ! *Down with . . . !*
  Je vous verrai là-bas. *I'll see you over there.*
bascule *f. weighing-machine, scale.*
base *f. base; basis.*
baser *to base.*
  Sur quoi base-t-il son opinion? *On what does he base his opinion?*
bas-relief *m. bas-relief.*
bassin *m. basin; pool.*
bataille *f. battle.*
batailler *to battle.*
BATEAU *m. boat.*
BÂTIMENT *m. building.*
  Où est le bâtiment de l'administration? *Where is the administration building?*
BÂTIR *to build, erect.*
  Faire bâtir. *To have (something) built.*
bâton *m. stick; spoke.*
battement *m. beating.*
BATTRE *to beat.*
  Battre des oeufs. *To beat (up) eggs.*
  Ils ont battu des mains. *They clapped their hands. They applauded.*
  Le coeur lui bat. *His heart is beating. His heart is in his mouth.*
  Il a battu le record de l'année dernière. *He beat last year's record.*
  Ils ont battu en retraite. *They beat a retreat.*
  Il faut battre le fer pendant qu'il est chaud. *One must strike while the iron is hot.*

SE BATTRE *to fight.*
bavard(e) *m. and f. a gossip.*
bavard *adj. talkative.*
bavardage *m. gossip.*
bavarder *to chatter, gossip.*
beau *m. beauty; dandy.*
BEAU (bel *before a vowel or "mute"* h, belle *f.*, beaux *m. pl.*, belles *f. pl.*) *adj. beautiful, pretty, nice.*
  Que c'est beau! *It's really very nice! How lovely!*
  Elle a une belle écriture. *She has a nice handwriting.*
  Il y a de belles maisons dans notre rue. *There are some beautiful houses on our street.*
  Les beaux-arts. *The fine arts.*
  Un beau geste. *A nice gesture.*
  Un beau parleur. *A smooth-talker.*
  Le temps se met au beau. *The weather is getting nice. The weather is clearing up.*
  Je l'ai rencontré un beau jour. *I ran into him one fine day. I met him unexpectedly.*
  Il a beau faire. *He's making a useless effort.*
  Vous avez beau dire, je ne le crois pas. *Say what you will, I still don't believe it.*
  Ils ont beau dire et beau faire, ça m'est égal. *They can say or do what they want to; I don't care.*
  J'aurai beau lui parler, il n'écoute personne. *There's no use of my talking to him; he won't listen to anyone.*
  J'en entends de belles sur votre compte! *I've heard some pretty stories about you! Nice things I hear about you!*
  Ah! La belle affaire! *Well, a fine thing!*
  Il fait beau. *The weather is good.*
BEAUCOUP *much; many.*
  Le malade est beaucoup plus mal. *The patient is much worse.*
  C'est beaucoup dire. *That's saying a lot.*
  Je vous remercie beaucoup. *Thanks very much. Thanks a lot.*
  Beaucoup d'entre nous. *Many of us.*
  Beaucoup d'argent. *A lot of money.*
beau-fils *m. son-in-law* (belle-fille *f. daughter-in-law*).
beau-frère *m. brother-in-law* (belle-soeur *f. sister-in-law*).
beau-père *m. father-in-law* (belle-mère *f. mother-in-law*).
beauté *f. beauty.*
bébé *m. baby.*
bec *m. beak, bill.*
bégayer *to stammer.*
beige *adj. beige.*
bel *adj. See* beau.

C'est un bel homme. *He's a handsome man.*
Tout cela est bel et bon mais . . . *That's all very well but . . .*
Il est bel et bien ruiné. *He's completely ruined.*
belge *m. and f. noun and adj. Belgian.*
belle *See beau.*
bénéfice *m. profit, benefit.*
bénéficier *to profit.*
bénir *to bless.*
berceau *m. cradle.*
berger *m. shepherd.*
bergère *f. shepherdess; easy chair.*
besogne *f. work.*
Il abat de la besogne. *He gets through a great deal of work quickly.*
BESOIN *m. need.*
Il a ce dont il a besoin. *He has what he needs.*
J'en ai un besoin urgent. *I need it badly.*
Il est dans le besoin. *He's very poor. He's in dire need.*
J'interviendrai si besoin est. *I'll intervene if need be (in case of need).*
Au besoin. *If need be.*
En cas de besoin. *In case of need.*
bétail *m. cattle.*
bête *f. animal, beast.*
bête *adj. stupid, silly.*
bêtise *f. stupidity.*
Quelle bêtise! *What nonsense! How silly! How stupid!*
C'est une bêtise. *It's silly (stupid).*
Ne perdez donc pas votre temps à ces bêtises. *Don't waste your time on that nonsense (those stupidities).*
J'ai fait une bêtise. *I did a stupid thing.*
béton *m. cement, concrete.*
BEURRE *m. butter.*
Donnez-moi du beurre, s'il vous plaît. *Please let me have some butter.*
bibelot *m. curio, knickknack, trinket.*
bibliothèque *f. library; bookcase.*
bicyclette *f. bicycle.*
Se promener à bicyclette. *Go bicycle riding, take a bicycle ride.*
bidon *m. can, tin.*
BIEN *well; very, very much; comfortable.*
Très bien! *Very well! Fine! Good!*
C'est bien tard. *It's very late.*
C'est bien ça! *That's right! That's it!*
Bien entendu. *Of course.*
Bien sûr! *Of course! Surely!*
Bien des fois. *Many times. Many a time. Often.*
Eh bien, quoi de neuf? *Well, what's new?*
C'est bien de votre part d'avoir fait ça. *It was very nice of you to do that. ("It's very nice of you to have done that.")*

Bien qu'il fasse mauvais temps, je sortirai tout de même. *Although the weather's bad, I'll go out anyway.*
Bien de l'inspiration. *Plenty of inspiration.*
C'était bien pire. *That was much worse.*
Je crois bien! *I should think so!*
On est bien ici. *It's nice here; one is comfortable here.*
Ou bien. *Or (else).*
Tout est bien qui finit bien. *All's well that ends well.*
Voudriez-vous bien? *Would you please?*
Vous feriez bien. *You'd be doing a good thing; it would be a good idea.*
bien *m. good, welfare; virtue; pl. property.*
Le bien et le mal. *Good and evil.*
Faire le bien. *To do good.*
Homme de bien. *Upright man.*
Biens de consommation. *Consumer goods.*
Biens d'équipement. *Capital goods.*
C'est pour votre bien. *It's for your own good.*
On dit beaucoup de bien de lui. *He's very highly spoken of.*
Ils ont des biens en France. *They have some property in France.*
C'est un marchand de biens. *He's a real-estate agent.*
bienfaisance *f. charity.*
bienfait *m. kindness, good turn; blessing.*
BIENTÔT *soon.*
Nous partons bientôt à la campagne. *We'll soon be leaving for the country. We're soon leaving for the country.*
A bientôt. *See you soon.*
bienveillance *f. kindness, benevolence.*
Il l'a fait par bienveillance. *He did it out of kindness.*
bienvenu (bienvenue *f.*) *noun and adj. welcome.*
Vous serez toujours le bienvenu ici. *You're always welcome (the welcome one) here.*
Ils sont bienvenus partout. *They're welcome everywhere.*
Soyez le bienvenu! *Welcome!*
bienvenue *f. welcome.*
Le président a dit quelques paroles de bienvenue. *The president said a few words of welcome.*
bière *f. beer.*
La bière blonde (brune). *Light (dark) beer.*
bière *f. coffin, casket.*
bijou *m.* (bijoux *pl.*) *jewel.*
bijouterie *f. jewelry.*
bijoutier *m. jeweler.*
bilan *m. balance sheet.*

bille *f. billiard ball; small ball; marble.*
Le stylo à bille. *Ball-point pen.*
BILLET *m. ticket (subway, train, theatre, etc.); bill.*
Quel est le prix des billets? *How much are (the) tickets?*
Un billet d'aller. *A one-way ticket.*
Un billet d'aller et retour. *A round-trip ticket.*
Voulez-vous me faire la monnaie de ce billet? *Can you change this bill for me? ("Will you give me change for this bill?")*
Payez-vous sur ce billet et rendez-moi la monnaie. *Take it out of this bill and let me have the change.*
Prendre un billet. *To buy a ticket.*
biographie *f. biography.*
biologie *f. biology.*
bis *Again! Encore!*
biscuit *m. biscuit.*
Des biscuits secs. *Crackers.*
bizarre *adj. strange, odd.*
C'est bizarre! *It's strange (queer, funny)!*
blague *f. tobacco pouch; joke, hoax.*
Blague à tabac. *Tobacco pouch.*
Quelle blague! *What a joke!*
Sans blague! *No kidding! No fooling!*
Blague à part. *All joking aside.*
blaguer *to joke.*
blâme *m. blame.*
Rejeter le blâme sur quelqu'un. *To throw the blame on someone.*
blâmer *to blame.*
blanc *m. blank; linen.*
Laissez quelques lignes en blanc. *Leave a few blank lines.*
De but en blanc. *Abruptly. Point-blank.*
Vous trouverez cela au rayon de blanc. *You'll find that in the linen department.*
Regarder quelqu'un dans le blanc des yeux. *To look someone straight in the eye.*
BLANC (blanche *f.*) *adj. white.*
Vous nous servirez une bouteille de vin blanc? *Will you give ("serve") us a bottle of white wine?*
Vous avez carte blanche. *You have a free hand. You have carte blanche.*
Elle a passé une nuit blanche. *She spent a sleepless night. She pulled an all-nighter.*
Le film en noir et blanc. *The black-and-white film.*
blanchir *to whiten.*
blanchissage *m. laundering, washing.*
Envoyez tout ça au blanchissage. *Send all that to the laundry.*
blanchisserie *f. hand laundry.*
La blanchisserie est au coin de la rue. *The laundry is on the corner ("of the street").*

blanchisseuse *f. laundress.*
blé *m. wheat.*
blessé *noun (m.) and adj. wounded.*
blesser *to wound, hurt.*
se blesser *to hurt oneself.*
blessure *f. wound.*
BLEU *noun (m.) and adj. blue.*
Bleu marine. *Navy blue.*
Des yeux bleus. *Blue eyes.*
La robe bleue. *The blue dress.*
bloc *m. block.*
En bloc. *In bulk.*
blond (blonde *f.*) *noun and adj. blond; light (beer).*
bloquer *to block; tighten.*
se blottir *to squat; nestle; snuggle down.*
Elle se blottit dans le fauteuil. *She snuggled down in the armchair.*
blouse *f. blouse; smock.*
bobard *m. lie, fib.*
Ne me racontez pas de bobards (*fam.*) *Tell it to the Marines! Tell it to your grandmother! You expect me to believe that!*
bobine *f. spool, reel.*
bocal *m. (bocaux pl.) glass jar.*
BOEUF *m. (boeufs pl.) ox; beef.*
Vous mettez la charrue devant les boeufs. *You're putting the cart before the horse. ("You're putting the plow before the oxen.")*
Du boeuf à la mode. *Pot roast.*
Donnez-moi un filet de boeuf. *Give me a steak tenderloin.*
BOIRE *to drink.*
Que voulez-vous boire? *What would you like (to have) to drink?*
Versez-moi à boire. *Pour me a drink.*
On sert à boire et à manger. *Food and drinks are served here.*
Buvons à votre santé. *Let's drink to your health.*
bois *m. wood; woods.*
Bois de chauffage. *Firewood.*
Allons faire un tour dans le bois. *Let's go for a walk in the woods.*
boisson *f. drink.*
C'est une boisson rafraîchissante. *It's a refreshing drink.*
Un débit de boissons. *A liquor store.*
boîte *f. box.*
Je lui ai envoyé une boîte de chocolats. *I sent him a box of chocolates.*
Des boîtes de conserves. *(Tin) cans.*
Boîte à chapeau. *Hatbox.*
Boîte d'accus. *f. Storage battery.*
N'oubliez pas de mettre la lettre dans la boîte (aux lettres). *Don't forget to put the letter in the mailbox.*

Boîte de nuit. *Nightclub.*

boiter *to limp, be lame.*

bol *m. bowl, basin.*

bombarder *to bomb, shell.*

bombe *f. bomb.*

Faire la bombe. *To go on a spree. To paint the town red.*

bon *m. bond; premium; order, voucher.*

Bon de poste. *Money order.*

Bon du Trésor. *Treasury bond.*

Bon de caisse. *Cash voucher.*

Bon de livraison. *Delivery order.*

Après cent francs d'achat, vous recevrez un bon. *If you buy a hundred francs worth of merchandise you get a premium.*

BON (bonne *f.*) *adj. good.*

Est-ce bon à manger? *Is this good to eat?*

Ça sent bon. *It smells nice. It has a nice smell.*

C'est bon. 1. *That's good (fine).* 2. *Enough said! That will do!*

Il n'est bon à rien. *He's good-for-nothing.*

Il a une bonne nature. *He's good-natured.*

A quoi bon? *What's the use? What for? What's the good of it?*

C'est un bon garçon. *He's a decent (nice) fellow.*

Bonne année! *Happy New Year!*

Bon voyage! *Bon voyage! Pleasant journey!*

Ça ne me dit rien de bon. *I don't think anything good will come of it. It looks rather bad.*

Il fait bon ici. *It's nice (comfortable) here.*

De bonne heure. *Early.*

Voici quelque chose de bon marché. *Here's something cheap.*

Bonne chance! *Good luck!*

Bon nombre de. *A number of, a good many.*

Bon séjour! *Have a pleasant stay!*

Le bon chemin (sens). *The right way, road (direction).*

bonbon *m. candy.*

bond *m. bound, leap.*

bondé *adj. crowded, packed.*

bondir *to bound, leap.*

Bondir d'indignation. *To be filled with indignation.*

BONHEUR *m. happiness.*

Par bonheur. *Luckily.*

Porter bonheur. *To bring luck.*

Au petit bonheur. *In a happy-go-lucky way. In a carefree way.*

boniment *m. smooth talk; patter.*

Faire le boniment. *To give a sales talk.*

BONJOUR *m. Good morning. Good afternoon. Good day. Hello.*

bonne *f. maid.*

bonnet *m. cap.*

BONSOIR *m. Good evening. Good night.*

BONTÉ *f. goodness, kindness.*

Ayez la bonté de me faire savoir. *Please let me know. ("Have the goodness to . . .")*

bord *m. edge, border; shore.*

Le bord d'un verre. *The rim of a glass.*

Il est tombé par-dessus bord. *He fell overboard.*

Aller au bord de la mer. *To go to the seashore.*

A bord. *On board (ship).*

Aux bords du Rhône. *On the banks of the Rhone.*

Le dessin du bord. *Border design.*

borne *f. limit, boundary.*

Cela dépasse toutes les bornes! *That's the limit!*

bosse *f. bump.*

bossu *noun (m.) and adj.* (bossue *f.*) *hunchback.*

botte *f. boot.*

Bottin *m. French telephone directory.*

BOUCHE *f. mouth; entrance.*

Il est resté bouche bée. *He stood gaping ("with his mouth wide open").*

Où est la bouche de métro la plus proche? *Where is the nearest subway entrance?*

bouchée *f. mouthful.*

boucher *m.* (bouchère *f.*) *butcher.*

boucher *to stop, cork; block up.*

boucherie *f. butcher shop.*

bouchon *m. cork.*

boucle *f. buckle; curl.*

Boucles d'oreilles. *Earrings.*

bouder *to sulk.*

boue *f. mud, dirt.*

bouger *to move, stir.*

Ne bougez pas! *Don't move! Don't budge!*

bougie *f. candle; spark plug.*

bouillir *to boil.*

Faites bouillir l'eau. *Boil the water.*

L'eau a-t-elle bouilli? *Has the water boiled?*

Commencer à bouillir. *To come to a boil.*

bouillon *m. bubble; bouillon.*

Un bouillon de légumes. *Vegetable broth.*

boulangerie *f. bakery.*

boule *f. ball.*

boulevard *m. boulevard.*

bouleverser *to overthrow, upset.*

Il a été bouleversé par les évènements. *The events upset him.*

bouquet *m. cluster, bunch; bouquet.*

Ça, c'est le bouquet *(fam.)*! *That tops everything! That's the limit!*

bouquiniste *m. secondhand bookseller.*

bourdonnement *m. humming, buzzing; dial tone (telephone).*

bourgeois *noun and adj. middle-class, bourgeois.*

Cuisine bourgeoise. *Good plain cooking.*

bourgeoisie *f. middle class.*
bourse *f. purse; stock exchange.*
bousculer *to upset; hustle.*
BOUT *m. end, extremity.*
D'un bout à l'autre. *From beginning to end.*
("From one end to the other.")
Il est à bout de patience. *He's at the end of his patience. His patience is exhausted.*
Au bout d'une heure. *After an hour. In an hour. ("At the end of an hour.")*
Joindre les deux bouts. *To make ends meet.*
Au bout du compte. *After all. In the end.*
Savoir sur le bout du doigt. *To have at one's fingertips.*
A tout bout de champ. *Frequently. Repeatedly.*
bouteille *f. bottle.*
boutique *f. store, shop.*
bouton *m. button; knob.*
Voulez-vous me recoudre ce bouton? *Will you please sew this button on (for me)?*
Ce bouton vient de sauter. *This button has just come off.*
Veston à deux boutons. *Two-button jacket.*
Où sont mes boutons de manchettes? *Where are my cuff links?*
Tournez le bouton, s.v.p. (s'il vous plaît). *Please turn the knob.*
boutonner *to button.*
boutonnière *f. buttonhole.*
bracelet *m. bracelet.*
branche *f. branch.*
branler *to shake.*
BRAS *m. arm.*
Accueillir à bras ouverts. *To receive with open arms.*
Ils marchaient bras dessus, bras dessous. *They walked arm-in-arm.*
Avoir quelque chose sur les bras. *To have something on one's hands.*
brave *adj. (following noun) brave; (before noun) honest, good.*
C'est un homme brave. *He's a brave man.*
C'est un brave garçon. *He's a good fellow.*
bravo *m. bravo; applause.*
brèche *f. breach, gap.*
BREF (brève *f.*) *adj. brief, short.*
Il a la parole brève. *He always gives curt answers.*
Répondre d'un ton bref. *To give a curt answer.*
En bref. *In brief. In short.*
Il a dû partir à bref délai. *He had to leave on short notice.*
brevet *m. patent; certificate.*
bridge *m. bridge (cards).*
Jouer au bridge. *To play bridge.*
brillant *adj. brilliant, shiny.*
briller *to shine, glitter.*

Tout ce qui brille n'est pas or. *All that glitters is not gold.*
brin *m. blade of grass; a little bit.*
Un brin d'herbe. *A blade of grass.*
Faire un brin de causette. *To have a little chat.*
brique *f. brick.*
brise *f. breeze.*
briser *to break (something).*
se briser *to break into pieces, be broken into pieces.*
broche *f. brooch.*
brochure *f. pamphlet, brochure.*
broder *to embroider.*
bronze *m. bronze.*
brosse *f. brush.*
La brosse du peintre. *Paintbrush.*
La brosse à chaussures. *Shoebrush.*
La brosse à cheveux. *Hairbrush.*
La brosse à habits. *Clothesbrush.*
Donnez un coup de brosse à mon pardessus. *Brush my coat.*
brosser *to brush.*
brouillard *m. fog.*
Il fait du brouillard. *It's foggy (out).*
brouille *f. quarrel.*
se brouiller *to quarrel.*
brouillon *m. rough draft.*
BRUIT *m. noise; rumor.*
Le bruit m'a empêché de dormir. *The noise kept me from sleeping.*
En ville le bruit court qu'ils vont partir. *There's a rumor in the city that they're going to leave.*
Beaucoup de bruit pour rien. *Much ado about nothing.*
BRÛLER *to burn.*
se brûler *to burn.*
Vous vous brûlerez les doigts. *You'll burn your fingers.*
BRUN *noun (m.) and adj.* (brune *f.*) *brown; dark (beer).*
brusque *adj. sudden, abrupt.*
brusquement *bluntly; suddenly.*
Brusquement, ils l'aperçurent. *Suddenly, they saw him.*
brut *adj. raw; gross.*
Matière brute. *Raw material.*
Dix pour-cent brut. *Ten percent gross.*
brutal (brutaux *pl.*) *adj. brutal, rough, rude.*
brute *f. rough person, brute.*
Quelle brute! *What a beast!*
bu *drunk (p.p. of* boire).
bûche *f. log.*
budget *m. budget.*
buffet *m. sideboard; refreshment room.*
Vous pouvez avoir quelque chose à manger au buffet de la gare. *You can get something to eat in the station*

restaurant *("in the refreshment room of the station").*

buisson *m. bush.*

bulle *f. bubble.*

bulletin *m. bulletin.*

Suivant le bulletin météorologique, il pleuvra demain. *According to the weather report, it will rain tomorrow.*

C'est le bulletin mensuel de notre association. *It's the monthly bulletin of our association.*

Le bulletin de vote. *Ballot.*

BUREAU *m. office; desk.*

A partir de demain, le bureau ferme à cinq heures. *Beginning tomorrow, the office will close at five.*

Pouvez-vous me dire où se trouve le bureau des renseignements? *Can you tell me where the information bureau is?*

Envoyez ceci à l'adresse de mon bureau. *Send this to my business address.*

Le bureau de poste se trouve à côté de la gare. *The post office is next to the railroad station.*

Le bureau de tabac est au coin de la rue. *The tobacco store is on the corner ("of the street").*

Ramassez tous ces papiers qui traînent sur votre bureau. *Gather up the papers that are scattered on your desk.*

buste *m. bust.*

but *m. goal, purpose.*

Je ne puis deviner son but. *I can't guess (make out) his purpose (aim).*

Il est allé droit au but. *He went straight to the point.*

buvard *m. blotting paper, blotter.*

C

ÇA *(contraction of* cela*) that.*

C'est ça! *That's it! That's right!*

Qu'est-ce que c'est que ça? *What's that?*

C'est toujours ça! *That's so much to the good! At least we have that!*

Ça ne fait rien. *That doesn't matter. That's unimportant.*

Comment vont les affaires?—Comme ci, comme ça. *How are things? (How's business?)—So, so.*

Ça et là. *Here and there.*

Ça ne presse pas. *There's no hurry.*

Ça va. *It's all right, O.K.; that's enough.*

Ça y est! *That's it!*

C'est ça. *That's it, that's right.*

cabine *f. cabin; booth.*

Une cabine de première classe. *First-class cabin (on a ship).*

Où se trouvent les cabines téléphoniques? *Where are the telephone booths?*

cabinet *m. closet, small room; cabinet.*

Ce cabinet sert de débarras. *This closet is used for storage. This is a storage closet.*

Il est dans son cabinet de travail. *He's in his study.*

Il a un cabinet d'avocat. *He's an attorney.*

Le docteur est dans son cabinet. *The doctor is in his office.*

Les cabinets sont au fond du couloir. *The washrooms are at the end of the hall.*

Le nouveau cabinet a été formé. *The new cabinet has just been formed.*

câble *m. cable.*

câbler *to cable.*

cacher *to hide.*

se cacher *to hide oneself.*

cachet *m. seal, stamp; pill; style.*

Cachet d'oblitération. *Postmark.*

Avez-vous un cachet d'aspirine? *Do you have an aspirin?*

Cela a beaucoup de cachet. *That's quite stylish.*

cachette *f. hiding place.*

En cachette. *Secretly.*

cadavre *m. corpse; cadaver.*

cadeau (cadeaux *pl.*) *present, gift.*

cadet *m.* (cadette *f.*) *noun and adj. younger, youngest, junior.*

Il est le cadet. *He's the youngest.*

Ma fille cadette. *My youngest daughter.*

C'est le cadet de mes soucis. *That's the least of my worries.*

cadre *m. frame; company executive.*

cadre (pour tableaux). *(Picture) frame.*

cafard *m. cockroach; the blues (slang).*

CAFÉ *m. coffee; café.*

Un café nature. *Black coffee.*

Donnez-moi un café au lait. *Give me a coffee with milk.*

Allons au café. *Let's go to the café.*

Garçon de café. *Waiter.*

cafetière *f. coffeepot.*

cage *f. cage.*

cahier *m. notebook.*

caillou *m.* (cailloux *pl.*) *pebble.*

caisse *f. box; crate; cash register; cash-window, teller (in a bank), pay-office.*

J'ai mis mon argent à la caisse d'épargne. *I put my money in the savings bank.*

La caisse ferme à trois heures. *The pay-office (cash-window) closes at three p.m.*

caissier (caissière *f.*) *cashier; teller (bank).*

cajoler *to cajole.*

calamité f. calamity.

calcul m. calculation, arithmetic.

calculer to calculate.

calendrier m. calendar.

câlin noun (m.) and adj. (câline f.) caressing, cuddly.

câliner to cajole; to cuddle.

calmant noun (m.) and adj. (calmante f.) sedative; calming, soothing.

CALME noun (m.) and adj. calm, quiet, mild.

Du calme! Be quiet

calmer to calm, relieve.

se calmer to become calm, quiet down.

Calmez-vous. Calm down. Compose yourself.

La tempête s'est calmée. The storm has blown over.

calomnie f. calumny, slander.

calomnier to slander.

camarade m. friend, pal.

C'est un bon camarade. He's a good friend. He's a pal.

Un camarade d'école. A schoolmate.

cambrioleur m. burglar, thief.

camelote f. trash, junk.

caméra f. movie camera.

camion m. truck.

camp m. camp.

CAMPAGNE f. country; field; campaign.

Nous habitons la campagne à présent. We live in the country now.

Mener une campagne contre quelqu'un. To conduct a campaign against someone.

camper to camp.

canadien (canadienne f.) noun and adj. Canadian.

canal m. (canaux pl.) canal.

canapé m. sofa; canapé.

canard m. duck; hoax.

Il fait un froid de canard. It's bitter cold.

canari m. canary.

cancer m. cancer.

candeur f. candor.

candidat m. candidate, examinee.

candidature f. candidacy.

candide adj. candid.

caniche m. poodle.

canif m. penknife.

canne f. stick, cane.

canon m. gun, cannon, barrel.

canot m. canoe, boat, rowboat.

caoutchouc m. rubber; rubber band.

Une balle en caoutchouc. A rubber ball.

Mettez vos caoutchoucs. Put on your rubbers.

cap m. cape (geog.).

CAPABLE adj. capable, able, qualified.

Pensez-vous qu'il soit capable de faire le travail? Do you think he's able to do the job?

Il en est bien capable! He's very capable of (doing) it! I wouldn't be surprised if he did it!

capacité f. capacity.

cape f. cape (cloak).

capitaine m. captain.

capital m. (capitaux pl.) capital.

CAPITAL (capitaux pl.) adj. main, chief, principal, essential.

Ce que je vous dis là est capital! What I'm telling you now is essential (important).

Peine capitale. Capital punishment.

capitale f. capital (of a country).

capitulation f. capitulation.

capituler to capitulate, surrender.

caprice m. caprice, whim.

Avoir des caprices. To be fickle.

capricieux (capricieuse f.) adj. capricious.

captif (captive f.) noun and adj. captive.

capturer to capture, seize.

CAR for, because, as.

CARACTÈRE m. character.

caractéristique adj. characteristic.

carafe f. jug.

caramel m. caramel.

cardinal m. (cardinaux pl.) cardinal.

cardinal (cardinaux pl.) adj. chief, cardinal.

Points cardinaux. Cardinal points.

caresse f. caress, endearment.

caresser to caress; cherish.

carié adj. decayed.

carnet m. small notebook; book of tickets; customs permit (for car).

Carnet d'adresses. Address book.

Carnet de chèques. Checkbook.

carotte f. carrot.

carpe f. carp.

Il est muet comme une carpe. He doesn't open his mouth. ("He's as mute as a carp.")

carré m. square.

carré adj. square.

carreau m. square; paving tile; windowpane; diamond (cards).

carrefour m. crossroads, intersection.

carrément squarely, flatly.

carrière f. career; track, ground.

Soldat de carrière. Professional (regular) soldier.

Donner libre carrière à son imagination. To give free rein to one's fancy.

carrosse m. coach, carriage.

carrousel m. merry-go-round.

carrure f. breadth.

Il a une belle carrure. He's well-built.

CARTE f. card; menu; map.

C'est une bonne carte dans son jeu. That's one of his strongest cards.

Donnez-moi la carte. *May I have the menu, please.*

Une carte postale. *A postcard.*

Des cartes de visite. *Calling cards.*

Je me suis fait tirer les cartes hier soir. *Last night I had my fortune told.*

On lui a donné carte blanche. *He was given carte blanche. They gave him a free hand.*

Jouer aux cartes. *To play cards.*

La carte d'invitation. *(Printed) invitation.*

La carte routière. *Road map.*

carton *m. cardboard.*

cartouche *f. cartridge.*

CAS *m. case, event, occasion.*

Malheureusement ce n'est pas toujours le cas. *Unfortunately that isn't always the case.*

Le cas échéant. *If that should be the case.*

C'est le cas ou jamais de le faire. *It must be done now or never.*

C'est bien le cas de le dire. *One may indeed say so.*

En tout cas. *At all events. In any case.*

En aucun cas. *On no account.*

On fait grand cas de lui. *He's highly thought of.*

Je fais peu de cas de son opinion. *I don't value his opinion very much.*

En cas d'urgence. *In case of (an) emergency.*

En ce cas-là. *In that case.*

cascade *f. cascade, waterfall.*

caserne *f. barracks.*

casier *m. registry, records, rack, compartment.*

cassé *adj. broken.*

CASSER *to break; annul; dismiss.*

Ça ne casse rien. *It's nothing special.*

se casser *to break.*

Il s'est cassé le bras. *He broke his arm.*

casserole *f. pan.*

cassette *f. casket, case; cassette tape.*

catalogue *m. catalogue.*

catastrophe *f. catastrophe, accident.*

catégorie *f. category.*

catégorique *adj. categorical, clear, explicit.*

Un refus catégorique. *A flat refusal.*

cathédrale *f. cathedral.*

catholique *noun and adj. Catholic, catholic.*

cauchemar *m. nightmare.*

CAUSE *f. cause, motive; lawsuit, case.*

Il n'y a point d'effet sans cause. *There is no effect without a cause.*

La partie a été reportée à cause de la pluie. *The game was postponed on account of rain.*

Et pour cause! *For a very good reason! With good reason!*

Mettre en cause la probité de quelqu'un. *To question someone's honesty.*

Questions hors de cause. *Irrelevant questions.*

J'ai obtenu gain de cause. *I won my case.*

Connaissez-vous tous les faits de la cause? *Do you know the facts of the case?*

CAUSER *to cause.*

CAUSER *to talk, converse.*

On en cause. *People are talking about it.*

causerie *f. talk; informal lecture.*

caution *f. bail; security.*

cave *f. cellar, cave.*

cavité *f. cavity.*

CE (cet *before vowels and "mute"* h; cette *f.,* ces *pl.*) *adj. this, that, these, those.*

J'ai été en retard ce matin. *I was late this morning.*

Prenez ce verre-ci. *Take this glass.*

C'est ce livre-là. *It's that book.*

Cette situation est gênante. *This situation is embarrassing.*

Un de ces jours. *One of these days.*

CE (c' *before vowels*) *pron. he, she, it, this, that.*

Ce n'est pas vrai. *It's (that's) not true.*

Est-ce assez? *Is that enough?*

C'est bien. *Good.*

C'est moi. *It's I (me).*

A ce qu'il me semble. *As it seems to me.*

Voici ce dont il s'agit. *Here's the point.*

Ce qu'il a grandi! *How he's grown!*

Sur ce, il s'en alla. *Thereupon he left.*

Il tient à ce que vous veniez. *He insists on your coming.*

Pour ce qui est de cela. *For that matter.*

Qu'est-ce que c'est? *What is it?*

CECI *this.*

Que veut dire ceci? *What does this mean?*

Ecoutez bien ceci. *Listen to this.*

céder *to yield, give in.*

ceindre *to gird; encircle.*

ceinture *f. belt.*

CELA *that.*

Cela n'a pas d'importance. *That doesn't matter. That's not important.*

C'est pour cela que je viens. *That's why I've come.*

C'est bien cela. *That's right. That's it.*

Cela ne vous regarde pas. *That's no business of yours.*

célèbre *adj. famous.*

célébrer *to celebrate, praise; to practice (religion).*

On célèbre tous les cultes. *All religions are practiced.*

célibataire *m. and f. bachelor, single woman; adj. single, unmarried.*

cellule *f. cell*

CELUI (celle *f.,* ceux *m. pl.,* celles *f. pl.*) *that one; those.*

Voilà celui que je préfère. *There's the one I prefer.*

Celle-ci me paraît meilleure. *This one seems better to me.*

Ceux-ci sont plus cher. *These are more expensive.*

Préféreriez-vous celui-ci? *Would you prefer this one?*

Celui-ci est meilleur que celui-là. *This one is better than that one.*

Je n'aime ni celui-ci ni celui-là. *I don't like either one. ("I don't like this one or that one.")*

cendre *f. ash, ashes.*

cendrier *m. ashtray.*

censé *adj. supposed, reputed.*

Je ne suis pas censé le savoir. *I'm not supposed to know it.*

Nul n'est censé ignorer la loi. *Ignorance of the law is no excuse. ("No one is supposed to be ignorant of the law.")*

censure *f. censorship.*

CENT *noun (m.) and adj. hundred.*

Il a cent fois raison. *He's absolutely right.*

Cinq cents francs. *Five hundred francs.*

cent *m. cent ($^1/_{100}$ euro).*

centaine *f. about a hundred.*

centième *noun and adj. hundredth.*

centimètre *m. centimeter (0.394 inch).*

central *(centraux pl.) adj. central.*

centrale *f. station.*

Centrale électrique. *Powerhouse.*

CENTRE *m. center.*

Le centre de la France. *The center of France.*

Centre de villégiature. *Holiday resort.*

Lyon est un centre industriel et commercial. *Lyons is an industrial and commercial center.*

Au centre. *In the center.*

CEPENDANT *nevertheless, however.*

Cependant j'aurais bien voulu y aller. *Nevertheless I should like to have gone there. ("Nevertheless I would have wished to go there.")*

CERCLE *m. circle; club.*

Cercle vicieux. *Vicious circle.*

Cercle littéraire. *Literary circle. Literary club.*

Aller au cercle. *To go to the club.*

cercueil *m. coffin.*

cérémonie *f. ceremony.*

Ne faites donc pas de cérémonies. *Don't make such a fuss. Don't stand so much on ceremony.*

cérémonieux *(cérémonieuse f.) adj. ceremonious, formal.*

cerf *m. deer.*

cerise *f. cherry.*

cerner *to encircle, close in upon.*

Avoir les yeux cernés. *To have rings under one's eyes.*

CERTAIN *adj. certain, sure.*

De cela, j'en suis certain. *I'm certain of that.*

Je tiens ces renseignements pour certains. *I'm sure of this information. ("I consider this information to be certain.")*

C'est un homme d'un certain âge. *He's middle-aged.*

Un certain nombre de personnes. *A certain number of persons.*

C'est un indice certain. *It is a sure indication.*

Ce qu'il y a de certain, c'est que . . . *One thing is certain, namely . . . What is certain is that . . .*

certainement *certainly.*

Viendrez-vous?—Mais certainement. *Will you come?—Certainly.*

certains *certain people.*

Certains le disent. *Some say so. Certain people say so.*

certificat *m. certificate.*

certifier *to certify, attest.*

certitude *f. certainty.*

J'en ai la certitude. *I'm sure of it.*

cerveau *m. (cerveaux pl.) brain.*

J'ai un rhume de cerveau. *I have a head cold.*

cervelle *f. brain.*

Il se creuse la cervelle. *He's racking his brains.*

cesse *f. ceasing; respite.*

Sans cesse. *Ceaselessly. Continually. Constantly.*

Il le répète sans cesse. *He keeps repeating it.*

CESSER *to cease, stop.*

La pluie a cessé. *The rain (has) stopped. It's stopped raining.*

Ce chien ne cesse d'aboyer. *This dog doesn't stop barking. This dog keeps on barking.*

Cessez de crier. *Stop shouting.*

Cessez le feu! *Cease fire!*

C'EST-À-DIRE *that is to say.*

CET *See ce.*

Ceux *See celui.*

CHACUN *adj. and pron. each, each one.*

Chacun de nous pensait de même. *Each one of us thought the same.*

Cinq francs chacun. *Five francs each. Five francs apiece.*

Chacun pour soi. *Everyone for himself.*

Chacun (à) son goût. *Everyone to his taste.*

Chacun (à) son tour. *Everyone in his turn.*

chagrin *m. grief, sorrow.*
  Avoir du chagrin. *To be sad.*
chagriner *to grieve, cause grief.*
se chagriner *to grieve, worry about.*
chahut *m. row, racket.*
chahuter *to make a lot of noise.*
chaine *f. chain; channel (television).*
CHAIR *f. flesh.*
chaire *f. chair (in a university); pulpit.*
CHAISE *f. chair.*
  Chaise-longue. *Chaise-longue. Lounging chair.*
chaland *m. barge.*
chalet *m. country cottage.*
CHALEUR *f. heat.*
  Par une chaleur écrasante. *In stifling heat.*
chaleureux (chaleureuse *f.*) *adj. warm; ardent.*
  Un accueil chaleureux. *A hearty welcome.*
se chamailler *to quarrel, bicker.*
chambarder *to upset, disturb.*
CHAMBRE *f. room; bedroom.*
  La chambre des machines. *The engine room.*
  Cette chambre a besoin d'être aérée. *This room needs airing.*
  Faites la chambre, s'il vous plaît. *Will you please clean the room?*
  Chambre sur la rue. *Room facing the front.*
  Chambre sur la cour. *Room facing the back (rear).*
  Chambre à louer. *Room to let.*
  Chambre d'ami. *Spare (bed) room. Guest room.*
  Chambre d'enfants. *Nursery.*
  Musique de chambre. *Chamber music.*
  La Chambre des Députés. *The Chamber of Deputies.*
chameau *m.* (chameaux *pl.*) *camel.*
chamois *m. chamois.*
  Peau de chamois. *Chamois (cloth).*
CHAMP *m. field.*
  Il vient d'acheter un champ adjacent au mien. *He just bought a field next to mine.*
  Champ de blé. *Field of wheat.*
  Le champ est libre, allez-y! *The coast is clear. Go ahead!*
  Nous y sommes allés sur-le-champ. *We went there at once (right away).*
  A tout bout de champ. *Repeatedly.*
  Champ de courses. *Race track.*
  Champ de bataille. *Battlefield.*
champagne *m. champagne.*
champêtre *adj. rural, rustic.*
champignon *m. mushroom.*
champion *m.* (championne *f.*) *champion.*
championnat *m. championship.*
CHANCE *f. luck.*
  Je n'ai pas de chance. *I don't have any luck.*

Si vous réussissez vous aurez de la chance. *If you succeed you'll be lucky.*
Il a toutes les chances pour lui. *The odds are in his favor.*
La chance a tourné. *The tables are turned.*
Je vais courir la chance. *I'll take the chance.*
Elle a des chances d'arriver. *She has good chances of succeeding.*
Voyez ce que c'est que la chance! *That's what you call luck!*
Bonne chance! *Good luck!*
Pas de chance! *No luck! Rotten luck!*
Quelle chance! *What luck! What a stroke of luck!*
chancelant *adj. staggering, unsteady.*
  Santé chancelante. *Delicate health.*
chanceler *to stagger, be unsteady.*
  Chanceler dans sa résolution. *To waver in one's resolution.*
chanceux (chanceuse *f.*) *adj. lucky.*
  C'est un hasard chanceux. *It's a stroke of luck.*
chandelle *f. candle.*
  Brûler la chandelle par les deux bouts. *To burn the candle at both ends.*
  Voir trente-six chandelles. *To see stars.*
  Je vous dois une fière chandelle (*fam.*). *I ought to be very grateful to you.*
CHANGE *m. exchange.*
  Vous aurez des francs contre vos dollars au bureau de change. *You can get your dollars changed into francs at an exchange office.*
  Agent de change. *Stockbroker.*
  Quel est le cours du change aujourd'hui? *What is the rate of exchange today?*
  Gagner au change. *To gain on the exchange.*
  Le guichet de change. *(Money) exchange window.*
changeant *adj. changing, variable.*
  D'humeur changeante. *Fitful.*
CHANGEMENT *m. change.*
  Changement de propriétaire. *Under new management. ("Change of ownership.")*
  Il vous faudrait un changement d'air. *You need a change.*
  La situation est sans changement. *The situation remains unchanged.*
  Changement de vitesse. *Gearshift.*
CHANGER *to change.*
  Ça change tout. *That alters matters. That changes everything.*
  Changez les draps. *Change the sheets.*
  Il a changé de nom. *He changed his name.*
  Le temps va changer. *The weather's changing.*
  Changeons de conversation. *Let's change the subject.*

Pour changer. *For a change.*

Plus ça change plus c'est la même chose. *The more things change, the more they're the same.*

On change de train pour . . . *Change here for . . .*

Faire changer l'huile. *To have the oil changed.*

se changer *to change, to change one's clothes.*

Nous devons nous changer pour le dîner. *We have to change for dinner.*

CHANSON *f. song.*

C'est toujours la même chanson. *It's always the same old story.*

chant *m. song, singing.*

chantage *m. blackmail.*

CHANTER *to sing.*

Qu'est-ce que vous me chantez *(fam.)*? *What sort of a story are you telling me?*

Je le ferai si ça me chante *(fam.)*. *I'll do it if it suits me.*

chanteur *m.* (chanteuse *f.*) *singer.*

chantier *m. yard.*

Chantier de construction. *Shipyard.*

Chantier de bois. *Lumberyard.*

Mettre un bateau en chantier. *To lay the keel of a ship.*

Mettre un bâtiment en chantier. *To put up the framework of a building.*

Avoir un ouvrage sur le chantier. *To have a piece of work in hand. To have some work in progress.*

chantonner *to hum.*

chantre *m. cantor.*

chanvre *m. hemp.*

chaos *m. chaos, confusion.*

CHAPEAU *m.* (chapeaux *pl.*) *hat.*

Oter (enlever) son chapeau. *To take one's hat off.*

chapelet *m. rosary.*

chapelle *f. chapel.*

chaperon *m. hood; chaperon.*

CHAPITRE *m. chapter.*

CHAQUE *adj. each, every.*

La situation empire chaque jour. *The situation is getting (growing) worse every day.*

Chaque chose en son temps. *There's a time for everything. ("Everything in its time.")*

Chaque chose à sa place. *Everything has its place.*

char *m. chariot, wagon.*

Char d'assaut. *Tank.*

charade *f. charade.*

charbon *m. charcoal.*

Etre sur des charbons ardents. *To be on pins and needles.*

charcuterie *f. delicatessen.*

chardon *m. thistle.*

CHARGE *f. charge; burden; position; extras (rent).*

Il est à ma charge. *I'm supporting him.*

Les devoirs de ma charge. *The duties of my position.*

Le loyer est de dix mille francs plus les charges. *The rent is 10,000 francs plus extras.*

Il est revenu à la charge. *He tried again. He made another attempt.*

Femme de charge. *Housekeeper.*

Entrer en charge. *To take up one's duties.*

Les témoins à charge. *The witnesses for the prosecution.*

La prise en charge. *Taking over (a rented car).*

chargé *m. a person entrusted with certain duties (functions, etc.).*

Le chargé d'affaires. *The chargé d'affaires.*

chargement *m. lading, loading.*

CHARGER *to load, increase; entrust; charge.*

Charger une voiture de malles. *To load a truck with trunks.*

Cela charge mon budget. *That increases my expenses.*

On m'a chargé de cette mission. *I have been entrusted with this mission.*

Je vous charge de me remplacer. *I'd like you to take my place. I choose you as my substitute.*

Il est chargé de mes intérêts. *He's taking care of my interests. I've entrusted my interests to him.*

se charger *to undertake, to take upon oneself.*

Je m'en charge. *I take it upon myself (to do it). I'll undertake it (to do it). I'll take charge of it. I'll make it my business (to do it).*

chariot *m. wagon.*

charitable *adj. charitable, kind.*

charité *f. charity, alms.*

charmant *adj. charming.*

charme *m. charm.*

charmer *to charm, delight.*

charnière *f. hinge.*

charnu *adj. fleshy, plump.*

charrette *f. cart.*

charrier *to cart, transport.*

charrue *f. plough, plow.*

charte *f. charter.*

chasse *f. hunting; pursuit.*

chasser *to chase, hunt; discharge.*

chasseur *m. hunter; bellboy.*

châssis *m. frame.*

CHAT *m.* (chatte *f.*) *cat.*

Ils s'accordent comme chien et chat. *They fight like cats and dogs.*

Il n'y avait pas un chat. *There wasn't a living creature there.*

Je donne ma langue au chat. *Cat's got my tongue.*

J'ai d'autres chats à fouetter. *I have other fish to fry.*

Les enfants jouent à chat perché. *The children are playing tag.*

Ne réveillez pas le chat qui dort. *Let sleeping dogs lie.*

La nuit tous les chats sont gris. *All cats are gray in the dark.*

châtaigne *f. chestnut.*

châtain *adj. brown (of hair).*

Elle a les cheveux châtains. *She has brown hair.*

château *m.* (châteaux *pl.*) *castle, manor.*

châtier *to punish.*

Qui aime bien châtie bien. *Spare the rod and spoil the child.*

châtiment *m. punishment.*

chatouiller *to tickle.*

chatouilleux (chatouilleuse *f.*) *adj. ticklish.*

CHAUD *m. heat.*

Il ne craint ni le chaud ni le froid. *He's afraid of nothing. ("He fears neither heat nor cold.")*

"Tenir au chaud." *"Keep in a warm place."*

CHAUD *adj. warm, hot.*

Faites attention, c'est chaud. *Be careful, it's hot.*

Eau chaude. *Hot water.*

Une boisson chaude. *A warm drink.*

J'ai chaud. *I'm warm.*

Cela ne me fait ni froid ni chaud. *It's all the same to me. It makes no difference to me.*

Pleurer à chaudes larmes. *To weep bitterly.*

Il fait chaud. *The weather is warm, hot.*

chaudière *f. boiler.*

chauffage *m. heating.*

Chauffage central. *Central heating.*

chauffer *to warm, heat.*

se chauffer *to warm oneself, get warm.*

chauffeur *m. chauffeur.*

chaussée *f. highway; embankment.*

Rez-de-chaussée. *Ground floor.*

chausser *to put on shoes.*

Du combien chaussez-vous? *What size shoe do you wear?*

chaussette *f. sock.*

CHAUSSURE *f. shoe.*

Une paire de chaussures. *A pair of shoes.*

Un magasin de chaussures. *A shoe store.*

Quelle est la pointure de vos chaussures? *What size shoe do you wear?*

Nettoyez mes chaussures, s'il vous plaît. *Will you please shine my shoes?*

chauve *adj. bald.*

chaux *f. lime.*

chavirer *to capsize, turn upside down.*

CHEF *m. manager, director, chief, leader, head.*

Le chef de bureau. *The chief clerk.*

Ingénieur en chef. *Chief engineer.*

Le chef d'orchestre. *The orchestra leader. The conductor.*

Chef de gare. *Stationmaster.*

C'est un chef-d'oeuvre. *It's a masterpiece.*

Chef d'équipe. *Captain of a team.*

Il l'a fait de son propre chef. *He did it on his own authority.*

CHEMIN *m. way, road.*

Ce chemin va à la ville. *That road leads to the town.*

Comment avez-vous trouvé votre chemin par la ville? *How did you find your way about the town (around town)?*

Il a fait son chemin. *He's succeeded in life. He's made his way in the world.*

Il est toujours dans mon chemin. *He's always in my way.*

L'affaire est en bon chemin. *The matter is progressing nicely.*

En chemin de fer. *By train.*

Billet de chemin de fer. *Railroad ticket.*

Le bon chemin. *The right way.*

Envoyer par chemin de fer. *To send by railway.*

Voyager en chemin de fer. *To travel by train.*

Perdre son chemin. *To lose one's way, get lost.*

Rebrousser (refaire le) chemin. *To retrace one's steps, turn back, start over again.*

cheminée *f. chimney, fireplace.*

cheminer *to tramp, walk.*

CHEMISE *f. shirt; folder (for papers).*

Chemise de nuit. *Nightgown.*

chemisier *m. woman's (tailored) blouse.*

chêne *m. oak.*

chenille *f. caterpillar.*

CHÈQUE *m. check.*

Avez-vous endossé le chèque? *Did you endorse the check?*

J'ai oublié mon carnet de chèques à la maison. *I left my checkbook at home. ("I forgot my checkbook at home.")*

Toucher un chèque. *To cash a check.*

Le chèque de voyage. *Traveler's check.*

CHER (chère *f.*) *adj. dear, beloved; expensive.*

(Mon) Cher . . . *(My) Dear . . . (in a letter).*

C'est mon voeu le plus cher. *It's my most cherished dream.*

La vie est-elle chère là? *Are living expenses high there?*

Il me le payera cher! *He'll pay dearly for that!*

CHERCHER to seek, search; try to, go and get.

Je l'ai cherché de tous côtés. *I looked for him everywhere.*

Allez chercher un taxi, s'il vous plaît. *Please (go and) get a cab.*

Il cherche à entrer. *He's trying to get in.*

chéri (chérie f.) noun and adj. beloved, darling.

chérir to cherish.

chétif (chétive f.) adj. puny, weak.

CHEVAL m. (chevaux pl.) horse.

Monter à cheval. *To go horseback riding.*

Fer à cheval. *Horseshoe.*

Monter sur ses grands chevaux. *To get up on one's high horse.*

chevelure f. hair.

chevet m. the head of the bed.

Rester au chevet de quelqu'un. *To remain at a person's bedside. Not to leave someone's bedside.*

CHEVEU m. (cheveux pl.) hair.

Je désire me faire couper les cheveux. *I want to have my hair cut. I want a haircut.*

C'est tiré par les cheveux. *That's farfetched.*

Etre à un cheveu de la ruine. *To be within a hairbreadth of disaster.*

Il se fait des cheveux blancs. *He's worrying himself gray.*

A faire dresser les cheveux. *Terrifying. Enough to make one's hair stand on end.*

cheville f. ankle; peg.

chèvre f. goat.

chevreau m. kid.

La peau de chevreau. *Kid(skin).*

chevreuil m. roebuck, roe; venison.

CHEZ at, in, at the house of.

Venez chez nous. *Come over to our place.*

Je vous verrai chez les Durand. *I'll see you at the Durands'.*

Nous étions chez des amis. *We were at the home of some friends.*

Monsieur Durand est-il chez lui? *Is Mr. Durand at home?*

Il faut que j'aille chez le médecin. *I have to go to the doctor's.*

Achetez cela chez l'épicier. *Buy that at the grocer's.*

Il demeure chez nous. *He lives with us.*

Faites comme chez vous. *Make yourself at home.*

C'est devenu une habitude chez lui. *It's become a habit with him.*

chic m. trick, knack, style.

Le chic parisien. *Parisian style.*

Elle a du chic. *She has style (chic).*

Il a un chic pour faire ça. *He has a knack for that sort of thing.*

CHIEN m. dog.

Chien de garde. *Watchdog.*

Chien qui aboie ne mord pas. *Barking dogs seldom bite.*

Quel temps de chien (fam.)! *What terrible (awful) weather!*

chiffon m. rag; scrap of paper.

Donnez-donc un coup de chiffon à mes chaussures. *Please shine my shoes.*

Le chiffon pour les meubles. *Dustcloth.*

chiffonner to crumple up; ruffle.

CHIFFRE m. figure, number.

Des chiffres romains. *Roman numerals.*

Des chiffres arabes. *Arabic numerals.*

Voulez-vous vérifier l'exactitude de ces chiffres? *Will you please check these figures?*

Les chiffres ne concordent pas. *The figures don't agree (tally).*

chimère f. chimera, idle fancy.

Se forger des chimères. *To have (entertain) illusions.*

chimie f. chemistry.

Chine f. China.

chinois noun and adj. Chinese.

chirurgie f. surgery.

chirurgien m. surgeon.

choc m. shock, blow, collision.

CHOCOLAT m. chocolate.

Une tablette de chocolat. *A chocolate bar.*

Une glace au chocolat. *Chocolate ice cream.*

Un chocolat chaud. *A cup of hot chocolate.*

choeur m. choir, chorus.

Un enfant de choeur. *An altar boy; choirboy.*

choir to fall.

Laisser choir. *To drop.*

choisi adj. selected, chosen.

Un recueil de morceaux choisis. *Collection of selected pieces (poems, essays, etc.). An anthology.*

CHOISIR to choose.

Il n'y a pas à choisir. *There's nothing to choose from. There is no choice left.*

CHOIX m. choice.

Avez-vous fait votre choix? *Have you chosen (decided, made your choice)?*

Vous n'avez pas le choix. *You have no choice. You haven't any alternative. It's not up to you.*

C'est à votre choix. *It's up to you to choose. It's up to you. As you choose.*

Articles de choix. *Choice articles.*

De tout premier choix. *Of the best quality.*

chômage m. unemployment.

choquer to shock, offend.

se choquer to be shocked, offended.

CHOSE f. thing.

Tout ça c'est la même chose. *It all ("All that") comes to the same thing.*

Je voudrais quelque chose de bon marché. *I'd like something reasonable (cheap).*

Chose curieuse, il se taisait. *Curiously enough, he didn't say anything ("he was silent").*

Chaque chose en son temps. *Everything in its proper time.*

Toutes choses étant égales, je préfère cette solution. *Other things being equal, I prefer this solution.*

Dites-lui bien des choses de ma part. *Remember me to him (her).*

Que vous a-t-il dit?—Peu de chose. *What did he tell you?—Nothing of importance. Nothing very important.*

Ce n'est pas chose aisée. *It's no easy matter.*

La chose publique. *The public welfare.*

chou *m.* (choux *pl.*) *cabbage; dearest.*

Une soupe aux choux. *Cabbage soup.*

Des choux-fleurs. *Cauliflower.*

Mon petit chou! *Dearest!*

chouette *adj.* (*fam.*) *great, neat, terrific.*

chrétien *m.* (chrétienne *f.*) *Christian.*

chronique *f. chronicle*

Chronique musicale. *Musical news. News about the world of music.*

chuchoter *to whisper.*

chut! *shh!*

chute *f. fall; downfall.*

CI *here.*

Par ci, par là. *Here and there.*

Ci-gît . . . *Here lies . . .*

Comme dit ci-après. *As is said further on (hereafter).*

Ci-joint vous trouverez . . . *Enclosed (herewith) you will find . . .*

Voir ci-dessous. *See below.*

Voir carte ci-contre. *See map on opposite page.*

Ce livre-ci. *This book.*

A cette heure-ci. *At this very hour.*

Voir ci-dessus. *See above.*

cible *f. target.*

cicatrice *f. scar.*

cidre *m. cider.*

CIEL *m.* (cieux *pl.*) *sky; heaven.*

Il n'y a pas un nuage dans le ciel. *There isn't a cloud in the sky.*

A ciel ouvert. *Under the open sky.*

Tomber du ciel. *To come as a godsend (windfall).*

C'est tombé du ciel. *It's a stroke of good fortune. It's a windfall.*

Remuer ciel et terre. *To move heaven and earth.*

Le ciel m'est témoin. *Heaven is my witness.*

Aide-toi, le ciel t'aidera. *God helps those who help themselves.*

Que le ciel m'en préserve! *God forbid!*

Ciel! *Heavens!*

Bleu ciel. *Sky blue.*

cierge *m. candle or taper used for religious purposes.*

CIGARE *m. cigar.*

CIGARETTE *f. cigarette.*

ci-inclus *enclosed (herewith).*

cil *m. eyelash.*

cime *f. summit, top.*

ciment *m. cement.*

cimetière *m. cemetery.*

CINÉMA *m. movies.*

Faire du cinéma. *To act in the movies.*

cinématographique *adj. cinematographic.*

cingler *to lash, whip.*

CINQ *noun and adj. five.*

cinquantaine *f.* (about) *fifty; fiftieth year.*

CINQUANTE *noun and adj. fifty.*

cinquantième *noun and adj. fiftieth.*

CINQUIÈME *fifth.*

cintre *m. curve, bend; clothes hanger.*

cirage *m. waxing; shoe polish.*

circonférence *f. circumference.*

CIRCONSTANCE *f. circumstance.*

Le tribunal a tenu compte des circonstances atténuantes. *The court took into consideration the extenuating circumstances.*

Qu'auriez-vous fait en pareille circonstance? *What would you have done in a similar case?*

Etre à la hauteur des circonstances. *To be equal to the occasion.*

Paroles de circonstance. *Words suited to the occasion.*

circuit *m. circuit.*

Cinq mètres de circuit. *Five meters in circumference.*

Mettre une ligne en court-circuit. *To short-circuit a line.*

circulaire *noun (f.) and adj. circular.*

circulation *f. circulation; traffic.*

La circulation du sang. *Blood circulation.*

Il y a très peu de circulation dans cette rue. *There is very little traffic in this street.*

Accidents de la circulation. *Traffic accidents.*

Circulation interdite. *No thoroughfare.*

circuler *to circulate, move around.*

Circulez! *Move on! Keep moving!*

Faire circuler une nouvelle. *To spread a piece of news.*

cire *f. wax.*

cirer *to wax.*

Cirer des souliers. *To shine (polish) shoes.*

cirque *m. circus.*

CISEAUX m. pl. scissors.

ciseler to engrave, chisel.

citadin (citadine f.) noun and adj. pertaining to a city; city-dweller.

citation f. quoting; citation.

cité f. city.

Cité ouvrière. 1. Block of tenement houses. 2. Garden city for workers.

Cité universitaire. Student housing.

citer to cite, quote.

Citez-m'en un passage. Quote a passage of it to me.

Il a été cité à l'ordre du jour. He has been cited for bravery.

Il fut cité en justice. He was summoned to court (as a witness or as a defendant).

citerne f. cistern, tank.

citoyen m. (citoyenne f.) citizen.

citron m. lemon.

Citron pressé. Lemonade.

citronnade f. lemonade.

citrouille f. pumpkin.

civière f. stretcher.

civil adj. civil.

civilisation f. civilization.

civiliser to civilize.

civilité f. politeness.

clair m. light, shine.

Au clair de lune. In the moonlight.

Il a tiré l'affaire au clair. He cleared up the matter.

CLAIR adj. clear, light (in color).

C'est clair comme le jour. It's as clear as day.

Le temps est clair. The weather's clear.

J'aime cette couleur bleu clair. I like this light blue.

clair adv. clear.

Je commence à voir clair. I'm beginning to understand.

Voir clair dans l'esprit de quelqu'un. To read someone's mind.

clairement clearly, plainly.

clairon m. bugle.

clairvoyance f. perspicacity, clear-sightedness.

clairvoyant adj. perspicacious, clear-sighted.

clameur f. clamor, uproar.

clan m. clan.

clandestin adj. clandestine, secret.

claquer to clap, smack, slam.

Il claque des dents. His teeth are chattering.

Il a claqué la porte en partant. He slammed the door when (as) he left.

clarifier to clarify.

clarinette f. clarinette.

clarté f. light, brightness.

CLASSE f. class.

Une classe de français. A French class.

En quelle classe voyagez-vous? What class are you traveling?

Aller en classe. To go to school.

Les classes moyennes. The middle classes.

classement m. classification, filing.

classer to classify.

classeur m. rack, file.

classification f. classification.

classifier to classify.

classique noun (m.) and adj. classic(al).

clause f. clause.

clavier m. keyboard (of a piano, computer, typewriter, etc.)

CLÉ (clef) f. key.

Fermer une porte à clé. To lock a door.

clément adj. clement, lenient.

clergé m. clergy.

cliché m. cliché; negative (photography).

client m. client, customer.

clientèle f. clientele, customers.

cligner to blink.

Cligner de l'oeil. To wink.

clignoter to twitch.

climat m. climate.

climatisation f. air-conditioning.

climatiseur m. air conditioner.

clin d'oeil m. wink.

clinique f. nursing home.

cloche f. bell.

clocher m. belfry; steeple.

clochette f. small bell.

cloison f. partition, interior wall.

cloître m. cloister.

clôture f. enclosure, fence; closing.

Mur de clôture. Enclosing wall.

clôturer to close.

Clôturer la séance. To bring the meeting to an end. To close the meeting.

clou m. nail.

clouer to nail, fix.

Etre cloué sur place. To be rooted to the spot. To stand stock-still. ("To be nailed to the spot.")

cloué adj. studded (with nails).

Passage clouté. Pedestrian crossing.

club m. club.

coaguler to coagulate, curdle.

coalition f. coalition, alliance.

cocasse adj. funny, comical.

C'était tout à fait cocasse (fam.). It was very funny (a scream).

coche m. stagecoach.

Manquer le coche. To miss the boat.

cocher m. coachman.

cochon m. pig.

code m. law, code.

Code de la route. Traffic regulations.

coefficient m. coefficient.

COEUR m. heart.

Il a une maladie de coeur. *He has a heart condition.*

Il en a eu le coeur brisé. *It broke his heart.*

Avoir mal au coeur. *To feel nauseous.*

En avoir le coeur net. *To clear up a matter. To get to the bottom of something.*

Je vous remercie de tout mon coeur. *I thank you from the bottom of my heart.*

Cela me fend le coeur. *That breaks my heart.*

Partir le coeur léger. *To set out with a light heart.*

Avoir le coeur gros. *To be sad at heart.*

Si le coeur vous en dit. *If you feel like it.*

Vous le prenez trop à coeur. *You're taking it too much to heart.*

Apprendre par coeur. *To learn by heart.*

Faire contre mauvaise fortune bon coeur. *To keep a stiff upper lip. To put a good face on a bad matter.*

Rire de bon coeur. *To laugh heartily.*

Il a son bureau au coeur du quartier des affaires. *He has his office in the heart of the business section.*

coffre *m. chest, box, trunk (car).*

coffre-fort *m. safe-deposit box.*

coffret *m. small box.*

cognac *m. brandy.*

cognement *m. knocking.*

cogner *to bump.*

cohue *f. crowd, mob.*

Quelle cohue! *What a mob!*

coiffer *to do someone's hair.*

se coiffer *to do one's hair.*

Se faire coiffer. *To have one's hair done.*

coiffeur (coiffeuse *f.*) *barber; hairdresser.*

coiffure *f. hairdo.*

Sa nouvelle coiffure lui va bien. *Her new hairdo is very becoming (becomes her).*

Salon de coiffure. *Beauty parlor.*

COIN *m. corner.*

Il y a un kiosque à journaux au coin de la rue. *There's a newsstand on the corner.*

Je l'ai cherché dans tous les coins. *I looked for it everywhere.*

Regarder du coin de l'oeil. *To look out of the corner of one's eye. To give a side glance.*

coincer *to wedge; corner; arrest (fam.).*

coïncidence *f. coincidence.*

col *m. collar.*

Un col souple. *A soft collar.*

Un col raide. *A hard (stiff) collar.*

Un faux col. *A detachable collar.*

colère *f. anger.*

Entrer en colère. *To be angry.*

colis *m. package, parcel.*

Par colis postal. *By parcel post.*

collaborateur *m.* (collaboratrice *f.*) *collaborator.*

collaboration *f. collaboration.*

collaborer *to collaborate.*

colle *f. paste, glue.*

collection *f. collection.*

collectioner *to collect; gather.*

collège *m. middle school; preparatory school.*

coller *to stick, paste, glue.*

collier *m. necklace.*

colline *f. hill.*

collision *f. collision.*

colonel *m. colonel.*

colonie *f. colony.*

coloniser *to colonize.*

colonne *f. column.*

colorer *to color.*

Elle sait colorer son récit. *She knows how to color her story.*

colossal *adj. colossal.*

Une fortune colossale. *An immense fortune.*

combat *m. fight, combat, battle.*

Engager le combat. *To go into action.*

combattre *to fight, combat, battle.*

COMBIEN *how many, how much.*

C'est combien? (Combien est-ce?) *How much is it?*

Combien vous dois-je? *How much do I owe you?*

Le combien sommes-nous? *What's the date today?*

Combien y a-t-il d'ici au parc? *How far is it from here to the park?*

Il est à combien le dollar? *What's the rate of exchange for the dollar?*

combinaison *f. combination, arrangement; slip (for women).*

combiner *to combine; scheme, contrive.*

J'ai combiné un nouveau plan. *I devised (worked out) a new project.*

comble *m. summit, top.*

De fond en comble. *From top to bottom. Completely.*

Ça c'est le comble! *That's the limit! That's the last straw!*

Pour comble de malheur. *To crown everything. To add to my troubles. ("For/As the height of misfortune.")*

Faire salle comble. *To draw a full house (theatre, etc.).*

combler *to heap, fill up; load, overload.*

Vous me comblez! *You overwhelm me! You're spoiling me!*

combustible *m. fuel.*

combustible *adj. combustible.*

comédie *f. comedy, play.*

Cessez cette comédie! *Stop acting!*

comédien (comédienne *f.*) *actor, player (any kind of play).*

comestible *noun (m.) and adj. victuals, food; eatable.*

comité *m. committee.*

commandant *m. commanding (officer).*

commande *f. order; control.*
Passer une commande. *To place an order.*

commander *to command, order.*
Commander à quelqu'un de faire quelque chose. *To command someone to do something.*
Commander quelque chose. *To order something.*

COMME *as, like.*
Il lui a dit cela comme ami. *He told that to him as a friend.*
Il a agi comme un enfant. *He acted like a child.*
Comment ça va?—Comme ci, comme ça. *How are things?—So, so.*
A-t-il été nommé?—Non, mais c'est tout comme. *Has he been appointed?—No, but he's as good as (appointed).*
Comme il est tard! *How late it is!*
Il est très comme il faut. *He's very proper (well-bred). He's a gentleman.*
Comme cela. *Like that, that way.*
Qu'est-ce qu'il nous faut comme papiers? *What do we need in the way of documents?*

commencement *m. beginning.*
Au commencement j'ai cru qu'il plaisantait. *At first I thought he was joking.*
Dès le commencement ça m'a déplu. *I disliked it from the start.*

COMMENCER *to begin.*
Il a commencé à travailler. *He started to work.*
Pour commencer. *First of all. To begin with.*
Commencer par. *To begin with, by.*

COMMENT *how.*
Comment ça va? *How are you?*
Comment? *What did you say? I beg your pardon?*
Mais comment donc! *By all means!*
Comment! *What!*
Comment fait-on pour . . . *How does one go about . . .*

commentaire *m. commentary; comment.*
Ceci se passe de commentaire. *This speaks for itself. ("No comment is necessary.")*

commenter *to comment.*

commerçant *m. merchant, dealer.*

commerce *m. trade.*

commercial (commerciaux *pl.*) *adj. commercial.*

commettre *to commit.*
Vous avez commis une erreur. *You've made a mistake.*

commis *m. clerk.*

commissaire *m. commissary, commissioner.*

commissariat *m. commissionership used in the following expression:*
Le commissariat de police. *Police headquarters. The central police station of a precinct.*

commission *f. commission; committee; message; errand.*
Sa commission sur l'affaire est de 5%. *His commission on the deal is 5%.*
Commission d'enquête. *Board of inquiry.*
Puis-je faire une commission? *Is there any message? Can I take a message (for you)?*
Voulez-vous me faire une commission? *Would you please do (run) an errand for me?*

commissionnaire *m. commission agent; messenger.*

commode *f. chest of drawers, bureau.*

commode *adj. practical, convenient.*
C'est commode. *It's convenient (handy). It's comfortable.*
Il est très commode. *He's very pleasant (good-natured, easygoing).*

commodité *f. convenience, comfort.*
Vivre dans la commodité. *To live in comfort.*

commotion *f. commotion, shock.*

commun *m. common; commonplace; the common run.*
Cela tombe dans le commun. *It's becoming commonplace.*

COMMUN *adj. common.*
C'est très commun. *That's very common.*
Amis communs. *Mutual friends.*
Avoir des intérêts communs. *To have common interests.*
D'un commun accord. *By common consent.*
Faire cause commune avec quelqu'un. *To make common cause with someone.*
Le sens commun. *Common sense.*
Nom commun. *Common noun.*
N'avoir rien de commun avec quelqu'un. *To have nothing in common with someone.*
Lieux communs. *Commonplaces. Commonplace (trivial) remarks.*
Expression peu commune. *Unusual expression.*
Ce sont des gens très communs. *They're very common (people).*

communal (communaux *pl.*) *adj. communal.*

communauté *f. community.*

commune *f. smallest territorial district in France.*

communication *f. communication.*
Communication d'idées. *Exchange of ideas.*
Je me suis mis en communication avec eux. *I got in touch with them.*
Communication téléphonique. *Telephone call.*

Vous avez la communication. *Your call is ready. Here's your party.*

communion *f. communion.*

communiqué *m. communiqué, official news.*

communiquer *to communicate.*

Je lui ai communiqué votre note. *I gave him your note.*

Les chambres communiquent. *The rooms are adjoining (communicating).*

Je n'ai pas encore pu communiquer avec lui. *I haven't yet been able to get in touch with him.*

communisme *m. communism.*

communiste *m. and f. noun and adj. communist.*

compact *m. CD*

compagne *f. (female) companion.*

COMPAGNIE *f. company.*

Dupont et Cie. (et Compagnie). *Dupont and Co.*

Je me plais en sa compagnie. *I like his company.*

Je vous tiendrai compagnie. *I'll keep you company.*

Il nous a faussé compagnie. *He left us suddenly. He deserted us. He left us in the lurch.*

compagnon *m. companion.*

Compagnon de travail. *Fellow worker.*

Compagnon d'infortune. *Companion in misfortune.*

comparable *adj. comparable.*

COMPARAISON *f. comparison.*

Hors de toute comparaison. *Beyond comparison.*

Etablir une comparaison entre deux choses. *To draw a parallel between two things.*

comparaître *to appear.*

Vous devez comparaître en personne. *You have to appear in person.*

comparatif (comparative *f.*) *adj. comparative.*

comparativement *comparatively.*

COMPARER *to compare.*

compartiment *m. compartment.*

Compartiment de première classe. *First-class compartment.*

C'est un compartiment de non-fumeurs. *No smoking in this compartment.*

compas *m. compass.*

compassion *f. compassion, pity.*

Faire compassion. *To arouse compassion.*

compatible *adj. compatible.*

compatir *to sympathize with.*

Je compatis à votre chagrin. *I sympathize with you in your grief.*

compatissant *adj. compassionate, sympathizing.*

compatriote *m. and f. compatriot, fellow-countryman.*

compensation *f. compensation*

compenser *to compensate for.*

compétent *adj. competent.*

compétition *f. competition.*

complainte *f. complaint.*

complaire *to please, humor.*

Il lui complaît. *He humors him.*

se complaire *to take delight in, derive pleasure from.*

Se complaire à faire quelque chose. *To take pleasure in doing something.*

complaisance *f. complacence; kindness.*

Auriez-vous la complaisance de . . . ? *Would you be so kind as to . . . ?*

complaisant *adj. obliging, willing.*

complet *m. suit.*

Je viens de m'acheter un complet marron. *I just bought (myself) a brown suit.*

COMPLET (complète *f.*) *adj. full, complete.*

C'est complet. *There's no more room. It's full.*

Manque complet de. *Complete (utter) lack of.*

Un repas complet. *A full meal.*

COMPLÈTEMENT *fully, completely.*

Il est complètement ruiné. *He's completely ruined.*

COMPLÉTER *to complete, finish.*

complet-veston *m. business suit.*

complexe *noun (m.) and adj. complex.*

complication *f. complication.*

Entrer dans des complications. *To meet with complications.*

complice *m. a party to, accomplice.*

compliment *m. compliment; congratulations; regards.*

Je vous fais mes compliments. *I congratulate you. Congratulations!*

Mes compliments chez vous. *Remember me at home. Give my regards to your family.*

compliqué *adj. complicated.*

compliquer *to complicate.*

se compliquer *to become complicated, involved.*

Cela se complique. *It's getting involved (complicated).*

complot *m. plot, conspiracy.*

comploter *to plot, scheme.*

comporter *to allow; include.*

Cette règle comporte des exceptions. *This rule has exceptions.*

Je le ferai malgré les inconvénients que cela comportera. *I'll do it in spite of the difficulties which it will entail.*

se comporter *to behave.*

composer *to compose.*

Composer un numéro. *To dial a number.*

se composer *to consist of, be composed of, be made up of.*

L'appartement se compose de huit pièces et deux salles de bains. *The apartment consists of eight rooms and two bathrooms.*

compositeur *m.* (compositrice *f.*) *composer.*

composition *f. composition, essay.*

compote *f. compote, stewed fruit.*

compréhension *f. understanding.*

Avoir la compréhension facile. *To understand things right away. To have a quick mind.*

COMPRENDRE *to include; understand.*

Tout est compris. *Everything is included.*

Ce prix ne comprend pas les rectifications. *This price doesn't include alterations.*

Y compris. *Including.*

Il est facile de comprendre pourquoi. *It's easy to understand why.*

Il ne comprend pas l'anglais. *He doesn't understand English.*

Je n'y comprends rien. *I can't understand it at all. I can't make it out.*

C'est à n'y rien comprendre. *It's beyond me. I can't understand it. It doesn't make sense.*

Cela se comprend. *That's easy to understand. Naturally. Of course.*

Je peux tout juste me faire comprendre en français. *I can just about make myself understood in French.*

Je lui ai fait comprendre que . . . *I made it clear to him that . . .*

comprimé *m. pill.*

comprimer *to compress; curb, repress.*

compromettre *to commit; compromise.*

Ne me compromettez pas là-dedans. *Don't involve me in it.*

compromis *m. compromise.*

Mettre une affaire en compromis. *To submit an affair for arbitration.*

comptabilité *f. bookkeeping, accounting.*

comptable *m. bookkeeper, accountant.*

comptant *m. cash.*

Au comptant ou à crédit. *In cash or on credit.*

Payable au comptant. *Terms, cash.*

comptant *adj. in cash.*

Argent comptant. *Ready money. Spot cash.*

Payer comptant. *To pay cash.*

Ne prenez pas tout pour argent comptant. *Don't take everything for gospel truth.*

COMPTE *m. account; calculation; amount.*

Créditez-en mon compte. *Credit this to my account.*

Faites-vous ouvrir un compte à la banque. *Open a bank account.*

Faites le compte des recettes. *Add up the receipts.*

Tenez compte de tout ça. *Take all that into account.*

Un compte-rendu. *A report.*

Les bons comptes font les bons amis. *Short reckonings make long friends.*

J'ai un compte à régler avec lui. *I have a bone to pick with him.*

Je m'en rends compte. *I understand that. I'm aware of that.*

Son compte est bon. *Now he's in for it.*

Régler de vieux comptes. *To pay off old scores.*

Il ne doit de comptes à personne. *He is answerable to nobody.*

Elle est inquiète sur son compte. *She is worried about him.*

Pour mon compte. *As far as I'm concerned.*

En fin de compte. *After all. In the end. When all is said and done.*

compte-gouttes *m. dropper.*

COMPTER *to count.*

L'enfant est en train d'apprendre à compter. *The child is just learning how to count.*

Nous serons dix sans compter l'hôte. *We'll be ten, not counting the host.*

A compter de demain. *Counting from tomorrow.*

Puis-je compter sur vous? *Can I count (depend, rely) on you?*

Vous pouvez y compter. *You may depend upon it.*

J'avais compté sur quelque chose de mieux. *I counted on something better. I had expected something better.*

Je vous compterai cet article trente francs. *I'll charge you thirty francs for this item.*

Ça ne compte pas. *That doesn't matter. That doesn't count.*

compteur *m. meter (taxi).*

comptoir *m. counter.*

concéder *to concede, grant, admit.*

Je concède que j'ai eu tort. *I admit I was wrong.*

Je vous concède ce point. *I grant you that point.*

concentré *adj. concentrated.*

se concentrer *to concentrate.*

Se concentrer en soi-même. *To retire within oneself.*

conception *f. conception.*

concerner *to concern.*

Cela ne vous concerne pas. *That doesn't concern you.*

Est-ce que cela le concerne? *Is that any of his business?*

En ce qui me concerne. *As far as I'm concerned.*

Concernant. *In regard to. Regarding.*

concert *m. concert.*
Dépêchez-vous si vous ne voulez pas être en retard pour le concert. *Hurry up if you don't want to be late for the concert.*
Nous devons agir de concert. *We have to act together.*
se concerter *to consult one another.*
concession *f. concession.*
concevoir *to conceive.*
Cela se conçoit facilement. *That's easily understood.*
concierge *m. and f. janitor, superintendent.*
concilier *to reconcile, conciliate.*
concis *adj. concise, terse.*
concision *f. brevity.*
CONCLURE *to conclude.*
Conclure la paix. *To conclude peace.*
Il faut conclure maintenant. *It's time to come to a conclusion.*
Une entente a été conclue. *An understanding has been reached (arrived at).*
C'est une affaire conclue. *The matter's closed. That's settled. It's a bargain.*
Que concluez-vous de ce fait? *What do you infer (conclude) from that? What do you think that means?*
conclusion *f. conclusion.*
concorde *f. concord; harmony.*
concours *m. meeting; assistance, help; contest.*
Point de concours. *Point of convergence.*
Prêter son concours à quelqu'un. *To help someone. To collaborate with someone.*
Par le concours de. *Through the help of.*
Hors de concours. *Not competing (on account of acknowledged excellence). Beyond comparison. In a class by itself.*
Concours d'admission. *Entrance examination.*
concret (concrète *f.*) *adj. concrete.*
concurrence *f. competition.*
concurrent *m. competitor.*
concurrent *adj. competitive.*
condamnation *f. condemnation.*
condamner *to sentence, condemn, blame.*
condenser *to condense.*
condescendre *to condescend.*
CONDITION *f. condition.*
A condition que (de). *Provided that.*
Dans ces conditions. *Under these conditions. Under these circumstances.*
Dans les conditions actuelles. *Under present conditions.*
J'accepte mais à condition que . . . *I accept with the condition that . . .*
J'accepte mais à une seule condition. *I accept but on one condition.*

Les conditions étaient raisonnables. *The terms were reasonable.*
Se rendre sans condition. *To surrender unconditionally.*
conditionnel (conditionnelle *f.*) *adj. conditional.*
condoléance *f. condolence.*
Veuillez agréer mes sincères condoléances. *Please accept my heartfelt sympathy.*
conducteur *m.* (conductrice *f.*) *conductor.*
Un conducteur d'autobus. *A bus conductor.*
CONDUIRE *to drive; lead.*
Un permis de conduire. *A driving license.*
Savez-vous conduire? *Do you know how to drive?*
Conduire une armée. *To lead an army.*
Il l'a conduite chez elle. *He took her home.*
Il conduit bien sa barque. *He manages his affairs well.*
Le cuivre conduit l'électricité. *Copper conducts electricity.*
SE CONDUIRE *to behave.*
Il ne sait pas se conduire. *He doesn't know how to behave.*
Quelle manière de se conduire! *What a way to behave! What behavior!*
conduit *m. passage, channel.*
Conduit souterrain. *Drain.*
conduite *f. conduct; command.*
Sa conduite est irréprochable. *His conduct is irreproachable (perfect).*
N'avez-vous pas honte de votre conduite? *Aren't you ashamed of your behavior?*
Changer de conduite. *To turn over a new leaf.*
Conduite d'eau. *Waterpipe.*
cône *m. cone.*
confection *f. construction; ready-to-wear clothes.*
La confection de cette machine est très chère. *This machine is very expensive to construct.*
Acheter une robe de confection. *To buy a ready-made dress.*
confectionner *to make, manufacture.*
conférence *f. conference; lecture.*
Il est en conférence avec le docteur Dupont. *He's conferring (in conference) with Dr. Dupont.*
Il a fait une conférence excellente. *He gave an excellent lecture.*
conférencier (conférencière *f.*) *lecturer.*
conférer *to confer.*
confesser *to confess.*
confession *f. confession, avowal.*
confiance *f. trust, confidence.*
J'ai entière confiance en lui. *I have complete confidence in him.*

C'est une personne de confiance. *He (she) is a trustworthy person.*

Abus de confiance. *Breach of trust.*

confidence *f. confidence; secret.*

confidentiel (confidentielle *f.*) *adj. confidential.*

A titre confidentiel. *Confidentially.*

confier *to trust, entrust; confide.*

se confier *to confide in, trust to.*

confiner *to border upon.*

confirmation *f. confirmation.*

En confirmation de votre commande, ayez l'obligeance de nous envoyer une lettre. *Please send us a letter in confirmation of your order.*

En confirmation de mon coup de téléphone de ce matin. *Confirming my telephone call of this morning.*

Confirmation d'un traité. *Ratification of a treaty.*

confirmer *to confirm.*

L'exception confirme la règle. *The exception proves the rule.*

confiscation *f. confiscation, seizure.*

confiserie *f. candy store.*

confisquer *to confiscate.*

confiture *f. jam, preserves.*

conflit *m. conflict.*

Conflit d'opinions. *Conflict of opinion.*

confondre *to confuse.*

Je confonds toujours ces deux personnes. *I always get those two people mixed up. I always mistake one for the other.*

Confondre des noms. *To confuse names. To get names confused.*

Il est confus. *He's baffled.*

Il en est confus. *He's very sorry (about it).*

se confondre *to become confused.*

Se confondre en excuses. *To apologize profusely.*

confondu *adj. confused, disconcerted, abashed.*

Je suis confondu de votre bonté. *I'm overwhelmed by your kindness. I don't know what to say (how to express my gratitude).*

Il a été confondu. *He was confused (disconcerted, abashed).*

conforme *adj. according, consistent.*

Une copie conforme à l'original. *A copy corresponding to the original.*

Leurs goûts sont conformes aux nôtres. *Their tastes are similar to (agree with) ours.*

Leurs actions ne sont pas conformes à leurs principes. *Their actions (acts) aren't in conformity with their principles.*

conformément *in accordance with, in conformity with, in compliance with.*

Conformément à vos ordres. *In accordance with your instructions ("orders").*

conformer *to form, shape.*

Conformer sa conduite à ses paroles. *To suit his actions to his words.*

se conformer *to comply with.*

Il s'est conformé à ses ordres. *He complied with his instructions.*

conformité *f. conformity.*

Ses vues sont en conformité avec les miennes. *His views agree with mine.*

En conformité de (avec). *In accordance with.*

CONFORT *m. comfort.*

Une maison avec confort moderne. *A house with all modern conveniences.*

Le niveau du confort. *The standard of living.*

CONFORTABLE *adj. comfortable.*

Ce fauteuil est très confortable. *This armchair is very comfortable.*

confronter *to confront.*

confus *adj. confused; embarrassed.*

Je suis tout confus. *I'm terribly sorry. I'm very embarrassed.*

Il en est confus. *He's very sorry. He doesn't know how to apologize.*

Il est confus. *He's baffled. He doesn't know how to act (what to do).*

Vous me rendez confus. *You embarrass me.*

Des voix confuses. *Indistinct voices.*

Notions vagues et confuses. *Vague and confused ideas.*

Souvenirs confus. *Blurred memories.*

confusion *f. confusion.*

Tout était en confusion. *Everything was in confusion (in a confused state).*

Mettre tout en confusion. *To upset everything. To put everything in disorder.*

Confusion de noms. *A mistake in names.*

Etre rouge de confusion. *To blush with embarrassment.*

congé *m. leave; discharge.*

Il a obtenu un congé de huit jours. *He received (got) a week's vacation. He got a week off.*

On a donné congé au locataire. *The tenant was given notice.*

Nous avons pris congé d'eux. *We took leave of them.*

congédier *to dismiss, fire.*

Ils ont congédié la bonne. *They dismissed the maid.*

conglomération *f. conglomeration.*

congrès *m. congress, assembly, conference.*

Le congrès international des étudiants. *International Students Congress.*

conjugaison *f. conjugation.*

conjuger *to unite; conjugate.*

conjurer *to plot; entreat; ward off.*

Ils ont conjuré sa défaite. *They plotted his defeat.*

Je vous en conjure. *I entreat (implore) you.*

Il a conjuré la ruine de son ami. *He prevented (averted, staved off) his friend's ruin.*

CONNAISSANCE *f. acquaintance; knowledge.*

Amenez vos amis et connaissances. *Bring your friends and acquaintances.*

Nous sommes en pays de connaissance. *We are with old friends.*

Enchanté de faire votre connaissance. *Glad (happy) to know you.*

Je suis très content d'avoir fait leur connaissance. *I'm very glad to have met them.*

En connaissance de cause. *With full knowledge of the facts. On good grounds.*

A ma connaissance, l'affaire n'est pas encore conclue. *To my knowledge (as far as I know), the matter isn't settled yet.*

Il n'en a pas la moindre connaissance. *He doesn't know (understand) the least thing about it. He doesn't have the slightest knowledge of the subject.*

Sans connaissance. *Unconscious.*

connaisseur *m. expert, connoisseur.*

CONNAÎTRE *to know.*

Je ne veux pas les connaître. *I don't want to meet them (to be acquainted with them).*

Je connais bien son caractère. *I know (understand) his character very well.*

Il s'y connaît. *He has great experience in the matter.*

Il s'est fait connaître. 1. *He introduced himself.* 2. *He made himself known. He made a name for himself.*

Il en connaît bien d'autres. *He has many more tricks up his sleeve.*

se connaître en. *To be a connoisseur of, an expert at.*

connexion *f. connection.*

connivence *f. connivance.*

Agir de connivence avec quelqu'un. *To act in complicity with someone.*

conquérir *to conquer, capture.*

Il a conquis l'estime de ses chefs. *He won the esteem of his superiors.*

conquête *f. conquest.*

Vous avez fait sa conquête. *You've won his (her) heart.*

consacrer *to dedicate, devote.*

Je ne puis vous consacrer que quelques minutes. *I can spare you only a few minutes.*

conscience *f. conscience.*

Une conscience droite. *A clear conscience.*

Cas de conscience. *Point of conscience.*

C'est une affaire à votre conscience. *Follow your conscience.*

Par acquit de conscience. *For conscience' sake. To salve one's conscience.*

Cela lui pèse sur la conscience. *It's weighing on his conscience.*

Il travaille avec conscience. *He works conscientiously.*

Il a conscience de ses erreurs. *He's aware of his errors (mistakes).*

consciencieux *(consciencieuse f.) adj. conscientious.*

conscient *adj. conscious.*

Je suis conscient de la gravité de la situation. *I'm aware (conscious) of the gravity of the situation.*

consécutif *(consécutive f.) adj. consecutive.*

CONSEIL *m. advice, counsel; council.*

Donnez-moi un conseil. *Give me your advice.*

Je vais prendre conseil de mon avocat. *I'm going to ask the advice of my lawyer.*

Je viens sur le conseil de . . . *I've come at the advice of . . .*

Le conseil municipal. *The city council.*

La nuit porte conseil. *Sleep on it. ("Night brings counsel.")*

Passer en conseil de guerre. *To be court-martialed.*

conseiller *m. counselor, adviser.*

conseiller *to advise.*

Que me conseillez-vous de faire? *What do you advise me to do?*

consentement *m. consent, assent.*

Je vous donne mon consentement. *You have my consent. I give you my consent.*

consentir *to consent, agree.*

Il a consenti à venir. *He agreed to come.*

CONSÉQUENCE *f. consequence, result.*

Les conséquences se feront sentir sous peu. *The consequences will soon become apparent (make themselves felt).*

C'est une affaire sans conséquence. *It's an unimportant matter.*

En conséquence. *Consequently. As a result.*

conséquent *adj. consistent.*

Il n'est pas conséquent avec lui-même. *He's not consistent.*

Par conséquent. *Consequently. As a result.*

conservateur *m. keeper, guardian, commissioner.*

Conservateur d'un musée. *Curator of a museum.*

conservateur (conservative *f.*) *adj.*
conservative.

conservation *f.* conservation, preservation.
Instinct de la conservation. *Instinct of self-preservation.*

conservatoire *m.* conservatory.

conserve *f.* preserves.
Boîtes de conserve. *(Tin) cans.*
Mettre en conserve. *To can.*

conserver to preserve, keep, maintain, save
(tooth).
Conservez-le avec soin. *Take good care
of it.*
Il a conservé son sang-froid. *He kept his
head. He didn't lose his head.*

se conserver to keep.
Articles qui ne se conservent pas.
*Perishable goods. ("Articles that
don't keep.")*

CONSIDÉRABLE *adj.* considerable.
Une quantité considérable. *A considerable
quantity.*
Elle m'a rendu un service considérable. *She
did me a great favor.*

CONSIDÉRATION *f.* consideration.
Il n'a de considération pour personne. *He
has no consideration for anyone.*
Je le prendrai en considération. *I'll take it
into consideration.*
Agréez, Monsieur, l'assurance de ma
parfaite considération. *Very truly yours
(in a letter).*

CONSIDÉRER to consider.
Ce n'est pas à considérer. *It's not to be
thought of. It's not even to be
considered.*
Il faut considérer que . . . *It must be borne in
mind that . . .*
Il est très considéré dans notre milieu. *He is
highly thought of in our circle.*
Nous sommes considérés responsables. *We
are held liable (considered
responsible).*

consignation *f.* consignment, deposit.

CONSIGNE *f.* orders, instructions;
regulations; baggage room, check
room.
Il a manqué à la consigne. *He disobeyed
orders.*
Je ne connais que la consigne. *Orders are
orders. ("I don't know anything but the
orders.")*
Etre de consigne. *To be on duty.*
Nous avons mis les bagages à la consigne.
We left our baggage in the check room.

consigner to deposit; register.
Consigner ses bagages. *To leave one's
luggage in the check room.*

consistance *f.* consistency.

CONSISTER to consist of.
En quoi cela consiste-t-il? *What does it
(this) consist of?*

consolation *f.* consolation.

consoler to console, comfort.

se consoler to be consoled.
Consolez-vous! *Cheer up!*

consolider to consolidate, strengthen.
Bilan consolidé. *Consolidated balance
sheet.*

consommateur *m.*, consommatrice *f.*
consumer.

consommation *f.* consummation;
consumption; drinks.
Biens de consommation. *Consumer goods.*
Payer pour les consommations. *To pay for
the drinks.*

consommer to consume, use up.

consonne *f.* consonant.

conspirateur *m.* (conspiratrice *f.*) conspirator.

conspiration *f.* conspiracy.

conspirer to conspire, plot.

CONSTAMMENT constantly.
Il se disputent constamment. *They're
constantly (continually) arguing.*

constance *f.* constancy, persistence.

constant *adj.* constant.

constatation *f.* establishment, verification.

constater to state; ascertain; verify.
Constater un fait. *To establish a fact.*
Il a constaté que tout marchait mal. *He
noticed that things were going badly.*
Ils étaient contents de constater de pareils
progrès. *They were glad (happy) to see
such rapid progress.*
Vous pouvez constater! *You can see for
yourself!*

consterné *adj.* astonished, dismayed,
appalled.
Il le regardait d'un air consterné. *He looked
at him with an air of amazement.*

consterner to astonish.
Nous en étions consternés. *We were
appalled by it (staggered by it,
dismayed at it).*

constituer to constitute, form.
Ils constituent une société littéraire. *They're
forming a literary society.*

constitution *f.* constitution.
Avoir une bonne constitution. *To have a
good constitution.*

constitutionnel (constitutionnelle *f.*) *adj.*
constitutional.

CONSTRUCTION *f.* building, structure;
construction.

CONSTRUIRE to build.

consul *m.* consul.

consulat *m.* consulate.

consultation *f.* consultation.

Heures de consultation. *Consulting hours (at a doctor's office). Doctor's hours.*

CONSULTER *to consult.*

Il faut consulter un médecin. *You'd better (we'd better) consult a doctor.*

Consulter un dictionnaire. *To consult a dictionary.*

se consulter *to consult one another; be consulted.*

Ils se consultent. *They're deliberating. They're putting their heads together.*

consumer *to consume.*

L'incendie a tout consumé. *The fire destroyed everything.*

CONTACT *m. contact, touch.*

Il est entré en contact avec lui. *He was (got) in contact (came into contact) with him.*

J'évite tout contact avec eux. *I'm avoiding all contact with them.*

Mettre le contact. *To turn (switch) on (the light, etc.).*

Couper le contact. *To turn (switch) off.*

contagieux (contagieuse *f.*) *adj. contagious.*

contagion *f. contagion.*

conte *m. story, tale.*

Un conte de fées. *A fairy tale.*

contemplation *f. contemplation; meditation.*

contempler *to contemplate, ponder, look intently at.*

contemporain *adj. contemporary.*

contenance *f. countenance; capacity, extent.*

Faire bonne contenance. *To keep one's countenance. To put a good face on a bad matter. To make the best of a bad bargain. To keep smiling.*

Perdre contenance. *To be put out of countenance. To become embarrassed (flustered).*

Faire perdre contenance à quelqu'un. *To stare someone out of countenance. To embarrass someone.*

Quelle est la contenance de ce réservoir? *What's the capacity of this reservoir (tank)?*

CONTENIR *to contain.*

Que contient ce paquet? *What does this package contain?*

Ce rapport contient beaucoup d'erreurs. *This report has many mistakes in it.*

se contenir *to contain oneself, control oneself.*

Il n'a pu se contenir. *He couldn't control himself.*

content *m. sufficiency, enough of.*

Manger tout son content. *To eat one's fill.*

Il en a son content. *He's gotten enough of it. That's enough for him. He has had his fill.*

CONTENT *adj. glad, happy, satisfied, content.*

Je suis content de vous voir. *(I'm) Glad to see you.*

Etes-vous content du résultat de votre travail? *Are you pleased (satisfied) with the result of your work?*

contentement *m. contentment.*

SE CONTENTER *to be content with, satisfied with.*

J'ai dû me contenter de cela. *I had to be content (satisfied) with that. I had to content myself with that.*

Il sait se contenter de peu. *He's satisfied with little.*

CONTENU *m. contents.*

Le contenu d'une lettre. *The contents of a letter.*

Le contenu de ce paquet paraît être avarié. *The contents of this package seem damaged.*

conter *to tell, relate.*

contestation *f. dispute.*

contester *to contest, dispute.*

Je ne conteste pas ce fait. *I'm not disputing the fact.*

continent *m. continent.*

contingent *m. contingent, quota.*

CONTINU *adj. continuous.*

Une ligne continue. *A continuous (unbroken) line.*

Est-ce que le courant est alternatif ou continu? *Is the current alternating or direct?*

continuation *f. continuation.*

CONTINUEL (continuelle *f.*) *adj. continual.*

Un bruit continuel. *A continual noise. A noise that doesn't stop.*

continuellement *continually.*

CONTINUER *to continue.*

Continuez votre récit. *Go on with your story.*

Cela continuera longtemps. *It will last (for) a long time.*

La neige continue de (à) tomber. *It's still snowing. It keeps on snowing. The snow's still falling.*

contour *m. contour, outline.*

contourner *to go around.*

Contourner la loi. *To get around (evade) the law.*

contraceptif *m. contraceptive.*

contraception *f. contraception.*

contracter *to contract.*

Contracter une assurance. *To take out an insurance policy.*

Contracter une habitude. *To acquire a habit.*

contraction *f. contraction.*

contradiction *f. contradiction.*

Il a l'esprit de contradiction. *He's very*

contrary. He contradicts everything you say.

contradictoire *adj. contradictory, opposing.*

contraindre *to compel, force.*
Il fut contraint d'obéir. *He was forced to obey.*

contrainte *f. restraint; coercion.*
Parler sans contrainte. *To speak without restraint. To speak frankly.*

CONTRAIRE *adj. opposite.*
Il est d'un avis contraire. *He's of the opposite opinion.*
Contraire à la raison. *Against all common sense.*
Sauf avis contraire. *Unless advised to the contrary.*
Au contraire. *On the contrary.*
Au contraire de. *Contrary to.*
Le lait lui est contraire. *Milk disagrees with him.*

CONTRAIREMENT *contrary; on the contrary.*
Contrairement à ce que je pensais. *Contrary to what I thought.*

contrariant *adj. trying; annoying.*
Comme c'est contrariant! *What a nuisance! How annoying!*

contrarié *adj. annoyed, upset.*

contrarier *to oppose; provoke.*
Pourquoi toujours le contrarier? *Why do you always oppose (provoke, cross) him?*
Contrarier les desseins de quelqu'un. *To interfere with someone's schemes. To thwart someone's plans.*

contrariété *f. annoyance, vexation.*
Quelle contrariété! *What a nuisance! How annoying!*
Eprouver une vive contrariété. *To be very much (highly) annoyed.*

contraste *m. contrast.*
contraster *to contrast.*
contrat *m. contract.*
Rupture de contrat. *Breach of contract.*

contravention *f. misdemeanor, police offense; fine, ticket.*

CONTRE *against.*
Ils se sont alliés contre l'ennemi. *They made an alliance (united) against the enemy.*
Il a dressé une échelle contre le mur. *He placed a ladder against the wall.*
Le pour et le contre de cette question. *The pros and cons of this question.*
Il y a du pour et du contre. *There's something to be said on both sides.*
Il se tenait tout contre lui. *He was standing very near him.*
S'assurer contre l'incendie. *To insure against fire.*
Envers et contre tous. *Against all comers.*

Il l'a fait à contre-coeur. *He did it reluctantly (unwillingly).*
Contre toute attente. *Contrary to all expectation.*
Livraison contre remboursement. *Cash on delivery.*
Par contre. *On the other hand.*

contrebande *f. contraband, smuggling.*
contrebandier *m. smuggler.*
contredire *to contradict.*
contrée *f. region.*
contrefaçon *f. counterfeiting.*
contrefaire *to counterfeit; imitate.*
contre-ordre *m. counter-order, countermanding.*
Sauf contre-ordre. *Unless I hear to the contrary.*
contresigner *to countersign.*
contretemps *m. wrong time; piece of bad luck.*
A contretemps. *At the wrong time.*
C'est arrivé à contretemps. *It happened at a bad moment.*
Un fâcheux contretemps. *An annoying occurrence.*
contrevenir *to contravene.*
CONTRIBUER *to contribute.*
Je contribuerai à la dépense. *I'll contribute toward the expenses.*
contribution *f. contribution, tax.*
Contributions directes. *Direct taxation.*
contrit *adj. contrite, penitent.*
D'un air contrit. *Penitently. In a contrite spirit.*
CONTRÔLE *m. control.*
Il a perdu tout contrôle sur lui-même. *He lost his self-control.*
Contrôle postal. *Postal censorship.*
contrôler *to control; check; punch (tickets).*
se contrôler *to control oneself.*
contrôleur *m. inspector; conductor (of a trolley, train, etc.).*
Contrôleur des contributions. *Inspector of taxes.*
CONVAINCRE *to convince.*
J'en suis convaincu. *I'm sure of it. I'm convinced of it.*
convaincu *adj. convinced, full of conviction, earnest.*
Parler d'un ton convaincu. *To speak with conviction.*
convalescence *f. convalescence.*
convalescent (convalescente *f.*) *noun and adj. convalescent.*
CONVENABLE *adj. suitable, becoming; decent, proper.*
Ce n'est pas très convenable. *That's not nice (proper).*
Vous devriez choisir un moment plus

convenable pour y aller. *You should find a more suitable time to go there.*
Croyez-vous qu'il soit convenable que j'y aille? *Do you think it's all right (proper) for me to go there?*
Je n'ai rien de convenable à me mettre. *I haven't anything decent to put on.*

convenablement *suitably, properly, fitly.*
Faites-le convenablement. *Do it right. Do it well.*

convenance *f. suitability, fitness, convenience; decency.*
Ces conditions sont-elles à votre convenance? *Are these terms acceptable to you?*
C'était un mariage de convenance. *It was a marriage of convenience.*

CONVENIR *to suit, fit; be right, proper; agree, admit.*
Cet emploi m'aurait convenu. *This job (position) would have suited me (been just right for me).*
Il ne vous convient pas de . . . *It's not advisable (proper, suitable) for you to . . .*
Si cela vous convient. *If it's convenient for you. If it suits your convenience. If it's agreeable to you.*
Il convient de ne pas en parler. *It's not proper (right) to speak about it.*
Je conviens que j'ai eu tort. *I admit that I was wrong.*
A l'heure convenue. *At the hour agreed (fixed, set) upon.*
C'est convenu. *It's agreed. Settled.*
Convenir (à). *To suit, be suitable.*

convention *f. convention, agreement; standard.*
La convention de Genève. *The Geneva Convention.*
Les conventions sociales. *The social conventions.*

conventionnel (conventionnelle *f.*) *adj. conventional.*

conversation *f. conversation.*
Lier conversation avec quelqu'un. *To enter (get) into a conversation with someone.*
Faire tous les frais de la conversation. *To do all the talking.*

converser *to converse, talk with.*
conversion *f. conversion.*
convertir *to convert; turn into.*
se convertir *to become converted, become a convert.*
conviction *f. conviction.*
Une conviction inébranlable. *A firm (unshakable) conviction.*
Pièce à conviction. *Piece of evidence.*
convier *to invite.*
convive *m. and f. guest (at the table).*

convocation *f. convocation, convening.*
convoi *m. convoy.*
convoiter *to covet, desire.*
convoitise *f. covetousness.*
convoquer *to summon, call together.*
Avez-vous été convoqué à la réunion? *Were you asked to the meeting?*
convulsion *f. convulsion.*
coopération *f. cooperation.*
coopérer *to cooperate.*
coordination *f. coordination.*
coordonner *to coordinate, arrange.*
copie *f. copy.*
copier *to copy.*
copieux (copieuse *f.*) *adj. copious.*
coq *m. rooster.*
Fier comme un coq. *Proud as a peacock.*
coque *f. shell.*
Oeufs à la coque. *Soft-boiled eggs.*
coquet (coquette *f.*) *adj. coquettish; elegant, smart, stylish; dainty.*
coquette *f. coquette, flirt.*
coquetterie *f. coquetry, coquettishness; smartness, stylishness.*
coquillage *m. shellfish; shell.*
coquille *f. shell.*
corbeau *m.* (corbeaux *pl.*) *crow.*
corbeille *f. basket.*
Corbeille à papier. *Wastepaper basket.*
Corbeille à pain. *Bread-basket.*
Corbeille à ouvrage. *Work-basket.*
corbillard *m. hearse.*
corde *f. cord, rope.*
Corde à linge. *Clothesline.*
Corde à sauter. *Skipping rope.*
Instrument à cordes. *Stringed instrument.*
Etre au bout de sa corde. *To be at the end of one's rope.*
Usé jusqu'à la corde. *Threadbare.*
cordial (cordiaux *pl.*) *adj. cordial.*
Un accueil cordial. *A hearty welcome.*
cordialement *cordially.*
Cordialement à vous. *Sincerely yours.*
cordon *m. cord, string, band; ribbon.*
Cordon de sonnette. *Bellrope.*
Cordon bleu. *First-rate cook (used only of a woman).*
Tenir les cordons de la bourse. *To hold the purse strings.*
Cordon, s'il vous plaît! *Door, please! (Said to the concierge when you want the door opened late at night).*
cordonnier *m. shoemaker.*
corne *f. horn.*
Bêtes à cornes. *Horned beasts.*
Rentrer les cornes. *To draw in one's horns.*
cornet *m. small horn, trumpet; telephone receiver.*
corporel (corporelle *f.*) *adj. corporal.*

Châtiment corporel. *Corporal punishment.*
CORPS *m. body.*
Le corps humain. *The human body.*
Garde du corps. *Bodyguard.*
Corps liquide. *Liquid body.*
Lutter corps à corps avec quelqu'un. *To come to grips with someone. ("To fight body to body.")*
Il a le diable au corps. *He's very wild. He's full of devilment. Nothing can stop him. ("He has the devil in his body.")*
Prendre corps. *To assume shape.*
Se donner corps et âme à quelque chose. *To be entirely devoted to something.*
corpulence *f. corpulence, stoutness.*
correct *adj. correct, exact.*
Est-ce que c'est correct? *Is that correct?*
Votre réponse est correcte. *Your answer is right.*
correction *f. correction, accuracy.*
Avez-vous fait toutes les corrections nécessaires? *Did you make (have you made) all the necessary corrections?*
Maison de correction. *Reformatory. House of Correction.*
correspondance *f. correspondence; connection, change (subway).*
Il a ouvert sa correspondance. *He opened his mail.*
Prendre la correspondance. *To change trains (subway).*
correspondant *m. correspondent; party (telephone).*
Il est le correspondant étranger de ce journal. *He's the foreign correspondent of this paper.*
correspondre *to correspond, agree.*
Je corresponds avec elle. *I correspond with her. I write to her.*
La théorie ne correspond pas aux faits. *The theory doesn't square with the facts.*
corridor *m. corridor, passage.*
corriger *to correct.*
corroborer *to corroborate, confirm.*
corrompre *to corrupt, deprave; bribe.*
Corrompre un témoin. *To bribe a witness.*
corrompu *adj. corrupt, depraved.*
corruption *f. corruption.*
corsage *m. bodice, body (of a dress).*
corset *m. corset.*
cortège *m. procession.*
Cortège nuptial. *Wedding procession.*
Cortège funèbre. *Funeral procession.*
corvée *f. forced labor; drudgery.*
Etre de corvée. *To be on duty.*
Quelle corvée! *How tiresome! What a nuisance!*
cosmopolite *m. and f. noun and adj. cosmopolitan.*

costaud *(fam.) noun (m.) and adj. strong, strapping fellow; husky fellow.*
costume *m. suit, costume, outfit.*
Costume de ski. *Ski outfit, ski clothes.*
cote *f. quota, quotation.*
côte *f. rib; shore.*
On lui compterait les côtes, il est tellement maigre. *He's so thin you can count the bones ("the ribs").*
Ils se tenaient côte à côte. *They were standing side by side.*
Nous nous tenions les côtes de rire. *We split our sides laughing.*
Le bateau a été jeté sur la côte par la tempête. *The boat was cast ashore by the storm.*
Côte d'Azur. *French Riviera.*
côté *m. side, direction.*
C'est à côté. *It's nearby, next door.*
C'est son côté faible. *That's his weak spot.*
Prendre les choses par le bon côté. *To look on the bright side of things.*
Il a mis de l'argent de côté. *He has put some money aside.*
Ils s'en sont allés chacun de son côté. *Each went his way.*
Répondre à côté. *To miss the point (in an answer). To give an answer that is beside the point.*
De ce côté-ci. *On this side, in this direction.*
De côté. *On the side (seats).*
De l'autre côté de. *On the other side of.*
De quel côté? *In which direction?*
Du côté de la Sorbonne. *Toward the Sorbonne.*
côtelette *f. chop.*
cotisation *f. contribution; dues.*
se cotiser *to contribute; pay dues.*
coton *m. cotton.*
Des bas de coton. *Cotton stockings.*
Du coton hydrophile. *Absorbent cotton.*
Filer un mauvais coton. *To be in a bad way.*
côtoyer *to border on, keep close to.*
COU *m. neck.*
L'enfant s'est jeté au cou de sa mère. *The child hugged his mother ("threw himself on his mother's neck").*
Prendre ses jambes à son cou. *To take to one's heels.*
Etre dans les dettes jusqu'au cou. *To be up to one's ears in debt.*
couchage *m. bedding.*
Le sac de couchage. *Sleeping bag.*
couche *f. bed; couch.*
Couche de houille. *Coal-bed.*
coucher *to sleep.*
On a couché à la belle étoile. *We slept in the open air.*
se coucher *to go to bed.*

Il s'est couché tard. *He went to bed late.*

Couche-toi. *Go to bed.*

couchette *f. berth, bunk (on a ship).*

coude *m. elbow.*

Coude à coude. *Side by side.*

Jouer des coudes à travers la foule. *To shoulder (elbow) one's way through the crowd.*

coudoyer *to elbow, rub shoulders with.*

coudre *to sew.*

Coudre un bouton. *To sew a button on.*

Machine à coudre. *Sewing machine.*

coulant *adj. flowing.*

Noeud coulant. *Slip knot.*

Il est coulant en affaires. *He's very accommodating. He's easy to do business with.*

couler *to flow; sink.*

Faites couler l'eau. *Let the water run.*

Le navire a coulé. *The ship sank.*

couleur *f. color.*

Il m'en a fait voir de toutes les couleurs (*fam.*). *He gave me plenty of trouble.*

Le film en couleurs. *Color film.*

couleuvre *f. garter snake.*

coulisse *f. groove; wings (theatre).*

Porte à coulisse. *Sliding door.*

Fenêtre à coulisse. *Sliding window.*

Les coulisses. *The wings (in a theatre).*

Savoir ce qui se passe dans les coulisses. *To know what's happening behind the scenes.*

couloir *m. corridor, passageway, hallway.*

COUP *m. blow; stroke.*

Il lui a donné un coup. *He struck him.*

Un coup de tonnerre. *A thunderclap.*

Un coup de soleil. *Sunburn.*

Ce fut un coup dur pour sa famille. *It was a heavy blow to his family.*

Donner un coup de main. *To lend (give) someone a hand. To help someone out.*

Un coup de tête. *An impulsive act. Something done on the spur of the moment.*

Faire quelque chose par un coup de tête. *To act on impulse (impulsively).*

Un sale coup. *A dirty trick.*

Tenir le coup. *To withstand the blow. To hold out.*

Coup de téléphone. *Telephone call.*

Il a été tué sur le coup. *He was killed on the spot.*

Tout à coup. *All of a sudden. Suddenly. All at once.*

Le coup de coude. *Nudge.*

Le coup d'envoi. *Kickoff (soccer).*

Le coup de pied. *Kick.*

Le coup de sifflet. *Whistle (-blast).*

Le coup-franc. *Free kick (soccer).*

Un coup de fil. *A telephone call.*

Un coup d'oeil. *A glance.*

Un coup de peigne. *A quick haircombing.*

Les trois coups. *The three knocks (theatre).*

coupable *m. a guilty person.*

coupable *adj. guilty.*

coupe *f. cup; cutting.*

La coupe de cheveux. *Haircut.*

coupe-papier *m. paper knife.*

couper *to cut.*

Il lui a coupé la parole. *He interrupted him.*

Ne coupez pas. *Hold the wire. Don't hang up.*

se couper *to cut oneself.*

Il s'est coupé le doigt. *He cut his finger.*

Se faire couper les cheveux. *To have one's hair cut, have a haircut.*

couple *m. pair, couple.*

coupon *m. cutting; coupon; remnant.*

Coupon de rationnement. *Rationing stamp (coupon).*

coupure *f. cut, gash; small banknote.*

Coupure de journal. *Newspaper clipping.*

Coupure de courant. *Electrical outage.*

Donnez-moi quelques petites coupures, s'il vous plaît. *Give me some small bills, please.*

COUR *f. court; courtship; yard.*

Cour de justice. *Court of justice.*

Faire la cour à une jeune fille. *To court a girl.*

Cour d'un immeuble. *Courtyard (of a building).*

COURAGE *m. courage.*

Perdre courage. *To lose heart.*

Prendre son courage à deux mains. *To pluck up courage. ("To take one's courage into one's hands").*

Bon courage! *Good luck!*

Du courage! *Cheer up!*

Le courage lui manqua. *His courage failed him.*

courageux (courageuse *f.*) *adj. courageous.*

COURAMMENT *easily, fluently; generally.*

Il parle anglais couramment. *He speaks English fluently.*

Ce mot s'emploie couramment. *This word is in current use.*

COURANT *noun (m.) and adj. current; running.*

Eau courante. *Running water.*

Le courant d'une rivière. *The current of a river.*

La monnaie courante. *Legal tender.*

J'ai reçu votre lettre du vingt courant. *I received your letter of the 20th (of this month).*

Donnez-moi vos prix courants. *What are your prices? May I see your list of prices?*

Courant électrique. *Electric current.*

Il y a un courant d'air ici. *There's a draft here.*

Dans le courant de la semaine. *Some day this week.*

Je ne suis au courant de rien. *I don't know anything about it.*

Tenez-moi au courant. *Keep me informed.*

courbature *f. stiffness, tiredness.*

Avoir une courbature. *To be stiff (aching) all over.*

courbaturer *to tire oneself out.*

Je me sens tout courbaturé. *I feel stiff all over. My whole body aches.*

courbe *f. curve.*

courber *to bend, curve*

se courber *to bend, stoop.*

COURIR *to run.*

Courez vite après lui. *Run after him quickly.*

Vous courez un grand risque. *You're running a great risk.*

Par le temps qui court. (Par les temps qui courent.) *Nowadays. As things are at present.*

Faire courir un bruit. *To spread a rumor.*

couronne *f. wreath, crown.*

couronnement *m. crowning.*

couronner *to crown.*

COURRIER *m. mail; column, report (newspaper, magazine).*

Y a-t-il du courrier pour moi? *Is there any mail for me?*

Faites-le-moi savoir par retour du courrier. *Let me know by return mail.*

courrier électronique *m. e-mail.*

courroie *f. strap.*

courroucé *adj. angry.*

courroux *m. anger, wrath.*

Etre en courroux. *To be angry.*

COURS *m. course; flow; currency; rate, price.*

Avoir cours. *To be legal tender.*

Cours du soir. *Evening courses.*

En cours de route. *While traveling.*

Les cours d'eau navigables. *Navigable streams.*

Le cours du marché. *The market prices.*

Cette pièce n'a pas cours. *This coin is not legal (is no longer current).*

Il donne libre cours à sa joie. *His happiness is unrestrained.*

Le cours du change. *Rate of exchange.*

course *f. run; race; course.*

Course de chevaux. *Horse race.*

Faire des courses. *To go out shopping.*

Garçon de courses. *Errand boy.*

COURT *adj. short.*

Une courte phrase. *A short sentence.*

Elle a la vue courte. *She's shortsighted.*

Tout court. *That's all. Just that.*

De courte durée. *Short-lived.*

Rester court. *To stop short.*

Couper court. *To put an end to. To cut short.*

Elle est toujours à court d'argent. *She's always short of money.*

court-circuit *m. short circuit.*

court-circuiter *to bypass.*

courtier *m. broker.*

courtiser *to court.*

courtois *adj. courteous.*

courtoisie *f. courtesy, politeness.*

COUSIN *m.* (cousine *f.*) *cousin.*

Cousin germain. *First cousin.*

Cousins issus de germains. *Second cousins.*

coussin *m. cushion.*

COÛT *m. cost.*

Le coût de la vie. *The cost of living.*

COUTEAU *m. knife.*

COÛTER *to cost.*

Ceci coûte dix francs. *This costs ten francs.*

Il me le faut, coûte que coûte. *I must have it at any cost.*

Cela m'a coûté les yeux de la tête. *That cost me a mint of money (a small fortune).* *("That cost me the eyes of the head.").*

coûteux (coûteuse *f.*) *adj. costly, expensive.*

Peu coûteux. *Inexpensive.*

COUTUME *f. custom, habit.*

Cette coutume existe encore. *This custom still exists.*

J'ai coutume de lire avant d'aller me coucher. *I'm in the habit of reading before going to bed.*

Comme de coutume. *As usual.*

coutumier (coutumière *f.*) *adj. in the habit of; customary.*

couture *f. sewing, needlework.*

Nous avons été battus à plate couture. *We were completely beaten.*

couturier *m.* (couturière *f.*) *dressmaker.*

couvent *m. convent.*

couver *to hatch (eggs); brood.*

couvercle *m. lid, cover.*

couvert *m. cover; things on the table for a meal.*

Sous le couvert de la nuit. *Under cover of night.*

Mettez le couvert pour le dîner. *Set the dinner table.*

Oter le couvert. *To clear the table.*

couverture *f. cover; covering; blanket.*

couvre-lit *m. bedspread.*

COUVRIR *to cover.*

Couvrez cette casserole. *Cover this pot.*

Elle a couvert ses plans. *She concealed (hid) her plans.*

Le bruit couvrait ma voix. *The noise drowned out my words.*

se couvrir *to cover oneself; to be covered.*

Couvrez-vous bien. *Dress yourself warmly.*

Se couvrir le visage. *To cover (hide) one's face.*

crabe *m. crab.*

crachat *m. spittle.*

cracher *to spit.*

Défense de cracher. *No spitting.*

C'est son père tout craché (*fam.*). *He's the spitting image of his father.*

craie *f. chalk.*

CRAINDRE *to fear.*

Il ne craint personne. *He's not afraid of anyone.*

Il n'y a rien à craindre. *There is nothing to be afraid of (to fear).*

Je ne crains pas de le dire. *I'm not afraid to say so.*

CRAINTE *f. fear, dread.*

Soyez sans crainte. *Have no fear.*

Surveillez-le de crainte qu'il ne s'en aille. *Watch him lest he leave.*

craintif (craintive *f.*) *adj. timid, apprehensive.*

cramoisi *adj. crimson.*

crampe *f. cramp.*

se cramponner *to hold on to, clutch.*

Elle se cramponnait à sa mère. *She held on to her mother.*

cran *m. notch; spirit.*

Cran de sûreté. *Safety-notch.*

Il ne le lâche pas d'un cran (*fam.*). *He won't leave him for a moment.*

Il a du cran. *He has a lot of self-assurance.*

Il manque de cran. *He has no spirit.*

crâne *m. skull, cranium.*

Il avait le crâne fracassé. *He had a fractured skull.*

crapaud *m. toad.*

craquer *to crack.*

Faire craquer les doigts. *To crack one's fingers.*

CRAVATE *f. tie.*

Avez-vous une cravate pour aller avec ce costume? *Do you have a tie to go with this suit?*

Rajustez votre cravate. *Fix your tie.*

CRAYON *m. pencil.*

Vous pouvez écrire au crayon ou à l'encre. *You can write in pencil or ink.*

créance *f. trust, belief; credit.*

Lettres de créance. *Credentials.*

créancier *m. creditor.*

créateur (créatrice *f.*) *noun and adj. creator; creative.*

Le Créateur. *The Creator. God.*

Créateur d'un article. *Inventor of an article.*

création *f. creation.*

créature *f. creature.*

C'est une bonne créature. *He's (she's) a nice person.*

crèche *f. crib; day nursery.*

crédit *m. credit.*

A crédit. *On credit.*

Il achète à crédit et vend comptant. *He buys on credit and sells for cash.*

créditer *to credit.*

crédule *adj. credulous, gullible.*

Ne soyez donc pas aussi crédule. *Don't believe everything you're told.*

crédulité *f. credulousness.*

CRÉER *to create; establish.*

Il s'est créé beaucoup d'ennemis. *He made many enemies for himself.*

CRÈME *f. cream.*

crêpe *f. crepe; pancake.*

crépiter *to crackle.*

crépuscule *m. twilight.*

crête *f. crest.*

creuser *to hollow out; dig; to drill (tooth).*

Se creuser la tête. *To rack one's brains.*

creux (creuse *f.*) *noun (m.) and adj. hollow.*

crevaison *f. puncture, flat (tire).*

crevasse *f. crack, split.*

crève-coeur *m. bitter disappointment, heartbreak.*

crever *to burst, break out.*

Le torrent a crevé la digue. *The flood burst the dam.*

Le nuage a crevé. *There was a cloudburst.*

Il en crèvera de dépit (*fam.*). *He'll be very disappointed. ("He'll burst with spite.")*

Cela crève les yeux. *You can't help noticing it. It stares you in the face.*

Je suis crevé! *I'm beat!*

Le pneu crevé. *Flat tire.*

crevette *f. shrimp.*

CRI *m. scream.*

Pousser un cri aigu. *To scream.*

A grands cris. *With loud cries.*

Le dernier cri. *The latest style. The latest rage. The last word.*

criard *adj. shrill; gaudy.*

cribler *to riddle with.*

CRIER *to cry, scream.*

Ne criez pas si fort. *Don't shout so loud! Don't yell like that!*

Il a crié "Au feu, au feu." *He cried: "Fire, fire!"*

Sans crier gare. *Without a word of warning.*

Il criait à tue-tête. *He cried (out) at the top of his lungs. He screamed (yelled). He shouted as loud as possible.*

Crier misère. *To complain of poverty.*

crime *m. crime.*

criminel (criminelle *f.*) *noun and adj. criminal.*

crin *m. horsehair.*

crinière *f. mane (of a horse, lion, etc.).*

crise *f. crisis; fit; attack.*

Crise politique. *Political crisis.*
Une crise de nerfs. *A fit of hysterics.*
Une crise cardiaque. *A heart attack.*
crisper *to contract, clench.*
cristal *m.* (cristaux *pl.*) *crystal.*
cristalliser *to crystallize.*
critique *m. critic.*
critique *f. criticism.*
critique *adj. critical, decisive.*
Etre dans une situation critique. *To be in a
   critical situation.*
critiquer *to criticize.*
croc *m. canine tooth.*
crochet *m. hook; crochet.*
crocheter *to crochet.*
crochu *adj. hooked.*
crocodile *m. crocodile.*
CROIRE *to believe.*
Croire en Dieu. *To believe in God.*
Je vous crois! *I should say so!*
C'est à croire. *It's credible. It's believable.
   It's something you can believe.*
Moi, je ne le crois pas. *I don't think so. I
   don't believe it.*
Croyez bien. (Croyez-le bien). *Depend on it.*
Croyez bien que je suis navré. *Believe me,
   I'm terribly sorry.*
A l'en croire, on pourrait penser qu'il est
   quelqu'un. *To listen to him you would
   think that he's really somebody.*
se croire *to believe oneself, to consider oneself.*
Il se croyait tout permis. *He thought he
   could do anything.*
Il se croit (un) malin. *He thinks he's clever
   (smart).*
Cela se croit aisément. *That's easy to
   believe.*
croisement *m. crossing.*
"Croisement dangereux." *"Dangerous
   crossroads."*
croiser *to cross.*
Les mots croisés. *Crossword puzzle.*
croisière *f. cruise.*
croissance *f. growth.*
croître *to grow; increase.*
Mauvaise herbe croît toujours. *Ill weeds
   grow apace.*
CROIX *f. cross.*
croquer *to crunch; sketch.*
croquis *m. sketch.*
crouler *to collapse; give way.*
croustillant *adj. crisp.*
croûte *f. crust.*
croyant *adj. believing.*
cru *adj. raw; crude.*
Légumes crus. *Raw vegetables.*
cruauté *f. cruelty.*
cruche *f. pitcher; jug.*
Tant va la cruche à l'eau qu'à la fin elle se

casse. *The pitcher goes so often to the
   well that at last it breaks.*
cruel (cruelle *f.*) *adj. cruel.*
cruellement *cruelly, bitterly.*
crustacés *m. pl. shellfish.*
cube *m. cube.*
cubiste *m. cubist (painting).*
cueillir *to gather, pick.*
cuiller *f.* (*also spelled* cuillère) *spoon.*
Cuiller à soupe. *Tablespoon.*
cuillerée *f. spoonful.*
cuir *m. leather.*
En cuir. *In, of leather.*
CUIRE *to cook.*
Faire cuire. *To cook (something).*
La bonne fait cuire le dîner dans la cuisine.
   *The maid is cooking dinner in the
   kitchen.*
Le pain cuit. *The bread is baking.*
Les yeux me cuisent. *My eyes are smarting.*
Il vous en cuira. *You'll smart for it. You'll be
   sorry for it. You'll suffer for it.*
CUISINE *f. kitchen; cuisine.*
Articles de cuisine. *Cooking utensils.*
J'adore la cuisine française. *I'm fond of (I
   like) French cooking.*
Ma mère a d'excellentes recettes de cuisine.
   My mother has some excellent recipes.
Livre de cuisine. *Cookbook.*
Elle fait bien la cuisine. *She is a good cook.
   She cooks well.*
cuisiner *to cook.*
cuisinier *m.* (cuisinière *f.*) *cook.*
cuisinière *f. stove, range (top).*
cuisse *f. thigh.*
cuit *adj. cooked.*
Bien cuit. *Well-cooked, well-done (meat).*
cuivre *m. copper.*
culbute *f. somersault.*
culbuter *to turn a somersault; upset.*
culinaire *adj. culinary.*
culminant *adj. culminating.*
culotte *f. breeches.*
culte *m. worship; cult, creed, religion;
   Protestant church service.*
cultivateur *m. cultivator; farmer.*
cultivé *adj. cultured.*
cultiver *to cultivate.*
culture *f. culture.*
cumulatif (cumulative *f.*) *adj. cumulative.*
cupide *adj. greedy.*
cupidité *f. cupidity, greed.*
cure *f. treatment, cure.*
curé *m. priest.*
cure-dents *m. toothpick.*
curer *to pick, clean.*
Se curer les ongles. *To clean one's nails.*
curieux (curieuse *f.*) *noun and adj. curious;
   curious person.*

Un attroupement de curieux. *A crowd of interested spectators.*

Il était curieux de le savoir. *He was curious to know it.*

Il a une curieuse façon de parler. *He has a curious way of speaking.*

curiosité *f. curiosity.*

Cette visite inopinée a piqué sa curiosité. *That unexpected visit excited his curiosity.*

Les curiosités de la ville. *The sights of the town.*

cuve *f. tank, cistern.*

cuvette *f. washbasin.*

cycle *m. cycle.*

cyclisme *m. cycling.*

Faire du cyclisme. *To ride a bicycle.*

cycliste *adj. of cycling.*

La course cycliste. *Bicycle race.*

cygne *m. swan.*

cylindre *m. cylinder.*

cynique *m. and f. noun and adj. cynical, cynic.*

D

d' *See* de.

dada *m. hobby.*

Chacun a son dada. *Everyone has his fad (pet hobby, pet subject).*

daigner *to deign, condescend.*

daim *m. buck; buckskin, suede.*

dame *f. lady.*

Priez la dame d'entrer. *Ask the lady to come in.*

Elle fait la grande dame. *She puts on airs.*

Jeu de dames. *Checkers.*

DANGER *m. danger.*

A l'abri du danger. *Safe.*

Courir un danger. *To be in danger. To run a risk.*

Pas de danger (*fam.*)! *No fear! Not very likely!*

dangereux (dangereuse *f.*) *adj. dangerous.*

danois *noun and adj. Danish.*

DANS *in.*

Mettez-le dans votre poche. *Put it in your pocket.*

Portez ce paquet dans ma chambre, s'il vous plaît. *Please take this parcel to my room.*

Ce n'est pas dans mon pouvoir. *It's not within my power.*

Il est dans son droit. *He's within his rights.*

Dans l'ensemble. *On the whole. Everything taken together.*

Je reviendrai dans trois jours. *I'll come back in three days.*

Vous les aurez dans la journée. *You'll have them the same day.*

danse *f. dance, dancing.*

danser *to dance.*

darder *to dart, shoot forth.*

DATE *f. date.*

Sa lettre porte la date du cinq juin. *The letter is dated June the fifth.*

Une amitié de vielle date. *A friendship of long standing. An old friendship.*

dater *to date.*

A dater de ce jour. *From today on.*

Dater de loin. *To be of long standing.*

DAVANTAGE *more, further.*

Je n'en dis pas davantage. *I'll say no more.*

Je ne resterai pas davantage. *I won't stay any longer.*

Bien davantage. *Much more.*

DE (d', du, des) *of, from.*

De jour en jour. *From day to day.*

Du matin au soir. *From morning till night.*

De haut en bas. *From top to bottom.*

De mal en pis. *From bad to worse.*

Un morceau de pain. *A piece of bread.*

Ce tableau est de Renoir. *This painting is by Renoir.*

J'ai changé d'avis. *I changed my mind.*

C'est à vous de jouer. *It's your turn to play.*

Avez-vous du vin? *Have you any wine?*

dé *m. thimble; dice.*

débâcle *f. downfall, collapse.*

déballer *to unpack.*

débandade *f. disbanding, stampede.*

A la débandade. *In confusion.*

débarquement *m. landing, disembarkment.*

Quai de débarquement. *Arrival platform.*

débarquer *to land; unload.*

débarras *m. riddance.*

Bon débarras! *Good riddance!*

débarrasser *to rid, clear up; clear (a table).*

J'en suis enfin débarrassé. *At last I'm rid of it.*

Débarrassez la table. *Clear the table.*

se débarrasser *to get rid of, shake off.*

Je ne puis me débarrasser de lui. *I can't get rid of him.*

débarrer *to unbar; uncap (lens of camera).*

débat *m. debate.*

débattre *to debate, discuss.*

se débattre *to struggle.*

débit *m. (retail) store.*

Débit de tabac. *Tobacco store.*

Débit de vin. *Wine shop.*

débiter *to sell retail; debit.*

Veuillez en débiter mon compte. *Please charge it to my account.*

déblayer *to clear away.*

déboire *m. disappointment, failure.*

Avoir des déboires. *To meet with failure.*

Il a eu des déboires dans la vie. *He's had his disappointments in life.*

déboîter *to dislocate.*

Il s'est déboîté l'épaule en tombant. *He fell and dislocated his shoulder.*

débonnaire *adj. meek, mild.*

Il est débonnaire. *He's good-natured.*

débordant *adj. overflowing.*

Débordant de santé. *Bursting with health.*

Joie débordante. *Bubbling over with joy.*

débordement *m. overflow, flood.*

déborder *to overflow.*

Plein à déborder. *Full to overflowing.*

Il déborde de vie. *He's full of vitality.*

Je suis débordé de travail. *I'm swamped with work.*

déboucher *to uncork.*

débourser *to pay out (money), spend.*

Sans rien débourser. *Without spending a penny.*

DEBOUT *upright, standing.*

Se mettre debout. *To stand up.*

Allons, debout! *Come on, get up!*

Il dormait debout. *He couldn't keep his eyes open. He was asleep on his feet.*

Il n'est pas encore debout. *He's not up yet.*

Une histoire à dormir debout. *A dull tale.*

Cela ne tient pas debout. *It's preposterous.*

déboutonner *to unbutton.*

débraillé *adj. untidy, slovenly.*

débrayer *to change gear.*

débris *m. pl. debris.*

Débris d'un naufrage. *Remains of a wreck.*

débrouillard *m. a resourceful person.*

débrouillard *adj. resourceful.*

se débrouiller *to manage, get along.*

Je me débrouille tant bien que mal. *I manage (get along) as best I can.*

Il sait se débrouiller. 1. *He can take care of himself. He can stand on his own two feet.* 2. *He knows his way around. He knows how to get out of difficulties.*

début *m. start, beginning; debut.*

Il n'est pas à son début. *He's not a beginner. He's no novice.*

Elle a fait ses débuts au théâtre. *She made her debut on the stage.*

débutant *m. beginner.*

débuter *to begin.*

Il débute à quatre cents francs par mois. *He's starting at four hundred francs a month.*

décadence *f. decadence, decline.*

décamper *to decamp, make off.*

décapotable *f. convertible (car).*

décédé *m. a deceased person.*

décédé *adj. deceased.*

décéder *to die.*

DÉCEMBRE *m. December.*

décemment *decently.*

décence *f. decency, modesty.*

Il n'a aucune décence. *He has no modesty.*

décent *adj. decent, modest, proper.*

déception *f. deception, disappointment.*

Il a éprouvé une cruelle déception. *He met with a sad disappointment.*

décès *m. decease, death.*

décevoir *to deceive, disappoint.*

Cet aboutissement inattendu l'a déçu. *That unexpected outcome (result) disappointed him.*

déchaînement *m. breaking loose, outburst.*

déchaîner *to unchain, let loose.*

Il est déchaîné (fam.). *Nothing will stop him.*

décharge *f. unloading; relief; outlet.*

A la décharge de l'accusé. *In favor of the defendant.*

décharger *to unload; relieve.*

Décharger sa conscience. *To relieve one's conscience.*

déchéance *f. fall, downfall.*

déchet *m. waste, refuse.*

Déchets de viande. *Meat scraps.*

Déchets radioactifs. *Radioactive waste.*

déchiffrer *to decipher.*

Je ne sais pas déchiffrer cette lettre. *I can't read this letter.*

déchiqueter *to cut, tear.*

déchirement *m. tearing.*

Déchirement de coeur. *Heartbreak.*

déchirer *to tear.*

Ma jupe est déchirée. *My skirt is torn.*

Il est déchiré par le remords. *He's torn with remorse.*

déchirure *f. tear, rip.*

déchoir *to fall.*

Sa popularité déchoit. *His popularity is falling off.*

déchu *adj. fallen.*

décidé *adj. resolute, determined.*

Chose décidée. *Settled matter.*

C'est un homme très décidé. *He's very resolute.*

décidément *decidedly.*

Décidément je n'ai pas de chance. *I really haven't any luck.*

DÉCIDER *to decide.*

Voilà qui décide tout! *That settles it!*

Qu'avez-vous décidé? *What have you decided?*

Je suis décidé à le faire. *I'm determined to do it.*

SE DÉCIDER *to make up one's mind, resolve, be decided.*

Il a fini par se décider. *He finally made up his mind.*

Il est long à se décider. *He is slow in*

*making decisions. It takes him a long
time to decide.*

décimal (décimaux *pl.*) *adj. decimal.*

décisif (décisive *f.*) *adj. decisive.*
Au moment décisif. *At the crucial moment.*
Argument décisif. *Decisive argument.*

décision *f. decision.*

déclamation *f. elocution, oratory.*
Discours plein de déclamation. *Bombastic
speech.*

déclamatoire *adj. declamatory, high-flown.*

déclamer *to declaim, recite.*

déclaration *f. declaration, proclamation.*
Déclaration de guerre. *Declaration of war.*
Déclaration en douane. *Customs
declaration.*

déclarer *to declare; state.*
La guerre a été déclarée. *War was declared.*
Il a déclaré ses intentions. *He made his
intentions known.*
Avez-vous quelque chose à déclarer? *Have
you anything to declare (at the
customs)?*

déclenchement *m. starting.*
Déclenchement d'une attaque. *Launching of
an attack.*

déclencher *to start, launch.*
Déclencher les hostilités. *To open hostilities.*

déclencheur *m. shutter release.*

déclin *m. decline, decay.*

déclinaison *f. declination; declension.*

décliner *to decline, refuse.*

décoiffé *adj. disheveled (hair).*

décoller *to loosen, disengage.*
Il ne décolle pas (*fam.*). *He won't budge
from here.*

décolleté *adj. cut low in the neck (of a dress).*

décolorer *to fade, discolor.*

décombres *m. pl. debris, rubbish.*

décommander *to cancel, countermand.*
Décommander une réunion. *To cancel a
meeting.*

décomposer *to decompose, decay.*

décompte *m. deduction.*
Faire le décompte. *To make a deduction
from a sum to be paid.*

déconcerté *adj. disconcerted.*
Il avait l'air déconcerté. *He looked abashed
(put out, baffled).*

déconcerter *to disconcert, baffle.*
Cette réponse le déconcerta. *The answer
upset him (took him aback, put him out
of countenance, disconcerted him).*

déconfire *to put out of countenance.*

déconfit *adj. crestfallen.*

déconseiller *to advise against.*
Je vous déconseille de le faire. *I advise you
against doing it.*

décontenancé *adj. confused, abashed.*

décontenancer *to put out of countenance,
abash.*
Il ne s'est pas décontenancé. *He wasn't put
out of countenance. He didn't lose his
self-assurance.*

déconvenue *f. disappointment.*
Quelle déconvenue! *What a disappointment!*

décor *m. decorations; show; setting, scenery.*
Changement de décor. *Change of scenery.*
Tout cela n'est qu'une façade pour le décor.
*All that's nothing but window-dressing.
All that's nothing but show.*

décoratif (décorative *f.*) *adj. decorative,
ornamental.*

décoration *f. decoration, medal.*

décorer *to decorate; confer an honor on.*
Décorer une chambre. *To decorate a room.*
Il a été décoré. *He received a decoration.*

découper *to slice, carve.*
Découper de la viande. *To slice meat.*
Découper un article dans le journal. *To cut
out an article in a newspaper.*
Découper une volaille. *To carve a fowl.*

découragement *m. discouragement.*

décourager *to discourage.*
Il m'a découragé de le faire. *He
discouraged me from doing it.*

se décourager *to be disheartened.*
Il n'est pas homme à se décourager. *He's
not a man to lose courage easily. He's
not the sort of person to get
discouraged easily.*

décousu *adj. unsewn; disconnected.*
Une conversation décousue. *A rambling
conversation.*

découvert *m. noun and adj. overdraft, deficit;
uncovered; brought to light.*
Mettre quelque chose à découvert. *To
uncover something. To bring something
to light.*
Avoir la tête découverte. *To be bareheaded.*

découverte *f. discovery.*

DÉCOUVRIR *to discover.*

décrépit *adj. decrepit.*

décrépitude *f. decrepitude, decay.*

décret *m. decree, order.*

décréter *to decree, issue.*

décrier *to disparage, discredit.*

DÉCRIRE *to describe.*

décrocher *to unhook, take off; lift (telephone
receiver).*

décroître *to decrease.*
Aller en décroissant. *To keep decreasing.*

dédaigner *to disdain, scorn.*

dédaigneux (dédaigneuse *f.*) *adj. disdainful.*
Il fait le dédaigneux. *He turns up his nose.*

dédain *m. disdain, scorn.*
Avec dédain. *Scornfully.*

DEDANS *inside, within.*

Au dehors et au dedans. *Outside and inside.*

Je l'ai mis là-dedans. *I put it in there.*

Il a tenté de me mettre dedans. *He tried to get the better of me.*

dédicacer *to dedicate; autograph.*

dédier *to dedicate.*

se dédire *to take back.*

Il s'est dédit de sa promesse. *He broke his promise.*

Je ne puis m'en dédire. *I can't go back on my word.*

dédommagement *m. indemnity, compensation.*

dédommager *to indemnify, compensate.*

déduction *f. deduction, inference.*

Faire une déduction. 1. *To deduct.* 2. *To deduce. To infer.*

Pouvez-vous me faire une déduction? *Can you give me a discount? Can you let me have it a little cheaper?*

déduire *to deduce, infer, deduct.*

défaillance *f. failing, failure.*

Moment de défaillance. *Weak moment.*

Sans défaillance. *Unflinching. Without flinching.*

défaillant *adj. failing, faltering.*

Défaillant de fatigue. *Dropping with fatigue.*

Mémoire défaillante. *Faltering memory.*

défaillir *to become weak, lose strength.*

Ses forces commencent à défaillir. *His strength is beginning to fail.*

Sans défaillir. *Without flinching.*

Elle se sentait prête à défaillir. *She felt about to faint.*

défaire *to defeat; undo.*

L'ennemi a été défait. *The enemy was beaten (defeated).*

Il défait tout ce que je fais. *He undoes all that I do.*

Défaire les bagages. *To unpack the bags.*

se défaire *to get rid of.*

Il faut vous défaire de cette habitude. *You must get out of that habit.*

Il ne veut pas s'en défaire. *He won't part with it.*

Je n'ai pu me défaire de lui. *I couldn't get rid of him.*

défait *adj. undone, loose; discomposed.*

Il avait le visage défait. *His face was drawn.*

Elle avait les cheveux défaits. *Her hair was disheveled.*

défaite *f. defeat, excuse.*

Essuyer une défaite. *To suffer a defeat.*

DÉFAUT *m. defect, fault; deficiency.*

C'est là son moindre défaut. *That's the least of his (her) faults.*

Sa mémoire lui fait souvent défaut. *His memory often fails him.*

A défaut de mieux. *For want of something better.*

défaveur *f. disfavor, discredit.*

Tomber en défaveur. *To fall out of favor.*

défavorable *adj. unfavorable.*

Des conditions défavorables. *Unfavorable conditions.*

défectueux (défectueuse *f.*) *adj. defective, faulty.*

DÉFENDRE *to defend, protect, forbid.*

Défendre sa patrie. *To defend one's country.*

Il sait défendre son opinion. *He can hold his own.*

C'est défendu. *That's not allowed. That's forbidden.*

Je vous le défends bien. *I forbid you to do it.*

se défendre *to defend oneself.*

Il est homme à se défendre. *He's the kind of man who fights back.*

Ne vous en faites pas pour lui, il saura se défendre. *Don't worry about him; he can take care of himself.*

Il n'a pas pu s'en défendre. *He couldn't resist the temptation.*

DÉFENSE *f. fortification; prohibition.*

Les défenses de la ville. *The fortifications of the city.*

Défense de marcher sur le gazon. *Keep off the grass.*

Une défense absolue. *A strict prohibition.*

Défense de stationner ici. *No loitering. No parking.*

Défense de fumer. *No smoking.*

Défense d'afficher. *Post no bills.*

Défense d'entrer. *No admittance.*

défenseur *m. protector, defender; supporter.*

défensif (défensive *f.*) *adj. defensive.*

défensive *f. defensive.*

Se tenir sur la défensive. *To be on the defensive.*

déférence *f. deference, respect.*

déférer *to submit, refer.*

défi *m. challenge.*

Jeter un défi à quelqu'un. *To challenge someone.*

Relever un défi. *To take up a challenge.*

En défi de quelque chose. *In defiance of something.*

défiance *f. distrust, suspicion.*

déficit *m. deficit.*

défier *to defy.*

se défier *to distrust, be distrustful.*

Se défier de quelqu'un. *To distrust someone.*

défilé *m. defile, gorge, mountain pass; marching past; parade, procession.*

Défilé de mannequins. *Fashion show.*

défiler *to march past, parade.*

Les troupes défilèrent. *The troops paraded.*

défini *adj. definite.*

définir *to define, describe.*

C'est difficile à définir. *It's hard to define.*

définitif (définitive *f.*) *adj. definitive, final.*

Résultat définitif. *Final result.*

En définitive. *In short.*

définition *f. definition.*

Quelle est la définition de ce mot? *What's the definition of this word?*

définitivement *definitely, finally.*

Elle est partie définitivement. *She left for good.*

déformer *to deform, put out of shape.*

défraîchi *adj. soiled, faded.*

Des fleurs défraîchies. *Faded flowers.*

se défraîchir *to fade.*

défunt *m. deceased.*

dégagé *adj. easy, free, offhand, flippant.*

D'un air dégagé. *In an offhand manner.*

dégager *to redeem, release, clear.*

Je l'ai dégagé de sa parole. *I released him from his promise.*

se dégager *to free oneself, break loose.*

Se dégager d'une promesse. *To get out of a promise.*

Enfin la vérité se dégage. *At last the truth is coming out.*

dégât *m. damage, devastation.*

dégel *m. thaw.*

dégeler *to thaw.*

dégénéré *noun and adj. degenerate.*

dégouliner *to trickle.*

dégoût *m. disgust, loathing.*

dégoûtant *adj. disgusting.*

dégoûter *to disgust.*

Elle en est dégoûtée. *She's disgusted by it. She's sick of it.*

dégrader *to degrade, lower.*

dégraissage *m. (dry) cleaning.*

dégraisser *to remove the fat.*

Faire dégraisser. *To have (something) cleaned.*

degré *m. degree, extent.*

dégringoler *to fall, tumble down.*

Il dégringola en bas des escaliers. *He tumbled (came tumbling) down the stairs.*

déguenillé *adj. ragged, tattered.*

déguisement *m. disguise, fancy dress.*

se déguiser *to disguise oneself, put on fancy dress.*

déguster *to taste, sample.*

dehors *m. appearance, exterior.*

Personne aux dehors aimables. *Person who makes a nice appearance.*

Sous des dehors trompeurs. *Under false colors. Not to be what one pretends to be. ("Under deceitful appearances.")*

DEHORS *outside, out, out of doors.*

Il fait froid dehors. *It's cold out.*

Mettre quelqu'un dehors. *To throw (put) someone out.*

Ne pas se pencher au dehors. *Do not lean out of the window.*

En dehors de la maison. *Outside the house.*

Au dehors de ce pays. *Outside this country.*

DÉJÀ *already.*

Il est déjà là. *He's already there.*

Je l'ai déjà vu. *I've seen him before.*

DÉJEUNER *m. lunch.*

Où prend-il son déjeuner? *Where does he eat lunch?*

Le petit déjeuner. *Breakfast.*

DÉJEUNER *to have lunch.*

Je n'ai qu'une demi-heure pour déjeuner. *I have only half an hour for lunch.*

DELÀ *beyond.*

Au-delà. *Farther. Beyond.*

C'est aller au-delà de mes désirs. *It's more than I hoped for.*

Par delà les mers. *Beyond the seas.*

délabré *adj. shattered, crumbling, dilapidated.*

Sa santé est bien délabrée. *Her health has become greatly impaired.*

DÉLAI *m. delay, postponement, fixed time.*

Sans délai. *Without delay.*

Dans le(s) plus bref(s) délai(s). *As soon as possible.*

délaisser *to forsake, abandon.*

délassement *m. rest, relaxation.*

La pêche est mon délassement préféré. *Fishing is my favorite pastime.*

se délasser *to relax.*

délégation *f. delegation.*

délégué *m. delegate, representative.*

déléguer *to delegate.*

délibération *f. deliberation.*

délibérément *deliberately, intentionally.*

délibérer *to deliberate.*

délicat *adj. delicate*

Une situation délicate. *A delicate situation.*

délicatesse *f. delicacy, refinement.*

Il manque de délicatesse. *He lacks refinement.*

délices *m. pl. delight, pleasure.*

délicieux (délicieuse *f.*) *adj. delicious; delightful.*

délier *to untie.*

délirant *adj. delirious, frantic.*

délire *m. delirium.*

délirer *to be delirious.*

délit *m. offense.*

Il a été pris en flagrant délit. *He was caught in the act. He was caught red-handed.*

délivrance *f. deliverance, release.*

délivrer *to free, release.*

Les prisonniers étaient délivrés. *The prisoners were released.*

Délivrer une marchandise. *To deliver goods.*

déloyal (déloyaux *pl.*) *adj. unfaithful, disloyal.*

déluge *m. deluge*

"Après nous le déluge." *When we are gone, come what may. ("After us, the deluge.")*

DEMAIN *tomorrow.*

Au revoir, à demain. *See you tomorrow. ("Good-bye until tomorrow.")*

Demain matin. *Tomorrow morning.*

DEMANDE *f. request, application.*

J'espère qu'on fera droit à ma demande. *I hope my request will be granted.*

Sur demande. *On request.*

DEMANDER *to ask.*

On vous demande au téléphone. *You're wanted on the telephone.*

Quand vous la verrez, demandez-lui de nous écrire. *When you see her, ask her to write to us.*

Vous m'en demandez trop! *That's asking too much of me! You expect too much from me!*

L'affaire demande à être éclaircie. *The affair needs to be cleared up.*

Je vous demande un peu! *I ask you! Did you ever!*

Demander un conseil. *To ask for advice.*

On ne demande pas mieux. *One couldn't ask for anything better.*

se demander *to wonder.*

démangeaison *f. itch.*

démanger *to itch.*

Se langue lui démange (*fam.*). *He's itching to speak.*

se démaquiller *to remove makeup.*

La crème à démaquiller. *Cold cream, cleansing cream.*

démarcation *f. demarcation.*

démarche *f. gait, walk; proceeding, step.*

Faire des démarches. *To take steps.*

démarrer *to start, move off.*

Le moteur ne veut pas démarrer. *The motor won't start.*

Il n'en démarrera pas. *He won't budge from his position (alter his stand, change his mind).*

démarreur *m. starter (car).*

démasquer *to unmask.*

démêlé *m. dispute, quarrel.*

Avoir des démêlés avec la justice. *To be up against the law.*

démêler *to unravel, disentangle.*

Démêler un malentendu. *To clear up a misunderstanding.*

déménagement *m. moving.*

Une voiture de déménagement. *A moving van.*

Trois déménagements valent un incendie. *Three moves are as bad as a fire.*

déménager *to move, change one's residence.*

Nous avons déménagé hier. *We moved yesterday.*

se démener *to struggle, strive.*

Se démener pour réussir. *To strive hard to succeed.*

démenti *m. denial.*

Donner un démenti. *To deny, to refute.*

démentir *to give the lie to, contradict, belie.*

Ses actions démentent ses paroles. *His actions belie his words.*

demeure *f. dwelling, residence.*

Il y a établi sa demeure. *He established residence there.*

Il a été évincé de sa demeure. *He was evicted from his home.*

DEMEURER *to live, reside.*

Je ne sais pas au juste où il demeure. *I don't know exactly where he lives.*

L'affaire n'en demeurera pas là. *The affair won't stop there. The matter won't rest there.*

S'il en était demeuré là. *If he had stopped there. If he hadn't gone any further.*

DEMI *half.*

Il est une heure et demie. *It is half-past one.*

Ne faire les choses qu'à demi. *To do things halfway (by halves). To leave things half done.*

Il ne fait que des demi-journées. *He works only half a day.*

Faire demi-tour. *To turn around.*

Un demi de blonde. *A half-liter of light beer.*

Une demi-douzaine de. *Half a dozen of.*

démission *f. resignation.*

Il donne sa démission. *He's resigning.*

A-t-il offert sa démission? *Has he handed in his resignation?*

démissionner *to resign.*

démobiliser *to demobilize.*

démocratie *f. democracy.*

démodé *adj. old-fashioned, out of style.*

Cette robe est démodée. *This dress is out of style.*

demoiselle *f. young lady, miss.*

Demoiselle d'honneur. *Bridesmaid.*

démolir *to demolish.*

La maison a été démolie. *The house was demolished (torn down).*

démon *m. devil, imp.*

démonétiser *to call in (of money).*

démonstratif (démonstrative *f.*) *adj. demonstrative.*

démonstration *f. demonstration, exhibition.*

Faire une démonstration. *To demonstrate.*

démonté *adj. dismounted; upset, raging.*

se démonter *to come apart; be abashed.*

Cette machine se démonte facilement. *This machine can be taken apart (comes apart, can be dismantled) easily.*

Il ne se démonte pas facilement. *He's not easily upset.*

démontrer *to demonstrate, prove.*

démoralisé *adj. demoralized.*

démoraliser *to demoralize.*

démordre *to let go, give up.*

Il n'en démordra pas d'un iota. *He won't back down an inch.*

dénaturer *to distort, misrepresent.*

dénicher *to find out, discover.*

Où a-t-il déniché cela (fam.)? *Where did he find that out? Where did he unearth that?*

dénier *to deny.*

Dénier toute responsabilité. *To disclaim all responsibility.*

dénigrer *to disparage, speak ill of.*

Il dénigre tout le monde. *He speaks ill of everyone (knocks, disparages, runs everyone down).*

dénommer *to denominate, name.*

dénoncer *to denounce, tell on.*

dénonciation *f. denunciation.*

dénoter *to denote; indicate; point out.*

Pouvez-vous dénoter la différence? *Can you tell (indicate, point out) the difference?*

Cela dénote de l'ignorance. *That shows (reveals) ignorance.*

dénouement *m. outcome, ending (play).*

dénouer *to untie, loosen.*

Dénouer une intrigue. *To untangle a plot.*

se dénouer *to be cleared up, be unraveled, be settled.*

L'affaire se dénouera en justice. *The affair will be settled ("cleared up") in court.*

denrée *f. ware, food.*

Denrées alimentaires. *Food products.*

Denrées coloniales. *Colonial products.*

dense *adj. dense, compact, thick.*

densité *f. density.*

DENT *f. tooth.*

J'ai mal aux dents. *My teeth hurt.*

Les dents de lait. *Milk teeth.*

L'enfant fait ses dents. *The child is cutting his teeth.*

Une dent cariée. *A decayed tooth.*

Armé jusqu'aux dents. *Armed to the teeth.*

Dent de sagesse. *Wisdom tooth.*

N'avoir rien à se mettre sous la dent. *To have nothing to eat.*

Il a une dent contre lui. *He has a grudge against him.*

Rire à belles dents. *To laugh heartily.*

Il n'a pas desserré les dents. *He didn't say a word. He didn't open his mouth.*

Il est sur les dents. *He's on the alert. He doesn't know what to do first.*

Cela fait grincer les dents. *It's enough to make you grind your teeth (set your teeth on edge).*

Il ment comme un arracheur de dents (fam.). *He's a great liar.*

Il parle entre ses dents. *He mumbles. ("He speaks between his teeth.")*

dentelle *f. lace.*

dentifrice *noun (m.) and adj. dentifice.*

La pâte dentifrice. *Toothpaste.*

La poudre dentifrice. *Toothpowder.*

L'eau dentifrice. *Mouthwash.*

dentiste *m. and f. dentist.*

dénué *adj. destitute; devoid.*

Dénué d'intérêt. *Devoid of interest. Completely lacking in interest.*

dénuement *m. extreme poverty.*

Etre dans le dénuement. *To be in want.*

dépareillé *adj. odd, unmatched.*

départ *m. departure.*

Un départ inopiné. *Sudden (unexpected) departure.*

Quelle est l'heure de départ du train? *When does the train leave?*

Point de départ. *Starting point.*

département *m. department.*

dépasser *to surpass, go beyond, overtake.*

Ça dépasse mes moyens. *It's beyond my means. I can't afford it.*

Ce travail dépasse mes forces. *This work is too much for me ("beyond my strength").*

Ça me dépasse! *That's beyond me! That beats me! That's too much for me!*

dépaysé *adj. out of one's element; out of place.*

Il se sent tout dépaysé. *He feels out of place.*

dépêche *f. a telegram.*

Envoyer une dépêche. *To send a telegram.*

se dépêcher *to hasten, hurry.*

Dépêchez-vous. *Hurry up.*

Il faut qu'il se dépêche. *He has to hurry. He'd better hurry up.*

dépeindre *to depict, describe.*

dépendance *f. dependence.*

Etre sous la dépendance de quelqu'un. *To be under someone's domination.*

dépendre *to depend, be dependent.*

Tout dépend des circonstances. *Everything depends on the circumstances.*

Cela ne dépend pas de nous. *That's not up to us. That doesn't depend on us.*

Cela dépend. *That depends.*

dépens *m. costs, expense.*

A ses frais et dépens. *At his own expense.*

Apprendre à ses dépens. *To learn to one's cost.*

dépense *f. expense.*
Faire des dépenses. *To incur expenses.*
Regarder à la dépense. *To be thrifty.*
DÉPENSER *to spend.*
Nous avons dépensé en tout à peine vingt francs. *Altogether we spent less than twenty francs.*
Il dépense au-delà de ses revenus. *He lives beyond his means. He spends more than he makes.*
se dépenser *to exert oneself, not to spare oneself.*
dépensier (dépensière *f.*) *adj. extravagant, spendthrift.*
dépérir *to waste away, decay.*
se dépeupler *to become depopulated.*
dépit *m. spite, resentment.*
Masquer son dépit. *To conceal one's resentment.*
Par dépit. *Through spite. Out of spite.*
Il a agi en dépit du bon sens. *He acted contrary to good sense. He didn't use common sense.*
dépiter *to vex, upset.*
Je suis fort dépité. *I'm very much annoyed.*
se dépiter *to take offense, be annoyed.*
déplacement *m. displacement, traveling.*
déplacé *adj. out of place, misplaced.*
déplacer *to displace, shift, move, to paste (computer)*
se déplacer *to change one's place, move about.*
déplaire *to displease, be unpleasant.*
Cela me déplaît. *I dislike that. I don't like that.*
Ne vous en déplaise. *No offense meant. With all due respect to you.*
déplier *to unfold.*
déplorable *adj. deplorable, lamentable.*
déplorer *to deplore, lament.*
déployer *to display, spend, exhibit.*
déposer *to put down.*
Déposez la valise ici. *Put the suitcase down here.*
Ils ont déposé les armes. *They've surrendered. They've laid down their arms.*
dépositaire *m. depository, trustee.*
déposséder *to dispossess, oust.*
dépôt *m. deposit; depot.*
Un dépôt d'autobus. *A bus terminal.*
En dépôt. *In custody. In safekeeping.*
dépouiller *to deprive, strip.*
Dépouiller quelqu'un de ses droits. *To deprive someone of his rights.*
Dépouiller le courrier. *To open the mail.*
dépourvu *adj. bereft, devoid of.*
Dépourvu d'argent. *Short of cash.*
Etre pris au dépourvu. *To be taken unaware.*

déprimé *adj. depressed.*
Se sentir déprimé. *To feel depressed.*
DEPUIS *since.*
J'y habite depuis vingt ans. *I've lived there twenty years.*
Vous avez grossi depuis un an. *You've put on weight in this last year.*
Mon bail est expiré depuis hier. *My lease expired yesterday.*
Depuis lors. *Since that time.*
Depuis quand m'attendez-vous?—Peut-être depuis dix minutes. *How long have you been waiting for me?—About ten minutes. ("Probably since ten minutes.")*
député *m. deputy, delegate.*
déraciné *adj. uprooted.*
Se sentir déraciné. *To feel like a fish out of water.*
dérailler *to be derailed; talk nonsense (fam.).*
déraisonnable *adj. unreasonable.*
dérangement *m. disturbance, trouble.*
Causer du dérangement à quelqu'un. *To disturb someone.*
déranger *to disturb, inconvenience.*
Se cela ne vous dérange pas. *If it doesn't inconvenience you.*
Cela dérange tous mes plans. *That upsets (spoils) all my plans.*
Il ne dérange jamais personne. *He never bothers anyone.*
se déranger *to inconvenience oneself, take the trouble.*
Ne vous dérangez pas. *Don't trouble. Don't bother.*
déraper *to skid.*
déréglé *adj. out of order.*
se dérider *to cheer up.*
dérision *f. mockery.*
Quelle dérision! *What a mockery!*
dérisoire *adj. derisive, ridiculous.*
Vendre quelque chose à un prix dérisoire. *To sell something at a ridiculously low price.*
dérive *f. drift.*
Aller à la dérive. *To drift.*
dériver *to derive.*
Ce mot dérive du latin. *This word is derived from Latin.*
DERNIER (dernière *f.*) *adj. last; noun m. and f. youngest child; the last one; the latter.*
C'est mon dernier souci. *That's the least of my worries. ("That's my last worry.")*
C'est sa dernière carte. *It's his last card.*
C'est du dernier ridicule. *That's utterly ridiculous.*
Il est toujours au courant des dernières nouvelles. *He always knows the latest*

news. *He's always informed about the latest news.*

C'est de la dernière imprudence. *Nothing could be more imprudent.*

Etre du dernier bien avec quelqu'un. *To be on the very best terms with someone.*

Il veut toujours avoir le dernier mot. *He must always have the last word.*

Voilà le dernier cri. *That's the latest rage.*

Mon petit dernier. *My youngest child.*

Le dernier. *The latter.*

L'année dernière. *Last year.*

dernièrement *lately.*

dérober *to steal, make away with; hide.*

On lui a dérobé son argent. *His money has been stolen.*

se dérober *to escape, steal away, shun.*

Se dérober à ses créanciers. *To avoid one's creditors.*

se dérouler *to unroll, unfold.*

déroute *f. rout.*

derrière *m. back, rear.*

Les derrières d'une armée. *The rear of an army.*

DERRIÈRE *behind; back.*

Il a certainement quelque chose derrière la tête. *He certainly has something in the back of his mind.*

Je l'ai laissé bien loin derrière moi. *I left him (quite, very) far behind me.*

DÈS *from.*

Dès à présent. *Henceforth.*

Dès son retour. *On his return.*

Dès qu'il le saura. *As soon as he knows (learns) it.*

Dès lors. *Ever since.*

désaccord *m. disagreement, clash.*

Ils sont toujours en désaccord. *They always disagree.*

désagréable *adj. disagreeable, unpleasant.*

Nouvelle désagréable. *Unwelcome news.*

Personne désagréable. *Unpleasant person.*

désapprouver *to disapprove.*

désarmement *m. disarmament, disarming.*

désarmer *to disarm.*

désarroi *m. disorder, confusion.*

Mettre tout en désarroi. *To turn everything upside down.*

désastre *m. disaster.*

désastreux (désastreuse *f.*) *adj. disastrous.*

désavantage *m. disadvantage, drawback.*

Avoir le désavantage. *To be at a disadvantage.*

A son désavantage. *To his (her) disadvantage.*

désavantageux (désavantageuse *f.*) *adj. disadvantageous.*

se désavouer *to retract, go back on one's word.*

descendant *m. descendant.*

DESCENDRE *to descend, go down.*

Lorsque vous descendrez, regardez s'il y a du courier. *When you go downstairs, see if there is any mail.*

Combien de marches y a-t-il à descendre? *How many steps are there to go down?*

Envoyez-moi quelqu'un pour descendre mes valises. *Send someone to carry down my bags.*

A quel arrêt dois-je descendre? *At what stop (bus, streetcar) do I get off?*

A quel hôtel êtes-vous descendu? *At what hotel are you stopping?*

Tout le monde descend! *All off! Last stop! All change!*

descente *f. slope, descent.*

Une descente rapide. *A steep slope.*

Descente de police. *Police raid.*

descriptif (descriptive *f.*) *adj. descriptive.*

description *f. description.*

désemparé *adj. helpless, in distress.*

déséquilibré *adj. out of balance.*

désert *m. desert.*

désert *adj. deserted.*

L'endroit était désert. *The place was deserted.*

déserter *to desert, abandon.*

déserteur *m. deserter.*

désespéré *adj. desperate.*

désespérer *to despair, give up.*

Ne désespérez pas. *Don't give up. Don't lose courage.*

désespoir *m. despair, grief, hopelessness.*

Je suis au désespoir. *I'm in despair.*

Coup de désespoir. *Act of despair.*

En désespoir de cause. *As a last resort.*

se déshabiller *to undress.*

se déshabituer *to break oneself of a habit.*

déshériter *to disinherit.*

déshonnête *adj. improper, immodest.*

déshonneur *m. dishonor, disgrace.*

déshonorant *adj. dishonorable, shameful.*

déshonorer *to dishonor, disgrace.*

désigner *to designate, point out.*

Désigner quelque chose du doigt. *To point at something.*

désillusion *f. disillusion.*

désillusionner *to disillusion.*

désintéressé *adj. disinterested; unselfish.*

se désintéresser *to lose one's interest in.*

désinvolte *adj. easy, unconstrained, unembarrassed.*

désinvolture *f. unconstraint, ease.*

désir *m. desire, wish.*

désirable *adj. desirable.*

DÉSIRER *to desire, wish.*

Je désire vous voir. *I'd like to see you.*

Que désirez-vous de plus? *What else would you like? What do you want besides?*

Je désire recommander ma lettre. *I'd like to have my letter registered.*

Cela laisse à désirer. *It's not quite satisfactory. That leaves something to be desired.*

Je n'ai plus rien à désirer. *I can't (couldn't) wish for anything else. I've nothing left to wish for.*

Elle se fait désirer. *She keeps people waiting.*

Madame désire? *What would you like, madam?*

Qu'est-ce que vous désirez? *May I help you? What would you like? What can I do for you?*

désireux (désireuse *f.*) *adj. desirous.*

Il est désireux de plaire. *He's anxious to please.*

se désister *to relinquish a right, waive a claim, withdraw a legal action or one's candidacy.*

Se désister d'une demande. *To waive a claim.*

Se désister d'une promesse. *To break a promise. Not to keep a promise.*

désobéir *to disobey.*

désobéissance *f. disobedience.*

désobligeance *f. unkindness, disagreeableness.*

désobliger *to offend.*

désoeuvré *adj. unoccupied, idle.*

désolation *f. desolation, grief.*

désolé *adj. desolate; very sorry.*

Je suis désolé. *I'm very sorry.*

Je suis désolé de l'entendre. *I'm sorry to hear it.*

désoler *to ravage, devastate.*

désordonné *adj. disorderly.*

désordre *m. disorder.*

Nous avons tout trouvé en désordre. *We found everything in disorder (topsy-turvy).*

désorganisé *adj. disorganized.*

désorienté *adj. bewildered.*

désormais *henceforth, from now on.*

desséché *adj. dry.*

dessein *m. design, scheme, aim.*

A dessein. *Intentionally. Designedly.*

desserrer *to loosen.*

dessert *m. dessert.*

desservir *to serve; clear (the table).*

dessin *m. drawing, sketch.*

Dessin animé. *Animated cartoon.*

dessiner *to draw.*

se dessiner *to stand out, be outlined.*

Mes projects se dessinent. *My plans are taking shape.*

dessous *m. lower part, bottom.*

Un dessous de bouteille. *A coaster.*

Avoir le dessous. *To have (get) the worst of it. To be defeated.*

Le pauvre, il a eu le dessous. *The poor fellow got the worst of it (was defeated).*

Il y a là un dessous que nous ne comprenons pas. *There's something (some mystery) about it which we don't understand.*

En dessous. *Below; next smaller (size).*

DESSOUS *under, below.*

Regardez en-dessous de la chaise. *Look under the chair.*

C'est là, en-dessous. *It's there below.*

C'est au-dessous de moi. *It's beneath me. It's beneath my dignity.*

Il y a quelque chose là-dessous. *There's something behind it.*

dessus *m. top.*

Le dessus de lit. *Bedspread.*

Le dessus de la main. *The back of the hand.*

Le dessus du panier. *The cream (pick) of the crop.*

Il a gagné le dessus. *He won the upper hand.*

DESSUS *on, over, above, on top.*

Le livre se trouve au-dessus de l'étagère. *The book's on top of the bookshelf.*

Qui habite à l'étage du dessus? *Who lives on the floor above?*

Il y a beaucoup à dire là-dessus. *A lot can be said about that. There's a good deal to say (to be said) about that.*

Ils vont bras dessus, bras dessous. *They're walking arm in arm.*

Il est en dette par-dessus la tête. *He is up to his neck in debt.*

Cette nouvelle l'a mis sens dessus dessous. *The news upset him. He was bowled over by the news.*

Il a mis le doigt dessus. *He put his finger on it. He hit the nail on the head.*

destin *m. fate, destiny.*

destinataire *m. addressee, recipient.*

destination *f. destination.*

Arriver à destination. *To arrive at a destination.*

Trains à destination de Toulouse. *Trains to Toulouse.*

destinée *f. destiny.*

destiner *to destine; intend.*

Il est destiné à devenir célèbre. *He's destined to become famous.*

Ceci vous était destiné. *This was meant for you.*

se destiner *to intend to enter a profession.*

Il se destine à la médecine. *He intends to be a doctor.*

destitué *adj. deprived of, lacking.*

destruction *f. destruction.*

désunion *f. disunion, dissension.*

détaché *adj. loose; indifferent; detached.*
D'un air détaché. *In a casual manner.*

détachement *m. indifference, detachment.*

détacher *to loosen, untie; detach.*

se détacher *to get loose, be separated; stand out.*
Se détacher sur l'horizon. *To stand out against the horizon.*

DÉTAIL *m. detail; retail.*
Vendre au détail. *To sell retail.*
Prix de détail. *Retail price.*
Donner tous les détails. *To give full particulars.*

détaillé *adj. detailed.*
Un compte-rendu détaillé. *A detailed account.*

détailler *to detail, enumerate.*

déteindre *to fade, lose color.*
Déteindre au lavage. *To run (fade) in the wash.*

se détendre *to relax, loosen.*

détente *f. relaxation, loosening.*

détention *f. holding; detention.*

détériorer *to spoil.*

détermination *f. determination.*

déterminé *adj. determined, definite; resolute.*

déterminer *to determine.*
Je suis déterminé à faire cela. *I'm determined to do it.*

détestable *adj. detestable, hateful.*

détester *to hate.*
Il le déteste. *He hates him.*

détour *m. deviation, turn.*
La route fait un brusque détour. *The road makes a sharp turn.*
Faire un détour. *To make a detour.*

détourner *to divert, avert.*
Détourner l'attention de quelqu'un. *To divert someone's attention.*
Détourner les soupçons. *To avert suspicion.*

détraqué *adj. out of order.*
Ma montre est détraquée. *My watch is out of order.*
Il est un peu détraqué (fam.). *He's a little unbalanced (crazy).*

détraquer *to put out of order, spoil, ruin.*

détresse *f. distress, affliction.*
Navire en détresse. *Ship in distress.*
Sa détresse fait pitié à voir. *Her (his) plight is pitiful.*

détriment *m. detriment.*
Il l'a appris à son détriment. *He found it out to his cost.*

détruire *to destroy.*

DETTE *f. debt.*
Il a payé les dettes les plus criardes. *He paid the most pressing debts.*

Il m'a remis une reconnaissance de dette. *He gave me an I.O.U.*

deuil *m. mourning, grief.*
Prendre le deuil. *To go into mourning.*
Porter le deuil. *To be in mourning.*

D.E.U.S.T. *m. Diplôme d'études universitaires scientifiques et techniques.*

DEUX *noun and adj. two.*
Il est deux heures et quart. *It is a quarter past two.*
Les enfants étaient tous deux fatigués. *Both children were tired.*
Voici le fait en deux mots. *Briefly, the matter is this. This is the matter in a nutshell ("in two words").*
Ils se ressemblent comme deux gouttes d'eau. *They're as alike as two peas in a pod ("as two drops of water").*
Il l'a vu de ses deux yeux. *He saw it with his own ("two") eyes.*
Cette classe a lieu un jeudi sur deux. *This class meets on alternate Thursdays.*
Il est entre deux âges. *He's middle-aged.*
Elle regarde à deux sous. *She thinks twice before spending anything. She pinches pennies (is penny-pinching).*
A deux pas d'ici. *Right near here, nearby, very close by.*
(Tous) les deux. *Both (of them, of us).*
Toutes les deux semaines. *Every other week.*
Vous deux. *The two of you, both of you.*

DEUXIÈME *noun and adj. second.*
C'est la deuxième maison à droite. *It's the second house to your right.*

devancer *to precede.*

devant *m. front.*
Je ne suis pas encore prêt, prenez les devants. *I'm not ready yet, go on ahead.*

DEVANT *before, in front of.*
Il a pris un autobus qui l'a emmené juste devant l'immeuble. *He took a bus which brought him right in front of the building.*
Egaux devant la loi. *Equal before the law.*
Aller au-devant de ses amis. *To go to meet one's friends (as a courtesy).*
Aller au devant des ennuis. *To borrow trouble.*
Aller droit devant soi. *To go straight ahead. To follow one's nose.*

dévalorisation *f. depreciation.*

dévaluation *f. devaluation, depreciation.*

se dévaluer *to devalue.*

devanture *f. shop window.*

dévastation *f. devastation.*

dévaster *to devastate.*

déveine *f. bad luck.*
J'ai de la déveine aujourd'hui (fam.). *I have no luck today. My luck's bad today.*

développement *m. development.*
développer *to develop.*
Faire développer. *To have developed (film).*
DEVENIR *to become.*
Devenir grand. *To grow tall. To grow up.*
Il devient vieux. *He's growing (getting) old.*
Que devenez-vous ces jours-ci? *What are you doing these days?*
J'ai failli en devenir fou. *It nearly drove me mad.*
Que va-t-il devenir? *What is to (will) become of him?*
Je ne sais que devenir. *I don't know what is to become of me.*
Qu'il est devenu gros! *How fat he's gotten! He's certainly gotten fat!*
Devenir blanc de rage. *To turn white with anger.*
Il en est devenu amoureux. *He fell in love with her.*
se dévêtir *to undress, strip.*
déviation *f. deviation.*
dévier *to deviate, diverge.*
deviner *to guess.*
Vous avez deviné juste. *That's right. You've guessed right.*
devinette *f. riddle.*
dévisager *to stare.*
devise *f. motto; currency.*
Des devises étrangères. *Foreign bills.*
devoir *m. duty, obligation.*
C'est son devoir. *It's his (her) duty.*
Faire son devoir. *To do one's duty.*
Payer ses devoirs à quelqu'un. *To pay one's respects to someone.*
DEVOIR *to owe; have to; must.*
Il me doit beaucoup d'argent. *He owes me a lot of money.*
Je crois devoir rentrer à la maison. *I believe I'll have to go home.*
Il doit y avoir quelqu'un. *Someone must be there.*
Il devait lui écrire. *He was supposed to write to him.*
Il devrait lui écrire. *He ought to write to him.*
Tout doit finir. *Everything is bound to come to an end.*
Nous devons le faire. *We must do it.*
Il doit y aller. *He has to go there.*
devoirs *m. pl. homework.*
Mon fils a beaucoup de devoirs à faire. *My son has a lot of homework to do.*
dévorer *to devour, eat greedily.*
dévot *adj. devout, pious.*
dévotion *f. devotion.*
dévoué *adj. devoted, faithful.*
Votre tout dévoué. *Yours very truly.*
dévouement *m. devotion; self-sacrifice.*

dévouer *to dedicate, consecrate.*
Dévouer son énergie à une cause. *To devote one's energy to a cause.*
se dévouer *to devote oneself.*
dextérité *f. dexterity, skill.*
diable *m. devil.*
C'est un pauvre diable. *He's a poor devil.*
C'est un assez bon diable. *He's not a bad fellow.*
Il tire le diable par la queue. *He lives from hand to mouth. He's hard up.*
Que diable voulez-vous en faire (*fam.*)? *What on earth do you want to do with it?*
Ce n'est pas le diable. *It's not so very difficult.*
diagonale *f. diagonal.*
dialogue *m. dialogue.*
diamant *m. diamond.*
diaphragme *m. diaphragm.*
diapositive *f. transparency, slide (photography).*
diarrhée *f. diarrhea.*
dichotomie *f. dichotomy.*
dictateur *m. dictatrice f. dictator.*
dicter *to dictate, suggest.*
Dictez-moi. J'écrirai. *Dictate ("to me") and I'll take it down ("I'll write").*
DICTIONNAIRE *m. dictionary.*
diesel *m. diesel.*
diète *f. diet.*
Diététicien m., diététicienne f. *dietician.*
Diététique *f. dietetics.*
Magasin diététique. *Health food store.*
DIEU *m. God.*
Dieu sait ce qu'il en sera! *God knows what will come of it!*
Que Dieu me soit en aide! *So help me God!*
Pour l'amour de Dieu! *For goodness' sake!*
Grâce à Dieu, je n'y suis pas allé. *Thank heavens I didn't go.*
C'est une punition du bon Dieu. *It's a judgment of God.*
diffamer *to defame, slander.*
DIFFÉRENCE *f. difference.*
Cela fait une grande différence. *That makes a lot of difference.*
différend *m. disagreement.*
DIFFÉRENT *adj. different.*
Celui-ci est bien différent de l'autre. *This one is quite different from the other one.*
DIFFÉRER *to differ.*
DIFFICILE *adj. difficult, hard.*
C'est un problème difficile. *It's a difficult problem.*
Il est difficile. *He's a difficult person.*
DIFFICULTÉ *f. difficulty.*
Il fait naître des difficultés. *He creates (he's always creating) difficulties.*

Ils se sont heurtés à de sérieuses difficultés. *They encountered serious obstacles.*

digérer *to digest, swallow.*

digne *adj. worthy.*

Je l'en trouve digne. *I consider him worthy of it. I think he deserves it.*

Cela est bien digne de lui. *That's just like him.*

dignité *f. dignity.*

digression *f. digression.*

dilapider *to waste, squander.*

dilater *to dilate, expand.*

dilemme *m. dilemma.*

diligence *f. diligence, application.*

Faire diligence. *To hurry.*

diligent *adj. diligent, industrious.*

diluer *to dilute.*

DIMANCHE *m. Sunday.*

Le(s) dimanche(s). *On Sundays.*

dimension *f. dimension, size.*

diminuer *to lessen, diminish.*

Diminuer les prix. *To reduce prices.*

Diminuer à vue d'oeil. *To diminish visibly.*

diminutif (diminutive *f.*) *adj. diminutive.*

diminution *f. diminishing, reduction.*

dinde *f. turkey.*

dindon *m. turkey.*

dîner *m. dinner.*

dîner *to dine.*

Nous dînerons en tête à tête. *We'll have dinner alone (just the two of us, privately).*

Qui dort dîne. *Sleeping makes one forget one's hunger.*

diplomatique *adj. diplomatic.*

diplôme *m. diploma, degree.*

Obtenir un diplôme. *To get a degree.*

diplômer *to grant a diploma to.*

DIRE *to say.*

L'art de bien dire. *The art of speaking well.*

Dites-donc, quand viendrez-vous chez nous? *Well, when will you come to our place?*

Aussitôt dit, aussitôt fait. *No sooner said than done.*

Que dites-vous de cela? *What do you think of that?*

On dirait qu'il va faire beau aujourd'hui. *It looks as if it will be a beautiful day.*

Alors, c'est dit? *Then it's settled?*

Il lui a fait dire de venir. *He sent him word to come.*

Que voulez-vous dire? *What do you mean?*

Que veut dire cette attitude? *What is the meaning of your attitude?*

Je veux dire que . . . *I mean that . . .*

A vrai dire. *To tell the truth.*

Soit dit entre nous. *Between ourselves.*

Non, je ne tiens pas à y aller, cela ne me dit rien. *No I don't feel like going there.*

The idea doesn't appeal to me. *It doesn't appeal to me.*

Quand je vous le disais! *I told you so!*

C'est-à-dire. *That is (to say), I (you) mean, in other words.*

Comme on dit. *As they say.*

Entendre dire (que). *To hear (that).*

Il n'y a pas à dire. *There's no doubt.*

Il m'a dit de partir. *He told me to leave.*

Je dirais. *I'd say.*

se dire *to be said, call oneself.*

Cela se dit, mais ne s'écrit pas. *That's said but it's never written.*

Il se dit votre ami. *He calls himself your friend.*

Cela se dit tout bas. *That should be whispered. That shouldn't be said aloud.*

DIRECT *adj. direct, straight.*

Impôts directs. *Direct taxes.*

Train direct. *Express train.*

Complément direct. *Direct object (grammar).*

directement *directly.*

directeur *m.* (directrice *f.*) *director.*

DIRECTION *f. direction; management.*

Changer de direction. 1. *To change the management.* 2. *To change direction. To go in another direction.*

directrice *f. directress.*

diriger *to direct; lead, rule.*

se diriger (**vers**) *to head for, make for a place.*

discernement *m. perception; discernment.*

discerner *to discerne, distinguish.*

Discerner le bien du mal. *To tell right from wrong.*

discipline *f. discipline.*

discipliner *to discipline.*

discorde *f. discord, strife.*

discours *m. speech.*

Prononcer un discours. *To make a speech.*

discret *adj. discreet.*

discrètement *discreetly.*

discrétion *f. discretion, tact.*

discussion *f. discussion.*

La discussion s'envenima. *The discussion became bitter.*

Une discussion orageuse. *A stormy discussion (debate).*

DISCUTER *to discuss, argue.*

Nous avons discuté pendant des heures entières. *We argued for hours on end.*

Il n'y a pas à discuter. *There's no question about it.*

DISPARAÎTRE *to disappear.*

Mon livre a disparu. *My book has disappeared.*

dispenser *to dispense; exempt.*

Je vous dispense de ces observations. *You may keep those remarks to yourself.*

se dispenser *to excuse oneself from.*

se disperser *to disperse, scatter.*

disponible *adj. available, at one's disposition.*

Il a peu d'argent disponible. *He doesn't have very much money available (at his disposal).*

DISPOSER *to dispose, arrange; have at one's disposal.*

Vous pouvez disposer librement de mon appartement. *You can make (free) use of my apartment.*

Il dispose de grands moyens d'action. *He possesses (has at his disposal) considerable resources ("means of action").*

Il est mal disposé à mon égard. *He's not well-disposed toward me.*

disposition *f. disposal, disposition.*

Je suis tout à votre disposition. *I am entirely at your disposal. I'm at your complete disposal.*

dispute *f. dispute, quarrel.*

disputer *to dispute, contest.*

se disputer *to quarrel.*

Ne vous disputez pas. *Don't quarrel.*

disque *m. disc, record.*

Microsillon, stéréo, de 33 tours. *Microgroove, stereo, 33 r.p.m.*

Disque compact. *Compact disc.*

Disque souple; disquette *f. Floppy disk.*

disséminer *to sow, scatter, disseminate.*

dissension *f. dissension, discord.*

dissoudre *to dissolve, disperse.*

dissuader *to dissuade.*

DISTANCE *f. distance; interval.*

A peu de distance. *At a short distance.*

Tenez-vous à distance. *Keep at a distance.*

distant *adj. distant; aloof.*

distinct *adj. distinct.*

distinctement *distinctly.*

distinctif (distinctive *f.*) *adj. distinctive.*

Trait distinctif. *Distinguishing feature. Characteristic.*

distinction *f. distinction.*

On doit faire une distinction entre ces deux choses. *One must make a distinction (distinguish) between these two things.*

Sans distinction. 1. *Indiscriminately. Without (any) discrimination.* 2. *Without distinction. Undistinguished.*

Un homme sans distinction. *An undistinguished man.*

distingué *adj. distinguished.*

distinguer *to distinguish, discriminate.*

se distinguer *to distinguish oneself.*

distraction *f. amusement; recreation; inattention.*

J'aime bien ces distractions. *I like these amusements/activities.*

Il est sujet à des distractions. *He's frequently very absent-minded.*

distraire *to divert; distract, amuse.*

Venez avec nous, cela vous distraira. *Come with us. It will cheer you up (it will be a pleasant change for you).*

distrait *adj. absent-minded.*

distribuer *to distribute, give out.*

distribution *f. distribution.*

divaguer *to digress, wander.*

divan *m. divan, sofa.*

DIVERS *adj. various, several, different.*

Il fabrique des objets divers. *He manufacturers various kinds of articles.*

A diverses reprises. *Several times.*

Faits divers. *News items.*

diversion *f. diversion, change.*

diversité *f. diversity, difference.*

divertir *to divert; entertain.*

se divertir *to amuse oneself.*

Il a l'air de se divertir. *He seems to be enjoying himself.*

divertissement *m. entertainment.*

dividende *m. dividend.*

divin *adj. divine, holy.*

diviser *to divide.*

division *f. division.*

divorce *m. divorce.*

divorcer *to divorce.*

divulguer *to divulge, reveal.*

DIX *noun and adj. ten.*

DIX-HUIT *noun and adj. eighteen*

DIX-HUITIÈME *noun and adj. eighteenth.*

DIXIÈME *noun and adj. tenth.*

DIX-NEUF *noun and adj. nineteen.*

DIX-NEUVIÈME *noun and adj. nineteenth*

DIX-SEPT *noun and adj. seventeen*

DIX-SEPTIÈME *noun and adj. seventeenth.*

dizaine *f. about ten.*

docile *adj. docile, submissive.*

DOCTEUR *m. doctor.*

Docteur en médecine. *Doctor. Physician, M.D.*

doctorat *m. Doctorate degree.*

document *m. document.*

documenter *to document, supply information about.*

se documenter *to gather documentary evidence.*

DOIGT *m. finger.*

Mon doigt me fait mal. *My finger hurts.*

Savoir quelque chose sur le bout des doigts. *To have something at one's fingertips.*

Doigt de pied. *Toe.*

Il se met le doigt dans l'oeil. *He's fooling (deceiving) himself. He is grossly (entirely) mistaken.*

Il s'en mord les doigts. *He's sorry he did it. He regrets having done it. He's repentant (now).*

Il lui obéit au doigt et à l'oeil. *He's at his beck and call.*

Mon petit doigt me l'a dit. *A little bird told me.*

Il était à deux doigts de la ruine. *He came near being ruined. He was on the very brink of ruin. He came within an ace of being ruined.*

dollar *m. dollar.*

domaine *m. domaine; estate.*
Ce n'est pas de mon domaine. *That's not within my province.*

domestique *m. servant.*

domestique *adj. domestic.*
Animal domestique. *Domestic animal.*

domicile *m. residence.*
Quel est votre domicile personnel? *What is your home address?*
Il a élu son domicile chez son père. *He established legal residence at the home of his father.*

domination *f. domination.*

dominer *to dominate, rule.*
Dominer ses scrupules. *To overcome one's scruples.*

se dominer *to control oneself.*
Il ne sait pas se dominer. *He has no self-control.*

dommage *m. damage; wrong.*
Payer les dommages-intérêts. *To pay the damages.*
C'est dommage. *It's a pity (a shame). It's too bad.*

dompter *to tame; overcome.*

don *m. gift.*
Le don des langues. *A gift for languages.*
Il a le don de l'à-propos. *He has the knack of always saying the right thing.*

DONC *so, therefore, indeed, accordingly.*
Notre travail est fini, donc nous pouvons partir. *Our work is finished, so (therefore, consequently) we can go (leave).*
Il n'a pas dit non, donc je pense qu'il est d'accord. *He didn't say no, so (therefore) I think he agrees.*
Vous aviez donc oublié? *So you forgot, didn't you?*
Pensez donc! *Just think!*
Allons donc! *Nonsense! You don't really mean that. You can't really be serious.*
Dites donc. *Say! Say there!*
Dites donc, ça suffit! *Look here, that's enough.*
Mais comment donc? *But how?*

Qu'y a-t-il donc? *What's the matter anyhow?*

données *f. data.*

DONNER *to give.*
Donnez-moi le menu, s'il vous plaît. *May I have the menu, please?*
Donnez-moi la main. *Give me your hand.*
Cet arbre donne des prunes. *This tree yields plums.*
Donnez-moi un acompte. *Pay me a part. Let me have a down payment.*
Il m'a donné à entendre que . . . *He intimated that . . . ("He gave me to understand that . . .")*
Donnez-nous de vos nouvelles. *Let's hear from you.*
Le chien lui donna un coup de patte. *The dog clawed (scratched) him.*
Il donne du fil à retordre. *He gives one a lot of trouble. He's not easy to manage (he puts up a lot of resistance).*
Je vous donnerai un coup de main. *I'll lend (give) you a hand. I'll help you.*
Il a donné à côté. *He missed (his aim).*
Pourquoi lui avez-vous donné le change? *Why did you put him on the wrong scent (mislead him)?*
Les fenêtres de la maison donnent sur le parc. *The windows (of the house) face the park.*
Il me donne gain de cause. *He sides with me. He decides in my favor.*
C'est à vous à donner. *It's your turn to deal the cards.*
Ce n'est pas donné à tout le monde. *That's not given to everyone (to be able to do something). Not everybody can do it.*
On lui a donné l'éveil. *They put him on his guard.*
Donner satisfaction à quelqu'un. *To please someone.*
Donner des ennuis à quelqu'un. *To cause someone trouble.*
Donner un coup de fil à. *To call, ring up (telephone).*
Donner un coup d'oeil à. *To glance, take a look at.*

se donner *to give oneself, devote oneself.*
Donnez-vous la peine d'entrer. *Will you please come in?*
Il se donne pour noble. *He passes himself off as a nobleman.*
Se donner une entorse. *To sprain, twist one's ankle.*

DONT *whose; of whom, of which.*
Le monsieur dont j'ai oublié le nom. *The gentleman whose name I've forgotten.*
Nous nous sommes arrêtés à un village dont j'ai oublié le nom. *We stopped at a*

*village the name of which I've
forgotten.*

C'est un homme dont il faut se méfier. *He's
a man you can't trust (you have to be
careful of).*

Voici ce dont il s'agit. *This is what it's all
about.*

doré *adj. gilded.*

dorénavant *from now on, henceforth.*

DORMIR *to sleep.*

Je n'ai pas dormi de la nuit. *I didn't sleep
all night.*

Il dormait comme une souche. *He was
sleeping like a log.*

Il dort debout. *He can't keep his eyes
open.*

Laissez dormir cette affaire jusqu'à lundi.
*Let the matter rest (wait) until
Monday.*

DOS *m. back.*

J'ai mal au dos. *My back aches.*

Il n'a rien à se mettre sur le dos. *He hasn't
a shirt to his back.*

Il m'a mis cela sur le dos. *He gave me the
responsibility.*

Il se met tout le monde à dos. *He turns
everybody against him.*

Il me tourne le dos. *He turns his back on
me.*

Il est toujours sur mon dos. *He's always at
my side telling me what to do.*

Il a bon dos. *They put all the blame on him.
They blame him for everything.*

J'en ai plein le dos (*fam*). *I'm fed up with it.*

dose *f. dose, share.*

dossier *m. back; record; file.*

Le dossier d'une chaise. *The back of a chair.*

Apportez les dossiers de l'affaire X. *Bring
the files on the X case.*

dot *f. dowry.*

douane *f. customs; customhouse; duty.*

Droits de douane. *Custom duties.*

Bureau de douane. *Customs house.*

La déclaration en douane. *Customs
declaration.*

Passer à la douane. *To clear, go through
customs.*

Le poste de douane. *Customs house.*

douanier *m. customs officer.*

double *adj. double.*

Mot à double sens. *Ambiguous word.*

Fermer une porte à double tour. *To double-
lock a door.*

doubler *to double.*

Le prix de la viande a doublé. *The price of
meat has doubled.*

Défense de doubler. *No passing on this road.*

doublure *f. lining.*

DOUCEMENT *slowly, gently.*

Allez-y (plus) doucement. *Act prudently. Go
easy.*

Doucement, ne nous échauffons pas. *Take it
easy, let's not get excited.*

Ça va tout doucement. *Things are so-so.
Things aren't too bad.*

douceur *f. sweetness, softness.*

douche *f. shower.*

Prendre une douche. *To take a shower.*

doué *adj. gifted.*

Il est doué pour la musique. *He has a gift
for music.*

douillet (douillette *f.*) *adj. soft, overdelicate.*

DOULEUR *f. pain, ache; grief.*

Ce médicament adoucira votre douleur. *This
medicine will relieve your pain.*

Elle est abîmée dans sa douleur. *She is
overwhelmed by grief.*

douloureux (douloureuse *f.*) *adj. painful.*

DOUTE *m. doubt.*

Avoir des doutes au sujet de quelque chose.
*To doubt something. To have doubts
about something.*

Cela est hors de doute. *There is no question
about it.*

Il n'y a pas l'ombre d'un doute. *There is not
a shadow of a doubt.*

Sans doute. *Of course. Doubtlessly.*

DOUTER *to doubt.*

Je doute qu'il accepte. *I don't think he'll
accept. I doubt whether he'll accept.*

se douter *to suspect; think.*

Je m'en doutais bien. *I thought so. I thought
(guessed) as much.*

Il ne se doutait de rien. *He suspected
nothing. He had no inkling (of what
was going on, etc.). He hadn't the
slightest suspicion (notion, idea).*

douteux (douteuse *f.*) *adj. doubtful.*

DOUX (douce *f.*) *adj. soft, gentle, easy.*

Il est doux comme un mouton. *He's as
gentle as a lamb.*

C'est doux au toucher. *It feel soft (to the
touch).*

Il n'a pas la main douce. *He's rough. He
doesn't use kid gloves.*

Filer en douce. *To leave on the sly. To steal
away.*

Elle lui fait les yeux doux. *She's making
eyes at him (looking sweet at him).*

Il fait doux. *The weather is mild.*

DOUZAINE *f. dozen.*

DOUZE *noun and adj. twelve.*

DOUZIÈME *noun and adj. twelfth.*

dramatique *adj. dramatic.*

L'art dramatique. *The drama.*

Situation dramatique. *Dramatic situation.*

dramatiser *to dramatize.*

drame *m. drama.*

drap *m. sheet; cloth.*

Ce drap est à raccommoder. *This (bed) sheet has to be mended.*

Les voilà dans de beaux draps. *They're in a fine pickle. They're in a fine mess.*

drapeau *m.* (drapeaux *pl.*) *flag.*

dresser *to erect.*

Il dresse l'oreille. *He's on the alert ("He pricks up his ears.")*

On lui avait dressé un piège. *They had set a trap for him.*

Dresser un acte de décès. *To make out a death certificate.*

drogue *f. drug.*

trafiquant de drogue. *Drug pusher.*

se droguer. *To take drugs.*

DROIT *m. right; law; duty.*

La force prime le droit. *Might is right.*

Il a reconnu mon droit. *He recognized my claim.*

C'est mon droit. *It's my privilege.*

Il a droit à la retraite. *He's entitled to a pension.*

Droits d'entrée. *Import duties.*

Droits de sortie. *Export duties.*

Le droit d'inscription. *Registration fee.*

Le droit d'entrée est cher. *The entrance fee is expensive.*

Droits de succession. *Inheritance tax.*

Il fait son droit à Paris. *He's studying law in Paris.*

Le droit des gens. *International law.*

Le droit d'aînesse. *Birthright.*

DROIT *adj. right, straight.*

Une ligne droite. *A straight line.*

Tenez-vous droit. *Stand (up) straight.*

Aller droit au fait. *To go straight to the point.*

C'est le bras droit du patron. *He's the boss's right-hand man.*

DROITE *f. right hand.*

Elle était assise à ma droite. *She sat on my right.*

Tenir sa droite. *To keep to the right.*

DRÔLE *adj. funny, amusing.*

Comme c'est drôle! *How strange!*

Cela m'a fait un drôle d'effet. *It gave me a funny feeling.*

Quelle drôle d'idée! *What a funny idea!*

C'est un drôle de personnage (*fam.*). *He's an odd fellow.*

Ce fromage a un drôle d'aspect. *This cheese doesn't look right.*

DU *See* de. *from the, of the, some.*

Je veux du pain. *I'd like some bread.*

Il revient de la Côte d'Azur. *He just came back from the Riviera.*

Pas du tout. *Not at all.*

dû *m. due.*

Il réclame son dû. *He claims his due.*

dû (due *f.*) *adj. due, owed.*

L'acte est en bonne et due forme. *The deed is in proper form.*

duquel (de laquelle *f.*, desquels *m. pl.*, desquelles *f. pl.*) *of which, whom.*

Duquel s'agit-il? *Which one is it a question of?*

DUR *adj. hard, rough.*

Ce lit est trop dur. *This bed is too hard.*

Oeufs durs. *Hard-boiled eggs.*

Il est dur d'oreille. *He's hard of hearing.*

Il a la tête dure. *He's thick-headed (stubborn).*

Travailler dur. *To work hard.*

DURANT *during.*

Durant sa vie. *During his lifetime.*

Durant son voyage, il est tombé malade. *He became sick during his trip.*

Je l'ai attendu trois heures durant. *I waited for him three whole hours.*

durcir *to harden.*

durée *f. duration.*

De courte durée. *Short-lived.*

La durée de la guerre. *The duration of the war.*

DURER *to last.*

J'ai peur que cela ne dure pas. *I'm afraid it won't last.*

dureté *f. hardness.*

dynamite *f. dynamite.*

dysenterie *f. dysentery.*

E

EAU *f.* (eaux *pl.*) *water.*

Cours d'eau. *Waterway.*

Jet d'eau. *Fountain.*

C'est une goutte d'eau dans la mer. *It's like a drop in the ocean. It's a drop in the bucket.*

eau-de-vie *f. brandy.*

eau-forte *m.* (eaux-fortes *pl.*) *etching.*

ébahi *adj. amazed, dumbfounded.*

ébaucher *to sketch.*

éblouir *to dazzle.*

éblouissant *adj. dazzling.*

ébranlement *m. shock, concussion.*

ébranler *to shake.*

L'explosion ébranla la maison. *The explosion shook the house.*

Sa raison en fut ébranlée. *His mind was unsettled by it.*

écaille *f. scale, shell; tortoiseshell.*

écart *m. deviation; digression.*

Il se tient à l'écart. *He keeps in the background.*

écarter *to separate; move aside.*

Ecarter les obstacles. *To brush the obstacles aside.*

s'écarter *to move aside; diverge; deviate.*

échafaud *m. scaffold.*

échafaudage *m. scaffolding.*

échancrer *to indent, notch.*

échancrure *f. indentation, groove.*

échange *m. exchange.*

En échange de. *In exchange for.*

Faire un échange. *To exchange.*

échanger *to exchange.*

échantillon *m. sample.*

échapper *to escape, overlook.*

Il a échappé à la mort. *He escaped death.*

Il a laissé échapper toute l'histoire. *He blurted out the whole story.*

Nous l'avons échappé belle. *We had a narrow escape.*

s'échapper *to escape.*

écharpe *f. scarf.*

s'échauffer *to become overheated, warm up.*

échéance *f. date; term (of payment).*

Payable à l'échéance. *Payable at maturity.*

échéant *adj. falling due.*

Le cas échéant. *In that case.*

échec *m. failure, defeat.*

Subir un échec. *To suffer defeat. To meet with failure.*

échecs *m. pl. chess.*

Faisons une partie d'échecs. *Let's play a game of chess.*

échelle *f. ladder; scale.*

échelon *m. step (of a ladder).*

Monter par échelons. *To rise by degrees.*

échelonner *to space out, spread out.*

échevelé *adj. disheveled.*

écho *m. echo.*

Faire écho. *To echo.*

échoir *to fall to one's lot.*

Le devoir m'a échu de le lui dire. *It fell to me to tell him.*

échouer *to fail.*

Mon plan a échoué. *My plan failed.*

Il a échoué à son examen. *He failed in his examination.*

éclaboussement *m. splashing.*

éclabousser *to splash.*

éclaboussure *f. splash.*

éclair *m. lightning, flash.*

Il a passé comme un éclair. *He shot by like lightning.*

Vif comme l'éclair. *Quick as lightning. Quick as a flash.*

C'était un éclair de génie. *It was a stroke of genius.*

éclairage *m. lighting, illumination.*

Eclairage des rues. *Street lighting.*

éclaircir *to clear up, become brighter; lighten (color).*

Le temps s'éclaircit. *The weather's clearing up.*

éclairer *to light, illuminate.*

Cette lampe n'éclaire pas. *This lamp gives a poor light.*

éclat *m. burst; glitter.*

Son mariage se fit sans éclat. *His (her) marriage took place quietly. He (she) had a quiet wedding.*

Une action d'éclat. *A brilliant feat.*

Partir d'un éclat de rire. *To burst into laughter. To burst out laughing.*

éclatant *adj. loud, ringing.*

éclater *to split, burst.*

Un incendie éclata. *A fire broke out.*

Eclater de rire. *To burst into laughter. To burst out laughing.*

ÉCOLE *f. school, schoolhouse.*

Se rendre à l'école. *To go to school.*

Maître d'école. *Schoolteacher.*

Ecole maternelle. *Day care; nursery school.*

Ecole mixte. *Coed school.*

Ecole de cours moyen. *Junior high school.*

Ecole privée. *Private school.*

Ecole secondaire. *High school.*

écolier *m. (écolière f.) schoolboy, schoolgirl.*

éconduire *to show to the door.*

économe *adj. thrifty.*

ÉCONOMIE *f. economics; thrift; pl. savings.*

Economie politique. *Political economy.*

Par économie de temps. *To save time.*

Faire des économies. *To save money. To put money aside.*

économique *adj. economical.*

économiser *to save.*

Economiser pour l'avenir. *To save up for the future.*

écorce *f. bark; rind, peel.*

écorcher *to peel off, graze.*

Il écorche le français. *He murders French.*

écossais *noun and adj. Scottish.*

écouler *to flow out, run out.*

Faire écouler l'eau. *To drain off the water.*

écoute *f. listening-place.*

Se tenir aux écoutes. *To keep one's ears open. To eavesdrop.*

ÉCOUTER *to listen to.*

Maintenant je suis tout à vous, je vous écoute. *Now I'm at your disposal; I'm listening.*

Ecoutez! *Look here! I'll tell you what!*

Ecoutez-moi. *Take my advice. Listen to me.*

J'écoute. *Number, please? (telephone).*

écran *m. screen.*

écrasant *adj. crushing.*

écraser *to crush, run over.*

Vous allez vous faire écraser. *You'll be run over (You'll get yourself run over).*

Je suis écrasé de travail. *I'm swamped with work.*

s'écraser *to collapse.*

s'écrier *to cry out, exclaim.*

ÉCRIRE *to write.*

Je lui ai écrit un mot. *I dropped him a line.*

J'écris toujours toutes mes lettres à la machine. *I always type my letters.*

Machine à écrire. *Typewriter.*

Comment écrit-on ce mot en français? *How do you write (spell) this word in French?*

écriteau *m. poster, notice.*

ÉCRITURE *f. handwriting.*

Il a une belle écriture. *He has good handwriting.*

ÉCRIVAIN *m. writer.*

s'écrouler *to collapse, fall to pieces.*

Tous leurs plans s'écroulèrent. *All their plans collapsed.*

écume *f. foam.*

écureuil *m. squirrel.*

écurie *f. stable.*

édifice *m. building.*

édifier *to erect; edify, enlighten.*

Il m'a édifié sur cette affaire. *He enlightened me about the matter.*

éditer *to publish.*

éditeur *m. publisher.*

édition *f. publication, edition.*

Edition épuisée. *Out of print.*

Maison d'édition. *Publishing house.*

éditorial (éditoriaux *pl.*) *adj. editorial.*

ÉDUCATION *f. education; breeding, manners.*

Ils ont reçu une excellente éducation. *They received an excellent education.*

C'est un homme sans éducation. *He's an ill-bred person. He's a boor.*

Il n'a pas d'éducation. *He has no breeding.*

effacé *unobtrusive, retiring.*

Manières effacées. *Retiring manners.*

effacer *to erase, obliterate, to cut (computer).*

s'effacer *to fade, wear away, stand aside.*

Les souvenirs s'effacent vite. *Memories fade rapidly.*

effaré *frightened, dismayed.*

s'effarer *to be frightened, startled.*

effaroucher *to startle.*

effectif (effective *f.*) *adj. effective.*

effectivement *effectively; in reality, actually.*

Cela est arrivé effectivement. *It really (actually) happened.*

effectuer *to effect, carry out.*

Effectuer une réconciliation. *To bring about a reconciliation.*

effervescence *effervescence.*

effervescent *adj. effervescent.*

EFFET *m. impression, effect.*

Prendre effet. *To take effect. To go into effect.*

Il me fait l'effet d'un ignorant. *He strikes me as being very ignorant.*

A cet effet. *To this end.*

Mon conseil a produit l'effet voulu. *My advice had the desired effect.*

Cela fait de l'effet. 1. *That is effective.* 2. *That has the right effect. That looks well. That attracts attention.*

En effet. *As a matter of fact.*

Sans effet. *Ineffective.*

Il a manqué son effet. *He failed to make the impression (he was supposed to).*

effets *m. pl. possessions, belongings.*

Faites vos effets. *Pack up your things.*

Ces effets ont été portés. *These clothes have been worn.*

efficace *adj. effective, adequate.*

efficacité *f. effectiveness.*

effigie *f. effigy.*

effiler *to taper.*

effleurer *to touch lightly.*

s'effondrer *to fall in, break down.*

Le plafond s'effondra. *The ceiling collapsed.*

s'efforcer *to endeavor, strive.*

EFFORT *m. effort.*

Malgré tous nos efforts. *Despite all our efforts.*

Faire un effort sur soi-même. *To exercise self-control.*

effrayer *to frighten.*

effroi *m. fright, terror, fear.*

effronté *adj. brazen-faced, shameless.*

effronterie *f. impudence.*

effroyable *adj. frightful.*

effusion *f. effusion, overflowing.*

Avec effusion. *Effusively.*

EGAL (égale, égales *f.*, égaux *m. pl.*) *noun and adj. equal.*

Sous ce rapport, il est sans égal. *In that respect he has no equal.*

C'est égal! N'importe! *It doesn't matter! Never mind!*

Ça m'est bien égal. *I don't care. It's all the same to me.*

Tout cela lui est bien égal. *All that's the same to him. All that makes no difference to him. He's indifferent to all that.*

Cela vous est-il égal que je ferme la porte? *Do you mind if I shut the door?*

ÉGALEMENT *equally; also.*

J'irai également. *I'll go too. I'll also go.*

égaler *to equalize, equal.*

égaliser *to equalize.*

égalité *f. equality, evenness.*

EGARD *m. regard.*

N'ayez aucune crainte à cet égard. *Have no fear on that score.*

Avoir des égards. *To be considerate.*

Eu égard aux circonstances. *All things considered. Considering the circumstances.*

Il a manqué à sa parole à mon égard. *He didn't keep his word to me.*

Qu'avez-vous à dire à son égard? *What do you have to say concerning (about) him?*

égarer *to misplace, lose.*

J'ai égaré ma montre. *I misplaced my watch.*

s'égarer *to get lost.*

Je me suis égaré. *I got lost.*

égayer *to cheer up.*

église *f. church.*

égoïsme *m. egoism, selfishness.*

égoïste *m. and f. noun and adj. egoist; selfish.*

Agir en égoïste. *To act selfishly.*

Une personne égoïste. *A selfish person.*

égorger *to butcher, slaughter.*

égout *m. drain, sewer.*

égoutter *to drain.*

Faire égoutter des légumes. *To strain vegetables.*

égratigner *to scratch.*

élan *m. spring, bound; outburst; impulse.*

D'un seul élan. *At one bound.*

Elan de l'imagination. *Flight of the imagination.*

élancé *adj. tall and slim.*

s'élancer *to rush, rise.*

Il s'élança à sa poursuite. *He dashed after him.*

élargir *to widen, stretch.*

élastique *m. and f. noun and adj. elastic.*

élection *f. election.*

électricité *m. electricity.*

élégance *f. elegance.*

élégant *adj. elegant; stylish.*

élément *m. element.*

Il est dans son élément. *He's in his element.*

élémentaire *adj. elementary.*

éléphant *m. elephant.*

élevage *m. breeding, raising (of animals).*

élévation *f. elevation; rise.*

élève *m. and f. student, pupil.*

élevé *adj. high; brought up, reared.*

Bien élevé. *Well-bred.*

Mal élevé. *Ill-bred.*

élever *to bring up; raise, erect.*

Elever des enfants. *To rear (raise) children.*

On lui a élevé un monument. *They erected a monument to him.*

s'élever *to rise, arise.*

éliminer *to eliminate.*

élire *to elect.*

élite *f. elite.*

ELLE (elles *pl.*) *she; it; her.*

Vous pouvez vous fier à elle. *You can trust her. You can have confidence in her.*

Chez elle. *At her house.*

Chacune d'elles. *Each of them.*

elle-même *herself.*

elles-mêmes *(f. pl.) themselves.*

éloge *m. praise.*

Adresser des éloges à quelqu'un. *To praise someone.*

Faire l'éloge de quelqu'un. *To sing someone's praises.*

élogieux (élogieuse *f.*) *adj. laudatory, flattering.*

Il parla de lui en termes élogieux. *He spoke highly of him.*

éloigné *adj. far, distant, remote.*

Le plus éloigné. *The furthermost.*

Avenir peu éloigné. *Near future.*

Rien n'est plus éloigné de mes intentions. *Nothing is further from my intentions.*

Parent éloigné. *Distant relative.*

éloignement *m. absence, removal.*

éloigner *to move away.*

Eloigner les soupçons. *To avert suspicion.*

Eloigner une pensée. *To dismiss a thought.*

s'éloigner *to move off, withdraw.*

S'éloigner de tout le monde. *To shun everybody.*

éloquence *f. eloquence.*

éloquent *adj. eloquent.*

émail *m. enamel.*

émancipation *f. emancipation.*

émanciper *to emancipate.*

s'émanciper *to gain one's freedom.*

émaner *to emanate, issue forth.*

emballage *m. packing, wrapping.*

Papier d'emballage. *Wrapping paper.*

emballer *to pack.*

s'emballer *to be carried away.*

Ne vous emballez pas! *Keep cool!*

S'emballer pour quelque chose. *To be keen on something.*

embarcadère *m. pier.*

embargo *m. embargo.*

embarquement *m. embarking.*

embarquer *to take on board; involve.*

Ce sont eux qui l'ont embarqué dans cette affaire. *They're the ones who got him involved in that affair.*

s'embarquer *to go on board, start upon.*

Ils se sont embarqués à Marseille. *They embarked at Marseilles.*

embarras *m. obstacle; difficulty, trouble.*

Se trouver dans l'embarras. *To be in difficulties.*

Se tirer d'embarras. *To get out of a difficulty.*

Faire des embarras. *To be fussy (particular).*

Je n'ai que l'embarras du choix. *I have too much to choose from.*

embarrassant *adj. cumbersome; perplexing.*
Une situation embarrassante. *An embarrassing position.*

embarrassé *adj. perplexed, embarrassed.*

embarrasser *to embarrass.*
Il n'est jamais embarrassé. *He's never at a loss.*
Que cela ne vous embarrasse pas. *Don't let that trouble you (bother you, put you out). Have no fear on that score.*
Il est embarrassé d'un rien. *He makes a mountain out of a molehill.*
Cette question m'embarrasse. *That question puzzles me.*

embaucher *to hire.*

embellir *to embellish; grow more beautiful.*
Comme elle a embelli! *How beautiful she's become!*

embêtant *adj. (fam.) boring; annoying.*

embêter *(fam.) to annoy.*

s'embêter *(fam.) to be bored.*

emblée *used only in the following phrase:*
D'emblée. *At once. Right away.*

emblème *m. emblem.*

embonpoint *n. stoutness, weight.*

embouteillage *m. traffic jam, tie-up.*

embranchement *m. branching off; branch.*

embrasser *to embrace, kiss.*
N'embrassez pas trop à la fois. *Don't undertake too much at once. Don't try to do too many things at the same time.*
Embrasser une autre religion. *To adopt another religion.*

embrayage *m. clutch (car).*

embrouiller *to entangle; confuse.*

s'embrouiller *to get confused.*

embûche *f. pitfall; trap.*

embuscade *f. ambush, snare.*

émeraude *f. emerald.*

émerveillé *adj. amazed, filled with wonder.*

émetteur (émettrice *f.*) *adj. broadcasting.*

émettre *to emit, issue; express.*
Emettre une opinion. *To express an opinion.*

émeute *f. riot, outbreak.*

émigrant *m. emigrant.*

émigration *f. emigration.*

émigré *m. refugee.*

émigrer *to emigrate, migrate.*

éminence *f. eminence.*

éminent *adj. eminent.*

émissaire *m. emissary.*

émission *f. emission, issue; radio broadcast.*

emmagasiner *to store (goods).*

emmêler *to entangle, mix up.*

emmener *to lead away, take out.*

émoi *m. agitation, excitement.*

émotion *f. emotion, stir.*

émotionner *to move, stir (emotionally), thrill.*

s'émotionner *to be moved, stirred, roused; get excited.*

émouvant *adj. moving, touching.*

émouvoir *to move, rouse.*
Elle était émue jusqu'aux larmes. *She was moved to tears.*

empaqueter *to pack, make into a parcel.*

s'emparer *to take hold of.*

empêchement *m. hindrance, impediment, bar.*

EMPÊCHER *to prevent, keep from.*
Empêchez-les de faire cela. *Prevent (keep) them from doing that.*
Il faut souffrir ce que l'on ne peut empêcher. *What can't be cured must be endured.*
Qu'est-ce qui vous a empêché de venir? *What kept you from coming?*

s'empêcher *to refrain from.*

empereur *m. emperor.*

empesé *adj. stiff, starched.*

empeser *to starch.*
Faire empeser. *To have (something) starched.*

empester *to stink, reek.*

emphase *f. pomposity, bombast.*

empiéter *to encroach upon, infringe.*

empiler *to stack.*

empire *m. empire.*

empirer *to get worse.*

emplacement *m. site, location.*

emplette *f. purchase.*
J'ai fait des emplettes. *I've been shopping.*

EMPLOI *m. employment, function.*
Mode d'emploi. *Directions for use.*
Il est apte à tous les emplois. *He's well qualified for every occupation.*
Etre sans emploi. *To be out of work.*

employé *m. employee.*

EMPLOYER *to use.*
Ils ont employé tous les moyens. *They've tried everything. They've tried all possible means.*

empocher *to pocket.*

empoigner *to grasp, seize.*

empoisonnement *m. poisoning.*

empoisonner *to poison.*
Elle empoisonne sa vie. *She makes life unbearable for him (her).*

emportement *m. transport, anger.*

EMPORTER *to carry away.*
Le vent a emporté mon chapeau. *The wind blew my hat away.*
Emportez tout cela. *Take all that away.*
Il a été emporté par la fièvre thyphoïde. *He died of typhoid. He was carried off by thyphoid.*
Restez calme, ne vous laissez pas emporter. *Remain calm, don't lose control of yourself.*

L'emporter sur quelqu'un. *To get the best of someone.*

Il a été emporté par l'enthousiasme. *He was carried away by enthusiasm.*

s'emporter *to run away; fly into a passion.*

Les chevaux se sont emportés. *The horses ran away.*

Il s'est emporté. *He flew into a rage.*

empreindre *to imprint.*

empreinte *f. impression, print.*

Empreintes digitales. *Fingerprints.*

empressé *adj. eager, zealous.*

empressement *m. eagerness, readiness.*

Mettre beaucoup d'empressement à faire quelque chose. *To be more than willing to do something.*

s'empresser *to hurry, hasten.*

emprise *f. expropriation; influence.*

Il a beaucoup d'emprise sur lui. *He has a lot of influence over him.*

emprisonnement *m. imprisonment.*

emprisonner *to imprison.*

emprunt *m. borrowing, loan.*

emprunter *to borrow.*

ému *adj. moved, touched.*

EN *into, in, to, within.*

Aller en ville. *To go into town.*

Venir en auto. *To come by car.*

Aller en Amérique. *To go to America.*

En son honneur. *In his honor.*

En été. *In the summer.*

Il est né en 1912. *He was born in 1912.*

En son absence. *In his absence.*

En vacances. *On vacation.*

Montre en or. *Gold watch.*

De mal en pis. *From bad to worse.*

De jour en jour. *From day to day.*

On apprend en vieillissant. *We learn as we grow older.*

Voyager en auto (avion, bateau, train, taxi, voiture). *To travel by auto (plane, boat, railway, taxi, car).*

En deux jours. *In (within) two days.*

EN *some, any; of him, of her, of it, of them; from there.*

En avez-vous? *Do you have any (of it, of them)?*

En voulez-vous? *Do you want some (of it, of them)?*

A-t-il de l'argent?—Oui, il en a. *Does he have any money?—Yes, he has some.*

Donnez-en à Jean. *Give some to John.*

Avez-vous besoin de mon livre?—Oui, j'en ai besoin. *Do you need my book?—Yes, I need it.*

Ont-ils des livres?—Ils en ont beaucoup. *Do they have any books?—They have many of them.*

Vient-il de Paris?—Il en vient directement.

Is he coming from Paris?—He's coming directly from there.

Qu'en pensez-vous? *What do you think of (about) it?*

S'en aller. *To go away.*

S'en faire. *To worry.*

Ne t'en fais pas. *Don't worry.*

encadrer *to frame.*

enceinte *f. enclosure, walls.*

enceinte *adj. pregnant.*

encercler *to encircle.*

enchaînement *m. linking-up; connection.*

enchaîner *to chain; link; connect.*

enchanter *to enchant, charm.*

Je suis enchanté de vous revoir. *I am delighted to see you again.*

Ça ne m'enchante pas. *It doesn't appeal to me.*

Permettez-moi de vous présenter à M. Lardieu.—Enchanté. *I'd like to introduce you to Mr. Lardieu.—Glad to know you.*

enchère *f. bid.*

Vente aux enchères. *Auction sale. Sale by auction.*

enchevêtré *adj. tangled, involved.*

enchevêtrer *to entangle, ravel.*

enclin *adj. inclined, apt.*

encolure *f. neck-opening.*

encombre *m. hindrance.*

Nous sommes arrivés sans encombre. *We arrived without difficulty.*

encombrement *m. obstruction; crowd.*

encombrer *to encumber.*

ENCORE *yet, still.*

Quoi encore? *What else?*

Encore une fois. *Once more.*

Attendons encore un peu. *Let's wait a little longer.*

Hier encore je lui ai parlé. *I spoke to him only yesterday.*

Il n'est pas encore là. *He hasn't come yet.*

encourageant *adj. encouraging.*

encouragement *m. encouragement.*

encourager *to encourage.*

encourir *to incur.*

encre *f. ink.*

encrier *m. inkwell.*

encyclopédie *f. encyclopedia.*

endormi *adj. asleep.*

endormir *to put to sleep.*

s'endormir *to fall asleep.*

Elle s'est endormie de fatigue. *She was so tired that she fell asleep.*

ENDROIT *m. place.*

Quel joli endroit! *What a beautiful place!*

Cette pièce est très amusante par endroits. *This play is very amusing in places.*

L'endroit faible. *The weak spot.*

Il a mal agi à mon endroit. *He didn't act well toward me. He didn't treat me right.*

enduire *to smear, cover.*

endurance *f. endurance.*

endurcir *to harden.*

endurer *to endure, bear.*

énergie *f. strength, energy.*

énergique *adj. energetic.*

énervant *adj. irritating.*

énervé *adj. irritated, exasperated, on edge.*

énerver *to get on someone's nerves, upset someone.*

s'énerver *to become irritated, exasperated; get nervous.*

enfance *f. childhood.*

enfant *m. child.*

enfantillage *m. childishness.*

enfantin *adj. childish.*

enfer *m. hell.*

enfermer *to lock up, lock away.*

ENFIN *at last, finally, after all.*

Il y est enfin arrivé, il le mérite bien. *He finally succeeded—he certainly deserves to.*

Je suis heureux d'être reçu enfin à mon examen. *I'm glad I finally passed that examination.*

enflammer *to inflame.*

enfler *to swell.*

enfoncer *to drive in, push in.*

s'enfoncer *to penetrate, go deep into.*

enfouir *to bury in the ground.*

s'enfuir *to flee.*

engagé *adj. stuck, jammed (mechanism).*

engagement *m. obligation; pledge; pawning.*

engager *to pledge, promise, bind; engage; urge.*

Cela n'engage à rien. *That's not binding.*

s'engager *to enlist, pledge.*

engin *m. engine.*

englober *to include, take in.*

engloutir *to swallow; engulf.*

s'engouffrer *to be engulfed.*

engourdi *adj. numb.*

engourdir *to make numb.*

engourdissement *m. numbness.*

engraisser *to fatten; gain weight.*

enivrer *to go to one's head, intoxicate.*

enjamber *to step over, stride.*

enjeu *n. (enjeux pl.) stake.*

enjoindre *to enjoin; to order.*

enlacer *to entwine, clasp.*

enlever *to remove, wipe off, clear away.*

Enlevez toutes ces choses. *Remove all these things. Take all these things away.*

ennemi *noun (m.) and adj. enemy.*

ENNUI *m. nuisance, trouble, bother.*

Il lui a causé beaucoup d'ennuis. *He caused him a lot of trouble.*

Cela a amené des ennuis. *That caused all sorts of trouble.*

Je regrette si je vous ai causé un ennui quelconque. *I'm sorry if I caused you any inconvenience.*

Mourir d'ennui. *To be frightfully bored.*

Quel ennui! *What a nuisance!*

ennuyant *adj. annoying, vexing.*

ennuyer *to bore, bother.*

Cela vous ennuierait-il d'attendre un peu? *Would you mind waiting a little?*

Je suis très ennuyé. *I'm very much worried. I have a lot of trouble (a lot of worries).*

s'ennuyer *to be bored.*

ennuyeux (ennuyeuse *f.*) *adj. boring, tedious.*

énorme *adj. enormous.*

énormément *enormously, extremely.*

Je le regrette énormément. *I'm extremely sorry.*

énormité *f. enormousness; enormity.*

s'enquérir *to inquire.*

enquête *f. inquiry.*

Faire une enquête. *To hold an inquiry.*

enragé *adj. rabid, mad.*

enrager *to enrage, fume.*

enregistrer *to register; to record; to save (on a computer).*

s'enrhumer *to catch a cold.*

s'enrichir *to grow (get) rich.*

s'enrôler *to enlist.*

enroué *adj. hoarse, husky.*

enrouler *to roll up, wind.*

enseigne *f. sign; token.*

Nous sommes tous logés à la même enseigne. *We're all in the same boat.*

enseignement *m. teaching, education.*

enseigner *to teach.*

ENSEMBLE *noun m. and adv. together, whole.*

L'ensemble du travail est bon. *The work is good on the whole.*

Vue d'ensemble. *General view. All-round picture.*

Etre bien ensemble. *To be on good terms.*

Ils sont arrivés ensemble. *They arrived together.*

ensevelir *to bury.*

ensoleillé *adj. sunny, sunlit.*

ensorceler *to bewitch.*

ENSUITE *then, afterwards.*

Allons d'abord déjeuner, ensuite nous irons au musée. *Let's first have lunch; afterwards we'll go to the museum.*

Et ensuite? *And what else? And then what?*

s'ensuivre *to follow, ensue.*

entamer *to begin, start.*

Il a entamé la conversation. *He opened the conversation.*

entasser *to heap up.*

ENTENDRE *to hear, understand.*

J'entends un bruit. *I hear a noise.*

Il entend mal. *He's hard of hearing (he doesn't hear well).*

Elles ne veulent pas en entendre parler. *They won't hear of it. They refuse to consider it.*

Il n'y entend rien. *He can't make it out.*

Il ne veut rien entendre. *He won't listen.*

J'ai entendu dire que . . . *I've heard it said that . . .*

Faire entendre raison à quelqu'un. *To bring someone to reason.*

A l'entendre. *To listen to (him). From what (he) says.*

Faites comme vous l'entendez. *Do what you think best. Do it your own way. Do it any way you please.*

Vous entendez tout de travers. *You misunderstand the whole thing. You've got everything wrong.*

Je n'entends pas que vous fassiez cela. *I won't allow you to do that. I won't hear of your doing that.*

Il n'y entend pas malice. *He means well. He doesn't mean any harm.*

C'est entendu. *That's settled. It's a bargain. Agreed. All right. Very well, it's a deal.*

Bien entendu. *Of course.*

S'ENTENDRE *to be audible; understand; agree to get along.*

On ne s'entend pas ici. *There's so much noise you can't hear anything. You can't hear yourself talk here.*

Ils s'entendent à demi-mot. *They know at once what the other is going to say.*

Lui et moi nous finissons toujours par nous entendre. *We always agree in the end.*

Ils ne s'entendent pas bien. *They don't get along well together.*

Cela s'entend. *It goes without saying.*

Il s'entend aux affaires. *He's a born businessman. He has a good business head.*

entente *f. understanding; agreement; meaning.*

Ils sont arrivés à une entente. *They reached an agreement.*

Mot à double entente. *Word with a double meaning.*

enterrement *m. burial.*

enterrer *to bury.*

entêté *adj. stubborn.*

s'entêter *to be stubborn.*

enthousiasme *m. enthusiasm.*

enthousiasmer *to make someone enthusiastic.*

s'enthousiasmer *to become enthusiastic.*

J'en ai été enthousiasmé. *I was very enthusiastic about it.*

ENTIER (entière *f.*) *adj. entire, whole.*

La famille entière est allée en promenade. *The whole family went for a walk.*

Ce savon se vend dans le monde entier. *This soap is sold all over the world.*

entièrement *entirely, wholly.*

entorse *f. sprain, strain.*

entourer *to surround, encircle.*

entr'acte *m. intermission (theatre).*

s'entraider *to help one another.*

entrain *m. heartiness, spirit.*

Il a de l'entrain. *He's full of energy. He's full of life.*

entraînement *m. training.*

entraîner *to draw along, sweep away; involve; train for sports.*

ENTRE *between, among.*

Tout est fini entre nous. *It's all over between us.*

Nous sommes entre amis. *We are among friends.*

Parler entre les dents. *To mumble.*

Il est entre bonnes mains. *He's in good hands.*

ENTRÉE *f. entrance.*

Entrée interdite. *No admittance.*

Entrée libre. *Admission free.*

Droit d'entrée. *Import duty.*

entrefaite *f. (usually in the pl.) meantime.*

Il est arrivé sur ces entrefaites. *He arrived in the meantime.*

entremise *f. intervention.*

entreprendre *to undertake, attempt.*

entreprise *f. enterprise, undertaking.*

Entreprise commerciale. *Business concern.*

ENTRER *to enter, come in.*

Entrez. *Come in.*

Défense d'entrer. *No admittance.*

Entrez dans cette chambre-ci. *Go into this room.*

Entrer à l'école. *To enter (begin) school.*

Entrer à l'université. *To enter the university.*

Entrer en fonctions. *To take up one's duties.*

Il ne m'était pas entré dans l'idée que . . . *It never entered my mind that . . .*

entresol *m. mezzanine.*

entretenir *to keep up, maintain, entertain, support.*

entretien *m. upkeep; conversation.*

Frais d'entretien. *Cost of maintenance.*

J'ai eu un entretien avec elle. *I had a talk with her.*

entrevoir *to catch a glimpse of.*

Je n'ai fait que l'entrevoir. *I only caught a glimpse of him (her).*

entrevue *f. interview.*

énumérer *to enumerate.*

envahir *to invade.*

enveloppe *f. envelope.*

envelopper *to wrap up, surround.*

envergure *f. spread, span.*
De grande envergure. *Far-reaching.*

envers *m. wrong side, back.*
Mettre sa robe à l'envers. *To put on one's dress inside out.*

envers *toward, to.*
Envers et contre tous. *Against everyone. Against all comers.*

ENVIE *f. envy; wish.*
Par envie. *Through jealousy.*
Cela vous donne envie de rire. *It (that) makes you want to laugh. It's enough to make you laugh.*
Elle mourait d'envie d'y aller. *She was dying to go there.*
Avec envie. *Longingly.*
J'en ai envie. *I'd like to have it. I feel like it.*
Je n'ai pas envie d'y aller. *I don't feel like going there.*

envier *to envy, covet.*

envieux (envieuse *f.*) *adj. envious.*

environ *around; nearly*
Il doit être environ cinq heures. *It must be about five o'clock.*
J'ai environ cent francs. *I have about a hundred francs.*

environs *m. pl. vicinity; neighborhood.*
Il habite dans les environs de Paris. *He lives near Paris. He lives in the vicinity of Paris.*

envisager *to face; consider.*

envoi *m. parcel.*
Nous avons reçu son envoi. *We received his parcel.*

s'envoler *to fly away.*

envoyé *m. envoy, delegate.*

ENVOYER *to send.*
Il a envoyé chercher le médicin. *He sent for the doctor.*
Elle vous envoie ses meilleures amitiés. *She sends you her best regards.*
Envoyez-moi un mot. *Drop me a line.*
Je vous envoie toutes mes pensées affectueuses. *Affectionately yours (in a letter).*
Envoyez-le promener (*fam.*) *Send him about his business.*

épais (épaisse *f.*) *adj. thick, dense, heavy.*

épaisseur *f. thickness; depth; density.*

épanchement *m. pouring out; effusion.*

épancher *to pour out.*

s'épanouir *to open out; beam.*

épargne *f. saving, thrift.*
Caisse d'épargne. *Savings bank.*

épargner *to spare; save.*

éparpiller *to scatter, disperse.*

épars *adj. scattered, dispersed; disheveled.*
Cheveux épars. *Disheveled hair.*

épatant *adj. wonderful, stunning.*
C'est épatant (*fam.*)! *That's wonderful! That's swell!*

épater *to astound, amaze.*

épaule *f. shoulder.*

épée *f. sword.*

épeler *to spell.*

éperdu *adj. distressed, dismayed.*

éperdument *desperately.*

épeuré *adj. frightened.*

épice *f. spice.*

épicerie *f. grocery store.*

épicier *m. grocer.*

épidémie *f. epidemic.*

epidémique *adj. epidemic.*

épier *to watch, spy upon.*

épilepsie *f. epilepsy.*

épilogue *m. epilogue.*

épinard *m. spinach.*

épine *f. thorn, spine; obstacle.*

épineux (épineuse *f.*) *adj. thorny, ticklish.*

épingle *f. pin.*
Une épingle à nourrice. *A safety pin.*

épisode *m. episode.*

éploré *adj. weeping.*

éplucher *to peel, clean, sift.*

épluchure *f. piece of peel.*

éponge *f. sponge.*

époque *f. period, time.*

épouse *f. wife.*

épouser *to marry.*

épouvantable *adj. dreadful, appalling, frightful.*

épouvante *f. fright, terror.*

épouvanter *to terrify, dismay.*

époux *m. husband.*

s'éprendre *to fall in love.*

épreuve *f. proof, test, trial, ordeal; print (photography).*

éprouver *to try; experience.*
J'éprouve du plaisir à vous voir. *I'm very happy to see you.*
Eprouver une perte. *To suffer a loss.*
Je l'ai éprouvé par moi-même. *I went through the same experience myself.*

épuisement *m. draining off; exhaustion.*

épuiser *to exhaust.*
Il a épuisé ma patience. *He exhausted my patience.*
Ce livre est épuisé. *That book is out of print.*

équilibre *m. equilibrium, balance.*

équilibrer *to balance.*

équipage *m. crew.*

équipe *f. team.*
Chef d'équipe. *Foreman.*
L'esprit d'équipe. *Team spirit.*

équiper *to equip.*

équivalent *noun (m.) and adj. equivalent.*

équivoque *adj. equivocal.*

éreintement *m. exhaustion.*

éreinter *to exhaust.*

s'éreinter *to tire oneself out.*

ériger *to erect.*

errant *adj. wandering, roving.*

errer *to wander, go astray; err, make a mistake.*

Nous avons erré toute la nuit. *We wandered around the whole night.*

Tout le monde peut errer. *Anyone is likely to make a mistake.*

erreur *f. mistake, error.*

erroné *adj. erroneous, wrong, mistaken.*

éruption *f. eruption.*

escadre *f. squadron.*

escale *f. call, stop.*

Vol sans escale. *Nonstop flight.*

escalier *m. staircase, stairs.*

escargot *m. snail.*

esclavage *m. slavery.*

esclave *m. and f. slave.*

escompte *m. discount, rebate.*

A l'escompte. *At a discount.*

escompter *to discount.*

escorte *f. escort; convoy.*

escorter *to escort, convoy.*

escrime *m. fencing.*

escroc *m. swindler, crook.*

escroquer *to steal, swindle.*

espace *m. area, space.*

espacé *adj. far-apart.*

Espagne *m. Spain.*

En Espagne. *In, to Spain.*

espagnol *noun (m.) and adj. Spanish.*

espèce *f. species, kind, sort.*

L'espèce humaine. *Mankind.*

Une espèce de. *A sort of.*

En espèces. *In cash.*

espérance *f. hope.*

espérer *to hope, expect.*

espiègle *adj. mischievous.*

espièglerie *f. prank.*

espion *m. spy.*

espoir *m. hope.*

ESPRIT *m. spirit, mind; sense, wit.*

Il se met l'esprit à la torture. *He's racking his brains.*

Quand est-ce que cette idée vous est venue à l'esprit? *When did you get that idea?*

Il a de l'esprit. *He's witty (clever).*

Avez-vous perdu l'esprit? *Have you lost your senses?*

C'est un esprit léger. *He's a superficial person.*

Avoir l'esprit des affaires. *To have a good business head.*

Présense d'esprit. *Presence of mind.*

Etat d'esprit. *State of mind.*

esquisse *f. sketch.*

esquisser *to sketch, outline.*

esquiver *to elude; dodge.*

s'esquiver *to slip off.*

essai *m. attempt, trial.*

C'était son coup d'essai. *It was his first attempt.*

Prendre à l'essai. *To take on approval.*

Mettre à l'essai. *To put to the test.*

Essai de vitesse. *Speed test.*

Faire un essai. *To try (something) out.*

essayage *m. fitting; testing.*

Le salon d'essayage. *Fitting room.*

ESSAYER *to try, try on.*

Laissez-moi essayer. *Let me try.*

Essayer une robe. *To try on a dress.*

essence *f. essence; gas.*

Vérifier le niveau d'essence. *To check the gas gauge.*

essentiel *m. essential.*

L'essentiel. *The main point.*

essentiel (essentielle *f.*) *adj. essential.*

essoufflé *adj. out of breath.*

essouffler *to put out of breath.*

s'essouffler *to be out of breath.*

essuie-glace *m. windshield wiper.*

essuie-main *m. hand towel.*

essuyer *to wipe; to suffer, undergo (a loss, blow, etc.)*

Essuyer la vaisselle. *To dry the dishes.*

Essuyez votre figure. *Wipe your face.*

Essuyer un refus. *To meet with a refusal.*

Essuyer une perte. *To suffer a loss.*

estimation *f. estimation, appraising.*

estime *f. esteem, regard.*

estimer *to estimate, value.*

estomac *m. stomach.*

J'ai mal à l'estomac. *I have a stomachache.*

estrade *f. platform, stage.*

estropié *adj. crippled, disabled.*

estropier *to cripple.*

ET *and.*

Deux et deux. *Two and two.*

Je n'ai pas faim. Et vous? *I'm not hungry. How about you?*

étable *f. stable.*

ÉTABLIR *to establish, set up; lay down, settle.*

Son père l'a établi à Paris. *His father started him in business in Paris.*

Etablir un prix. *To fix a price.*

On ne pouvait pas établir son identité. *They couldn't identify him.*

s'établir *to establish oneself.*

Il s'est établi à son compte. *He's in business for himself.*

établissement *m. establishment, premises.*

Etablissement de charité. *Charitable institution.*

étage *m. floor, flight, story.*

étagère f. rack, shelf.

étain m. tin.

étalage m. display, shopwindow.

étaler to spread out, unfold; show off.

étancher to quench; stanch.

étang m. pond; pool.

étape f. stage, halting-place, lap (of race).

ÉTAT m. state, condition.

Il y a du mieux dans son état. There is some improvement in his health.

Il est en état de payer. He's in position to pay.

Il était en état de légitime défense. It was a case of legitimate self-defense.

Faire grand état de quelque chose. To make a lot of fuss about something.

Ses états de service sont bons. His record is satisfactory.

Un état lucratif. A well-paid job.

Les bureaux de l'état. Government bureaus.

Les Etats-Unis m. pl. The United States.

Aux Etats-Unis. In (to) the United States.

ÉTÉ m. summer.

été been.

éteindre to put out, extinguish, cancel.

s'éteindre to die out.

étendre to spread out, stretch out; extend, expand.

s'étendre to extend, stretch.

étendue f. expanse, extent.

éternel (éternelle f.) adj. eternal.

éternité f. eternity.

éternuer to sneeze.

étincelant adj. sparkling.

étinceler to sparkle.

étincelle f. spark.

étiquette f. label, tag; etiquette.

étoffe f. material.

étoile f. star.

étonnant adj. amazing; wonderful.

étonnement m. amazement; surprise.

étonner to surprise, amaze.

étouffer to suffocate; deaden; stifle; hush up.

étourderie f. thoughtless action; blunder.

étourdi adj. careless, thoughtless.

étourdissement m. dizziness; shock.

étrange adj. strange; foreign.

étranger m. (étrangère f.) foreigner; abroad.

Vivre à l'étranger. To live abroad.

Il y a beaucoup d'étrangers à Paris. There are many foreigners in Paris.

étranger (étrangère f.) adj. foreign.

étrangler to strangle.

être m. being, creature.

Un être humain. A human being.

Le bien-être. Well-being.

ÊTRE to be.

Etre fatigué. To be tired.

Etre à l'heure. To be on time.

C'est vrai. It's true.

A qui est ceci? To whom does this belong?

Qu'est-ce que c'est? What is it?

Il est à Paris. He is in Paris.

Il est arrivé hier. He arrived yesterday.

J'y suis. I understand. I get it.

Vous n'y êtes pas. You don't understand.

Ainsi soit-il. So be it.

Etant donné votre refus. Given your refusal.

Ça y est! That's it!

C'est, ce sont. It (he, she, this, that) is; they are.

étreindre to clasp, embrace.

étreinte f. embrace.

étrennes f. pl. New Year's gift.

étroit adj. narrow, limited.

étroitesse f. narrowness.

ÉTUDE f. study.

L'étude des langues. The study of languages.

Ce notaire a vendu son étude. That notary has sold his practice.

A l'étude. Under consideration (of a project, etc.).

Il y a fait ses études de droit. He studied law there.

étudiant m. (étudiante f.) student.

Etudiant en médecine. Medical student.

étudier to study.

étui m. case, sheath.

Etui à cigarettes. Cigarette case.

eu had.

euro m. euro (currency).

EUX they, them.

eux-mêmes (m. pl.) themselves.

évacuer to evacuate.

s'évader to escape, get away.

évaluation f. evaluation.

évaluer to value, estimate.

s'évanouir to faint.

évanouissement m. fainting spell.

s'évaporer to evaporate.

évasif (évasive f.) adj. evasive.

évasion f. escape, flight.

éveil m. alarm, awakening.

éveillé adj. lively, wide-awake.

éveiller to wake, arouse.

Cela a éveillé mon attention. That aroused my attention.

Le bruit m'a éveillé. The noise woke me up.

s'éveiller to wake up.

événement m. event.

Le cours des événements. The course of events.

Cela fera événement. That will cause quite a stir.

éventuel (éventuelle f.) adj. possible, likely to happen.

éventuellement possibly, on occasion.

évêque *m. bishop.*
évidemment *evidently; naturally.*
  Evidemment, il faut y aller. *Of course, we have to go.*
évidence *f. evidence, conspicuousness.*
  En évidence. *Conspicuous.*
  Mettre en évidence. *To make evident.*
évident *adj. evident.*
évier *m. kitchen sink.*
éviter *to avoid, prevent.*
évoluer *to develop, evolve.*
évolution *f. evolution.*
évoquer *to evoke.*
EXACT *adj. exact, true, correct.*
  C'est exact. *It's a fact.*
  Il n'est jamais exact. *He is never on time.*
exactement *exactly.*
exactitude *f. correctness, accuracy.*
exagérer *to exaggerate.*
exalter *to exalt, extol.*
s'exalter *to grow excited, enthusiastic.*
examen *m. examination.*
examiner *to examine, investigate.*
exaspération *f. exasperation.*
exaspérer *to exasperate.*
s'exaspérer *to become exasperated.*
exaucer *to fulfill, grant.*
excéder *to exceed.*
EXCELLENT *adj. excellent.*
excentricité *f. eccentricity.*
excentrique *m. and f. noun and adj. eccentric.*
excepté *excepting, besides.*
exception *f. exception.*
  Sans exception. *Without exception.*
exceptionnel (exceptionnelle *f.*) *adj. exceptional.*
excès *m. excess, intemperance.*
excessif (excessive *f.*) *adj. excessive.*
exciter *to excite, stir up, arouse.*
exclamation *f. exclamation.*
  Point d'exclamation. *Exclamation mark.*
s'exclamer *to exclaim, cry out.*
exclure *to exclude.*
exclusion *f. exclusion.*
exclusivement *exclusively.*
exclusivité *f. exclusiveness.*
excursion *f. excursion, tour.*
excusable *adj. excusable.*
excuse *f. excuse, apology, pretense.*
EXCUSER *to excuse.*
  Excusez-moi. *Excuse me. Pardon me.*
S'EXCUSER *to apologize.*
  Je m'excuse, cela m'est sorti de la tête. *I'm sorry. It slipped my mind.*
exécuter *to perform, carry out, execute.*
exécution *f. execution, performance; enforcement.*
  Mettre un projet en exécution. *To carry out a plan.*

exemplaire *m. pattern; sample.*
  En double exemplaire. *In duplicate.*
EXEMPLE *m. example.*
  Donner l'exemple. *To set the example.*
  Suivre l'exemple de quelqu'un. *To follow someone's example.*
  Que ceci vous serve d'exemple. *Let this be a lesson (warning) to you.*
  Supposons à titre d'exemple. *Let's suppose for argument's sake.*
  Joindre l'exemple à la parole. *To suit the action to the word.*
  Etre un exemple de vertu. *To be a model of virtue.*
  Par exemple! *Really! How do you like that!*
  Ça, par exemple, c'est trop fort. *That, really, is too much.*
  Par exemple. *For example.*
exempt *adj. exempt.*
  Exempt de droits. *Duty-free.*
exercer *to exercise, practice, exert.*
s'exercer *to drill, practice.*
exercice *m. exercise, practice.*
  Exercice d'une profession. *Practice of a profession.*
  Faire l'exercice. *To drill.*
exhaler *to exhale; give vent to.*
exhiber *to show, produce.*
exhibition *f. exhibition.*
exigeant *adj. exacting, demanding.*
  Elle est exigeante. *She's too hard to please.*
exigence *f. exactingness; exigence.*
  Satisfaire les exigences. *To meet the requirements.*
exiger *to exact, require.*
  Qu'exigez-vous encore de moi? *What more do you expect (want) from me?*
  L'honneur l'exige. *Honor demands it.*
exil *m. exile.*
exilé *noun and adj. exile; exiled.*
exiler *to exile.*
existence *f. existence; life.*
  Moyens d'existence. *Means of subsistence.*
exister *to exist, live.*
expansion *f. expansion.*
expatrier *to expatriate.*
expédier *to send off, forward; ship.*
expéditeur *m.* (expéditrice *f.*) *shipper, sender.*
expédition *f. expedition; shipment.*
expérience *f. experience.*
  Faire une expérience. *To experience. To have an experience.*
expert *m. and f. noun and adj. expert.*
expiation *f. expiation.*
expier *to expiate, atone for.*
expiration *f. expiration.*
expirer *to expire; die.*
explication *f. explanation.*
expliquer *to explain.*

s'expliquer *to understand.*
> Je ne m'explique pas comment il a pu le faire. *I can't understand how he was able to do it.*

exploit *m. exploit, feat, achievement.*

exploitation *f. exploitation.*

exploiter *to exploit, take advantage of; improve.*

explorer *to explore, search.*

explosion *f. explosion.*
> Faire explosion. *To blow up.*

exportateur *m. exporter.*

exportation *f. export.*

exporter *to export.*

exposé *m. statement, report.*
> Faire l'exposé de. *To give an account of.*

exposer *to show, state; expose, endanger.*
> Exposer sa vie. *To risk one's life.*

exposition *f. exhibition; exposition, account.*
> Salle d'exposition. *Showroom.*

exprès *on purpose, purposely.*
> Tu fais ça exprès! *You're doing that on purpose.*

exprès (expresse *f.*) *adj. express.*
> Par exprès. *Special delivery.*

expression *f. expression.*

exprimer *to express.*

exquis *adj. exquisite.*

extase *f. ecstasy, rapture.*

s'extasier *to go into raptures.*

extension *f. extension, extent.*

s'exténuer *to wear oneself out.*

extérieur *noun (m.) and adj. exterior.*
> A l'extérieur. *Outside.*

extérieurement *externally.*

exterminer *to exterminate, annihilate.*

extra *m. extra.*

extraire *to extract, draw out.*

extrait *m. extract.*

extraordinaire *adj. extraordinary.*

extravagance *f. extravagance.*

extravagant *adj. extravagant.*

extrême *m. extreme, utmost.*

extrêmement *extremely.*

extrémité *f. extremity.*

exubérance *f. exuberance.*

exubérant *adj. exuberant, immoderate.*

F

fable *f. fable.*

fabricant *m. manufacturer; mill owner.*

fabrication *f. manufacture.*

fabrique *f. factory; manufacture.*
> La marque de fabrique. *The trademark.*
> C'est le prix de fabrique. *It's the cost price.*

fabriquer *to manufacture.*

> Il fabrique des autos. *He manufactures cars.*
> Qu'est-ce que vous êtes en train de fabriquer (*fam.*)? *What are you doing? What are you up to?*

fabuleusement *fabulously.*

fabuleux (fabuleuse *f.*) *adj. fabulous.*

façade *f. front, facade.*

face *f. face.*
> Face à face. *Face to face.*
> Il faut considérer ce problème sur toutes ses faces. *We must consider this problem in all its aspects.*
> Pile ou face. *Heads or tails.*
> Regardez en face. *Look on the opposite side.*
> Ma maison fait face à la poste. *My house faces the post office.*

facétieux (facétieuse *f.*) *adj. facetious.*

fâché *adj. offended, vexed, angry.*

fâcher *to offend, displease.*
> Vous le fâcherez en faisant cela. *You will offend him (make him angry) by doing that.*
> Soit dit sans vous fâcher. *I hope you won't feel offended by what I say. Please don't take offense (at what I'm going to say).*

se fâcher *to take offense; get angry.*
> Il s'est fâché tout rouge. *He lost his temper completely. He flared up.*
> Il se fâche pour un rien. *He takes offense at the least little thing.*
> Ne vous fâchez pas. *Don't get angry.*

fâcheux (fâcheuse *f.*) *adj. annoying.*
> Un incident fâcheux. *An awkward incident.*

FACILE *adj. easy.*
> C'est plus facile à dire qu'à faire. *It's easier said than done.*
> Il est facile à vivre. *He's easy to get along with.*

FACILEMENT *easily.*

facilité *f. facility, ease.*
> Il fait tout avec facilité. *He does everything with ease.*
> Facilités de paiements. *Easy terms.*

faciliter *to facilitate, make easy.*

FAÇON *f. manner.*
> De façon à. *So as to.*
> D'une façon ou d'une autre. *Some way or other. One way or another.*
> En aucune façon. *By no means.*
> De cette façon, je vous attends demain. *Then I'll expect you tomorrow.*
> De toute façon, je vous verrai demain. *Anyhow, I'll see you tomorrow.*
> Ne faites pas tant de façons. *Don't stand on ceremony.*
> C'est sa façon de parler. *That's his way of speaking. That's the way he speaks.*
> Je vais lui dire ma façon de penser. *I'll give him a piece of my mind.*

Sans façon. *Simply. Informally. Without any fuss.*

Je n'aime pas la façon de cette robe. *I don't like the cut (make) of this dress.*

Qu'est-ce que c'est que ces façons? *What sort of manners are these? What kind of behavior is this? Is this the way to behave?*

façonner *to work, shape.*

fac-similé *m. facsimile, fax.*

facteur *m. factor; postman.*

Il est important de prendre tous ces facteurs en considération. *It's important to take all these factors into consideration.*

A quelle heure vient le facteur? *What time does the postman come?*

faction *f. sentry duty*

facture *f. bill, invoice.*

facultatif (facultative *f.*) *adj. optional.*

faculté *f. faculty.*

La faculté de droit. *The law faculty.*

Il a encore toutes ses facultés. *He's still in possession of all his faculties.*

fade *adj. insipid.*

FAIBLE *adj. weak.*

faiblesse *f. weakness.*

faiblir *to weaken.*

faïence *f. pottery.*

faillir *to fail, err; be on the point of; go bankrupt.*

En cela, il a failli. *He failed in that.*

Elle a failli tomber. *She came near falling. She almost fell.*

faillite *f. bankruptcy.*

FAIM *f. hunger.*

Assouvir sa faim. *To satisfy one's hunger.*

J'ai une faim de loup. *I'm terribly hungry.*

Je mourais de faim. *I was starved.*

fainéant *noun and adj. lazy, idle.*

FAIRE *to do, make.*

Que faites-vous demain? *What are you doing tomorrow?*

Il a fait cette radio lui-même. *He built this radio himself.*

Faites comme vous voudrez. *Do as you like.*

Faites-le-moi voir. *Show it to me. Let me see it.*

Il a fait son devoir. *He did his duty.*

Il a fait son chemin. *He made his way in the world.*

Il a fait beaucoup d'argent l'an passé. *He made a lot of money last year.*

Il fait ses études à Londres. *He's studying in London.*

Qu'est-ce que vous voulez que j'y fasse? *What can I do about it?*

Vous pouvez faire usage de ma voiture. *You can use my car.*

Faire une promenade. *To go for a walk.*

Toute réflexion faite. *All things considered.*

Il ne sait que faire. *He doesn't know what to do.*

Il n'y a rien à faire. *There's nothing to be done.*

Qu'est-ce que ça fait? *What does it matter?*

Ça ne fait rien. *It doesn't matter. It doesn't make any difference.*

Deux et deux font quatre. *Two and two are four.*

Il fait nuit. *It's dark (night).*

Il n'en fait qu'à sa tête. *He does as he pleases.*

Il lui a fait dire de venir. *He sent him word to come.*

Faites-le entrer. *Show him in.*

Cela fait soixante-douze francs. *That's seventy-two francs.*

Comment fait-on pour . . . *How does one go about . . .*

Elle ne fait que parler. *She does nothing but talk.*

Faire à sa tête. *To do as one pleases.*

Faire attention. *To pay attention.*

Faire de l'autostop. *To hitchhike.*

Faire bon voyage. *To have a good trip.*

Faire de l'alpinisme. *To go mountain climbing.*

Faire de la peine. *To distress, grieve.*

Faire de son mieux. *To do one's best.*

Faire des courses. *To go shopping.*

Faire des photo(graphie)s. *To take photos (pictures).*

Faire des repas légers. *To take light meals.*

Faire des sports d'hiver. *To practice (engage in) winter sports.*

Faire dix minutes de marche. *To walk for ten minutes.*

Faire du cyclisme. *To ride a bicycle.*

Faire du ski (nautique). *To go (water-) skiing.*

Faire l'affaire de. *To meet the needs of.*

Faire la connaissance de. *To make the acquaintance of.*

Faire la quête. *To take up a collection (church).*

Faire la queue. *To stand on line.*

Faire le plein (d'essence). *To fill up (with gasoline).*

Faire mal. *To hurt.*

Faire mieux de. *To do better to.*

Faire partie de. *To be part of.*

Faire salle comble. *To draw a full house (theatre).*

Faire signe à. *To motion to.*

Faire une commission. *To take, deliver a message.*

Faire un essai. *To try (something) out.*

Faire un prix global. *To make a total price.*

Faire un tour (un voyage). *To take a trip.*

Faire une tournée. *To go on tour (theatre).*

Fait à la main. *Handmade.*

Il fait beau (chaud, doux, du soleil, du vent, frais, froid, mauvais). *The weather is fine (warm, mild, sunny, windy, cool, cold, bad).*

Pourquoi faire? *What for?*

Tout à fait. *Quite, entirely, altogether.*

s'en faire *to worry.*

Ne t'en fais pas. *Don't worry.*

se faire *to be made; be done; get used to.*

Il se fait du mauvais sang. *He worries himself sick.*

Il s'est fait naturaliser Américain. *He became a naturalized American citizen.*

On se fait à tout. *One gets used to everything.*

Il se fait tard. *It's getting late.*

Comment se fait-il qu'elle ne soit pas ici? *How come she's not here?*

Cela ne se fait pas. *People don't do that. That's not done.*

faire faire *to have done.*

Faire faire le graissage. *To have a lubrication job done.*

se faire faire *to have something done or made for oneself.*

Se faire faire les ongles (une mise en plis). *To have one's nails done (one's hair set).*

faiseur *m.* (faiseuse *f.*) *maker.*

Un faiseur de projets. *A schemer.*

C'est un faiseur! *He's a bluffer!*

FAIT *m. fact; act.*

Un fait accompli. *A fait accompli. An accomplished fact. A thing already done.*

Il était bien au courant du fait. *He was well aware of the fact.*

Allons au fait. *Let's come to the point.*

Je vais vous mettre au fait. *I'll acquaint you with the matter.*

Ces faits sont assez rares. *These occurrences are rather rare. These things seldom happen (occur).*

Si fait, si fait. *Yes, indeed.*

Au fait. *By the way.*

fait *done, made.*

faîte *f. top, summit.*

falaise *f. cliff.*

FALLOIR *to be necessary.*

Nous avons tout ce qu'il nous faut. *We've everything we need.*

Merci, c'était juste ce qu'il me fallait. *Thanks a lot, that's just what I needed.*

Il s'en est fallu de peu pour que je réussisse. *I nearly succeeded.*

Il faut que vous y alliez. *You must go there.*

Il faut avouer que c'est un peu de notre faute. *We must admit that it's partly our fault.*

Il fallait voir ça, ça valait mille! *You ought to have seen it, it was worth a fortune!*

Il faudra que j'y aille. *I'll have to go there.*

Vous l'avez fait?—Il a bien fallu. *Did you do it?—I didn't have any choice. I had to.*

C'est un jeune homme comme il faut. *He's a well-bred young man.*

Combien de temps faudra-t-il? *How much time (how long) will it take?*

Il ne faut pas tout croire. *You mustn't believe everything.*

S'il le faut. *If necessary.*

Tout ce qu'il vous faut. *Everything you need.*

fameusement *famously; awfully.*

FAMEUX (fameuse *f.*) *adj. famous.*

familiariser *to familiarize.*

familiarité *f. familiarity.*

familier *m. close friend, a friend of the family.*

Il est un des familiers de la maison. *He's a friend of the family.*

familier (familière *f.*) *adj. familiar.*

Très vite le nouveau système lui est devenu familier. *He soon became accustomed to the new system.*

Ce visage m'est familier. *I've seen that face before.*

familièrement *familiarly.*

FAMILLE *f. family.*

Toute ma famille était là. *My whole family was there.*

Quel est votre nom de famille? *What's your last name?*

Ils ont un air de famille. *They have (bear) a family resemblance.*

famine *f. starvation.*

fanatique *m. and f. noun and adj. fanatic, fan.*

Un fanatique du cinéma. *A movie fan.*

se faner *to wither, fade.*

fanfaron *m.* (fanfaronne *f.*) *boaster.*

Il fait le fanfaron. *He's bragging.*

fange *f. mud.*

fantaisie *f. fancy, imagination; humor, whim, caprice.*

fantastique *adj. fantastic.*

fantôme *m. ghost.*

farce *f. joke.*

fard *m. make-up for the face.*

Il l'a dit sans fard. *He said it plainly.*

fardeau *m.* (fardeaux *pl.*) *burden.*

se farder *to put on make-up.*

farine *f. flour.*

Ce sont des gens de la même farine. *They're birds of a feather.*

farouche *adj. wild, savage.*

fasciner *to fascinate.*

fastidieux (fastidieuse *f.*) *adj. tedious, dull, wearisome.*

fat *noun (m.) and adj. conceited, vain.*

fatal *adj. fatal.*

fatalité *f. fate, fatality, calamity.*

fatigant *adj. tiring.*

fatigue *f. fatigue, weariness.*

  Tomber de fatigue. *To be dead tired. ("To drop with fatigue.")*

  Je suis mort de fatigue. *I'm dead tired.*

  Habits de fatigue. *Working clothes.*

fatigué *adj. tired.*

fatiguer *to tire, wear out.*

fatuité *f. self-conceit.*

faubourg *m. suburb, outlying part of a city.*

se faufiler *to slip in or out of a place.*

fausser *to falsify, distort.*

  Fausser une clé. *To bend a key.*

  Fausser une serrure. *To tamper with a lock.*

fausseté *f. falsehood; falseness.*

FAUTE *f. lack, need; mistake; fault.*

  Faire faute. *To be lacking.*

  Il leur a fait faute. *He let them down.*

  Sans faute. *Without fail.*

  Je viendrais sans faute. *I'll come without fail.*

  Il parle français sans faute. *He speaks French without any mistakes.*

  Corrigez mes fautes, s'il vous plaît. *Please correct my mistakes.*

  Il est en faute. *He made a mistake. He's guilty.*

  Ce n'est pas (de) sa faute. *It's not his fault.*

  A qui la faute? *Whose fault is it?*

  Faire une faute. *To make a mistake.*

  Faute d'orthographe. *Spelling mistake.*

  Faute de jugement. *A mistake in judgment. An error of judgment.*

  Faute d'inattention. *A slip.*

  Faute de mieux. *For want of something better.*

fauteuil *m. armchair.*

  Le fauteuil d'orchestre. *Orchestra seat.*

fautif (fautive *f.*) *adj. faulty.*

FAUX (fausse *f.*) *adj. false.*

  Il fait fausse route. *He took the wrong road. He is on the wrong track.*

  C'est un faux bonhomme. *He's a hypocrite.*

  Il a fait un faux-pas. *He committed a faux-pas (an error of conduct). He made a mistake (blunder).*

  Un faux numéro. *Wrong number (telephone).*

FAVEUR *f. favor, good will.*

  Une faveur insigne. *A special favor.*

  Cette mode a pris faveur. *This fashion is in vogue.*

  Un billet de faveur. *A free ticket. A free pass.*

favorable *adj. favorable.*

favorablement *favorably.*

favori (favorite *f.*) *noun and adj. favorite.*

favoriser *to be partial to.*

fécond *adj. fruitful, fertile.*

fédération *f. federation*

fée *f. fairy.*

féerique *adj. fairylike, enchanting.*

feindre *to pretend, feign.*

feinte *f. pretense.*

félicitation *f. congratulation.*

féliciter *to congratulate.*

  Permettez-moi de vous féliciter. *Allow me to congratulate you.*

se féliciter *to be pleased with something.*

femelle *f. female.*

féminin *adj. feminine.*

FEMME *f. woman, wife.*

fendre *to split.*

FENÊTRE *f. window.*

fente *f. crack, slit, slot.*

  La fente latérale. *The side slash (man's suit jacket).*

FER *m. iron.*

  Partez-vous par chemin de fer? *Are you going by train?*

  Voulez-vous donner un coup de fer à ma cravate, je vous prie. *Please press my tie.*

ferme *f. farm.*

ferme *adj. firm, steady.*

fermement *firmly.*

FERMER *to close, shut.*

  Fermez la porte. *Close (shut) the door.*

  Fermer une lettre. *To seal a letter.*

  J'ai fermé l'eau (le gas). *I turned off the water (the gas).*

  Il n'a pu fermer l'oeil de la nuit. *He couldn't sleep a wink last night.*

  On ferme. *It's closing time.*

fermeté *f. firmness, hardness.*

fermeture *f. closing.*

  Heure de fermeture. *Closing time.*

  Une fermeture éclair. *A zipper.*

fermier *m.* (fermière *f.*) *farmer.*

féroce *adj. ferocious.*

ferraille *f. scrap iron.*

fertile *adj. fertile, fruitful.*

fertilité *f. fertility.*

fervent *noun and adj. enthusiast; fervent.*

ferveur *f. fervor.*

fessée *f. spanking.*

festin *m. feast.*

festival *m.* (festivaux *pl.*) *festival.*

FÊTE *f. holiday; name day; festivity.*

  Que lui offrirez-vous pour sa fête? *What will you give him for his name day?*

Ce n'est pas tous les jours fête. *Christmas comes but once a year. We'll make this an occasion.*

On lui fera fête. *We'll give him a hearty welcome.*

Ce serait une fête de les voir. *It would be a treat to see them.*

La fête bat son plein. *The festival is at its height. The celebration is in full swing.*

fêter *to celebrate.*

FEU *m. fire, heat, flame; traffic light.*

Voulez-vous me donner du feu, s'il vous plaît? *May I have a light, please?*

Au feu! *Fire!*

Jeter de l'huile sur le feu. *To add fuel to the fire.*

C'est un feu de paille. *It's only a flash in the pan.*

Il n'y voit que du feu. *He doesn't see the trick.*

J'en mettrais ma main au feu. *I could swear to it.*

Il a le visage en feu. *His face is flushed.*

Feu de camp. *Campfire.*

Le feu passe au rouge. *The traffic light changes to red.*

feu *adj. late, deceased.*

feuille *f. leaf, sheet.*

feuilleter *to turn over the pages of a book, leaf through a book.*

feuilleton *m. feuilleton, serial.*

feutre *m. felt.*

Un chapeau de feutre. *A felt hat.*

FÉVRIER *m. February.*

fiançailles *f. pl. engagement.*

fiancé *m. (fiancée f.) fiancé.*

se fiancer *to become engaged.*

fiasco *m. fiasco.*

fibre *f. fiber.*

Fibre optique. *Optical fiber.*

Fibre de verre. *Fiberglass.*

ficeler *to tie up.*

ficelle *f. string.*

fiche *f. slip; file.*

fiction *f. fiction.*

fidèle *adj. faithful.*

fidélité *f. faithfulness, fidelity.*

La haute fidélité. *High fidelity.*

fier *(fière f.) adj. proud.*

Etre fier de quelqu'un. *To be proud of someone.*

Il est fier comme Artaban. *He's as proud as Lucifer.*

J'ai eu une fière peur. *I was really frightened.*

se fier *to trust.*

Il ne fait pas bon se fier à lui. *He's not to be trusted. Don't depend on him.*

Fiez-vous à moi. *Leave it to me.*

fierté *f. pride, vanity.*

fièvre *f. fever.*

fiévreux *(fiévreuse f.) adj. feverish.*

figer *to congeal, set.*

Il est resté figé sur place. *He was rooted to the spot.*

figue *f. fig.*

figure *f. form, shape; face, looks.*

Il fait bonne figure. *He cuts a good figure. He makes a good impression.*

Il fait triste figure. *He cuts a sorry figure.*

Il a fait longue figure. *He pulled a long face.*

Sa figure ne me revient pas. *I don't like his looks.*

Je ne savais trop quelle figure faire. *I didn't know how to look (what countenance to assume).*

Il le lui a jeté à la figure. *He threw it up to him. He insulted him.*

figurer *to appear, figure in.*

Il n'a pas voulu que son nom figure dans l'affaire. *He didn't want his name to appear in the matter.*

se figurer *to imagine.*

S'il se figure cela, il s'abuse. *If he imagines that, he is only deceiving (fooling) himself.*

Ne vous figurez pas que les alouettes vont vous tomber toutes rôties dans la bouche. *Don't expect a fortune to drop into your lap.*

Figurez-vous que vous êtes en Inde. *Imagine yourself in India.*

FIL *m. thread, wire.*

Donnez-moi du fil et une aiguille. *Give me some thread and a needle.*

Du fil de fer barbelé. *Barbed wire.*

Donnez du fil à retordre. *To cause a lot of trouble.*

Ce rasoir a perdu son fil. *This razor has lost its edge.*

Sa vie ne tenait qu'à un fil. *His life hung by a thread.*

Cette malice est cousue de fil blanc. *This trick is too obvious.*

De fil en aiguille. *One thing led to another.*

Il tient le fil de l'intrigue. *He knows all about the intrigue.*

Donnez-moi un coup de fil. *Give me a ring.*

Qui est au bout du fil? *Who's speaking (telephone)?*

file *f. row, line.*

filer *to spin; to follow; leave.*

Filer du lin. *To spin flax.*

Le train filait le long du fleuve. *The train was running along the river.*

Le bateau file quinze noeuds à l'heure. *The boat makes fifteen knots an hour.*

Le voleur est filé par la police. *The thief is being shadowed by the police.*

Allez, filez (*fam.*)! *Get out! On your way!*

filet *m. net.*

Auriez-vous l'obligeance de descendre le sac jaune du filet? *Would you mind taking down the yellow bag from the rack?*

FILLE *f. daughter; girl.*

Il n'a des yeux que pour sa fille. *His daughter is the apple of his eye.*

Comment écrit-on votre nom de jeune fille? *How do you spell your maiden name?*

C'est une vieille fille. *She's a spinster (old maid).*

filleul *m.* (filleule *f.*) *godchild.*

film *m. film, movie, picture.*

Le film en couleurs (en noir et blanc). *Color (black-and-white) film.*

Le grand film. *Main feature.*

filou *m. thief, swindler.*

FILS *m. son.*

Il est fils de son père. *He resembles his father. He's a chip off the old block.*

Il est le fils de ses oeuvres. *He is a self-made man.*

filtre *m. filter, strainer.*

FIN *f. end.*

Mettre fin à. *To put an end to. To stop.*

Tirer à sa fin. *To come to an end.*

Ça n'a pas de fin. *There's no end to it.*

Sans fin. *Endless. Endlessly.*

Il a mené cette affaire à bonne fin. *He brought the affair to a successful conclusion.*

A cette fin. *To that end. For that purpose.*

A la fin. *In the end.*

A la fin des fins. *In the end. When you come down to it.*

A la fin du compte. *In the end. When all is said and done. To make a long story short.*

Payable fin courant. *Payable at the end of the current month.*

Qui veut la fin veut les moyens. *Where there's a will, there's a way.*

Ceci se passait vers fin 1930. *This happened toward the end of 1930.*

FIN *adj. fine, refined; slender; subtle.*

C'est un fin gourmet. *He's a real gourmet.*

Il n'est pas fin. *He's not shrewd.*

Bien fin qui m'y prendra. *(No one will) Catch me doing that!*

C'est trop fin pour moi. *That's too subtle for me. I don't get the joke.*

Il a l'oreille fine. *He has a good ear.*

Ils jouent au plus fin. *They're trying to outsmart each other.*

final *adj. final.*

finalement *finally.*

finance *f. finance; cash, ready money.*

Etre à court de finance. *To be short of cash.*

financier *m. financier.*

financier (financière *f.*) *adj. financial.*

finesse *f. finesse, fineness, shrewdness, wit.*

Elle a beaucoup de finesse. *She has a lot of wit.*

Il entend finesse à tout ce qu'on dit. *He gives a malicious slant to everything you say.*

FINIR *to end, finish.*

Il finit par nous dire ce que nous voulions savoir. *In the end he told us what we wanted to know.*

Quand il s'y met, il n'en finit plus. *Once he starts, he never stops.*

C'est fini entre eux. *It's all over between them.*

Il a fini par y arriver. *He finally succeeded.*

Tout est bien qui finit bien. *All's well that ends well.*

fisc *m. the treasury.*

Les agents du fisc. *Tax collectors.*

fiscal (fiscaux *pl.*) *adj. fiscal.*

fixation *f. fixing.*

fixe *adj. fixed.*

Un prix fixe. *A fixed price.*

fixement *fixedly, steadfastly.*

Regarder quelque chose fixement. *To stare at something.*

fixer *to fix.*

Fixer les yeux sur quelqu'un. *To stare at someone.*

Maintenant je suis fixé. *Well, now I know what's what. That settles it.*

Nous y avons fixé notre résidence. *We have settled (set up residence) there.*

se fixer *to settle, set up residence.*

flacon *m. flask.*

flageolet *m. kidney bean.*

flagrant *adj. flagrant.*

En flagrant délit. *In the very act. (Caught) Red-handed.*

flair *m. sense of smell; intuition.*

Cet homme a du flair. *This man has a gift for finding things out.*

flairer *to scent, smell.*

flamand *noun and adj. Flemish.*

flambant *adj. blazing.*

flambeau *m.* (flambeaux *pl.*) *torch.*

flamber *to flame, flame up.*

flamboyant *adj. flaming.*

flamboyer *to blaze.*

flamme *f. flame.*

flanc *m. flank, side.*

flanelle *f. flannel.*

Un costume de flanelle grise. *A gray flannel suit.*

flâner *to lounge about, be idle.*

flash *m. flash (photography).*

flatter *to flatter.*

se flatter *to delude oneself, imagine.*

flatterie *f. flattery, compliment.*

flatteur *m. (flatteuse f.) adj. flattering.*

fléau *m. (fléaux pl.) plague, curse.*

flèche *f. arrow.*

fléchir *to bend; yield, give way; move, touch.*

Se laisser fléchir. *To relent. To yield. To give in.*

flegmatique *adj. phlegmatic.*

flegme *m. phlegm; coolness, imperturbability.*

Il est d'un grand flegme. *He's very cool.*

flemme *f. (fam.) laziness.*

Il a la flemme de la faire. *He's too lazy to do it.*

flétrir *to wither, fade.*

fleur *f. flower.*

fleurir *to bloom.*

fleuriste *m. florist.*

fleuve *m. river.*

flexible *adj. flexible.*

flocon *m. flake.*

flot *m. wave.*

Il revient à flot. *He's making a new start in business. He's getting on his feet again.*

flottant *adj. floating.*

flotte *f. fleet.*

flotter *to float.*

flou *adj. soft, fluffy (of hair); blurred.*

fluctuation *f. fluctuation.*

fluet *(fluette f.) adj. thin, delicate.*

fluide *noun (m.) and adj. fluid.*

flûte *f. flute.*

flux *m. flow.*

Un flux de paroles. *A flow of words.*

fluxion *f. fluxion.*

foi *f. faith, trust, belief.*

J'ai foi en lui. *I have faith in him.*

On ne peut ajouter foi à ce qu'il dit. *You can't believe (rely upon) what he says.*

Il n'a ni foi ni loi. *He follows neither law nor gospel.*

Ma foi, tant pis. *Well, never mind.*

Etre de bonne foi. *To be sincere.*

foie *m. liver.*

Mal au foie. *Liver complaint.*

foin *m. hay.*

foire *f. fair.*

La foire de Lyon. *The Lyons Fair.*

FOIS *f. time, turn.*

Deux fois. *Twice.*

Je l'ai vue une fois avec lui. *I once saw her with him.*

Je vous raconterai ça une autre fois. *I'll tell you about it some other time.*

Maintes et maintes fois. *Again and again. Many times.*

Il y a regardé à deux fois avant de commencer. *Before he started, he thought about it twice.*

Une fois pour toutes. *Once and for all.*

Une fois n'est pas coutume. *Once does not make a habit.*

Une bonne fois. *Once for all.*

Des fois qu'il viendrait vous voir (fam.) *In case he should come to see you.*

Il était une fois ... *Once upon a time ...*

Une fois par semaine (jour, an, mois). *Once a week (day, year, month).*

Une fois arrivé, vous ... *Once you arrive, you ...*

foison *m. plenty, abundance.*

foisonner *to abound.*

folâtre *adj. playful.*

folichon *(folichonne f.) adj. playful.*

folie *f. madness, extravagance.*

Faire des folies. *To squander money.*

folle *See fou.*

follement *madly.*

fomenter *to foment, excite, stir up.*

foncé *adj. dark (of a color).*

Vert foncé. *Dark green.*

foncer *to dash, rush.*

foncier *(foncière f.) adj. based on land; fundamental.*

foncièrement *fundamentally, essentially, basically.*

fonction *f. function, duty, office.*

Faire fonction de. *To act as.*

Entrer en fonctions. *To take up one's duties.*

fonctionnaire *m. civil servant.*

fonctionner *to work, to operate, to function.*

Cette machine ne fonctionne pas. *This machine doesn't work.*

Le métro ne fonctionne plus. *The subway trains aren't running.*

FOND *m. bottom, back, rear; background.*

De fond en comble. *From top to bottom.*

Au fond. *At bottom. Basically. On the whole. In the main. After all.*

Le fond d'une boutique. *The back of a shop.*

On ne peut faire fond sur lui. *One can't depend on him. You can't rely on him.*

A fond de train. *At full speed.*

Au fond du coeur il était très fier de ce qu'il avait fait. *Deep down ("at the bottom of his heart"), he was very proud of what he had done.*

Je l'ai trouvé au fin fond de mon tiroir. *I found it at the very bottom of my drawer.*

Il faut aller au fond de cette affaire. *We must get to the root of that matter.*

Il connaît l'histoire à fond. *He has a thorough knowledge of history.*

Un article de fond. *An editorial.*

fondamental *adj. fundamental.*

fondateur *m.* (fondatrice *f.*) *founder.*

fondation *f. foundation.*

fondé *m. agent, proxy.*

Fondé de pouvoir. *Agent.*

fondé *adj. well-founded, justified.*

Ses soupçons ne sont pas fondés. *His suspicions are groundless (have no basis).*

fondement *m. foundation, base.*

Une rumeur sans fondement. *An unfounded rumor.*

fonder *to found, establish.*

fondre *to melt.*

fonds *m. funds, capital.*

Etre en fonds (*fam.*). *To be in funds.*

fontaine *f. spring, fountain.*

fonte *f. melting.*

forçat *m. convict.*

Il mène une vie de forçat. *He works very hard. He slaves (away).*

FORCE *f. strength, force.*

Il est à bout de force. *He's exhausted.*

Il n'a pas la force de parler. *He's too weak to speak.*

Il est un joueur de tennis de première force. *He's a first-rate tennis player.*

Il a crié de toutes ses forces. *He shouted with all his might.*

Il le fera de gré ou de force. *He'll have to do it whether he wants to or not. He'll have to do it willy-nilly.*

Vous n'êtes pas de sa force. *You're no match for him.*

Ici les fermiers sont la force du pays. *Here the farmers are the backbone of the country.*

Par force. *Under compulsion.*

Il est entré par force dans la maison. *He forced his way into the house.*

Les agents de la force publique. *The police force.*

Les forces aériennes. *Air force.*

De force égale. *Evenly matched.*

force *adj. a great deal, many.*

Il reçut force compliments. *He received many compliments.*

forcément *under compulsion, necessarily, forcibly.*

forcené *m. and f. madman, madwoman.*

forcené *adj. frantic, mad.*

forcer *to force, break open.*

On devait forcer la porte. *They had to force the door.*

On lui a forcé la main. *They forced his hand.*

Ne forcez pas votre talent. *Don't overestimate your ability. Don't try to do things that are beyond your ability.*

forêt *f. forest.*

forfait *m. contract; crime.*

Travailler à forfait. *To work on a contract basis. To work for a fixed fee.*

Il a commis un forfait. *He committed a crime.*

forge *f. forge.*

forger *to forge.*

Cette lettre a été forgée. *This letter has been (is) forged.*

forgeron *m. blacksmith.*

formalité *f. formality, red tape.*

format *m. format.*

Format de poche. *Pocket size.*

formation *f. formation, training.*

FORME *f. form, shape; etiquette, manners.*

En bonne et due forme. *In due and proper form.*

Il l'a fait pour la forme. *He did it for form's sake.*

Prendre forme. *To take shape.*

Etre en forme. *To be in form.*

Sous toutes les formes. *In all aspects.*

formel (formelle *f.*) *adj. formal.*

formellement *formally, expressly, explicitly.*

former *to form, create.*

se former *to form, to take form.*

formidable *adj. formidable; wonderful, tremendous, unbelievable.*

J'ai une idée formidable. *I have a brilliant idea.*

C'est formidable tout de même! *That's really something!*

Formidable! *Great!*

formulaire *m. printed form.*

formule *f. formula, printed form.*

formuler *to formulate.*

fort *m. strong point; fort, fortress.*

C'est son fort. *That's his forte. That's his strong point. That's what he does (knows) best.*

FORT *adj. strong; loud.*

C'est un esprit fort. *He has a strong mind.*

Parlez plus fort, s'il vous plaît. *Please speak louder.*

Il a trouvé plus fort que lui. *He found his match.*

J'aurai fort à faire en cela. *I'll have a great deal to do (in that). That will give me a lot of work (trouble).*

Ça ne marche pas fort. 1. *I'm not feeling too well.* 2. *It's not going too well.*

C'est trop fort! *That's too much!*

C'est plus fort que moi. *I can't help it.*

forteresse *f. fortress.*

fortifiant *m. tonic.*

fortification *f. fortification.*

fortifier *to strengthen; fortify.*

fortune *f. fortune, chance, fate; wealth.*
Un coup de fortune. *A stroke of luck.*
Il a amassé une grande fortune. *He made a fortune.*
Ils ont perdu leur fortune. *They lost all their money.*
Faire contre mauvaise fortune bon coeur. *To make the best of a bad job. To put a good face on a bad matter.*

fortuné *adj. fortunate, lucky.*

fosse *f. pit, hole.*

fossé *m. ditch.*

fossette *f. dimple.*

fou (folle *f.*) *noun and adj. mad, insane.*
Elle est folle de joie. *She's overjoyed ("mad with joy").*
Etre fou de quelqu'un. *To be crazy (mad) about someone.*

foudre *f. lightning.*
avoir un coup de foudre. *To have a crush.*

foudroyer *to crush, overwhelm.*

fouet *m. whip, rod.*

fouetter *to whip.*

fougue *f. spirit, passion.*

fougueux (fougueuse *f.*) *adj. impetuous.*

fouiller *to dig, investigate, search.*

fouillis *m. mess.*

foulard *m. scarf.*

foule *f. crowd.*

fouler *to tread; sprain.*
Se fouler le poignet. *To sprain one's wrist.*

foulure *f. sprain.*

four *m. oven.*
La pièce a fait four. *The play was a flop.*

fourbe *m. rogue, cheat.*

fourberie *f. cheating, deceit.*

fourbu *adj. overtired.*
Je suis fourbu (*fam.*). *I'm dead tired.*

fourche *f. fork, point of bifurcation.*

fourchette *f. fork.*

fourgon *m. van.*

fourmi *f. ant.*

fourmiller *to swarm.*

fourneau *m.* (fourneaux *pl.*) *furnace.*

fournir *to furnish.*

fournisseur *m. supplier.*

fourniture *f. supplies, material.*

fourreur *m. furrier.*

fourrure *f. fur.*

foyer *m. hearth.*

fracas *m. crash; fracas, uproar.*

fracasser *to smash.*

fraction *f. fraction.*

fracture *f. fracture.*

fracturer *to fracture.*

fragile *adj. fragile.*

fragilité *f. fragility.*

fragment *m. fragment.*

fraîcheur *f. coolness.*

frais *m. pl. expenses; efforts.*
A grands frais. *At a great cost (expense).*
Il en est pour ses frais. *He had all that trouble for nothing.*
Ne vous mettez pas en frais pour moi. *Don't put yourself out for me.*
Les frais de retour. *Charge for returning (rented car).*

frais (fraiche *f.*) *adj. cool, fresh.*
Pas frais. *Stale.*
Mettre au frais. *To put in a cool place.*
De fraîche date. *Recent.*
Il fait frais. *The weather is cool.*

fraise *f. strawberry.*

framboise *f. raspberry.*

franc (franche *f.*) *adj. frank, loyal; genuine.*
Franc comme l'or. *As frank (open) as a child ("as gold").*
Jouer franc jeu. *To play fair. To be fair and square. To be on the level.*

français *m. French (language).*
En français. *In French.*

FRANÇAIS *adj. French.*

Français *m. Frenchman.*

FRANCE *f. France.*

franchement *frankly, openly.*

franchir *to cross.*
L'avion a franchi l'Atlantique en un temps record. *The plane crossed the Atlantic in record time.*

franchise *f. frankness; exemption.*

franco *free.*
Livré franco. *Delivery free of charge.*

franc-parler *m. candor, frankness.*

frange *f. fringe.*

frapper *to strike; surprise.*
Frapper à la porte. *To knock at the door.*
Cette remarque m'avait frappé. *I was struck by that remark.*

fraternel (fraternelle *f.*) *adj. fraternal.*

fraternité *f. fraternity.*

fraude *f. fraud.*

frauder *to smuggle.*

fraudeur *m. smuggler.*

frayer *to open up, clear.*
Se frayer un passage. *To clear a way for oneself.*

frayeur *f. fright, fear, terror.*

fredonner *to hum.*

frein *m. brake; curb.*

frêle *adj. weak, frail.*

frémir *to vibrate, quiver.*
Ça me fait frémir quand j'y pense. *It gives me the shivers to think of it.*

frémissement *m. quiver, shudder.*

frénésie *f. frenzy.*

fréquent *adj. frequent.*

fréquenter *to frequent, keep company with.*

FRÈRE *m. brother.*
    Beau-frère. *Brother-in-law.*

frétiller *to wriggle.*

friandise *f. dainty, delicacy.*

friction *f. friction, rubbing.*

frileux (frileuse *f.*) *adj. chilly, sensitive to cold.*

friper *to rumple.*

fripon *m.* (friponne *f.*) *rogue.*

frire *to fry.*

frise *f. frieze.*

friser *to curl, wave.*

frisson *m. shiver.*

frissonner *to shiver, shudder.*

frite *f. French fried potato.*

friture *f. fried food.*

frivole *adj. frivolous.*

frivolité *f. frivolity.*

FROID *noun (m.) and adj. cold; coldness.*
    Il fait froid aujourd'hui. *It's cold today.*
    Cela ne me fait ni chaud ni froid. *It's all the same to me. It makes no difference to me one way or the other.*
    Il n'a pas froid aux yeux. 1. *He's very determined.* 2. *He's not at all shy.*

froidement *coldly.*

froideur *f. coldness.*

froisser *to crease, rumple; hurt (one's feelings).*

fromage *m. cheese.*

froncer *used in the following expression:*
    Froncer les sourcils. *To frown.*

front *m. forehead; front.*

frontière *f. border, frontier.*

frottement *m. rubbing.*

frotter *to rub.*

fructueux (fructueuse *f.*) *adj. fruitful.*

fruit *m. fruit.*

frustrer *to frustrate.*

fugitif *m.* (fugitive *f.*) *fugitive, runaway.*

fuir *to flee; avoid; leak.*

fuite *f. flight, evasion.*

fumée *f. smoke.*

fumer *to smoke, fume.*

fumier *m. manure.*

funèbre *adj. mournful, dismal.*

funérailles *f. pl. funeral rites.*

funeste *adj. deadly, fatal.*

fur *m. used in the following expression:*
    Au fur et à mesure. *Gradually. Proportionately. In proportion (as). As soon (as). As far (as). In succession.*

fureur *f. fury.*
    Il s'est mis en fureur. *He flew into a rage.*
    Cette pièce fait fureur. *This play is a hit.*

furie *f. fury, rage.*

furieusement *furiously.*

furieux (furieuse *f.*) *adj. furious, enraged.*

furtif (furtive *f.*) *adj. furtive.*

furtivement *furtively.*

fuselage *m. fuselage.*

fusil *m. gun.*

fusiller *to shoot.*

fusion *f. fusion, melting.*

futile *adj. futile, trifling.*

futilité *f. futility.*

futur *noun (m.) and adj. future (grammatical).*

fuyard *m. fugitive.*

G

gâcher *to spoil, make a mess of.*

gâchis *m. slush; mess; wet mortar.*

gaffe *f. blunder.*

gage *m. pledge, deposit, security.*
    Mettre en gage. *To pawn.*
    En gage d'amitié. *In token of friendship.*

gager *to wager, bet.*

gagne-pain *m. livelihood.*

gagner *to gain, earn, win, save (time); reach.*
    Il gagne son pain. *He just about makes a living.*
    C'est autant de gagné! *So much to the good!*
    Il a gagné la porte. *He reached the door. He got to the door.*
    Gagné par le sommeil. *Overcome by sleep.*

gai *adj. gay, cheerful.*

gaiement *gaily.*

gaieté *f. mirth.*

gaillard *m. jolly fellow, daring fellow.*

gaillard *adj. strong, vigorous.*

gain *m. gain, profit; success.*

gala *m. gala; celebration.*

galant *adj. gallant, courteous.*

galanterie *f. courtesy, politeness.*

galerie *f. gallery.*

galet *m. pebble.*

galoche *f. rubber; pl. rubbers, overshoes.*

galon *m. stripe.*

galop *m. gallop.*

gamin *m.* (gamine *f.*) *youngster.*

gamme *f. scale; range.*

gant *m. glove.*

garage *m. garage.*

garant *m. surety, bail.*

garantie *f. guarantee; security, pledge*

garantir *to guarantee; certify.*

GARÇON *m. boy; bachelor; fellow.*
    C'est un bon garçon. *He's a good fellow.*
    C'est un vieux garçon. *He's an old bachelor.*

garde *f. guard, defense.*
    Etre sur ses gardes. *To be on one's guard.*

garde *m. guard, attendant.*
GARDER *to keep.*
Il garde le lit. *He's confined to bed.*
Il garde la chambre. *He stays (is staying) in his room.*
Voulez-vous garder cet enfant? *Will you take care of (watch) this child?*
Je le garderai comme souvenir. *I'll keep it as a souvenir.*
Il n'a pas pu garder le sérieux. *He couldn't keep a straight face.*
Garder rancune. *To bear a grudge against.*
Dieu m'en garde! *God forbid!*
se garder *to beware; watch out; keep from.*
Gardez-vous de tomber. *Watch out, don't fall. Take care not to fall.*
Je m'en garderai bien. *I'll take good care not to do that.*
gardien *m. (gardienne f.) guardian, warden.*
gare *f. railroad station.*
Où se trouve la gare? *Where's the station?*
Par la gare (par chemin de fer). *By railway.*
gare! *Look out! Out of the way!*
se gargariser *to gargle.*
garni *m. furnished rooms.*
garnir *to furnish; adorn, decorate*
garnison *f. garrison.*
garniture *f. ornaments, trimmings.*
La garniture d'intérieur. *Upholstery (car).*
gars *m. fellow.*
gaspillage *m. waste, squandering.*
gaspiller *to waste, squander.*
gâté *adj. spoiled.*
Un enfant gâté. *A spoiled child.*
gâteau *m. (gâteaux pl.) cake.*
gâter *to spoil, soil; waste.*
se gâter *to go wrong, get bad, spoil.*
Les affaires se gâtent. *Business is taking a turn for the worse. Business is getting bad.*
Le temps se gâte. *It's getting cloudy. It's going to rain.*
GAUCHE *m. and f. noun and adj. left side; left; awkward.*
Aller à gauche. *To go to the left.*
Il emprunte à droite et à gauche. *He borrows left and right.*
Il a dû se lever du pied gauche. *He got up on the wrong side of the bed.*
Il est gauche. *He's very awkward (clumsy).*
La Rive Gauche. *The Left Bank (Paris).*
La toile de gauche. *The canvas on the left.*
gaucherie *f. awkwardness.*
gaz *m. gas.*
gaze *f. gauze.*
gazette *f. gazette, news sheet.*
gazeux *(gazeuse f.) adj. effervescent.*
Eau gazeuse. *Soda water.*
gazon *m. grass, lawn.*

géant *noun (m.) and adj. giant.*
gelée *f. frost.*
geler *to freeze.*
gémir *to groan, moan.*
gémissement *m. groan, moan.*
gênant *adj. annoying.*
Ça a dû être gênant. *That must have been awkward.*
gencive *f. gums (of the mouth).*
gendarme *m. gendarme.*
gendre *m. son-in-law.*
gêne *f. uneasiness; inconvenience.*
Il est sans gêne. *He has a free and easy (offhand) manner. He doesn't stand on ceremony.*
Cela ne me cause aucune gêne. *It doesn't inconvenience me in the least.*
Ils sont dans la gêne. *They're in (great) difficulties.*
gêné *adj. uneasy, embarrassed.*
GÊNER *to inconvenience; prevent, hinder.*
Sa présence me gênait pour parler librement. *His presence prevented me from speaking freely.*
Cela vous gêne-t-il? *Does it bother you? Is it in your way?*
Il est gêné dans ses affaires. *His affairs are not quite in order.*
SE GÊNER *to inconvenience oneself, trouble oneself.*
Je ne me suis pas gêné pour le lui dire. *I made no bones about telling him so.*
Ne vous gênez pas! *Make yourself at home!*
général *m. general.*
GÉNÉRAL *adj. general.*
En général. *Generally. In general.*
généralement *generally.*
généraliser *to generalize.*
génération *f. generation.*
généreusement *generously.*
généreux *(généreuse f.) adj. generous.*
générosité *f. generosity.*
génial *(géniaux pl.) adj. inspired, full of genius; fantastic.*
Une idée géniale. *A brilliant idea.*
génie *m. genius.*
genou *m. (genoux pl.) knee.*
GENRE *m. kind, class; gender.*
Quel genre de livres aimez-vous? *What kind of books do you like?*
C'est plus dans mon genre. *That's more in my line.*
Ce genre de maladie est courant ici. *This type of illness is quite common here.*
C'est de très mauvais genre. *It's very bad form.*
Se donner un genre. *To pose. To give oneself airs.*
GENS *m. pl. people, persons.*

Ce sont des gens bien. *They're nice people.*

Beaucoup de jeunes gens y vont. *A lot of young people go there.*

GENTIL (gentille *f.*) *adj. kind, nice.*

Ils ont tous été très gentils. *They were all very nice.*

C'est gentil à vous de penser à moi. *It's kind of you to remember me.*

gentillesse *f. graciousness.*

Auriez-vous la gentillesse de fermer la fenêtre? *Would you be kind enough to close the window? Would you be so kind as to close the window?*

gentiment *kindly, pleasantly.*

géographie *f. geography.*

geologie *f. geology.*

géométrie *f. geometry.*

gérance *f. management.*

gérant *m.* (gérante *f.*) *manager.*

gerbe *f. sheaf.*

gercer *to chap.*

Mains gercées. *Chapped hands.*

gerçure *f. chap, crack.*

gérer *to manage, take care of.*

germain *adj. used in the following expression:*

Cousin germain. *First cousin.*

germe *m. germ.*

germer *to germinate.*

gérondif *m. gerund.*

geste *m. gesture; action.*

gesticuler *to gesticulate.*

gibier *m. game (animals).*

gifle *f. slap in the face.*

gifler *to slap.*

gigot *m. leg of lamb.*

gilet *m. vest.*

Gilet de sauvetage. *Life jacket.*

gîte *m. home, lodging.*

glace *f. ice; ice cream.*

glacer *to freeze.*

glacial *adj. icy.*

glacière *f. icebox.*

glissant *adj. slippery.*

glisser *to slide; slip out; pass over.*

Il lui en a glissé un mot. *He gave him a hint (about it).*

global *adj. global, total.*

globe *m. globe.*

gloire *f. glory, fame.*

glorieux (glorieuse *f.*) *adj. glorious.*

glorifier *to praise.*

glouton (gloutonne *f.*) *adj. gluttonous.*

gloutonnerie *f. greediness.*

gluant *adj. sticky.*

goguenard *adj. sneering.*

gomme *f. eraser.*

gonflé *adj. swollen.*

gonfler *to swell.*

gorge *f. throat; gorge; groove.*

Mal à la gorge. *A sore throat.*

gorgée *f. mouthful.*

gorille *m. gorilla.*

gosier *m. throat.*

gosse *m. (fam.) kid, brat.*

gouache (gouache *f.*) *painting.*

gourmand *adj. greedy.*

gourmet *m. gourmet.*

GOÛT *m. taste, flavor, liking.*

C'est une affaire de goût. *It's a matter of taste.*

Il y prend goût. *He's taken a liking to it.*

Je lui trouve un petit goût salé. *It tastes a little too salty to me.*

Chacun à son goût. *To each his own.*

goûter *m. five-o'clock tea, snack.*

goûter *to taste, appreciate; to have tea.*

goutte *f. drop; gout.*

Il n'y entend pas goutte. *He doesn't understand the least thing about it.*

Je n'y vois goutte. *I can't see at all. I can hardly see.*

gouttière *f. gutter.*

gouvernante *f. governess.*

gouvernement *m. government.*

gouverner *to govern.*

gouverneur *m. governor.*

grâce *f. mercy; thanks; grace.*

Grâce à Dieu! *Thank God!*

Faire quelque chose de bonne grâce. *To do something readily (willingly, with good grace).*

gracieux (gracieuse *f.*) *adj. graceful, courteous.*

grade *m. rank, grade.*

grain *m. grain; bit; bead.*

graine *f. seed.*

graissage *m. greasing, lubrication.*

graisse *f. grease, fat.*

graisser *to grease; bribe.*

graisseux (graisseuse *f.*) *adj. greasy.*

grammaire *f. grammar.*

gramme *m. gram.*

gramophone *m. phonograph.*

GRAND *adj. great, large, tall.*

C'est un grand homme sec. *He's a tall thin man.*

Elle est aussi grande que moi. *She's as tall as I.*

Grand-père (mère). *Grandfather (mother).*

Ma grande soeur. *My big (older) sister.*

Grand froid. *Severe cold.*

Au grand jour. *Publicly. In public.*

De grande taille. *Of large size.*

grand'chose *much.*

Ce n'est pas grand'chose. *It's not very important. It doesn't matter.*

grandeur *f. size, greatness.*
grandiose *adj. grandiose.*
grandir *to grow, increase.*
grand-père *m. grandfather.*
grappe *f. bunch.*
gras (grasse *f.*) *adj. fat, oil, greasy.*
gratification *f. gratuity, tip, bonus.*
gratin *m. gratin (covered with bread crumbs and grated cheese and then baked.)*
    Des pommes de terres au gratin. *Potatoes au gratin.*
gratis *free of charge.*
    Entrée gratis. *Admission free.*
gratte-ciel *m. skyscraper.*
gratter *to scratch.*
gratuit *adj. free.*
    Entrée gratuite. *Admission free.*
gratuitement *without charge.*
grave *adj. grave, serious.*
gravement *seriously.*
graver *to engrave, carve.*
gravier *m. gravel.*
gravir *to climb.*
gravité *f. gravity.*
gravure *f. engraving, print.*
gré *m. pleasure, gratitude.*
    Je lui en sais un gré infini. *I'm very grateful to him for that.*
    Elle n'en fait qu'à son gré. *She does as she pleases.*
    Bon gré mal gré. *Willy-nilly. Whether one likes it or not.*
grec (grecque *f.*) *noun and adj. Greek.*
grêle *f. hail.*
grêle *adj. slender, slim.*
grêler *to hail.*
grelotter *to shiver with cold.*
grenier *m. garret, attic.*
grenouille *f. frog.*
grève *f. strike.*
    Se mettre en grève. *To go on strike.*
gribouiller *to scribble.*
grief *m. grievance.*
    Le seul grief que j'ai. *The only objection I have.*
    Il a un grief contre moi *He has a grievance against me.*
griffe *f. claw.*
griffonner *to scribble.*
grignoter *to nibble.*
gril *m. broiler.*
grille *f. iron gate.*
griller *to toast, broil.*
    Pain grillé. *Toast.*
grimace *f. grimace.*
grimper *to climb.*
grincement *m. grinding.*
grincer *to grind.*
grincheux (grincheuse *f.*) *adj. grumpy.*

grippe *f. grippe, flu; dislike.*
    Avoir la grippe. *To have the grippe.*
    Elle m'a pris en grippe. *She's taken a dislike to me.*
gris *adj. gray.*
grogner *to groan, grunt.*
grognon *adj. grumbling.*
grondement *m. roaring; rumbling.*
gronder *to roar; scold.*
groom *m. bellboy.*
gros *m. mass; wholesale.*
    En gros et au détail. *Wholesale and retail.*
    Le gros de l'armée n'est pas encore passé. *The main body of the army hasn't passed yet.*
    Voici, en gros, ce que j'ai compris. *Here is roughly what I understood.*
GROS (grosse *f.*) *adj. stout, fat, thick, big, coarse.*
    Une grosse corde. *A thick rope.*
    Il est trop gros. *He's too fat (stout).*
    Gros rire. *Loud laugh.*
grossier (grossière *f.*) *adj. coarse, rude.*
grossièreté *f. coarseness; rudeness.*
grossir *to enlarge, increase; grow bigger, gain weight.*
grotesque *adj. absurd, ridiculous.*
grotte *f. cave.*
grouillement *m. swarming.*
grouiller *to swarm.*
groupe *m. group.*
groupement *m. group, association.*
grouper *to groupe.*
guenille *f. old rag.*
guêpe *f. wasp.*
GUÈRE *not much, only a little, hardly, scarcely.*
    Je ne l'aime guère. *I don't really like him (her).*
    Il ne la voit guère. *He hardly ever sees her.*
    Je ne suis guère content. *I'm hardly satisfied. I'm not at all satisfied.*
    Il n'y a guère plus de trois ans. *It's barely more than three years ago.*
    Est-il ruiné?—Il ne s'en faut guère. *Is he bankrupt?—Pretty nearly.*
guérir *to heal, get well.*
guérison *f. recovery.*
guerre *f. war.*
guet *m. watch, lookout.*
    Il a l'oeil et l'oreille au guet. *He keeps his eyes and ears open.*
    Il fait le guet. *He's keeping watch. He's on the alert.*
guet-apens *m. ambush.*
guetter *to watch.*
gueule *f. mouth (used only of animals).*
guichet *m. ticket window.*
guide *m. guide, guidebook.*

guider *to lead.*
guidon *m. handlebar.*
guigne *f. bad luck.*
guignol *m. Punch and Judy show.*
guillemets *m. pl. quotation marks.*
guillotine *f. guillotine.*
guillotiner *to guillotine.*
guise *f. manner, way.*
   Il n'en fait qu'à sa guise. *He does just as he pleases.*
   A votre guise! *As you please!*
guitare *f. guitar.*
guitariste *m. guitar player, guitarist.*
guttural *(gutturaux pl.) adj. guttural.*
gymnastique *f. physical training.*

H

Note: Words marked with a dot have an aspirated "h." Aspirated h nouns take the complete singular article (le or la) instead of l' (i.e., le héros). The plural article les has no liaison with its noun.

habile *adj. clever, skillful, able, competent.*
habileté *f. skillfulness.*
habillé *adj. dressed; dressy.*
habiller *to dress, clothe.*
S'HABILLER *to dress.*
   Elle est en train de s'habiller. *She's getting dressed.*
habit *m. coat; full dress; pl. clothes.*
habitant *m. (habitante f.) inhabitant, resident.*
habitation *f. dwelling.*
HABITER *to inhabit, dwell in, live.*
   Où habitez-vous maintenant? *Where are you living now? Where do you live now?*
habits *m. pl. clothes.*
HABITUDE *f. habit.*
   D'habitude ils arrivent toujours en retard. *They're generally late.*
   Venez comme d'habitude. *Come as usual.*
habitué *m. and f. person who frequents a place, regular customer.*
habituel *(habituelle f.) adj. habitual, usual, customary.*
habituellement *habitually, usually.*
s'habituer *to get used to.*
   On s'y habitue peu à peu. *One gradually gets used to it.*
• **hache** *f. axe.*
• **hacher** *to chop.*
• **hagard** *adj. haggard.*
• **haie** *f. hedge.*
• **haillon** *m. rag.*
   Il est en haillons. *He's in rags and tatters.*
• **haine** *f. hatred.*

• **haineux** *(haineuse f.) adj. hateful.*
• **haïr** *to hate.*
haleine *f. breathe.*
   Je suis hors d'haleine. *I'm out of breath.*
   Elle a lu ce livre tout d'une haleine. *She read that book in one sitting.*
   Il nous a tenus en haleine. *He kept us in suspense.*
   C'est un récit de longue haleine. *That's a long-winded story.*
• **haletant** *adj. panting.*
• **haleter** *to pant.*
hallucination *f. hallucination.*
halluciner *to hallucinate.*
• **halte** *f. halt.*
   Halte là! *Stop there!*
hameçon *m. fishhook.*
• **hanche** *f. hip.*
• **handicap** *m. handicap.*
• **hangar** *m. hangar.*
• **hanter** *to haunt.*
• **hantise** *f. obsession.*
• **harangue** *f. harangue.*
• **haranguer** *to harangue.*
• **harasser** *to harass, tire out.*
• **harceler** *to annoy, bother, pester.*
• **hardi** *adj. bold.*
• **hardiesse** *f. boldness, daring.*
• **hareng** *m. herring.*
• **hargneux** *(hargneuse f.) adj. peevish, surly.*
• **haricot** *m. bean.*
harmonie *f. harmony.*
harmonieux *(harmonieuse f.) adj. harmonious.*
• **harnais** *m. harness.*
• **harpe** *f. harp.*
• **HASARD** *m. risk, peril, chance.*
   Je l'ai rencontré par hasard. *I met him by accident.*
   Le hasard a fait que j'ai réussi. *I succeeded by mere luck.*
   Il court le hasard de perdre gros. *He runs the risk of losing heavily.*
   Il ne faut rien laisser au hasard. *It's best to leave nothing to chance.*
se • **hasarder** *to risk.*
• **hasardeux** *(hasardeuse f.) adj. hazardous, risky.*
• **hâte** *f. hurry, speed.*
   Je l'ai écrit à la hâte. *I wrote it in a hurry.*
   J'ai hâte de le revoir. *I'm eager to see him again. I can't wait to see him again.*
• **hâter** *to hasten, hurry up.*
   Hâtez-vous! *Hurry up!*
• **hâtivement** *hastily.*
   Il s'habilla hâtivement. *He dressed in a hurry.*
• **hausse** *f. rise.*
• **hausser** *to raise, lift up.*
se • **hausser** *to raise oneself.*

- **HAUT** *noun (m.) and adj. top, summit; high.*
  Aller en haut. *To go upstairs.*
  Allez voir là-haut si vous le trouvez. *See if you can find it up there.*
  A marée haute. *At high tide.*
  La haute mer. *The high seas.*
  Penser tout haut. *To think aloud.*
  Voir plus haut. *See above.*
- **hautain** *adj. haughty.*
- **hauteur** *f. height.*
- **haut-parleur** *m. loudspeaker.*
hebdomadaire *n. and adj. weekly.*
héberger *to shelter.*
hébété *adj. dazed.*
  Un regard hébété. *A bewildered expression.*
hébreu (hébraïque *f.*) *noun and adj. Hebrew.*
hectare *m. hectare.*
- **hein** *what?*
hélas *alas.*
hémisphère *m. hemisphere.*
herbe *f. grass, herb.*
héréditaire *adj. hereditary.*
hérédité *f. heredity.*
héritage *m. inheritance.*
hériter *to inherit.*
héritier *m.* (héritière *f.*) *heir.*
héroïne *f. heroine.*
héroïque *adj. heroic.*
- **héros** *m. hero.*
hésitation *f. hesitation, wavering.*
hésiter *to hesitate.*
HEURE *f. hour; time.*
  D'heure en heure la situation empirait. *The situation was growing worse every hour.*
  Je serai prête dans une demi-heure. *I'll be ready in half an hour.*
  Mettez votre montre à l'heure. *Set your watch.*
  A dix heures pile. *At ten sharp.*
  A la bonne heure! *Excellent! Good! Fine!*
  Il l'a fait sur l'heure. *He did it right away.*
  Tout à l'heure. *Right away. In a moment.*
  Bon, à tout à l'heure. *Good, see you later.*
  A neuf heures quinze du matin. *At 9:15 A.M.*
  A quelle heure? *At what time?*
  A sept heures et demie. *At 7:30.*
  A vingt et une heures. *At 9:00 P.M.*
  Cent kilomètres à l'heure. *A hundred kilometers an hour.*
  De (très) bonne heure. *(Very) early.*
  L'heure d'affluence. *Rush hour.*
  L'heure d'arrivée (de départ). *Arrival (departure) time.*
  Payer à l'heure. *To pay by the hour.*
  Quelle heure est-il? *What time is it?*
  Se faire réserver une heure. *To make an appointment (hairdresser, etc.).*
  (Etre) à l'heure. *(To be) On time.*

heureusement *happily, luckily, fortunately.*
HEUREUX (heureuse *f.*) *adj. happy, lucky, fortunate.*
- **heurt** *m. shock, blow.*
- **heurter** *to knock against, collide (with); hurt someone's feelings.*
- **hideux** (hideuse *f.*) *adj. hideous, frightful.*
HIER *m. yesterday.*
  Il y est allé hier soir. *He went there last night.*
- **hiérarchie** *f. hierarchy.*
hilarité *f. hilarity.*
hirondelle *f. swallow (bird).*
- **hisser** *to hoist*
HISTOIRE *f. history, story, tale.*
  Un cours d'histoire. *A history course.*
  Raconter une histoire. *To tell a story.*
  Histoire de rire. *For the fun of it. Just for fun.*
historien *m. historian.*
historique *adj. historical.*
hiver *m. winter.*
  Faire des sports d'hiver. *To practice, engage in winter sports.*
- **hocher** *to shake (one's head), nod.*
- **homard** *m. lobster.*
homicide *m. homicide.*
hommage *m. homage, respect.*
HOMME *m. man.*
  Un homme comme il faut. *A well-bred man. A gentleman.*
  Un brave homme. *A nice fellow.*
  Un homme de tous métiers. *A jack-of-all-trades.*
homosexuel *m.* (homosexuelle *f.*) *homosexual*
homosexualité *homosexuality.*
honnête *adj. honest, loyal, polite.*
honnêteté *f. honesty.*
HONNEUR *m. honor.*
  C'est beaucoup d'honneur pour moi. *It is a great honor to me.*
  Il a agi en tout bien tout honneur. *He acted honestly. He acted with the best intentions.*
  Elle fait les honneurs de la maison. *She's doing the honors ("of the house").*
  Parole d'honneur! *On my word of honor!*
  On a donné une réception en son honneur. *They gave a party for him.*
  Le diplôme d'honneur. *Certificate of honor.*
honorable *adj. honorable.*
honorablement *honorably.*
honoraires *m. pl. fees (to professionals).*
honorer *to pay honor; do credit to.*
- **honte** *f. shame, disgrace, confusion.*
  N'avez-vous pas honte de faire cela? *Aren't you ashamed to do that?*
  J'ai honte de vous faire attendre. *I'm sorry to make you wait. I'm sorry to keep you waiting.*

Il fait honte à sa famille. *He's the black sheep of the family.*

Quelle honte! *How disgraceful!*

• **honteusement** *disgracefully.*

• **honteux** (honteuse *f.*) *adj. ashamed.*

Il en a été tout honteux. *He was very ashamed about (of) it.*

hôpital *m. hospital.*

• **hoquet** *m. hiccup.*

horaire *m. timetable.*

horizon *m. horizon.*

horizontal (horizontaux *pl.*) *adj. horizontal.*

horloge *f. clock.*

horloger *m. watchmaker.*

hormis *except, save.*

Ils étaient tous là hormis trois. *They were all there but three.*

horreur *f. horror, dread.*

Juste ciel! Quelle horreur! *Heavens! How awful!*

Il me fait horreur. *He horrifies me. I find him repulsive.*

J'ai horreur de. *I loathe. I have a horror of.*

horrible *adj. horrible.*

horrifier *to horrify.*

• **HORS** *out of, outside, beside.*

Hors d'usage. *No longer used.*

C'est hors (de) pair. *It's beyond comparison.*

Ici tout est hors de prix. *Everything is terribly expensive here.*

Il est hors de lui. *He's beside himself.*

C'est tout à fait hors de question. *It's altogether out of the question.*

• **hors-d'oeuvre** *m. hors-d'oeuvre.*

hospice *m. poorhouse; charitable institution.*

hospitalier (hospitalière *f.*) *adj. hospitable.*

hospitalité *f. hospitality.*

hostile *m. adj. hostile.*

hostilité *f. hostility; pl. hostilities.*

hôte *m.* (hôtesse *f.*) *host, guest.*

HÔTEL *m. hotel.*

Ils sont descendus à l'hôtel. *They stopped at the hotel.*

L'hôtel de ville. *The city hall.*

hôtellerie *f. inn.*

• **houille** *f. coal.*

Houille blanche. *Water power.*

• **houleux** (houleuse *f.*) *adj. heavy, surging.*

• **houppe** *f. puff.*

• **housse** *f. cover.*

• **huer** *to boo.*

huilage *m. lubrication.*

huile *f. oil.*

La peinture à l'huile. *Oil painting.*

• **HUIT** *noun and adj. eight.*

Huit jours. *A week.*

• **huitaine** *f. about eight.*

• **HUITIÈME** *noun and adj. eighth.*

huitre *f. oyster.*

humain *adj. human.*

Le genre humain. *Mankind.*

humanité *f. humanity.*

humble *adj. humble, lowly.*

humblement *humbly.*

humeur *f. humor, disposition, temper, mood.*

Avec humeur. *Crossly.*

Il est d'une humeur massacrante. *He's as cross as can be.*

Elle était de bonne humeur. *She was in a good mood.*

humide *adj. damp, wet.*

humidité *f. humidity.*

humiliant *adj. humiliating.*

humiliation *f. humiliation.*

humilier *to humilitate.*

humilité *f. humility.*

humour *m. humor.*

• **hurlement** *m. howl.*

• **hurler** *to yell, scream.*

hygiène *f. hygiene.*

hygiénique *adj. hygienic.*

hymne *m. hymn.*

hypnotiser *to hypnotize.*

hypnotisme *m. hypnotism.*

hypocrisie *f. hypocrisy.*

hypocrite *m. and f. noun and adj. hypocrite; hypocritical.*

hypothèque *f. mortgage.*

hypothèse *f. hypothesis, assumption.*

hystérie *f. hysteria.*

hystérique *adj. hysterical.*

I

ICI *here, in this place; now, this time.*

Par ici la sortie. *This way out.*

Il fait bon ici. *It's comfortable (nice) here.*

A combien d'ici est l'école? *How far is the school from here?*

Je ne suis pas d'ici. *I'm a stranger here.*

Jusqu'ici. *Up to here. Up to now.*

D'ici là. *Between now and then. In the meanwhile. Until then.*

D'ici peu. *Before long.*

Je dois quitter New York d'ici une semaine. *I have to leave New York within a week.*

Ici Charles Lewis. *This is Charles Lewis speaking (on telephone).*

Par ici. *This way.*

idéal *noun (m.) and adj.* (idéal, idéales *f.*) *ideal. (The m. plural of the adjective is* idéaux; *the plural of the noun is usually* idéaux, *though the form* idéals *sometimes occurs.)*

idéalisme *m. idealism.*

idéaliste *m. and f. idealist.*
idée *f. idea, conception, plan.*
    Quelle drôle d'idée! *What a funny idea!*
    Une idée fixe. *An obsession.*
    Se faire des idées. *To imagine things.*
    Faites à votre idée. *Do as you see fit (think right).*
    L'idée me vient que . . . *It occurs to me that . . . The thought occurs to me that.*
    Elle a des idées noires. *She has the blues.*
identification *f. identification.*
identifier *to identify.*
identique *adj. identical.*
identité *f. identity.*
    Les pièces d'identité. *Identification (papers).*
idiome *m. language, dialect.*
idiot (idiote *f.*) *noun and adj. idiot; idiotic, stupid.*
    Si vous êtes assez idiot pour le faire (*fam.*). *If you're stupid enough to do it.*
idolâtrer *to worship, idolize.*
idole *f. idol*
ignoble *adj. vile, base.*
ignominie *f. shame, disgrace.*
ignominieux (ignominieuse *f.*) *adj. disgraceful.*
ignorance *f. ignorance.*
ignorant *adj. ignorant, illiterate.*
ignorer *to be ignorant of, be unaware.*
    Il ignorait tout ce qui s'était passé. *He didn't know anything about what had taken place. He knew nothing of what had happened.*
    Je n'ignore pas que . . . *I'm not unaware that . . .*
IL *he, it.*
    Faites-le monter quand il viendra. *Send (show) him up when he comes.*
    Il pleut. *It's raining.*
    Il est tard. *It's late.*
    Il y a une erreur. *There's a mistake.*
    Il y a longtemps. *A long time ago.*
    Il y en a d'autres. *There are others.*
île *f. island.*
illégal (illégaux *pl.*) *adj. illegal.*
illégitime *adj. illegitimate, unlawful.*
illicite *adj. unlawful.*
illimité *adj. boundless.*
illisible *adj. illegible.*
illogique *adj. illogical.*
illumination *f. illumination.*
illusion *f. illusion, delusion.*
s'illusionner *to delude oneself.*
illustration *f. illustration.*
illustre *adj. illustrious, renowned.*
illustrer *to illustrate; explain.*
s'illustrer *to become famous.*
image *f. image, picture, likeness.*

imaginaire *adj. imaginary.*
imagination *f. imagination; fancy.*
imaginer *to imagine, conceive.*
s'imaginer *to imagine, believe.*
    Il ne faut pas vous imaginer que . . . *You mustn't imagine (believe) that . . .*
imbécile *adj. fool.*
imbécilité *f. stupidity.*
imbiber *to soak.*
imbu *adj. imbued.*
    Il est imbu de lui-même. *He's conceited. He's impressed with his own importance.*
imitateur *m.* (imitatrice *f.*) *imitator.*
imitation *f. imitation, copy.*
imiter *to imitate.*
immaculé *adj. immaculate.*
immatriculation *f. matriculation, registration.*
immatriculer *to matriculate, register.*
immédiat *adj. immediate.*
immédiatement *immediately.*
immémorial (immémoriaux *pl.*) *adj. immemorial.*
immense *adj. huge.*
immerger *to immerse.*
IMMEUBLE *m. building.*
immigrant *m. immigrant.*
immigration *f. immigration.*
immigré *m. immigrant.*
immigrer *to immigrate.*
imminent *adj. imminent.*
immobile *adj. motionless.*
    Un visage immobile. *Immobile features.*
    Rester immobile. *To stand still.*
immobilier (immobilière *f.*) *adj. immovable, real.*
    Biens immobiliers. *Real estate.*
    Agence immobilière. *Real estate agency.*
immobilité *f. immobility.*
immodéré *adj. immoderate.*
immodeste *adj. immodest.*
immonde *adj. filthy.*
immoral (immoraux *pl.*) *adj. immoral.*
immortalité *f. immortality.*
immortel (immortelle *f.*) *adj. immortal.*
immunité *f. immunity.*
impair *adj. odd.*
    Un nombre impair. *An odd number.*
impardonnable *adj. unpardonable.*
imparfait *adj. imperfect, unfinished.*
impartial (impartiaux *pl.*) *adj. impartial.*
impasse *f. blind alley; difficulty.*
impassible *adj. impassive.*
impatience *f. impatience.*
impatient *adj. restless, impatient.*
impatienter *to exhaust someone's patience.*
    Il m'impatiente. *He makes me lose my patience.*
s'impatienter *to grow impatient.*

impayable *adj. priceless, very funny.*
> Il est impayable dans ce rôle. *He's perfect (excellent, very funny) in that part. He's tops in that role.*

impeccable *adj. impeccable, faultless.*

impénétrable *adj. impenetrable, inscrutable.*

impératif *noun (m.) and adj. (impérative f.) imperative.*

imperceptible *adj. imperceptible.*

imperfection *f. imperfection, incompletion.*

impérialisme *m. imperialism.*

impérieux *(impérieuse f.) adj. imperative.*
> Il est impérieux que j'y aille. *It's absolutely necessary for me to go there.*

imperméable *m. raincoat.*

imperméable *adj. impermeable.*

impertinence *f. impertinence.*

impertinent *adj. impertinent, fresh.*

impétueux *(impétueuse f.) adj. impetuous.*

impétuosité *f. impulsiveness.*

impitoyable *adj. pitiless.*

implacable *adj. implacable, relentless.*

implicite *adj. implicit.*

impliquer *to involve.*
> Il y est impliqué. *He's involved (mixed up) in it.*

implorer *to implore, beseech, beg.*

impoli *adj. impolite.*
> Il a été impoli envers nous. *He was rude to us.*

impolitesse *f. impoliteness, rudeness.*

impopulaire *adj. unpopular.*

IMPORTANCE *f. importance.*
> Je n'y attache aucune importance. *I don't attach any importance to it (that). I don't consider it important.*
> Cela n'a aucune importance. *It doesn't matter at all.*

IMPORTANT *adj. important.*

importation *f. importation; pl. imports.*

importer *to import.*

IMPORTER *to matter.*
> N'importe. *Never mind. It's not important.*
> N'achetez pas n'importe quoi. *Don't buy just anything at all.*
> N'importe quand. *No matter when.*
> Faites-le n'importe comment. *Do it some way or other.*
> Mais qu'importe? *But what of it? What difference does it make?*
> N'importe qui vous le dira. *Anyone will tell you.*
> N'importe où. *Anywhere.*
> N'importe quel(le). *Any . . . at all.*

importun *adj. importunate, tiresome, bothersome, unwelcome.*

importuner *to bother.*

imposant *adj. imposing.*

imposer *to impose; inflict; levy, tax.*

> Il a imposé des conditions. *He imposed conditions.*
> Prix imposé par le fabricant. *Retail price set by the manufacturer.*
> Son âge impose le respect. *His age commands respect.*
> Imposer une punition. *To inflict (a) punishment.*

s'imposer *to impose oneself.*

impossibilité *f. impossibility.*

IMPOSSIBLE *noun (m.) and adj. impossible.*
> Il tente l'impossible. *He attempts the impossible.*
> Je ferai l'impossible pour vous. *I'll do my utmost to help you. I'll do anything for you.*
> Il est impossible (fam.). *He's impossible.*

imposteur *m. impostor.*

imposture *f. imposture.*

impôt *m. tax.*
> Impôt sur le revenu. *Income tax.*

impotence *f. impotence, helplessness.*

impotent *adj. helpless.*

impraticable *adj. impracticable.*

impression *f. impression.*
> L'impression d'ensemble. *The general impression.*
> Il a fait impression. *He made quite an impression.*

impressionnant *adj. impressive.*

impressionner *to impress.*

impressionniste *impressionist (painting).*

imprévu *adj. unexpected.*
> Des difficultés imprévues. *Unforeseen difficulties.*

imprimante *f. printer.*

imprimante à laser *f. laser printer.*

imprimer *to print.*

imprimerie *f. printing plant.*

imprimés *m. pl. printed matter.*

imprimeur *m. printer.*

improbabilité *f. improbability, unlikelihood.*

improbable *adj. unlikely.*

impromptu *adj. impromptu.*

impropre *adj. incorrect.*
> Une expression impropre. *An incorrect expression.*

improviser *to improvise.*

(à l') improviste *unexpectedly.*
> Il est venu à l'improviste. *He came unexpectedly.*

imprudence *f. imprudence.*

imprudent *adj. imprudent, incautious.*

impuissance *f. importance; powerlessness.*

impuissant *adj. powerless.*

impulsif *(impulsive f.) impulsive.*

impur *adj. impure; foul.*

imputer *to impute.*

inaccessible *adj. inaccessible.*

inaccoutumé *adj. unaccustomed, unusual.*
inachevé *adj. unfinished.*
inactif (inactive *f.*) *adj. inactive.*
inadmissible *adj. inadmissible.*
inanimé *adj. lifeless.*
inaperçu *adj. unseen.*
   Il passait inaperçu. *He escaped notice.*
inapte *adj. unfit.*
inaptitude *f. unfitness.*
inattentif (inattentive *f.*) *adj. inattentive*
inattention *f. lack of attention, heedlessness.*
inauguration *f. inauguration.*
inaugurer *to inaugurate.*
incalculable *adj. incalculable.*
incapable *adj. incapable.*
incapacité *f. incapacity.*
incassable *adj. unbreakable.*
incendie *m. fire.*
incendier *to set on fire.*
incertain *adj. uncertain, doubtful.*
incertitude *f. incertitude, doubt.*
incessamment *incessantly; at once, right away.*
   Il parle incessamment. *He speaks constantly.*
   Il arrivera incessamment. *He'll be there right away.*
incident *m. incident, occurrence.*
incinérer *to burn to ashes.*
incision *f. incision.*
inciter *to incite, instigate.*
incliner *to bend; incline toward.*
   Incliner la tête. *To bend one's head.*
   Incliner à faire quelque chose. *To feel inclined to do something.*
   Elle incline pour la couleur bleue. *She likes blue. Blue is her favorite color.*
s'incliner *to slant, slope; bow to, yield to, submit to.*
   S'incliner devant les faits. *To bow to the inevitable.*
inclus *adj. included, enclosed.*
   Ouvert toute la semaine, dimanche inclus. *Open daily and Sundays. ("Open all week, including Sundays.").*
   Ci-inclus. *Enclosed herewith.*
incognito *adj. incognito.*
incohérence *f. incoherence.*
incohérent *adj. incoherent.*
incomber *to be incumbent on; devolve on.*
incommode *adj. inconvenient, uncomfortable, unhandy.*
   Un homme incommode. *An unpleasant man.*
incommoder *to inconvenience, trouble.*
   Cela vous incommoderait-il de remettre notre rendez-vous? *Would it inconvenience you to postpone our appointment?*

incomparable *adj. incomparable, matchless.*
incompatible *adj. incompatible.*
incompétence *f. incompetency.*
incompétent *adj. incompetent.*
incompréhensible *adj. incomprehensible.*
incompréhension *f. lack of understanding.*
inconcevable *adj. inconceivable.*
incongru *adj. incongruous, out of place.*
inconnu *m. stranger.*
inconnu *adj. unknown.*
   Ce lieu m'est inconnu. *This place is unfamiliar to me.*
inconscient *adj. unconscious.*
inconséquent *adj. inconsistent.*
inconsidération *f. lack of consideration, thoughtlessness.*
inconsolable *adj. inconsolable.*
incontestable *adj. undeniable.*
inconvenance *f. impropriety.*
inconvénient *m. inconvenience, disadvantage, objection.*
   Il n'y a pas d'inconvénient à cela. *There's no objection to that.*
   Je n'y vois pas d'inconvénient. *I see no objection to that.*
   Il a évité un inconvénient. *He avoided a difficulty.*
incorporer *to incorporate.*
incorrect *adj. incorrect.*
   C'est incorrect. *It isn't true.*
incrédule *adj. incredulous.*
incrédulité *f. incredulity.*
incriminer *to accuse, indict.*
incroyable *adj. incredible.*
incruster *to encrust.*
inculpé *m. defendant.*
inculper *to indict, charge.*
incurable *adj. incurable.*
indécence *f. indecency.*
indécent *adj. indecent.*
indécis *adj. uncertain, undecided; indistinct.*
indécision *f. indecision.*
indéfini *adj. indefinite.*
indélicatesse *f. indelicacy, tactlessness.*
indemne *adj. uninjured, unharmed, safe and sound.*
indemnité *f. indemnity.*
indépendance *f. independence, freedom.*
indépendant *adj. independent.*
indication *f. indication.*
   A titre d'indication. *For your guidance.*
   J'ai suivi les indications données. *I did as directed.*
indice *m. sign, mark.*
indifférence *f. indifference.*
indifférent *adj. indifferent.*
   Ça m'est indifférent. *I don't care (either) one way or the other. It's all the same to me.*

Il m'est indifférent. *He's nothing to me. I don't care about him.*

Ils ont parlé de choses indifférentes. *They talked about the weather.*

indigence *f. poverty, want.*

indigent *adj. poor, destitute.*

indignation *f. indignation.*

indigne *adj. unworthy.*

indigner *to rouse indignation.*

Cela m'indigne. *It makes my blood boil.*

s'indigner *to become indignant.*

indiquer *to indicate.*

Pouvez-vous m'indiquer la rue de Rivoli? *Could you please tell me how to get to Rivoli Street?*

Cela indique sa bêtise. *It only shows his stupidity.*

indirect *adj. indirect.*

indiscret (indiscrète *f.*) *adj. indiscreet.*

indiscrétion *f. indiscretion.*

Sans indiscrétion, qu'est-il arrivé? *If you don't mind my asking, what happened?*

indispensable *adj. indispensable.*

indisposer *to indispose.*

individu *m. fellow.*

C'est un drôle d'individu. *He's a funny (queer) fellow.*

C'est un misérable individu. *He's an awful (miserable) person. He's a scoundrel.*

Quel sale individu (fam.)! *What a nasty fellow!*

individuel (individuelle *f.*) *adj. individual.*

indocile *adj. disobedient.*

indolent *adj. indolent, indifferent, apathetic.*

indu *adj. undue, not right.*

Rentrer à une heure indue. *To come home very late.*

induire *to induce, lead, infer.*

Induire en erreur. *To mislead.*

Induire en tentation. *To lead into temptation.*

indulgence *f. indulgence, leniency.*

indulgent *adj. indulgent, lenient.*

industrie *f. industry; skill.*

L'industrie minière. *The mining industry.*

Un chevalier d'industrie. *A confidence man. A swindler.*

Il vit d'industrie. *He lives by his wits.*

industriel *m. manufacturer.*

industriel (industrielle *f.*) *adj. industrial.*

industrieux (industrieuse *f.*) *adj. busy.*

inébranlable *adj. unshakable.*

inédit *adj. unpublished.*

inégal (inégaux *pl.*) *adj. unequal, uneven.*

inégalité *f. lack of equality.*

inepte *adj. inept, foolish, stupid, absurd.*

inerte *adj. inert, dull.*

inévitable *adj. inevitable, unavoidable.*

inévitablement *inevitably.*

inexact *adj. inaccurate.*

inexactitude *f. inaccuracy.*

inexorable *adj. inexorable.*

inexpérience *f. inexperience.*

infaillible *adj. infallible.*

infanterie *f. infantry.*

infatuer *to infatuate.*

infect *adj. filthy, foul.*

infecter *to infect, taint.*

infection *f. infection.*

inférieur *adj. inferior.*

infériorité *f. inferiority.*

infidèle *adj. unfaithful, faithless.*

infidélité *f. faithlessness.*

infime *adj. lowest, extremely trifling.*

infini *adj. infinite, boundless.*

infiniment *infinitely, extremely.*

Je regrette infiniment, mais je ne peux pas venir cet après-midi. *I'm terribly sorry but I won't be able to come this afternoon.*

infirme *m. and f. noun and adj. cripple; infirm, crippled.*

infirmière *f. nurse.*

inflammable *adj. flammable.*

infliger *to inflict.*

INFLUENCE *f. influence; authority.*

INFLUENCER *to influence.*

informaticien, ne *m., f. computer programmer.*

INFORMATION *f. information, news; inquiry.*

Je vous envoie ceci pour votre information. *I'm sending you this for your information.*

Informations de la dernière heure. *Latest bulletins (news).*

Nous avons pris des informations sur lui. *We made inquiries about him.*

informatique *f. computer science.*

Langage informatique. *Computer language.*

Programme informatique. *Computer program.*

s'informer *to inquire, investigate.*

Il s'est informé de votre santé à plusieurs reprises. *He asked (inquired) about your health several times.*

infortune *f. misfortune, calamity.*

infortuné *adj. unfortunate, ill-fated.*

s'ingénier *to tax one's ingenuity, contrive.*

ingénieur *m. engineer.*

ingénieux (ingénieuse *f.*) *adj. ingenious, clever.*

ingrat *adj. ungrateful.*

ingratitude *f. ingratitude.*

ingrédient *m. ingredient.*

inhabile *adj. inapt, unskilled.*

inhabitable *adj. uninhabitable.*

inhumain *adj. inhuman.*

inhumer *to bury.*

inimaginable *adj. unimaginable.*

inimitié *f. enmity, hatred.*

ininflammable *adj. uninflammable.*

inintelligence *f. lack of intelligence.*

ininterrompu *adj. uninterrupted.*

initial (initiale, *f.* initiales, *f.*, *pl.*, initiaux *m.*, *pl.*) *noun* (*f.*) *and adj. initial.*

initiation *f. initiation, introduction.*

initiative *f. initiative.*

initier *to initiate, teach.*

injure *f. insult, abuse.*

injurier *to insult, call names.*

injuste *adj. unjust.*

injustice *f. injustice, unfairness.*

innocence *f. innocence.*

innocent *adj. innocent; simple, foolish.*
> Aux innocents les mains pleines. *The fools have all the luck. Fortune is kind to fools.*

innombrable *adj. numberless.*

inoculer *to inoculate.*

inoffensif (inoffensive *f.*) *adj. harmless.*

inondation *f. flood.*

inonder *to flood.*

inopiné *adj. unexpected.*

inouï *adj. unheard of; wonderful, extraordinary.*

inquiet (inquiète *f.*) *adj. uneasy, restless, worried.*
> Je suis très inquiet à son sujet. *I'm very worried about him (her).*

inquiéter *to worry (someone), alarm, make uneasy.*

s'inquiéter *to worry.*
> Ne vous inquiétez pas pour cela. *Set your mind at rest (at ease) about that. Don't worry about that. Don't let that worry you.*
> Il n'y a vraiment pas lieu de s'inquiéter. *There is no reason to worry. There's really no cause for concern (for alarm).*

inquiétude *f. anxiety, restlessness, uneasiness.*

insanité *f. insanity.*

inscription *f. inscription, registration.*

inscrire *to write down; register.*
> Inscrivez tout ce que je vais dire. *Write down everything I'm going to say.*

s'inscrire *to write down one's name, register, matriculate, to enroll.*

inscrit *adj. inscribed; registered, indicated, shown.*

insensé *adj. insane, mad, rash.*

insensible *adj. insensible, indifferent (to), unmoved (by).*

inséparable *adj. inseparable.*

insérer *to insert.*

insidieux (insidieuse *f.*) *adj. insidious.*

insigne *m. emblem.*

insigne *adj. distinguished, remarkable.*

insinuation *f. insinuation.*

insinuer *to insinuate.*

insistance *f. insistence.*

insister *to insist.*
> Il a spécialement insisté sur ce point. *He laid stress on that point.*

insolation *f. sunstroke.*

insolence *f. insolence.*

insolent *adj. insolent, rude.*

insomnie *f. insomnia.*

insouciance *f. unconcern.*

insouciant *adj. careless, unconcerned.*

inspecter *to inspect.*

inspecteur *m. inspector.*

inspection *f. inspection, survey.*

inspiration *f. inspiration, suggestion.*
> Sous l'inspiration du moment. *On the spur of the moment.*

inspirer *to inhale; inspire.*

instabilité *f. instability.*

instable *adj. unstable, unsteady, fickle.*

installation *f. installation.*

installer *to install.*

instamment *eagerly, earnestly.*
> Prier instamment. *To beg. To entreat. To request earnestly.*

instance *f. entreaty, solicitation, request.*
> Etre en instance de départ pour. *To be on the point of leaving for.*
> Se rendre aux instances de quelqu'un. *To yield to someone's entreaties.*

INSTANT *m. instant, moment.*
> Je suis à vous dans un instant. *I'll be with you in a moment.*
> Un instant! *Just a minute!*
> Il va arriver d'un instant à l'autre. *He'll be here any minute.*

instantané *m. snapshot.*

instantanément *instantaneously.*

instar *used in the following expression:*
> A l'instar de. *Like. After the fashion of. In imitation of.*

instigateur *m.* (instigatrice *f.*) *instigator.*

instigation *f. instigation.*

instiller *to instill.*

instinct *m. instinct.*
> L'instinct de conservation. *The instinct of self-preservation.*

instinctif (instinctive *f.*) *adj. instinctive.*

instituer *to institute.*

institut *m. institute.*

instituteur *m.* (institutrice *f.*) *schoolteacher in elementary school.*

institution *f. institution; boarding school.*

instruction *f. instruction; education.*
> Manquer d'instruction. *To lack education.*
> Suivez les instructions données. *Follow the directions (instructions).*

INSTRUIRE *to instruct, teach; inform.*
instruit *adj. well-educated, well-informed.*
instrument *m. instrument, tool.*
INSU *m. unawareness.*
> A l'insu de. *Unknown to. Without the knowledge of.*
> Il l'a fait à l'insu de ses parents. *He did it without his parents' knowledge.*
> Pourquoi l'avez-vous fait à mon insu? *Why did you do it behind my back?*

insubordination *f. insubordination.*
insubordonné *adj. insubordinate.*
insuccès *m. failure.*
insuffisance *f. insufficiency, deficiency, incompetence.*
insuffisant *adj. insufficient, incompetent.*
insulte *f. insult.*
insulter *to insult.*
insupportable *adj. unbearable.*
s'insurger *to rebel, revolt.*
insurrection *f. insurrection.*
intact *adj. intact.*
intarissable *adj. inexhaustible.*
intégral (intégraux *pl.*) *adj. integral, entire.*
intégrité *f. integrity.*
intellectuel (intellectuelle *f.*) *noun and adj. intellectual.*
intelligemment *intelligently.*
intelligence *f. intelligence.*
> Intelligence artificielle. *Artificial intelligence.*
> Etre d'intelligence avec. *To have an understanding with. To be in league with. To be hand in glove with.*

intelligent *adj. intelligent, clever.*
intempérance *f. intemperance.*
intense *adj. intense.*
intensité *f. intensity.*
INTENTION *f. intention, purpose.*
> Vous vous méprenez sur ses intentions. *You're mistaken about his intentions.*
> Avez-vous l'intention d'y aller? *Do you intend to go there?*
> Il l'a fait avec intention. *He did it on purpose.*

intercéder *to intercede.*
intercepter *to intercept.*
interdire *to forbid.*
> C'est interdit. *That's not allowed. That's prohibited.*
> Les chiens sont interdits. *No dogs allowed.*

interdit *adj. forbidden; confused.*
> Entrée interdite sous peine de poursuite. *No admittance under penalty of law.*
> Passage interdit. *No thoroughfare.*
> Sens interdit. *One way.*
> Elle demeurait tout interdite. *She stood there completely confused (taken aback, speechless).*

INTÉRESSANT *adj. interesting.*
INTÉRESSER *to interest, concern; give a share.*
> En quoi tout cela vous intéresse-t-il? *How does all that concern you?*
> On l'a intéressé dans l'affaire. *He'll receive his share of the profits.*

INTÉRÊT *m. interest, share.*
> Les intérêts du prêt s'accumulent. *The interest on the loan is accruing.*
> J'ai intérêt à en acheter. *It's to my interest to buy some of it.*
> Il y aurait intérêt à. *It would be desirable (to our advantage) to.*
> Porter intérêt à quelqu'un. *To take an interest in someone.*
> Il paiera des dommages-intérêts. *He'll pay damages.*

intérieur *m. inside; home; home life.*
> Nous avons rendez-vous à l'intérieur du restaurant. *We're meeting inside the restaurant.*
> Ils n'ont pas d'intérieur à eux. *They have no home life.*

intérieur *adj. interior.*
intérim *m. interim.*
interloquer *disconcert.*
> Il en est resté tout interloqué (*fam.*). *He was completely disconcerted. He was taken aback. He was speechless.*

intermède *m. medium; interlude.*
> Par l'intermède de. *By means of. Through the medium (agency) of.*

intermédiaire *noun (m.) and adj. intermediary; intermediate.*
interminable *adj. interminable, endless.*
internat *m. boarding school.*
international (internationaux *pl.*) *adj. international.*
interne *m. boarder (at school); intern (hospital).*
interner *to intern.*
interpeller *to call upon.*
interprétation *f. interpretation.*
interprète *m. interpreter.*
interpréter *to interpret.*
interrogation *f. interrogation.*
> Point d'interrogation. *Question mark.*

interrogatoire *m. interrogatory.*
interroger *to examine, question.*
interrompre *to interrupt.*
> Excusez-moi de vous interrompre, mais on vous appelle au téléphone. *Pardon me for interrupting you, but you're wanted on the phone.*
> J'ai dû interrompre mes leçons d'anglais lorsque mon professeur est parti. *I had to discontinue my English lessons, when my teacher left.*

interruption *f. interruption.*
interurbain *adj. interurban, long-distance (telephone).*
    Un appel interurbain. *Long-distance telephone call.*
intervalle *m. interval.*
intervenir *to intervene, interfere.*
intervention *f. interference.*
interview *f. interview.*
intestin *m. intestine; pl. intestines.*
intimation *f. notification of an order.*
intime *adj. intimate, private.*
    Un ami intime. *An intimate (very close) friend.*
intimider *to intimidate.*
intimité *f. intimacy.*
intituler *to entitle.*
intolérable *adj. intolerable, unbearable.*
intolérance *f. intolerance.*
intolérant *adj. intolerant.*
intonation *f. intonation.*
intoxication *f. poisoning.*
intransigeance *f. intransigence, uncompromisingness.*
intransigeant *adj. uncompromising, intolerant.*
intrépide *adj. dauntless, bold.*
intrigant *m. intriguer, schemer, wire-puller.*
intrigue *f. intrigue, plot (of a book, etc.).*
intriguer *to plot; puzzle.*
    Cette affaire l'intrigue beaucoup. *This case (matter) puzzles him a lot.*
introduction *f. introduction.*
INTRODUIRE *to introduce.*
    Il a introduit beaucoup de réformes. *He introduced numerous reforms.*
    Il fut introduit au salon. *He was shown into the living (parlor) room.*
introuvable *adj. not to be found.*
    Cet article est introuvable. *This article is hard to find (not to be found).*
intrus *m. intruder.*
intuition *f. intuition.*
inutile *adj. useless.*
invalide *m. and f. noun and adj. invalid, cripple.*
invariable *adj. invariable.*
invasion *f. invasion.*
invective *f. invective.*
inventaire *m. inventory.*
inventer *to invent, devise.*
invention *f. invention.*
inverse *m. reverse, opposite.*
    Il fait toujours l'inverse de ce qu'on lui demande. *He always does the opposite of what you ask him.*
inverse *adj. reverse, contrary, opposite.*
    En sens inverse. *In the opposite direction.*
inversibles *m. pl. film (for transparencies).*

invincible *adj. invincible, unconquerable.*
invisible *adj. invisible.*
invitation *f. invitation.*
    Une carte d'invitation. *(Printed) invitation.*
invité *m. guest.*
inviter *to invite.*
involontaire *adj. involuntary.*
involontairement *involuntarily.*
invoquer *to call upon.*
invraisemblable *adj. unlikely, hard to believe.*
    Une histoire invraisemblable. *A told story.*
invulnérable *adj. invulnerable.*
iode *m. iodine.*
    Teinture d'iode. *Tincture of iodine.*
ironic *f. irony.*
ironique *adj. ironical.*
irréfléchi *adj. thoughtless, hasty, rash.*
irrégulier (irrégulière *f.*) *adj. irregular.*
irrémédiable *adj. irremediable.*
irréparable *adj. irreparable.*
irréprochable *adj. irreproachable.*
irrésistible *adj. irresistible.*
irrespectueux (irrespectueuse *f.*) *adj. disrespectful.*
irresponsable *adj. irresponsible.*
irrévocable *adj. irrevocable.*
irrigation *f. irrigation.*
irriguer *to irrigate.*
irritable *adj. irritable.*
irritant *adj. irritating.*
irriter *to irritate, annoy, anger.*
irruption *f. irruption, violent entry.*
    Faire irruption dans une salle. *To burst into a room.*
islamique *adj. Islamic.*
isolement *m. isolation, loneliness; insulation.*
isoler *to isolate, separate.*
israélite *m. and f. noun and adj. Jew. Jewish.*
issu *adj. born of, descended from.*
issue *f. issue, way out.*
Italie *f. Italy.*
italien (italienne *f.*) *noun and adj. Italian.*
item *ditto; likewise, also.*
itinéraire *m. itinerary, route.*
ivoire *m. ivory.*
ivre *adj. drunk.*
ivresse *f. drunkenness, intoxication; enthusiasm.*
ivrogne *m. drunkard.*

J

jadis *formerly, once.*
jaillir *to gush (out), spurt, burst forth.*
jalousie *f. jealousy, envy.*
jaloux (jalouse *f.*) *adj. jealous.*

JAMAIS (*with* ne) *never.*
　Je n'y ai jamais été. *I've never been there.*
　Jamais de la vie! *Never! Not on your life!*
jambe *f. leg.*
　Il a pris ses jambes à son cou (*fam.*). *He took to his heels.*
jambon *m. ham.*
JANVIER *m. January.*
japonais (japonaise *f.*) *noun and adj. Japanese.*
jaquette *f. jacket of a woman's suit.*
jardin *m. garden.*
　Jardin d'enfants. *Kindergarten.*
jardinier *m.* (jardinière *f.*) *gardener.*
jargon *m. jargon; slang; incorrect language.*
jarretière *f. garter.*
jaser *to chatter.*
jaunâtre *adj. yellowish.*
jaune *adj. yellow.*
　Jaune paille. *Straw-yellow, straw-colored.*
jaunir *to turn yellow.*
JE *I.*
jersey *m. woolen material.*
jet *m. throw, throwing; gush; jet; ray.*
　Un jet d'eau. *A fountain.*
jetée *f. jetty, pier.*
jeter *to throw.*
jeton *m. token*
jeu *m.* (jeux *pl.*) *game; play.*
　Etre en jeu. *To be at stake.*
　Un jeu de mots. *A pun.*
　Un jeu d'esprit. *A witticism.*
　Le jeu des acteurs. *Acting.*
　Les jeux d'eau. *Fountains (playing).*
　Les jeux de lumière. *Lighting (theatre).*
　Jeu-vidéo. *Video game.*
JEUDI *m. Thursday.*
　Le(s) jeudi(s). *On Thursdays.*
à jeun *fasting.*
　Prenez ce médicament à jeun. *Take this medicine on an empty stomach.*
JEUNE *adj. young; junior.*
　Jeune homme. *Young man.*
　Jeune fille. *Young lady.*
　Dubois jeune. *Dubois, Jr.*
jeûne *m. fast.*
jeûner *to fast.*
jeunesse *f. youth.*
joaillerie *f. jewelry.*
joie *f. joy.*
joindre *to join, unite.*
se joindre *to join; join in.*
joint *adj. joined, connected; enclosed; attached.*
joli *m. used in the following expression;*
　C'est du joli (*fam.*)! *That's a fine thing!*
JOLI *adj. pretty.*
　Une jolie femme. *A pretty woman.*
joliment *nicely.*

　Il nous a joliment trompés. *He really (certainly) took us in (fooled us).*
jonction *f. junction.*
joue *f. cheek.*
jouer *to play.*
　Jouer au bridge (au tennis). *To play bridge (tennis).*
　Jouer du piano (de la flûte, de la clarinette). *To play the piano (the flute, the clarinet).*
se jouer *to make game of; make light of.*
　Il se joue de tout le monde. *He makes game of everybody.*
　Se jouer des difficultés. *To overcome difficulties with the greatest ease. To make light of difficulties.*
jouet *m. toy.*
joueur *m.* (joueuse *f.*) *player, gambler.*
joufflu *adj. chubby.*
joug *m. yoke.*
jouir (de) *to enjoy, rejoice in.*
　Il jouit d'une bonne santé. *He enjoys good health.*
　Il sait jouir de la vie. *He knows how to enjoy life.*
jouissance *f. enjoyment.*
JOUR *m. day, daytime; daylight.*
　Quel jour sommes-nous? *What's today?*
　Je le vois tous les jours. *I see him every day.*
　De nos jours. *In our time. Nowadays. These days.*
　Sur ses vieux jours. *In his old age.*
　Il fait jour. *It's daylight.*
　Au petit jour. *At daybreak.*
　Jeter le jour dans. *To throw light on.*
　Du jour au lendemain. *Overnight. From one day to the next.*
　Ils vivent au jour le jour. *They live from hand to mouth.*
　A un de ces jours. *See you one of these days. So long.*
　Mettre un compte à jour. *To bring an account up to date.*
　Ces jours-ci. *These days.*
　Huit (quinze) jours. *One week (two weeks).*
　Payer par jour. *To pay by the day.*
　Plusieurs fois par jour. *Several times a day.*
journal *m.* (journaux *pl.*) *newspaper; diary.*
　Le marchand de journaux. *Newsvendor.*
　Journal parlé. *Radio newscast.*
　Journal télévisé. *TV newscast.*
journalier (journalière *f.*) *adj. daily.*
　Un travail journalier. *A daily task.*
journalisme *m. journalism.*
journaliste *m. journalist.*
journée *f. day.*
　Payé à la journée. *Paid by the day.*
　Dans la journée. *During the day.*

Vous les aurez dans la journée. *You'll have them the same day.*

jovial adj. *jovial, jolly.*

joyau m. (joyaux pl.) *jewel.*

joyeux (joyeuse f.) adj. *merry, jolly.*

jubiler *to be jubilant, rejoice, exult.*

judiciaire adj. *judicial.*

Une enquête judiciaire. *An official inquest.*

judicieux (judicieuse f.) adj. *judicious, sensible.*

juge m. *judge.*

jugement m. *judgment, sentence.*

juger *to judge.*

A en juger par. *Judging by.*

JUILLET m. *July.*

JUIN m. *June.*

jumeau (jumelle f., jumelles f. pl., jumeaux m. pl.) *noun and adj. twin.*

jumelles f. pl. *binoculars, opera glasses.*

jupe f. *skirt.*

jurer *to swear.*

juridiction f. *jurisdiction.*

juridique adj. *juridical, judicial.*

juron m. *oath, swear-word.*

jury m. *jury.*

jus m. *juice.*

Le jus de fruits. *Fruit juice.*

JUSQUE *till, until, as far as.*

Jusqu'ici. *Up to here. Up to now.*

Jusque là. *Up to there. Up to then.*

Du matin jusqu'au soir. *From morning till night.*

Jusqu'où allez-vous? *How far are you going?*

Jusqu'à un certain point, il a raison. *He's right up to a certain point.*

Attendez jusqu'après la fin du mois. *Wait till the end of the month.*

Jusqu'à quel âge avez-vous vécu à Paris? *How old were you when you left Paris? ("Up to what age did you live in Paris?")*

JUSTE adj. *just, fair, exact.*

Un homme juste. *An upright man.*

Rien de plus juste. *Nothing could be fairer.*

C'est juste ce qu'il me faut. *It's just what I want (need).*

Quelle est l'heure juste? *What is the correct time?*

Je ne sais au juste s'il est parti. *I don't know for sure whether he left.*

Son vêtement est trop juste. *His coat is too tight.*

Comme de juste. *Of course.*

justement *exactly.*

C'est justement ce que je vous disais. *That's exactly what I was telling you.*

justesse f. *exactness, accuracy.*

La justesse d'une opinion. *The soundness of an opinion.*

Il est arrivé de justesse. *He arrived just in time.*

justice f. *justice, jurisdiction; courts of justice.*

justification f. *justification.*

justifier *to justify.*

se justifier *to justify oneself.*

juvénile adj. *juvenile.*

juxtaposer *to place side by side.*

K

képi m. *cap, kepi.*

kilo m. (*abbreviation of* kilogramme) *kilogram.*

kilométrage m. *distance in kilometers (f. mileage).*

kilomètre m. *kilometer.*

kiosque m. *stand; newsstand.*

klaxon m. *automobile horn.*

L

l' *See* le.

la *See* le.

LÀ *there, to there.*

Ça et là. *Here and there.*

Il est allé là. *He went there.*

LÀ-BAS *over there.*

Regardez là-bas. *Look over there.*

labeur m. *labor, toil.*

laboratoire m. *laboratory.*

laborieux (laborieuse f.) adj. *laborious, industrious.*

labour m. *plowing.*

labourage m. *plowing.*

labourer *to plow.*

laboureur m. *plowman.*

labyrinthe m. *labyrinth.*

lac m. *lake.*

lacer *to lace, tie.*

Lacez vos souliers. *Tie your shoelaces.*

lacet m. *lace.*

lâche m. *coward.*

lâche adj. *loose; cowardly.*

lâchement *in a cowardly way.*

lâcher *to loosen, relax, release.*

lâcheté f. *cowardice.*

lâcheur m. (lâcheuse f.) *quitter.*

lacune f. *gap; blank.*

là-dessus *on that, on it, thereupon.*

laid adj. *ugly.*

laideur f. *ugliness.*

laine f. *wool.*

En laine. *In, of wool.*

laisse f. *leash.*

LAISSER *to leave.*
  Laissez ça là. *Leave it (that) there.*
  Laissez-moi tranquille. *Leave me alone.*
  Laissez donc! *Please don't trouble yourself. Don't bother.*
  Laissez voir. *Let's see, let me see (it).*
  Vous me la laissez à 60 francs? *Will you give it to me for 60 francs?*
se laisser *to let oneself, allow oneself.*
  Elle se laisse abattre. *She lets herself get depressed. She lets herself get discouraged.*
  Je ne me suis pas laissé faire. *I didn't let myself be taken in.*
  Ils ne se le laisseront pas dire deux fois. *They won't have to be told twice.*
laisser-aller *m. taking things easy, slackness, neglect, listlessness.*
  Il est d'un laisser-aller incroyable! *He's unbelievably negligent (careless, sloppy)!*
laisser-faire *m. non-interference, non-intervention.*
laisser-passer *m. pass.*
LAIT *m. milk.*
  Café au lait. *Coffee (with milk).*
  Dents de lait. *First teeth. Milk teeth.*
  Soeur de lait. *Foster sister.*
laiterie *f. dairy.*
laitier *m.* (laitière *f.*) *dairyman, dairywoman.*
laiton *m. brass.*
laitue *f. lettuce.*
lambeau *m.* (lambeaux *pl.*) *scrap, shred.*
  Mes vêtements sont en lambeaux. *My clothes are in rags.*
  Mon pardessus tombe en lambeaux. *My overcoat is falling to pieces.*
lame *f. blade, plate, sheet, wire.*
  Lame de rasoir. *Razor blade.*
lamentable *adj. deplorable, pitiful.*
lamentation *lamentation.*
se lamenter *to lament.*
lampe *f. lamp.*
lampe-éclair *f. flashbulb.*
lance *f. spear.*
lancer *to throw, fling; emit; issue (a warrant, etc.).*
se lancer *to rush, dash.*
LANGAGE *m. language.*
langoureux (langoureuse *f.*) *adj. languishing, languid; yearning, pining.*
langouste *f. rock lobster.*
LANGUE *f. tongue; language.*
langueur *f. langor.*
languide *adj. languid, weary, listless.*
languir *to languish, pine.*
languissant *adj. languid, languishing.*
lanterne *f. lantern.*
lapider *to lapidate, stone.*

lapin *m. rabbit.*
laps *m. lapse (time).*
lapsus *m. lapse, error, slip.*
larcin *m. larceny, petty theft.*
lard *m. pork fat.*
large *m. breadth, width; open sea.*
large *adj. broad, wide; extensive; generous.*
largesse *f. liberality.*
largeur *f. width; broadness.*
larme *f. tear.*
larmoyant *adj. weeping, tearful.*
larron *m. robber, thief.*
larynx *m. larynx.*
las (lasse *f.*) *adj. tired, weary; disgusted, fed up.*
  Je suis très las. *I'm very tired.*
  Je suis bien las de cela. *I'm sick and tired of that.*
lasser *to tire, fatigue, bore.*
se lasser *to tire, grow weary.*
latéral (latéraux *pl.*) *adj. lateral.*
latin *noun and adj. Latin.*
latitude *f. latitude.*
laurier *m. laurel; glory.*
lavabo *m. washbasin, washstand; lavatory, washroom.*
lavage *m. washing.*
laver *to wash, bathe.*
SE LAVER *to wash oneself.*
laverie *f. machine laundry.*
lavette *f. washcloth.*
layette *f. layette.*
LE (la *f.*, les *pl.*, l' *before vowels and "mute" h*) *the.*
  Le livre. *The book.*
  La lettre. *The letter.*
  L'homme. *The man.*
  Les hommes. *The men.*
LE (la *f.*, les *pl.*, l' *before vowels and "mute" h*) *him, her, it.*
  Faites-le tout de suite! *Do it right away.*
  Je la vois assez souvent. *I see her quite often.*
  Je l'ai commandé. *I ordered it.*
  Je le veux. *I want it.*
lécher *to lick.*
leçon *f. lesson.*
  Etudiez vos leçons. *Study your lessons.*
  Il lui a fait la leçon. *He lectured him. He gave him a lecture.*
lecteur *m.* (lectrice *f.*) *reader.*
lecteur de disques *m. hard drive.*
lecture *f. reading.*
légal (légaux *pl.*) *adj. legal.*
légalité *f. legality.*
légation *f. legation.*
légendaire *adj. legendary, fabulous.*
légende *f. legend.*
LEGER (légère *f.*) *adj. light (in weight).*

légèrement *lightly.*

légèreté *f. lightness.*

légion *f. legion.*

La légion d'honneur. *The Legion of Honor.*

La Légion Etrangère. *The Foreign Legion.*

législatif (législative *f.*) *adj. legislative.*

législation *f. legislation.*

législature *f. legislature, legislative body.*

légitime *adj. legitimate, justifiable.*

legs *m. legacy.*

léguer *to bequeath.*

légume *m. vegetable.*

LENDEMAIN *m. the next day.*

LENT *adj. slow.*

LENTEMENT *slowly.*

lenteur *f. slowness.*

lentille *f. lentil, lens.*

LEQUEL (laquelle *f.*, lesquels *m. pl.*, lesquelles *f. pl.*) *who, which one.*

Je ne sais lequel choisir. *I don't know which one to choose.*

Laquelle voulez-vous? *Which one do you want?*

lesbienne *f. lesbian.*

lessive *f. washing.*

lessiver *to wash (clothes, etc.).*

leste *adj. nimble.*

lestement *briskly, nimbly.*

léthargie *f. lethargy.*

LETTRE *f. letter.*

La lettre recommandée. *Registered letter.*

LEUR *their; to them.*

Cela leur appartient. *That belongs to them.*

levain *m. yeast.*

levant *m. Levant.*

levée *f. removal, collecting; trick (in cards).*

La levée postale. *Mail collection.*

lever *m. rising, getting up.*

A quelle heure est le lever du rideau? *(At) what time does the curtain go up?*

Le lever du soleil. *Sunrise.*

LEVER *to raise, lift.*

Lever la tête. *To raise one's head. To look up.*

Il n'est pas encore levé. *He isn't up yet. He hasn't gotten up yet.*

La séance a été levée à trois heures. *The meeting was adjourned at three o'clock.*

SE LEVER *to get up.*

Je dois me lever de bonne heure demain matin. *I have to get up early tomorrow morning.*

Le vent se lève. *The wind is rising.*

levier *m. lever.*

lèvre *f. lip.*

Il l'a dit du bout des lèvres. *He said it half-heartedly.*

Je l'ai sur le bord des lèvres. *I have it on the tip of my tongue.*

Du rouge à lèvres. *Lipstick.*

lézard *m. lizard.*

liaison *f. joining, binding.*

liasse *f. bundle.*

libéral (libéraux *pl.*) *adj. liberal.*

libéralité *f. liberality, generosity.*

libération *f. liberation.*

libérer *to set free.*

liberté *f. liberty, freedom.*

libraire *m. bookseller.*

librairie *f. bookshop.*

LIBRE *adj. free.*

Etes-vous libre ce soir? *Are you free tonight?*

Il n'a pas un moment de libre. *He hasn't a free moment. He hasn't a minute to himself.*

Libre à vous. *Do it if you wish. It's up to you.*

Avez-vous une chambre libre? *Do you have a vacant room?*

Avoir du temps libre. *To have some free time.*

librement *freely.*

licence *f. license, permission; Master's degree.*

Il a passé sa licence de droit. *He received a law degree.*

La licence d'exportation. *Export license.*

lie *f. dregs.*

liège *m. cork.*

lien *m. tie, bond.*

lier *to bind, tie.*

LIEU *m.* (lieux *pl.*) *place.*

Au lieu de. *In place of. Instead of.*

En premier lieu. *In the first place.*

Avoir lieu. *To take place.*

Tenir lieu de. *To take the place of.*

Lieu commun. *Commonplace. Trite saying.*

Etre sur les lieux. *To be on the spot.*

lieutenant *m. lieutenant.*

lièvre *m. hare.*

LIGNE *f. line, row, rank.*

La ligne est occupée, raccrochez. *The line is busy, hang up (telephone).*

Suivez la ligne du chemin de fer. *Follow the railroad track.*

Cette question vient en première ligne. *This question is of primary importance.*

Prenez cela en ligne de compte. *Take that into account. Take that into consideration.*

Ecrivez-moi quelques lignes. *Drop me a few lines.*

A la ligne. *New paragraph (in dictating).*

En ligne. *In line, lined up.*

ligue *f. league.*

lime *f. file.*

limer *to file.*

limitation *f. limitation, restriction.*

limite *f. limit.*
limiter *to bound.*
Limoges *m. Limoges porcelain.*
limonade *f. lemon drink (carbonated).*
limpide *adj. limpid, clear.*
lin *m. flax; linen.*
linge *m. linen; laundry.*
lingerie *f. linen manufacture; linen room; lingerie.*
linguiste *m. and f. linguist.*
lion *m. lion.*
liqueur *f. liquor, liqueur.*
liquidation *f. liquidation; clearance sale.*
liquide *adj. liquid.*
liquider *to liquidate.*
LIRE *to read.*
  Avez-vous jamais lu ce livre? *Have you ever read this book?*
  Je sais lire en français mais je ne sais pas le parler. *I can read French but I can't speak it.*
lisible *adj. legible.*
lisiblement *legibly.*
lisse *adj. smooth, polished.*
liste *f. list.*
LIT *m. bed; layer.*
  Garder le lit. *To stay in bed.*
LITRE *m. liter (measure).*
littéraire *adj. literary.*
littéral *adj. literal.*
  Sens littéral. *Literal meaning.*
littéralement *literally.*
littérature *f. literature.*
livide *adj. livid.*
livraison *f. delivery.*
LIVRE *m. book.*
livrer *to deliver.*
se livrer *to give way to; devote one's attention to.*
livret *m. small book; bankbook.*
local *m. (locaux pl.) premises.*
local *(locaux pl.) adj. local.*
localité *f. locality, place, spot.*
locataire *m. tenant.*
location *f. hiring, renting.*
  Prix de location. *Rent.*
  Location de livres. *Lending library.*
  Bureau de location. *Box office.*
locomotive *f. locomotive, engine.*
locution *f. expression, phrase.*
loge *f. lodge; loge, box.*
logement *m. lodging, housing.*
loger *to reside; put up, accommodate.*
logiciel *m. software.*
logique *adj. logical; f. logic.*
logiquement *logically.*
logis *m. home, house.*
  Il garde le logis. *He stays at home.*
LOI *f. law.*

LOIN *far.*
  Les voyez-vous là-bas au loin? *Do you see them over there in the distance?*
  Loin de là. *Far from it.*
  De loin en loin. *At long intervals.*
  Cet artiste ira loin. *This artist will go far.*
  Ne pas voir de loin. *To lack foresight.*
lointain *m. distance.*
  On peut le voir dans le lointain. *You can see it in the distance.*
loisir *m. leisure.*
  A ses moments de loisir. *In his spare time.*
long *m. and f. long.*
  Le long de la Seine. *Along the Seine.*
  Il s'est promené le long de la rivière. *He walked along the river.*
  Au long de. *Alongside of. Along.*
  A la longue. *In the long run.*
  Etendu de tout son long *(fam). Lying at full length.*
  Se promener de long en large. *To walk to and fro.*
  Cinq mètres de long. *Five meters long.*
LONG *(longue f.) adj. long.*
  Avoir la vue longue. *To be farsighted.*
  En long. *Lengthwise.*
  De longues années. *Many years.*
longitude *f. longitude.*
LONGTEMPS *a long time.*
  Il y a longtemps que je l'attends. *I've been waiting for him a long time.*
longuement *for a long time.*
longueur *f. length, duration.*
loque *f. rag.*
  En loques. *In rags.*
lorgnette *f. opera glasses.*
lorgnon *m. lorgnette.*
LORS *then.*
  Dès lors. *From that time.*
  Depuis lors. *Since then.*
LORSQUE *when.*
  Lorsque j'ai voulu m'en aller . . . *When I wanted to go . . .*
lot *m. lot, share, prize.*
loterie *f. lottery.*
lotion *(pour les cheveux) f. (hair) lotion.*
louable *adj. laudable, praiseworthy.*
louange *f. praise.*
louche *adj. Cross-eyes; squinting; shady, suspicious.*
loucher *to be cross-eyed.*
LOUER *to praise; rent, lease.*
  Il l'a loué. *He praised him.*
  Louer une voiture à l'heure. *To hire a car by the hour.*
  Chambres à louer. *Rooms to let. Rooms for rent.*
loup *m. wolf.*
  J'ai une faim de loup. *I have a ravenous*

appetite. ("*I have the hunger of a wolf.*")

Il est connu comme le loup blanc. *Everybody knows him.*

loupe *f. magnifying glass.*

LOURD *adj. heavy.*

Ça pèse lourd. *It's heavy. It weighs a lot.*

Il fait lourd aujourd'hui. *It's sultry (close, humid) out today.*

J'ai la tête lourde. *My head feels heavy.*

Il a fait une lourde erreur. *He made a grave mistake.*

lourdaud *adj. awkward, clumsy.*

loyal (loyaux *pl.*) *adj. honest, fair.*

loyauté *f. honesty.*

loyer *m. rent.*

lu *(have) read.*

lubie *f. whim.*

lucide *adj. clear.*

lucratif (lucrative *f.*) *adj. profitable.*

lueur *f. gleam.*

lugubre *adj. dismal, gloomy.*

LUI *him, her, it.*

Je me souviens de lui. *I remember him.*

Lui aussi me l'a dit. *He also told it to me.*

lui-même *himself.*

LUMIÈRE *f. light.*

Il n'y a pas assez de lumière. *There isn't enough light.*

Les jeux de lumière. *Lightning (theatre).*

lumineux (lumineuse *f.*) *adj. light.*

lunatique *m. and f. noun and adj. eccentric person, capricious.*

LUNDI *m. Monday.*

LUNE *f. moon.*

lunettes *f. pl. glasses.*

lustre *m. gloss, luster, brilliance; chandelier.*

luthérien (luthérienne *f.*) *noun and adj. Lutheran.*

lutte *f. fight.*

lutter *to wrestle, struggle.*

luxe *m. luxury, splendor.*

luxueux (luxueuse *f.*) *adj. luxurious, sumptuous.*

lycée *m. secondary school.*

lycéen *m.* (lycéene *f.*) *pupil attending the lycée.*

M

MA *See* mon.

Ma soeur va au lycée. *My sister goes to the lycée.*

macabre *adj. macabre, gruesome.*

Un humour macabre. *Grim humor.*

macadam *m. macadam.*

macaron *m. macaroon.*

mâcher *to chew.*

Mâchez votre nourriture. *Chew your food.*

Il ne mâche pas ses mots. *He doesn't mince words.*

Son frère lui a mâché tout son travail. *His work has been prepared for him by his brother.*

machin *m. what's-his-name; what-do-you-call-it, thingamajig, thingamabob.*

C'est machin qui l'a dit. *What's-his-name said so.*

Qu'est-ce que c'est que ce machin-là? *What's that gadget?*

machinal (machinaux *pl.*) *adj. mechanical; instinctive.*

machinalement *mechanically, instinctively.*

MACHINE *f. machine, engine.*

Une machine infernale. *A time bomb.*

La machine à écrire. *Typewriter.*

La machine à coudre. *Sewing machine.*

Machine à vapeur. *Steam engine.*

Les machines. *The machinery.*

Faites machine en arrière. *Reverse the engine.*

A la machine. *By machine.*

machiner *to plot.*

Machiner la perte de quelqu'un. *To plot someone's ruin.*

Qu'est-ce qu'il machine encore? *What else is he up to? What's he up to now?*

machinerie *f. machinery.*

mâchoire *f. jaw.*

Il s'est cassé la mâchoire. *He broke his jaw.*

mâchonner *To chew with difficulty; mumble.*

maçon *m. mason.*

maçonnerie *f. masonry.*

MADAME *f.* (mesdames *pl.*) *Madam, Mrs.*

Si madam permet. *If madam will permit.*

Pardon, madame.—Du tout, monsieur. *I beg your pardon, madam.—Not at all.*

Eh bien, mesdames, nous ferions mieux d'entrer. *Well, ladies, we'd better go in.*

Comment va madame votre mère? *How's your mother?*

Madame est servie. *Dinner is served.*

Mme (*abbreviation of* madame). *Mrs.*

MADEMOISELLE *f.* (mesdemoiselles *pl.*) *Miss.*

Bonsoir, mademoiselle. *Good evening, Miss.*

Mlle (*abbreviation of* mademoiselle). *Miss.*

MAGASIN *m. store, shop.*

Ce magasin est bien monté. *This store's well stocked.*

Elle court les magasins. *She goes from one shop to another. She makes the rounds of the stores.*

Il tient un magasin d'épicerie. *He has a grocery store.*

Un magasin de nouveautés. *A novelty shop.*

Le grand magasin. *The department store.*

magazine *m. magazine.*

magicien *m.* (magicienne *f.*) *magician.*

magie *f. magic; charm.*
La magie noire. *Black magic.*
La magie de son sourire. *The charm of her smile.*

magique *adj. magic.*

magistral (magistraux *pl.*) *adj. magisterial, masterly.*

magistrat *m. magistrate.*

magistrature *f. magistracy; the bench.*
La magistrature assise. *The judges. The bench.*

magnanime *adj. magnanimous, generous.*
C'est une personne magnanime. *He's (she's) very magnanimous.*

magnanimité *f. magnanimity.*

magnétique *adj. magnetic.*
La bande (le ruban) magnétique. *The tape.*

magnétisme *m. magnetism; hypnotism.*

magnétophone *m. tape recorder.*

magnificence *f. magnificence, splendor.*
La magnificence de la réception a ébloui les invités. *The splendor of the reception dazzled the guests.*
Telle magnificence n'avait jamais été vue. *Such splendor (magnificence) had never been seen before.*

MAGNIFIQUE *adj. magnificent, splendid.*
Il fait un temps magnifique. *It's a glorious day.*
Un repas magnifique. *An excellent (a wonderful) meal.*

mahométan *noun and adj. Mohammedan.*

MAI *m. May.*

maigre *adj. lean, thin.*
Elle est maigre comme un clou. *She's as thin as a rail.*
Ses appointements sont maigres. *His salary is low.*
Un jour maigre. *A fast day. A day of fasting.*
Une majorité de cinq voix, c'est maigre. *A majority of five votes—that's not very much.*

maigrir *to grow thinner, lose weight.*
Elle a maigri et pâli. *She's grown thinner and paler.*

maille *f. stitch.*
Tricoter deux mailles à l'envers et deux à l'endroit. *Purl two, knit two.*

maille *f. an old copper coin.*
Il n'a ni sou ni maille. *He hasn't a penny to his name.*
Il a eu maille à partir avec lui. *He had a bone to pick with him.*

maillot *m. tights.*
Un maillot de bain. *A bathing suit.*

MAIN *f. hand.*

J'ai mal aux mains. *My hands hurt. My hands are sore.*

Il a les mains nettes dans cette affaire. *His hands are clean in this affair.*

Je m'en lave les mains. *I wash my hands of it.*

Il a eu la main heureuse. 1. *He was lucky.* 2. *He had a lucky hand (in cards).*

Elle lui a accordé sa main. *She agreed to marry him. ("She gave him her hand.")*

On a mis la dernière main à ce travail. *They put the finishing touches on this piece of work.*

L'argent ne lui tient pas dans les mains. *He's (she's) a spendthrift.*

Ils vont la main dans la main. *They always agree with each other. ("They always go hand in hand.")*

Je lui ai payé cette somme de la main à la main. *I paid this sum to him in person (in cash and without receipt).*

Il s'est défendu les armes à la main. *He offered armed resistance.*

Il n'y va pas de main morte. *He goes at it tooth and nail.*

Donner un coup de main. *To lend a hand. To help.*

Il fait sentir sa main. *He exercises his authority. He makes his authority felt.*

Nous avons tout de première main. *We buy from the producer.*

Je l'ai acheté de seconde main. *I bought it secondhand.*

J'ai quelqu'un sous la main. *I have someone I can use. I have someone who can help me.*

Ils ont agi en sous main. *They've acted secretly. They've acted in an underhanded manner.*

Il a été pris la main dans le sac. *He was caught in the act. He was caught red-handed.*

Ils en sont venus aux mains. *They came to blows over it.*

On le lui a remis en mains propres. *It was delivered to him personally.*

C'était préparé de longue main. *It was provided for long in advance.*

On lui a mis le marché en mains. *He was told to take it or leave it.*

Il a mis la main à la pâte. *He joined in to help. He lent a hand.*

Il dépense son argent à pleines mains. *He spends his money freely.*

C'est fait de main de maître. *It has the touch of the master.*

J'en mettrais ma main au feu. *I could swear to it.*

Il a un poil dans la main. *He's very lazy.*

("*Hair grows in the palm of his hands.*")

Il a fait des pieds et des mains pour réussir. *He did everything in his power to succeed.*

Il a le coeur sur la main. 1. *He's generous (open-hearted).* 2. *He wears his heart on his sleeve.*

Fait à la main. *Handmade.*

Laver à la main. *To wash by hand.*

main-d'oeuvre *f. manpower.*

Le main-d'oeuvre est abondante dans la région. *Manpower is plentiful in this region. There is an abundant labor supply in this region.*

maint *adj. many a.*

Je le lui ai dit maintes fois. *I told it to him many a time (many times).*

maintenance *f. maintenance.*

MAINTENANT *now.*

Que devons-nous faire maintenant? *What shall we do now?*

Elle a bonne mine maintenant. *She looks well now.*

A vous maintenant. *It's your turn now.*

Maintenant même. *Right now.*

MAINTENIR *to maintain.*

Il maintient ce qu'il a dit. *He maintains (sticks to) what he said.*

Maintenir l'ordre. *To preserve order.*

Maintenir les prix bas. *To keep prices down.*

se maintenir *to keep oneself; keep up, last.*

Il se maintient dans les bonnes grâces du patron. *He keeps in his boss's favor.*

Vous croyez que cela va se maintenir? *Do you think it's going to last long?*

maintien *m. maintenance; behavior.*

MAIRE *m. mayor.*

Le maire et ses adjoints. *The mayor and his deputies.*

Monsieur le Maire. *Mr. Mayor.*

MAIRIE *f. city hall.*

Pourriez-vous me dire où se trouve la mairie? *Can you tell me where City Hall is?*

MAIS *but.*

Mais certainement! *(But) Of course! Why, certainly!*

Mais oui! *Why, certainly! Why, of course!*

Mais si! *(denies or contradicts a previous negative statement) But it's so. But it's true. I tell you yes. Yes, indeed!*

Mais non! *Of course not! I should say not! No, indeed!*

Je le ferai, mais il faut que vous m'aidiez. *I'll do it but you'll have to help me.*

J'accepte, mais à charge de revanche. *I accept but on condition that you let me do the same for you sometime.*

Mais qu'avez-vous donc? *Why, what's the matter (with you)? Why, what's the trouble?*

Non seulement . . . mais encore . . . *Not only . . . but also . . .*

maïs *m. corn.*

MAISON *f. house.*

Meubler une maison. *To furnish a house.*

A la maison. *At home.*

Il est de la maison. *He's one of the family.*

Cette maison se spécialise dans ces machines. *This firm specializes in these machines.*

Maison René Dubois. *The firm of René Dubois.*

On a fait maison nette. *They made a clean sweep of all the employees.*

MAÎTRE *m.* (maîtresse *f.*) *master; teacher.*

Son père est allé voir son maître. *His father went to see his teacher.*

En France, les avocats sont appelés "maître". *In France, lawyers are addressed as "maître."*

Ce fut un coup de maître. *It was a masterly stroke.*

Il parle en maître. *He speaks with authority.*

Il ne faut pas le blâmer, il n'est pas maître de ses actes. *There's no point blaming him (throwing the blame on him); he's not responsible for his actions (for what he does).*

maîtresse *adj. chief, principal.*

Une oeuvre maîtresse. *Masterwork.*

maîtriser *to master; overcome; overpower.*

Maîtrisez votre envie de rire. *Keep a solemn face. Try to keep from laughing.*

Deux hommes ont essayé de le maîtriser. *Two men tried to overpower him.*

majesté *f. majesty.*

Il a des allures pleines de majesté. *He has a very stately bearing.*

majestueux (majestueuse *f.*) *adj. stately, majestic.*

majeur *adj. major, greater; of age.*

La majeure partie du temps il est au bureau. *Most of the time he's at the office.*

Sons fils est majeur depuis deux mois. *His son came of age two months ago.*

Ceci est un cas de force majeure. *It's a case of absolute necessity.*

major *m. major.*

majorité *f. majority; coming of age.*

Je me rallie au point de vue de la majorité. *I side with the majority.*

La majorité absolue. *Absolute majority.*

Il a atteint sa majorité. *He came of age.*

majuscule *adj. capital letter.*

Ce mot ne s'écrit pas avec une majuscule. *This word isn't capitalized.*

MAL *m.* (mau**x** *pl.*) *evil, wrong.*

Discerner le bien du mal. *To tell right from wrong.*

C'est peut-être un bien pour un mal. *Perhaps it's a blessing in disguise.*

Elle a eu du mal à le retenir à la maison. *She had trouble keeping him home.*

J'ai mal partout. *I ache all over.*

Je l'ai dit sans penser à mal. *I didn't mean any harm by it. I didn't mean any offense.*

J'ai mal à la gorge. *I have a sore throat.*

J'ai mal aux dents. *I have a toothache. My teeth hurt.*

Cette dent me fait mal. *This tooth hurts me.*

J'ai un mal de tête affreux. *I have a frightful headache.*

Il avait le mal du pays. *He was homesick.*

Mal au coeur. *Nausea, upset stomach.*

mal *adj. bad.*

Bon gré mal gré. *Willy-nilly.*

MAL *adv. bad, badly.*

Il a pris très mal la chose. *He took the thing very badly.*

Il y avait pas mal de monde. *There was quite a crowd there. There were a good many people there.*

Ce titre s'adapte mal au roman. *That title doesn't suit (isn't appropriate to) the novel.*

malade *m. or f. patient.*

Comment va le malade aujourd'hui? *How's the patient today?*

MALADE *adj. sick, ill.*

Alors qu'il était malade. *When he was ill.*

Il est tombé malade hier. *He was taken ill yesterday.*

Il en est malade. *He's very upset about it. It's made him sick.*

maladie *f. sickness.*

Il sort de maladie. *He's just getting over (recovering from) his illness.*

maladif (maladive *f.*) *adj. sickly.*

maladresse *f. blunder.*

Il a commis une maladresse. *He made a blunder.*

maladroit *adj. awkward, clumsy.*

Il est maladroit. *He's clumsy.*

Il a la main maladroite. *His fingers are all thumbs.*

malaise *m. discomfort; uncomfortableness; uneasiness.*

Il a un léger malaise. *He's slightly indisposed.*

malappris *m. ill-bred person.*

Ne fréquentez pas ces malappris. *Don't go around with those ill-bred people.*

malchance *f. ill luck, bad luck.*

La malchance s'acharne après eux. *They're*

very unlucky. They have very bad luck. *("Bad luck pursues them relentlessly.")*

Par malchance, je n'étais pas là. *As ill luck would have it, I wasn't there.*

maldonne *f. misdeal.*

Il y a maldonne. *It's a misdeal. The cards haven't been dealt right.*

mâle *m. male.*

Mâle ou femelle. *Male or female.*

mâle *adj. male, masculine, virile.*

C'est un enfant mâle. *It's a boy.*

Une voix mâle. *A manly voice.*

malédiction *f. curse.*

malentendu *m. misunderstanding.*

Il y a un malentendu en cela. *There's some misunderstanding there.*

malfaire *to do ill, do mischief.*

malfaisant *adj. mischievous; injurious.*

malfaiteur *m. thief.*

MALGRÉ *in spite of, notwithstanding.*

Malgré tout. *In spite of everything.*

Malgré tous ses défauts, nous l'aimons bien quand même. *In spite of all his faults we still like him very much.*

MALHEUR *m. unhappiness; bad luck; calamity.*

Il m'est arrivé un malheur. *Something terrible happened to me.*

Jouer de malheur. *To be unlucky.*

Pour comble de malheur. *To crown one's troubles.*

A quelque chose malheur est bon. *It's an ill wind that blows no good.*

Le grand malheur! *That's nothing much to complain about. That's not such a great tragedy.*

malheureusement *unfortunately.*

MALHEUREUX (malheureuse *f.*) *adj. unhappy; unfortunate; wretched, poor.*

Il est très malheureux. *He's very unhappy.*

Il a la main malheureuse. *He's unlucky.*

malhonnête *adj. dishonest; rude.*

Un malhonnête homme. *A dishonest man.*

Des paroles malhonnêtes. *Rude words.*

malhonnêtement *dishonestly, rudely.*

malhonnêteté. *f. dishonesty; rudeness.*

malice *f. spite, mischief, slyness; trick.*

Par malice. *Maliciously. Through spite.*

D'un air plein de malice. *With a sly grin.*

Il lui a fait une malice. *He played a trick on him.*

malicieux (malicieuse *f.*) *adj. malicious.*

malin (maligne *f.*) *adj. clever, sly, shrewd, malicious; malignant.*

C'est un malin. *He has his wits about him. He's a shrewd fellow. He knows a trick or two. He has a trick or two up his sleeve. He knows what's what.*

Ce n'est pas malin! *That's not so clever! That's not very difficult! That's easy enough!*

Une fièvre maligne. *A malignant fever.*

malingre *adj. puny, weak.*

malle *f. trunk.*

Il fait sa malle. *He's packing his trunk.*

malpropre *adj. unclean; indecent.*

malpropreté *f. dirt, dirtiness, uncleanliness.*

malsain *adj. unhealthy, unwholesome.*

malséant *adj. unbecoming, improper.*

maltraiter *to mistreat.*

malveillance *f. malevolence; spite.*

malveillant *adj. malevolent, ill-disposed, evil-minded.*

malvenu *adj. unwelcome.*

maman *f. mother, ma, mom.*

manche *m. handle, holder.*

manche *f. sleeve.*

Aux manches courtes. *With short sleeves, short-sleeved.*

manchette *f. cuff; wristband (shirt).*

mandat *m. mandate; warrant; money order.*

mandataire *m. mandatory; proxy, attorney.*

mandat-carte *m. a money order in the form of a postcard.*

mandat-poste *m. postal money order.*

mander *to inform; write to say; to send word; send for.*

On l'a fait mander. *He was sent for.*

manège *m. riding school; merry-go-round; maneuver.*

MANGER *to eat.*

Que désirez-vous manger? *What would you like to eat?*

Il donne à manger. *He has (keeps) a restaurant.*

La salle à manger était très grande. *The dining room was very large.*

Il mange ses mots. *He clips his words.*

Manger à sa faim. *To eat one's fill.*

Manger de tout. *To eat everything, anything, all sorts of things.*

mangeur *m. (mangeuse f.) eater, one who eats.*

Un mangeur de livres. *A bookworm.*

maniable *adj. easy to handle.*

maniaque *adj. eccentric, crotchety.*

manie *f. mania, passion, hobby.*

maniement *m. handling.*

manier *to handle, use.*

Savoir manier la parole. *To know how to handle words.*

Il manie bien la langue. *He expresses himself well.*

Il a bien manié l'affaire. *He handled the deal very well.*

MANIÈRE *f. manner, way, fashion.*

D'une manière ou d'une autre il faut le

faire. *It has to be done one way or another (by hook or by crook).*

Il a de très bonnes manières. *He has very good manners.*

En aucune manière. *By no means. In no manner (way).*

maniéré *adj. affected.*

maniérisme *m. mannerism.*

manifestation *f. manifestation, demonstration.*

manifeste *adj. evident, clear.*

manifester *to make clear.*

Il a manifesté ses intentions. *He made his intentions clear.*

manigance *f. trick.*

manipuler *to manipulate, handle.*

manivelle *f. handle.*

mannequin *m. mannequin, model, dummy.*

manoeuvre *f. action, maneuver.*

manoeuvrer *to manage, drill.*

MANQUE *m. want, lack.*

Manque de goût. *Lack of taste.*

C'est un manque d'égards. *That shows lack of respect (consideration).*

manqué *adj. unsuccessful; would-be.*

Un peintre manqué. *A would-be painter.*

C'est un garçon manqué. *She ought to have been a boy. She's a tomboy.*

manquement *m. omission, lack.*

MANQUER *to miss; lack; be wanting.*

Le temps me manque. *I haven't enough time. I haven't much time.*

Ne manquez pas de venir. *Don't fail to come. Be sure to come.*

Elle a manqué de se noyer. *She almost drowned. She barely escaped drowning.*

Il manque à sa parole. *He breaks his word. He doesn't keep his word.*

Vous nous manquez. *We miss you.*

mansarde *f. garret, attic.*

manteau *m. (manteaux pl.) coat.*

manucure *m. manicure.*

manuel *(manuelle f.) adj. manual.*

manufacture *f. manufacture; making; factory.*

manufacturer *to make, manufacture.*

manuscrit *m. copy; manuscript.*

maquillage *m. make-up.*

se maquiller *to put make-up on.*

marais *m. marsh, swamp.*

maraude *f. plundering.*

marbre *m. marble.*

MARCHAND(E) *m. or f. merchant, storekeeper.*

marchand *adj. saleable; having to do with trade.*

Prix marchand. *Market price.*

Un navire marchand. *A merchant ship. A merchantman.*

marchandage *m. bargaining; haggling.*

marchander *to bargain, haggle.*

marchandise *f. goods, merchandise.*

MARCHE *f. walk, movement; progress; step; march.*

Faites marche arrière; la rue est barrée. *Back up. The road is blocked.*

Il a vingt minutes de marche. *It's a twenty-minute walk from here.*

Quelques marches plus bas. *A few steps farther down.*

Marches militaires. *Military marches.*

Faire dix minutes de marche. *To walk for ten minutes.*

MARCHÉ *m. market; marketing; bargain.*

Etre sur le marché. *To be on the market.*

Faire le marché. *To do the marketing.*

Par-dessus le marché. *Besides (that). In addition (to that).*

Cet article est bon marché. *This article is very cheap.*

Le marché noir. *Black market.*

Le Marché aux Puces. *Flea Market.*

Analyse de marché. *Market analysis.*

Besoins du marché. *Market demand.*

Etude de marché. *Market research.*

Valeur du marché. *Market value.*

marchepied *m. running board.*

MARCHER *to walk; progress; work (of machines)*

Marchons plus vite. *Let's walk faster.*

L'affaire marche bien, je crois. *I believe the business (matter, affair) is coming along nicely.*

Cette machine ne marche pas. *This machine doesn't work.*

La pendule marche-t-elle? *Is the clock going?*

Qu'est-ce qui ne marche pas? *What's wrong? What's the matter?*

MARDI *m. Tuesday.*

Mardi Gras. *Shrove Tuesday.*

marécage *m. marsh.*

marée *f. tide.*

margarine *f. margarine.*

marge *f. margin, border.*

MARI *m. husband.*

mariage *m. marriage.*

se marier *to marry, get married.*

marin *m. sailor, seaman.*

marin *adj. marine, nautical.*

Il a le pied marin. *He has good sea legs.*

marionnette *f. marionnette, puppet.*

marital (maritaux *pl.*) *adj. marital.*

maritime *adj. maritime.*

marketing *m. marketing.*

marmelade *f. marmalade.*

marmite *f. saucepan, pot.*

marmotter *to mumble.*

marotte *f. whim, hobby.*

Chacun a sa marotte. *Everyone has his hobby (whim, fad). Everyone has a weakness for something.*

marque *f. mark; scar; stamp; brand.*

Une marque d'affection. *A mark of affection.*

Une marque d'estime. *A token of esteem.*

Une liqueur de marque. *A very fine liquor. A liquor of superior quality.*

marquer *to mark, stamp.*

Ma montre marque midi. *It's noon by my watch.*

marrant *adj. (fam.) funny.*

marron *m. chestnut.*

marronnier *m. chestnut tree.*

MARS *m. March.*

marteau *m. hammer.*

martial *adj. martial.*

martyr *m. martyr.*

martyre *m. martyrdom.*

martyriser *to make a martyr of, persecute.*

mascarade *f. masquerade; pretense.*

masculin *noun (m.) and adj. masculine, manly.*

masque *m. mask, face, countenance.*

masqué *adj. disguised.*

masquer *to conceal.*

massacrant *adj. cross.*

Il est d'une humeur massacrante. *He's very cross (in an awful mood, in a vile temper).*

massacre *m. massacre, slaughter.*

massacrer *to massacre, slaughter.*

massage *m. massage.*

masse *f. mass, heap, lump.*

En masse. *By bulk. In great quantity.*

Les masses. *The masses.*

massif (massive *f.*) *adj. massive, bulky, solid.*

massue *f. club.*

match (de football) *m. (football) game, match.*

matelas *m. mattress.*

matelot *m. sailor.*

mater *to break someone in.*

Il a finalement été maté. *He was finally broken in.*

matériaux *m. pl. materials.*

matériel *m. equipment; implements; hardware.*

maternel (maternelle *f.*) *adj. maternal, motherly.*

mathématiques *f. pl. mathematics.*

MATIÈRE *f. matter, subject matter; theme; cause; contents.*

En matière de. *In matters of.*

Entrer en matière. *To broach a subject.*

La table des matières. *The table of contents.*

MATIN *m. morning.*

Comment cela s'est-il passé ce matin? *How did it go this morning?*

Demain matin. *Tomorrow morning.*

Le samedi matin. *On Saturday morning(s).*

Neuf heures du matin. *Nine A.M.*

matinal (matinaux *pl.*) *adj. early rising.*

Vous êtes bien matinal aujourd'hui *You certainly got up early today. You're certainly up early today!*

MATINÉE *f. morning.*

Y a-t-il un train pour Paris dans la matinée? *Is there a train for Paris in the morning?*

maudire *to curse.*

maudit *adj. accursed.*

MAUVAIS *adj. bad.*

Des mauvaises nouvelles. *Bad news.*

Passer un mauvais quart d'heure. *To spend an uncomfortable quarter of an hour.*

Il parle un mauvais français. *He speaks (a) broken French.*

Il a très mauvaise mine. *He doesn't look well at all. He looks quite ill.*

Le mauvais sens. *The wrong direction.*

maximum *m. maximum, highest point.*

mayonnaise *f. mayonnaise.*

ME (m' *before vowels*) *me, to me, myself.*

Ça ne me plaît pas. *I don't like that.*

Je me lave les mains. *I'm washing my hands.*

méchanicien *m. mechanic.*

méchanique *noun (f.) and adj. mechanics; mechanical.*

méchanceté *f. wickedness, malice, spite.*

Par pure méchanceté. *Out of pure spite.*

méchant *adj. wicked, naughty; sorry, disagreeable.*

Il n'est pas si méchant qu'il en a l'air. *He's not as bad as he looks.*

Un méchant enfant. *A naughty child.*

Une méchante affaire. *An unpleasant business.*

Elle portait ce méchant manteau. *She was wearing that shabby coat.*

mèche *f. wick.*

Il a vendu la mèche. *He let the cat out of the bag.*

Eventer la mèche. *To discover a plot.*

méconnaissable *adj. unrecognizable.*

méconnaître *to disregard, slight.*

mécontent *adj. displeased, dissatisfied.*

Il est très mécontent de lui. *He's very displeased with him.*

Il n'a pas sujet d'être mécontent. *He has no reason to be dissatisfied.*

médaille *f. medal.*

MÉDECIN *m. doctor, physician.*

médecine *f. medicine (profession).*

médical (médicaux *pl.*) *adj. medical.*

médicament *m. medicine.*

médiocre *adj. mediocre.*

médiocrité *f. mediocrity.*

médire *to slander.*

méditation *f. meditation.*

méditer *to meditate; plot.*

méfait *m. misdeed.*

méfiance *f. distrust.*

se méfier *to be suspicious, mistrust, be on one's guard against.*

Il ne se méfie de rien. *He doesn't suspect anything.*

mégarde *f. inadvertence.*

Il l'a fait par mégarde. *He didn't mean to do it. He didn't do it purposely. He did it by mistake.*

MEILLEUR *adj. better, best; preferable.*

Celui-là est meilleur. *That one is better.*

Mon meilleur ami. *My best friend.*

mélancolie *f. melancholy, sadness.*

mélancolique *adj. melancholy.*

mélange *m. mixture.*

mélanger *to mix.*

mêlée *f. mêlée, scramble, free-for-all.*

mêler *to mix.*

Il est mêlé à une mauvaise affaire. *He got himself involved (mixed up) in an unpleasant affair ("in a bad business").*

Mêlez les cartes. *Shuffle the cards.*

se mêler *to be mixed; get mixed up in.*

Mêlez-vous de ce qui vous regarde. *Attend to (mind) your own business.*

mélodie *f. melody.*

mélodieux (mélodieuse *f.*) *adj. melodious.*

melon *m. cantaloupe.*

membre *m. member; limb.*

MÊME *noun and adj. same, the same.*

C'est la même chose. *It's the same thing.*

Je le ferai moi-même. *I'll do it myself.*

Cela revient au même. *It amounts to the same thing.*

C'est la bonté même. *He (she) is very kind ("is kindness itself").*

Aujourd'hui même. *Today, this very day.*

Dans Paris même. *Within Paris itself.*

Moi-même, lui-même, soi-même. *Myself, himself, oneself.*

MÊME *even, also.*

Même s'il pleut, nous irons. *We'll go even if it rains.*

Même lui était d'accord. *Even he agreed.*

Il n'est même pas venu nous voir. *He didn't even come to see us.*

Vous auriez pu me le dire, tout de même! *Still, you could have told me!*

Vous auriez tout de même pu le faire. *You still could have done it.*

Nous devrons tout de même le faire. *We'll have to do it anyway.*

Etre à même de. *To be able to. To be in a position to.*

mémoire f. memory.

menace f. threat.

menacer to threaten.

ménage m. housekeeping; household; married couple.

Avez-vous fait le ménage? *Have you finished (done) the housework?*

Le jeune ménage est très heureux. *The newlyweds are very happy.*

ménager to economize, be careful of; treat with respect; arrange, bring about.

Vous devez ménager votre santé. *You ought to take care of yourself (of your health).*

Ménager quelqu'un. *To spare someone. To be considerate of someone.*

Il ne ménage pas assez ses expressions. *He's not careful enough about his speech.*

Elle lui ménageait une surprise. *She prepared a surprise for him. She had a surprise in store for him.*

ménagère f. housekeeper.

mendiant m. beggar.

mendier to beg, ask for alms.

MENER to lead.

Où mène ce chemin? *Where does this road lead?*

Cela ne mènera à rien. *That won't lead to anything.*

Mener une affaire à bien. *To bring a matter to a successful conclusion.*

mensonge m. lie.

mensuel (mensuelle f.) adj. monthly.

mensuellement monthly.

mental (mentaux pl.) adj. mental.

mentalité f. mentality, way of looking at things.

menteur m. (menteuse f.) liar.

mention f. mention.

Faire mention de. *To mention.*

mentionner to mention.

mentir to lie.

menton m. chin.

menu m. menu.

Donnez-moi le menu, s'il vous plaît. *May I please have the menu?*

menu adj. small.

Chaque semaine il reçoit de l'argent pour ses menus plaisirs. *Every week he receives some pocket money.*

menuisier m. carpenter.

se méprendre to make a mistake, be mistaken about.

Il s'est mépris sur mes intentions. *He misunderstood my intentions.*

Quant à son but, il n'y a pas à s'y méprendre. *There can be no mistake about his purpose (object).*

mépris m. contempt.

méprise f. mistake.

Il l'a fait par méprise. *He did it by mistake.*

mépriser to despise.

MER f. sea.

Par mer. *By sea.*

Cette année nous n'allons pas à la mer. *We're not going to the seashore this year.*

Les bananes viennent d'outre-mer. *Bananas come from overseas.*

mercerie f. haberdashery.

MERCI f. thanks; mercy.

C'est bon, merci. *That will do, thank you.*

Dieu merci, il est sain et sauf! *Thank God, he's all right!*

Etre à la merci de. *To be at the mercy of.*

Sans merci. *Without mercy. Merciless.*

Il a accordé merci aux prisonniers. *He showed mercy to the prisoners.*

Merci (bien, beaucoup). *Thank you (very much).*

MERCREDI m. Wednesday.

Le mercredi des cendres. *Ash Wednesday.*

MÈRE f. mother.

Ma mère est sortie. *Mother isn't in. Mother's gone out.*

La mère Durand fait son marché (fam.). *Old Mrs. Durand is doing her marketing.*

La maison mère se trouve à 12 rue Caumartin. *The main office is at 12 Caumartin Street.*

mérite m. merit, worth.

mériter to deserve.

merveille f. wonder, miracle.

Ça va?—Ça va à merveille. *How are things?—Fine! Couldn't be better.*

MERVEILLEUX (merveilleuse f.) adj. wonderful, excellent.

mésaventure f. misadventure, misfortune.

mésinterpréter to misinterpret, misconstrue.

mesquin adj. stingy, petty.

Elle est mesquine. *She's stingy.*

Elle a l'esprit mesquin. *She's very petty.*

C'est très mesquin de sa part. *That's very cheap of him (her).*

message m. message.

Portez ce message à monsieur Dubois. *Take this message to Mr. Dubois.*

messagerie f. transport service.

messe f. (eccles.) mass.

MESURE f. measure.

Prendre la mesure de quelque chose. *To measure (take the measurement of) something.*

Il a pris toutes les mesures nécessaires. *He took all the necessary measures.*

Je vous aiderai dans la mesure du possible. *I'll help you as much as I can.*

Il est en mesure de le faire rapidement. *He's prepared to do it quickly.*

Le parlement a approuvé la mesure. *Parliament ratified the bill.*

Au fur et à mesure. *Gradually. In proportion (to). In the measure that. In succession. As soon as. As fast as.*

Au fur et à mesure que vous recevrez de la marchandise, envoyez-la moi. *As you get the goods in, send them to me.*

Battre la mesure. *To beat time.*

Ce costume a été fait sur mesure. *This suit was made to order.*

mesurer *to measure.*

se mesurer *to measure oneself against someone.*

métal *m. (métaux pl.) metal.*

métallurgie *f. metallurgy.*

métaphore *f. metaphor, image.*

méthode *f. method, way, custom.*

méticuleux (méticuleuse *f.*) *adj. meticulous.*

MÉTIER *m. trade, employment.*

Quel est son métier? *What's his trade?*

Il est menuisier de son métier. *He's a carpenter by trade.*

MÈTRE *m. meter.*

métro (politain) *m. subway (Paris).*

METTRE *to put.*

Mettez ça ici. *Put that here.*

Mettre la dernière main à quelque chose. *To put the finishing touches on something.*

Je n'ai plus rien à me mettre. *I don't have a thing left to wear.*

Je ne peux pas mettre la main sur mon chapeau. *I can't find my hat.*

Nous y avons mis deux heures. *We spent two hours on it. It took us two hours.*

SE METTRE *to place oneself, sit down; begin, set about.*

Allons nous mettre à table. *Let's sit down to dinner (lunch, breakfast, etc.). ("Let's sit down to the table.")*

Se mettre au lit. *To go to bed. To get into bed.*

Ils se sont mis à rire. *They all started to laugh.*

Le temps se met au beau. *The weather's getting nice.*

Mettons-nous au travail. *Let's begin (get down) to work.*

Mets-toi ici. *Stand here.*

MEUBLE *m. piece of furniture.*

Les meubles de style. *Period furniture.*

meubler *to furnish.*

meunier *m. miller.*

meurtre *m. murder.*

meurtrier (meurtrière *f.*) *adj. murderous, deadly.*

Une arme meurtrière. *A deadly weapon.*

meute *f. pack (of dogs, etc.).*

mezzanine *f. mezzanine.*

mi-chemin *halfway.*

Ce restaurant se trouve à mi-chemin de Bordeaux. *The restaurant is halfway to Bordeaux.*

micmac *m. underhand intrigue; mess.*

Il y a un micmac là-dedans. *There's something fishy about it.*

Quel micmac (fam.)! *What a mess!*

(à) mi-côte *halfway.*

Ils sont descendus de bicyclettes à mi-côte. *Halfway up the hill they got off their bicycles.*

micro *m. microphone.*

Il parle au micro. *He speaks on the air (radio).*

microbe *m. microbe.*

microscope *m. microscope.*

microsillon *m. microgroove (record).*

MIDI *m. noon; the South of France.*

Il est près de midi. *It's nearly noon. It will soon be noon.*

Il part demain dans le Midi. *He's leaving tomorrow for the South (South of France).*

miel *m. honey.*

mielleux (mielleuse *f.*) *adj. honeyed.*

MIEN *m. (mienne f.) mine.*

A qui appartient ce livre?—C'est le mien. *Whose book is this?—It's mine.*

miette *f. crumb.*

MIEUX *better.*

Tant mieux. *So much the better.*

J'aimerais mieux pas. *I'd rather not.*

Vous aimez mieux rester ou partir? *Would you rather stay or go?*

Mieux vaut tard que jamais. *Better late than never.*

Le mieux est de ne pas en parler. *The best thing is to say nothing about it. It's best not to talk about it.*

Cela (ça) vaudrait mieux. *That would be better.*

Faire de son mieux. *To do one's best.*

Je ferais mieux d'attendre. *I'd better wait.*

Mieux vaut les faire réparer. *It's better to have them repaired.*

On ne demande pas mieux. *One couldn't ask for anything better.*

mignon (mignonne *f.*) *adj. dainty, cute.*

migraine *f. headache.*

mijoter *to simmer.*

mil *thousand. See mille.*

En l'an mil neuf cent quarante-deux. *During the year 1942. In 1942.*

MILIEU *m. middle; environment; sphere.*

Mettez cette table au milieu de la chambre. *Put this table in the middle of the room.*

Couper par le milieu. *To cut in half.*

Il n'appartient pas à notre milieu. *He doesn't belong to our circle.*

militaire *m. soldier.*

militaire *adj. military.*

MILLE *adj. thousand.*

Merci mille fois. *Thanks very much. ("Thanks a thousand times.")*

millier *m. about a thousand.*

Des milliers de choses. *Thousands of things.*

million *m. million.*

millionnaire *m. and f. noun and adj. millionaire.*

mince *adj. thin, slender.*

mine *f. look, bearing.*

Vous avez bonne mine. *You look well (fine).*

Il a fait mine de ne pas me voir. *He pretended not to see me.*

Avoir mauvaise mine. *To look bad.*

mine *f. mine.*

Une mine de fer. *An iron mine.*

mineur *m. miner.*

mineur *adj. under age.*

Il est mineur. *He's under age. He's a minor.*

miniature *f. miniature.*

minime *adj. small, tiny.*

minimum *m. minimum.*

ministère *m. ministry.*

Le Ministère de la Guerre. *The War Department.*

ministre *m. minister.*

MINITEL *m. electronic network similar to the Internet.*

minois *m. face, pretty face.*

minorité *f. minority.*

minuit *m. midnight.*

minuscule *adj. tiny.*

Un salon minuscule. *A tiny living room.*

Des lettres minuscules. *Lower case (letters).*

MINUTE *f. minute.*

Faites-le à la minute. *Do it right away.*

Attendez une minute, je viens. *Wait a minute, I'm coming.*

Minute! *Wait a minute! Just a minute! In a minute!*

minutieux (minutieuse *f.*) *adj. meticulous; careful.*

miracle *m. miracle.*

mirage *m. mirage.*

mirobolant (*fam.*) *adj. astounding.*

miroir *m. mirror.*

miroiter *to flash, glitter, reflect light.*

mise *f. putting, manner of dressing.*

Ce n'est pas de mise. *It's not proper.*

Mise en action. *Realization.*

Cette affaire a été mise au point. *This matter was clarified and settled.*

Mise en vigueur. *Enforcement. Putting into effect.*

Mise en vente. *Sale (in a store).*

Mise en plis. *Hair setting.*

misérable *adj. miserable.*

misère *f. misery.*

miséricorde *f. mercy.*

mission *f. mission.*

mitaine *f. mitten.*

mi-temps *f. half-time (sports).*

mitrailler *to shoot with a machine gun.*

mitrailleuse *f. machine-gun.*

(à) mi-voix *under one's breath.*

Il parle à mi-voix. *He speaks under his breath.*

mixte *adj. mixed.*

mixture *f. mixture.*

mobile *adj. mobile, movable.*

mobilier *m. furniture.*

mobilisation *f. mobilization.*

mobiliser *to mobilize.*

moche *adj. (fam.) ugly.*

MODE *f. fashion; custom; millinery.*

Ce n'est plus à la mode. *This has gone out of fashion. It (this) is no longer fashionable.*

Magasin de modes. *Millinery store.*

modèle *m. model, pattern, design.*

modeler *to model, shape.*

modération *f. moderation.*

modéré *adj. moderate.*

modérer *to moderate.*

MODERNE *adj. modern.*

modeste *adj. modest, unassuming.*

modestie *f. modesty.*

modifier *to modify.*

modiste *f. milliner.*

moëlle *f. marrow.*

moeurs *f. pl. manners; morals.*

Autres temps, autres moeurs. *Manners change with the times.*

Un certificat de bonne vie et moeurs. *A certificate of good character.*

MOI *me.*

C'est moi. *It's me (I).*

C'est à moi. *It's mine.*

Asseyez-vous près de moi. *Sit near me.*

Donnez-le-moi. *Give it to me.*

Moi-même. *Myself.*

MOINDRE *adj. less; the least.*

Je n'ai pas le moindre doute à ce sujet. *I don't doubt that in the least. I haven't the least doubt about it.*

Il a choisi le moindre de deux maux. *He chose the lesser of the two evils.*

C'est très gentil de votre part d'avoir fait ça.—Mais non, c'est bien la moindre des choses. *That's very kind of you.— Not at all. It's nothing.*

Le moindre bruit le dérange. *The least noise disturbs him.*

moine *m. monk.*

MOINS *m. less; fewer; minus.*

Il est une heure moins le quart. *It's a quarter to one. ("It's an hour less a quarter.")*

Pas le moins du monde. *Not at all. Not in the least.*

Au moins. *At least.*

A moins que. *Unless.*

MOIS *m. month.*

moisir *to become moldy.*

moisson *f. harvest.*

moissonner *to reap.*

moite *adj. moist.*

MOITIÉ *f. half.*

Voulez-vous la moitié de cette pomme? *Do you want half of this apple?*

Ne faites pas les choses à moitié. *Don't do things halfway.*

molaire *f. molar.*

mollesse *f. softness; flabbiness.*

moment *m. moment.*

Il sera là dans un moment. *He'll be there in a moment.*

C'est le bon moment. *Now is the time.*

On l'attend d'un moment à l'autre. *We expect him any moment now.*

Du moment que ça ne vous intéresse pas. *Since it doesn't interest you.*

C'est le moment de . . . *It's the moment to, it's time to . . .*

En ce moment. *(Just) now, at this moment.*

Par moments. *At times, occasionally.*

(Pas) pour le moment. *(Not) for the moment.*

momie *f. mummy.*

MON *m. (ma f., mes pl.) my.*

Mon père et ma mère sont en voyage. *Both Dad and Mother are away.*

Mes livres ne sont pas ici. *My books aren't here.*

monarchie *f. monarchy.*

monarque *m. monarch.*

monastère *m. monastery.*

mondain *adj. worldly, fashionable.*

mondanités *f. pl. society news.*

MONDE *m. world, universe; people, crowd.*

Il court le monde. *He travels all over the world.*

Elle a mis au monde une fille. *She gave birth to a daughter.*

Il n'y avait pas grand monde. *There weren't many people there (present).*

Nous attendons du monde. *We're expecting company.*

Tout le monde en parle. *Everyone is talking about it.*

Le beau monde. *Society. The fashionable set.*

Je ne le ferais pour rien au monde. *I wouldn't do it for anything in the world.*

Partout au monde. *Everywhere in the world.*

Que de monde! *What a crowd!*

monétaire *adj. monetary.*

MONNAIE *f. coin; small change; currency.*

Avez-vous de la petite monnaie? *Have you any small change?*

La monnaie de ce pays. *The currency of this country.*

monnayeur *m. one who coins (mints) money.*

Faux monnayeur. *Counterfeiter.*

monocle *m. monocle.*

monologue *m. monologue, soliloquy.*

monopole *m. monopoly.*

monopoliser *to monopolize.*

monorail *m. monorail vehicle.*

monotone *adj. monotonous.*

monotonie *f. monotony.*

MONSIEUR *m. (messieurs pl.) Mr.*

Bonjour, monsieur Dupont. *Hello, Mr. Dupont. Good day, Mr. Dupont.*

Qui est ce monsieur? *Who is that gentleman?*

Monsieur chose. *Mister what's-his-name?*

Dites à ces messieurs d'entrer. *Ask the (these) gentlemen to come in.*

Monsieur 'dame. *Sir, madam (addressing a man and woman together).*

Le monsieur. *Man, gentleman.*

monstre *m. monster.*

monstrueux *(monstrueuse f.) adj. monstrous, huge.*

mont *m. mountain, mount.*

montagne *f. mountain.*

montant *m. total, sum total, amount.*

montant *adj. rising.*

La marée montante. *The rising tide.*

MONTER *to go up.*

Le train va partir, vous feriez mieux de monter dedans. *You'd better get on the train—it's about to leave.*

Monter à l'échelle. *To climb the ladder.*

Il est monté en grade. *He has been promoted. He has risen in grade.*

Le vin lui est monté à la tête. *The wine went to his head.*

Monter la tête à quelqu'un. *To get someone worked up. To work on someone's feelings.*

se monter *to provide oneself; amount to; get excited.*

Il s'est bien monté pour son voyage. *He provided himself with everything he needed for his trip.*

A combien se monte la facture? *What does the bill amount to?*

Il se monte la tête. *He's getting himself (all) worked up (excited).*

MONTRE *f. watch; show.*
J'ai cassé ma montre. *I broke my watch.*
Il a fait montre d'un grand courage. *He displayed great courage.*
montre-bracelet *f. wristwatch.*
MONTRER *to show.*
Montrez-le-moi. *Show it to me.*
Montrer du doigt quelque chose à quelqu'un. *To point out something to someone.*
se montrer *to appear.*
Il s'est montré à la fenêtre. *He appeared at the window.*
Il s'est montré sous son vrai jour. *He showed himself in his true colors (in his true light).*
Il s'est montré très gentil. *He was very nice.*
monture *f. setting, mounting, frame.*
monument *m. monument.*
se moquer *to laugh at, make fun of, ridicule.*
Il s'est bel et bien moqué de nous. *He certainly made us look like fools.*
Je m'en moque comme de l'an quarante. *I don't give a hang. I don't care a straw about it.*
En tout cas il s'en moque. *Anyway, he doesn't care.*
C'est se moquer du monde! *That's the height of impertinence! That's taking people for fools!*
moqueur (moqueuse *f.*) *adj. mocking, jeering, derisive.*
moral *noun (m.) and adj.* morale *f. morale, mind, spirit; moral.*
Remontez-lui le moral. *Encourage him. Help his morale.*
Un conte moral. *A story with a moral.*
morale *f. morality, ethics.*
Il lui a fait la morale pendant deux heures. *He lectured him (gave him a lecture) for two hours.*
moralement *morally.*
moralité *f. morality; moral.*
Sa moralité est douteuse. *His honesty (morality) is questionable.*
La moralité de cette histoire. *The moral of this (the) story.*
moratorium *m. moratorium.*
morbide *adj. morbid.*
MORCEAU *m.* (morceaux *pl.*) *piece.*
Prenez un morceau de pain. *Take a piece of bread.*
Le vase a été mis en morceaux. *The vase broke into pieces.*
Il a vendu sa voiture pour un morceau de pain. *He sold his car for a song (for next to nothing).*
Un morceau pour piano à quatre mains. *A four-hand piano piece.*

morceler *to cut up in small pieces.*
mordant *adj. mordant, biting, caustic.*
Paroles mordantes. *Biting (cutting) words.*
mordicus *stoutly.*
Il l'a nié mordicus. *He denied it stoutly.*
Il a défendu son opinion mordicus. *He defended his position tooth and nail.*
mordiller *to nibble.*
mordre *to bite.*
se mordre *to bite.*
Il s'en mord les doigts. *He regrets what he did.*
Il s'en mord la langue. *He regrets what he said.*
morgue *f. pride, haughtiness, arrogance.*
morgue *f. morgue.*
moribond *m. moribund, dying.*
morne *adj. gloomy, dismal, dull.*
morose *adj. morose, gloomy.*
mors *m. bit (of a bridle).*
morsure *f. bite.*
mort *m. dead person, casualty.*
MORT *f. death.*
Il a vu la mort de près. *He nearly died. He came very near dying.*
Un silence de mort. *Dead silence.*
MORT *adj. dead.*
mortalité *f. mortality, death rate.*
mortel (mortelle *f.*) *adj. mortal.*
morte-saison *f. slack season.*
mortifier *to mortify; humiliate.*
mortuaire *adj. mortuary.*
mosquée *f. mosque.*
MOT *m. word.*
Traduisez-moi ça mot à mot. *Translate that for me word for word.*
Je vais vous envoyer un mot à ce sujet. *I'll let you know about it. I'll drop you a line about it.*
Mots d'esprit. *Witticisms. Witty remarks.*
Un bon mot. *A pun.*
Il ignore le premier mot de la biologie. *He doesn't know the first thing about biology.*
Pour vous dire tout en deux mots. *To be brief. ("To tell you everything in two words.")*
Il a toujours le mot pour rire. *He's always cracking jokes (telling funny stories). He's fond of a joke.*
Laisser un mot. *To leave a message.*
Les mots croisés. *Crossword puzzle.*
moteur *m. motor, engine.*
Un moteur électrique. *An electric motor.*
Un moteur Diesel. *A Diesel engine.*
Un moteur à vapeur. *A steam engine.*
moteur (motrice *f.*) *adj. motive, propulsive, driving (power).*
motif *m. motive, cause.*

Pour quel motif? *On what ground? For what reason?*

Sans motif. *Without a motive. Without any reason (cause).*

Avoir un motif pour faire quelque chose. *To have a motive for doing something.*

Pour des motifs de jalousie. *Out of jealousy. ("For reasons of jealousy.")*

Leurs motifs sont bons. *Their motives are good.*

Sous aucun motif. *On no account.*

motion *f. motion.*

motiver *to motivate.*

Sur quoi motivez-vous votre décision? *On what do you base your decision?*

Ce discours a motivé beaucoup de critiques. *This speech led to (caused) a lot of criticism.*

motocyclette *f. motorcycle.*

mou (mol *before a vowel or "mute" h,* molle *f.* moux *m. pl.,* molles *f. pl.*) *adj. soft.*

Un lit mou. *A soft bed.*

Un chapeau mou. *A felt hat.*

Une personne molle. *A spineless person.*

Temps mou. *Humid (close, sticky) weather.*

mouche *f. fly.*

Agaçant comme une mouche. *Very irritating.*

Quelle mouche vous a piqué (*fam.*)? *What's the matter with you? What's wrong with you? What's come over you?*

C'est une fine mouche. *He's (she's) a sly one.*

Faire d'une mouche un éléphant. *To make a mountain out of a molehill.*

Elle a pris la mouche. *She was offended.*

se moucher *to blow one's nose.*

mouchoir *m. handkerchief.*

moudre *to grind.*

moue *f. pout.*

Elle fait la moue. *She's pouting.*

mouiller *to soak, wet.*

Leurs vêtements étaient tout mouillés. *Their clothes were all wet (soaked).*

moulage *m. casting.*

moule *m. mold.*

mouler *to cast, mold, shape.*

moulin *m. mill.*

Un moulin à café. *A coffee mill.*

mourant *m.* (mourante *f.*) *a dying person; adj. dying.*

mourir *to die.*

Il est mort avant-hier. *He died the day before yesterday.*

Mourir de rire. *To die with laughter.*

Mourir de froid. *To perish from cold.*

Je m'ennuie à mourir. *I'm bored to death.*

mousse *f. moss.*

mousseline *f. muslin.*

mousser *to foam.*

Faites mousser cette crème. *Whip (up) the cream.*

moustache *f. mustache.*

moustique *m. mosquito.*

moutarde *f. mustard.*

mouton *m. sheep.*

Revenons à nos moutons. *Lets get back to the subject (to the point).*

mouvement *m. movement, motion, impulse.*

Mettre en mouvement. *To start. To put in motion.*

Etre en mouvement. *To be in motion.*

Ils ont souvent des mouvements de colère. *They often have fits of anger (angry moods).*

Une symphonie en trois mouvements. *A symphony in three movements.*

Elle l'a fait de son propre mouvement. *She did it of her own accord.*

mouvementé *adj. animated.*

mouvoir *to move.*

Le bateau est mû à la vapeur. *This boat is driven by steam.*

Il est mû par l'intérêt. *He's acting out of self-interest. ("He's motivated by interest.")*

Mû par la pitié. *Moved by pity.*

moyen *m. means.*

Voies et moyens. *Ways and means.*

La fin justifie les moyens. *The end justifies the means.*

Il a employé les grands moyens. *He took extreme measures.*

Au moyen de . . . *By means of . . .*

Il n'en a pas les moyens. *He hasn't the means. He can't afford it.*

moyen (moyenne *f.*) *adj. mean, middle, medium.*

Le Moyen Age. *The Middle Ages.*

Le Français moyen. *The average Frenchman.*

moyennant *provided that.*

moyenne *f. average, medium.*

En moyenne. *On the average.*

muer *to molt, cast, slough off (of animals); break (of voice).*

muet (muette *f.*) *adj. mute, speechless.*

Un film muet. *A silent film.*

Etre sourd-muet. *To be deaf and dumb.*

Muet comme la tombe. *As silent as the grave.*

mugir *to low; bellow.*

mugissement *m. lowing; roaring.*

mulâtre *m.* (mulâtresse *f.*) *mulatto.*

mule *f. mule.*

multiplet *m. byte.*

multiplication *f. multiplication.*

multiplier *to multiply.*

se multiplier *to multiply.*
  Leurs difficultés se sont multipliées. *Their difficulties increased as they went along.*
multitude *f. multitude.*
  Il a adressé la multitude. *He addressed the crowd.*
  J'ai reçu une multitude de cartes de Noël. *I received lots (loads) of Christmas cards.*
municipal (municipaux *pl.*) *adj. municipal.*
se munir *to provide oneself.*
  Se munir de provisions. *To provide oneself with food. To take along provisions.*
  Munissez-vous de monnaie. *Take some small change along.*
munition *f. ammunition.*
mur *m. wall.*
mûr *adj. ripe, mature, matured.*
muraille *f. high, defensive wall.*
mural (muraux *pl.*) *adj. mural.*
mûrir *to ripen; mature.*
murmure *m. murmur, whispering.*
murmurer *to murmur, whisper.*
muscle *m. muscle.*
museau *m. muzzle, snout.*
musée *m. museum.*
  Le musée (d'art). *The (art) museum.*
muselière *f. muzzle.*
muser *to idle, dawdle.*
musical (musicaux *pl.*) *adj. musical.*
music-hall *m. music hall.*
musicien *m.* (musicienne *f.*) *musician.*
musique *f. music*
  La musique de chambre. *Chamber music.*
mutilation *f. mutilation.*
mutilé *m. mutilated; disabled.*
  C'est un mutilé de guerre. *He's a disabled war veteran.*
mutiler *to maim.*
se mutiner *to mutiny.*
mutuel (mutuelle *f.*) *adj. mutual.*
myope *adj. myopic, shortsighted.*
myopie *f. myopia.*
mystère *m. mystery.*
  Il a résolu le mystère. *He solved the mystery.*
  Il fait grand mystère de tout. *He makes a great mystery out of everything.*
  Il n'en fait pas mystère. *He makes no secret of it (no mystery about it).*
mystérieux (mystérieuse *f.*) *adj. mysterious.*
mystifier *to mystify, hoax.*
mythe *m. myth, legend.*
mythologie *f. mythology.*

N

nacre *f. mother-of-pearl.*
nage *f. swimming; perspiration.*

A la nage. *By swimming.*
Il est tout en nage. *He's bathed in perspiration.*
nageoire *f. fin.*
nager *to swim.*
  Sait-il nager? *Does he know how to swim?*
  Il sait nager. 1. *He can swim.* 2. *He can manage, take care of himself, get along.*
  Ils nagent dans l'opulence. *They're swimming in wealth. They're rolling in riches.*
nageur *m.* (nageuse *f.*) *swimmer.*
naguère *not so long ago.*
naïf (naïve *f.*) *adj. naive, artless; silly.*
  Avoir un air naïf. *To look innocent (naive).*
  Quel naïf! *What a fool! What a simpleton!*
nain *m.* (naine *f.*) *dwarf.*
naissance *f. birth, beginning.*
  Elle a donné naissance à un fils. *She gave birth to a son.*
  Il est Français de naissance. *He's French by birth.*
  Cette rumeur a pris naissance récemment. *This rumor sprang up recently.*
NAÎTRE *to be born.*
  Il est né coiffé. *He was born with a silver spoon in his mouth.*
  Lucienne Durand, née Legroux. *Lucienne Durand, née Legroux (i.e. whose maiden name was Legroux).*
  Cela fit naître des soupçons. *That made people suspicious. That aroused suspicion.*
  Faire naître le mépris. *To breed contempt.*
  Je ne suis pas né d'hier. *I wasn't born yesterday.*
naïvement *naively.*
  J'ai pensé naïvement qu'ils tiendraient leur promesse. *I naively thought they would keep their promise.*
naïveté *f. naivete.*
  Elle a eu la naïveté de le croire. *She was naive enough to believe that.*
nantir *to secure, provide.*
  Il l'a nanti de vêtements. *He provided him with clothes.*
nantissement *m. pledge, security.*
naphtaline *f. naphthaline.*
nappe *f. tablecloth.*
narcotique *m. narcotic.*
narguer *to scorn, sneer.*
narine *f. nostril.*
narquois *adj. sly.*
  Un sourire narquois. *A sly smile.*
  Une remarque narquoise. *A sly (ironical, bantering) remark.*
narrateur *m.* (narratrice *f.*) *narrator.*
narration *f. narration.*

nasal (nasaux *pl.*) *adj. nasal.*

nasillard *adj. nasal.*

natal (nataux *pl.*) *adj. native.*
Son pays natal. *His native country.*

natalité *f. birthrate.*

natation *f. swimming.*

natif (native *f.*) *adj. native.*

nation *f. nation.*

national (nationaux *pl.*) *adj. national.*

nationalisme *m. nationalism.*

nationalité *f. nationality.*
Quelle est votre nationalité? *What nationality are you?*

naturalisation *f. naturalization.*

naturaliser *to naturalize.*

NATURE *f. nature.*
La nature l'a bien partagée. *She's very talented.*
Une nature-morte. *A still-life painting.*
Elle est d'une nature douce. *She has a nice disposition.*
Payer en nature. *To pay in kind.*
Un café nature. *Black coffee.*
Tout cela n'est certainement pas de nature à nous rassurer. *That's certainly not very reassuring.*
Contre nature. *Unnatural.*

naturel *m. naturalness; native disposition.*
Voir les choses au naturel. *To see things as they are.*
Etre d'un bon naturel. *To have a good disposition.*
Etre d'un mauvais naturel. *To be ill-natured.*
Un heureux naturel. *A cheerful disposition.*

NATUREL (naturelle *f.*) *adj. natural.*
Histoire naturelle. *Natural history.*
Les sciences naturelles. *The natural sciences.*
Mort naturelle. *Natural death.*
Elle est très naturelle. *She's very unaffected.*
Son explication m'a paru très naturelle. *His explanation seemed very straightforward (honest, reasonable) to me.*
De grandeur naturelle. *Life-size.*
Il trouve ça tout naturel. *He takes it for granted.*
Ce vêtement est en soie naturelle, non pas en soie artificielle. *This garment is made of real silk, not rayon.*

NATURELLEMENT *naturally.*
Ses cheveux bouclent naturellement. *Her hair is naturally curly.*
A-t-il été fâché lorsqu'il l'a appris?—Naturellement! *Was he angry when he heard about it?—Naturally!*
Naturellement je le ferai. *Naturally I'll do it. Of course I'll do it.*

naufrage *m. shipwreck, wreck.*
Il a fait naufrage au port. *He fell just short of success (of his goal). He failed just when it looked as though he'd succeed. He failed with his goal in sight. ("He was shipwrecked in sight of the harbor.")*

nauséabond *adj. nauseous, foul.*

nausée *f. nausea, nauseousness.*

naval *adj. naval.*

navet *m. turnip; bore; third-rate film.*

navette *f. shuttle.*
Il fait la navette entre Paris et Tours. *He travels back and forth between Paris and Tours.*

navigateur *m. navigator.*

navigation *f. navigation, sailing.*

naviguer *to sail.*
Naviguer au long cours. *To be a merchant seaman.*
Il a navigué sur toutes les mers. *He's sailed the seven seas.*
Il navigue à l'aventure. *He tramps about (goes from one place to another as the fancy takes him).*
Ici il faut naviguer avec prudence. *We must tread lightly here (proceed with caution).*

NAVIRE *m. ship.*
Le navire faisait eau. *The ship had sprung a leak.*
Navire de guerre. *A warship.*
Un navire à vapeur. *A steamer.*

navrant *adj. heart-rending.*
C'est une histoire navrante. *It's a heart-rending story.*

navrer *to distress.*
Je suis navré, mais je ne puis accepter votre invitation. *I'm terribly sorry but I can't accept your invitation.*
J'ai été navré d'apprendre la grande perte que vous venez de subir. *I was very sorry to hear of your loss (the loss you have just suffered).*

NE (n' *before vowels and "mute"* h) *not, no.*
Je ne sais pas. *I don't know.*
Je n'ai que cent mille francs. *I have only 100,000 francs.*
Il n'accepte aucune observation. *He doesn't like to be criticized. He never accepts any criticism.*
Je crains qu'il ne revienne plus. *I'm afraid he won't come back (again).*
Ils ne tarderont guère à venir. *It won't be long before they'll be here (come).*
Il est plus intelligent qu'il n'en a l'air. *He's more intelligent than he looks.*
Il agit autrement qu'il ne parle. *His actions don't agree with his words. He speaks*

one way and acts another. ("He acts otherwise than he speaks.")

Ne ... à peine. *Hardly, scarcely.*

Ne ... jamais. *Never.*

N'est-ce pas? *Isn't that so?*

Il m'a prié de ne pas parler. *He begged me not to speak.*

Ne ... point. *Not at all.*

Elle ne fait que parler. *She does nothing but talk.*

Ne ... rien. *Nothing.*

Ne ... ni ... ni ... *Neither ... nor ...*

N'importe où. *Anywhere.*

N'importe quelle banque. *Any bank.*

NÉANMOINS *however, nevertheless.*

Néanmoins je le ferai. *Nevertheless I'll do it.*

NÉANT *m. nothing, nought, nothingness.*

Néant. *None. Nothing to report (in filling out a form).*

Le néant de la gloire. *The emptiness of glory.*

Il est sorti du néant. *He rose from obscurity.*

Réduire quelque chose à néant. *To reduce to nothing (nought). To annihilate.*

nébuleux (nébuleuse *f.*) *adj. cloudy; nebulous.*

nécessaire *m. what is necessary, necessity.*

Il n'a que le strict nécessaire. *He only has the bare necessities.*

Elle se prive du nécessaire pour ses enfants. *For the sake of her children she deprives herself even of necessities.*

Nous faisons le nécessaire. *We're doing whatever is necessary. We're taking all necessary measures.*

Un nécessaire à ouvrage. *A sewing kit.*

Un nécessaire de toilette. *A toilet case.*

NÉCESSAIRE *adj. necessary.*

C'est nécessaire. *It (this) is necessary.*

Il est nécessaire que vous le fassiez. *It's necessary that you do it.*

Des mesures nécessaires. *Necessary measures.*

Il s'est rendu nécessaire à son patron. *He made himself indispensable to his boss.*

NÉCESSITÉ *f. necessity; need.*

Denrées de première nécessité. *Essential foodstuffs.*

Faire quelque chose par nécessité. *To be compelled to do something. To do something out of necessity.*

Se trouver dans la nécessité de faire quelque chose. *To find oneself obliged to do something.*

Il est de toute nécessité de le faire. *It's absolutely essential that it be done.*

La nécessité est mère de l'invention. *Necessity is the mother of invention.*

Nécessité n'a pas de loi. *Necessity knows no law.*

Faire de nécessité vertu. *To make a virtue of necessity.*

nécessiter *to necessitate.*

Ceci va nécessiter notre départ. *This will oblige (make it necessary for) us to leave.*

néfaste *adj. unlucky; harmful.*

négatif (négative *f.*) *adj. negative.*

négligeable *adj. negligible.*

négligence *f. neglect, negligence; mistake; carelessness.*

Négligence à faire quelque chose. *Carelessness in doing something.*

Par négligence. *Through carelessness. Through an oversight.*

négligent *adj. careless.*

Ne soyez pas si négligent. *Don't be so careless.*

D'un air négligent. *Carelessly. Nonchalantly. Casually.*

négliger *to neglect.*

se négliger *to neglect oneself.*

négoce *m. trade, business.*

négociant *m. merchant.*

négociation *f. negotiation.*

négocier *to negotiate.*

NEIGE *f. snow.*

neiger *to snow.*

néon *m. neon.*

Une enseigne au néon. *A neon sign.*

NERF *m. nerve; tendon; vigor, energy.*

Elle a ses nerfs aujourd'hui. *She's nervous (jumpy, jittery, irritable) today.*

Il me tape sur les nerfs (*fam.*) *He exasperates me.*

Ce bruit vous agace les nerfs. *That noise irritates (gets on) one's nerves.*

nerveux (nerveuse *f.*) *adj. nervous.*

nervosité *f. nervousness, irritability.*

net (nette *f.*) *adj. clean, neat; net.*

C'est clair et net. *There's no doubt about it. It's very clear.*

Il le lui a refusé tout net. *He refused him flatly.*

Je veux en avoir le cœur net. *I want to know the truth about it. I want to get to the bottom of it.*

Quel a été votre bénéfice net? *What was your net profit?*

J'ai reçu mille francs net. *I received a clear 1,000 francs.*

Il veut en avoir le cœur net. *He wants to get to the bottom of it. He wants to clear the matter up.*

nettement *clearly.*

netteté *f. neatness, cleanliness, clearness.*

nettoyage *m. cleaning.*

Nettoyage à sec. *Dry cleaning.*

nettoyer *to clean, sweep.*

Faire nettoyer à sec. *To have something dry-cleaned.*

neuf *m. what is new; novelty.*

Quoi de neuf? *What's new?*

NEUF (neuve *f.*) *adj. new.*

NEUF *noun and adj. nine.*

neutralité *f. neutrality.*

neutre *adj. neutral.*

NEUVIÈME *noun and adj. ninth.*

neveu *m. nephew.*

névralgie *f. neuralgia.*

névrose *f. neurosis.*

NEZ *m. nose.*

Saigner du nez. *To bleed from the nose. To have a nosebleed.*

Parler du nez. *To talk through one's nose.*

Il ne voit pas plus loin que le bout de son nez. *He can't see any farther than the end of his nose.*

Il lui a ri au nez. *He laughed in his face.*

Elle a le nez retroussé. *She has a turned-up nose.*

NI *nor.*

Ni celui-ci, ni celui-là. *Neither this one, nor that one.*

niais *adj. simple, foolish.*

niaiserie *f. foolishness.*

niche *f. dog kennel; trick.*

se nicher *to build a nest, nestle.*

nid *m. nest.*

nièce *f. niece.*

nier *to deny.*

nigaud *adj. simpleton.*

niveau *m. level.*

Vérifier le niveau d'essence. *To check the gas gauge.*

noble *m. and f. noble; nobleman or noblewoman.*

noble *adj. noble.*

noblesse *f. nobility.*

noce *f. wedding.*

Ils sont partis en voyage de noces. *They left for their honeymoon.*

Il a fait la noce. *He went on a spree.*

noceur *m.* (noceuse *f.*) *dissipated person.*

Noël *m. Christmas.*

Le Père Noël. *Santa Claus.*

noeud *m. knot, bow.*

NOIR *noun (m.) and adj.* (noire *f.*) *black.*

Elle est vêtue de noir. *She's dressed in black.*

Voir tout en noir. *To see the dark side of everything.*

Il a l'oeil au beurre noir. *He has a black eye.*

C'est ma bête noire. *It's my pet aversion.*

Il est dans la misère noire. *He's in dire poverty.*

noirceur *f. blackness; slander.*

noircir *to blacken.*

noix *f. walnut, nut.*

NOM *m. name; noun.*

Votre nom ne lui revient pas. *He doesn't recall your name.*

Il l'a fait en mon nom. *He did it on my behalf.*

Son nom de famille est Durand. *His surname is Durand.*

Un nom de guerre. *A pseudonym. An assumed name, especially in time of war.*

Se faire un nom. *To win (make) a name for oneself.*

NOMBRE *n. number.*

Un bon nombre de gens sont du même avis. *A good many people are of the same opinion.*

Ils sont au nombre de dix. *They're ten in number.*

Compter quelqu'un au nombre de ses amis. *To count someone as one of (among) one's friends.*

nombreux (nombreuse *f.*) *adj. numerous.*

C'est un de ses nombreux admirateurs. *He's one of his many admirers.*

nomination *f. appointment.*

nommer *to name, call; appoint.*

Peut-il nommer la personne qui lui a dit cela? *Can he name the person who told him that?*

Il vient d'être nommé directeur. *He was just named director.*

NON *no, not.*

Je pense que non. *I think not.*

Mais non! *(But) No! Certainly not!*

nonchalance *f. nonchalance.*

nonchalant *adj. nonchalant.*

NORD *noun (m.) and adj. north.*

L'Amérique du Nord. *North America.*

Il ne perd pas le nord, celui-là. *He's never at a loss. ("He never loses his bearings.")*

Le pôle nord. *The North Pole.*

normal (normaux *pl.*) *adj. normal.*

Elle n'est pas dans son état normal. *She isn't her usual self.*

NOS *See* notre.

nostalgie *f. nostalgia.*

notable *adj. notable, important.*

notaire *m. notary; solicitor.*

notamment *in particular, among others.*

notariat *m. profession of notary.*

notarié *m.* **acte notarié.** *deed.*

note *f. note; remark, observation; bill.*

Il y a une note dans le journal à ce sujet. *There is a notice in the paper about that.*

Prendre note de quelque chose. *To take note (notice) of something. To bear something in mind.*

Prendre des notes. *To take notes.*

L'explication se trouve dans les notes au bas de la page. *The explanation is given ("is found") in the footnotes.*

Le docteur a envoyé sa note. *The doctor sent his bill.*

C'est un mauvais élève. Il ne récolte que des mauvaises notes. *He's a poor student. He gets only bad marks.*

Le pianiste a fait une fausse note. *The pianist hit a wrong note.*

noter *to notice, note; to mark.*

Notez bien que je n'en suis pas certain! *Mind. I'm not sure about it!*

Ce sont des choses à noter pour plus tard. *These are things to watch for later on.*

Avez-vouz noté l'adresse? *Did you mark down the address?*

J'ai noté le passage d'un trait rouge. *I marked that passage in red.*

notice *f. notice, short account.*

Notice biographique. *Biographical sketch.*

notifier *to notify.*

notion *f. notion, idea.*

notoriété *f. notoriety.*

NÔTRE (le nôtre *m.*, la nôtre *f.*, les nôtres *m. and f.*) *ours.*

NOTRE (notre *f.*, nos *pl.*) *adj. our.*

Notre chose à nous. *Our own thing.*

nouer *to knot, tie.*

nourrir *to feed, nourish.*

nourriture *f. food.*

NOUS *we, us.*

nous-mêmes *ourselves.*

NOUVEAU (nouvel *m.* used before a vowel or "*mute*" h, nouvelle *f.*, nouveaux *m. pl.*, nouvelles *f. pl.*) *adj. new.*

Je ne suis pas encore installé dans mon nouvel appartement. *I'm not settled yet in my new apartment.*

C'est la nouvelle mode. *That's the latest fashion.*

De nouveau. *Again, once more.*

nouveauté *f. newness, novelty.*

NOUVELLE *f. a piece of news, information; short story; pl. news.*

Demander des nouvelles de la santé de quelqu'un. *To ask after someone's health.*

De qui tenez-vous cette nouvelle? *Who gave you that information? Who told you the news?*

Il a écrit des nouvelles pour les journaux. *He's written short stories for the newspapers.*

Il aura de mes nouvelles! *He'll hear from me!*

Pas de nouvelles, bonnes nouvelles. *No news is good news.*

nouvelliste *m. short-story writer.*

NOVEMBRE *m. November.*

novice *m. novice.*

novocaïne *f. novocaine.*

noyau *m. stone (of a fruit).*

noyer *to drown.*

se noyer *to drown oneself.*

nu *adj. naked, bare, undressed.*

Il est sorti nu-tête. *He went out bareheaded.*

nuage *m. cloud.*

nuance *f. shade, hue, nuance.*

nucléaire *adj. nuclear.*

Arme nucléaire. *Nuclear weapon.*

Energie nucléaire. *Nuclear energy.*

Industrie nucléaire. *Nuclear industry.*

Reacteur nucléaire. *Nuclear reactor.*

nue *f. high cloud.*

On le porte jusqu'aux nues. *They praise him to the skies.*

nuire *to harm, injure.*

Il cherche à me nuire auprès d'eux. *He's trying to put me in bad with them. He's trying to hurt me in their opinion.*

nuisible *adj. harmful, injurious.*

NUIT *f. night, darkness.*

A la nuit tombante. *At nightfall.*

Bonne nuit. *Good night.*

Elle a passé une nuit blanche. *She had a sleepless night.*

nul (nulle *f.*) *adj. no one; nobody; null.*

A l'impossible nul n'est tenu. *No one can be expected to do the impossible.*

Nul et non avenu. *Null and void.*

Nulle part. *Nowhere.*

nullité *f. invalidity; emptiness; nonentity.*

NUMÉRO *m. number; edition (publication).*

Vous m'avez donné un faux numéro. *You gave me the wrong number.*

Je lui ai donné votre numéro de téléphone. *I gave him your telephone number.*

numéroter *to number.*

nuptial (nuptiaux *pl.*) *adj. bridal.*

nuque *f. the nape of the neck.*

nutrition *f. nutrition.*

obéir *to obey, be obedient.*

Je lui obéis. *I obey him (her).*

J'y obéis. *I obey it.*

obéissance *f. obedience.*

obéissant *adj. obedient.*

obèse *adj. fat, stout.*

obésité *f. obesity.*

obituaire *noun (m.) and adj. obituary.*

objecter *to object.*

Je n'y objecte pas. *I don't object to it. I have no objection (to raise).*

objectif *m. objective, aim, goal; lens (camera).*

Atteindre son objectif. *To attain one's object (goal).*

objectif (objective *f.*) *adj. objective.*

objection *f. objection.*

OBJET *m. object, thing, article, purpose.*

Emballez ces objets. *Pack up these things.*

Dans cet objet. *With this end in view.*

Objet direct. *Direct object (grammar).*

obligation *f. obligation; bond.*

obligatoire *adj. obligatory, compulsory.*

obligeance *f. kindness.*

Auriez-vous l'obligeance de sonner? *Would you mind ringing the bell?*

obliger *to oblige, compel; please.*

Je suis obligé de vous quitter. *I'm obliged (I have) to leave you.*

Le devoir m'y oblige. *Duty compels me to do it.*

Vous l'avez obligé, il vous en est reconnaissant. *You've been of service to him; he's very grateful ("for it").*

oblique *adj. oblique.*

oblitérer *to obliterate.*

obscène *adj. obscene.*

obscur *adj. dark, dim, gloomy.*

Il fait obscur ici. *It's dark here.*

Il est de naissance obscure. *He comes from an obscure family. ("He is of obscure birth.")*

obscurcir *to obscure, dim.*

s'obscurcir *to grow dim, become cloudy.*

obscurité *f. obscurity, darkness.*

obséder *to obsess.*

obsèques *f. pl. funeral.*

observation *f. observation, lookout; remark, hint.*

observatoire *m. observatory.*

observer *to observe, examine, look at; remark, notice.*

Observez strictement votre régime. *Keep strictly to your diet.*

On vous observe, prenez garde. *Be careful, you're being watched.*

Comme vous me l'avez fait observer. *As you pointed out to me.*

obsession *f. obsession.*

obstacle *m. obstacle.*

obstiné *adj. obstinate, stubborn.*

s'obstiner *to be obstinate, persist in.*

obstruer *to obstruct.*

obtenir *to obtain.*

obtus *adj. dull.*

Il a l'esprit obtus. *He's dull-witted.*

obus *m. shell (artillery).*

OCCASION *f. occasion, opportunity; reason, motive; bargain.*

Nous avons rarement l'occasion d'y aller. *We rarely have occasion to go there.*

Profiter de l'occasion. *To take advantage of the opportunity.*

A l'occasion. *If need be. On occasion. When the opportunity occurs.*

Je le vois par occasion. *I see him from time to time.*

D'occasion. *Secondhand, used.*

occasionner *to cause.*

Occident *m. Occident, West.*

occidental (occidentaux *pl.*) *adj. occidental, western.*

occupation *f. occupation, pursuit, employment, work.*

Armée d'occupation. *Army of occupation.*

Si mes occupations me le permettent, je viendrai. *I'll come if my work permits.*

Il est sans occupation. *He's out of work.*

occuper *to occupy, take up; preoccupy; reside in; busy.*

L'ennemi a occupé la ville. *The enemy occupied the town.*

Toutes les places sont occupées. *There aren't any vacant seats. All the seats are taken.*

Occuper une place importante dans le gouvernement. *To hold an important position in the government.*

La ligne est occupée. *The (telephone) line is busy.*

s'occuper *to busy oneself with, take care of, be engaged in.*

Est-ce qu'on s'occupe de vous? *Are you being waited on? Is someone waiting on you?*

Voulez-vous être assez aimable de vous occuper de moi? *Would you mind waiting on me?*

Je m'en occuperai. *I'll see to it.*

Il s'occupe de tout. *He's attending to everything.*

océan *m. ocean.*

OCTOBRE *m. October.*

octroyer *to grant.*

oculiste *m. oculist.*

odeur *f. odor, scent.*

odieux (odieuse *f.*) *adj. odious, hateful.*

odorat *m. sense of smell.*

OEIL *m.* (yeux *pl.*) *eye, sight.*

Loin des yeux, loin du coeur. *Out of sight, out of mind.*

Il n'a pas froid aux yeux. 1. *He's very determined.* 2. *He's not at all shy.*

Cela saute aux yeux. *It's as clear as daylight. It's so obvious it almost hits you in the eye. It stares you in the face.*

Cela lui crève les yeux. *It's right before his eyes.*

Elle le voit d'un mauvais oeil. *She looks unfavorably upon it.*

Cela coûte les yeux de la tête. *It costs a mint of money. It costs a small fortune.*

Il ne dort que d'un oeil. *He sleeps with one eye open. He's always on the alert.*

Il ne peut en croire ses yeux. *He can't believe his eyes.*

Il y tient comme à la prunelle de ses yeux. *He values it as the apple of his eye.*

Jetez un coup d'oeil sur son travail. *Take a look at his work.*

OEUF *m. egg.*

Comment préférez-vous vos oeufs; à la coque, brouillés ou sur le plat? *How do you like your eggs—boiled, scrambled or fried?*

OEUVRE *f. work.*

Il faut les voir à l'oeuvre! *You should see them at work!*

Il est fils de ses oeuvres. *He's a self-made man.*

Il a mis tous les moyens en oeuvre. *He left no stone unturned.*

Ses oeuvres ont beaucoup de succès. *His works are very popular.*

Oeuvres de bienfaisance. *Works of charity.*

A l'oeuvre on connaît l'artisan. *A carpenter is known by his chips. A man is known by what he does. The proof of the pudding is in the eating.*

Chef-d'oeuvre. *Masterpiece.*

Oeuvre maîtresse. *Masterwork.*

offense *f. offense.*

offenser *to offend, shock.*

s'offenser *to be offended.*

Il s'offense d'un rien. *He takes offense at the least thing.*

office *m. duty, functions.*

Faire office de secrétaire. *To act as a secretary.*

C'est mon office de . . . *It's my duty to . . .*

Il m'a rendu un mauvais office. *He did me a bad turn.*

Office divin. *Religious service.*

officiel (officielle *f.*) *adj. official.*

officier *m. officer.*

officieux (officieuse *f.*) *adj. officious; unofficial, informal.*

Commission officieuse. *Informal commission.*

offrande *f. offering.*

offre *f. offer, tender.*

Voici ma dernière offre. *Here's my last offer.*

Il lui a fait des offres de service. *He offered to help him.*

offrir *to offer, present; give a present.*

Il lui a offert une montre pour son anniversaire. *He gave him (her) a watch for his (her) birthday.*

s'offrir *to propose oneself, offer.*

s'offusquer *to be offended, shocked.*

oie *f. goose.*

Bête comme une oie. *Silly as a goose.*

oignon *m. onion.*

oindre *to rub with oil.*

oiseau *m.* (oiseaux *pl.*) *bird.*

oisif (oisive *f.*) *adj. idle.*

oisiveté *f. idleness.*

olive *f. olive.*

ombrage *m. shade; offense.*

ombrageux (ombrageuse *f.*) *adj. touchy, easily offended.*

ombre *f. shade, shadow, spirit, obscurity, shelter, cover.*

Mettons-nous à l'ombre. *Let's get out of the sun. Let's get in the shade.*

Il n'y a pas l'ombre de vérité en cela. *There isn't a bit (shred, shadow) of truth in that.*

Il a été mis à l'ombre. *He was put in jail.*

omelette *f. omelet.*

omettre *to omit.*

omission *f. omission.*

ON *one, we, people, they.*

On ne sait jamais. *One never knows.*

On dit que . . . *It's said that . . . People say that . . .*

On m'a volé ma montre. *My watch has been stolen. Someone stole (has stolen) my watch.*

Où va-t-on? *Where are we going?*

On sonne. *Someone's ringing.*

oncle *m. uncle.*

onde *f. wave.*

ondoyer *to wave, undulate.*

onduler *to undulate.*

ongle *m. fingernail, toenail.*

Il est artiste jusqu'au bout des ongles. *He's an artist to his fingertips. He's every inch an artist.*

Il le sait sur le bout des ongles. *He knows it perfectly.*

Il se ronge les ongles. *He's very impatient. ("He is biting his nails.")*

onguent *m. ointment, unguent, salve.*

ONZE *noun and adj. eleven.*

ONZIÈME *noun and adj. eleventh.*

opéra *m. opera.*

opération *f. operation, performance.*

opérer *to operate.*

opérette *f. operetta.*

opiniâtre *adj. obstinate.*

s'opiniâtrer *to be stubborn, obstinate; cling to an opinion.*

opinion *f. opinion.*

opportun *adj. timely, opportune.*
opportunité *f. opportunity.*
opposé *noun (m.) and adj. (opposée f.) opposite; adverse.*
   C'est tout l'opposé! *It's quite the contrary (opposite, reverse)!*
opposer *to oppose.*
s'opposer *to oppose, object to.*
opposition *f. opposition.*
oppresser *to oppress.*
oppression *f. oppression.*
opprimer *to oppress.*
opter *to decide upon, chose.*
optimisme *m. optimism.*
optimiste *m. optimist.*
optimiste *adj. optimistic.*
option *f. option, choice.*
optique *adj. optic.*
opulence *f. opulence, wealth.*
opulent *adj. opulent, wealthy.*
OR *m. gold.*
   Une bague en or. *A gold ring.*
   C'est de l'or en barre. *It's as good as gold.*
   Il a un coeur d'or. *He has a heart of gold.*
   C'est une affaire d'or! *It's a gold mine!*
or *now, but.*
   Or ça. *Now then.*
   Or donc . . . *Well then . . .*
oracle *m. oracle.*
orage *m. storm.*
orageux (orageuse *f.*) *adj. stormy.*
oraison *f. oration; prayer.*
oral (oraux *pl.*) *adj. oral.*
ORANGE *noun (f.) and adj. orange (fruit).*
orange *noun (m.) and adj. orange (color).*
orateur *m.* (oratrice *f.*) *orator.*
orbite *f. orbit.*
orchestre *m. orchestra.*
   Un chef d'orchestre. *An orchestra leader.*
   A l'orchestre. *In the orchestra (seats).*
   Le fauteuil d'orchestre. *Orchestra seat.*
ordinaire *m. usual way.*
   D'ordinaire. *Usually. As a rule.*
   Cela sort de l'ordinaire. *That's unusual.*
   Faites-le comme à l'ordinaire. *Do it as usual. Do it the usual way.*
   Plus qu'à l'ordinaire. *More than usual.*
   Au-dessus de l'ordinaire. *Out of the ordinary.*
   C'est un homme au-dessus de l'ordinaire. *He's an unusual man.*
   Par avion ou ordinaire? *Airmail or regular?*
ORDINAIRE *adj. ordinary, common.*
   En temps ordinaires. *In ordinary times.*
   C'est un homme ordinaire (Il est très ordinaire.) *He's very ordinary (common).*
   Il a répondu avec sa politesse ordinaire. *He answered with his usual politeness.*

ORDINATEUR *m. computer.*
   Micro-ordinateur. *Microcomputer.*
   Ordinateur personnel. *Personal computer.*
ordonnance *f. order; ordinance, regulation; prescription.*
   Il a rendu une ordonnance. *He issued an order.*
   Une ordonnance de police. *A police regulation.*
   Le docteur a donné une ordonnance au malade. *The doctor gave the patient a prescription.*
ordonner *to order, set in order.*
ORDRE *m. order.*
   Un numéro d'ordre. *A serial number.*
   Remettez de l'ordre dans vos affaires. *Tidy up your belongings. Put your things in order.*
   Passons à l'ordre du jour. *Let's proceed with the order of the day.*
   De premier ordre. *First rate.*
   Payez à l'ordre de. *Pay to the order of.*
ordure *f. dirt; pl. garbage.*
OREILLE *f. ear, hearing.*
   Il a de l'oreille. *He has a musical ear.*
   Ça lui entre par une oreille et ça lui sort par l'autre. *It goes in one ear and out the other.*
   Faire la sourde oreille. *To turn a deaf ear.*
   Vous pouvez dormir sur vos deux oreilles. *You've nothing to worry about. You can sleep soundly.*
   Il ne s'est pas fait tirer l'oreille. *He didn't have to be asked twice. He didn't have to be coaxed.*
   L'oreille fine. *Acute hearing.*
oreiller *m. pillow.*
orfèvrerie *f. goldsmith's work.*
organe *m. organ (of the body).*
organisation *f. organization.*
organiser *to organize.*
organisme *m. organism.*
orge *f. barley.*
orgue *m. organ (mus).*
orgueil *m. pride, arrogance.*
   Rabaisser l'orgueil de quelqu'un. *To take someone down a peg or two.*
   Il y a mis son orgueil. *He took pride in doing it.*
orgueilleux (orgueilleuse *f.*) *adj. proud, arrogant.*
Orient *m. Orient, East.*
oriental (orientaux *pl.*) *adj. oriental.*
orientation *f. orientation.*
   Il a perdu le sens de l'orientation. *He lost his sense of direction.*
orienter *to orient.*
orifice *m. aperture.*
originaire *adj. originating.*

Il est originaire de Tours. *He comes from Tours.*

original (originaux *pl.*) *adj. original.*

originalité *f. originality, oddity.*

origine *f. origin, source, birth.*

Dès l'origine. *From the outset.*

ornement *m. ornament.*

orner *to adorn, trim.*

ornière *f. rut.*

Il est sorti de l'ornière. *He got out of the rut.*

orphelin *m.* (orpheline *f.*) *orphan.*

orphelinat *m. orphanage.*

orthographe *f. spelling.*

Des fautes d'orthographe. *Spelling mistakes.*

OS *m. bone.*

Ils ont été trempés jusqu'aux os. *They were soaked to the skin ("to the bones.")*

Il n'a que les os et la peau. *He's only skin and bones.*

osciller *to oscillate.*

oser *to dare.*

Si j'ose m'exprimer ainsi. *If I may take the liberty of saying so.*

osseux (osseuse *f.*) *adj. bony.*

ostentation *f. ostentation, show.*

otage *m. hostage.*

ÔTER *to take away, take off.*

Oter les taches de graisse. *To remove grease stains.*

Tenez, ôtez-moi cela de là. *Here, take this away.*

Il lui a ôté son chapeau. *He raised his hat to him (her).*

OU *or.*

Ou . . . ou . . . *Either . . . or . . .*

Ou (bien). *Or (else).*

OÙ *where.*

Où serez-vous? *Where will you be?*

Où allons-nous? *Where are we going?*

Où en sont les choses? *How do matters stand? What's the situation?*

N'importe où. *Anywhere.*

Où vous voudrez. *Wherever you wish.*

ouate *f. cotton.*

ouater *to pad; line.*

oubli *m. forgetting, neglect.*

OUBLIER *to forget.*

J'ai oublié de lui demander. *I forgot to ask him.*

J'ai oublié mes gants chez vous. *I forgot my gloves at your house.*

s'oublier *to forget oneself.*

OUEST *m. west.*

OUI *yes, so, indeed.*

Mais oui! *Why certainly! Of course!*

ouïe *f. hearing.*

ouragan *m. hurricane.*

ouriet *m. hem.*

ours *m. bear.*

outil *m. tool.*

outiller *to supply, equip.*

outrage *m. insult.*

outrager *to insult.*

outrageusement *insultingly.*

outrance *f. excess.*

A outrance. *To excess. To the bitter end. Beyond all measure.*

Ils se battirent à outrance. *They fought desperately.*

OUTRE *beyond.*

Outre mesure. *Beyond measure.*

Outre cette somme. *In addition to that sum.*

Il passa outre. *He went on.*

outrepasser *to overstep, go beyond, exceed.*

OUVERT *adj. open; frank, sincere.*

Le musée est-il ouvert aujourd'hui? *Is the museum open today?*

Il parle à coeur ouvert. *He speaks very frankly (openly).*

ouvertement *openly, frankly.*

ouverture *f. opening; overture.*

L'ouverture d'un crédit. *The opening of an account.*

Il a profité de la première ouverture pour y aller. *He seized the first opportunity to go there.*

OUVRAGE *m. work, performance.*

Il abat de l'ouvrage comme quatre. *He does a great deal of work. ("He works for four.")*

Ils se sont mis à l'ouvrage. *They set to work.*

Il a du coeur à l'ouvrage. *He works with a will.*

Un ouvrage d'art. *A work of art.*

Ouvrages publics. *Public works.*

Un bel ouvrage. *A nice piece of work.*

ouvreuse *f. usherette.*

ouvrier *m. workman, artisan.*

OUVRIR *to open; begin.*

Ouvrez la fenêtre. *Open the window.*

Ils ont ouvert des négociations. *They opened (began) negotiations.*

Ouvrir l'appétit. *To sharpen the appetite.*

s'ouvrir *to open.*

ovale *adj. oval.*

oxygène *noun and adj. oxygen.*

P

pacifier *to pacify, appease.*

pacifique *adj. pacific, peaceful, peaceable.*

pacifiste *m. pacifist.*

pacotille *f. cheap wares.*

pacte *m. pact, contract.*

pactiser *to make an agreement, come to terms, compromise.*

pagaille *f. disorder.*
> Tout était en pagaille. *Everything was in disorder.*

page *f. page.*
> En première page. *On the front page.*

paiement *See* payement.

paillasse *f. straw mattress.*

paillasson *m. doormat.*

paille *f. straw.*
> Jaune paille. *Straw-yellow, straw-colored.*

paillette *f. spangle.*

PAIN *m. bread, loaf.*
> Donnez-moi du pain et du vin. *Give me some bread and wine.*
> Ça se vend comme des petits pains. *It's selling like hot cakes.*
> Je l'ai eu pour une bouchée de pain. *I got it for almost nothing (for a song).*
> Il ne vaut pas le pain qu'il mange. *He isn't worth his salt.*

pair *noun (m.) and adj. equal, even.*
> Il est sans pair. *He's without a peer.*
> Un écrivain hors de pair. *An incomparable writer.*
> Il marche de pair avec son époque. *He keeps abreast of the times.*
> Une domestique engagée au pair. *A maid receiving room and board but no salary.*
> Un nombre pair. *An even number.*

paire *f. pair, couple.*
> Je voudrais une paire de gants. *I'd like a pair of gloves.*
> Les deux font la paire. *They are two of a kind.*

paître *to graze.*

paix *f. peace.*
> Il a cédé pour avoir la paix. *He gave in just to have peace.*
> Fichez-moi la paix (fam.)! *Let me alone! Don't bother me!*

palais *m. palace; palate.*
> Le Palais de Justice. *Law Courts.*

pâle *adj. pale.*

palette *f. palette.*

palier *m. landing of a flight of stairs.*

pâlir *to turn pale.*

palissade *f. fence.*

palmier *m. palm tree.*

palper *to feel.*

palpitation *f. palpitation.*

palpiter *to palpitate.*

se pâmer *to faint; be enraptured.*

pamplemousse *m. grapefruit.*

panier *m. basket.*
> Un panier à papiers. *A wastepaper basket.*

panique *f. panic.*

panne *f. breakdown.*
> L'auto est en panne. *The car broke down.*
> Avoir une panne d'essence (une panne sèche). *To be, run out of gasoline.*
> La panne d'allumage. *Ignition trouble.*
> La panne de moteur. *Engine trouble.*

panneau *m. (panneaux pl.) panel; trap.*
> Le panneau de la porte. *The door panel.*
> Il a donné dans le panneau. *He fell into the trap.*

panorama *m. panorama.*

panoramique *adj. panoramic.*

pansement *m. bandage.*

panser *to bandage.*

pantalon *m. pants, trousers.*

pantelant *adj. panting, gasping.*

pantomine *f. pantomime, mime show.*

pantoufle *f. slipper.*

papa *m. daddy, father.*

pape *m. pope.*

paperasses *f. pl. old wastepaper, scribbled papers; red tape.*

papeterie *f. stationery store.*

PAPIER *m. paper; document.*
> Papier à lettres. *Writing paper.*
> Papier d'emballage. *Wrapping paper.*
> Vos papiers sont en règle. *Your papers are in order.*
> Il est dans ses petits papiers (fam.) *He stands well (is in good) with him.*
> Rayez cela de vos papiers. *Don't count on any such thing.*

papillon *m. butterfly.*

papotage *m. gossip.*

papoter *to gossip.*

paquebot *m. liner.*

Pâques *m. pl. Easter.*

paquet *m. package, parcel, bundle.*

PAR *by, by means of, across, through.*
> Par contre. *On the other hand.*
> Par ici. *This way.*
> Par la suite. *In the course of time.*
> A en juger par. *Judging by.*
> Par la gare (chemin de fer), avion, bateau. *By, via railway, air(mail), ship.*
> Par exemple. *For example, for instance.*
> Par exprès. *Special delivery.*
> Par moments. *At times, occasionally.*
> Par une chaleur écrasante. *In stifling heat.*
> Par un si beau dimanche. *On such a beautiful Sunday.*
> Payer par heure (jour, semaine). *To pay by the hour (day, week).*
> Une fois par semaine (jour, mois, an). *Once a week (day, month, year).*

parachute *m. parachute.*

parade *f. parade.*

parader *to parade.*

paradis *m. paradise.*

paradoxe *m. paradox.*
paragraphe *m. paragraph.*
PARAÎTRE *to appear; be published.*
Vous paraissez être tout chose. *You seem out of sorts (not yourself, out of spirits).*
Un sourire parut sur ses lèvres. *A smile came to his lips.*
Il laisse trop paraître ses sentiments. *He betrays his feelings too much.*
A ce qu'il paraît. *Apparently.*
Quand ce livre paraîtra-t-il? *When will the book appear (be published)?*
Oui, paraît-il. *Yes, so it seems.*
parallèle *m. and f. noun and adj. parallel.*
paralyser *to paralyze.*
paralysie *f. paralysis.*
paralytique *m. and f. noun and adj. a paralytic; paralyzed.*
parapet *m. parapet.*
paraphrase *f. paraphrase.*
parapluie *m. umbrella.*
parasite *m. parasite, sponger.*
parasol *m. parasol.*
paratonnerre *m. lighting rod.*
parc *m. park.*
parcelle *f. particle.*
PARCE QUE *because, on account of.*
Je n'y ai pas été parce que j'étais fatigué. *I didn't go because I was tired.*
J'ai dû partir parce qu'il se faisait tard. *I had to leave because it was getting late.*
parchemin *m. parchment.*
parcimonie *f. stinginess.*
parcimonieux (parcimonieuse *f.*) *adj. stingy.*
parcourir *to travel through, run through.*
Il a parcouru le monde dans tous les sens. *He has been all over the world.*
J'ai parcouru le journal. *I glanced at (had a look at) the paper.*
Un frisson m'a parcouru. *A shiver ran up and down my spine.*
parcours *m. course, distance covered.*
Effectuer le parcours. *To cover the distance.*
PAR-DESSOUS *under.*
PAR-DESSUS *over.*
pardessus *m. overcoat.*
PAR-DEVANT *in front of.*
PARDON *m. pardon.*
Je vous demande pardon. *I beg your pardon. Pardon me.*
Pardon? *I didn't quite catch that. What did you say?*
pardonnable *adj. pardonable, excusable.*
PARDONNER *to pardon, forgive.*
Pardonnez-moi. *Pardon me.*
PAREIL (pareille *f.*) *adj. like, similar.*
En pareil cas. *In such cases. In a similar case.*

Un pareil travail. *A similar job. A job of this sort.*
pareille *f. the like.*
Je n'ai jamais vu la pareille. *I never saw the like.*
Ne manquez pas de lui rendre la pareille. *Be sure to pay him back in his own coin.*
pareillement *likewise; in the same manner.*
Et moi pareillement. *And so do I. (And so am I, etc.)*
parent *m. relative; pl. parents.*
parenté *f. relationship.*
parenthèse *f. parenthesis.*
parer *to adorn.*
paresse *f. laziness.*
paresseux (paresseuse *f.*) *adj. lazy, idle.*
PARFAIT *adj. perfect; finished.*
Parfait sous tous les rapports. *Perfect in every respect.*
Parfait! *Fine! Good!*
Voilà qui est parfait! *That's wonderful! That's perfect!*
C'est un parfait raseur (*fam.*) *He's a terrible bore.*
parfaitement *perfectly; exactly.*
Parfaitement, c'est ce que j'ai dit. *Exactly, that's just what I said.*
PARFOIS *sometimes.*
parfum *m. perfume.*
se parfumer *to use perfume.*
pari *m. bet.*
paria *m. outcast.*
parier *m. to bet.*
parité *f. equality.*
parjure *f. perjury.*
pariementer *to negotiate, parley.*
PARLER *to talk.*
Vous parlez trop vite. *You speak (you're speaking) too fast.*
On parle de vous. *People are talking about you.*
Parlez-vous sérieusement? *Are you serious?*
Parlez-moi de votre voyage. *Tell me about your journey (trip).*
se parler *to speak to each other.*
Ils ne se parlent plus. *They are no longer on speaking terms.*
parloir *m. parlor.*
PARMI *among.*
paroi *f. partition wall.*
paroisse *f. parish.*
PAROLE *f. word, speech.*
Avoir la parole. *To have the floor.*
La parole est à lui. *It's his turn to speak.*
Ce sont des paroles en l'air. *It's just idle talk. It's all talk. It's just a lot of talk.*
Parole d'honneur. *Word of honor. I give you my word of honor.*
Tenir sa parole. *To keep one's word.*

Rendre sa parole à quelqu'un. *To release someone from a promise.*

parquet *m. floor.*

parrain *m. godfather.*

parsemer *to stew.*

PART *f. share, portion, part.*

Il s'est attribué la meilleure part. *He took the best part for himself. ("He assigned the best part to himself.")*

Il n'est pas là, il a dû partir quelque part. *He isn't there. He must have gone somewhere.*

Dites-leur bien des choses aimables de notre part. *Give them our best regards.*

Ça c'est un cas à part. *That's quite another question.*

Et à part ça, quoi de neuf? *Apart from that, what else is new?*

C'est de la part de qui? *Who's calling? (telephone).*

Nulle part. *Nowhere.*

partage *m. share, division.*

Nous en avons fait le partage. *We divided it equally.*

partager *to share, divide, distribute.*

Partager en deux. *To divide in two.*

Voulez-vous partager notre dîner? *Will you share our dinner? Will you have a bite with us?*

partenaire *m. partner.*

parterre *m. flower bed.*

parti *m. party, side; decision.*

Un parti politique. *A political party.*

J'en ai pris mon parti. *I have made up my mind.*

Parti pris. *Preconceived notion. Prejudice.*

Tirer bon parti de quelque chose. *To turn something to good advantage.*

Il a pris parti pour lui. *He sided with him.*

Il ne sait quel parti prendre. *He doesn't know what to do.*

partial (partiaux *pl.*) *adj. partial.*

partialité *f. partiality.*

participation *f. participation.*

participe *m. participle.*

participer *to take part, participate in.*

particulier (particulière *f.*) *adj. particular, private.*

Je n'ai rien de particulier à vous dire. *I've nothing special to tell you.*

J'ai des raisons particulières pour ne pas y aller. *I have personal reasons for not going there.*

particulièrement *particularly, in particular.*

PARTIE *f. part, game.*

La plus grande partie de la journée. *The greater part of the day.*

En grande partie. *To a great (large) extent. In a large measure.*

Faire partie de. *To belong to. To be a member of.*

Il s'en est fallu de peu que je n'aie gagné la partie. *I came very near winning the game.*

Perdre la partie. *To lose the game.*

Partie nulle. *Game that ends in a draw.*

C'est une partie remise. *The pleasure is only deferred.*

Voulez-vous être de la partie? *Will you join us? Will you be one of us?*

PARTIR *to start; leave.*

A partir de demain. *Starting from tomorrow. Beginning tomorrow.*

Il est parti pour Paris. *He left for Paris.*

Partir en France. *To leave for France.*

Il partit d'un éclat de rire. *He burst out laughing.*

Votre raisonnement part d'un principe faux. *The basis of your argument is wrong. ("Your argument is based on a wrong foundation.")*

Il est parti de rien. *He rose from nothing.*

Il a maille à partir avec lui. *He has a bone to pick with him.*

partisan *m. partisan; advocate of, one in favor of.*

partition *f. partition.*

PARTOUT *everywhere.*

parure *f. jewelry; set.*

Une parure de diamants. *A set of diamonds.*

parvenir *to reach.*

Votre lettre m'est enfin bien parvenue. *Your letter finally reached me.*

Il est parvenu à ses fins. *He achieved his purpose. He attained his end.*

Parvenir à entrer. *To manage to get in.*

Il parviendra à le faire. *He'll succeed in doing it. He'll manage to do it.*

PAS *m. step; pace; footprint.*

Accélérons le pas. *Let's walk faster.*

Il a fait un faux pas. *He stumbled. He made a blunder.*

Il n'y a qu'un pas. *It's only a few steps away.*

Il habite à deux pas d'ici. *He lives a few steps away.*

A pas de loup. *By stealth. Stealthily.*

Il l'a tiré d'un mauvais pas. *He got him out of a fix.*

Il n'y a que le premier pas qui coûte. *Getting started is the only hard part. The beginning is the only difficulty.*

Le Pas de Calais. *The straits of Dover.*

PAS *not.*

Pourquoi pas? *Why not?*

Pas moi. *Not I.*

Pas si bête. *I'm not such a fool. I'm not that much of a fool.*

Ne . . . pas. *Not.*

Non pas. *Not.*

Pas du tout! *Not at all! No indeed!*

Pas pour le moment. *Not for the moment.*

Pas que je sache. *Not that I know (of).*

passable *adj. passable, fairly good.*

Le dîner était passable. *The dinner was fairly good.*

passade *f. short stay.*

passage *m. passage.*

Passage interdit au public. *No thoroughfare.*

On avait barré le passage. *They blocked the way.*

Le passage clouté. *Pedestrian crossing.*

passager *m. (passagère f.) passenger.*

passager *(passagère f.) adj. fleeting, transitory.*

passant *m. passerby.*

passe *f. pass.*

Le mot de passe. *Password.*

Il est dans une passe difficile. *He's in a difficult situation. He's in a tight corner (spot).*

passé *m. past, past things.*

Dans le passé. *In the past.*

passe-partout *m. passkey.*

passeport *m. passport.*

PASSER *to pass.*

Il est passé sur le quai. *He passed on to the platform.*

Passez me voir quand vous aurez le temps. *Look me up when you have time.*

J'ai passé l'été dernier à la même plage. *I spent last summer at the same beach.*

On ne passe pas. *No thoroughfare.*

Il sont passés maîtres dans cet art. *They are past masters in that art.*

Comme le temps passe! *How (quickly) time flies!*

Passons maintenant à un autre chapitre, voulez-vous? *Let's change the subject (drop the matter), shall we?*

Cette pièce est passée à la télévision. *This play is shown on television.*

Je passerai au bureau. *I'll stop in at the office.*

Je te passerai les mots croisés. *I'll give you the crossword puzzle.*

On peut passer? *Can we go through?*

Passer l'après-midi (la nuit). *To spend the afternoon (the night).*

Passer à la douane. *To clear, go through customs.*

Passer par le portillon automatique. *To go through the automatic gate.*

Passer par un magasin. *To stop at a store.*

Passez à la caisse. *Go to the cashier's desk.*

Passez-moi le 48.62.57 à Bordeaux. *Connect me with 48.62.57 (telephone) in Bordeaux.*

"Passez piétons." *"Pedestrians Walk" (traffic sign).*

Regarder passer les gens. *To watch the people passing by.*

SE PASSER *to happen; do without.*

Cela se passe couramment tous les jours. *It (that) takes place (happens) every day.*

Qu'est-ce qui se passe? *What's going on?*

Il faudra vous en passer. *You'll have to do without (dispense with) it.*

Je ne puis m'en passer. *I can't do without it.*

passerelle *f. footbridge, bridge (on a ship), gangway.*

passif *m. debts, liabilities; passive (grammar).*

L'actif et le passif. *Assets and liabilities.*

passif *(passive f.) adj. passive; on the debit side.*

passion *f. passion.*

passionnant *adj. thrilling.*

Une histoire passionnante. *A thrilling story.*

passionner *to excite.*

passoire *f. strainer.*

pasteur *m. pastor.*

patauger *to splash and flounder.*

pâte *f. paste; dough.*

pâté *m. patty; block; blot.*

Un pâté de maisons. *Block of buildings.*

J'ai fait un pâté. *I made a blot.*

patelin *m. small locality.*

patente *f. patent.*

patenté *adj. licensed.*

paternel *(paternelle f.) adj. paternal.*

paternité *f. fatherhood.*

pâteux *(pâteuse f.) adj. pasty, doughy, sticky, viscous, clammy.*

pathétique *adj. pathetic.*

pathos *m. affected pathos, bathos.*

patience *f. patience.*

Je suis à bout de patience. *("I'm at the end of my patience.") My patience is at an end. I've lost patience.*

patient *adj. patient.*

patin *m. skate.*

Des patins à roulettes. *Roller skates.*

Des patins à glace. *Ice skates.*

patinage *m. skating.*

patiner *to skate.*

pâtir *to suffer.*

Il a pâti la faim. *He suffered hunger.*

pâtisserie *f. pastry; pastry shop.*

patrie *f. native country.*

patrimoine *m. inheritance.*

patriote *m. and f. patriot.*

patriote *adj. patriotic.*

patriotisme *m. patriotism.*

patron *m. patron; employer, boss; pattern.*

Il est bien vu de son patron. *His employer (boss) thinks well of him.*

J'aime ce patron. *I like this pattern.*
patronage *m. patronage.*
patrouille *f. patrol.*
patrouiller *to patrol.*
patte *f. paw.*
pâturage *m. pasture.*
pâturer *to pasture.*
paume *m. palm.*
paupière *f. eyelid.*
pause *f. pause.*
pauvre *adj. poor.*
pauvrement *poorly.*
pauvreté *f. poverty.*
pavé *m. pavement.*
pavillon *m. pavilion; flag.*
payable *adj. payable.*
payant *adj. paying.*
Entrée payante. *No free admission.*
paye *f. pay.*
C'est le jour de paye, aujourd'hui. *Today's payday.*
payement *m. payment.*
payer *to pay.*
Il l'a payé de la même monnaie. *He paid him back in his own coin.*
Payez-lui son dû. *Give him his due.*
Faire payer les frais. *To have the expenses paid.*
PAYS *m. country.*
Voir du pays. *To travel.*
Elle a le mal du pays. *She's homesick.*
Il est en pays de connaissance. *He feels at home. He's among friends.*
paysage *m. landscape; scenery.*
paysan *m. peasant.*
peau *f. skin; peel.*
Il n'a que les os et la peau. *He's just skin and bone.*
Il a sauvé sa peau. *He saved his own skin.*
pêche *f. peach.*
pêche *f. fishing.*
péché *m. sin.*
pêcher *to fish.*
pécher *to sin.*
pécuniaire *adj. pecuniary, having to do with money.*
pédant *m. and f. noun and adj. pedant, pedantic.*
peigne *m. comb.*
Donner un coup de peigne. *To run the comb through the hair.*
peigner *to comb.*
peignoir *m. dressing gown.*
peindre *to paint, portray.*
PEINE *f. punishment; pain; trouble.*
Peine capitale. *Capital punishment.*
On lui a remis sa peine. *He was pardoned.*
Entrée interdite sous peine d'amende. *No admittance under penalty of law.*

Rien ne peut adoucir sa peine. *Nothing can relieve her sorrow.*
Cela m'a fait de la peine. *I feel sorry about that.*
Votre absence m'a mis en peine. *Your absence got me into (caused me a lot of) trouble.*
A grand-peine. *With much difficulty. With great difficulty.*
Ce n'est pas la peine. *It's not worthwhile. It's not worth the trouble.*
Il a peine à se soutenir. *He can hardly stand up (keep on his feet).*
Je le connais à peine. *I hardly know him.*
J'ai peine à croire que ce soit vrai. *I can hardly believe that's true.*
Il a de la peine à rester éveillé. *He can hardly remain awake.*
Avoir de la peine. *To grieve, be in sorrow.*
Ne vous donnez pas la peine. *Don't trouble.*
peintre *m. painter.*
peinture *f. painting; paint; picture.*
La peinture à l'huile. *Oil painting.*
péjoratif (péjorative *f.*) *adj. disparaging.*
pêle-mêle *pell-mell, in disorder, helter-skelter.*
peler *to peel.*
pèlerin *m. pilgrim.*
pèlerinage *m. pilgrimage.*
pelle *f. shovel.*
pellicule *f. film.*
Le rouleau de pellicules. *Roll of film.*
pelote *f. ball.*
pelouse *f. lawn.*
pelure *f. peel, skin.*
pénalité *f. penalty.*
penalty *m. penalty (soccer).*
penaud *adj. crestfallen.*
Il en est resté tout penaud. *He looked sheepish.*
penchant *m. slope; inclination, bent.*
Il est sur le penchant de sa ruine. *He's on the brink of ruin.*
Elle a un penchant pour la danse. *She likes to dance.*
pencher *to incline, bend, lean.*
se pencher *to lean.*
Ne vous penchez pas à la fenêtre. *Don't lean out of the window.*
PENDANT *during, while.*
J'ai été en Angleterre pendant huit jours. *I was in England for a week.*
Pendant que vous y êtes . . . *While you're on the subject . . . While you're at (about) it . . .*
pendre *to hang.*
Pendez ce tableau au mur. *Hang this picture on the wall.*
pendule *f. clock.*
pénétrer *to penetrate.*

pénible *adj. painful, difficult.*

Il m'est pénible de devoir dire cela. *It's painful for me (I hate) to have to say this.*

péniblement *painfully.*

péninsule *f. peninsula.*

pénitence *f. penitence; punishment.*

pensée *f. thought.*

Elle est absorbée dans ses pensées. *She's absorbed in her thoughts.*

Je l'ai fait avec la pensée que . . . *I did it with the thought in mind that . . .*

PENSER *to think, consider, intend.*

Y pensez-vous! *What an idea!*

Vous n'y pensez pas! *You don't mean it! You don't intend to do it!*

Ça me fait frémir quand j'y pense. *It gives me the shivers just to think about it.*

Quand pensez-vous faire un voyage au Canada? *When do you expect to take a trip to Canada? When are you planning to go to Canada?*

Faites-moi penser à cela. *Remind me of that.*

Qu'est-ce que vous pensez d'elle? *What's your opinion of her?*

Pensez donc! *Just imagine! Just think of it!*

Je pense à lui. *I'm thinking of him (her).*

J'y pense. *I'm thinking of it.*

Nous pensions louer une voiture. *We were thinking of renting a car.*

penseur *m. thinker.*

pensif (pensive *f.*) *adj. pensive.*

pension *f. pension; boardinghouse; board.*

Je suis en pension chez Mme. Dupont. *I'm boarding at Mrs. Dupont's.*

La pension est-elle bonne ici? *Is the food good in this boardinghouse? ("Is the board good here?")*

Elle a mis son fils en pension. *She sent her son to a boarding school.*

pensionnaire *m. boarder.*

pensionnat *m. boarding school.*

pente *f. slope, descent.*

pénurie *f. scarcity, dearth.*

pépin *m. pit, kernel.*

perçant *adj. piercing.*

percer *to pierce.*

PERDRE *to lose.*

Nous n'avons pas de temps à perdre. *We have no time to lose.*

Vous ne perdez rien pour attendre. *You'll lose nothing by waiting.*

Ne perdez donc pas votre temps à ces bêtises. *Don't waste your time on that nonsense.*

Perdre la raison. *To go mad. To lose one's mind (reason).*

Il courait à perdre haleine. *He ran until he was out of breath.*

PÈRE *m. father.*

M. Dupont père. *Mr. Dupont, senior.*

Il est bien le fils de son père. *He's a chip off the old block.*

perfection *f. perfection.*

A la perfection. *Perfectly.*

perfectionner *to perfect, improve.*

perfide *adj. perfidious, deceiving.*

perfidie *f. perfidy, treachery.*

perforer *to perforate.*

péril *m. danger, hazard.*

Faites-le à vos risques et périls. *Do it at your own risk.*

Il l'a aidé au péril de sa vie. *He helped him at the risk of his life.*

Mettre en péril. *To endanger. To imperil. To jeopardize.*

périlleux (périlleuse *f.*) *adj. perilous, risky.*

périmé *adj. out-of-date.*

période *f. period, age.*

périodique *noun (m.) and adj. periodic; periodical.*

péripétie *f. adventure.*

périr *to perish.*

perle *f. pearl.*

permanence *f. permanence.*

permanent *adj. permanent.*

PERMETTRE *to permit.*

Permettez-moi de vous présenter à ma soeur. *Allow me to introduce you to my sister.*

Permettez que je vous accompagne. *May I go along with you? May I accompany you? ("Allow me to accompany you.")*

Vous permettez?—Faites donc! *May I?—Of course!*

Me permettez-vous de fumer? *Do you mind my smoking? Do you mind if I smoke?*

Cet argent lui permit de faire un long voyage. *That money enabled him to take a long trip.*

Il se croyait tout permis. *He thought he could do anything.*

Permis à vous de ne pas me croire. *You're free to believe me or not.*

Permettez! 1. *Excuse me! Allow me!* 2. *Wait a minute! Not so fast!*

Si madame permet. *If madame will permit.*

se permettre *to allow oneself, take the liberty.*

Il se permet beaucoup trop de choses. *He takes too many liberties.*

Si je peux me permettre de vous faire une observation. *If I may take the liberty of remarking.*

Je ne peux pas me le permettre. *I can't afford it.*

permis *m. license, permit.*

permission *f. permission; leave, furlough.*

Vous avez ma permission. *You have my permission.*

Demander la permission. *To ask permission.*

Il est en permission. *He's on leave (on furlough).*

pernicieux (pernicieuse *f.*) *adj. pernicious.*

perpendiculaire *adj. perpendicular.*

perpétuel (perpétuelle *f.*) *adj. perpetual, everlasting, endless.*

perpétuellement *perpetually.*

perpétuité *f. perpetuity.*

Prison à perpétuité. *Life imprisonment.*

perplexe *adj. puzzled.*

perquisition *f. search.*

Un mandat de perquisition. *A search warrant.*

La police a fait une perquisition chez lui. *The police searched his house.*

perquisitionner *to make a search.*

perroquet *m. parrot.*

perruque *f. wig.*

persécuter *to persecute.*

persécution *f. persecution.*

persévérance *f. perseverance.*

persévérer *to persevere, persist.*

persistance *f. persistence.*

persister *to persist.*

personnage *m. person; distinguished person; a somebody; character (play)*

personnalité *f. personality.*

PERSONNE *f. person, individual.*

La personne dont je vous ai parlé . . . *The person I spoke to you about . . .*

Les enfants ne sont admis qu'accompagnés par de grandes personnes. *Children must be accompanied by adults.*

Une personne de marque. *A man of note. An important (outstanding) man.*

PERSONNE *anyone, anybody, no one, nobody.*

Heureusement, personne n'a été blessé dans l'accident. *Fortunately, no one was hurt (injured) in the accident.*

Je n'y suis pour personne. *I'm not at home to anybody.*

Personne n'est venu. *Nobody came. No one came.*

Qui est venu?—Personne. *Who came?—No one.*

personnel *m. staff, personnel.*

personnel (personnelle *f.*) *adj. personal.*

personnellement *personally.*

personnifier *to personify; impersonate.*

Elle est la bonté personnifiée. *She's kindness itself.*

perspective *f. perspective.*

perspicace *adj. perspicacious, shrewd.*

perspicacité *f. perspicacity, insight.*

persuader *to persuade, convince.*

Il est persuadé qu'il réussira. *He imagines (he's sure, convinced) he'll succeed.*

Nous sommes persuadés que vous nous aiderez. *We feel confident that you'll help us.*

persuasif (persuasive *f.*) *adj. persuasive.*

persuasion *f. persuasion.*

perte *f. loss.*

Profits et pertes. *Profit and loss.*

A perte de vue. *As far as the eye can reach.*

Il raisonne toujours à perte de vue. *He never stops arguing.*

pertinent *adj. pertinent, relevant.*

perturbation *f. perturbation, disturbance.*

pervers *adj. perverse, depraved, wicked.*

pervertir *to corrupt.*

pesant *adj. heavy, weighty.*

peser *to weigh.*

Combien cela pèse-t-il? *How much does it (this) weigh?*

Pesez bien vos paroles. *Weigh your words carefully.*

peste *f. plague.*

pétard *m. firecracker.*

pétillement *m. crackling, sparkling.*

pétiller *to crackle.*

Le bois pétille. *The wood is crackling.*

Elle pétille d'esprit. *She's very witty.*

PETIT *adj. small.*

Un petit bout, s'il vous plaît. *A little bit, please.*

Petit à petit. *Bit by bit. Little by little.*

Ne faites pas la petite bouche. *Don't mince matters. Don't beat about the bush.*

La petite monnaie. *Small change.*

PETIT DÉJEUNER *m. breakfast.*

pétition *f. petition.*

pétrifier *to petrify.*

pétrin *m. kneading-trough.*

Eh bien, il est dans un beau pétrin (*fam.*) *Well, he's in a fine mess (fix).*

pétrole *m. petroleum, oil.*

Une lampe à pétrole. *A kerosene lamp.*

pétulance *f. petulance, liveliness.*

PEU *m. a little; a few.*

J'en ai peu. *I have a few. I've got a few.*

Peu à peu. *Little by little.*

Ce chapeau est un peu juste. *This hat is a little too tight.*

Faites voir un peu. *Just show me.*

Ne vous inquiétez donc pas pour si peu de chose. *Don't let such trifles disturb you.*

Il y a un peu plus de trois semaines. *A little over three weeks ago.*

Je vous demande un peu! *I ask you! How do you like that!*

Mais pourquoi, je vous demande un peu! *But why, I'd like to know.*

Ce n'est pas peu dire. *That's saying a good deal.*

En peu de mots, voilà l'histoire. *Here's the story in a nutshell ("in a few words").*

Un tout petit peu. *Just a little bit.*

peuple *m. people, nation.*

PEUR *f. fear, fright, terror.*

Il a peur. *He's afraid.*

Il en a été quitte pour la peur. *He got off with just a fright.*

Il en est presque mort de peur. *He nearly died of fright. It nearly frightened him to death.*

J'ai peur qu'il ne vienne pas. *I'm afraid he won't (may not) come.*

De peur que. *For fear that.*

peureux (peureuse *f.*) *adj. easily frightened.*

PEUT-ÊTRE *maybe, perhaps.*

phare *m. lighthouse; headlight.*

pharmacie *f. pharmacy, drugstore.*

pharmacien *m. pharmacist, druggist.*

phénomène *m. phenomenon.*

philosophe *m. philosopher.*

philosophie *f. philosophy.*

phonographe *m. record player, phonograph.*

photo *f. photo.*

photocopie *f. photocopy.*

photocopieur *m. photocopier.*

photographe *m. photographer.*

photographie *f. photography.*

Le magasin de photographie. *Camera shop.*

photographier *to photograph, take a snapshot.*

photographique *adj. photographic.*

Un appareil photographique. *A camera.*

phrase *f. sentence.*

physionomie *f. face.*

physique *f. physics.*

physique *adj. physical.*

pianiste *m. and f. pianist.*

piano *m. piano.*

Jouer du piano. *To play the piano.*

pic *m. pick; peak.*

PIÈCE *f. piece; room; play; coin.*

Il l'a mis en pièces. *He broke it to pieces.*

Des pièces de rechange. *Spare parts.*

Ça rafraîchira la pièce. *That will cool the room.*

Cette pièce est très courue. *This play is very popular.*

Il lui rendra la monnaie de sa pièce. *He'll pay him back in the same coin.*

Les pièces d'identité. *Identification papers.*

PIED *f. foot.*

Mon pied a glissé et je suis tombé. *My foot slipped and I fell.*

Un coup de pied. *A kick.*

A pied. *By foot. On foot.*

Combien y a-t-il à pied d'ici à la gare? *How long does it take to walk from here to the station?*

Doigt de pied. *Toe.*

Sur la pointe des pieds. *On tiptoe.*

Ne vous laissez pas marcher sur les pieds. *Don't let people take advantage of you (step all over you).*

Il était armé de la tête aux pieds. *He was armed to the teeth.*

On l'a mis au pied du mur. *He was cornered. He was with his back to the wall. They had him with his back to the wall.*

Il a mis l'affaire sur pied. *He got the business started.*

Il a dû se lever du pied gauche. *He must have gotten up on the wrong side of the bed.*

Le tour (la promenade) à pied. *Walk, stroll.*

piège *m. trap, snare.*

PIERRE *f. stone, flint, rock.*

Il a un coeur de pierre. *He has a heart of stone. He is merciless (heartless).*

L'âge de pierre. *The Stone Age.*

Il gèle à pierre fendre. *It's freezing (out).*

Une pierre à briquet. *A flint (for a lighter).*

piété *f. piety.*

piétiner *to trample, stamp.*

piéton *m. pedestrian.*

piètre *adj. paltry, poor.*

C'est un piètre nageur. *He's a poor swimmer.*

pieux (pieuse *f.*) *adj. pious, devout.*

pigeon *m. pigeon.*

pile *f. heap; reverse (of coin).*

Une pile de livres. *A pile of books.*

Pile ou face. *Heads or tails.*

pilier *m. pillar.*

pillage *m. pillage, looting.*

piller *to plunder.*

pilote *m. pilot.*

piloter *to pilot; to lead, guide, show around; to show someone the way.*

pilule *f. pill.*

pince *f. grip; pincers.*

pinceau *m. (pinceaux pl.) paintbrush.*

pincer *to pinch.*

Ping-Pong *m. Ping-Pong.*

pipe *f. pipe.*

pique *m. spade (cards).*

pique-assiette *m. sponger.*

piquer *to prick, stitch; excite, pique, nettle.*

Les moustiques m'ont piqué cette nuit. *I was bitten up by mosquitoes last night.*

Cela a piqué sa curiosité. *That aroused his curiosity.*

Ella a été piquée au vif par ces paroles. *She was greatly piqued (nettled) by this remark.*

se piquer *to pride oneself; pretend.*

Il se pique de son savoir. *He likes to think he knows it all.*

piqûre *f. sting; injection.*

PIRE *m. adj. worst; worse.*

Le pire c'est que . . . *The worst part is . . . The worst is that . . .*

Ce qu'il y a de pire . . . *What's worse . . .*

C'était bien pire. *That was much worse.*

PIS *worse.*

Il met les choses au pis. *He assumes the worst.*

En mettant les choses au pis, on ne perdra pas tout. *If worse comes to worst, we won't lose anything.*

Chaque jour cela va de mal en pis. *It gets worse daily. Everyday it goes from bad to worse.*

piscine *f. swimming pool.*

piste *f. track.*

Être sur la piste de. *To be on the track of.*

Nous faisons fausse piste. *We're on the wrong track.*

pistolet *m. pistol, gun.*

piston *m. piston.*

Il a du piston. *He has pull.*

piteux (piteuse *f.*) *adj. pitiful, sorry.*

Ils sont revenus dans un piteux état. *They came back in a very sorry condition.*

Il fait une assez piteuse figure. *He was a pretty sorry figure.*

PITIÉ *f. pity.*

Il me fait pitié. *I feel sorry for him.*

Il l'a pris en pitié. *He took pity on him.*

Quelle pitié! *What a pity!*

pitoyable *adj. pitiable, wretched.*

pitoyablement *woefully.*

pittoresque *adj. picturesque, quaint.*

pivot *m. pivot.*

Un point de pivot dans l'histoire. *A turning point in history.*

pivoter *to pivot.*

placard *m. poster; cupboard.*

PLACE *f. place, spot; seat.*

Il ne peut pas rester en place. *He can't stand still.*

Je vais essayer d'avoir des places. *I'll try to get seats.*

A votre place, je n'accepterais pas. *If I were in your place, I wouldn't accept.*

Je ne voudrais pas être à sa place. *I wouldn't like to be in his shoes (place).*

Je viens à la place de mon frère. *I've come instead of my brother.*

Faites place! *Make room!*

Remettre quelqu'un à sa place. *To put someone in his place. To take someone down a peg or two.*

Il est sans place. *He's out of a job.*

Une place assise. *Seat (bus).*

On fait tout sur place. *Everything is done on the premises.*

placement *m. placing; investment.*

Bureau de placements. *Employment agency.*

Il a fait un placement avantageux. *He made a good investment.*

PLACER *to place.*

Placez cela sur la table. *Put that on the table.*

Cet article est difficile à placer. *This article (item) is hard to sell.*

Impossible de placer un mot! *It's impossible to get a word in edgewise!*

Placer son argent à l'intérêt. *To invest one's money at interest.*

plafond *m. ceiling.*

plage *f. beach.*

plaider *to plead.*

plaie *f. wound.*

plaindre *to pity.*

Elle est bien à plaindre. *You really have to feel sorry for (pity) her.*

se plaindre *to complain.*

Il est toujours en train de se plaindre. *He's always complaining.*

Je vois ce dont vous vous plaignez. *I see what you're complaining of.*

plaine *f. plain.*

plainte *f. complaint.*

Formulez vos plaintes par écrit. *State your complaints in writing.*

plaintif (plaintive *f.*) *adj. plaintive.*

plaire *to be pleasant, please.*

Ça ne me plaît pas. *I don't like that.*

Plaît-il? *I didn't quite catch that. Will you please say that again?*

S'il vous plaît. *Please.*

Comme il vous plaira. *As you please. As you wish.*

se plaire *to like, enjoy.*

Il s'y plaît. *He likes it there.*

Il se plaît à contrarier les gens. *He takes pleasure in contradicting people.*

plaisant *adj. pleasant, agreeable.*

plaisanter *to joke.*

Vous plaisantez! *You're joking! You don't really mean it!*

Il ne plaisante jamais en affaires. *He takes his business matters very seriously. ("He never trifles about business.")*

plaisanterie *f. joke.*

Il entend la plaisanterie. *He can take a joke.*

Il l'a fait par plaisanterie. *He did it in jest (as a joke).*

Tourner une chose en plaisanterie. *To laugh a thing off.*

PLAISIR *m. pleasure, amusement; consent.*

Train de plaisir. *Excursion train.*

C'était plaisir de l'entendre. *It was a pleasure to hear him.*

Faire plaisir à quelqu'un. *To please someone.*

Voulez-vous me faire un plaisir? *Will you please do me a favor?*

Je le ferai avec plaisir. *I'll be glad to do it.*

plan *m. plan, design, scheme.*

Leurs plans ont échoué. *Their plans failed (fell through).*

Il m'a laissé en plan (*fam.*). *He left me in the lurch.*

Le premier plan. *Foreground (painting).*

planche *f. board, plank; shelf.*

plancher *m. floor.*

planer *to soar.*

planète *f. planet.*

plante *f. plant; sole of the foot.*

planter *to plant.*

plaque *f. plate, sheet.*

plastique *adj. plastic.*

plat *m. dish.*

Ce plat est bien assaisonné. *This dish (food) is well seasoned.*

Il a mis les pieds dans le plat. *He made a blunder. He put his foot in it.*

Quel est le plat du jour? *What's the special on today's menu? What's today's special?*

plat *adj. flat, plain, dull.*

Il a les pieds plats. *He has flat feet.*

Plat comme une galette. *As flat as a pancake.*

Elle a les cheveux plats. *She has straight hair.*

Un pneu à plat. *Flat tire.*

plateau *m. tray.*

platine *m. platinum.*

platitude *f. platitude.*

plâtre *m. plaster.*

plausible *adj. plausible.*

plein *m. full part; height.*

Le plein de la mer. *High tide.*

La fête bat son plein. *The festival is at its height.*

PLEIN *adj. full, filled, complete.*

Plein de monde. *Crowded.*

Observation pleine d'esprit. *Witty remark.*

Il est plein de vie. *He's full of life.*

En plein air. *In the open air, out of doors.*

Faire le plein (d'essence). *To fill up (with gasoline).*

pleur *m. tear.*

pleurard *adj. whining.*

pleurer *to cry, weep.*

pleurnicher *to whimper.*

pleutre *m. coward.*

pleuvoir *to rain.*

Il recommence à pleuvoir. *It's starting to rain again.*

Pleuvoir à verse. *To pour.*

Les lettres de félicitation pleuvèrent. *Congratulatory notes poured in.*

pli *m. fold, crease.*

Une mise en plis. *A hair-setting.*

plier *to fold, bend.*

Il a plié son journal. *He folded his paper.*

Il a plié bagage et est parti. *He packed (up) and left.*

Tout plie devant lui. *He carries all before him.*

plomb *m. lead.*

plomber *to fill (tooth).*

plombier *m. plumber.*

plongée *f. dive.*

La plongée sous-marine. *Scuba diving.*

plongeon *m. dive; diving; plunge.*

Faire un plongeon. *To dive.*

plonger *to plunge, dive.*

se plonger *to plunge.*

ployer *to bend, bow.*

plu *pleased.*

PLUIE *f. rain.*

Une pluie torrentielle. *A heavy rain. A heavy downpour.*

Parler de la pluie et du beau temps. *To talk about the weather.*

plume *f. feather, quill; pen.*

plumeau *m. (plumeaux pl.) feather duster.*

plupart *f. the greater part.*

La plupart d'entre eux sont d'accord avec moi. *Most of them agree with me.*

La plupart du temps. *Generally. Most of the time.*

pluriel *m. plural.*

PLUS *more, most, farther, further.*

Je ne lui en donnerai plus. *I don't give him any more.*

Elle a tout au plus vingt ans. *She is twenty at most.*

Plus j'essaie moins je réussis. *The more I try the less I succeed.*

Vous auriez pu venir plus tôt. *You might have come sooner.*

En plus. *Extra, additional.*

Ne . . . plus. *No longer, no more.*

Plus de trois minutes. *More than three minutes.*

PLUSIEURS *several, many, some.*

Plusieurs fois. *Several times.*

Plusieurs personnes. *Several people.*

J'en ai plusieurs. *I have several (of them).*

PLUTÔT *sooner, rather.*

Il fait plutôt froid. *It's rather cold.*

Plutôt que. *Rather than.*

Plutôt mourir! *I'd sooner die!*

pneu *m. tire.*

pneumonie *f. pneumonia.*

poche *f. pocket.*

Format de poche. *Pocket-sized.*

C'est dans la poche. *It's in the bag.*

poêle *m. stove; f. frying pan.*

poésie *f. poetry.*

poète *m. poet.*

poétique *adj. poetical.*

poids *m. weight, heaviness, gravity, burden.*

poignant *adj. poignant, heart-gripping.*

poignard *m. dagger.*

poignée *f. handful.*

poignet *m. wrist.*

poil *m. hair, fur.*

poinçonner *to punch.*

poing *m. fist.*

POINT *m. point; period.*

Point de vue. *Point of view.*

Mettre au point. *To perfect.*

Jusqu'à un certain point je suis d'accord. *Up to a certain point, I agree.*

Sur ce point. *On that score.*

Point. *Period.*

Deux points. *Colon.*

Point virgule. *Semicolon.*

Point d'interrogation. *Question mark.*

Point d'exclamation. *Exclamation mark.*

Le point du jour. *Dawn.*

POINT *no, not, not at all.*

Peu ou point. *Little or none at all.*

Je n'en veux point. *I don't want that at all. I don't like that at all.*

Ce n'est point de mon ressort. *It's not at all in my province.*

pointe *f. point.*

Sur la pointe des pieds. *On tiptoe.*

pointiller *to dot.*

pointilliste *noun (m. and f.) and adj. pointillist (painting, artist).*

pointu *adj. sharp, pointed.*

pointure *f. size (shoes, socks, stockings, gloves, hats).*

poire *f. pear.*

pois *m. pea.*

Des petits pois. *Green peas.*

poison *m. poison.*

poisson *m. fish.*

poitrine *f. chest.*

poivre *m. pepper.*

pôle *m. pole.*

poli *adj. polite.*

police *f. police; policy.*

poliment *politely.*

polir *to polish; refine.*

polisson (polissonne *f.*) *adj. naughty child.*

politesse *f. politeness.*

politicien (politicienne *f.*) *noun and adj. politician.*

politique *f. politics, policy.*

politique *adj. political.*

poltron (poltronne *f.*) *adj. cowardly.*

POMME *f. apple.*

Ces pommes sont aigres. *These apples are sour.*

Pommes de terre frites. *French-fried potatoes.*

pompe *f. pomp, ceremony.*

pompe *f. pump.*

pompeux (pompeuse *f.*) *adj. pompous.*

pompier *m. fireman.*

ponctuel (ponctuelle *f.*) *adj. punctual.*

ponctuer *to punctuate.*

pondre *to lay (eggs).*

pont *m. bridge.*

populaire *adj. popular.*

population *f. population.*

porc *m. pig; pork.*

Côtelettes de porc. *Pork chops.*

porcelaine *f. porcelain.*

pore *m. pore.*

port *m. harbor, port, shelter; bearing; carrying.*

Ils sont arrivés à bon port. *They arrived safe and sound.*

Faire naufrage au port. *To fail with one's goal in sight. To be shipwrecked in port (in sight of the harbor).*

Franco de port. *Postage prepaid. Delivery free.*

Elle a un port de reine. *She has a very stately appearance (bearing).*

portant *adj. bearing, carrying.*

Il n'est pas bien portant. *His health is poor.*

Il a tiré sur lui à bout portant. *He shot at him point-blank.*

portatif *m. laptop*

PORTE *f. door.*

Fermez la porte. *Close the door.*

porte-bagages *m. luggage rack (car).*

porte-bonheur *m. good-luck charm.*

porte-cigare *m. cigar holder; pl. cigar case.*

porte-cigarette *m. cigarette holder; pl. cigarette case.*

porte-clefs *m. pl. keyring.*

portefaix *m. porter.*

portefeuille *m. wallet; briefcase; portfolio.*

portemanteau *m. coat-stand; coat-hanger.*

porte-mine *m. automatic pencil.*

porte-monnaie *m. purse.*

porte-parole *m. spokesperson.*

PORTER *to bear, carry; wear.*

Je ne peux pas porter ce paquet, il est trop lourd. *I can't carry this package—it's too heavy.*

Toutes deux portaient des jupes bleues. *Both were wearing blue skirts.*

SE PORTER *to be worn; to go; to be (of health).*

C'est tout ce qui se porte en ce moment. *That's the latest fashion. Everyone's wearing that now.*

Il s'est porté à son secours. *He went to his aid.*

Je ne m'en porte pas plus mal. *I'm none the worse for it.*

Comment vous portez-vous? *How are you?*

Je me porte à ravir. *I'm in excellent health.*

porteur *m. bearer; porter.*

Payable au porteur. *Payable to bearer.*

Un porteur portait leurs valises. *A porter carried their suitcases.*

portière *f. carriage door, car door.*

portillon (automatique) *m. (automatic) gate (subway).*

portion *f. portion, helping.*

portrait *m. portrait, picture.*

pose *f. attitude, posture; exposure (photography).*

pose-mètre *m. exposure meter, light meter.*

POSER *to place, lay down; pose; ask (a question).*

Posez le paquet sur la table. *Put this package on the table.*

Il pose. *He's very affected. He shows off.*

Je vais vous poser une question. *I'm going to ask you a question.*

Ce problème qui se pose à nous est ardu. *We have a difficult problem before us.*

poseur (poseuse *f.*) *adj. person who poses, affected person.*

position *f. position.*

posséder *to possess, own.*

possession *f. possession, property.*

possibilité *f. possibility.*

POSSIBLE *adj. possible.*

Est-ce qu'il vous sera possible de venir avec nous? *Will it be possible for you to come with us?*

postal *adj. postal.*

La carte postale. *Postcard.*

POSTE *f. post office; mail.*

Le bureau de poste. *The post office.*

Vous trouverez la poste dans la première rue à droite. *The post office is on the first street to your right.*

La poste aérienne. *Airmail.*

Le bureau des P. et T. (Postes et Télécommunications). *Post office.*

La poste restante. *General delivery.*

poste *m. post, station.*

Le poste de douane. *Customs station, customs house.*

postérieur *adj. posterior.*

postérité *f. posterity.*

posthume *adj. posthumous.*

post-scriptum *m. postscript.*

posture *f. posture.*

pot *m. jug, can, jar.*

Sourd comme un pot. *As deaf as a doorknob.*

Ne tournez pas autour du pot! *Don't beat around the bush!*

potable *adj. drinkable; good enough.*

L'eau est potable. *The water is drinkable.*

Le travail est potable. *The work is fairly good.*

potage *m. soup.*

poteau *m. (poteaux pl.) post, stake.*

potence *f. gallows.*

potentiel (potentielle *f.*) *adj. potential.*

potin *m. gossip; row, rumpus.*

Elles font des potins. *They're gossiping.*

Il fait du potin. *He's raising a rumpus.*

potion *f. potion, medicine.*

poubelle *f. garbage can.*

pouce *m. thumb.*

poudre *f. powder, dust, gunpowder.*

poudrer *to powder.*

pouffer *to burst out.*

Il a pouffé de rire (*fam.*) *He burst out laughing.*

poule *f. hen, fowl.*

poulet *m. chicken.*

poulie *f. pulley.*

pouls *m. pulse.*

poumon *m. lung.*

poupée *f. doll.*

POUR *for, for the sake of, on account of, on the part of, toward.*

Faites cela pour moi. *Do it for me (for my sake).*

J'en ai pour un mois. *It will take me a month.*

Le pour et le contre. *The pros and cons.*

Pour ainsi dire. *As it were. So to speak.*

Comment fait-on pour . . . *How does one go about . . .*

Pour commencer. *To begin with.*

Pour toujours. *Forever.*

S'arranger (avec quelqu'un) pour . . . *To arrange (with someone) to . . .*

Pour que. *So that, in order that.*

pourboire *m. tip.*

pour cent *m. percentage.*

pourcentage *m. percentage.*

pourchasser *to pursue.*

pourparler *m. negotiation.*

Entrer en pourparlers. *To enter into negotiations.*

POURQUOI *why.*

Pourquoi pas? *Why not?*

C'est pourquoi je vous demande d'y aller. *That's why I ask (I'm asking) you to go there.*

Pourquoi faire? *Why? What for?*

pourrir *to rot, decay.*

pourriture *f. rotting, decay, rot.*

poursuite *f. pursuit, lawsuit.*

poursuivre *to pursue.*

POURTANT *however, yet, still.*

Il habite la France depuis peu de temps et pourtant il parle très bien le français. *He's been in France for only a short while, yet he speaks French very well.*

Il a beaucoup de talent et pourtant il n'a jamais rien fait. *He's talented, yet he's never managed to achieve anything. Though he's very talented, he's never accomplished anything.*

Pourtant vous progressez, cela ne fait pas de doute. *Still you're progressing, there's no doubt of that.*

Pourtant j'aurais bien voulu la voir. *Still I should like to have seen her.*

Pourtant vous avez raison. *You're right, nevertheless.*

C'est comme ça pourtant. *Believe it or not.*

pourvoir *to provide.*

pourvu que *provided that.*

Je viendrai pourvu que je finisse mon travail. *I'll come provided I finish my work.*

Pourvu qu'il revienne vite. *I hope he'll return very soon.*

Pourvu que nous puissions monter! *I only hope we can get on!*

pousser *to push, shove; to grow (hair, etc.).*

Poussé par la pitié. *Prompted by pity.*

Il lui a poussé la main. *He forced his hand.*

L'herbe pousse très vite. *The grass grows very quickly.*

poussière *f. dust.*

poutre *f. beam.*

POUVOIR *m. power, ability, authority.*

Pouvoir d'achat. *Purchasing power.*

Il a un grand pouvoir sur lui. *He has a great influence over him.*

Il exerce un pouvoir. *He has power of attorney.*

POUVOIR *to be able, have power, be allowed.*

Je ne peux (puis) pas venir. *I can't come.*

Cela se peut bien. *It's quite possible.*

On n'y peut rien. *There's nothing that can be done. It can't be helped.*

Si vous ne pouvez pas, dites-le. *If you can't, say so.*

Pouvez-vous m'indiquer où se trouve la poste? *Can you tell me where the post office is?*

Je n'en peux plus. *I'm exhausted.*

Vouloir c'est pouvoir. *Where there's a will there's a way.*

En quoi pourrais-je vous servir? *What can I do for you?*

En quoi puis-je vous être utile? *What can I do for you?*

Est-ce que je peux? *May I?*

Pourriez-vous . . . *Could you . . .*

se pouvoir *to be possible.*

Il se peut qu'il soit parti. *He may have gone (left). It's possible that he's gone.*

Ça se peut. *That's possible.*

prairie *f. meadow.*

pratique *f. practice, performance.*

pratique *adj. practical.*

Il a beaucoup de sens pratique. *He has a great deal of common sense. He's very practical.*

pratiquer *to practice; carry out; make; play (sports).*

Voilà comment il faut pratiquer. *This is how the thing is done. This is the way you have to go about it.*

Pratiquer sa religion. *To practice one's religion.*

pré *m. meadow.*

préalable *m. first of all.*

Au préalable, allez-lui parler. *First of all, go (to) speak to him.*

précaire *adj. precarious.*

précaution *f. precaution.*

précédent *adj. preceding.*

Il m'a téléphoné le jour précédent. *He called me up the day before.*

précéder *to precede; take precedence.*

C'est dans le chapitre qui précède. *It's in the preceding chapter. It's in the chapter before this one.*

précepteur *m. (préceptrice f.) private tutor.*

prêcher *to preach.*

précieux *(précieuse f.) adj. precious, costly; affected.*

précipice *m. precipice.*

précipiter *to precipitate, hurl, throw down, plunge; hurry, hasten.*

Précipiter ses pas. *To hurry along.*

Il ne faut rien précipiter. *Never do things in a hurry. You mustn't hurry things. Let things take their course.*

se précipiter *to rush down; rush on; hurry.*

précis *adj. precise, accurate, concise.*

A vingt et une heures précises. *At exactly 9:00 P.M.*

précisément *precisely.*

préciser *to specify.*

précision *f. precision, accuracy.*

précoce *adj. precocious.*

précocité *f. precociousness.*

précurseur *m. forerunner, precursor.*

prédécesseur *m. predecessor.*

prédestiné *adj. predestined.*

prédiction *f. prediction.*

prédilection *f. predilection, preference.*

prédire *to predict, foretell.*

prédominant *adj. prevailing.*

prédominer *to prevail.*

préface *f. preface.*

préférable *adj. preferable.*
préféré *adj. favorite.*
préférence *f. preference.*
De préférence. *Preferably.*
PRÉFÉRER *to prefer.*
Laquelle préférez-vous? *Which (one) do you prefer?*
préjudice *m. prejudice, damage, harm.*
préjugé *m. presumption; prejudice.*
se prélasser *to enjoy comfort, lounge around; take things (life) easy.*
prélever *to deduct; to withdraw (money).*
préliminaire *adj. preliminary.*
prélude *m. prelude.*
prématuré *adj. premature.*
préméditation *f. premeditation.*
préméditer *to premeditate.*
PREMIER (première *f.*) *adj. first; former (of two).*
A la première occasion. *At the first opportunity.*
Matières premières. *Raw materials.*
Le premier rôle. *The leading role.*
En première. *In first class.*
En première page. *On the front page.*
Le premier plan. *Foreground (painting).*
Les quatre premières places. *The first four seats.*
se prémunir (contre) *to protect oneself from, guard against.*
PRENDRE *to take, grasp, seize, catch; to have (food, drink).*
Prenez-en. *Take some.*
Prenez tout cela en considération. *Take all that into consideration.*
Je sais comment le prendre. *I know how to manage him (deal with him).*
Où avez-vous pris cela? *Where did you get that idea?*
Il s'est laissé prendre. *He let himself be caught.*
Je vous prendrai en passant. *I'll call for you (pick you up) on the way.*
Qu'est-ce qui le prend? *What's the matter with him? What's come over him? What's gotten into him?*
Qu'est-ce que vous allez prendre! *You're in for it!*
Il a pris du poids. *He has gained weight.*
Prendre un billet. *To buy, get a ticket.*
Prendre la correspondance. *To change trains (subway).*
Prendre des renseignements. *To get information.*
se prendre *to be caught; set about.*
Il s'est pris d'amitié pour lui. *He took a liking to him.*
Il s'y est bien pris. *He set about it the right way.*

Il s'en est pris à lui. *He blamed him. He picked on him.*
prénom *m. Christian name, first name.*
préoccupation *f. preoccupation.*
préoccuper *to absorb one's thought, engross one's mind, preoccupy.*
Ses affaires le préoccupent. *He's engrossed in his business.*
se préoccuper *to give one's attention to, see to a matter, trouble oneself about.*
préparatifs *m. pl. preparations.*
préparation *f. preparation.*
préparer *to prepare, to make ready.*
Faire préparer une ordonnance. *To have a prescription filled.*
se préparer *to get ready.*
Je m'étais préparé à partir. *I had gotten ready to leave.*
Un orage se prépare. *A storm is gathering (brewing).*
prépondérant *adj. preponderant.*
PRÈS *near.*
Versailles est près de Paris. *Versailles is near Paris.*
Tout près. *Quite near. Close by.*
De près et de loin. *Near and far.*
A peu près. *Nearly. Almost. About.*
Il y avait à peu près vingt personnes. *There were about twenty people.*
Il y a près de deux ans. *Nearly two years ago.*
prescription *f. prescription.*
prescrire *to prescribe.*
présence *f. presence, attendance.*
Il l'a dit en ma présence. *He said it in my presence.*
Je ferai acte de présence. *I'll put in an appearance.*
présent *m. present (time).*
A présent. *Just now, at present.*
présent *adj. present.*
présentable *adj. presentable.*
présentation *f. presentation.*
Payable à présentation. *Payable on demand.*
Lettre de présentation. *Letter of introduction.*
présenter *to present, offer, introduce; deliver.*
se présenter *to present oneself, appear, occur.*
L'affaire se présente bien. *The business (affair, deal) sounds very promising.*
Une difficulté s'est présentée. *A difficulty arose.*
Si jamais le cas se présente. *If the case ever arises (comes up).*
Il s'est présenté chez elle. *He called on her.*
préservatif *m. condom, sheath.*
préservation *f. preservation.*
préserver *to preserve.*
présidence *f. presidency, chairmanship.*

président *m. president, chairman.*
  Président-Directeur Général (P-DG).
    Chairman.
présidentiel (présidentielle *f.*) *adj.*
    presidential.
présider *to preside.*
présomption *f. presumption.*
présomptueux (présomptueuse *f.*) *adj.*
    presumptuous.
PRESQUE *almost, nearly, all but.*
  C'est presque fini. *It's almost finished.*
  Il a presque réussi. *He almost succeeded.*
  Je ne le vois presque jamais. *I hardly ever*
    see him.
  Je l'ai eu pour presque rien. *I got it for*
    almost nothing (for a song).
pressant *adj. pressing, urgent.*
  C'est un cas pressant. *It's an urgent case.*
presse *f. haste; crowd; press.*
  Il n'y a pas de presse. *There's no hurry.*
  La presse quotidienne. *The daily press.*
pressentiment *m. foreboding.*
pressentir *to have a foreboding.*
presser *to squeeze; hasten; hurry.*
  Ça ne presse pas. *There's no hurry.*
  Je suis très pressé. *I'm in a great hurry.*
  C'est une affaire qui presse. *It's an urgent*
    matter.
  Un citron pressé. *Lemonade.*
se presser *to hurry.*
  Pressez-vous! *Hurry up!*
pressing *m. (dry) cleaner.*
pression *f. pressure.*
prestige *m. prestige.*
présumer *to presume, suppose.*
prêt *m. loan.*
prêt (à) *adj. ready (to).*
prétendre *to pretend; maintain; aspire to.*
  Il prétend que ce n'est pas vrai. *He*
    maintains that it isn't true.
  Prétendre à faire quelque chose. *To aspire to*
    do something.
prétentieux (prétentieuse *f.*) *adj. pretentious.*
prétention *f. pretention; claim.*
PRÊTER *to lend.*
  Pouvez-vous me prêter un livre? *Can you*
    lend me a book?
se prêter *to lend itself.*
  Cet appartement se prête à nos besoins. *This*
    apartment is suited to (suits) our needs.
prétexte *m. pretext, pretense.*
prêtre *m. priest.*
preuve *f. proof, evidence.*
prévaloir *to prevail.*
prévenant *adj. obliging, nice.*
prévenir *to anticipate; notify in advance;*
    forestall, ward off; warn.
  Prévenir les désirs de quelqu'un. *To*
    anticipate someone's wishes.

Prévenez-moi d'advance. *Let me know in*
    advance.
  En cas d'accident, prévenez ma famille. *In*
    case of accident, notify my family.
  Prévenir une maladie. *To ward off a*
    sickness.
prévision *f. anticipation; forecast.*
  Contre toute prévision. *Contrary to all*
    expectations.
prévoir *to forecast, foresee, look forward to.*
  Il a prévu tout ce qui est arrivé. *He foresaw*
    everything that happened.
  La réunion prévue pour demain n'aura pas
    lieu. *The meeting scheduled for*
    tomorrow will not take place.
  C'était à prévoir. *That was to be expected.*
prévoyance *f. forethought, precaution.*
prier *to pray, beg.*
  Entrez, je vous en prie. *Please come in.*
  Puis-je ouvrir la fenêtre?—Je vous en prie.
    May I open the window?—Please do.
    Of course.
  Il aime se faire prier. *He likes to be coaxed.*
prière *f. prayer, request, petition.*
primaire *adj. primary, elementary.*
prime *f. premium, bonus.*
prime *adj. first, early.*
  De prime abord. *At first. At first sight.*
primitif (primitive *f.*) *adj. primitive.*
prince *m. prince.*
principal *m. principal thing.*
  Le principal est de réussir. *The main thing is*
    to succeed.
principal (principaux *pl.*) *adj. principal, chief,*
    head.
principauté *f. principality.*
principe *m. principle; basis; rule.*
  C'est un de ses principes. *It's one of his*
    principles.
  En principe je ne le fais pas. *As a rule I*
    don't do it.
PRINTEMPS *m. spring.*
priorité *f. priority.*
pris *adj. caught.*
  Se trouver pris. *To be (get) caught.*
pris *f. taking, capture.*
  La prise de vue. *Shot (photography).*
  La prise en charge. *Taking over (rented car).*
prison *f. prison.*
prisonnier *m. prisoner.*
privation *f. privation, hardship.*
privé *adj. private.*
priver *to deprive.*
  Je ne vous en prive pas? *Can you spare it?*
privilège *m. privilege.*
privilégié *adj. privileged.*
PRIX *m. price, cost; prize, reward.*
  Il faut à tout prix que nous le fassions. *We*
    have to do it at any cost.

Articles de prix. *Expensive goods (merchandise).*

Le prix de rachat. *Resale price.*

Le prix global. *Total price.*

Le prix unitaire. *Unit price.*

probabilité *f. probability.*

PROBABLE *adj. probable, likely.*

PROBABLEMENT *probably.*

PROBLÈME *m. problem, puzzle.*

procédé *m. process; behavior.*

procéder *to proceed.*

procédure *f. procedure.*

procès *m. lawsuit, trial.*

processeur *m. word processor.*

procession *f. procession.*

procès-verbal *m. (official) report, written report of proceedings, minutes of a meeting, record (of evidence).*

PROCHAIN *adj. next, coming.*

La semaine prochaine. *Next week.*

La prochaine fois. *Next time.*

prochainement *shortly, soon.*

proche *adj. near, close at hand, approaching.*

proclamation *f. proclamation.*

proclamer *to proclaim.*

procurer *to procure, obtain, acquire.*

Pouvez-vous me procurer cela? *Can you get that for me?*

procureur *m. attorney.*

Procureur général. *Attorney General.*

Procureur de la République. *District attorney.*

prodigalité *f. prodigality, lavishness.*

prodige *m. marvel, wonder, prodigy.*

prodigieux (prodigieuse *f.*) *adj. prodigious, wonderful.*

prodigue *adj. prodigal, lavish.*

prodiguer *to squander, be lavish, give freely.*

production *f. production.*

produire *to produce.*

Quel effet a-t-elle produit sur lui? *What impression did she make on him?*

Cela n'a produit aucun effet. *It had no effect.*

Produire un titre. *To show one's title deeds.*

produit *m. produce; product; production.*

Il importe des produits étrangers. *He imports foreign products.*

Il est dans les produits alimentaires. *He's in the food business.*

profane *adj. profane.*

profaner *to profane, desecrate, violate, defile.*

professer *to profess.*

professeur *m. and f. teacher, professor.*

profession *f. profession; declaration.*

professionel (professionnelle *f.*) *adj. professional.*

professorat *m. professorship.*

profil *m. profile.*

profit *m. profit, gain, advantage.*

Profits et pertes. *Profit and loss.*

Faites-en votre profit. *Make the best of it.*

profitable *adj. profitable, advantageous.*

profiter *to profit, benefit; grow.*

PROFOND *adj. deep; dark.*

profondément *profoundly, deeply.*

profondeur *f. depth; profundity.*

profusion *f. profusion.*

programme *m. program.*

progrès *m. progress.*

progresser *to progress.*

progressif (progressive *f.*) *adj. progressive.*

prohiber *to prohibit.*

prohibition *f. prohibition.*

proie *f. prey.*

projet *m. project, scheme, design.*

prologue *m. prologue.*

prolonger *to prolong.*

promenade *f. walk, stroll; ride.*

Faire une promenade (à pied, en voiture). *To take (a walk or stroll, a ride).*

promener *to take (out) for a walk.*

Faire promener un chien. *To take a dog out for a walk.*

Il l'a envoyé promener. *He sent him packing.*

se promener *to go for a walk, ride.*

Se promener à bicyclette (à cheval). *To go bicycle (horseback) riding.*

promesse *f. promise.*

promettre *to promise.*

promotion *f. promotion.*

prompt *adj. prompt, quick, sudden, swift.*

Il est très prompt. *He's very prompt.*

Avoir la répartie prompte. *To be quick at repartee.*

Avoir l'esprit prompt. *To have a quick mind. To have a ready wit. To catch on quickly.*

promptement *promptly.*

Il a répondu promptement. *He answered promptly.*

promptitude *f. promptness.*

promulguer *to promulgate, issue.*

pronom *m. pronoun.*

prononcer *to pronounce.*

Comment le prononcez-vous? *How do you pronounce it?*

Est-ce que je le prononce bien? *Do I pronounce it right? Am I pronouncing it right?*

se prononcer *to declare.*

prononciation *f. pronunciation.*

propagande *f. propaganda.*

propager *to propagate, spread.*

prophète *m. prophet.*

prophétie *f. prophecy.*

propice *adj. propitious, favorable.*

proportion f. proportion; dimensions.
   Toutes proportions gardées. *Due allowance being made.*
propos m. purpose; talk.
   A propos, est-ce que vous venez avec nous? *By the way, are you coming with us?*
   Vous arrivez bien à propos. *You've come just in time.*
   Il est à propos. *It's desirable.*
   Mal à propos. *At the wrong time.*
   A propos de . . . *Speaking of . . .*
proposer to propose, offer.
se proposer to intend.
   Que se propose-t-elle de faire? *What does she intend to do?*
proposition f. proposition, offer, proposal.
PROPRE adj. own; clean, neat.
   A sa propre surprise. *To his own surprise.*
   Ses propres paroles. *His own words. His very words.*
   Le sens propre d'un mot. *The right meaning of a word.*
   Biens propres. *Personal property.*
   Un propre à rien. *A good-for-nothing.*
   Pas propre. *Not clean. Dirty.*
propreté f. cleanliness, neatness.
propriétaire m. proprietor, landlord.
propriété f. property.
prose f. prose.
prospère adj. prosperous.
prospérer to prosper.
prospérité f. prosperity, success.
protecteur (protectrice f.) noun and adj. protector; protective.
protection f. protection.
protéger to protect.
protestant m. Protestant.
protestation f. protestation.
protester to protest.
protocole m. protocol.
prouesse f. prowess.
prouver to prove, show.
provenir to proceed, result.
proverbe m. proverb.
providence f. providence.
province f. province.
   Une vie de province. *Country life.*
provision f. provision, stock.
provisoire adj. provisional, temporary.
   Un emploi provisoire. *A temporary job.*
provocant adj. provoking.
provocation f. provocation.
provoquer to provoke, stir up.
proximité f. proximity.
prudemment prudently, discreetly.
prudence f. prudence.
prudent adj. prudent, cautious.
prune f. plum.
pruneau m. prune.

prunier m. plum tree.
pseudonyme m. pseudonym.
psychiatre m. psychiatrist.
psychiatrie f. psychiatry.
psychologie f. psychology.
psychologique adj. psychological.
   Au moment psychologique. *At the psychological moment.*
psychologue m. psychologist.
pu been able.
public m. the public.
   Il l'a fait en public. *He did it publicly.*
publicité f. publicity, advertising, commercial.
publier to publish, make public.
puce f. flea.
   Le Marché aux Puces. *Flea Market.*
pudeur f. modesty.
puéril adj. puerile, childish.
PUIS then, afterwards; besides.
   Nous mangerons d'abord, puis nous irons au théâtre. *First we'll eat, then we'll go to the theatre.*
   Il est venu une fois nous voir, puis on ne l'a plus jamais revu. *He came to see us once and then we never saw him again.*
   Et puis? *What's next? What then?*
PUISQUE since, as.
   Puisqu'il ne vient pas, commençons sans lui. *Since he isn't coming, let's start without him.*
   Je n'y suis pas allé puisque vous me l'avez déconseillé. *I didn't go since you had advised me not to.*
puissance f. power.
puissant adj. powerful.
puits m. well.
punir to punish.
punition f. punishment.
pupille m. ward, minor in the charge of a guardian.
pupitre m. student's desk.
pur adj. pure.
purée f. purée, mash.
   Purée de pommes de terre. *Mashed potatoes.*
purement purely.
pureté f. purity.
purge f. purgative.
purification f. purification.
purifier to purify.
putride adj. putrid.
pyjama m. pajamas.

Q

quadruple m. quadruple, fourfold.
quai m. platform (train); wharf; embankment.

Je vous retrouverai sur le quai (d'une gare). *I'll meet you on the platform (of a railroad station).*

qualifier *to qualify.*

qualité *f. quality.*

QUAND *when.*

Quand viendrez-vous? *When will you come?*

Venez n'importe quand. *Come (at) any time.*

Quand même, vous n'auriez pas dû le faire. *Nevertheless you shouldn't have done it.*

Quand je vous le disais! *Didn't I tell you so!*

QUANT À *as for, as to.*

Quant à moi. *As for me.*

Quant à cela. *As for that.*

QUANTITÉ *f. quantity, abundance.*

QUARANTAINE *f. about forty.*

QUARANTE *noun and adj. forty.*

quarantième *noun and adj. fortieth.*

quart *m. quarter.*

Il est une heure moins le quart. *It's a quarter to one.*

Les trois quarts du temps, il ne fait rien. *Most of the time he does nothing.*

quartier *m. quarter; neighborhood.*

Coupez cette pomme en quartiers. *Cut this apple into quarters.*

J'habite dans ce quartier-ci. *I live in this neighborhood.*

QUATORZE *noun and adj. fourteen.*

QUATORZIÈME *noun and adj. fourteenth.*

QUATRE *noun and adj. four.*

Venez vers les quatre heures. *Come about four o'clock.*

Je demeure à quatre pas d'ici. *I live close by.*

Je me tenais à quatre pour ne pas éclater de rire. *It was all I could do to keep from laughing.*

quatre-vingt-cinq *noun and adj. eighty-five.*

QUATRE-VINGTIÈME *noun and adj. eightieth.*

QUATRE-VINGTS *noun and adj. eighty.*

QUATRIÈME *noun and adj. fourth.*

QUE *that, which.*

Je pense que c'est vrai. *I think that it's true.*

Je pense que non. *I think not.*

Les objets que vous voyez ici lui appartiennent. *The things which you see here belong to him.*

Ce que. *That which, what.*

QUE *than, that, as, what.*

Il est plus grand que sa soeur. *He's taller than his sister.*

Ne . . . que. *Only.*

Elle ne fait que parler. *She does nothing but talk.*

Que c'est ennuyeux! *How boring that is! What a bore!*

Que de monde! *What a crowd!*

Que de richesses! *What riches!*

QUEL (quelle *f.*) *adj. which, which one, what.*

Quel livre voulez-vous? *Which book do you want?*

Quel est son nom? *What's his name?*

Quelle heure est-il? *What time is it?*

Quel que soit le résultat, je le ferai. *Whatever the outcome may be, I'll do it.*

Quel âge avez-vous? *How old are you?*

Quelle est sa nationalité? *What is his nationality?*

Quel luxe! *What (a) luxury!*

QUELCONQUE *adj. any.*

Un livre quelconque. *Any book.*

Il est très quelconque. *He's very ordinary (common).*

C'est très quelconque. *It's very ordinary (common).*

QUELQUE *adj. some, any.*

Quelques amis sont venus hier soir. *Some friends came last night.*

Je l'ai vu il y a quelques jours. *I saw him a few days ago.*

J'ai vu quelque chose d'amusant. *I saw something amusing.*

Quelques-uns. *Some (things, people).*

A quelque chose malheur est bon. *It's an ill wind that blows nobody good.*

Quelque chose de meilleur (de différent). *Something better (different).*

QUELQUEFOIS *sometimes.*

Je le vois quelquefois. *I see him sometimes.*

QUELQUE PART *somewhere.*

QUELQU'UN *someone, somebody.*

querelle *f. quarrel.*

quereller *to quarrel.*

QU'EST-CE QUE *what.*

Qu'est-ce que c'est? *What's this? What is it?*

Qu'est-ce que c'est que cela? *What's that?*

QUESTION *f. question.*

Poser une question. *To ask a question.*

Sortir de la question. *To be beside the point.*

La personne en question. *The person in question.*

Il n'en est pas question. *It's out of the question.*

questionner *to question.*

quête *f. search; collection.*

Faire la quête. *To take up a collection (church).*

queue *f. tail; line.*

Il fait la queue. *He's waiting in line. He's waiting for his turn.*

A la queue leu leu. *One behind the other.*

Une histoire sans queue ni tête. *A senseless, disconnected story.*

Un piano à queue. *A grand piano.*

QUI *who, whom, which, that.*

Qui est-ce? *Who is he? Who is it?*

Qui désirez-vous voir? *Whom do you want to see?*

A qui est-ce? *Whose is this? To whom does this belong?*

A qui le tour? *Whose turn is it?*

quiconque *whoever.*

Quiconque veut venir. *Whoever wants to come.*

quille *f. ninepin.*

quincaillerie *f. hardware store.*

QUINZAINE *f. about fifteen.*

Dans une quinzaine. *In two weeks ("fifteen days").*

Une quinzaine (d'années). *About fifteen (years).*

QUINZE *noun and adj. fifteen.*

D'aujourd'hui en quinze. *Two weeks from today.*

QUINZIÈME *noun and adj. fifteenth.*

quittance *f. receipt.*

quitte *adj. free, out of debt; to be quits with.*

Etre quitte de dettes. *To be out of debt.*

Il en est quitte pour la peur. *He escaped with a good fright.*

Il en est quitte à bon marché. *He got off cheaply.*

Il est quitte envers vous. *He owes you nothing. He's even with you.*

QUITTER *to leave.*

Quitter la chambre. *To leave the room.*

A quelle heure quittez-vous votre travail? *At what time do you leave work?*

Il a quitté Paris. *He left Paris.*

Il a quitté prise. *He let go.*

Quitter ses habits. *To take off one's clothes.*

Ne le quittez pas des yeux. *Keep your eyes on him.*

Ne quittez pas. *Hold on, just a moment (telephone).*

qui-vive *m. alert.*

Il est sur le qui-vive. *He's on the alert.*

QUOI *what, which.*

Quoi? Vous dites? *What did you say?*

A quoi pensez-vous? *What are you thinking about?*

A propos de quoi? *What's it in regard to? What's it about?*

Avez-vous de quoi écrire? *Do you have anything to write with?*

N'importe quoi. *No matter what. Anything.*

En quoi pourrais-je vous servir? *What can I do for you?*

En quoi puis-je vous être utile? *What can I do for you?*

QUOIQUE *although, though.*

Je serai là quoique je puisse être en retard.

I'll be there although I may be a little late.

Quoiqu'il en soit. *Be that as it may.*

quotidien (quotidienne *f.*) *adj. daily.*

quotidien *m. daily newspaper.*

R

rabâcher *to repeat over and over again, keep harping on.*

rabais *m. reduction in price, discount.*

Il l'a eu au rabais. *He got it at a reduced price.*

rabaisser *to lower, reduce.*

se rabaisser *to lower oneself.*

rabat-joie *m. wet blanket.*

rabattre *to beat down; reduce.*

Il lui faudra en rabattre. *He'll have to lower his pretentions (come down a peg or two).*

Il n'en rabattra pas un sou. *He won't take a cent off. He won't reduce his price a cent.*

se rabattre *to fall back on.*

rabbin *m. rabbi.*

raccommodage *m. darning.*

raccommoder *to darn, repair; reconcile.*

Mes chaussettes ont besoin d'être raccommodées. *My socks need darning.*

se raccommoder *to make up, settle one's differences.*

raccourci *m. shortcut.*

raccourcir *to shorten.*

Je viens de raccourcir ma nouvelle robe. *I just shortened my new dress.*

Les jours raccourcissent. *The days are growing shorter.*

Son tricot a raccourci. *His sweater shrank.*

raccrocher *to hang up (again).*

Raccrochez et refaites votre numéro. *Hang up and dial again.*

se raccrocher *to clutch, hold.*

Elle se raccroche toujours à cette espérance. *She still clings to that hope.*

race *f. race; breed.*

rachat *m. buying back.*

Le prix de rachat. *Resale price.*

racheter *to buy back, redeem.*

racine *f. root, origin.*

râclée *f. thrashing, licking.*

râcler *to scrape.*

racontar *m. idle talk.*

RACONTER *to tell, relate.*

Raconter une histoire. *To tell a story.*

Qu'est-ce que vous racontez là? *What are you talking about?*

C'est ce qu'on raconte. *That's what people say.*

radeau *m. raft.*

radiateur *m. radiator.*

radieux (radieuse *f.*) *adj. radiant, beaming, shining.*

radio *f. radio.*

radiodiffuser *to broadcast.*

radiographie *f. X-ray picture.*

radiographier *to X ray.*

radis *m. radish.*

radotage *m. twaddle, nonsense.*

radoter *to talk nonsense.*

se radoucir *to grow milder.*

Le temps a l'air de s'être radouci. *The weather seems to have become milder.*

rafale *f. squall.*

raffermir *to strengthen, fortify.*

se raffermir *to grow stronger, improve.*

Sa santé se raffermit de jour en jour. *Her health is improving every day.*

raffiné *adj. refined, subtle.*

raffiner *to refine.*

Raffiner du sucre. *To refine sugar.*

Vous raffinez! *You're too subtle!*

raffoler *to be very fond of.*

Il en raffole. *He's crazy about it.*

rafraîchir *to refresh, cool, freshen.*

Rafraîchir la mémoire de quelqu'un. *To refresh someone's memory.*

se rafraîchir *to get cooler.*

Le temps se rafraîchit. *It's getting cooler.*

rafraîchissement *m. refreshment.*

rage *f. rage.*

Il est fou de rage. *He's very angry. He's in a rage.*

Accès de rage. *Fit of madness.*

J'ai une violente rage de dents. *I have a terrible toothache.*

Cela fait rage. *It's quite the rage.*

rager *to rage.*

ragoût *m. stew.*

raide *adj. stiff, tight.*

Des cheveux raides. *Straight hair.*

Ça c'est un peu raide! *That's a little too much!*

raideur *f. stiffness.*

se raidir *to stiffen, become stiff.*

raie *f. line, stripe; part (in hair).*

rail *m. rail.*

railler *to mock, make fun of.*

raillerie *f. banter.*

raisin *m. grapes.*

Des raisins secs. *Raisins.*

RAISON *f. reason.*

Les raisons qu'il a données ne tiennent pas debout. *The reasons he gave don't make sense.*

Sans rime ni raison. *Without cause.*

Il lui a donné raison. *He backed him up. He sided with him. He said he was right.*

A raison de. *At the rate of.*

Il est revenu à la raison. *He came to his senses.*

Avez-vous perdu votre raison? *Are you out of your mind?*

Avoir raison. *To be right.*

raisonnable *adj. reasonable.*

Il m'a fait des prix raisonnables. *He gave me a fair price. The prices he asked were reasonable.*

raisonnement *m. reasoning, reason.*

Son raisonnement est sain. *His argument (reasoning) is sound.*

Pas de raisonnement! *Don't argue!*

raisonner *to argue; reason.*

Raisonnez moins et travaillez davantage. *Argue less and work more.*

Elle raisonne comme un enfant. *She reasons like a child.*

rajeunir *to grow young again.*

Vous rajeunissez tous les jours. *You look younger every day.*

Cette robe vous rajeunit. *That dress makes you look younger.*

rajustement *m. readjustment.*

ralentir *to slow down.*

Ralentissez, vous roulez trop vite. *Slow down, you're going too fast.*

"Ralentir!" *"Drive slowly!" "Slow down!"*

rallonge *f. extension-leaf.*

rallonger *to lengthen.*

rallumer *to relight; revive.*

ramasser *to gather up, collect, pick up.*

Ramassez vos papiers. *Pick up (collect) your papers.*

Il a ramassé sa monnaie et est parti. *He picked up his money and left.*

rame *f. oar.*

rameau *m.* (rameaux *pl.*) *twig.*

ramener *to bring back, bring home, restore.*

Il l'a ramené chez lui. *He brought him (her) back to his house.*

Il a ramené sa famille de la campagne. *He brought his family back from the country.*

Pouvez-vous me ramener chez moi? *Can you take me home?*

On l'a ramené à la vie. *They revived him.*

ramer *to row.*

ramification *f. ramification.*

ramifier *to ramify, branch out.*

se ramollir *to soften.*

rampe *f. banister.*

ramper *to crawl, creep; crouch.*

rance *adj. rancid.*

rancir *to grow rancid.*

rancoeur *f. rancor, bitterness.*

Il lui tient rancoeur. *He bears him a grudge. He has a grudge against him.*

rançon *f. ransom.*

rançonner *to set a ransom; cheat, exploit.*

On vous a rançonné dans cet hôtel-là. *They cheated you in that hotel.*

rancune *f. spite, grudge.*

Il lui en garde rancune. *He's bearing him a grudge. He has a grudge against him.*

Sans rancune! *No hard feelings! Let bygones be bygones!*

Par rancune. *Out of spite.*

rang *m. row, line, rank.*

Nous étions assis au premier rang. *We sat in the first row.*

Il a le rang de ministre. *He has the rank of minister.*

Tenir le premier rang. *To hold first place.*

Tenir son rang. *To live up to one's position.*

rangée *f. row, line.*

ranger *to put in order, arrange.*

Rangez vos livres par rang de taille. *Arrange your books by size.*

Faites ranger les curieux. *Keep (hold) the crowd back.*

se ranger *to side with; fall in line.*

Ils se sont tous rangés en ligne. *They all fell into line. They all lined up.*

Rangez-vous! *Get out of the way! Make way!*

Elle s'est rangée a mon avis. *She sided with me.*

ranimer *to revive; liven up.*

rapatriement *m. repatriation.*

rapatrier *to repatriate.*

râpé *adj. grated; shabby.*

Ses vêtements sont tout râpés. *His clothes are shabby.*

rapetisser *to reduce, shrink.*

rapide *m. express train.*

rapide *adj. rapid.*

rapidité *f. swiftness, rapidity.*

rappel *m. recall; repeal.*

rappeler *to recall, call back (telephone).*

L'ambassadeur a été rappelé. *The ambassador was recalled.*

Rappelez-moi à son bon souvenir. *Give him my regards. Remember me to him.*

SE RAPPELER *to remember, recollect.*

Je ne me le rappelle pas. *I don't recall it.*

Il se les rappelle. *He remembers them.*

Je me rappelle votre nom. *I remember your name.*

rapport *m. relation; report.*

Voulez-vous me faire un rapport sur la question? *Will you give me a report on the matter?*

Sous ce rapport, nous ne sommes pas d'accord. *In this respect we don't agree.*

Etre en mauvais rapport avec quelqu'un. *To be on bad terms with someone.*

rapporter *to bring back.*

Rapportez un pain. *Bring back a loaf of bread.*

Ne manquez pas de me rapporter les livres. *Be sure to return these books to me.*

Tout cela ne lui a rapporté que des ennuis. *All it brought him was a lot of trouble.*

Ça ne rapporte rien. *It doesn't pay.*

Ce placement rapporte trois pour cent. *This investment bears 3 percent interest.*

se rapporter *to refer.*

Cela se rapporte à autre chose. *That refers to something else.*

Je m'en rapporte à vous. *I leave it to you. I take your word for it.*

RAPPROCHER *to bring nearer, bring together.*

Rapprochez votre chaise de la table. *Move your chair nearer (to) the table.*

raquette *f. racket.*

Une raquette de tennis. *A tennis racket.*

rare *adj. rare.*

Un livre rare. *A rare book.*

Vous devenez rare! *You're (you've become) quite a stranger!*

rarement *rarely.*

ras *adj. close-cropped, close-shaven, smooth, bare, flat.*

Faire table rase. *To make a clean sweep.*

Ils étaient en rase campagne. *They were in the open country.*

raser *to shave.*

Se faire raser. *To have oneself shaved, get a shave.*

se raser *to shave oneself.*

rasoir *m. razor.*

La lame de rasoir. *Razor blade.*

se rassasier *to eat one's fill.*

rassemblement *m. gathering, assembly, crowd.*

se rassembler *to get together, assemble, gather.*

se rasseoir *to sit down again.*

rassis *adj. stale.*

rassurer *to reassure.*

se rassurer *to regain one's self-assurance, feel reassured.*

rat *m. rat.*

râtelier *m. rack; (fam.) a set of false teeth.*

rater *to fail; miss.*

Il a raté son examen. *He flunked his exam.*

Il s'en est fallu de peu que je rate le train. *I came very close to missing the train. I almost missed the train.*

rattacher *to tie up again.*

se rattacher *to join, adhere to.*

rattraper *to catch up, overtake.*

J'ai dû courir pour le rattraper. *I had to run to catch up with him.*

Allez-y, je vous rattraperai. *Go (on) ahead. I'll catch up to you.*

Il va falloir rattraper le temps perdu. *You'll have to make up for lost time.*

se rattraper *to recover.*

rature *f. erasing, crossing out, scratching out.*

raturer *to cross out, scratch out.*

rauque *adj. harsh, hoarse.*

ravage *m. ravage, havoc.*

ravager *to ravage, spoil, ruin.*

L'orage a ravagé le région. *The storm ravaged the region.*

ravaler *to swallow again.*

Il a dû ravaler ses mots. *He had to retract his words.*

ravir *to ravish, carry off; enrapture, delight.*

Je suis ravi de vous voir. *I'm delighted to see you.*

A ravir. *Admirably. Wonderfully well.*

Jouer du piano à ravir. *To play the piano very well.*

ravissant *adj. delightful, lovely.*

Elle est ravissante. *She's lovely.*

rayer *to cross out.*

Rayez ce mot. *Cross this word out.*

rayon *m. ray; radius; department (of a store); shelf.*

Des rayons de soleil. *Sunbeams.*

Où se trouve le rayon des chemises? *Where is the shirt department?*

rayonner *to radiate, shine.*

rayure *f. stripe.*

réaction *f. reaction.*

réagir *to react.*

réalisation *f. realization.*

réaliser *to realize, fulfill.*

réaliste *adj. realistic.*

réalité *f. reality.*

En réalité. *In reality. As a matter of fact.*

rebelle *adj. rebellious.*

se rebeller *to rebel.*

rébellion *f. rebellion.*

rebord *m. edge, brim.*

rebours *m. wrong way.*

A rebours. *Against the grain. The wrong way. Backwards.*

Au rebours de ce que j'ai dit. *Contrary to what I said.*

Il prend tout à rebours. *He misconstrues everything.*

reboutonner *to rebutton.*

rebrousser *to retrace.*

Il a rebroussé chemin. *He retraced his steps.*

rebut *m. scrap.*

recacheter *to seal again.*

récemment *lately.*

récent *adj. recent.*

récepteur *m. telephone receiver.*

réception *f. reception; hotel (reception) desk.*

Il nous ont fait bonne réception. *They gave us a warm welcome (reception).*

Accuser réception d'une lettre. *To acknowledge receipt of a letter.*

recette *f. receipt; recipe.*

Les recettes du jour. *The day's receipts. The money taken in during the day.*

La pièce fait recette. *The play is drawing well. The play is a box office success.*

Le garçon de recettes est venu encaisser la facture. *The collector came to collect the bill.*

receveur *m. receiver; collector; conductor (bus).*

RECEVOIR *to receive.*

Recevoir des ordres. *To receive orders.*

Recevoir un cadeau. *To receive a present.*

Nous avons bien reçu votre lettre. *We are in receipt of your letter.*

Recevoir quelqu'un à bras ouverts. *To welcome someone with open arms.*

Recevoir un mauvais accueil. *To receive a cold welcome.*

Ils reçoivent beaucoup. *They do a good deal of entertaining. They entertain a lot.*

Se faire recevoir avocat. *To be called to the bar.*

rechange *m. change.*

Une roue de rechange. *A spare wheel.*

La pièce de rechange. *Spare part.*

Le pneu de rechange. *Spare tire.*

recharger *to reload.*

Recharger un appareil. *To reload a camera.*

réchaud *m. portable stove.*

réchauffer *to warm up again; revive.*

recherche *f. research, investigation; studied elegance.*

Des recherches scientifiques. *Scientific research.*

Mis avec recherche. *Dressed with meticulous care.*

recherché *adj. in demand; select; mannered (painting).*

rechercher *to seek again, look for again; seek after.*

Rechercher un mot dans le dictionnaire. *To look up a word in the dictionary.*

Tout le monde le recherche. *He's very much sought after. People like his company.*

rechute *f. relapse.*

réciproque *adj. reciprocal, mutual.*

récit *m. tale; recital, narration.*

Faites-moi le récit de ce qui s'est passé. *Give me an account of what took place (happened).*

réciter *to recite, tell, relate.*

réclamation *f. claim, complaint, protest.*

réclame *f. advertisement, publicity.*

réclamer *to claim, require.*

Il en réclame la moitié. *He claims half of it.*

Réclamer de soins. *To require care.*

récolte *f. harvest, crop.*

récolter *to harvest.*

recommendation *f. recommendation, advice.*

Une lettre de recommendation. *A letter of recommendation.*

J'ai suivi ses recommendations. *I followed his advice.*

recommander *to recommend, register.*

Faites recommander cette lettre. *Have this letter registered. Register this letter.*

recommencer *to start again.*

récompense *f. reward; recompense.*

récompenser *to reward.*

réconciliation *f. reconciliation.*

réconcilier *to reconcile.*

reconduire *to drive back; take home.*

réconfort *m. comfort, relief.*

réconforter *to comfort, help.*

reconnaissance *f. recognition; gratitude; reconnaissance.*

Ils ont pour vous beaucoup de reconnaissance. *They're very grateful to you.*

Il lui a témoigné de la reconnaissance. *He showed his gratitude to him.*

Avec reconnaissance. *Gratefully. Thankfully. With thanks.*

reconnaissant *adj. grateful, thankful.*

Je vous suis reconnaissant de m'avoir aidé. *I'm very grateful to you for having helped me.*

Je vous serais très reconnaissant si vous pouviez le faire. *I would be very grateful to you if you could do it.*

reconnaître *to recognize.*

Je l'ai reconnu de suite. *I recognized him right away.*

Je vous reconnais bien là. *That's just typical of you. It's (that's) just like you.*

se reconnaître *to know (recognize) each other.*

Ils ne se sont pas reconnus. *They didn't recognize one another.*

Je ne m'y reconnais plus. *I'm completely at a loss. I'm completely confused.*

reconsidérer *to reconsider.*

record *m. record.*

Il détient le record. *He holds the record.*

se recoucher *to go to bed again.*

recoudre *to sew again, sew back on.*

recourir *to run again; turn to, resort to.*

recours *m. recourse.*

J'ai recours à vous pour . . . *I am applying to you for . . .*

recouvrir *to cover over, recover.*

Recouvert (de). *Upholstered (with, in).*

récréation *f. recreation, amusement; pastime.*

se récrier *to cry out.*

récrimination *f. recrimination.*

récrire *to rewrite.*

recrue *f. recruit.*

rectangle *m. rectangle.*

rectification *f. adjustment.*

rectifier *to rectify, correct.*

reçu *m. receipt.*

Voilà votre reçu. *Here's your receipt.*

Au reçu de votre lettre. *Upon receipt of your letter.*

recueil *m. collection.*

se recueillir *to collect oneself.*

reculer *to draw back, go backwards; put off; delay.*

(à) reculons *backwards.*

Marcher à reculons. *To walk backwards.*

récupérer *to recover.*

rédacteur *m. staff member of newspaper or magazine, editor.*

Le rédacteur en chef. *The editor-in-chief.*

Le rédacteur-gérant. *The managing editor.*

rédaction *f. writing; editing; editorial staff.*

rédiger *to draw up, write; edit.*

Cet article a été rédigé par le rédacteur en chef. *This article was written by the editor.*

redire *to say again.*

redoubler *redouble, increase.*

Redoubler d'efforts. *To redouble one's efforts.*

redoutable *adj. redoubtable, terrible, dreadful.*

redouter *to dread, fear.*

redresser *to straighten out, put to rights, reform.*

réduction *f. reduction.*

réduire *to reduce.*

Edition réduite. *Abridged edition.*

réel (réelle *f.*) *adj. real.*

réellement *really.*

refaire *to do over.*

Ça doit être refait. *It must be done over. That has to be redone.*

Vous avez été refait. *You were tricked.*

Refaire le chemin. *To start over again, retrace one's steps.*

référence *f. reference.*

Donner des références. *To give references.*

réfléchir *to reflect.*

Réfléchissez-y. *Think it over.*

C'est tout réfléchi! *My mind is made up! I've decided!*

réflexion *f. reflection.*

réforme *f. reform.*

réformer *to reform.*

refouler *to drive back.*

Il a été refoulé. *He was driven back.*

Elle a refoulé ses larmes. *She checked her tears.*

refrain *m. refrain.*
refroidir *to cool; to discourage.*
  Dépêchez-vous, le dîner va se refroidir.
    Hurry up, the food's getting cold.
refuge *m. refuge, shelter.*
se réfugier *to seek refuge, seek shelter.*
refus *m. refusal, denial.*
refuser *to refuse.*
  Il a refusé de le voir. *He refused to see him.*
  Il a été refusé à l'examen. *He failed the*
    examination.
regagner *to regain.*
régal *m. feast, treat.*
  Quel régal! *How delicious (of food)!*
se régaler *to treat oneself, give oneself a treat.*
regard *m. look, glance.*
  Attirer tous les regards. *To attract attention.*
  Suivre du regard. *To follow with one's eyes.*
  Au regard de. *In comparison with. With*
    regard to.
REGARDER *to look at.*
  Regardez ça. *Look at that.*
  Il ne regarde que ses intérêts. *He cares only*
    about his own interest.
  Cela ne me regarde pas. *That doesn't*
    concern me.
  Regarde donc! *Just look!*
régime *m. diet; administration.*
  Elle suit un régime. *She's on a diet.*
  Le régime de ce pays. *The administration of*
    this country.
région *f. region.*
règle *f. rule; ruler.*
  Il est de règle de. *It's customary to.*
  En règle générale. *As a general rule.*
  En règle. *In order, O.K.*
règlement *m. ruling, regulation.*
réglementaire *adj. according to regulation,*
  correct.
régler *to rule (paper); arrange, adjust.*
  Une affaire réglée. *A matter that has been*
    settled.
  Régler un compte. *To settle an account.*
  Régler une montre. *To set a watch.*
se régler *to be guided by.*
  Je me réglerai sur lui. *I'll follow his example.*
    I'll go (I'll be guided) by what he says.
règne *m. reign.*
régner *to reign, prevail.*
regret *m. regret, sorrow.*
  A mon grand regret. *To my great regret.*
    Much to my regret.
  A regret. *With regret.*
  J'en suis au regret. *I'm sorry.*
regrettable *adj. deplorable, regrettable.*
regretter *to regret, be sorry.*
  Je regrette de ne pouvoir accepter. *I'm sorry*
    I can't accept.
régularité *f. regularity.*

régulier (régulière *f.) adj. regular.*
rehausser *to raise up, heighten, enhance.*
rein *m. kidney.*
reine *f. queen.*
réinstaller *to reinstall, re-establish.*
réintégrer *to reinstate, restore.*
rejeter *to reject, throw back.*
  Il a rejeté son offre. *He rejected his offer.*
  Il a rejeté la faute sur lui. *He put the blame*
    on him.
rejoindre *to join again, reunite.*
se réjouir *to rejoice.*
  Je me réjouis de vous revoir. *I'm very glad*
    to see you again.
relâche *m. respite.*
  Travailler sans relâche. *To work without*
    stopping.
  Il y a relâche ce soir. *There's no*
    performance tonight.
relâcher *to loosen.*
relatif (relative *f.) adj. relative.*
relation *f. relation, acquaintance.*
  Il a de belles relations. *He has good*
    connections. ·
reléguer *to relegate.*
relever *to raise again; point out.*
  Il relève de maladie. *He's just getting over*
    his illness.
  Il a relevé des fautes. *He pointed out some*
    mistakes.
se relever *to get up again, rise again.*
relier *to bind.*
religion *f. religion.*
religieux (religieuse *f.) adj. religious.*
relire *to read again, reread.*
reliure *f. binding.*
reluire *to shine, be bright.*
remarquable *adj. remarkable.*
remarque *f. remark, notice.*
  Digne de remarque. *Noteworthy.*
  Une remarque piquante. *A stinging*
    remark.
remarquer *to remark; notice.*
  Je n'avais pas remarqué. *I hadn't noticed. I*
    didn't notice.
  Partout où il va, il se fait remarquer.
    Wherever he goes he makes himself
    conspicuous (attracts attention).
remboursable *adj. refundable.*
rembourser *to repay, refund.*
remède *m. remedy; cure.*
remédier *to remedy.*
remerciement *m. thanks.*
  Une lettre de remerciement. *A letter of*
    thanks. A thank-you note.
remercier *to thank; dismiss.*
  Je vous en remercie. *Thanks. Thank you*
    (for it).
  Je vous remercie beaucoup. *Thanks a lot.*

Je vous remercie de votre amabilité. *Thank you for your kindness.*

remettre *to put back, put back again, put on again.*

Il a remis son chapeau sur la tête. *He put his hat on again.*

L'air de la mer l'a remis complètement. *The sea air restored him completely.*

Remettez cette lettre en mains propres. *Deliver this letter to the addressee only.*

Il l'a remis à sa place. *He put him in his place. He took him down a peg or two.*

se remettre *to start again, recover.*

Se remettre à. *To start again. To set about again.*

Il s'est remis au travail. *He started to work again.*

Se remettre d'une maladie. *To recover from an illness.*

Il a eu une rechute, il a dû se remettre au lit. *He had a relapse and had to go back to bed again.*

Il se remet à sa place. *He's going back to his seat.*

Je m'en remets à vous. *I leave it to you.*

Remettez-vous-en à moi. *Leave it to me.*

remise *f. putting back.*

Faire une remise en état. *To put into shape, overhaul (car).*

remonter *to go up again.*

Remonter à sa chambre. *To go up to one's room again.*

remords *m. remorse.*

remorque *f. trailer.*

remplacer *to replace, substitute.*

remplir *to fill up; fulfill; fill out (form).*

Remplir d'allégresse. *To cheer up. To make happy. ("To fill with joy.")*

Remplir son devoir. *To fulfill one's duty.*

remporter *to take back; obtain.*

Il a remporté le premier prix. *He carried off the first prize.*

Remporter la victoire. *To win a victory.*

remue-ménage *m. bustle.*

remuer *to move, stir.*

Ne remuez pas tant. *Don't move around so much.*

Remuer ciel et terre. *To move heaven and earth.*

renard *m. fox.*

rencontre *f. meeting, encounter.*

RENCONTRER *to meet, come across.*

Je l'ai rencontré il y a à peu près dix jours. *I met him about ten days ago.*

Il a rencontré beaucoup de difficultés. *He encountered many difficulties.*

se rencontrer *to meet; be found.*

Nous nous rencontrons ce soir. *We're meeting tonight. We'll meet tonight.*

rendement *m. output.*

RENDEZ-VOUS *m. appointment.*

Prenons rendez-vous pour demain matin. *Let's make an appointment for tomorrow morning.*

Fixer un rendez-vous. *To make an appointment, date.*

se rendormir *to go to sleep again.*

RENDRE *to give back, return.*

Rendre un livre. *To return a book.*

Rendre de l'argent. *To pay back money.*

Rendre visite à quelqu'un. *To return someone's call.*

Rendre la monnaie d'une pièce d'un franc. *To give change for a franc.*

Rendre service à quelqu'un. *To do someone a favor.*

Vous m'avez rendu un grand service. *You've done me a great service (favor).*

La lettre l'a rendue heureuse. *The letter made her happy.*

se rendre *to surrender, yield; go (to a place).*

L'ennemi s'est rendu. *The enemy surrendered.*

Il se rend ridicule. *He's making himself ridiculous.*

Se rendre compte de quelque chose. *To realize (understand) something.*

Il s'y est rendu hier soir. *He went there last night.*

renfermer *to lock up again; contain.*

renfort *m. reinforcement.*

renier *to disown.*

renifler *to sniffle.*

renom *m. reputation.*

Un avocat de grand renom. *A very well-known lawyer.*

renommée *f. fame.*

renoncer *to renounce.*

renouveler *to renew.*

RENSEIGNEMENT *m. (piece of) information; pl. information.*

Ce renseignement m'a été très utile. *This piece of information was very useful to me.*

Fournir des renseignements sur quelque chose. *To give (furnish) information about something.*

Le service des renseignements. *Information (telephone).*

Prendre des renseignements. *To get information.*

renseigner *to give information.*

se renseigner *to make inquiries.*

rente *f. yearly income.*

rentrée *f. reentering, reopening.*

RENTRER *to go in, go or come home.*

Il est l'heure de rentrer. *It's time to go home.*

152

Ils sont rentrés à la maison. *They returned home.*

Rentrer dans les bonnes grâces de quelqu'un. *To regain favor with someone. To get into someone's good graces again.*

Il avait envie de rentrer sous terre. *He was terribly embarrassed.*

renverse *f. reversal.*

Il est tombé à la renverse. *He fell on his back.*

renverser *to overthrow; overturn, upset, knock down.*

renvoyer *to return, send back; dismiss, fire.*

Si ce livre ne vous plaît pas, renvoyez-le moi. *If you don't like the book, send it back to me.*

Il a été renvoyé. *He was fired.*

répandre *to pour, spill; spread.*

Répandre des larmes. *To shed tears.*

Elle a répandu la nouvelle. *She spread the news.*

se répandre *to spread.*

L'eau s'est répandu sur la table. *The water spread (ran) all over the table.*

Il s'est répandu en excuses. *He apologized profusely.*

Le bruit se répand que. *A rumor is being spread that. It's being rumored that.*

réparation *f. repair; reparation.*

réparer *to repair, mend.*

L'auto vient d'être réparée. *The car has just been repaired.*

Réparer les dégâts. *To make good the damage.*

Faire réparer. *To have (something) repaired, fixed.*

répartie *f. repartee.*

repas *m. meal.*

Faire des repas légers. *To take light meals.*

REPASSER *to pass again, call again; iron.*

Quand repassera-t-il? *When will he call again (stop by again)?*

Repassez cette chemise, je vous prie. *Will you please iron this shirt?*

Une planche à repasser. *An ironing board.*

Faire repasser. *To have (something) ironed.*

repentir *m. remorse.*

se repentir *to repent.*

RÉPÉTER *to repeat; rehearse.*

Veuillez répéter ce que vous avez dit. *Will you please repeat what you said?*

répétition *f. repetition.*

répit *m. respite.*

replier *to fold again.*

réplique *f. retort, repartee.*

Argument sans réplique. *Unanswerable argument.*

Il lui a donné la réplique. *He gave him the cue.*

Obéir sans réplique. *To obey without a word.*

répliquer *to retort, answer back.*

Ne répliquez pas! *Don't answer back!*

RÉPONDRE *to answer.*

Il n'a rien répondu. *He didn't answer.*

Cela ne répond pas à nos besoins. *That doesn't answer our needs.*

Je lui réponds. *I answer him, her.*

J'y réponds. *I answer it.*

répondeur automatique *m. answering machine.*

RÉPONSE *f. answer, reply.*

REPOS *m. rest, quiet, peace.*

Il vous faut prendre du repos. *You need some rest.*

Mettez-vous l'esprit en repos. *Set your mind at rest.*

C'est un placement de tout repos. *It's a safe investment.*

reposer *to put back again; rest, repose.*

Ici repose. *Here lies.*

se reposer *to rest; rely on.*

repousser *to push away, repulse, drive back; reject.*

reprendre *to take back, get back; resume.*

Reprenons à partir de la page 10. *Let's start again on page 10.*

On ne m'y reprendra plus, croyez bien. *You can be sure they won't catch me at it again.*

Reprendre la parole. *To begin talking again.*

Reprenez vos places. *Return to your seats.*

représaille *f. reprisal.*

représentant *m. representative, delegate.*

REPRÉSENTATION *f. exhibition; performance.*

La représentation commence à trois heures de l'après-midi. *The performance begins at 3 P.M.*

J'ai la représentation de cette maison. *I have the agency for this firm. I represent this firm.*

représenter *to represent.*

se représenter *to imagine.*

Représentez-vous ma surprise! *Imagine my surprise!*

réprimande *f. rebuke.*

réprimander *to rebuke.*

réprimer *to repress.*

REPRISE *f. recapture; resumption; pickup (of rented car).*

A deux reprises. *Twice.*

A plusieurs reprises. *Several times. Over and over again. Many times.*

réprobateur (réprobatrice *f.*) *adj. reproachful.*

reproche *m. reproach.*

reprocher *to reproach.*

se reprocher *to reproach oneself.*

république *f. republic.*

répugnance f. repugnance.

répugner to be repugnant, repulsive.

réputation f. reputation, fame, character.

requête f. request.

réquisition f. requisition.

rescousse f. rescue.

Venir à la rescousse. To come to the rescue.

réseau m. net; system; network.

Le réseau de chemins de fer. The railway system.

réservation f. reservation.

réserve f. reserve, reservation.

RÉSERVER to reserve.

Il faudra réserver vos chambres bien à l'avance. You'll have to reserve your rooms well in advance.

Tous droits réservés. All rights reserved.

Se faire réserver une heure. To make an appointment (hairdresser, etc.).

réservoir m. tank (gasoline).

résidence f. residence.

résider to reside.

résignation f. resignation.

se résigner to be resigned, resign oneself.

résistance f. resistance, opposition.

Faire résistance. To offer resistance.

Eprouver une résistance. To meet with resistance.

Le ragoût est la pièce de résistance. The main dish is the stew.

résister to resist.

résolu adj. resolute, determined.

resolution f. resolution.

résonner to resound, ring.

résoudre to resolve, solve.

Résoudre un problème. To solve a problem.

Il a résolu de partir. He resolved (made up his mind) to leave.

Cela ne résout pas la question. That doesn't solve the problem.

RESPECT m. respect.

Tenir en respect. To respect. To hold in respect.

Manquer de respect à quelqu'un. To lack respect for someone.

Respect de soi. Self-respect.

Veuillez bien présenter mes respects à madame votre mère. Please give my regards to your mother.

respecter to respect.

respectueux (respectueuse f.) adj. respectful, deferential.

respiration f. respiration, breathing.

respirer to breathe.

resplendir to shine, glitter.

replendissant adj. resplendent, shining.

responsabilité f. responsibility.

responsable adj. responsible, answerable.

ressemblance f. likeness.

ressembler to be like, look like.

Cela y ressemble beaucoup. It's very much like it. It resembles it a lot.

se ressembler to look alike.

Ils se ressemblent comme deux gouttes d'eau. They're as alike as two peas in a pod. They resemble each other like two drops of water.

Qui se ressemble s'assemble. Birds of a feather flock together.

ressentiment m. resentment.

ressentir to feel.

ressort m. spring; elasticity.

ressortir to bring out.

Faire ressortir le sens d'une phrase. To bring out the meaning of a sentence.

ressource f. resource, expedient; pl. means.

C'est un homme de ressources. He's a resourceful man.

En dernière ressource je le lui demanderai. I'll ask him as a last resort.

restant adj. remaining.

La poste restante. General delivery.

restaurant m. restaurant.

RESTE m. remains, rest.

Le reste de la famille. The rest of the family.

Le reste de la soirée. The rest of the evening.

Du reste. Besides. Moreover.

RESTER to remain, stay.

Je resterai là quelques jours. I'll stay there a few days.

Il nous reste encore quelques sous. We still have a few pennies left.

restriction f. restriction.

résultat m. result, consequence.

résulter to result.

Qu'en est-il résulté? What was the outcome? What was the result?

résumé m. summary, synopsis.

résumer to sum up, recapitulate.

Résumons. Let's sum up.

Voilà l'affaire résumée en un mot. That's the whole thing in a nutshell.

rétablir to re-establish, restore.

RETARD m. delay, slowness.

Je suis en retard. I'm late.

retarder to delay, be slow.

Ma montre retarde de vingt minutes. My watch is twenty minutes slow.

RETENIR to keep back, hold back; retain, reserve.

Retenez-le. Hold him back.

Retenir sa colère. To restrain (curb) one's anger.

Elle ne retient rien. She can't remember anything.

Qu'est-ce qui vous retient? What's keeping you?

J'ai retenu deux places pour ce soir. *I reserved two seats for this evening.*

retentir *to resound.*

retenue *f. reserve, moderation, caution, restraint.*

retirer *to draw back; retract.*

J'ai retiré mon argent. *I drew out my money.*

Retirer ses paroles. *To retract one's words.*

retomber *to fall again, have a relapse.*

retouche *f. alteration.*

RETOUR *m. return.*

Il est de retour. *He's back. He returned.*

Un billet d'aller et retour. *A round-trip ticket.*

Je vous répondrai par retour de courrier. *I'll answer you by return mail.*

Les frais de retour. *Charge for returning (rented car).*

retourner *to turn again, turn back, return.*

Il est retourné en arrière. *He turned back. He went back. He returned.*

Retourner sur ses pas. *To retrace one's steps.*

Je vous retourne votre livre. *I'm returning your book.*

se retourner *to turn around.*

Je n'ai même pas eu le temps de me retourner. *I didn't even have time to look around.*

retraite *f. retreat, shelter; retirement pension.*

retrécir *to shrink; become narrow.*

retroussé *adj. turned-up.*

Elle a le nez retroussé. *She has a turned-up nose.*

Le bas du pantalon retroussé? *Cuffs on the trousers?*

retrouver *to find again, recover, recognize.*

Je n'ai pas pu retrouver cet endroit. *I couldn't find that place again.*

Je l'ai retrouvé l'autre jour dans un café. *I ran into him the other day in a café.*

Je vous retrouverai ce soir. *I'll see you again this evening.*

se retrouver *to find one another again, meet; recognize.*

Retrouvons-nous à la gare. *Let's meet at the station.*

A la fin nous nous sommes retrouvés. *At last we found each other.*

réunion *f. meeting, reunion.*

réunir *to reunite, join together; gather.*

se réunir *to meet, gather together.*

RÉUSSIR *to succeed.*

Il n'a pas réussi à l'avoir. *He failed to get it. ("He didn't succeed in getting it.")*

Il n'a pas réussi le coup. *He didn't bring it off.*

Cela lui a mal réussi. *It turned out badly for him.*

revanche *f. revenge; return.*

En revanche. *On the other hand. In return.*

rêvasser *to daydream.*

rêve *m. dream.*

réveil *m. awakening, waking.*

A son réveil. *When he awoke.*

réveille-matin *m. alarm clock.*

réveiller *to wake, wake up, arouse.*

Réveillez-moi à huit heures. *Wake me at eight.*

SE RÉVEILLER *to wake up.*

Il faisait grand jour quand nous nous sommes réveillés. *It was broad daylight when we woke.*

Son courage s'est réveillé. *His courage revived.*

réveillon *m. Christmas Eve or New Year's Eve party.*

Le réveillon de Noël. *Christmas Eve.*

Le réveillon du jour de l'an. *New Year's Eve.*

révélation *f. revelation, disclosure.*

révéler *to reveal, betray.*

revendiquer *to lay claim to.*

revendre *to resell.*

REVENIR *to return, come back.*

Quand revenez-vous? *When will you return? When are you coming back?*

Je n'en reviens pas. *I can't get over it.*

Il revient de loin. *He has been at death's door.*

Ça revient au même. *That comes to the same thing. That amounts to the same thing.*

Il est revenu sur ses pas. *He retraced his steps.*

Il est revenu sur sa promesse. *He went back on his promise.*

Maintenant ça me revient. *Now I remember. Now it comes back to me.*

Sa tête ne me revient pas. *I don't like his looks.*

Cela (ça) revient moins cher. *That's cheaper. That comes to less.*

revenu *m. income.*

rêver *to dream.*

révérence *f. reverence.*

Avec révérence. *Reverently.*

Faire une révérence. *To curtsy.*

rêverie *f. reverie, daydreaming; daydream.*

revers *m. reverse, back.*

Eprouver des revers. *To suffer a loss. To meet with reverses.*

Les revers d'un veston. *The lapels of a coat.*

Le revers d'une robe. *The wrong side of a dress.*

reviser *to revise.*

révision *f. revision, reconsideration.*

revivre *to come to life again.*

REVOIR *m. meeting again.*

Au revoir. *Good-bye.*

revoir *to see again, meet again.*

Je l'ai revu l'autre jour. *I saw him again the other day.*

révolte *f. revolt.*

se révolter *to revolt.*

révolution *f. revolution.*

révoquer *to repeal, annul.*

revue *f. review, magazine.*

Les troupes ont été passées en revue. *The troops passed in review.*

Je lis cette revue chaque semaine. *I read this magazine every week.*

rez-de-chaussée *m. ground floor.*

rhumatisme *m. rheumatism.*

rhume *m. cold.*

Attraper un rhume. *To catch a cold.*

J'ai un rhume. *I have a cold.*

ricaner *to sneer.*

riche *adj. rich.*

richesse *f. riches; wealth.*

Que de richesses! *What riches!*

ride *f. wrinkle.*

rideau *m. (rideaux pl.) curtain, screen.*

ridicule *adj. ridiculous.*

ridiculiser *to ridicule.*

RIEN *m. trifle.*

C'est un rien. *It's a mere trifle.*

Il se fâche pour un rien. *He gets angry at the least little thing.*

Il faut y ajouter un rien de sel. *It needs just a trifle more salt.*

RIEN *anything; nothing.*

Je n'ai rien dit. *I didn't say anything.*

Qu'est-ce que vous avez dit?—Rien. *What did you say?—Nothing.*

Je n'ai rien à lire ce soir. *I have nothing to read tonight.*

Si cela ne vous fait rien. *If you don't mind.*

Rien d'autre. *Nothing else.*

De rien. *You're welcome. It's nothing. Not at all.*

rigide *adj. rigid.*

rigolo *(rigolote f.) adj. comical.*

rigoureux *(rigoureuse f.) adj. rigorous.*

rigueur *f. rigor, strictness, severity.*

A la rigueur. *Strictly speaking.*

C'est de rigueur. *It's compulsory.*

rime *f. rhyme.*

rincer *to rinse.*

RIRE *m. laughter.*

RIRE *to laugh.*

Ils ont éclaté de rire. *They burst out laughing. They burst into laughter.*

C'est à mourir de rire. *It's too funny for words. ("It's enough to make you die laughing.")*

Rire tout bas. *To laugh to one's self.*

Il a ri jaune. *He laughed out of the other side of his face.*

risque *m. risk, chance.*

Je ne veux pas prendre ce risque. *I don't want to take the chance (risk).*

Vous le faites à vos risques et périls. *You do it at your own risk.*

risquer *to risk.*

Qui ne risque rien, n'a rien. *Nothing ventured, nothing gained.*

rivage *m. bank, side.*

rival *m. (rivaux pl.) rival.*

rivalité *f. rivalry.*

rive *f. bank (of stream, pond, or lake).*

La Rive Gauche. *Left Bank (Paris).*

rivière *f. river, stream.*

riz *m. rice.*

robe *f. dress, gown.*

La robe de soie. *Silk dress.*

robinet *m. tap, faucet.*

robuste *adj. robust.*

rocher *m. rock, cliff.*

rôder *to prowl.*

roi *m. king.*

rôle *m. role, part.*

romain *(romaine f.) noun and adj. Roman.*

roman *m. novel.*

romantique *adj. romantic.*

rompre *to break; interrupt.*

Rompre des relations. *To break off relations.*

Il a rompu la conversation. *He interrupted the conversation.*

rond *m. round; ring, circle.*

rond *adj. round.*

ronfler *to snore.*

ronger *to gnaw.*

rose *f. rose.*

rose *adj. pink.*

rosée *f. dew.*

rossignol *m. nightingale; (colloq.) piece of junk, "lemon."*

rôti *m. roast.*

rôtir *to roast.*

roue *f. wheel.*

rouge *m. red color; redness; rouge.*

Un bâton de rouge. *Lipstick.*

ROUGE *adj. red; ruddy.*

rougir *to turn red, blush.*

rouille *f. rust.*

rouleau *m. roll.*

Le rouleau (de pellicules). *Roll (of film).*

rouler *to roll, roll up; drive.*

Il a roulé la feuille de papier soigneusement. *He carefully rolled up the sheet of paper.*

Rouler à toute vitesse. *To drive at full speed.*

roulette *f. small wheel.*

Ça marche comme sur des roulettes. *It's going like clockwork.*

ROUTE *f. road, highway.*

Où aboutit cette route? *Where does this road lead to?*

En route! *Let's be off!*

Frais de route. *Traveling expenses.*

routier *adj. of roads.*

La carte routière. *Road map.*

routine *f. routine.*

roux (rousse *f.*) *adj. red-haired, russet.*

royaliste *m. and f. noun and adj. royalist.*

royaume *m. kingdom, realm.*

ruban *m. ribbon; band.*

Le ruban magnétique. *Recording tape.*

rubis *m. ruby.*

rubrique *f. column (newspaper).*

La rubrique sportive. *Sports section.*

rude *adj. rough, harsh.*

RUE *f. street.*

Quel est le nom de cette rue? *What's the name of this street?*

Au bout de la rue, tournez à droite. *Turn right at the end of the street.*

Une telle occasion ne court pas les rues. *You don't get this opportunity every day.*

se ruer *to rush, dash.*

ruine *f. ruin.*

Il était à deux doigts de sa ruine. *He was on the very brink of (verge of) ruin. He came within an ace of being ruined.*

Ça tombe en ruines. *It's falling to pieces.*

ruiner *to ruin, destroy, spoil.*

Sa santé est ruinée. *His health is ruined.*

Il est bel et bien ruiné. *He's completely ruined.*

se ruiner *to ruin oneself.*

Il s'est ruiné la santé. *He ruined his health.*

ruisseau *m.* (ruisseaux *pl.*) *stream.*

ruisselant *adj. streaming.*

ruisseler *to stream down.*

rumeur *f. rumor.*

rupture *f. rupture; breaking-off.*

Une rupture définitive. *A final break.*

rural (ruraux *pl.*) *adj. rural.*

ruse *f. ruse, trick.*

ruser *to use craft.*

russe *m. and f. noun and adj. Russian.*

rustique *adj. rustic.*

rustre *m. boor.*

S

SA *See son.*

Où se trouve sa lettre? *Where is his (her) letter?*

Où se trouve sa bague? *Where is his (her) ring?*

sable *m. sand, gravel.*

sabotage *m. sabotage.*

saboteur *m. saboteur.*

SAC *m. bag, sack, pouch, pocketbook.*

L'affaire est dans le sac. *It's as good as settled. It's as good as done. It's a cinch. ("It's in the bag.")*

Il a été pris la main dans le sac. *He was caught red-handed.*

Mettre une ville à sac. *To sack a town.*

sacré *adj. sacred, holy.*

sacrement *m. sacrament.*

Le sacrement de mariage. *Sacrament of marriage.*

sacrifice *m. sacrifice.*

sacrifier *to sacrifice.*

sage *m. a wise man, a learned man.*

sage *adj. well-behaved (of children).*

Soyez sage! *Be good! Behave yourself! (Said to a child.)*

L'enfant est sage comme une image. *The child is very good (obedient).*

Une petite fille sage. *A good little girl.*

sagesse *f. wisdom; good behavior.*

saignant *adj. rare (of meat).*

saigner *to bleed.*

sain *adj. sound, healthy.*

saint *adj. holy, sacred.*

SAISIR *to seize.*

Je ne saisis pas. *I don't quite get (understand) it.*

Pardonnez-moi, je n'ai pas bien saisi votre nom. *Pardon me, I didn't quite catch your name.*

On a saisi ses biens. *His property was attached.*

SAISON *f. season.*

salade *f. salad.*

salaire *m. salary; wages.*

sale *adj. dirty.*

saler *to salt.*

saleté *f. dirt.*

salière *f. saltcellar.*

salir *to dirty, soil; defame.*

SALLE *f. hall, room.*

Une grande salle. *A large hall.*

Salle à manger. *Dining room.*

Salle de bains. *Bathroom.*

Salle d'attente. *Waiting room.*

Faire salle comble. *To draw a full house (theatre).*

La salle de concert. *Concert hall.*

salon *m. parlor, living room.*

Le salon d'essayage. *Fitting room.*

Le salon des dames (salon de beauté). *Beauty parlor.*

saluer *to pay one's respects, greet, take one's hat off to someone.*

salut *m. salvation, safety.*

salutation *f. salutation, greeting.*

Agréez mes sincères salutations (*in a letter*). *Best regards. ("Accept my kind regards.")*

SAMEDI *m. Saturday.*
sandale *f. sandal.*
sandwich *m. sandwich.*
SANG *m. blood.*
Il a le sang chaud. *He's quick-tempered.*
Bon sang ne peut mentir. *Blood will tell.*
Il se fait du mauvais sang. *He worries a lot.*
sang-froid *m. sang-froid, composure, coolness, self-control.*
sanglant *adj. bloody, blood-covered.*
sanglot *m. sob.*
sangloter *to sob.*
sanitaire *adj. sanitary.*
SANS *without.*
Sans amis. *Without friends. Friendless.*
Sans fin. *Without end.*
Sans blague! *No kidding! You're joking!*
Sans cesse. *Ceaselessly. Without stopping. Without a halt.*
Sans arrêt. *Without stopping.*
Il répète les mêmes mots sans arrêt. *He keeps repeating the same thing.*
Sans doute. *No doubt. Doubtless. Probably.*
Sans doute il viendra. *He'll probably (doubtlessly) come.*
Retrouvez-moi sans faute à six heures. *Meet me without fail at six o'clock.*
Bien entendu, cela va sans dire. *Of course, that goes without saying.*
Ne vous absentez pas sans le dire. *Don't leave without telling someone.*
N'y allez pas sans qu'on vous le dise. *Don't go unless you're told to.*
sans-façon *m. offhandedness, overfamiliarity; bluntness.*
C'est un sans-façon. *He has no manners. He's too familiar (too free and easy in his ways).*
C'est d'un sans-façon! *That's going a bit too far!*
sans-gêne *m. overfamiliarity, unceremoniousness, cheek, nerve.*
Votre ami est d'un sans-gêne. *Your friend is too familiar (takes too many liberties). Your friend is too free-and-easy (happy-go-lucky).*
sans-souci *m. and f. careless (easygoing) person.*
SANTÉ *f. health.*
Est-elle en bonne santé? *Is she in good health?*
Il respire la santé. *He looks the picture of health.*
A votre santé! *Here's to you! ("Your health!")*
saoul *adj. drunk.*
sarcasme *m. sarcasm, sarcastic remark.*
sarcophage *m. sarcophagus.*
sardine *f. sardine.*

satellite *m. satellite, follower.*
satin *m. satin.*
satire *f. satire.*
satisfaction *f. satisfaction.*
Il me donne satisfaction. *I'm satisfied with him.*
A la satisfaction de tous. *To everyone's satisfaction.*
satisfaire *to satisfy.*
satisfaisant *adj. satisfactory.*
Le résultat était très satisfaisant. *The result was very satisfactory.*
satisfait *adj. satisfied.*
Etes-vous satisfait de son travail? *Are you satisfied with his work?*
sauce *f. sauce, gravy.*
sauf (sauve *f.*) *adj. safe, unharmed.*
Nous en sommes sortis sains et saufs. *We came out of it safe and sound.*
SAUF *save, except.*
Nous les avons tous trouvés, sauf trois. *We found all of them except three.*
Tout le monde était là sauf lui. *Everybody was here except him.*
Sauf avis contraire. *Unless I (you) hear to the contrary.*
saumon *m. salmon.*
saut *m. leap, jump.*
sauter *to jump, leap; omit; come off.*
Vous avez sauté tout un paragraphe. *You've skipped a paragraph.*
Cela saute aux yeux. *It's as plain as can be. It's very conspicuous. It's very obvious. ("It leaps to the eye.")*
Il a sauté sur l'offre. *He leaped at the offer.*
Ce bouton vient de sauter. *This button has just come off.*
sautiller *to hop.*
sauvage *adj. savage, wild.*
sauvegarder *to safeguard.*
sauver *to save, rescue.*
Ils sont soucieux de sauver les apparences. *They're anxious to keep up appearances.*
se sauver *to save oneself, to take refuge; to leave.*
Il s'est sauvé à toutes jambes. *He ran away as fast as his legs could carry him.*
Il est tard, je me sauve. *It is late. I have to be going (I must be off).*
Sauve qui peut! *Every man for himself!*
sauvetage *m. rescue.*
Un bateau de sauvetage. *A lifeboat.*
savant *m. learned man, scholar.*
savant *adj. learned.*
SAVOIR *m. knowledge, erudition, learning.*
Il se targue de son savoir. *He boasts of his knowledge.*
Il n'a pas de savoir-vivre. 1. *He doesn't*

know how to live. 2. *He doesn't know how to behave.*

Il ne manque pas de savoir-faire. *He knows how to handle people. He has his wits about him.*

SAVOIR *to know.*

Je ne sais pas. *I don't know.*

Je ne le sais pas. *I don't know it.*

Je n'en sais rien. *I don't know anything about it.*

Savez-vous l'anglais? *Do you know English?*

Savez-vous l'heure qu'il est? *Do you know what time it is?*

Que désirez-vous savoir? *What do you want to know? What would you like to know?*

Faites-lui savoir que nous viendrons demain. *Inform him that we're coming tomorrow.*

Je ne sais pas pourquoi il est venu. *I don't know why he came (he's come).*

Pas que je sache. *Not that I know of. Not to my knowledge.*

Pour autant que je sache. *As far as I know.*

Un je ne sais quoi. *An indefinable something (quality).*

Comme vous devez le savoir. *As you must know.*

SAVON *m. soap.*

savourer *to taste, relish, enjoy (food, etc.).*

savoureux (savoureuse *f.*) *adj. tasty.*

scandale *m. scandal.*

scandaleux (scandaleuse *f.*) *adj. scandalous.*

scandaliser *to shock.*

scarlatine *f. scarlet fever.*

sceau *m.* (sceaux *pl.*) *seal.*

scélérat *m. villain, scoundrel, rascal.*

scellé *m. seal.*

scène *f. scene, stage (theatre).*

sceptique *adj. sceptical.*

sceptre *m. scepter.*

scie *f. saw.*

science *f. science.*

Sciences appliquées. *Applied sciences.*

Homme de science. *Scientist.*

scintillant *adj. scintillating.*

scintiller *to scintillate; sparkle, twinkle.*

scolaire *adj. pertaining to school.*

L'année scolaire commence le premier octobre. *The school year begins October 1st.*

scrupule *m. scruple.*

scrupuleux (scrupuleuse *f.*) *adj. scrupulous.*

scruter *to scrutinize; to examine closely.*

scrutin *m. ballot.*

sculpter *to sculpture.*

sculpteur *m. sculptor.*

sculpture *f. sculpture.*

SE *himself, herself, itself, oneself, themselves.*

Il se lave les mains. *He's washing his hands.*

Il se lève. *He's getting up.*

Ce mot se prononce ainsi. *That word is pronounced this way.*

Il se marie demain. *He's getting married tomorrow.*

La ville se voit d'ici. *The city can be seen from here.*

séance *f. meeting.*

La séance est levée. *The meeting is adjourned.*

SEC (sèche *f.*) *adj. dry.*

Faire nettoyer à sec. *To have (something) dry-cleaned.*

sèche-cheveux *m. hair dryer.*

sécher *to dry.*

SECOND *adj. second.*

SECONDAIRE *adj. secondary.*

SECONDE *f. second; second class.*

Attendez une seconde! *Wait a second!*

Je serai là dans une seconde. *I'll be there in a minute.*

Un carnet de secondes. *A book of second-class tickets.*

secouer *to shake.*

secours *m. help, assistance.*

Au secours! *Help!*

Ils ont accouru à son secours. *They ran to his aid. They came running to help him.*

Sortie de secours. *Emergency exit.*

secousse *f. shock, jolt.*

secret *m. secret.*

Je ne suis pas du secret. *I'm not in on the secret.*

C'est le secret de Polichinelle. *It's an open secret.*

secrétaire *m. writing desk.*

secrétaire *f. secretary.*

secteur *m. sector.*

section *f. section.*

sécurité *f. security.*

En sécurité. *In safety.*

sédition *f. sedition.*

séduire *to seduce; entice, attract, tempt.*

séduisant *adj. seductive, tempting, fascinating.*

Un sourire séduisant. *A bewitching smile.*

Une offre séduisante. *A tempting offer.*

seigneur *m. lord, nobleman.*

SEIZE *noun and adj. sixteen.*

SEIZIÈME *noun and adj. sixteenth.*

séjour *m. stay, visit.*

Un séjour de dix jours. *A ten-day visit.*

Il a fait un court séjour à Paris. *He stayed in Paris for a short time.*

Il faut que j'abrège mon séjour. *I'll have to cut my stay short. I'll have to leave earlier than I intended.*

Bon séjour! *(Have a) pleasant stay!*

séjourner *to stay, remain.*

SEL *m. salt.*

Voudriez-vous me passer le sel? *Would you mind passing me the salt?*

selle *f. saddle.*

SELON *according to.*

Selon ce qu'il dit. *According to what he says.*

Selon lui, vous avez tort. *According to him, you're wrong.*

Faites selon vos désirs. *Do as you wish.*

C'est selon. *That depends.*

Chacun vit selon ses moyens. *Everyone lives according to his means.*

SEMAINE *f. week.*

La semaine prochaine. *Next week.*

La semaine dernière. *Last week.*

Payer par semaine. *To pay by the week.*

Toutes les deux semaines. *Every other week.*

Une fois par semaine. *Once a week.*

SEMBLABLE *adj. alike, similar.*

A-t-on jamais vu rien de semblable? *Did you ever see such a thing?*

Rien de semblable! *Nothing of the sort!*

semblant *m. semblance, appearance.*

Il fait semblant de ne pas comprendre. *He pretends not to understand.*

SEMBLER *to seem, appear.*

Ceci semble très peu. *This seems very little.*

Il me semble que c'est plutôt cher. *It seems to me that it's rather expensive.*

A ce qu'il me semble c'est plutôt injuste. *It seems to me that's rather unfair.*

C'est ce qui lui semble. *It's just as he thought.*

SEMELLE *f. sole.*

semer *to sow.*

semestre *m. semester.*

SENS *m. sense; opinion; direction.*

Le sens figuré. *Figurative sense.*

Une expression à double sens. *A double-entendre. An ambiguous expression.*

Il a perdu ses sens. *He lost consciousness.*

Le bon sens. *Good sense.*

Cela n'a pas de sens commun. *That's absurd. That doesn't make sense.*

Il n'a pas de sens. *He has no common sense.*

Sens dessus-dessous. *Upside down.*

Attention, c'est une rue à sens unique. *Look out! This is a one-way street.*

Le bon (mauvais) sens. *The right (wrong) direction.*

sensation *f. sensation.*

sensé *adj. sensible, judicious.*

sensible *adj. sensitive.*

Il parle d'une manière sensible. *He speaks in a very sensitive way.*

C'est une âme sensible. *She's a sensitive person ("soul").*

Il est très sensible à la critique. *He's very sensitive to criticism.*

Il est sensible à l'adulation. *He's open to flattery. He's influenced by flattery.*

sentence *f. sentence.*

Il a reçu la sentence de mort. *He received the death sentence. He was sentenced to death.*

sentier *m. footpath.*

sentiment *m. feeling, sensation.*

Il n'a aucun sentiment. *He has no feeling.*

Nous partageons vos sentiments. *We share your views. We feel the way you do.*

Je voudrais savoir votre sentiment là-dessus. *I'd like to know what you think about it.*

Il est animé de bons sentiments. *He's well-meaning. His intentions are good.*

sentimental (sentimentaux *pl.*) *adj. sentimental.*

sentinelle *f. sentry.*

SENTIR *to perceive, feel; smell.*

On sent un courant d'air. *There's a draft. You can feel a draft.*

Il ne peut pas les sentir. *He can't stand them.*

Cela sent bon. *That smells nice.*

Cela ne sent pas bon. *I don't like the looks of it. It doesn't seem promising.*

se sentir *to feel.*

Elle ne se sent pas bien. *She doesn't feel well.*

Elle se sent faible. *She feels faint.*

Les effets se font encore sentir. *The effects are still being felt.*

séparation *f. separation.*

séparer *to separate, divide.*

SEPT *noun and adj. seven.*

SEPTEMBRE *m. September.*

SEPTIÈME *noun and adj. seventh.*

serein *adj. serene, calm.*

sérénité *f. serenity.*

sergent *m. sergeant.*

série *f. series, mass.*

Fait en série. *Mass production. ("Mass-produced.")*

Article hors série. *Specially manufactured article. Article made to order.*

sérieusement *seriously.*

SÉRIEUX (sérieuse *f.*) *adj. serious.*

Etes-vous sérieux? *Are you serious?*

C'est un jeune homme peu sérieux. *He's an irresponsible young man. He's not very serious.*

A demain les affaires sérieuses. *Let's enjoy ourselves today; business tomorrow.*

C'est bien autrement sérieux. *It's (that's) far more serious.*

serment *m. oath.*

sermon *m. sermon.*

serpent *m. snake.*

serré *adj. tight.*

On est un peu serré ici. *We're a little bit crowded in here.*

Il a le coeur serré. *He has a heavy heart.*

serrer *to press, squeeze, crush.*

Serrez-lui la main. *Shake hands with him.*

Cela serre le coeur. *That's heart-rending.*

Serrer les dents. *To clench one's teeth.*

Serrer les rangs. *To close ranks.*

Jouer serré. *To be cautious. To play a cautious game. To play the cards close to the chest.*

serrure *f. lock.*

serrurier *m. locksmith.*

servante *f. maid, servant.*

service *m. service; help.*

Qu'y a-t-il pour votre service? *What can I do for you?*

Rendez-moi ce service. *Do me a ("this") favor.*

Service militaire. *Military service.*

Chef de service. *Departmental head.*

A votre service. *At your service.*

serviette *f. napkin; towel; briefcase.*

Une serviette de toilette. *A (hand or face) towel.*

Une serviette éponge. *A Turkish towel.*

servir *to serve.*

On sert à boire et à manger. *Food and drink served here.*

Madame est servie. *Dinner is ready.*

Elle sert à table. *She waits on (the) table.*

Que cela vous serve de leçon. *Let that be a lesson to you.*

En quoi pourrais-je vous servir? *What can I do for you?*

Servir la messe. *To serve mass.*

se servir *to help oneself.*

Servez-vous. *Help yourself.*

Comme je n'avais pas de ciseaux je me suis servi d'un couteau. *Since I didn't have a pair of scissors, I used a knife.*

serviteur *m. servant.*

servitude *f. servitude, slavery.*

SES *See son.*

seuil *m. threshold.*

SEUL *adj. only, sole, single; alone.*

Mon seul et unique désir. *My only wish.*

Il aime rester seul. *He likes to be alone.*

SEULEMENT *only.*

Non seulement . . . mais encore . . . *Not only . . . but also . . .*

sévère *adj. severe, austere.*

sévérité *f. severity.*

sexe *m. sex.*

shampooing *m. shampoo.*

SI *whether; suppose that.*

Si on faisait une promenade? *How about taking a walk?*

Si on voulait la revendre? *Suppose we wanted to sell it back?*

SI *so.*

Ne parlez pas si haut. *Don't talk so loud.*

Il pleuvait si fort que nous ne pouvions sortir. *It rained so hard that we couldn't go out.*

Par un si beau dimanche. *On such a beautiful Sunday.*

SI *yes (in answering a negative question).*

N'avez-vous pas d'argent?—Si, j'en ai. *Don't you have any money?—Yes, I do.*

N'est-il pas encore parti?—Si, il est parti. *Hasn't he left yet?—Yes, he has.*

SIDA *m. AIDS.*

sideré *adj. dumbfounded.*

Il en resta tout sidéré. *He was completely dumbfounded.*

siècle *m. century.*

siège *m. siege; seat.*

siéger *to be seated.*

SIEN *(sienne f.) his, her, its.*

Ce n'est pas mon livre, c'est le sien. *It's not my book; it's his.*

Il a fait des siennes. *He's up to his old tricks again.*

sieste *f. nap, siesta.*

siffler *to whistle; hiss.*

sifflet *m. whistle; hiss.*

signal *m. signal.*

signaler *to point out.*

Je lui ai signalé l'erreur. *I drew his attention to the error.*

signature *f. signing, signature.*

signe *m. sign.*

Faire signe. *To make a sign. To signal. To gesture. To motion.*

Faire signe que oui. *To nod assent.*

signer *to sign.*

Signez ici. *Sign here.*

signification *f. meaning.*

SIGNIFIER *to mean.*

Qu'est-ce que ça signifie? *What does that mean?*

Qu'est-ce que ce mot signifie? *What does this word mean? What's the meaning of this word?*

SILENCE *m. silence.*

silencieux *(silencieuse f.) adj. silent.*

silhouette *f. silhouette, outline.*

similarité *f. similarity, likeness.*

SIMPLE *adj. simple.*

C'est simple comme bonjour. *As easy as falling off a log. As simple as ABC. As easy as anything.*

Un simple soldat. *A private.*

Ce sont des gens simples. *They're very simple people.*

simplement (tout simplement) *simply; just, only.*

simplicité *f. simplicity.*

simuler *to simulate, sham, pretend.*

sincère *adj. sincere.*

sincérité *f. sincerity.*

singe *m. monkey.*

singulier (singulière *f.*) *adj. singular; strange.*

Voici autre chose de plus singulier. *Here's something else that's even stranger.*

sinistre *adj. sinister.*

SINON *otherwise.*

sirop *m. syrup.*

sitôt *so soon.*

situation *f. situation.*

SIX *noun and adj. six.*

SIXIÈME *noun and adj. sixth.*

ski *m. ski, skiing.*

Faire du ski. *To ski.*

Faire du ski nautique. *To water-ski.*

slip *m. pair of (man's) shorts, bathing trunks.*

sobre *adj. sober, temperate, serious.*

sobriété *f. sobriety.*

sobriquet *m. nickname.*

social (sociaux *pl.*) *adj. social.*

socialisme *m. socialism.*

socialiste *m. and f. noun and adj. socialist.*

société *f. society.*

Il ne fréquente que la haute société. *He moves only in the best circles.*

La société fait un appel de capital. *The company is increasing its capital.*

Il s'affilia à une société sportive. *He joined an athletic club.*

J'ai eu le plaisir de sa société. *I have had the pleasure of his company.*

La Société Nationale des Chemins de Fer Français (S.N.C.F.). *French National Railways.*

SOEUR *f. sister.*

sofa *m. sofa.*

SOI *himself, herself, itself.*

Cela va de soi. *That goes without saying. Of course.*

Il n'a pas dix minutes à soi. *He hasn't ten minutes to himself.*

Chacun pour soi. *Every man for himself.*

Il ne pense qu'à soi. *He thinks only of himself.*

Soi-disant. *Would be.*

Un chez soi. *A home.*

soi-même *oneself.*

soie *f. silk.*

SOIF *f. thirst.*

J'ai soif. *I'm thirsty.*

soigner *to look after, take care of.*

Il faut bien les soigner. *We must take good care of them.*

SOIN *m. care.*

Prenez soin de ne pas réveiller les enfants. *Take care not to wake the children.*

Aux bons soins de. *In care of.*

Ce travail est fait sans soin. *This work is carelessly done.*

Elle a beaucoup de soin. *She's very tidy.*

Il est aux petits soins pour elle. *He shows her a lot of attention.*

SOIR *m. evening.*

A ce soir. *See you tonight. Until tonight.*

soirée *f. evening; party.*

soit *so be it; either . . . or . . .*

Je viendrai soit demain soit jeudi. *I'll come either tomorrow or Thursday.*

Vous venez avec moi?—Soit. *Are you coming with me?—All right.*

soixantaine *f. about sixty.*

SOIXANTE *noun and adj. sixty.*

soixante-dix (**-douze**) *seventy (seventy-two).*

soixantième *noun and adj. sixtieth.*

sol *m. ground.*

soldat *m. soldier.*

solde *m. sale.*

solde *f. pay.*

SOLEIL *m. sun.*

Il fait du soleil. *The weather is sunny.*

solennel (solennelle *f.*) *adj. solemn.*

solide *adj. solid, strong.*

Il est solide au poste. *He's strong. He's hale and hearty.*

Asseoir sur une base solide. *To establish on a solid basis.*

Il n'est pas solide sur ses jambes. *His legs are weak.*

solidifier *to solidify.*

solidité *f. solidity.*

solitaire *adj. solitary.*

solitude *f. solitude.*

soliciter *to entreat, beseech, ask earnestly.*

solution *f. solution.*

sombre *adj. dark, gloomy, somber.*

Il y fait sombre comme dans un four. *It's pitch-black. ("It's as black as an oven.")*

Une robe bleu sombre. *A dark-blue dress.*

sombrer *to sink.*

sommaire *m. summary, table of contents.*

sommaire *adj. summary, concise.*

Un repas sommaire. *A quick meal. A snack.*

sommation *f. summons.*

somme *m. nap.*

SOMME *f. sum.*

Sa somme s'élève à deux cent dix francs. *The total amounts to 210 francs.*

En somme. *On the whole. Finally. After all. In the end.*

SOMMEIL *m. sleep.*

J'ai sommeil. *I'm sleepy.*

Le sommeil le gagne. *He's becoming very sleepy.*

sommeiller *to doze.*

sommer *to summon.*

sommet *m. summit.*

somptueux (somptueuse *f.*) *adj. sumptuous.*

son *m. sound.*

SON (sa *f.*, ses *pl.*) *adj. his, hers, its.*

Il veut son livre. *He wants his book.*

Où est sa lettre? *Where's his (her) letter?*

Il cherche ses gants. *He's looking for his gloves.*

Des sons bruyants. *Noise.*

songe *m. dream.*

En songe. *In a dream.*

J'ai fait un drôle de songe. *I had a strange dream.*

songer *to dream; daydream.*

Songer à partir. *To think of leaving. To plan (intend) to leave.*

Nous songeons avec regret à votre départ. *We're sorry that you're leaving.*

sonner *to ring.*

On sonne. *Someone is ringing.*

Vous avez le temps de déjeuner avant que la cloche ne sonne. *You have time for lunch before the bell rings.*

sonnerie *f. ringing.*

sonnette *f. bell.*

sonore *adj. sonorous, resonant.*

sorcier *m.* (sorcière *f.*) *sorcerer; witch.*

sordide *adj. sordid, squalid, mean.*

sornette *f. nonsense, idle talk.*

sort *m. lot, fate.*

Les hommes sont rarement contents de leur sort. *People are seldom satisfied with their lot.*

On l'a abandonné à son sort. *He was left to his fate.*

Le sort en est jeté. *The die is cast.*

SORTE *f. manner, way.*

Toutes sortes de. *All kinds of.*

De toute sorte. *Of every kind.*

De telle sorte que. *In such a way that.*

En quelque sorte. *In some way. In a way. In some degree.*

D'aucune sorte. *Certainly not.*

Ne parlez pas de la sorte. *Don't speak like that (that way).*

Il parle avec un accent de sorte qu'il est difficile de le comprendre. *He speaks with such an accent that it's hard to understand him.*

sortie *f. exit.*

Par ici la sortie. *Exit (through here).*

SORTIR *to go out.*

Il vient de sortir. *He just went out. He just left.*

Vous sortez de la question. *You're getting away from the point.*

Sortez les mains de vos poches. *Take your hands out of your pockets.*

sottise *f. foolishness.*

Il ne fait que des sottises. *He's always doing something foolish. He's always making some blunder.*

Il est en train de débiter des sottises. *He's talking nonsense.*

SOU *m. penny.*

Nous étions sans le sou. *We were without a penny.*

Il n'a pas un sou vaillant. *He hasn't a penny to his name.*

Il n'a pas pour deux sous de courage. *He hasn't any courage.*

souche *f. stump; stock.*

Venir de bonne souche. *To come of good stock.*

Une souche. *A stub (of a ticket).*

SOUCI *m. worry, care.*

Il n'a aucun souci. *He has no worries.*

C'est le cadet de mes soucis. *That's the least of my worries.*

se soucier *to concern oneself, bother with.*

soucieux (soucieuse *f.*) *adj. anxious.*

Il est soucieux de faire son devoir. *He's anxious to do his duty.*

Il est peu soucieux de le revoir. *He isn't very eager to see him again.*

SOUDAIN *suddenly.*

Soudain, ils ont entendu un bruit. *Suddenly they heard a noise.*

SOUDAINEMENT *suddenly.*

Une idée lui vient à l'esprit soudainement. *Suddenly he gets an idea.*

souffle *m. breath.*

souffler *to breathe, blow.*

soufflet *m. slap.*

souffrance *f. suffering.*

Malgré ses souffrances. *In spite of his troubles.*

Cette affaire est en souffrance. *The matter has been postponed (is being held in abeyance).*

souffrant *adj. unwell.*

Il paraît souffrant. *He seems to be unwell. He seems to be suffering (in pain).*

souffrir *to suffer.*

Cela ne souffrira aucune difficulté. *There won't be the slightest difficulty.*

Je ne peux pas la souffrir. *I can't bear the sight of her.*

souhait *m. wish, desire.*

A souhait. *According to one's wishes. To one's liking.*

À vos souhaits! *Bless you (when someone sneezes)!*

souhaiter to wish.
Je vous souhaite un bon anniversaire. *(I wish you a) Happy Birthday!*
souiller to soil.
soulagement m. relief, alleviation (of pain).
soulager to ease; relieve, alleviate.
Il était soulagé. *He was relieved. His mind was set at ease.*
soulever to raise, lift; rouse, stir up.
Il ne pouvait pas soulever le paquet, c'était trop lourd. *He couldn't lift the package; it was too heavy.*
Cela me soulève le coeur. *That makes me sick. That makes me nauseous.*
soulier m. shoe.
Lacez vos souliers. *Tie your shoelaces.*
Il est dans ses petits souliers. *He's uneasy.*
souligner to underline.
se soumettre to submit.
Il a dû se soumettre à leur décision. *He had to abide by their decision.*
soumission f. submission; surrender.
soupçon m. suspicion; a little bit.
Rien ne justifiait ces soupçons. *Nothing justified these suspicions.*
Est-ce que vous voulez encore un peu de vin?—Juste un soupçon. *Do you want a little more wine?—Just a little bit more. Just a drop more.*
soupçonner to suspect.
soupe f. soup.
SOUPER to have supper.
Allons souper. *Let's have supper.*
Cette fois-ci j'en ai soupé *(fam.)*! *This time I'm fed up with it!*
soupir m. sigh.
soupirer to sigh.
souple adj. flexible, pliant.
Un bois souple. *Pliant wood.*
Un esprit souple. *A versatile mind.*
Un prix souple. *A price that is not fixed (that can be changed).*
Il est souple comme un gant. *He's easy to manage.*
source f. source.
Je le tiens de bonne source. *I have it on good authority (from a good source).*
Eau de source. *Spring water.*
sourcil m. eyebrow.
sourciller to frown, wince.
sourd adj. deaf.
Il est sourd comme un pot. *He's as deaf as a doorknob.*
Il fait la sourde oreille. *He turns a deaf ear.*
Sourd-muet: *Deaf-mute.*
sourdine f. mute.
En sourdine. *In secret. On the sly.*
souriant adj. smiling.
SOURIRE m. smile.

SOURIRE to smile; attract.
Il sourit tout le temps. *He's always smiling.*
Je dois avouer que l'idée me sourit. *I must admit that the idea attracts me (that I like the idea).*
souris f. mouse.
sournois adj. sly.
SOUS under, beneath.
Regardez sous la table. *Look under the table.*
C'est sous ce tas de papiers. *It's under this pile of papers.*
Cet acteur est connu sous le nom de Durand. *The stage name of this actor is Durand. ("This actor is known under the name of Durand.")*
Sous-directeur. *Assistant director.*
souscription f. subscription.
souscrire to subscribe.
Souscrire un chèque au porteur. *To make a check payable to bearer.*
sous-développer to underdevelop.
Pays sous-développé. *Underdeveloped country.*
sous-entendu m. double meaning.
Il le lui a fait comprendre par sous-entendus. *He hinted at it.*
sous-louer to sublet.
sous-main m. blotter.
soussigné adj. undersigned.
Je, soussigné. *I, the undersigned.*
sous-sol m. basement.
soustraction f. subtraction.
soustraire to subtract.
Soustrayez dix de vingt. *Subtract ten from twenty.*
Il a soustrait dix francs au cent qu'il me devait. *He took off ten francs from the 100 he owed me.*
soutenir to support, hold up; maintain.
Si on ne l'avait pas soutenu, il serait tombé. *If we hadn't held him up, he would have fallen.*
Il soutenait que je m'étais trompé. *He insisted (maintained) that I was mistaken.*
J'ai toujours soutenu son point de vue. *I've always supported his point of view.*
se soutenir to support oneself.
Il peut à peine se soutenir sur ses jambes. *He can hardly keep on his feet.*
soutenu adj. sustained.
souterrain m. underground.
souvenir m. remembrance.
En souvenir de. *In memory of.*
Son souvenir m'est resté. *I still remember him.*
SE SOUVENIR to remember.
Il se souvient toujours de vous. *He still remembers you.*

Je m'en souviens comme si ça m'était arrivé hier. *I can remember it as though it were yesterday.*

Je me souviens de votre nom. *I remember your name.*

SOUVENT *often.*

Est-ce que ceci arrive souvent? *Does this often happen?*

Je vais souvent chez lui. *I often go to his home.*

souverain *m. sovereign.*

souverain *adj. supreme.*

Un remède souverain. *A sure remedy.*

Il a un souverain mépris pour eux. *He has great contempt for them.*

spacieux (spacieuse *f.*) *adj. spacious.*

SPÉCIAL (spéciaux *pl.*) *adj. special.*

Un train spécial. *A special train.*

C'est une occasion spéciale. *It's a special occasion.*

Affectez cette dépense au compte spécial. *Put that expense on the special account.*

spécialiser *to specialize.*

se spécialiser *to specialize.*

spécialiste *m. and f. noun and adj. specialist; technician.*

spécialité *f. specialty.*

C'est une des spécialités de la maison. *This is one of the specialties of the house (in a restaurant).*

spécifier *to specify, be specific.*

Spécifiez! *Be specific!*

spécimen *m. specimen.*

spectacle *m. spectacle, show.*

Spectacle pour grandes personnes seulement. *Adults only.*

spectateur *m.* (spectatrice *f.*) *spectator; pl. audience.*

spectre *m. ghost.*

spéculateur *m. speculator.*

spéculer *to speculate.*

sphère *f. sphere; field, element.*

Là, il est hors de sa sphère. *He's out of his element there.*

spirituel (spirituelle *f.*) *adj. witty.*

spleen *m. spleen.*

splendide *adj. splendid.*

C'est splendide! *That's wonderful!*

Il fait un temps splendide, n'est-ce pas? *The weather's lovely, isn't it?*

spontané *adj. spontaneous.*

sport *m. sport.*

Faire des sports d'hiver. *To practice (engage in) winter sports.*

sportif (sportive *f.*) *adj. pertaining to sports.*

square *m. enclosed public garden.*

squelette *m. skeleton.*

stable *adj. stable, permanent.*

Un emploi stable. *A permanent position (job).*

stand *m. stand.*

station *f. standing; station, resort, stand.*

Il se tient là en station derrière la porte. *He's standing posted there behind the door.*

Une station balnéaire. *A seashore resort.*

La station de ski. *Ski resort.*

La station-service. *Service station.*

La tête de station. *Taxi stand.*

stationner *to stop, to park.*

Défense de stationner! *No parking! No loitering!*

statue *f. statue.*

stature *f. stature.*

statut *m. statute, bylaw.*

sténo *f. shorthand.*

sténographie *f. shorthand.*

stéréo (phonique) *adj. stereo(phonic).*

stérile *adj. sterile, barren.*

stimuler *to stimulate, spur on.*

stock *m. stock (in trade).*

store *m. window shade.*

stratagème *m. stratagem, trickery.*

strict *adj. strict.*

strictement *strictly.*

structure *f. structure.*

Une structure imposante. *An imposing structure. A huge building.*

studieux (studieuse *f.*) *adj. studious.*

studio *m. studio.*

stupéfaction *f. amazement.*

Imaginez-vous ma stupéfaction! *Imagine my amazement (surprise)!*

stupéfait *adj. amazed.*

J'en suis resté tout stupéfait. *I was completely dumbfounded.*

stupeur *f. stupor.*

Il fut frappé de stupeur. *He was dumbfounded.*

stupide *adj. stupid.*

stupidité *f. stupidity.*

style *m. style.*

Les meubles de style. *Period furniture.*

styler *to train.*

Votre domestique est bien stylée. *Your maid is well-trained.*

stylo *f. (fountain) pen.*

Le stylo à bille. *Ball-point pen.*

su *m. knowledge.*

Au vu et au su de tout le monde. *In public. Publicly.*

Il l'a fait au su de tout le monde. *He did it publicly.*

su *known.*

suave *adj. suave.*

subconscient *adj. subconscious.*

subdiviser *to subdivide.*

SUBIR *to undergo.*
  Il a subi une grave opération. *He underwent a serious operation.*
  Il n'est pas homme à subir un affront. *He isn't one to overlook an insult.*
  Il a subi un grand choc. *He received a great shock.*
subitement *suddenly.*
subjonctif (subjonctive *f.*) *noun* (*m.*) *and adj. subjunctive.*
subjuguer *to subdue, subjugate.*
sublime *adj. sublime.*
submerger *to submerge.*
subordonner *to subordinate.*
subside *m. subsidy.*
subsidiaire *adj. subsidiary, additional.*
subsistance *f. maintenance, subsistence.*
  Il gagne juste-assez pour sa subsistance. *He earns just enough for his subsistence.*
subsister *to subsist; continue to exist, remain.*
  Ce contrat subsiste toujours. *This contract still holds.*
substance *f. substance*.
  En substance. *In substance.*
  Certaines substances fermentent sous l'action de l'eau ou de la chaleur. *Certain substances ferment under the action of water or heat.*
  Un argument sans substance. *An argument without any weight.*
  La substance d'un article. *The gist of an article.*
substituer *to substitute.*
substitution *f. substitution.*
subterfuge *m. subterfuge.*
subtil *adj. subtle.*
subvenir *to provide.*
  Subvenir aux besoins de quelqu'un. *To provide for someone's needs.*
succéder *to succeed, follow after, take the place of.*
  Il succéda à son père. *He succeeded his father.*
succès *m. success.*
  Avec succès. *Successfully.*
  La pièce a eu un succès fou. *The play was a great success.*
  J'ai essayé sans succès. *I tried in vain.*
  Rien ne réussit comme le succès. *Nothing succeeds like success.*
successeur *m. successor.*
succession *f. succession.*
  Il a recueilli la succession de son père. *He inherited his father's money.*
  Il a pris sa succession. *He took over his business.*
  Droits de succession. *Inheritance taxes.*
succinct *adj. succinct, concise.*
succomber *to succumb, yield to.*

  Il a succombé à la tentation. *He yielded to temptation.*
  Succomber sous le poids de quelque chose. *To sink under the weight of something.*
  Je succombe de sommeil. *I'm dead tired. I can't keep my eyes open.*
  Succomber sous le nombre. *To yield to superior numbers. To be overpowered by numbers.*
succulent *adj. juicy.*
  Un repas succulent. *An appetizing meal.*
succursale *f. branch.*
  Cette banque a une succursale rue de Rivoli. *This bank has a branch on Rivoli Street.*
sucer *to suck.*
SUCRE *m. sugar.*
  Aimez-vous beaucoup de sucre dans votre café? *Do you like a lot of sugar in your coffee?*
  Elle est tout sucre et tout miel. *She's all honey.*
sucrier *m. sugar bowl.*
SUD *noun* (*m.*) *and adj. south.*
suer *to sweat, perspire.*
sueur *f. perspiration, sweat.*
SUFFIRE *to be sufficient.*
  Cela suffit. *That's enough.*
  Est-ce que cela suffit? *Is that enough?*
  Il suffit. *It's enough.*
  Une fois suffit, n'y revenez plus. *Once is enough. Don't try it again.*
  Il suffit qu'on lui dise de faire quelque chose pour qu'il fasse le contraire. *All you have to do is tell him to do something and he does the opposite. You have only to tell him to do something for him to do the opposite.*
suffisamment *sufficiently.*
  Suffisamment d'argent. *Enough money.*
SUFFISANT *adj. sufficient.*
  Ce n'est pas suffisant. *It's not enough.*
suffoquer *to suffocate.*
suffrage *m. suffrage.*
SUGGÉRER *to suggest.*
  Pouvez-vous suggérer quelque chose d'autre? *Can you suggest anything else?*
  Il a suggéré que nous attendions encore un mois. *He suggested that we wait another month.*
SUGGESTION *f. suggestion.*
  Puis-je offrir une suggestion? *May I make a suggestion?*
  Je crois que nous devrions adopter toutes ses suggestions. *I think we should adopt all of his suggestions.*
suicide *m. suicide.*
se suicider *to commit suicide.*

suie f. *soot.*

SUITE f. *(act of) following, sequence; pursuit; what follows; consequence, result.*

Revenez tout de suite. *Come back right away.*

Cinq fois de suite. *Five times in succession.*

Et ainsi de suite. *And so forth. And so on. Et cetera.*

Tout ce qu'on peut faire, c'est attendre la suite. *All we can do is to wait and see what happens.*

Comme suite à votre lettre du dix courant. *In reference to your letter of the tenth of this month.*

Il n'a pas de suite dans les idées. *He's inconsistent.*

La suite au prochain numéro. *To be continued in the next issue.*

La suite des événements. *The sequence (course) of events.*

Suite d'orchestre. *Suite for orchestra.*

Par suite de sa maladie il a dû partir dans le Midi. *Because of his illness he had to leave for the South.*

suisse m. and f. *noun and adj. Swiss.*

suivant (suivante f.) *noun and adj. following, next.*

Le suivant! *Next!*

Au suivant! *Next, please!*

Prenez le suivant. *Take the next one.*

SUIVANT *following, in conformance with, according to.*

J'agirai suivant la décision que vous prendrez. *I'll act according to your decision.*

Suivant le journal, le cabinet démissionera demain. *According to the newspaper, the cabinet will resign tomorrow.*

SUIVRE *to follow.*

Partez maintenant, je vous suis dans un moment. *You leave now. I'll follow you in a minute.*

Il le suit de près. *He's close on his heels.*

Son accent est si prononcé que j'ai beaucoup de mal à le suivre. *He has such a thick accent that it's hard for me to follow him.*

Oui, je vous suis. *Yes, I follow you.*

Il suit un cours de philosophie. *He attends a philosophy class. He's taking a course in philosophy.*

A suivre. *To be continued.*

A faire suivre. *Please forward.*

N'oubliez pas de suivre l'affaire. *Don't forget to follow the matter up.*

Une conséquence suit l'autre. *One thing leads to another.*

Il suit de là que . . . *It follows from this that . . .*

se **suivre** *to follow in order.*

Que s'en est-il suivi? *What came of it? What was the result?*

Cela posé, il s'en suit que nous nous étions trompés. *Once that is granted, it follows that we must have been mistaken.*

Les jours se suivent et ne se ressemblent pas. *There is no telling what tomorrow will bring.*

SUJET m. *subject.*

Quelle est le sujet de ce livre? *What's the subject of this book?*

Assez sur ce sujet. *That's enough about that (matter).*

Il n'a qu'une connaissance superficielle du sujet. *He has only a very superficial knowledge of the subject.*

Mauvais sujet. *A good-for-nothing. A rascal.*

Il était inquiet à son sujet. *He was worried about him (her).*

Au sujet de votre ami, il est revenu me voir hier. *As for your friend, he came back to see me yesterday.*

J'ai tout sujet de croire que c'est ainsi. *I have every reason to believe that it's so.*

sujet (sujette f.) *adj. subject to, inclined to, liable, exposed.*

Elle est sujette aux maux de têtes. *She's subject to headaches.*

super m. *special ("Super") gasoline.*

superbe adj. *superb.*

Il fait un temps superbe. *The weather is magnificent.*

Elle a un teint superbe. *She has a beautiful complexion.*

supercherie f. *deceit, fraud.*

superficie f. *surface, area.*

superficiel (superficielle f.) *adj. superficial.*

superflu adj. *superfluous.*

Il serait superflu d'en dire plus long. *It would be superfluous to say any more.*

supérieur adj. *superior.*

supériorité f. *superiority.*

superlatif noun (m.) *and adj.* (superlative f.) *superlative.*

superstitieux (superstitieuse f.) *adj. superstitious.*

superstition f. *superstition.*

suppléer *to take the place of; supply.*

Il s'est fait suppléer par un jeune homme. *He found a young man to replace him.*

Suppléez-nous de marchandise aussitôt que possible. *Supply us with more merchandise as soon as possible.*

supplément m. *supplement, extra.*

On paye un supplément pour le vin. *You have to pay extra for the wine.*

supplémentaire adj. supplementary.

Faire des heures supplémentaires. To work overtime.

On lui a demandé de rédiger un article supplémentaire. They asked him to write an additional article.

suppliant adj. pleading, suppliant.

supplication f. entreaty, plea.

supplice m. punishment, torture, agony.

supplier to beseech.

Je vous en supplie! I beg of you! Please!

support m. support, pillar, prop.

supportable adj. bearable, tolerable.

supporter to support; bear, suffer, put up with.

Je ne peux pas la supporter. I can't stand her.

supposer to suppose.

supposition f. supposition.

supprimer to suppress, cancel, abolish.

suprématie f. supremacy.

suprême adj. supreme, highest.

sur adj. sour.

SUR on, upon, above.

Mettez-le sur la table. Put it on the table.

Ne vous accoudez pas sur la table. Don't lean on the table.

Il a écrit un livre sur les Etats-Unis. He wrote a book about the United States.

Cette table a deux mètres sur cinq. This table is two meters by five.

Il était sur le point de partir. He was just about to leave.

Il arriva sur ces entrefaites. He arrived just at that moment.

Revenez sur vos pas. Retrace your steps.

Je n'ai pas d'argent sur moi. I have no money on (with) me.

SÛR adj. certain.

J'en suis sûr. I'm certain about it.

Il est toujours sûr de son fait. He always knows what he's talking about.

Bien sûr, j'ai compris. Of course, I understood.

Soyez sûr que je ne l'oublierai pas de sitôt. You may be sure that I won't forget it so soon.

Il est sûr de son affaire. 1. He's sure to succeed. 2. He's sure to get what he deserves. He's sure to get his.

surcharger to overload, overburden.

surchauffer to overheat.

surcouper to overtrump (cards).

surcroît m. addition.

Par surcroît. In addition.

Il a peur de faire un surcroît d'effort. He's afraid to exert himself ("make an extra effort.")

SÛREMENT surely.

Il va sûrement échouer. He'll surely fail. He's sure to fail.

Qui va lentement va sûrement. Slow and sure wins the race.

surenchère f. higher bid.

surestimer to overestimate.

sûreté f. safety.

Ne vous en faites pas, il est en sûreté. Don't worry, he's safe.

La Sûreté. The Criminal Investigation Department.

surface f. surface, area.

Il n'approfondit rien, il s'arrête toujours à la surface des choses. He never examines anything carefully. He never goes below the surface.

Quelle est la surface de ce terrain? What's the area of this piece of land?

surgir to spring up; appear.

Une voile surgit à l'horizon. A sail appeared on the horizon.

Faire surgir un souvenir. To evoke a memory.

surhumain adj. superhuman.

Un effort surhumain. A superhuman effort.

sur-le-champ at once, immediately.

Faites-le sur-le-champ. Do it right away.

surlendemain m. the day after.

surmener to overwork.

Surmener quelqu'un. To work someone too hard.

se surmener to overwork oneself.

surmontable adj. surmountable, that can be overcome.

Des difficultés surmontables. Surmountable obstacles. Difficulties that can be overcome.

surmonter to rise higher; surmount.

Il a surmonté tous ses ennuis. He overcame all his difficulties.

surnaturel (surnaturelle f.) adj. supernatural.

surnom n. nickname.

surpasser to surpass.

surpeuplé adj. overpopulated.

surplus m. surplus, excess.

Vous pouvez garder le surplus. You may keep the remainder (what's left over)

Au surplus, ayez la bonté de me taper deux lettres. In addition, please type two letters for me. Will you also type two letters for me, please?

surprenant adj. amazing, surprising.

SURPRENDRE to surprise.

Je ne suis pas du tout surpris. I'm not at all surprised.

Qu'il vous ait joué ce coup ne me surprend pas du tout. I'm not at all surprised that he played that trick on you.

Je l'ai surpris en flagrant délit. I caught him in the act.

L'orage nous a surpris. The storm overtook us.

SURPRISE *f. surprise.*
A ma grande surprise. *To my great surprise. Much to my surprise.*
Quelle bonne surprise! *What a pleasant surprise!*
Il nous a tous eu par surprise! *He took us all by surprise.*

surréaliste *adj. surrealistic.*

sursaut *m. jump; start.*
Il s'est éveillé en sursaut. *He awoke with a start.*

sursauter *to jump up; start (up).*
Il sursaute chaque fois qu'on ouvre la porte. *He jumps up every time the door opens.*
Pour un rien, elle sursaute. *She gets excited about the least little thing.*

sursis *m. respite.*
On lui a accordé un sursis. *He was granted an arrest of judgment.*

SURTOUT *above all, particularly, especially.*
Surtout, revenez à temps. *Be sure to come back on time. Above all, get back in time.*
Il lui a surtout demandé de ne pas en parler. *He especially asked him not to speak about it.*
Surtout n'allez pas là-bas. *Be sure not to go there.*
Surtout ne le laissez pas faire cela. *Whatever you do, don't let him do that.*

surveillance *f. supervision.*

surveillant *m. watchman; proctor, monitor (in a school).*

surveiller *to keep an eye on, watch.*

survenir *to arrive unexpectedly.*
Une tempête est survenue. *A heavy storm suddenly arose.*

survivant *m. survivor.*

survivre *to survive.*

susceptible *adj. susceptible.*
Je pense que ceci est susceptible de vous intéresser. *I think this may be of interest to you.*

susciter *to stir up, raise up, instigate, rouse, create, give rise to, cause.*

susdit *noun (m.) and adj. aforesaid.*

suspect (suspecte *f.*) *noun and adj. suspect.*

suspecter *to suspect.*

suspendre *to suspend.*
Le chandelier est suspendu au plafond. *The chandelier is suspended from the ceiling.*
A cause de la grève le travail a été suspendu. *Work has been suspended because of the strike.*

suspens *m. suspense.*
Ne nous tenez pas en suspens. *Don't keep us in suspense.*

suspension *f. suspension, cessation.*

suspicion. *f. suspicion.*

svelte *adj. slender, slim.*

S.V.P. *(abbreviation of* s'il vous plaît*) Please.*
Sonnez S.V.P. *Please ring the bell.*
R.S.V.P. *R.S.V.P. Please answer.*

syllabe *f. syllable.*

symbole *m. symbol.*

symbolique *adj. symbolic.*

symétrie *f. symmetry.*

symétrique *adj. symmetrical*

sympa *adj. (fam.) see* **sympathique.**

sympathie *f. sympathy.*
J'éprouve beaucoup de sympathie envers elle. *I've a great deal of sympathy for her.*
Il s'est aliéné les sympathies de tous. *He lost everybody's sympathy. He alienated everybody.*

sympathique *adj. congenial, likable, pleasant.*
C'est un homme très sympathique. *He's a very congenial (pleasant, nice, likable) fellow.*
Il m'est très sympathique. *I like him a lot.*

sympathiser *to sympathize.*

symphonie *f. symphony.*

symphonique *adj. symphonic.*

symptôme *m. symptom.*

synagogue *f. synagogue.*

syncope *f. fainting spell; syncopation (music).*

syndicat *m. (trade) union.*
Syndicat d'initiative. *Tourist (information) bureau.*

synonyme *adj. synonymous.*

syntaxe *f. syntax.*

système *m. system.*
Le système métrique. *Metric system.*
Le système nerveux. *The nervous system.*
Le système digestif. *The digestive system.*
Il s'est habitué rapidement au nouveau système. *He rapidly became accustomed to the new system.*
Il me tape sur le système (*fam.*). *He gets on my nerves.*
Par système. *Systematically.*

T

ta *See* ton.

tabac *m. tobacco.*

TABLE *f. table.*
Mettre la table. *To set the table.*
Mettons-nous à table. *Let's sit down to eat.*
Une table de quatre couverts, s'il vous plaît. *A table for four, please.*
Une table alphabétique. *An alphabetical list.*
Table des matières. *Table of contents.*

tableau *m. picture, painting.*
  Le tableau noir. *Blackboard.*
  Le cadre pour tableaux. *Picture frame.*
tablier *m. apron.*
tabouret *m. stool.*
tache *f. spot, stain.*
  Une tache de vin. *A wine stain.*
  Une tache de naissance. *Birthmark.*
  Des taches de rousseur. *Freckles.*
  Faire une tache. *To make a stain.*
TÂCHE *f. job, task.*
  Une tâche difficile. *A difficult task.*
  Mettez-vous à la tâche. *Get down to work.*
  Il prit à tâche de terminer le travail. *He made it his business to finish the work. He made it his job to get the work finished.*
  Un ouvrage à la tâche. *Piecework.*
  Ouvrier à la tâche. *A worker who does piecework.*
TACHER *to spot.*
TÂCHER *to try.*
  Tâchez d'y aller. *Try to go there.*
  Tâchez d'arriver de bonne heure. *Try to come early.*
  Tâchez de ne pas oublier. *Try not to forget.*
  Je tâcherai. *I'll try.*
tacite *adj. tacit, implied.*
taciturne *adj. taciturn, silent.*
tact *m. tact.*
taie *f. case, pillowcase.*
  Une taie d'oreiller. *A pillowcase.*
taille *f. cutting; height; waist; size (dresses, suits, coats, shirts).*
  C'est un homme de taille moyenne. *He's a man of average height.*
  Elle a une taille mince. *She's slender.*
  Quelle est votre taille? *What size do you wear? What's your size?*
  Il est de taille à se defendre. *He's capable of taking care of himself (defending himself).*
tailler *to sharpen.*
  Taillez votre crayon. *Sharpen your pencil.*
  On m'a taillé de la besogne. *I have my work cut out for me.*
tailleur *m. tailor; (woman's) suit.*
  Son tailleur a beaucoup de chic. *Her suit is very smart.*
taire *to say nothing of, keep quiet about, suppress.*
se taire *to be silent.*
  Taisez-vous! *Keep quiet! Shut up!*
  Vous n'avez plus qu'à vous taire. *You'd better not say anything. You'd better keep quiet.*
  Qui se tait consent. *Silence gives consent.*
talc *m. talc, talcum powder.*
talent *m. talent, skill.*

talon *m. heel.*
tambour *m. drum.*
tamis *m. sieve.*
tampon *m. plug, stopper.*
TANDIS QUE *while, whereas.*
  Il lisait tandis que je travaillais. *He was reading while I worked.*
  Il peut y aller tandis que nous devons rester ici. *He's able to go there whereas we have to stay here.*
tangible *adj. tangible.*
tanné *adj. sunburnt.*
TANT *so much.*
  Ne m'en donnez pas tant. *Don't give me so much.*
  J'ai tant de travail à faire! *I've so much work to do!*
  Je le lui ai répété tant de fois. *I've repeated it to him so many times.*
  Tant de monde. *So many people. Such a crowd.*
  Si vous réussissez, tant mieux. *So much the better if you succeed.*
  Tant pis! *Too bad! So much the worse.*
  Nous l'avons fait tant bien que mal. *We did it as well as we could.*
  Vous m'en direz tant! *You don't say so!*
tante *f. aunt.*
tantôt *in a little while, by and by, shortly, soon.*
  A tantôt. *See you later.*
tapage *m. racket, noise.*
taper *to tap, strike, beat; type.*
  Tapez cette lettre à la machine. *Type this letter.*
tapis *m. rug, carpet.*
tapisserie *f. tapestry.*
  Faire tapisserie. *To be a wallflower.*
tapissier *m. upholsterer.*
taquin *(taquine f.) noun and adj. teasing; a person who likes to tease.*
taquiner *to tease.*
TARD *late.*
  Il est rentré tard. *He came home late.*
  Il était plus tard qu'on ne le croyait. *It was later than we thought.*
  A plus tard. *See you later.*
  Mieux vaut tard que jamais. *Better late than never.*
  Il n'est jamais trop tard pour bien faire. *It's never too late to mend.*
tarder *to delay.*
  Sans tarder. *Without any delay.*
  Il me tarde de la revoir. *I can't wait to see her again.*
se targuer *to boast of, take pride in, plume oneself on.*
tarif *m. rate, scale of prices, price list.*
  Demi-tarif. *Half-fare (for a child).*

Quels sont vos tarifs? *What are your prices?*
Tarif des lettres. *Postal rate.*
Un paque affranchi au tarif des lettres. *A package sent as first-class mail.*
tarte *f. tart, pie.*
tas *m. pile, heap.*
Un tas de papiers. *A pile of papers.*
Regardez en-dessous de ce tas de lettres. *Look under this pile of letters.*
Un tas de foin. *A haystack.*
TASSE *f. cup.*
Voulez-vous encore une tasse de café. *Do you want another cup of coffee?*
Donnez-moi une demi-tasse. *Give me a demitasse.*
se tasser *to crowd together.*
tâter *to feel, handle, touch.*
tâtonner *to feel one's way, grope.*
(à) tâtons *gropingly.*
Il nous faut y aller à tâtons, il n'y pas de lumière. *There's no light. We'll have to grope our way in the dark.*
taureau *m. bull.*
Prendre le taureau par les cornes. *To take the bull by the horns.*
taux *m. rate of interest.*
Au taux de 4%. *At the rate of 4%.*
Le taux bancaire. *Bank rate.*
Le taux de change. *(Exchange) rate.*
Le taux d'intérêt. *Interest rate.*
taverne *f. tavern.*
taxe *f. tax.*
taxer *to tax.*
taxi *m. cab, taxi.*
En taxi. *By taxi.*
te *you, to you.*
technique *f. technique.*
technique *adj. technical.*
teindre *to dye.*
Se teindre les cheveux. *To tint, dye one's hair.*
teint *m. complexion.*
Avoir le teint clair. *To have a clear complexion.*
teinte *f. tint; touch.*
Demi-teinte. *Half-tint.*
Une légère teinte d'ironie. *A slight touch of irony.*
teinture *f. dye.*
TEL (telle *f.*) *adj. such.*
Une telle chose ne se voit pas tous les jours. *You don't see that sort of thing every day.*
Un tel garçon ira loin. *A boy (fellow) of this sort will go far.*
De tels moyens ne s'emploient pas. *Such means can't be used.*
De telle sorte que. *In such a way that (as to).*

Tel père, tel fils. *Like father, like son.*
télé-audio-conférence *m. teleconferencing.*
télécarte *f. phone card.*
télécommande *f. remote control.*
télé-communications *(f.) telecommunications.*
Le bureau des P et T (Postes et Télécommunications). *Post office.*
télécopieur *m. fax machine.*
télécopie *f. fax.*
TÉLÉGRAMME *m. telegram.*
télégraphie *f. telegraphy.*
Télégraphie sans fil (T.S.F.). *Radio.*
télégraphier *to telegraph.*
TÉLÉPHONE *m. telephone.*
Téléphone-répondeur. *Answering machine.*
Passez-moi l'annuaire du téléphone. *Please hand me the telephone book.*
Donnez-moi un coup de téléphone, n'est-ce pas? *Give me a ring, won't you?*
Le téléphone automatique. *Dial telephone.*
Parler au téléphone. *To speak on the telephone.*
téléphoner *to telephone.*
téléphonique *adj. telephonic.*
La cabine téléphonique. *Telephone booth.*
téléphoniste *m. and f. telephone operator.*
télévision *f. television.*
TELLEMENT *so much.*
Elle a tellement changé! *She changed so much!*
Il a tellement regretté de n'avoir pas pu venir. *He was so sorry he couldn't come.*
Il était tellement pressé qu'il a oublié sa clé. *He was so much in a hurry that he forgot his key.*
téméraire *adj. bold.*
témérité *f. temerity, boldness.*
témoignage *m. evidence.*
Vous serez appelé en témoignage. *You'll be called as a witness.*
Un faux témoignage. *A false witness. False evidence.*
En témoignage d'estime. *As a token of esteem.*
témoigner *to bear witness.*
témoin *m. witness.*
Je vous prends en témoin. *I call you to witness.*
Je tiens à vous parler sans témoins. *I'd like to speak to you privately.*
tempe *f. temple (of the head).*
tempérament *m. temperament.*
Il est actif par tempérament. *He's very active (by nature).*
température *f. temperature.*
tempête *f. storm.*
temple *m. temple, Protestant church.*

temporaire *m. adj. temporary.*

temporairement *temporarily.*

TEMPS *m. time; weather.*

C'était le bon vieux temps! *Those were the good old days!*

Je ne me sens pas très bien ces derniers temps. *I haven't been feeling very well lately.*

La plupart du temps. *Most of the time.*

Vous arrivez juste à temps. *You've come just in time.*

Dans le temps. *Formerly.*

Dans son temps. *In due course.*

Nous nous voyons toujours de temps en temps. *We still see one another from time to time.*

Entre temps. *Meanwhile.*

Tout ces choses prennent du temps. *All these things take time.*

En même temps. *At the same time.*

Par le temps qui court rien n'est surprenant. *Nothing is surprising nowadays.*

Que faire pour tuer le temps? *What shall we do to kill time?*

Le temps a l'air de se mettre au beau. *It looks as though the weather is going to be nice.*

Quel temps abominable! *What awful weather!*

De tous les temps. *Of all time.*

tenace *adj. obstinate.*

ténacité *f. tenacity, tenaciousness.*

tenailles *f. pl. pliers.*

tendance *f. tendency.*

tendon *m. tendon.*

tendre *adj. tender.*

Cette viande n'est pas assez tendre. *This meat isn't tender enough.*

Elle a le coeur trop tendre. *She's too tenderhearted.*

tendre *to stretch; hold out; put forth.*

Tendre la main. 1. *To lend a helping hand.* 2. *To beg alms.*

Quand j'ai eu besoin de lui, il m'a tendu la main. *When I needed him, he lent me a helping hand.*

Il lui a tendu la main. *He held out his hand to him.*

A quoi tendent ces paroles? *What are you driving at? ("What do these words mean?")*

tendrement *tenderly, affectionately.*

tendresse *f. tenderness, affection.*

Elle fit preuve d'une grande tendresse. *She showed great affection.*

TENIR *to hold.*

Tenez ce livre, je vous prie. *Please hold this book.*

Je tiens cela de bonne source. *I have it on the best authority.*

Tenir compte de quelque chose. *To take something into consideration (account).*

Je tiens à vous dire que . . . *I have to (must) tell you that . . .*

Il ne tient qu'à vous de le faire. *It's up to you to do it.*

Il le tiendra au courant des résultats. *He will keep him posted about the results.*

Tenir sa promesse. *To keep one's word.*

Tenir tête à. *To resist.*

Tenir lieu de. *To act as.*

Tiens, je n'aurais jamais cru cela. *Well, I would never have believed that.*

Tenez, le voilà! *Look, there he is!*

Tenez prenez-le. *Here, take it.*

Tenez, c'est pour vous. *Here, this is for you.*

Cela lui tient au coeur. *He's set his heart on it.*

Tenez ferme! *Hold fast! Hold out! Stick it out to the end!*

Je n'y tiens pas. *I don't particularly care about it. I don't particularly care to. I don't care for it. I would rather not.*

Votre raisonnement ne tient pas debout. *Your argument doesn't hold.*

Qu'à cela ne tienne. *Never mind that. Don't let that be an obstacle. That need be no objection.*

Si vous y tenez. *If you insist (on it).*

SE TENIR *to stay; keep from; refrain from.*

Se tenir chez soi. *To stay home.*

Tenez-vous debout. *Stand up.*

Tenez-vous tranquille. *Keep quiet.*

Il se tenaient les côtes de rire. *They split their sides laughing. ("They held their sides laughing.")*

Se tenir sur ses gardes. *To be on one's guard.*

Maintenant vous savez à quoi vous en tenir. *Now you know how things stand.*

Il s'en tient à ce qu'il dit. *He maintains what he said.*

tennis *m. tennis.*

tension *f. tension.*

tentant *adj. tempting.*

tentatif (tentative *f.*) *adj. tentative.*

tentation *f. temptation.*

tentative *f. attempt.*

La tentative a échoué. *The attempt failed.*

Après plusieurs tentatives. *After several attempts.*

tente *f. tent.*

tenter *to try; tempt.*

Je vais encore une fois tenter la chance. *I'm going to try my luck once again.*

Cela me tente. *That tempts me. That attracts me.*

J'ai été tenté de le faire. *I was tempted to do it.*

tenu *adj.* kept.

Une maison bien tenue. *A well-kept house.*

tenue *f.* holding.

La tenue des livres. *Bookkeeping.*

Ces enfants ont beaucoup de tenue. *These children are well brought up. These children are well behaved.*

Il a de la tenue. *He has very good (dignified) manners. He's well bred. He has a sense of decorum.*

Voyons, ayez de la tenue. *Come on, behave yourself.*

En tenue de soirée seulement (*in an invitation*). *Formal dress.*

En grande tenue. *In evening dress. In formal dress.*

terme *m.* term, boundary.

Il a mené cette affaire à bon terme. *He brought this deal to a successful conclusion.*

Il a avoué en termes propres. *He admitted (it) in so many words.*

Ménager ses termes. *To mince words.*

Etes-vous en bons termes avec eux? *Are you on friendly terms with them?*

Mettre un terme à. *To put an end to.*

Nous l'avons acheté à terme. *We bought it on the installment plan.*

Louer une maison pour un terme. *To rent a house for four months.*

Aux termes de . . . *By the terms of . . .*

terminaison *f.* termination, ending, end, conclusion.

TERMINER *to finish.*

Avez-vous terminé? *Have you finished? Are you through?*

C'est à peu près terminé. *It's almost (just about) finished.*

terminus *m.* terminus; end of the line (bus, etc.)

terne *adj.* dull.

Une couleur terne. *A dull color.*

ternir *to tarnish, stain.*

terrain *m.* ground.

Terrains à vendre. *Plots of land (building plots) for sale. Lots for sale.*

Il a acheté un terrain. *He bought a piece of ground.*

Il perd du terrain chaque jour. *He's losing ground every day.*

Là, il est sur son terrain. *There, he's in his element. He's at home there.*

Sonder le terrain. *To see how the land lies. To sound (someone) out.*

Tâter le terrain. *To feel one's way. To see how the land lies.*

terrasse *f.* terrace; pavement in front of a sidewalk café.

TERRE *f.* earth, land.

Sa terre lui rapporte un petit revenu. *His land yields him a small income.*

Remuer ciel et terre. *To move heaven and earth.*

Ne jetez pas de papier par terre. *Don't throw away any paper on the ground.*

Un tremblement de terre. *An earthquake.*

Etre terre à terre. *To be commonplace. To be vulgar. To be matter-of-fact. To be of the earth; earthy.*

terreur *f.* fear.

Il était pris de terreur. *He was terror-stricken.*

terrible *adj.* terrible, dreadful.

Quelque chose de terrible vient de lui arriver. *Something dreadful just happened to him.*

Un enfant terrible. *A little devil.*

terriblement *terribly.*

Je suis terriblement gênée. *I'm terribly embarrassed.*

terrifier *to terrify.*

territoire *m.* territory.

testament *m.* testament, will.

TÊTE *f.* head; mind.

Il a mal à la tête. *He has a headache.*

Il a perdu la tête. 1. *He lost his head.* 2. *He lost his mind.*

Quel est votre tour de tête? *What size hat do you wear?*

Crier à tue-tête. *To scream at the top of one's lungs.*

Donner tête baissée dans quelque chose. *To rush headlong into something.*

Elle fait la tête. *She's sulking.*

Il leur a tenu tête. *He held his own against them.*

J'en ai par-dessus la tête de toutes ses histoires. *I'm fed up with all his (her) stories.*

Elle se casse la tête. *She's racking her brain.*

Je ne sais où donner la tête. *I don't know which way to turn.*

Il se l'est mis dans la tête. *He took it into his head to do it.*

Avoir en tête. *To have in the back of one's mind.*

Se monter la tête. *To get excited.*

Il n'en fait qu'à sa tête. *He does just as he pleases.*

Un coup de tête. *A sudden rash act. An impetuous (impulsive) act.*

Il a pris la tête de la procession. *He headed the procession.*

Un tête à tête. *A private conversation.*

La tête de station. *Taxi stand.*

La tête me tourne. *My head is spinning.*

têtu *adj. subborn.*

texte *m. text.*

textile *m. textile.*

thé *m. tea.*

THÉÂTRE *m. theatre.*

Etes-vous allé au théâtre hier soir? *Did you go to the theatre last night?*

Un coup de théâtre. *An unexpected sensational event.*

Il veut faire du théâtre. *He wants to go on the stage.*

théière *f. teapot.*

thème *m. theme.*

théorie *f. theory.*

thermomètre *m. thermometer.*

thermos *m. thermos bottle.*

thèse *f. thesis.*

tic *m. nervous twitch.*

ticket *m. ticket (bus).*

tic-tac *m. tick-tock.*

tiède *adj. lukewarm.*

tiédeur *f. warmth, lukewarmness.*

TIEN (tienne *f.*) *yours.*

Est-ce que c'est le tien? *Is that yours?*

Il faut y mettre du tien. *You must contribute your share.*

Tu as encore fait des tiennes! *You've been up to your old tricks again!*

tiers *m. a third.*

tiers (tierce *f.*) *adj. third.*

Tiers monde. *Third World.*

Une tierce personne. *A third party.*

tige *f. stem.*

tigre *m. tiger.*

timbale *f. metal drinking cup.*

TIMBRE *m. postage stamp; bell.*

Avez-vous du papier à lettre, une enveloppe et un timbre? *Do you have some writing paper, an envelope, and a stamp?*

Le timbre a sonné. *The bell rang.*

timide *adj. timid, shy.*

timidité *f. timidity.*

tintamarre *m. racket, noise.*

Quel tintamarre! *What a racket!*

tinter *to ring, toll, knell.*

tir *m. shooting.*

tirade *f. tirade, speech.*

tirage *m. drawing; impression (print); circulation.*

Le tirage de la loterie nationale. *The drawing of the national lottery.*

Un tirage assez élevé. *A fairly wide circulation.*

Tirage à part. *Separate reprint (an article).*

Edition à tirage limité. *Limited edition.*

tirailler *to bother, pester.*

tiré *adj. drawn.*

Il est tiré à quatre épingles. *He's spick and span.*

Un visage tiré. *A drawn face. Drawn features.*

tire-bouchon *m. corkscrew.*

tirelire *f. money box.*

TIRER *to draw, pull; print (photography).*

Il sait tirer avantage de tout. *He knows how to turn everything to his advantage (to derive profit from everything, to turn everything to account).*

Elle s'est fait tirer les cartes. *She had her fortune told.*

Il l'a tiré d'erreur. *He undeceived him. He opened his eyes.*

Tirer les oreilles de quelqu'un. *To pull someone's ears.*

Il se fait tirer l'oreille. *He's very reluctant. He has to be coaxed.*

Tirer à la courte paille. *To draw straws.*

Tirer à blanc. *To fire a blank.*

Faire tirer un cliché. *To have a negative printed.*

se tirer *to get out of.*

tiroir *m. drawer.*

tisane *f. herbal tea.*

tisser *to weave.*

tissu *m. material.*

titre *m. title.*

Il l'a reçu titre gratuit. *He received it free.*

tituber *to stagger.*

titulaire *m. and f. noun and adj. head, chief; pertaining to a title, titular.*

toast *m. toast.*

toc *m. imitation jewelry; fake, sham, anything trashy.*

C'est du toc (*fam.*). 1. *It's imitation jewelry.* 2. *It's faked. It's a fake.*

tocsin *m. alarm.*

tohu-bohu *m. hurly-burly.*

TOI *you (familiar).* See tu.

Ils sont à tu et à toi. *They are on the most familiar terms.*

Qui est là, c'est toi? *Who's there? Is that you?*

toi-même *yourself (familiar).*

toile *f. linen; cloth; canvas (painting).*

Draps de toile. *Linen sheets.*

toilette *f. act of washing, dressing; dressing-up; washstand, dressing table; washroom.*

Vous voulez faire un brin de toilette avant de sortir? *Do you want to wash up a bit before going out?*

Une toilette ravissante. *A striking dress.*

Les articles de toilette. *Toilet accessories (articles).*

Où se trouve les toilettes? *Where is the washroom?*

toiser *to eye.*

Il l'a toisé avec dédain. *He looked him up and down contemptuously.*

toit *m. roof.*

tolérable *adj. tolerable, bearable.*

tolérance *f. tolerance.*

tolérant *adj. tolerant.*

tolérer *to tolerate.*

Je ne peux pas tolérer cet individu. *I can't stand that fellow.*

tomate *f. tomato.*

tombe *f. grave.*

tombeau (tombeaux *pl.*) *m. tomb.*

Il me mettra au tombeau. *He'll be the death of me.*

tombée *f. fall.*

A la tombée du jour. *At nightfall.*

A la tombée de la nuit. *At nightfall.*

TOMBER *to fall.*

Les feuilles commencent à tomber. *The leaves are starting to fall.*

Il tombe de l'eau. *It's raining.*

Tomber des nues. *To be astounded.*

On entendrait tomber une épingle. *You could hear a pin drop.*

Le projet est tombé à l'eau. *The project fell through. Nothing came of the project.*

Je tombe de sommeil. *I'm dead tired.*

Il est tombé malade. *He became sick.*

Il en est tombé amoureux. *He fell in love with her.*

tombola *f. charity lottery.*

tome *m. volume.*

Le tome premier n'est pas trouvable. *Volume one is missing (can't be found).*

ton *m. tone.*

Il changera bientôt de ton. *He'll soon change his tune.*

Prenez-le d'un ton un peu moins haut. *Come down a peg or two. Get off your high horse.*

Ses plaisanteries sont de très mauvais ton. *His jokes are in very bad taste.*

TON (ta *f.*, tes *pl.*) *your (familiar)*

Où est ton couteau? *Where's your knife?*

Ta soeur m'a téléphoné. *Your sister phoned me.*

Où sont tes livres? *Where are your books?*

tondeuse *f. (hair-) clippers.*

tondre *to clip.*

Tondre les cheveux. *To clip one's hair.*

tonique *adj. tonic.*

tonne *f. ton.*

tonneau *m. (tonneaux pl.) barrel.*

tonner *to thunder.*

tonnerre *m. thunder.*

torche *f. torch.*

torchon *m. dish towel.*

tordre *to twist, wring.*

Tordez ces vêtements. *Wring these clothes out.*

se tordre *to twist.*

Se tordre de rire (*fam.*). *To split one's sides laughing.*

torpeur *f. torpor.*

torpille *f. torpedo.*

torrent *m. torrent.*

Il pleut à torrent. *It's raining in torrents.*

Un torrent d'injures. *A stream of insults.*

Un torrent de larmes. *A flood of tears.*

torrentiel (torrentielle *f.*) *adj. torrential.*

Une pluie torrentielle. *A torrential rain.*

torride *adj. torrid; scorching.*

La zone torride. *The torrid zone.*

Il y faisait une chaleur torride. *The heat was scorching.*

torse *m. torso.*

TORT *m. wrong; error, fault.*

Vous avez tort. *You're wrong.*

Il est difficile de savoir qui a tort et qui a raison dans ce cas. *It's hard to know in this case who's right and who's wrong.*

Les absents ont toujours tort. *The absent are always in the wrong.*

Taisez-vous. Vous parlez à tort et à travers. *Keep quiet. You're talking nonsense.*

Vous lui avez fait beaucoup de tort. *You've done him a great deal of harm. You've wronged him.*

torticolis *m. stiff neck.*

tortue *f. turtle.*

Lent comme une tortue. *Slow as a snail ("as a turtle").*

torture *f. torture.*

Il a mis son esprit à la torture. *He racked his brains.*

torturer *to torture.*

TÔT *soon; early.*

Tôt ou tard. *Sooner or later.*

Il faudra quand même que vous le fassiez, tôt ou tard. *You'll have to do it sooner or later anyway.*

Nous avons l'habitude de nous réveiller tôt. *We're used to (accustomed to) getting up early.*

Pouvez-vous venir plus tôt? *Can you come earlier?*

Le plus tôt possible. *As soon as possible.*

total (totaux *pl.*) *noun (m.) and adj. (totale f.) total.*

Faites le total. *Add it up. Get the total.*

Le total s'élève à près de dix mille francs. *The whole sum amounts to 10,000 francs.*

totalement *totally.*

totalité *f. totality.*

En totalité. *As a whole.*

touchant *m. touching, pathetic.*

TOUCHER *to touch; to cash (check).*
   N'y touchez pas! *Don't touch that!*
   On ne touche pas! *Hands off! Don't touch!*
   En ce qui touche cette affaire . . . *As far as this question is concerned . . .*
   Ça lui a touché le coeur. *That affected (moved) him (her). ("It touched his [her] heart.")*
   Je vais lui en toucher un mot. *I'll mention it to him. I'll have a word with him about it. I'll drop him a hint (about it).*
se toucher *to border on each other.*
touffe *f. tuft, clump, wisp.*
touffu *adj. bushy, thick.*
   Cheveux touffus. *Bushy hair.*
   Bois touffus. *Thick woods.*
TOUJOURS *always; still.*
   Il vient toujours trop tôt. *He always comes too early.*
   Je suis toujours content de vous voir. *I'm always glad to see you.*
   Essayez toujours! *Keep trying!*
   Se trouve-t-il toujours à Paris? *Is he still in Paris?*
   Toujours est-il que je ne l'ai plus jamais revu. *The fact remains that I never saw him again.*
   Comme toujours. *As always, as usual.*
   Pour toujours. *Forever.*
toupet *m. toupee; nerve (fam.).*
   Quel toupet! *What nerve!*
   Il en a du toupet! *He has some nerve!*
tour *f. tower.*
TOUR *m. turn; tour; stroll; trick.*
   Faire un tour. *To take a walk.*
   A chacun son tour. *Every dog has his day.*
   Fermer à double tour. *To double-lock.*
   A tour de rôle. *In turn.*
   En un tour de main. *In the twinkling of an eye.*
   Quel est votre tour de tête? *What size hat do you wear?*
   Son sang n'a fait qu'un tour. *It gave him a dreadful shock.*
   Un tour de cartes. *A card trick.*
   Jouer un mauvais tour à quelqu'un. *To do someone a bad turn. To play someone a dirty trick.*
   Le tour à pied. *Walk, stroll.*
   Un disque de 33 tours. *33 r.p.m. record.*
   Votre tour dans la queue. *Your place in the line.*
tourbillon *m. whirlwind.*
tourisme *m. touring.*
   Bureau de tourisme. *Travel bureau. Travel agency.*
touriste *m. tourist.*
tourment *m. torment.*

Il a fait le tourment de ma vie. *He has been the bane of my existence.*
   Les tourments de la faim. *Hunger pangs.*
tourmente *f. storm.*
tourmenter *to torment.*
   Il le tourmente sans arrêt. *He keeps tormenting him.*
   Cet incident le tourmente. *This incident worries him.*
tournant *m. turning.*
   Les tournants de l'histoire. *The turning points of history.*
   J'ai pris le mauvais tournant. *I took the wrong turn.*
tourne-disque *m. record player.*
tournée *f. tour (theatre); round.*
   La tournée d'un agent de police. *A policeman's beat.*
   Il a payé une tournée à tout le monde. *He bought a round of drinks for everyone.*
   Faire une tournée. *To go on tour.*
tournemain *f. jiffy.*
   Il l'a fait en un tournemain. *He did it in a jiffy (in the twinkling of an eye, before you could say Jack Robinson).*
TOURNER *to turn.*
   Quand vous arrivez devant votre hôtel, tournez à gauche. *When you come to your hotel, turn to the left.*
   L'affaire a mal tourné. *The deal fell through.*
   Ma tête tourne. *I feel giddy. My head's swimming.*
   Il tourne autour du pot. *He's beating around the bush.*
   Elle lui a tourné la tête. *He became infatuated with her. ("She turned his head.")*
   Il l'a tourné en ridicule. *He made fun of him. He made him look ridiculous.*
   Tourner le dos à quelqu'un. *To give someone the cold shoulder.*
tournoi *m. tournament.*
tournure *f. shape, figure; turn, cast, appearance.*
   La tournure d'une phrase. *The construction of a sentence. Sentence construction.*
   Ses affaires ont pris une bien mauvaise tournure. *His affairs took a turn for the worse.*
TOUS *(plural of* tout) *all.*
   Ils sont tous partis. *They've all left.*
   Tous les deux. *Both.*
tousser *to cough.*
TOUT *(*toute *f.,* toutes *f. pl.,* tous *m. pl.) adj. and pron. all, any, every.*
   Tous les jours. *Every day.*
   Tout au moins. *At the very least.*
   Tout à fait. *Entirely.*
   Tout le monde est là. *Everybody's there.*

Elles sont toutes parties à la campagne. *They all left for the country.*

J'ai laissé toutes mes affaires à Paris. *I've left all my things in Paris.*

Rien du tout. *Nothing at all.*

Pas du tout. *Not at all.*

Voilà tout. *That's all.*

Par-dessus tout. *Above all.*

A tout à l'heure! *See you later!*

Tout d'un coup. *Suddenly.*

De tous les temps. *Of all time.*

Tous les deux. *Both (of them, of us).*

Tous les trois. *All three (of them, of us).*

Toute la journée. *The whole day, all day long.*

Toutes les deux semaines. *Every other week.*

Toutes sortes de. *All kinds of.*

Manger de tout. *To eat all sorts of things.*

Tout ce qu'il vous faut. *Everything you need.*

Tout ce qui peut intéresser une femme. *Everything that could interest a woman.*

Tout est bien qui finit bien. *All's well that ends well.*

tout *m. The whole thing; the entire amount.*

(Mais) pas du tout! *Not at all! No indeed! Certainly not!*

tout, toute *adv. very, quite, entirely, completely.*

Mes gencives sont toutes enflées. *My gums are all swollen.*

Tout à fait. *Quite, entirely, altogether.*

Tout à l'heure. *Presently, in a little while; a little while ago.*

Tout de suite. *Right away, immediately.*

Tout droit. *Straight ahead.*

Tout près d'ici. *Right near here.*

Tout simplement. *(Quite) simply; just, only.*

Un tout petit peu. *Just a little bit.*

Vous avez la gorge toute rouge. *Your throat is all red.*

TOUTEFOIS *nevertheless.*

Toutefois je ne suis pas d'accord avec vous. *Nevertheless, I don't agree with you.*

Toutefois ce n'est pas une raison pour que vous vous fâchiez. *That's still no reason for you to get angry.*

toux *f. cough.*

toxicomanie *f. drug addiction.*

trac *m. fear.*

J'ai le trac (*fam.*). *I'm afraid. I have cold feet.*

tracas *m. worry.*

Il a eu des tracas dernièrement. *He's been very worried lately.*

tracasser *to bother, pester.*

Il l'a tracassé du matin au soir. *He bothered him from morning till night.*

Ne vous tracassez pas. *Don't worry. Don't let it worry you.*

trace *f. track; footprint.*

Il suit les traces de son père. *He's following in his father's footsteps.*

Ce poème lui a laissé une trace profonde. *The poem made a deep impression on him.*

tracer *to trace.*

Tracer une carte. *To trace a map.*

Il faut tracer une ligne de conduite. *We must lay down (work out) a policy.*

tradition *f. tradition.*

C'est une vieille tradition. *It's an old tradition.*

traditionnel (traditionnelle *f.*) *adj. traditional.*

traducteur *m.* (traductrice *f.*) *translator.*

traduction *f. translation.*

traduire *to translate.*

trafic *m. traffic.*

Durant les heures d'affluence il y a beaucoup de trafic ici. *During rush hours there's a lot of traffic here.*

Les heures de fort trafic. *Busy hours. Peak hours.*

Les heures de faible trafic. *Slack hours.*

trafiquer *to trade in, deal in.*

tragédie *f. tragedy.*

tragique *noun (m.) and adj. tragic.*

Il prend tout au tragique. *He takes everything too seriously.*

trahir *to betray.*

trahison *f. treachery, betrayal.*

TRAIN *m. train; rate.*

J'ai manqué le train. *I missed the train.*

Le train doit arriver à midi. *The train is due at noon.*

Il a mené l'affaire à bon train. *He brought the deal to a successful conclusion.*

Au train où vous allez vous n'aurez pas encore fini dans dix ans. *At the rate you're going, you'll never finish.*

Il a mis l'affaire en train. *He prepared the deal. He got the deal started.*

Ils mènent grand train. *They live in grand style.*

A fond de train. *At full speed.*

Il est en train d'écrire des lettres. *He's busy writing letters.*

Il est en train de partir. *He's ready (about) to leave.*

Il est en train de s'habiller. *He's getting dressed.*

Elle est en train de préparer le dîner. *She's preparing dinner.*

traîne *f. train (of a dress).*

traîneau *m. sleigh.*

traîner *to drag; be scattered around.*

L'affaire traîne en longueur. *The matter (affair, business) is taking a long time ("is dragging out").*

Il laisse tout traîner. *He leaves everything lying about. He leaves things scattered about.*

Ne laissez pas traîner vos vêtements. *Don't leave your clothes lying about.*

Ramassez toutes les choses qui traînent. *Pick up everything that's scattered about.*

se traîner *to crawl along.*

train-train *m. routine.*

Les choses vont leur train-train. *Things are taking their course (moving slowly).*

traire *to milk.*

trait *m. used in the following expressions:*

Il a bu tout d'un trait. *He gulped it down. ("He drank it in one swallow.")*

Des traits réguliers. *Regular features.*

Un trait de génie. *A stroke of genius.*

Cela a trait à ce qu'on vient de dire. *That refers to what has already been said.*

Un trait d'union. *A hyphen.*

traite *f. stretch; draft; bill.*

Durant leur voyage ils ont fait 500 km. d'une traite. *During their trip they made 500 kilometers at a stretch.*

Ils l'ont fait tout d'une traite. *They did it straight off the bat.*

Accepter une traite. *To accept a note (draft).*

traité *m. treaty, treatise.*

traitement *m. treatment, salary.*

Traitement de l'information. *Data processing.*

Le traitement d'une maladie. *The treatment of a disease.*

Son traitement n'est pas très élevé. *His salary isn't very high.*

Il a subi des mauvais traitements. *He was mistreated. He was harshly treated.*

traiter *to treat.*

Il a traité cette affaire à la légère. *He treated the matter lightly. He didn't take the matter to heart.*

Traiter quelqu'un d'égal à égal. *To treat someone as an equal.*

Il l'a traité d'imbécile. *He called him a fool.*

traître *m. traitor.*

traître *adj. treacherous.*

Il ne m'en a pas dit un traître mot. *He didn't mention it to me. He didn't tell me the first thing (a single word) about it.*

trajet *m. journey.*

J'ai fait une partie du trajet en auto. *I drove part of the way.*

Ce n'est pas un long trajet. *It isn't a long trip.*

Un trajet de quatre heures. *A trip that takes four hours. A four-hour trip.*

trame *f. plot.*

tramer *to weave.*

tramway *m. trolley car, streetcar.*

Est-ce que le tramway s'arrête ici? *Does the trolley stop here?*

tranchant *m. edge.*

Epée à deux tranchants. *Two-edged sword.*

tranchant *adj. cutting, sharp.*

tranche *f. slice.*

Couper du pain en tranches. *To slice a loaf of bread.*

Une tranche de jambon. *A slice of ham.*

trancher *to cut, slice.*

Tranchons là. (Tranchons la question.) *Let's drop the subject.*

Il tranche sur tout. *He's very dogmatic.*

tranchée *f. trench.*

TRANQUILLE *adj. tranquil, calm.*

Tenez-vous tranquille. *Keep still. Keep quiet.*

Restez tranquille. *Keep still. Keep quiet.*

Maintenant j'ai l'esprit tranquille. *Now my mind is at ease.*

Les enfants sont très tranquilles. *The children are very quiet.*

Laissez-moi tranquille. *Leave me alone.*

C'est un homme très tranquille. *He's a very calm person.*

tranquillement *quietly, calmly.*

tranquilliser *to calm.*

se tranquilliser *to calm down, to feel calmer, to be easier in one's mind.*

tranquillité *f. tranquillity.*

transaction *f. transaction.*

transatlantique *noun (m.) and adj. transatlantic.*

Une chaise transatlantique. *A deck chair.*

transcription *f. transcription; transcript.*

transcrire *to transcribe.*

transe *f. anxiety.*

transférer *to transfer.*

transformation *f. transformation.*

transformer *to change.*

transfusion *f. transfusion.*

transi *adj. chilled, numb.*

Transi de froid. *He's numb with cold. He's frozen.*

Transi de peur. *He's petrified (with fear). He's frightened to death.*

transit *m. transit.*

Un visa de transit. *A transit visa.*

transitaire *m. forwarding agent.*

transition *f. transition.*

transmettre *to transmit.*

transparent *adj. transparent.*

transpercer *to pierce; penetrate.*

transpiration *f. perspiration.*

transpirer *to perspire.*

transport *to transport; transportation.*
   Frais de transport. *Freight charges.*
   Avec transport. *Enthusiastically.*

transporter *to transport.*
   Il a été transporté à l'hôpital. *He was carried to the hospital.*
   Etre transporté de joie. *To be beside oneself with joy.*

trappe *f. trap, pitfall.*

traquer *to track down.*

TRAVAIL *m.* (travaux *pl.*) *work.*
   Un travail difficile. *A difficult job.*
   Au travail maintenant! *Get to work! Let's get to work!*
   Il faut se mettre au travail. *We must get down to work.*
   Le Ministère du Travail. *Ministry of Labor. Labor Department.*
   Les travaux publics. *Public works.*
   Condamné aux travaux forcés. *Condemned to hard labor.*

TRAVAILLER *to work.*
   Ils travaillent trop. *They work too hard (much).*
   Il travaille à l'heure. *He works by the hour.*
   Quelque chose la travaille. *Something is preying on her mind.*

se travailler *to worry.*

travailleur *m. worker, industrious person.*

travailleur (travailleuse *f.*) *adj. industrious.*

TRAVERS *m. breadth, width.*
   A travers. *Across.*
   A travers champ. *Across country.*
   Passez au travers de ce champ. *Go through this field.*
   Elle fait tout de travers. *She does everything wrong.*
   Il l'a regardé de travers. *He gave him a black look.*
   Vous avez tout compris de travers. *You've misunderstood everything.*

traversée *f. crossing.*
   Avez-vous fait une bonne traversée? *Did you have a good crossing?*

TRAVERSER *to cross.*
   Traversons. *Let's cross over to the other side.*
   Elle a traversé la rue. *She crossed the street.*
   Une idée lui a traversé l'esprit. *An idea flashed through his (her) mind.*

travesti *adj. disguise.*
   Un bal travesti. *A fancy dress ball.*

travestir *to disguise.*

trébucher *to stumble.*

trèfle *m. clover; clubs (cards).*

TREIZE *noun and adj. thirteen.*

TREIZIÈME *noun and adj. thirteenth.*

tremblement *n. trembling.*
   Une tremblement de terre. *An earthquake.*

trembler *to tremble, shake.*

trempe *f. stamp; quality.*
   Un homme de sa trempe. *A man of his caliber.*

tremper *to soak.*
   J'étais trempé jusqu'aux os. *I was soaked to the skin ("bones").*

tremplin *m. springboard.*

trentaine *f. about thirty.*

TRENTE *noun and adj. thirty.*
   Il est six heures trente. *It's six-thirty.*
   J'ai vu trente-six chandelles. *I saw stars. ("I saw thirty-six candles.").*
   J'en ai assez de faire ses trente-six volontés. *I'm tired of catering to his whims.*
   Il n'y a pas trente-six façons de le faire. *There are no two ways about it.*
   Vous me l'avez déjà répété trente-six fois. *You've repeated it to me a hundred ("thirty-six") times.*

trentième *noun and adj. thirtieth.*

trépigner *to stamp one's feet.*

TRÈS *very.*
   Très bon. *Very good.*
   Très bien. *Very well.*
   Très peu. *Very little.*
   C'est très joli. *It's very pretty.*
   J'ai très froid. *I'm very cold.*
   De très bonne heure. *Very early.*

trésor *m. treasure.*

trésorerie *f. treasury.*

trésorier *m.* (trésorière *f.*) *treasurer.*

tressaillir *to start, give a start, quiver.*

tresse *f. braid.*

tresser *to weave.*

trêve *f. truce.*

triangle *m. triangle.*

tribu *f. tribe.*

tribunal *m.* (tribunaux *pl.*) *tribunal, court.*

tribut *m. tribute.*

tricher *to cheat.*

tricherie *f. cheating; trickery.*

tricheur *n.* (tricheuse *f.*) *cheat, trickster.*

tricot *m. sweater; knitting.*

tricoter *to knit.*

trier *to sort, sort out.*
   Aujourd'hui je vais trier mes lettres. *Today I'll sort my correspondence.*

trimbaler (fam.) *to drag.*

trimestre *m. three-month period.*

trinquer *to clink glasses.*

trio *m. trio.*

triomphal (triomphaux *pl.*) *adj. triumphal.*

triomphe *m. triumph.*

triompher *to triumph.*
   Il a triomphé de toutes les difficultés. *He overcame every difficulty.*

triple *adj. triple.*

tripoter *to paw, handle; meddle with, mess about, play with; speculate with.*

Ne tripotez pas mes affaires. *Don't tamper with (mess around with) my things.*

Il tripote l'argent des autres. *He speculates with other people's money.*

TRISTE *adj. sad.*

Elle a l'air triste. *She looks sad.*

J'étais bien triste d'apprendre que . . . *I was very sorry to hear that . . .*

Il lui a fait triste mine. *He received him without enthusiasm.*

tristesse *f. melancholy, sadness.*

Avec tristesse. *Sadly.*

trivial (triviaux *pl.*) *trivial.*

trivialité *f. triviality, triteness; vulgarity.*

Trève de trivialités! *Enough nonsense! Let's get serious!*

TROIS *noun and adj. three.*

Les trois quarts du temps. *Most of the time. ("Three quarters of the time.")*

Diviser en trois. *To divide into three parts.*

Le trois juillet. *July third.*

Tous les trois. *All three (of them, of us).*

Trois fois par jour. *Three times a day.*

TROISIÈME *noun and adj. third.*

trombe *f. whirlwind.*

Il est entré en trombe. *He came bursting in.*

trompe-l'oeil *m. deceptive appearance; deception, sham.*

Ces promesses ne sont qu'un trompe-l'oeil. *These are empty promises.*

Cette nouvelle loi n'est qu'un trompe-l'oeil. *This new law is just so much window-dressing (camouflage, bluff).*

tromper *to deceive.*

C'est ce qui vous trompe. *This is where you're mistaken. This is what fools you.*

Il se laisse tromper par les apparences. *He's taken in by appearances.*

Tromper la vigilance de quelqu'un. *To elude the vigilance of someone.*

SE TROMPER *to be mistaken.*

Vous vous trompez. *You're mistaken.*

Je me suis trompé à ce sujet. *I was mistaken about that.*

Il est facile de se tromper dans un cas pareil. *It's very easy to make a mistake in a case of this sort.*

A moins que je ne me trompe, c'est l'endroit même. *Unless I'm mistaken, this is the very spot.*

Il n'y a pas à s'y tromper. *There's no mistake about it.*

tromperie *f. deceit; deception.*

trompette *f. trumpet.*

Il partit sans tambour ni trompette. *He left quietly (without any fuss).*

trompeur (trompeuse *f.*) *noun and adj. deceitful, deceptive.*

Les apparences sont trompeuses. *Appearances are deceptive.*

A trompeur, trompeur et demi. *Set a thief to catch a thief.*

tronc *m. trunk.*

Le tronc de l'arbre. *The trunk of a tree.*

trône *m. throne.*

TROP *too.*

Trop tôt. *Too early.*

Trop tard. *Too late.*

N'allez pas trop loin. *Don't go too far.*

Il était de trop. *He was unwelcome. ("He was one too many.").*

C'en est trop! *This is too much! This is the last straw!*

Bien trop cher. *Much too expensive.*

Trop longtemps. *Too long.*

trophée *f. trophy.*

trot *m. trot.*

trotter *to trot.*

Elle est toujours à trotter. *She's always on the go.*

Cette chanson me trotte dans la tête. *That tune keeps running through my head.*

trottoir *m. sidewalk.*

trou *m. hole, opening.*

trouble *noun (m.) and adj. confusion, disorder.*

Etat de trouble. *State of agitation. Agitated state.*

Cause de trouble. *Disturbing factor.*

Des troubles de vision. *Trouble with one's eyesight. Eye trouble.*

Il lui a jeté le trouble dans l'esprit. *He made him uneasy.*

Il a une âme trouble. *His mind is uneasy.*

Il a une vision trouble. *He has poor vision.*

Pêcher dans l'eau trouble. *To fish in troubled waters.*

trouble-fête *m. kill-joy, wet blanket.*

troubler *to stir up; disturb.*

Cette situation est troublée. *The situation is confused.*

Troubler le bonheur de quelqu'un. *To mar someone's happiness.*

Troubler l'ordre public. *To disturb the peace.*

Elle est toute troublée. *She's flustered (confused, upset). She's all excited.*

se troubler *to become cloudy; to get dim, blurred; to get confused.*

Le temps commence à se troubler. *It's getting cloudy (overcast).*

L'orateur se troubla. *The speaker became confused (lost the thread of his speech).*

Sans se troubler. *Unruffled.*

Sans se troubler il continua son travail. *He continued his work calmly.*

troupe *f. troop, troops.*

troupeau *m.* (troupeaux *pl.*) *flock.*

trousse *f. bundle, package; case, kit; pl. heels.*

Une trousse d'outils. *A tool kit.*

Une trousse de toilette. *A case for toilet articles.*

Il était à ses trousses. *He was at his heels.*

trousseau *m.* (trousseaux *pl.*) *bunch (of keys); outfit, trousseau.*

Un trousseau de clés. *A bunch of keys.*

Elle achète son trousseau. *She's buying her trousseau.*

trouvaille *f. lucky find.*

Notre bonne est une trouvaille. *Our maid's a treasure.*

TROUVER *to find; to think, consider.*

L'avez-vous trouvé? *Did you find it?*

Vous trouverez le bureau au bout du couloir. *You will find the office at the end of the corridor.*

Venez me trouver jeudi. *Come to see me Thursday.*

Ne trouvez-vous pas qu'il a tort? *Don't you think (agree) he's wrong?*

Elle est jolie, vous ne trouvez pas? *She's pretty, don't you think?*

Vous trouvez? *You think so? Do you think so?*

Je le trouve sympathique. *I find him very pleasant (likable, nice).*

Je lui trouve mauvaise mine. *I don't think he looks well.*

Trouver plaisir à. *To take pleasure in.*

SE TROUVER *to be; to feel.*

Où se trouve la poste? *Where is the post office?*

Il se trouvait dans le besoin. *He was in need.*

Mon ancien professeur se trouvait là par hasard. *My former teacher happened to be there.*

Il se trouvait que je ne pouvais pas y aller. *It so happened that I couldn't go there.*

Je me trouve mieux. *I feel better.*

truc *m. knack; whatsis, gimmick.*

Avoir le truc pour faire quelque chose. *To have a knack for doing something.*

Il a trouvé le truc. *He got the knack.*

Il connaît les trucs du métier. *He knows all the tricks of the trade.*

truite *f. trout.*

truqueur *m.* (truqueuse *f.*) *faker, humbug, trickster, swindler.*

T.S.F. (télégraphie sans fil) *radio ("wireless").*

TU *you (familiar).*

Où vas-tu? *Where are you going?*

Que dis-tu? *What are you saying?*

tube *m. tube; hit song.*

tuberculose *f. tuberculosis.*

tuer *to kill.*

J'ai failli être tué. *I came very near being killed.*

Tuer le temps. *To kill time.*

L'ennui le tue. *He's bored to death.*

se tuer *to kill oneself.*

Il se tue au travail. *He's working himself to death.*

tue-tête *used in the following expression:*

Crier à tue-tête. *To shout at the top of one's lungs.*

tuile *f. tile.*

Quelle tuile (*fam.*)! *What bad luck.*

tumeur *f. tumor.*

tumulte *m. tumult; hustle and bustle.*

En tumulte. *In an uproar. In confusion.*

Un tumulte d'applaudissements. *Thunderous applause. A thunder of applause.*

tunnel *m. tunnel.*

turbulent *adj. turbulent, wild.*

turque *m. and f. noun and adj. Turkish.*

tutelle *f. guardianship.*

tuteur *m.* (tutrice *f.*) *guardian.*

se tutoyer *to be on familiar terms, to use "tu" to one another.*

tuyau *m.* (tuyaux *pl.*) *pipe.*

tweed *m. tweed.*

En tweed. *In, of tweed.*

tympan *m. eardrum.*

type *m. type; fellow.*

Le vrai type anglais. *The typical Englishman.*

C'est un drôle de type (*fam.*). *He's a strange fellow.*

J'ai connu un type qui . . . (*fam.*). *I once knew a fellow who . . .*

typhoïde *adj. typhoid.*

typique *adj. typical.*

tyran *m. tyrant.*

tyrannie *f. tyranny.*

tyranniser *to tyrannize.*

U

ulcère *m. ulcer.*

ultérieur *adj. ulterior; subsequent.*

Il a été élu dans une séance ultérieure. *He was elected at a later meeting.*

Attendez les ordres ultérieurs. *Wait for further orders.*

ultérieurement *later on, subsequently.*

Marchandises livrables ultérieurement. *Goods to be delivered later. Goods for future delivery.*

Cette partie du contrat a été ajoutée ultérieurement. *This part of the contract was added subsequently.*

ultimatum *m. ultimatum.*

ultra- *ultra-.*

UN (une *f.*) *adj. and pron. one.*

Ils arrivèrent un à un. *They arrived one by one.*

Vous ne pouvez les distinguer l'un de l'autre. *You can't tell (distinguish) one from the other. You can't tell which is which.*

Un de ces jours. *One of these days.*

L'un et l'autre. *Both (of them).*

Ni l'un ni l'autre. *Neither (of them).*

unanime *adj. unanimous.*

unanimité *f. unanimity.*

uni *adj. united, smooth, even, plain.*

unifier *to unify.*

Ces deux industries furent unifiées. *These two industries were consolidated.*

Unifiez vos idées. *Organize your ideas.*

uniforme *noun (m.) and adj. uniform.*

Une couleur uniforme. *A solid color.*

Il vit une vie uniforme. *He leads an uneventful life.*

union *f. union.*

unique *adj. unique, sole.*

Son unique plaisir. *His one (sole) pleasure.*

Il est fils unique. *He's an only son.*

Rue à sens unique. *One-way street.*

uniquement *solely.*

unir *to unite, join.*

Ces faits sont étroitement unis. *These facts are closely connected.*

Unir le geste à la parole. *To suit the action to the word.*

Les Etats-Unis. *The United States.*

unisson *m. unison.*

Chanter à l'unisson. *To sing in harmony.*

Ses goûts sont à l'unisson des miens. *His tastes are similar to mine.*

unité *f. unity; unit.*

univers *m. universe.*

universel (universelle *f.*) *adj. universal, worldwide.*

universitaire *adj. pertaining to a university.*

université *f. university, college.*

urbain *adj. urban.*

urgence *f. urgency.*

Il y a urgence à ce que ce soit fait immédiatement. *It's most important that this be done immediately.*

En cas d'urgence. *In case of emergency*

urgent *adj. urgent, pressing.*

J'en ai un besoin urgent. *I need it urgently.*

Il a du travail urgent à finir. *He has some urgent work to finish.*

USAGE *m. use; custom.*

Faites usage d'un antiseptique. *Use an antiseptic.*

Pour l'usage externe. *For external use only.*

C'est un article à son usage. *This is for his personal use.*

Usage personnel. *Personal use.*

Ce costume est hors d'usage. *This suit is worn out.*

Un mot hors d'usage. *An obsolete word.*

Des phrases d'usage. *Polite (conventional) expressions.*

Selon l'usage. *According to custom.*

Il est d'usage de. *It's customary to.*

Usages locaux. *Local customs.*

Il manque d'usage. *He lacks breeding.*

usé *adj. worn-out.*

Un costume usé. *A worn-out suit. An old suit.*

user *to use; wear out.*

Il a usé son pardessus. *His overcoat is worn out. He wore his coat out.*

Il a usé ses yeux à force de lire sans avoir assez de lumière. *He spoiled his eyes by reading in poor light.*

Il a usé de moyens peu honnêtes. *He used (resorted to) dishonest means.*

User de force. *To use force.*

User de son droit. *To avail oneself of one's rights. To take advantage of one's rights.*

Il a usé de tous les artifices pour réussir. *He used every trick in order to succeed.*

Est-ce ainsi que vous en usez avec eux? *Is that how you deal with them?*

s'user *to wear out.*

Sa vue s'use de plus en plus. *His eyesight is growing worse.*

usine *f. factory, plant.*

Un ouvrier d'usine. *A factory worker.*

ustensile *m. utensil.*

usuel (usuelle *f.*) *adj. usual, common.*

Une expression usuelle. *A common expression.*

usuellement *usually.*

usure *f. usury; wear.*

Cette étoffe résiste bien à l'usure. *This material wears well.*

usurper *to usurp.*

UTILE *adj. useful.*

En quoi puis-je vous être utile? *What can I do for you? Can I be of any help to you?*

Est-ce que cela pourrait vous être utile? *Can this be of any use to you? Can you use this?*

C'est un homme utile à connaître. *He's a useful man to know.*

Je le ferai en temps utile. *I'll do it in due time.*

utiliser *to utilize.*

utilité *f. utility.*

Ceci est d'une grande utilité. *This has many uses. This is very useful.*

Sans utilité. *Useless.*

V

vacance *f. vacancy; pl. vacation.*

Où partez-vous en vacances cette année? *Where are you going for your vacation this year?*

Les grandes vacances finissent le premier octobre. *The summer vacation ends October first.*

vacant *adj. vacant, unoccupied.*

vacarme *m. noise; uproar, hubbub.*

Ils font du vacarme. *They're making a racket.*

vacciner *to vaccinate.*

vache *f. cow.*

vacillant *adj. unsteady.*

vaciller *to be unsteady, waver, vacillate.*

Il vacille sur ses jambes. *He's unsteady on his legs.*

Je ne m'en rappelle plus bien; ma mémoire vacille sur ce sujet. *I can't recollect it very clearly; my memory is uncertain on that point.*

Il vacille entre les deux solutions. *He's hesitating between the two solutions. He can't make up his mind which solution to choose.*

va-et-vient *m. coming and going.*

vagabond *adj. vagabond, vagrant.*

vague *f. wave.*

Les vagues étaient très hautes. *The waves were very high.*

Une vague de chaleur. *A heat wave.*

vague *adj. vague, indefinite.*

Sa réponse était très vague. *His answer was very vague.*

Une couleur vague. *An indefinite color.*

Un regard vague. *A vacant glance.*

Je ne sais pas ce qu'il est, quelque vague acteur, je crois. *I don't know what he is—some sort of actor, I believe.*

vaguement *vaguely.*

vaillance *f. bravery.*

vaillamment *valiantly.*

vaillant *adj. brave, spirited.*

Elle n'a pas un sou vaillant. *She hasn't a penny.*

vain *adj. vain.*

De vaines promesses. *Empty promises.*

Elle est très vaine. *She's very vain.*

En vain. *In vain. Vainly.*

vaincre *to conquer.*

Il furent vaincus. *They were defeated.*

Il a vaincu sa frayeur. *He overcame his fear.*

Il a dû s'avouer vaincu. *He had to admit defeat.*

vainqueur *m. conqueror, victor.*

vaisseau *m. (vaisseaux pl.) vessel.*

Vaisseau spatial *m. Spaceship.*

vaisselle *f. plates and dishes.*

Faire la vaisselle. *To do the dishes.*

valable *adj. valid.*

Ces billets ne sont valables que pour deux mois. *These tickets are good for only two months.*

Une excuse valable. *A valid excuse.*

valet *m. valet.*

Le valet de pique. *The jack of spades.*

Il a une âme de valet. *He's very servile.*

VALEUR *f. value; pl. bonds, securities.*

C'est un bijou de valeur. *It's a very valuable jewel.*

C'est un homme de valeur. *He's very capable. He's a man of great abilities.*

Cela n'a pas grande valeur. *It isn't worth much.*

Attacher beaucoup de valeur à quelque chose. *To attach a great deal of importance to something. To set great store by something.*

Ces renseignements sont sans aucune valeur. *This information is completely valueless.*

Mettre en valeur. *To set off to best advantage.*

Il sait mettre ses connaissances en valeur. *He knows how to show off his knowledge.*

Mettre une propriété en valeur. *To improve the value of a property.*

Il a mis ce mot en valeur. *He emphasized that word.*

Ces valeurs sont d'un bon rapport. *These securities yield a good return.*

Un colis avec valeur déclarée. *A registered parcel.*

valeureux *(valeureuse f.) adj. brave, courageous.*

validité *f. validity.*

La validité de ce passeport est d'un an. *This passport is valid for a year.*

La validité d'un argument. *The validity of an argument.*

valise *f. valise, suitcase.*

Portez cette valise en haut. *Carry this suitcase upstairs.*

J'ai déjà fait mes valises. *I've already packed my bags.*

vallée *f. valley.*

La vallée de la Loire. *The Loire Valley.*

VALOIR *to be worth.*

Cela ne vaut rien. *It's (that's) not worth anything. It's (that's) worthless.*

Cela ne vaut pas grand'chose. *That's not very important. That's not worth very much.*

Il ne vaut pas mieux que son prédécesseur. *He's no better than his predecessor.*

Ce vaudrait mieux. *That would be better. That would be more advisable.*

Il vaudrait mieux rester ici pour le moment. *It would be better to stay here for the moment.*

Autant vaut retourner à la maison. *We may as well go home.*

Il sait se faire valoir. *He knows how to make the most of himself.*

Je trouve que cela vaut le coup. *I think it's worth trying.*

Cela ne vaut pas la peine. *It isn't worthwhile.*

Mieux vaut tard que jamais. *Better late than never.*

Ce n'est rien qui vaille. *It's not worth anything. It's not something of value.*

Mieux vaut les faire réparer. *It's better to have them repaired.*

valse *f. waltz.*

valser *to waltz.*

vanille *f. vanilla.*

vanité *f. vanity.*

vaniteux (vaniteuse *f.*) *adj. vain, conceited.*

vanter *to praise.*

se vanter *to boast.*

Il se vante de son succès. *He boasts about his success.*

Ce n'est pas quelque chose dont je me vanterais. *That's nothing to brag about. I wouldn't boast about anything of that sort.*

vapeur *f. steam, vapor.*

Vapeur d'eau. *Steam.*

Bateau à vapeur. *Steamer.*

vaquer *to be in recess; devote one's attention to.*

Il vaque à ses occupations. *He attends (devotes himself) to his business.*

variable *adj. variable, changeable.*

Un temps variable. *Changeable weather.*

Il est d'humeur variable. *He's very moody. His moods keep changing.*

variation *f. variation.*

Variation de temps. *Changes in the weather.*

VARIER *to vary, change.*

Les opinions varient à ce sujet. *Opinions vary on this subject.*

Ce tissu varie en qualité. *This cloth varies in quality.*

Le temps varie. *The weather is changing.*

variété *f. variety.*

Il n'y a pas grande variété ici. *There's very little variety here (in a store, restaurant, etc.).*

vase *m. vase.*

vaseline *f. vaseline.*

vaste *adj. vast, spacious.*

vaudeville *m. vaudeville.*

vau-l'eau *used in the following expressions:*

A vau-l'eau. *Downstream. Adrift.*

Tout va à vau-l'eau. *Everything is going to ruin.*

Aller à vau-l'eau. *To come to nothing.*

se vautrer *to sprawl.*

VEAU *m.* (veaux *pl.*) *calf.*

Un rôti de veau. *Roast veal.*

vécu *have lived.*

vedette *f. star.*

C'est une des dernières vedettes. *He's (she's) one of the recent stars (movies, theatre).*

Une vedette à moteur (or une vedette). *motorboat; patrol boat.*

végétation *f. vegetation; pl. adenoids.*

végéter *to vegetate.*

véhémence *f. vehemence.*

véhément *adj. vehement.*

véhicule *m. vehicle.*

veille *f. the state of being awake; day or evening before.*

La veille des élections. *The day before the election.*

Je l'ai vu la veille au soir. *I saw him last night.*

La veille de Noël. *Christmas eve.*

Il est à la veille de la ruine. *He's on the brink of ruin.*

VEILLER *to stay up; watch over.*

Elle a veillé très tard. *She sat up very late.*

Veiller aux intérêts de quelqu'un. *To look after someone's interests.*

Il veillera sur lui. *He'll look after him. He'll take care of him.*

Veillez à ce que mes ordres soient exécutés. *See to it that my orders are carried out.*

veilleur *m. watcher, night watchman.*

veilleuse *f. night light.*

Lumière en veilleuse. *Dim light. Light turned low.*

Il a mis l'électricité en veilleuse. *He dimmed the lights.*

Mettez vos phares en veilleuse. *Dim your headlights.*

VEINE *f. vein; luck.*

Il s'est coupé une veine. *He cut a vein.*

Il a de la veine. *He is lucky. He has luck.*

Ça a été un coup de veine. *It was a stroke of luck.*

Pas de veine! *Rotten luck!*

Il est en veine de plaisanterie. *He's in a humorous (joking) mood.*

vélo *m. (fam.) bicycle.*

vélocité *f. velocity.*

velours *m. velvet.*

vendange *f. grape harvest.*

vendeur *m.* (vendeuse *f.*) *person who sells; salesman, salesgirl; storekeeper.*

VENDRE *to sell.*

Ce magasin vend de tout. *This store sells (carries) everything.*

Maison à vendre. *House for sale.*

Cela se vend beaucoup. *That sells very well.*

VENDREDI *m. Friday.*

vénéneux (vénéneuse *f.*) *adj. poisonous (of plants).*

vénérable *adj. venerable.*

vénération *f. veneration, respect.*

vénérer *to revere, respect.*

vengeance *f. revenge.*

venger *to avenge.*

se venger *to get revenge.*

venimeux (venimeuse *f.*) *adj. poisonous.*

venin *m. venom.*

VENIR *to come.*

Venez avec nous. *Come with us.*

Quand pensez-vous venir? *When do you expect to come?*

Faites-le venir. *Have him come. Ask him to come. Get him to come.*

Il l'a fait venir. *He sent for him.*

Le voilà qui vient! *Here he comes!*

Je viens le voir. *I've come to see him.*

Il vient de sortir. *He just went out (left). He's just gone out.*

Où voulez-vous en venir? *What are you driving at?*

Maintenant je vous vois venir. *Now I see what you're driving at.*

D'où vient-il que vous n'alliez plus là? *How come you don't go there anymore?*

Il en était venu à sa fin. *He was at the end of his rope.*

Il me vient à l'idée que. *It occurs to me that.*

VENT *m. wind.*

Il fait du vent aujourd'hui. *It's windy today.*

Un coup de vent. *A gust of wind.*

Il est entré en coup de vent. *He dashed in.*

Il a jeté la paille au vent. *He trusted to luck.*

Regarder de quel côté souffle le vent. *To see how the land lies.*

Quel bon vent vous amène? *What lucky chance brings you here?*

Qui sème le vent récolte la tempête. *He that sows the wind shall reap the whirlwind.*

Il en a eu vent. *He got wind of it.*

Il a donné vent à sa colère. *He gave vent to his anger.*

VENTE *f. sale.*

Marchandise de bonne vente. *Goods that sell well.*

La vente ne va pas. *Business is slow.*

Hors de vente. *No longer on sale.*

Mise en vente. *For sale.*

En vente. *On sale.*

En vente à. *On sale at.*

ventilateur *m. ventilator, electric fan.*

VENTRE *m. belly, stomach.*

Il a mal au ventre (*fam.*). *He has a stomachache.*

Ventre affamé n'a point d'oreilles. *A hungry man doesn't listen to reason. ("A hungry stomach has no ears.")*

venu *m. one who comes.*

Le premier venu. *The first one who comes.*

Le dernier venu. *The last one who comes.*

venue *f. coming, arrival.*

Votre venue lui fera beaucoup de plaisir. *He'll be very happy (pleased) if you come. ("Your coming will give him a great deal of pleasure.")*

Avisez-moi de votre venue. *Let me know in advance when you'll arrive. ("Notify me in advance of your arrival.")*

Après plusieurs allées et venues . . . *After going back and forth several times . . .*

ver *m. worm.*

Un ver de terre. *An earthworm.*

Ver à soie. *Silkworm.*

véracité *f. veracity, truthfulness.*

verbal (verbaux *pl.*) *adj. verbal, oral.*

verbalement *verbally.*

VERBE *m. verb; tone of voice.*

Un verbe régulier. *A regular verb.*

Avoir le verbe haut. *To be dictatorial.*

verdict *m. verdict.*

verdir *to turn green.*

verdure *f. greenery.*

verge *f. rod, staff, switch, penis*

Verge d'or. *Goldenrod.*

verger *m. orchard.*

verglas *m. ice (on road).*

véridique *adj. veracious, true.*

vérification *f. verification.*

vérifier *to verify, adjust.*

Vérifier une référence. *To verify (check) a reference.*

Vérifier la tension artérielle. *To take one's blood pressure.*

Vérifiez si tout est prêt. *Make sure that everything is ready.*

Il faut vérifier les suffrages. *The votes have to be counted and checked.*

Ma montre a besoin d'être vérifiée. *My watch needs adjusting.*

véritable *adj. real.*

C'est un véritable diamant, et non pas due toc. *It's a real diamond, not an imitation.*

Il n'a fait que glisser sur le véritable sujet. *He barely touched on the real subject.*

Ce fut une véritable surprise. *It was a real surprise.*

Il a été un véritable ami. *He has been a true (real) friend.*

véritablement *truly, really.*

VÉRITÉ *f. truth.*

La vérité pure et simple. *The pure and simple truth.*

Dites la vérité. *Tell the truth.*

Ce que je vous dis là, c'est la vérité. *What I'm telling you is a fact (the truth).*

La vérité finit toujours par se découvrir. *The truth will come out.*

En vérité ça ne me dit rien. *To tell the truth it doesn't appeal to me.*

Je lui ai dit ses quatre vérités. *I told him a few home truths.*

vermine *f. vermin.*

vernir *to varnish.*

Les peintures viennent d'être vernies. *The paintings have just been varnished.*

Il a verni son récit. *He colored his story.*

vérole *f. pox.*

La petite vérole. *Smallpox.*

VERRE *m. glass.*

Boire dans un verre. *To drink from a glass.*

Mettre sous verre. *To keep under glass.*

Articles de verre. *Glassware.*

Papier de verre. *Sandpaper.*

J'ai pris un verre avec lui. *I had a drink with him.*

Vous voulez boire un petit verre? *Would you like a drink (of liquor)?*

verrou *m. bolt.*

vers *m. verse.*

VERS *prep. toward.*

Allons vers cette maison-là. *Let's go toward that house.*

Le voilà! Il vient vers nous. *There he is! He's coming toward us.*

Nous en reparlerons vers la fin de l'année. *We'll talk about it again toward the end of the year.*

Venez vers les deux heures. *Come about two.*

Il sera là vers trois heures. *He'll be there around three.*

(à) verse *pouring, emptying.*

A verse. *In torrents.*

La pluie tombe à verse. *It's pouring. It's raining in torrents. The rain's coming down in sheets. It's raining buckets. It's raining cats and dogs.*

versé *adj. experienced, versed in.*

VERSER *to pour; to deposit (money).*

Verser de l'eau. *To pour (some) water.*

Verser du café. *To pour (some) coffee.*

Versez-lui à boire. *Pour him a drink. Fill his glass.*

Verser une faible lumière. *To shed a dim light.*

Il a versé son argent à la banque. *He deposited his money at the bank.*

version *f. version.*

verso *m. back, reverse.*

Voir au verso. *See the reverse side.*

La réponse est écrite au verso. *The answer is written on the back.*

vert *m. green.*

VERT *adj. green.*

Légumes verts. *Green vegetables. Greens.*

Fruits verts. *Unripe fruit.*

Haricots verts. *String beans.*

Vert d'envie. *Green with envy.*

La verte jeunesse. *Callow youth.*

Vert clair (foncé). *Light (dark) green.*

vertical (verticaux *pl.*) *adj. vertical.*

vertige *m. dizziness, giddiness.*

Il fut pris de vertige. *He became dizzy.*

Cela m'a donné le vertige. *It made me dizzy.*

vertu *f. virtue, courage.*

Les quatre vertus cardinales. *The four cardinal virtues.*

Vivre dans la vertu. *To lead a good life.*

En vertu du contrat. *Under the terms of the contract.*

Faire de nécessité vertu. *To make a virtue of necessity.*

Plantes qui ont la vertu de guérir. *Plants that have healing properties.*

vertueux (vertueuse *f.*) *adj. virtuous.*

verve *f. zest, animation.*

Plein de verve. *Full of life. In lively spirits.*

Parler avec verve. *To speak in a lively manner.*

L'orateur était en verve aujourd'hui. *The speaker was in form today.*

veste *f. coat or jacket of a woman's suit.*

vestiaire *m. cloakroom.*

vestibule *m. hall, lobby.*

vestige *m. vestige, trace, remains.*

veston *m. coat, jacket (man's).*

Le complet-veston. *Business suit.*

Le veston à deux boutons. *Two-button jacket.*

vêtement *m. garment; pl. clothes.*

vétérinaire *m. veterinary.*

vêtir *to clothe, dress.*

Chaudement vêtu. *Warmly dressed.*

se vêtir *to be dressed in, put on.*

véto *m. veto.*

veuf *noun (m.) and adj. widower; widowed.*

veuve *noun (f.) and adj. widow, widowed.*

vexation *f. vexation.*

vexer *to vex, annoy.*
> Ça le vexe. *That annoys him.*
> Cela me vexe d'apprendre que . . . *I'm very sorry to hear that . . .*

viager *m. life interest.*
> Il a placé son argent en viager. *He invested his money in a life annuity.*

viager (viagère *f.*) *adj. for life.*
> Une rente viagère. *An income for life.*

VIANDE *f. meat.*

vibrant *adj. vibrating.*

vibrer *to vibrate.*

vice *m. vice.*

vice- *vice-.*
> Vice-président. *Vice-president.*

vice versa *vice versa.*

vicieux (vicieuse *f.*) *adj. vicious; incorrect use of a word or expression.*
> Un chien vicieux. *A vicious dog.*
> Cercle vicieux. *A vicious circle.*
> Une locution vicieuse. *An incorrect expression.*
> Usage vicieux d'un mot. *The wrong use of a word.*

vicissitude *f. vicissitude.*

victime *f. victim.*

victoire *f. victory.*

victorieux (victorieuse *f.*) *adj. victorious.*

victuaille *f. usually pl. victuals.*

vide *m. empty space, void, vacuum.*
> Regarder dans le vide. *To stare into space.*

VIDE *adj. empty.*
> J'ai l'estomac vide. *I'm hungry.*
> Un appartement vide. *An empty apartment.*
> Tête vide. *Empty-headed.*
> Paroles vides de sens. *Meaningless words. Words without any sense.*
> Des phrases vides. *Empty words.*
> Il est revenu les mains vides. *He came back empty-handed.*

vidéocassette *vidéocassette*

vider *to empty, clear out.*
> Videz vos verres! *Drink! ("Empty your glasses.")*
> Il fut forcé de vider les lieux. *He was compelled to vacate the premises.*

VIE *f. life.*
> Plein de vie. *Full of life.*
> Pour la vie. *For life.*
> Sans vie. *Lifeless.*
> Prix de la vie. *Cost of living.*
> Comment gagne-t-il sa vie? *What does he do for a living?*
> Jamais de la vie! *Never! It's out of the question!*

vieil *See* vieux.

vieillard *m. old man.*

vieille *f. old woman.*

vieillir *to grow old.*

vieillerie *f. old things, old rubbish, old clothes; old-fashioned idea.*

vieillesse *f. old age.*

vieux *m. old man.*
> Mon vieux. *My friend. Old chap.*

VIEUX (vieil *before masculine nouns beginning with a vowel or "mute" h*, vieille *f.*, vieilles *f. pl.*) *adj. old.*
> De vieilles habitudes. *Old habits.*
> Ça, c'est une vieille histoire. *That's an old story.*
> Une vieille fille. *An old maid.*
> Un vieux beau. *An old dandy.*
> Ses parents sont vieux jeu. *His parents are old-fashioned.*
> Un vieil homme. *An old man.*

VIF (vive *f.*) *adj. alive, living.*
> Chair vive. *The quick. Living flesh.*
> Vous l'avez blessé au vif. *You've wounded him to the quick.*
> Elle a la langue vive. *She has a sharp tongue.*
> Elle a l'humeur un peu vive. *She's short-tempered.*
> Il marchèrent à vive allure. *They walked at a brisk pace.*
> La discussion était très vive. *The discussion was very lively.*
> Un vert très vif. *Intense green. Very green.*
> Il est vif comme la poudre. *He's very excitable. He flares up easily.*
> A vif. *Exposed (nerve).*

vigie *f. lookout.*
> Il est de vigie. *He's on the lookout.*

vigilance *f. vigilance.*

vigilant *adj. vigilant.*

vigne *f. vine; vineyard.*

vigoureux (vigoureuse *f.*) *adj. vigorous.*

vigueur *f. vigor, strength.*
> Cette loi a été mise en vigueur. *This law is now in force.*

vil *adj. vile; cheap.*
> Je l'ai acheté à vil prix. *I bought it for a song (dirt-cheap).*
> Une vile calomnie. *A vile calumny.*

vilain *adj. nasty, villainous.*
> Ce sont de vilaines gens. *They're a bad lot.*
> Il lui joua un vilain tour. *He played a mean trick on him.*
> C'est une vilaine affaire. *It's an ugly (bad) business.*
> Un vilain incident. *An ugly incident.*
> Il fait vilain. *The weather's nasty.*

vilenie *f. meanness.*
> Il lui a fait des vilenies. *He played a mean trick on him.*

villa *f. villa.*

village *m. village.*

VILLE *f. town, city.*

Pouvez-vous m'indiquer comment je peux aller à la ville la plus proche? *Can you tell me how to get to the nearest town?*

Nous irons en ville cet après-midi faire des courses. *We're going to town this afternoon to do some shopping.*

Habiter hors de la ville. *To live out of town.*

Nous dînons en ville ce soir. *We're dining out tonight.*

villégiature *f. a stay in the country.*

Ils sont partis en villégiature. *They went to a summer resort.*

VIN *m. wine.*

Une bouteille de vin blanc. *A bottle of white wine.*

Une bouteille de vin rouge. *A bottle of red wine.*

vinaigre *m. vinegar.*

VINGT *noun and adj. twenty.*

A vingt et une heures. *At 9:00 P.M.*

vingtaine *f. about twenty.*

VINGTIÈME *noun and adj. twentieth.*

violation *f. violation.*

violemment *violently.*

violence *f. violence.*

violent *adj. violent.*

violer *to violate.*

VIOLET (violette *f.*) *adj. purple.*

violon *f. violin.*

vipère *f. viper.*

Elle a une langue de vipère. *She has a venomous tongue.*

virage *m. turning.*

Faites attention au virage. *Be careful, there's a curve in the road.*

virgule *f. comma.*

Point virgule. *Semicolon.*

viril *adj. manly, virile.*

vis *f. screw.*

visa *m. visa.*

Le visa d'entrée. *Entrance visa.*

VISAGE *m. face.*

Il a un visage aux traits accentués. *His face has strongly marked features.*

Il a le visage en feu. *His face is very red.*

Toute vérité a deux visages. *There are two sides to every question. ("Every truth has two aspects.")*

Faire bon visage à quelqu'un. *To smile at someone.*

Faire mauvais visage à quelqu'un. *To frown at someone.*

vis-à-vis *opposite; with regard to.*

Ils sont assis vis-à-vis l'un de l'autre. *They're sitting facing each other.*

Ses sentiments vis-à-vis de moi. *His feelings toward me.*

Vis-à-vis de moi il a toujours été très chic. *He has always been nice to me.*

Son respect vis-à-vis de lui diminuait chaque jour. *He respected him less and less. ("His respect toward him decreased every day.")*

viser *to aim; to visé, stamp (passport).*

Il a visé juste. *His aim was good. He hit the mark.*

A quoi vise tout cela? *What's the purpose of this? What's the object of this?*

Il a visé à ce but. *That was his goal (object, purpose).*

Je ne vise personne. *I'm not referring (alluding) to anyone in particular.*

Cette accusation le vise. *That accusation is directed against him.*

Elle vise toujours à l'effet. *She's always trying to create an impression.*

visible *adj. visible; easy to read.*

C'est très visible. *It's very conspicuous.*

Monsieur n'est pas visible. *Mr. X is not at home.*

Il ne sera pas visible avant deux heures. *He won't be able to see anyone before two o'clock.*

Ces objets d'art ne sont pas visibles. *These objects of art aren't open (accessible, on display) to the public.*

vision *f. vision.*

Sa vision n'est pas bonne. *He has poor vision.*

Il en a eu une vision momentanée. *He had (got) a glimpse of it.*

Une vision nette de quelque chose. *A clear view of something.*

VISITE *f. visit.*

Aller en visite. *To go visiting. To pay a call.*

Faire des visites. *To go visiting.*

Il lui a rendu visite. *He called on her.*

Qu'est-ce qui me vaut votre visite? *To what do I owe your visit?*

Une carte de visite. *A visiting card.*

Heures de visite. *Visiting hours.*

La visite des bagages. *Baggage inspection.*

La visite guidée (avec guide). *Guided tour.*

La visite-conférence. *Lecture tour.*

VISITER *to visit; examine.*

Visiter un malade. *To visit a patient.*

J'ai visité toutes les pièces. *I have been into every room.*

La douane a visité les malles. *The customs officials inspected the trunks.*

Faire visiter. *To show (someone) around.*

visiteur *m.* (visiteuse *f.*) *visitor.*

visser *to screw.*

vital (vitaux *pl.*) *adj. vital, essential.*

vitalité *f. vitality.*

VITE *swift, fast, quickly.*

Venez vite. *Come quickly!*

Faites vite! *Hurry up!*

Faites-le aussi vite que possible. *Do it as quickly as possible.*

vitesse *f. speed.*

A toute vitesse. *At full speed.*

Je vais expédier mon travail à toute vitesse. *I'm going to rush through my work. I'm going to get my work done as fast as possible.*

Il a expédié le colis en grande vitesse. *He sent the parcel by express.*

Changer de vitesse. *To change gears.*

Le changement de vitesse automatique. *Automatic transmission.*

vitre *f. pane (of glass).*

vitrine *f. shop window, showcase.*

vivace *adj. long-lived.*

Une haine vivace. *An undying hatred.*

Un préjugé vivace. *A deep-rooted prejudice.*

vivacité *f. vivaciousness, vivacity, liveliness; promptness.*

vivant *m. living being; lifetime.*

Les vivants et les morts. *The living and the dead. The quick and the dead.*

Du vivant de son père il n'aurait jamais osé. *He wouldn't have dared during his father's lifetime.*

En son vivant la maison était toujours remplie de monde. *During his lifetime the house was always full of company.*

C'est un bon vivant. 1. *He enjoys life. He knows how to live.* 2. *He's easygoing. He's a jolly fellow.*

vivant *adj. alive, living.*

Une langue vivante. *A living (modern) language.*

Pas une âme vivante. *Not a living soul.*

Il n'y a pas un homme vivant qui s'en souvient. *There isn't a man alive who remembers it.*

Il est le portrait vivant de son grand-père. *He's the living image of his grandfather.*

vivement *quickly, briskly, vigorously.*

Il entra vivement dans le magasin. *He hurried into the store.*

Sa mort les a vivement affligés. *They were deeply affected by his death.*

Il le ramassa vivement. *He snatched it up.*

Il a répondu vivement. *He answered warmly (with feeling).*

Vivement, on est en retard! *Hurry up, we're late!*

vivoter *to keep body and soul together.*

Ça va?—On vivote. *How are you getting along?—I just barely manage.*

Voilà deux ans qu'ils vivotent. *For two*

years now they've barely kept body and soul together.

VIVRE *to live.*

Vivre au jour le jour. *To live from day to day. To live from hand to mouth.*

Il n'a pas besoin de travailler pour vivre. *He doesn't have to work for a living.*

On peut vivre à très bon marché ici. *One can live very cheaply here.*

Ils vivent à Lyon. *They live in Lyons.*

Il fait bon vivre ici. *Life is pleasant here.*

Je n'ai pas rencontré âme qui vive. *I didn't meet a living soul.*

Il se laisse vivre. *He takes life easy.*

Il est commode à vivre. *He's easy to get on with.*

Qui vivra verra. *Live and learn. Time will tell.*

Vive la république! *Long live the Republic!*

vivres *m. pl. provisions, supplies.*

vocabulaire *m. vocabulary.*

vocation *f. vocation.*

vociférer *to shout, bawl, yell.*

voeu *m. (voeux pl.) vow; wish.*

Il est resté fidèle à son voeu. *He kept his vow.*

Son voeu a été accompli. *His wish was fulfilled.*

Tous mes voeux. *My best wishes.*

Mes voeux vous accompagnent. *My best wishes.*

Il a fait voeu de se venger. *He vowed vengeance.*

vogue *f. fashion.*

Ce chanteur est en vogue. *That singer is popular.*

La mode en vogue. *The prevailing fashion.*

C'est la vogue actuellement. *It's the latest rage. It's the rage at present.*

voguer *to row; sail.*

VOICI *here is, here are.*

Voici le livre. *Here's the book.*

Voici, monsieur. *Here you are, sir.*

En voici un autre. *Here's another one.*

Nous y voici. *Here we are. We've arrived.*

Je l'ai vu voici deux ans. *I saw him two years ago.*

Voici ce qu'il m'a dit. *Here's what he told me.*

Mon ami que voici vous le dira. *My friend here will tell you.*

Qu'est-ce qui vous est arrivé?—Voici. *What happened to you?—This is what happened.*

Voici . . . qui arrive. *Here comes . . .*

Vous voici. *Here you are.*

VOIE *f. way, road.*

Voie publique. *Public thoroughfare.*

Par voie de Paris. *Via Paris.*

Par voie de mer. *By sea.*

Voie ferrée. *Railroad track.*

Ligne à une voie. *Railroad line with a single track.*

Voie d'eau. *Waterway.*

Vous n'êtes pas dans la bonne voie. *You aren't on the right track.*

Il était en voie de guérison. *He was getting better. His health was improving.*

Etre en voie de réussir. *To be on the road to success.*

Obtenir par la voie de la persuasion. *To get by persuasion.*

Vous vous engagez dans une voie très dangereuse. *You're entering upon a very dangerous course.*

Ne vous en faites plus, l'affaire est en bonne voie. *Don't worry about it anymore, the affair (matter) is going well.*

VOILÀ *there is, there are.*

Le voilà. *Here he comes.*

Voilà tout. *That's all.*

A la bonne heure! Voilà ce qu'il y a de bon. *Good! That's one comfort.*

Voilà près d'un mois. *It's now nearly a month.*

Voilà ce qu'il m'a demandé. *That's what he asked me.*

Il est revenu voilà quatre ans. *He came back four years ago.*

En voilà un qui fera son chemin! *That fellow will go far!*

En voilà une idée! *What an idea!*

Voilà! *There! There you are!*

voile *f. sail.*

voile *m. veil.*

Prendre le voile. *To take the veil.*

voiler *to veil.*

voilette *f. veil of a woman's hat.*

VOIR *to see.*

Que voyez-vous? *What do you see?*

Je ne peux pas le voir d'ici. *I can't see it from here.*

Je l'ai vu partir. *I saw him leave.*

Voulez-vous voir si c'est fini? *Will you please see if it's finished?*

Je l'ai vu de mes propres yeux. *I saw it with my own eyes.*

Je verrai. *I'll see about it.*

C'est ce que nous verrons. *That remains to be seen.*

Il voit de loin. *He has foresight.*

Il fit voir son manuscrit à un ami. *He showed his manuscript to a friend.*

Nous avons été les voir. *We went to visit them.*

Il a vu rouge. *He saw red.*

Venez me voir quand vous serez à New York. *Look me up ("come to see me") when you're in New York.*

A le voir on dirait qu'il est très jeune. *To judge by his looks you'd say he's very young.*

Je le vois venir. *I see what he's driving at (what he's trying to do).*

Enfin, vous voyez où je veux en venir. *At any rate you understand just what I'm driving at.*

Cela n'a rien à voir à l'affaire. *That is entirely beside the point. That has nothing to do with the matter.*

Il n'a rien à voir là-dedans. *He has nothing to do with it.*

A ce que je vois, il n'a pas changé. *As far as I can see, he hasn't changed.*

Il s'est fait bien voir de son patron. *He gained the favor of his boss (chief, employer).*

Je ne peux pas le voir. *I can't stand him. I can't bear the sight of him.*

Il est bien vu de tout le monde. *He is highly esteemed by everybody.*

Vous n'y pensez pas, voyons! 1. *Come on, you don't really mean that!* 2. *Come on, you wouldn't really do it!*

Voyons, la dernière fois que je l'ai vu, c'était en 1942. *Let's see, the last time I saw him was in 1942.*

Voir c'est croire. *Seeing is believing. ("To see is to believe.")*

Laissez voir. *Let's see, let me see (it).*

se voir *to see oneself; see one another; be apparent or obvious.*

On s'y voit comme dans une glace. *You can see yourself there as in a mirror.*

Ils ne se voient plus. *They don't see each other anymore.*

Cela se voit. *That's obvious.*

Cela se voit tous les jours. *That happens every day. That's an everyday occurrence. You see that every day.*

voisin *m. neighbor.*

C'est mon voisin. *He's my neighbor. He's a neighbor of mine.*

Bon avocat, mauvais voisin. *A good lawyer makes a bad neighbor.*

voisin *adj. neighboring, adjacent, adjoining.*

Deux chambres voisines. *Two adjoining rooms.*

voisinage *m. proximity; vicinity, neighborhood.*

Tout le voisinage en parle. *The whole neighborhood is talking about it.*

voiture *f. car (subway, train); automobile.*

Ranger sa voiture. *To park one's car.*

Attention aux voitures. *Watch out for the cars.*

Nous sommes allés à Paris en voiture. *We drove down to Paris.*

Voiture d'enfant. *Baby carriage.*

En voiture! *All aboard!*

Voiture d'occasion. *Used car, secondhand car.*

Voyager en voiture. *To travel by car.*

VOIX *f. voice; vote.*

Il parle à haute voix. *He speaks in a loud voice.*

N'élevez pas la voix. *Don't raise your voice!*

De vive voix. *Viva voce. Orally.*

La voix du peuple. *Public opinion.*

Il a voix au chapitre. *He has a say in the matter.*

Il lui a donné sa voix. *He voted for him.*

vol *m. flight.*

vol *m. theft.*

volage *adj. fickle.*

volaille *f. poultry.*

volant *m. steering wheel.*

Au volant. *At the wheel.*

volcan *m. volcano.*

volée *f. flight.*

voler *to fly.*

Entendre voler une mouche. *To hear a pin drop.*

voler *to steal.*

Il ne l'a pas volé (*fam.*)! *He got what he deserved!*

volet *m. shutter.*

voleur *m.* (voleuse *f.*) *thief.*

volontaire *adj. voluntary.*

volontairement *voluntarily.*

volonté *f. will.*

A volonté. *At will.*

Prenez-en à volonté. *Take as much as you want.*

Il le fait à volonté. *He does it when he feels like it.*

Elle fait ses quatre volontés. *She does just as she pleases.*

Une volonté de fer. *An iron will.*

Faire acte de bonne volonté. *To show (prove) one's goodwill.*

Il l'a fait de sa propre volonté. *He did it of his own accord (of his own free will).*

Les dernières volontés. *Last will and testament.*

VOLONTIERS *gladly, with pleasure.*

Très volontiers. *With pleasure.*

Il consentait volontiers à le faire. *He readily consented to do it.*

Pouvez-vous m'indiquer comment je peux me rendre à cette adresse?—Volontiers. *Could you please tell me how to get to this address?—I'd be glad to.*

Je mangerais volontiers un dessert. *I could*

do with a dessert. *I'd like very much to have some dessert.*

On croit volontiers que . . . *One would like to believe that . . .*

volte-face *f. turning around.*

Il fit volte-face. *He turned around.*

volubilité *f. volubility.*

volume *m. volume.*

volumineux (volumineuse *f.*) *adj. bulky, voluminous.*

vomir *to vomit.*

vomissement *m. vomiting.*

voracité *f. voracity.*

vos *See* votre.

vote *m. vote, voting.*

Droit de vote. *Right to vote. Franchise.*

Bulletin de vote. *Ballot.*

Le vote d'une loi. *Passage of a law.*

Loi en cours de vote. *Bill before the House.*

voter *to vote.*

VOTRE (vos *m. and f. pl.*) *adj. your.*

Mettez votre chapeau. *Put your hat on.*

Faites votre choix. *Select (choose) what you want. Take your choice.*

Est-ce que ce sont vos livres? *Are those your books?*

Vos chemises sont prêtes. *Your shirts are ready.*

VÔTRE (la vôtre *f.*, les vôtres *m. and f. pl.*) *yours.*

Ce n'est pas la mienne, c'est la vôtre. *It isn't mine; it's yours.*

Son travail est aussi bien que le vôtre. *His work is as good as yours.*

Vous avez encore fait des vôtres. *You've been up to some of your old tricks again.*

A la vôtre! *To yours! (i.e., to your health, as a toast).*

vouer *to vow; dedicate.*

se vouer *to devote oneself to.*

VOULOIR *to want.*

Je veux sortir me promener. *I want to go out for a walk.*

Vous voulez venir? *Do you want to come?*

Si vous voulez, vous pouvez revenir demain. *If you like you can come back tomorrow.*

Il veut dix mille francs pour sa voiture. *He wants ten thousand francs for his car.*

Que voulez-vous dire? *What do you mean?*

Qu'est-ce que cela veut dire? *What does that mean?*

Que voulez-vous? 1. *What do you want? What can I do for you?* 2. *It can't be helped. What can you expect? What's to be done?*

Que me voulez-vous? *What do you want of me?*

Je veux bien. *I'd be glad to. I'm willing to. I have no objection.*

Je ne veux pas. *I don't want to.*

Vous l'avez bien voulu! *You asked for it!*

Je vous prie de bien vouloir m'attendre quelque instants. *Would you be good enough to wait for me for a few seconds?*

Il lui en veut. *He bears him a grudge. He has a grudge against him.*

Il faut savoir ce que l'on veut. *One has to make up one's mind.*

Je voudrais y aller. *I'd like to go there.*

Je voulais vous écrire là-dessus. *I meant to write you about it.*

Veuillez me faire savoir. *Please let me know.*

Veuillez faire ceci. *Please do this.*

Qu'il le veuille ou non, il faut qu'il le fasse. *Whether he wants to or not, he has to do it.*

Vouloir c'est pouvoir. *Where there's a will, there's a way.*

Veuillez agréer, Monsieur, l'assurance de ma plus parfaite considération. *Very truly yours.*

Où vous voudrez. *Wherever you wish.*

Tu veux? *How about it? Would you like to?*

Voudriez-vous (bien) . . . *Would you . . .*

voulu *wanted.*

VOUS *you.*

Vous désirez? *What would you like?*

Ce chapeau est à vous. *That's your hat.*

Faites comme chez vous. *Make yourself at home.*

Vous dites? *I beg your pardon? What did you say?*

De vous à moi. *Between you and me. Between the two of us.*

Vous deux. *You two, the two of you.*

vous-même(s) *yourself, yourselves.*

voûte *f. vault, arch.*

voûter *to vault, arch over.*

se voûter *to become round-shouldered or bent; stoop, be bent with age.*

VOYAGE *m. trip.*

Quand pensez-vous être de retour de votre voyage? *When do you expect to be back from your trip?*

Voyage de noces. *Honeymoon.*

Il est en voyage. *He's traveling.*

Bon voyage! *Pleasant journey!*

VOYAGER *to travel.*

J'aimerais voyager. *I'd like to travel.*

Voyager en train. *To travel by train.*

VOYAGEUR *m. (voyageuse f.) traveler, passenger.*

voyageur *(voyageuse f.) adj. traveling.*

Commis voyageur. *Traveling salesman.*

Pigeon voyageur. *Carrier pigeon.*

voyant *adj. showy, gaudy.*

Une couleur voyante. *A showy color.*

voyou *m. good-for-nothing.*

vrac *m. loose; in bulk.*

Il a acheté des livres en vrac. *He bought a job lot of books.*

vrai *m. truth.*

Le vrai de l'affaire, c'est que . . . *The truth of the matter is that . . .*

Est-elle revenue pour de vrai? *Did she really come back?*

A vrai dire . . . *To tell the truth. . . .*

VRAI *adj. true.*

Ma foi, c'est vrai! *It's really true!*

C'est un vrai bohême. *He's a real bohemian.*

Aussi vrai que je m'appelle Jacques. *As sure as my name is Jack.*

Tu le veux, vrai? *You want it, don't you?*

Vous me téléphonerez, pas vrai? *You'll phone me, won't you?*

VRAIMENT *really.*

Vraiment? *Really? Is that so?*

Vraiment, je ne pensais plus le revoir. *I really never expected to see him again.*

Vraiment, vous n'auriez pas dû vous donner tant de mal. *You really shouldn't have put yourself to all that trouble.*

J'ai appris quelque chose de vraiment drôle. *I just heard something really funny.*

vraisemblable *adj. probable, likely, credible.*

C'est très vraisemblable. *It's very probable (likely).*

Une histoire vraisemblable. *A story that sounds true.*

vu *seen, regarded.*

Etre bien vu. *To be respected.*

Mal vu. *Held in poor esteem.*

Ni vu ni connu (fam.). *Nobody will be any the wiser.*

Au vu et au su de tous. *Openly. To everybody's knowledge. As everybody knows.*

Vu que. *Since. Whereas. Seeing that.*

VUE *f. sight.*

Il a perdu la vue. *He lost his sight.*

Je ne le connais que de vue. *I only know him by sight.*

Il y a une très belle vue d'ici. *There's a very nice view from here.*

Nous nous sommes complètement perdus de vue. *We completely lost touch with one another.*

A première vue. *At first sight. Offhand.*

Mettre bien en vue. *To display prominently.*

Une vue saine. *A sound viewpoint.*

Il parle à perte de vue. *He talks endlessly.*

Il doit avoir quelque chose en vue. *He must have something in view.*

Avoir des vues sur quelque chose. *To have something in view (in mind). To have designs on something. To aim (be aiming) at something.*

Prise de vue. *Shot (photography).*

vulgaire *adj. vulgar; common.*

Une remarque vulgaire. *A vulgar remark.*

L'opinion vulgaire. *Public opinion.*

Le français vulgaire. *French slang.*

vulgarité *f. vulgarity.*

vulnérable *adj. vulnerable.*

W

wagon *m. carriage, coach.*

Un wagon-restaurant. *A dining car.*

Un wagon-lit. *A sleeper.*

Wagon de marchandises. *Freight car.*

watt *m. watt.*

Une ampoule de cinquante watts. *A fifty-watt bulb.*

w.-c. *water closet, toilet.*

week-end *m. weekend.*

Les Durand sont partis en week-end. *The Durands left for the weekend.*

whisky *m. whisky.*

Y

Y *there, to there.*

Allez-y! 1. *Go there.* 2. *Go right ahead!*

Nous nous y sommes perdus. *We got lost there.*

Revenons-y. *Let's go back there.*

La vie y est très chère. *Life there is very expensive.*

Il y a cinq personnes ici. *There are five people here.*

Il y avait beaucoup de monde. *There were a lot of people.*

Il y a quatre ans. *Four years ago.*

Il y a longtemps. *A long time ago.*

Il y a peu de temps. *A short while ago.*

Y a-t-il des lettres pour moi? *Are there any letters for me?*

J'y suis accoutumé maintenant. *I'm used to it now.*

Ah, j'y suis! *Oh, now I understand!*

Je n'y suis pas du tout. *I'm all at sea.*

Pendant que vous y êtes, donnez-moi un couteau. *While you're at it, get me a knife.*

Ça y est! *It's done! That's it!*

Je n'y suis pour rien. *I have nothing to do with it. I have no part in it.*

Il y a deux jours que j'ai mal aux dents. *I've had a toothache for two days.*

Il y en a d'autres. *There are others.*

J'y obéis. *I obey it.*

J'y pense. *I'm thinking about it.*

J'y réponds. *I answer it.*

J'y suis. *I understand. I get it.*

Nous y avons mis deux heures. *It took us two hours. We spent two hours on it.*

Y compris. *Including.*

yacht *m. yacht.*

yeux (*s.* oeil) *m. eyes.*

Coûter les yeux de la tête. *To cost a fortune.*

J'ai mal aux yeux. *My eyes hurt.*

Z

zèle *m. zeal.*

Brûler de zèle pour quelque chose. *To be very enthusiastic about something.*

Faire du zèle. *To show a lot of zeal (earnestness, enthusiasm).*

zélé *adj. zealous.*

zéro *m. zero.*

Le thermomètre est à zéro. *The thermometer is at zero.*

C'est un zéro. *He's of no account. He's a nonentity.*

Toute sa fortune a été réduite à zéro. *His fortune was reduced to nothing.*

zeste *m. peel.*

Le zeste d'une orange. *Orange peel.*

Cela ne vaut pas un zeste. *It isn't worth a straw.*

zézayer *to lisp.*

zigzag *m. zigzag.*

Il fait des zigzags. *He's staggering along.*

zinc *m. zinc.*

zone *f. zone.*

La zone torride. *The torrid zone.*

C'est un peintre de seconde zone. *He's a second-rate painter.*

zoo *m. zoo.*

zut *darn it.*

Zut alors! *Darn it!*

Zut, j'ai raté mon coup. *Darn it. I missed ("my shot").*

GLOSSARY OF PROPER NAMES

Alain	*Allan*
Alexandre	*Alexander*
Alice	*Alice*
André	*Andrew*
Anne	*Anna, Ann(e)*
Antoine	*Anthony*
Arthur	*Arthur*
Berthe	*Bertha*
Blanche	*Blanche*
Camille	*Camille*
Catherine	*Catherine*
Cécile	*Cecilia*
Charles	*Charles*
Christine	*Christine*
Christophe	*Christopher*
Claire	*Clara*
Claude	*Claude*
Claudine	*Claudine*
Colette	*Colette*
Daniel	*Daniel*
Denis	*Dennis*
Denise	*Denise*
Dominique	*Dominic*
Édouard	*Edward*
François	*Francis*
Frédéric	*Frederick*
Georges	*George*
Gérard	*Gerald*
Gustave	*Gustavus*
Guy	*Guy*
Hélène	*Helen*
Henri	*Henry*
Hubert	*Hubert*
Jacques	*Jack, James*
Jean	*John*
Jeanne	*Jane*
Julien	*Julian*
Léon	*Leo*
Lucien	*Lucian*
Marc	*Mark*
Marguerite	*Margaret*
Marie	*Mary*
Marthe	*Martha*
Maurice	*Maurice*
Michel	*Michael*
Monique	*Monique*
Olivier	*Oliver*
Paul	*Paul*
Pauline	*Pauline*
Pierre	*Peter*
Raymond	*Raymond*
René	*Rene*
Robert	*Robert*
Roger	*Roger*
Solange	*Solange*
Suzanne	*Susan*
Victor	*Victor*
Yvonne	*Yvonne*

GLOSSARY OF GEOGRAPHICAL NAMES

Afrique *f. Africa.*
Alger *m. Algiers.*
Algérie *f. Algeria, Algiers.*
Allemagne *f. Germany.*
(les) Alpes *f. pl. the Alps.*
Alsace *f. Alsace.*
Amérique *f. America.*
    L'Amérique du Nord. *North America.*
    L'Amérique du Sud. *South America.*
    L'Amérique Centrale. *Central America.*
    Les Etats-Unis d'Amérique. *The United States of America.*
Angleterre *f. England.*
Anvers *m. Antwerp.*
(l')Argentine *f. Argentina, the Argentine.*
Asie *f. Asia.*
(l')Atlantique *m. the Atlantic.*
Australie *f. Australia.*
Autriche *f. Austria.*
Belgique *f. Belgium.*
Bordeaux *m. Bordeaux.*
Brésil *m. Brazil.*
Bretagne *m. Brittany.*
Britanniques (Îles) *adj. the British Isles.*
Bruxelles *f. Brussels.*
Canada *m. Canada*
Chine *f. China.*
Danemark *m. Denmark.*
Douvres *m. Dover.*
Dunkerque *m. Dunkirk.*
Écosse *f. Scotland.*
Égypte *f. Egypt.*
Espagne *f. Spain.*
(les) États-Unis *m. pl. the United States.*
Europe *f. Europa; Europe.*
Genève *f. Geneva.*
Grande Bretagne *f. Great Britain.*
Grèce *f. Greece.*
(la) Havane *f. Havana.*
(le) Havre *m. Le Havre.*
(la) Hollande *f. Holland.*
(la) Hongrie *f. Hungary.*
Inde *f. India.*
Iran *m. Iran.*
Irlande *f. Ireland.*
Islande *f. Iceland.*
Israël *m. Israel.*
Italie *f. Italy.*
Japon *f. Japan.*
Londres *m. London.*

Luxembourg *m. Luxembourg.*
Lyon *m. Lyons.*
Maroc *m. Morocco.*
Marseille *m. Marseilles.*
(la) Méditerranée *f. the Mediterranean (Sea).*
Montréal m. Montreal.
Moscou *f. Moscow.*
Normandie *f. Normandy.*
Norvège *f. Norway.*
Océanie *f. Oceania.*
Paris *m. Paris.*
(les) Pays-Bas *m. pl. the Netherlands.*
Pérou *m. Peru.*
Pologne *f. Poland.*

Pyrénées *f. pl. Pyrenees.*
Roumanie *f. Rumania.*
Russie *f. Russia.*
Scandinavie *f. Scandinavia.*
Sibérie *f. Siberia.*
Sicile *f. Sicily.*
Suède *f. Sweden.*
Suisse *f. Switzerland.*
Syrie *f. Syria.*
Tanger *m. Tangier.*
Terre-Neuve *f. Newfoundland.*
Tunisie *f. Tunisia.*
Venise *f. Venice.*
Vienne *f. Vienna.*

English-French

A

a (an) un, une.
abandon (to) abandonner.
abbreviate abréger.
abbreviation abréviation f.
ability talent m.
able adj. capable.
able (be) pouvoir.
abolish abolir.
abortion avortement m.
about à propos de; autour de (*around*).
    What's it about? De quoi s'agit-il?
above au-dessus, en haut, dessus.
abroad à l'étranger.
absence absence f.
absent absent.
absolute absolu.
absorb absorber.
abstain from s'abstenir de.
abstract abstrait.
absurd absurde.
abundant abondant.
abuse abus m.
abuse (to) abuser.
academy académie f.
accent accent m.
accent (to) accentuer.
accept accepter.
acceptance acceptation f.
accident accident m.
accidental accidentel.
accidentally accidentellement.
accommodation arrangement m.
accommodate accommoder.
accompany accompagner.
accomplish accomplir.
accord accord m.
according (to) selon, suivant, d'après.
account récit m., compte m.
accuracy exactitude f., justesse f.
accurate juste, exact.
accuse accuser.
accustom accoutumer (à).
ache douleur f.
ache (to) avoir mal à.
achieve accomplir.
achievement accomplissement m.
acid acide, aigre.
acid acide m.
acknowledge reconnaître, convenir.
acknowledgment aveu m.; accusé de
    réception m.
acquaintance connaissance f.
acquire acquérir.
acre acre f.
across à travers.
act acte m.

act (to) agir.
action action f.
acting jeu m.
active actif.
activity activité f.
actor acteur m., comédien m.
actual réel, effectif.
actually effectivement.
acute aigu.
adapt adapter.
add ajòuter, additionner.
addition addition f.
address adresse f.
address (to) adresser.
addressee destinataire m.
adequate suffisant.
adjective adjectif m.
adhesive tape ruban adhésif m.
adjoining voisin.
administer administrer, distribuer.
admiral amiral m.
admiration admiration f.
admire admirer.
admission entrée f.
admit reconnaître, avouer; admettre; recevoir.
admittance entrée f.
    No admittance. Défense d'entrer. Entrée
      interdite.
adopt adopter.
adult adulte noun and adj.
advance progrès m.
advance (to) avancer.
advantage avantage m.
adventure aventure f.
adverb adverbe m.
advertise annoncer, afficher.
advertisement annonce f., affiche f.,
    réclame f.
advice conseil m.
advise conseiller.
affair affaire f.
affect intéresser; affecter.
affected affecté.
affection affection f.
affectionate affectueux.
affirm affirmer.
affluence affluence f.
afloat à flot.
afraid effrayé.
African africain.
after ensuite, après.
afternoon après-midi m.
afterwards après.
again encore, de nouveau.
against contre.
age âge m., époque f.
age (to) vieillir.
agency agence f.
agent agent m.

aggravate aggraver.
ago il y a.
   five years ago il y a cinq ans.
agree consentir à, être d'accord.
agreeable agréable.
agreed entendu, d'accord.
agreement pacte m., accord m.
agricultural agricole.
agriculture agriculture f.
ahead en avant.
aid aide f.
aid (to) aider.
   first aid les premiers soins.
   first-aid station station de secours.
AIDS SIDA m.
aim but m.
aim (to) viser.
air air m.
air conditioner climatiseur m.
airmail par avion.
airplane aéroplane m., avion m.
aisle passage m., allée f.
alarm alerte f., alarme f.
album album m.
alike pareil, semblable.
alive vivant, vif.
all tous, tout, toute, toutes.
   all right entendu, parfait.
alley allée f.
allow permettre.
allowed permis.
ally allié m.
almost presque.
alone seul.
along le long de.
alpaca alpaga m.
already déjà.
also aussi.
alter changer.
alternate (to) alterner.
alternately alternativement.
although bien que, quoique.
altitude élévation f.
always toujours.
amazed émerveillé, étonné.
amazed (be) être étonné.
amazement étonnement m.
amazing étonnant.
ambassador ambassadeur m.
ambitious ambitieux.
amend amender, corriger.
amends réparation f.
America Amérique f.
American américain.
among parmi.
amount somme f.
amount (to) revenir.
ample ample.
amuse amuser.

amusement amusement m.
amusing drôle.
analyze analyser.
ancestor ancêtre m.
anchor ancre f.
ancient ancien.
and et.
anecdote anecdote f.
anesthetic anesthésique.
angel ange m.
anger colère f.
anger (to) mettre en colère, fâcher.
angry en colère, courroucé, fâché.
   get angry se fâcher.
animal animal noun and adj.
animate animer.
animated animé.
annex annexe f.
annihilate anéantir.
anniversary anniversaire m.
announce annoncer.
annoy contrarier, ennuyer.
annual annuel.
annul annuler.
anonymous anonyme.
another un autre, une autre.
answer réponse f.
   answering machine téléphone-répondeur m.
answer (to) répondre.
antenna antenne f.
   dish antenna antenne parabolique f.
anterior antérieur (à).
anticipate anticiper, devancer.
antique antique.
anxiety anxiété f.
anxious inquiet.
any quelque.
anybody n'importe qui, personne.
anyhow n'importe comment.
anyone n'importe qui.
anything n'importe qui; quelque chose.
anyway n'importe comment.
anywhere n'importe où.
apart à part.
apartment appartement m.
apiece pièce, par tête.
apologize s'excuser.
apparent manifeste.
appeal (to) en appeler à, plaire.
appear apparaître.
appearance apparition f., air m.
appease apaiser.
appendix appendice m.
appetite appétit m.
applaud applaudir.
applause bravo m., applaudissement m.
apple pomme f.
application application f. (*diligence*),
   demande f. (*request*).

apply avoir rapport à (*be suitable*); solliciter (*apply for*); s'adresser à (*apply to*); appliquer (*administer*).
appoint désigner, nommer.
appointment rendez-vous m.; désignation f.
appreciate apprécier.
appreciation appréciation f.
approach abords m. pl., approche f.
appropriate convenable adj.
approval approbation f.
approve approuver.
April avril m.
apron tablier m.
arbitrary arbitraire.
arcade arcade f.
architect architecte m.
architecture architecture f.
ardent ardent.
area surface f.
argue discuter.
argument argument m.; dispute f.
arise se lever.
arm bras m.
    firearms arme f.
arm (to) armer.
armchair fauteuil m.
army armée f.
around autour de, alentour.
arouse soulever, éveiller.
arrange arranger.
arrangement disposition f.
arrest arrestation f.
arrest (to) arrêter.
arrival arrivée f.
arrive arriver.
art art m.
article article m.
artificial adj. artificiel.
artist artiste m.
artistic artistique.
as comme.
    as . . . as . . . aussi . . . que . . .
as for quant à.
as it were pour ainsi dire.
as little as aussi peu que.
as long as tant que.
as much autant.
as much as autant que.
as soon as dès que.
ascertain constater.
ash cendre f.
ashamed honteux.
aside de côté, à part, (en) aparté.
ask demander.
asleep endormi.
aspire aspirer à.
assault assaut m.
assemble réunir; rassembler.
assembly assemblée f.; congrès m.

assign assigner.
assist aider à.
assistance aide f.
assistant adjoint m.
associate associé m.
assume assumer, supposer.
assurance assurance f.
assure assurer.
astonish étonner.
astonishing étonnant.
astounded stupéfait.
astronaut astronaute m.
at à.
    at first d'abord.
    at last enfin.
    at once aussitôt.
    at the home of chez.
    at the place of business of chez.
    at the same time à la fois.
athlete athlète m. and f.
athletic athlétique, sportif.
athletics sports m. pl.
atmosphere atmosphère f.
atomic bomb bombe atomique f.
attach attacher.
attack attaque f.
attack (to) attaquer.
attain atteindre.
attempt essai m., tentative f.
attempt (to) essayer, tenter.
attend assister à.
attention attention f.
attic mansarde f.
attitude attitude f.
attorney avocat m., avoué m.
attract attirer.
attraction attraction f., attrait m.
attractive séduisant.
audience audience f., auditoire m.
August août m.
aunt tante f.
author auteur m.
authority autorité f.
authorize autoriser.
automatic automatique.
automobile automobile f., auto f., voiture f.
autumn automne m.
avenue avenue f.
average moyenne f.
    on the average en moyenne.
avoid éviter.
awake éveillé.
awake (be) être éveillé.
awake (to) réveiller, s'éveiller.
award récompense f.
award (to) accorder.
aware (be) se rendre compte de.
away absent.
    go away s'en aller.

awful affreux.
awhile pendant quelque temps.
awkward maladroit.
azure azur.

baby bébé m.
back dos m. (*body*); arrière m., derrière m., fond m.
background fond m.
backwards (en) arrière.
bacon lard fumé m.
bad mauvais.
badge insigne f.
bag sac m.
baker boulanger m.
bakery boulangerie f.
balance équilibre m.; solde m.
bald chauve.
ball balle f.
ball-point pen stylo à bille m.
balloon ballon m.
banana banane f.
band troupe f. (*troop*); lien m. (*tie*); orchestre m. (*orchestra*); ruban m.
bandage pansement m.
banister rampe f.
bank banque f.; bord m., rive f. (*river*).
  the Left Bank la Rive Gauche.
bank note billet de banque m.
bankruptcy banqueroute f.
banquet banquet m.
bar barre f.
barber coiffeur m.
bare nu, dégarni.
bargain occasion f.
  secondhand car voiture d'occasion.
barge chaland m.; péniche f.
barn grange f.
barrel tonneau m.
barren stérile.
bas-relief bas-relief m.
base bas, vil.
basin bassin m.
basis base f.
basket panier m.
bath bain m.
bathe baigner.
battery accu (mulateur) m.
battle bataille f., combat m.
be être.
  be ahead of devancer.
  be hungry avoir faim.
  be right avoir raison.
  be sleepy avoir sommeil.
  be sorry regretter.

  be thirsty avoir soif.
  be to blame être coupable.
  be wrong avoir tort.
beach plage f.
beaming radieux, rayonnant.
bean haricot m.
bear (to) porter, soutenir.
beat (to) battre; frapper (*strike*).
beautiful beau, belle.
beauty beauté f.
beauty parlor salon de beauté m., salon des dames, m.
because parce que.
because of à cause de.
become devenir.
becoming convenable; seyant.
bed lit m.
bedclothes couvertures f. pl.
bedding couchage m.
bedroom chambre à coucher f.
beef boeuf m.
beer bière f.
beet betterave f.
before avant (que).
beg mendier, supplier.
beggar mendiant m.
begin commencer.
beginning commencement m., début m.
behave se conduire.
behavior conduite f., tenue f.
behind en arrière, derrière.
Belgian belge.
belief croyance f.
believe croire.
bell cloche f.
belong appartenir.
below en-dessous, en bas, sous.
belt ceinture f.
bench banc m.
bend plier; courber, se pencher.
beneath dessous.
benefit bénéfice m., bienfait m.
benefit (to) bénéficier.
beside de plus, à part.
besides en outre.
best le meilleur.
bet pari m.
bet (to) parier.
betray trahir.
better meilleur, mieux.
between entre.
beware of se garder de, prendre garde à.
beyond plus loin, au delà de, hors de.
bicycle bicyclette f.
  bicycle race course cycliste f.
bid (to) ordonner, inviter, offrir.
big grand, gros.
bill facture f.; addition f. (*restaurant*); note f.
  bill of fare menu m.

billion milliard m.
bind lier.
biology biologie f.
bird oiseau m.
birth naissance f.
birthday anniversaire m.
biscuit biscuit m.
bishop évêque m.
bit (a) un peu.
bit morceau m.
bite morsure f., piqûre f.
bite (to) mordre.
bitter amer.
bitterness amertume f.
black noir.
blackbird merle m.
blade lame f.
blame blâme m.
blame (to) blâmer.
blank en blanc.
blanket couverture f.
bleed saigner.
bless bénir.
blessing bénédiction f.
blind adj. aveugle.
   a blind man un aveugle.
blind (to) aveugler.
block bloc m.
block (to) encombrer.
blond adj. blond.
   a blond un blond.
blood sang m.
blotter buvard m.
blouse blouse f., chemisier m. (*woman's*
    tailored).
blow coup m.
blue bleu, azur.
blush rougeur f.
blush (to) rougir.
board pension f. (*food*); planche f. (*plank*).
boardinghouse pension de famille.
boast se vanter.
boat bateau m., barque f., canot m.
body corps m.
boil (to) bouillir.
boiler chaudière f.
bold hardi.
bond lien m.; obligation f.
bone os m.
boo (to) huer.
book livre m.
   book of tickets carnet m.
booking location f.
booklet carnet m.
bookseller libraire m., bouquiniste m.
    (*secondhand*).
bookstore librairie f.
border frontière f., limite f. (*boundary*).
bored (be) s'embêter, s'ennuyer.

boring ennuyeux, embêtant.
born (be) naître.
borough arrondissement m. (*Paris*).
borrow emprunter.
both les deux.
bother ennui m.
bother (to) se tracasser; (se) déranger;
   ennuyer.
   Don't bother! Ne vous dérangez pas!
bottle bouteille f.
bottom bas m., fond m.
bough rameau m.
bounce (to) bondir.
boundary borne f., frontière f.
boundless illimité.
bowl écuelle f.
box boîte f., caisse f.
box office bureau de location m.
boy garçon m.
bracelet bracelet m.
braid natte f., tresse f.
brain cerveau m., cervelle f.
brake frein m.
branch branche f.
brave brave, courageux.
bread pain m.
breadth travers m.
   across à travers.
break (to) briser, rompre, casser.
   break out éclater.
breakdown panne f. (*mechanical*).
   engine trouble panne de moteur.
breakfast petit déjeuner m.
   have breakfast prendre le petit déjeuner.
breath souffle m., respiration f.
breathe respirer.
breeze brise f.
bribe (to) corrompre.
brick brique f.
bride mariée f.
bridge pont m.; bridge m. (*cards*).
brief bref.
bright clair.
brighten s'éclaircir.
brilliant éclatant.
bring apporter, amener.
bring together rapprocher.
bringing up éducation f.
British britannique.
broad large.
broil griller.
broken cassé.
bronze bronze m.
brook ruisseau m.
broom balai m.
brother frère m.
brother-in-law beau-frère m.
brown brun, marron.
bruise (to) meurtrir.

brush brosse f.
brute brute f.
bubble bulle f.
buckle boucle f.
bud bourgeon m.
budget budget m.
buffet (dresser) buffet m.
build construire, bâtir.
building construction f.; bâtiment m.
bulletin bulletin m.
bundle paquet m.
burden charge f.
bureau bureau m.
burn (to) brûler.
burst éclat m.
burst (to) éclater.
bus autobus m.; autocar m. (*outside city*).
bush buisson m.
bushel boisseau m.
business affaire f.
businessman homme d'affaires m.
businesswoman femme d'affaires f.
bust buste m.
busy occupé.
but mais.
butcher boucher m.
butcher shop boucherie f.
butter beurre m.
button bouton m.
buy (to) acheter.
buyer acheteur m.
buzzing bourdonnement m.
by par; à.
   by and by sous peu.
   by then d'ici là.
byte multiplet m.

C

cab taxi m.
cabbage chou m.
cabin cabine f.
cabinet cabinet m.
cable câble m.
cage cage f.
cake gâteau m.; pain m. (*of soap*).
calendar calendrier m.
calf veau m.
call appel m., cri m., visite f.
call (to) convoquer, appeler.
   call back rappeler.
   call forth évoquer.
   call out s'écrier.
calm calme.
camera appareil photographique m.; appareil
    cinématographique (*movie*).
camera shop magasin de photographie m.

camp camp m.
campfire feu de camp m.
camp (to) camper.
can bôite de conserve f.; bidon m.
can pouvoir (*be able*).
Canadian canadien.
cancel annuler.
candidate candidat m.
candle bougie f.
cantor chantre m.
canvas toile f. (*painting*).
cap casquette f.
capacity capacité f.
capital adj. capital.
capital capitale f. (*city*); capital m. (*money*).
capricious capricieux.
captain capitaine m.
captive captif.
capture (to) capturer.
car tramway m. (*streetcar*); voiture f.;
    wagon m.
carbon paper papier carbone m.
card carte f.
care soin m.
   In care of aux bons soins de (in a letter).
   take care of soigner, prendre soin de.
care (to)
   care about se soucier.
   care for aimer.
   care to avoir envie.
   I don't care. Ça m'est égal.
career carrière f.
careful soigneux.
careless négligent.
cares soucis m.; ennuis m.
caretaker concierge m., f.
carpenter menuisier m.; charpentier m.
carpet tapis m.
carry porter.
carry off emporter.
carry out exécuter.
cartoon (animated) dessin animé.
carve découper; sculpter.
carved sculpté.
case cas m.; étui m. (*container*); caisse f.
   in that case dans ce cas.
cash argent comptant m.
cash register caisse f.
cash (to) toucher.
cashier caissier m.
cask tonneau m.
cassette (tape) cassette f.
castle château m.
cat chat m.
catastrophe catastrophe f.
catch attraper.
category catégorie f.
Catholic catholique.
cattle bétail m.

cause raison f., cause f.
cause (to) causer.
cavalry cavalerie f.
cavity cavité f.
cease cesser.
ceiling plafond m.
celebrate célébrer; fêter.
cellar cave f.
cement ciment m.
cemetery cimetière m.
censorship censure f.
cent cent m., sou m.
center centre m.
centimeter centimètre m.
central central.
century siècle m.
cereal céréale f.
ceremony cérémonie f.
certain certain, sûr adj.
certainly certainement.
certainty certitude f.
certificate certificat m.
chain chaîne f.
chain (to) enchaîner.
chair chaise f.; chaire f.
chairman président m.
chalk craie f.
challenge défi m.
challenge (to) défier.
champion champion m.
chance hasard m., chance f.
change change m., transformation f.,
     changement m.; correspondance f.
     (*subway*).
change (to) changer.
chapel chapelle f.
chapter chapitre m.
character caractère m.; personnage m. (*in
     play*).
characteristic caractéristique noun and adj.
charge accusation f.; prix (demandé) m.;
     charge f.
     charge account *compte client m.*
charge (to) charger.
charitable charitable.
charity charité f.
charm charme m., grâce f.
charm (to) enchanter, charmer.
charming charmant, ravissant, délicieux.
charter charte f.
     charter flight avion charter m.
chase (to) poursuivre; chasser (*drive out*).
chat (to) bavarder.
cheap bon marché.
cheat (to) tricher, tromper.
check chèque m.
check (to) vérifier.
checkbook carnet de chèques m.
cheek joue f.

cheer (to) acclamer, encourager.
cheerful gai.
cheese fromage m.
chemical chimique.
chemist chimiste m.
chemistry chimie f.
cherish chérir.
cherry cerise f.
chest poitrine f. (*body*); coffre m. (*box*).
     chest of drawers commode f.
chestnut marron m., châtaigne f.
chew mâcher.
chicken poulet m.
chief adj. principal; maîtresse.
     masterwork oeuvre maîtresse f.
chief chef m. (*head*).
child enfant m., gosse m.
chime carillon m.
chimney cheminée f.
chin menton m.
china porcelaine f.
Chinese chinois.
chip jeton m.
chocolate chocolat m.
     chocolate bar tablette de chocolat.
choice adj. de choix.
choice choix m.
choir choeur m.
choke étrangler; étouffer.
choose choisir.
chop côtelette f. (*cut of meat*).
Christian chrétien noun and adj.
Christmas Noël f.
church église f., temple m. (*Protestant*).
cigar cigare m.
cigarette cigarette f.
cinematographic cinématographique.
circle cercle m.
circular circulaire m.
circulation circulation f.; tirage m.
     (*newspaper*).
circumstances circonstances f. pl.
citizen citoyen m.
city ville f.
city hall hôtel de ville.
civil civil.
civilization civilisation f., culture f.
civilize civiliser.
claim demande f., droit n.
claim (to) prétendre, réclamer, revendiquer.
clamor clameur f.
clap (to) applaudir.
clarinette clarinette f.
class classe f.
classic(al) classique.
classified advertisement petite annonce f.
classify classifier, classer.
clause clause f.
clean propre.

clean (to) nettoyer, degraisser.
  have (something) cleaned faire degraisser.
cleaning nettoyage m.
cleanliness propreté f.
clear clair, lucide.
clear (to) éclaircir; desservir (a table).
clearly clairement, ouvertement.
clerk employé de bureau m.
clever habile, adroit, intelligent.
climate climat m.
climb grimper.
clip attache f.
clip (to) attacher.
clippers tondeuse f.
cloak pèlerine f.
clock horloge f.
close auprès, tout près (near).
close (to) fermer.
closed fermé.
closet armoire f.
cloth étoffe f., toile f., tissu m.
clothe habiller.
clothes vêtement m., habits m. pl.
  clothes hanger cintre m.
cloud nuage m.
cloudy nuageux.
clover trèfle m.
club cercle m.; club m.
coach autocar m. (outside city).
coal charbon m.
coarse grossier.
coast côte f.
coat manteau m.; veste f.; veston m. (of suit).
cocoa chocolat chaud m.
code code m.
coffee café m.
coffeepot cafetière f.
coffin cercueil m.
coin pièce f.
cold froid adj.
cold cream crème à démaquiller.
coldness froideur f.
collaborate collaborer.
collar col m.; collier m. (dog).
collect réunir, assembler.
collection collection f.; quête f. (in church).
collective collectif.
college université f.
colonial colonial.
colony colonie f.
color couleur f.
color (to) colorer.
column colonne f.; rubrique f. (newspaper, magazine).
comb peigne m.
comb (to) peigner.
combination combinaison f.
combine combiner.
come venir.

come back revenir.
  come by again repasser.
comedy comédie f.
comet comète f.
comfort confort m.
comfort (to) consoler, rassurer.
comfortable confortable, à l'aise.
comma virgule f.
command commandement m.
command (to) commander.
commander commandant m.
commerce commerce m.
commercial adj. commercial
commercial publicité f.
commission commission f.
commit commettre.
common commun, ordinaire.
communicate communiquer.
communication communication f.
community communauté f.
compact disk, CD disque compact m.
companion camarade m. and f., compagnon m., compagne f.
company (guests) monde m., invités m. pl.
company (firm) compagnie f.
compare comparer.
comparison comparaison f.
compete faire concurrence.
competition concurrence f.
complain se plaindre.
complaint plainte f.
complete complet.
complex adj. complexe.
complexion teint m.
complicate compliquer.
complicated compliqué.
compliment compliment m.
compose composer.
composer compositeur m.
composition composition f.
compromise compromis m.
compromise (to) compromettre.
computer ordinateur m.
  microcomputer micro-ordinateur m.
  computer language language machine or de programmation.
  computer program programme informatique m.
portable computer portatif m.
computer science informatique f.
comrade camarade m.
conceit amour-propre m.
conceive concevoir.
concentrate concentrer.
concern maison f. (business); affaire f.; importance f.; anxiété f.
concern (to) concerner.
concert concert m.
concierge gardien m.

concrete concret adj.

condemn condamner.

condense condenser.

condition condition f., état m.

condom préservatif m.

conduct conduite f.

conduct (to) conduire, diriger (*music*).

conductor conducteur m.; receveur m. (*on train, bus, etc.*).

confess avouer.

confession aveu m.

confidence confidence f., confiance f.

confident confident.

confidential confidentiel.

confirm confirmer.

confirmation confirmation f.

confuse embrouiller; confondre (*one thing with another*).

confused dérouté (*person*); désorienté; embrouillé (*situation*).

confusing peu clair, déroutant.

congenial sympathique.

congratulate féliciter.

congratulation félicitation f.

connect unir, mettre en contact.

connection association f., relations f. pl.; correspondance f. (*subway*).

conquer conquérir.

conquest conquête f.

conscience conscience f.

conscientious consciencieux.

conscious conscient.

consent consentement m.

consent (to) consentir.

conservation conservation f.

conservative conservateur noun and adj.

consider considérer.

considerable considérable.

consideration réflexion f.; considération f.

consist (of) consister de.

consistent conséquent.

constant constant.

constantly constamment.

constitution constitution f.

constitutional constitutionnel.

consul consul m.

consumer consommateur m., consommatrice f.

consumer goods biens de consommation m. pl.

contagious contagieux.

contain contenir.

container récipient m.

contemporary contemporain.

contempt mépris m.

contend concourir.

content (be) être content, être satisfait.

content (to) satisfaire, contenter.

content(s) contenu m.

continent continent m.

continual continuel.

continue continuer.

contract contrat m.

contract (to) contracter.

contractor entrepreneur m.

contradict contredire.

contradiction contradiction f.

contradictory contradictoire.

contrary adj. contraire.

   contrary to contrairement.

contrary contraire m.

   on the contrary au contraire.

contrast contraste m.

contrast (to) contraster.

contribute contribuer.

contribution contribution f.

control contrôle m., autorité f.

control (to) gouverner, maîtriser, contrôler.

controversy polémique f.

convenience convenance f.

convenient commode.

convention réunion f., convention f.

conversation conversation f.

converse converser, causer.

convert (to) convertir.

convertible décapotable f. (*car*).

convict (to) convaincre, condamner.

conviction conviction f.

convince convaincre.

cook cuisinière f.

cook (to) cuire.

cooked cuit.

cool frais.

cool (to) refroidir.

copy exemplaire m., copie f.

copy (to) copier.

cork bouchon (*stopper*); liège m. (*material*).

cork (to) boucher.

corn maïs m.

corner coin m.; recoin m. (*nook*).

corporation corporation f.

correct correct, exact.

correct (to) corriger.

correction correction f.

correspond correspondre.

correspondence correspondance f.

correspondent correspondant m.

corresponding correspondant.

corrupt corrompre.

corruption corruption f.

cost coût m.

cost (to) coûter.

costly coûteux.

costs frais m. pl.

costume costume m.

cottage chaumière f.

cotton coton m. (*cotton thread, cotton material*); ouate f. (*medicine*).

couch canapé m.
cough toux f.
cough (to) tousser.
count comte m.
count (to) compter.
counter comptoir m. (*store*); guichet m.
countersign (to) contresigner.
countess comtesse f.
countless innombrable.
country province f.; campagne f.; patrie f. (*fatherland*).
country house maison de campagne f.
countryman compatriote m. and f., campagnard m.
couple couple m.
courage courage m.
course cours m.
court tribunal m.
courteous courtois.
courtesy courtoisie f.
courtyard cour f.
cousin cousin m.
cover couvercle m.
cover (to) couvrir.
   cover over recouvrir.
cow vache f.
crack fente f.
crack (to) craquer, fendre.
cradle berceau m.
craftsmen artisanat m.
crash fracas m.
crazy fou.
cream crème f.
   cleansing cream crème à démaquiller.
create créer.
creature créature f.
credit crédit m.
creditor créancier m.
creed culte m.
cricket grillon m.
crime crime m.
criminal criminel m.
crisis crise f.
   energy crisis crise d'énergie f.
crisp croustillant.
critic critique m.
crooked de travers.
crop moisson f.
cross adj. maussade, de mauvaise humeur.
cross croix f.
cross (to) croiser; rayer.
crossing passage m., traversée f.
   pedestrian crossing passage clouté.
cross-roads carrefour m.
crossword puzzle mots croisés m. pl.
crouch accroupir.
crow corbeau m.
crowd foule f., affluence f.
   rush hour l'heure d'affluence.

crowd (to) encombrer.
crowded rempli de monde, encombré (*streets, etc.*); bondé.
crown couronne f.
crown (to) couronner.
cruel cruel.
cruelty cruauté f., barbarie f.
crumb miette f.
crumbling effondrement m.
crushing écrasant.
crust croûte f.
crutch béquille f.
cry cri m.
cry (to) pleurer.
cubist cubist m.
cuff manchette f.
cult culte m.
cunning ruse f., artifice m.
cup tasse f.
cupboard placard m.
cure cure f.
cure (to) guérir.
curio bibelot m.
curiosity curiosité f.
curious curieux.
curl (to) boucler.
current adj. courant.
current cours m.
curtain rideau m.
curve courbe f.
cushion coussin m.
custom usage m.
customary habituel.
customer client m.
customs house douane f.
customs official douanier m.
customs permit carnet m.
cut (to) couper; effacer (computer)

D

dagger poignard m.
daily quotidien.
   daily newspaper quotidien m.
dainty délicat.
dairy laiterie f.
dam barrage m.
damage dommage m.
damage (to) endommager, avarier.
damp humide.
dance danse f.
dance (to) danser.
danger danger m.
dangerous dangereux.
Danish danois n. and adj.
dark noir, foncé.
darkness obscurité f.

dash se précipiter.
data données f. pl.
data processing traitement de l'information m.; informatique f.
date date f.
date (to) dater.
daughter fille f.
dawn aurore f., aube f.
day jour m., journée f.
   day after tomorrow après-demain m.
   day before veille f.
   day before yesterday avant-hier m.
dazzle éblouir.
dead mort.
deaf sourd.
deal opération f., affaire f.
dealer vendeur m., marchand m.
dear cher, coûteux (*expensive*).
death mort f.
debarkation débarquement m.
debatable discutable.
debate discussion f.
debate (to) discuter.
debris débris m. pl.
debt dette f.
debtor débiteur m.
decanter carafe f.
decay décadence f., ruine f.
decay (to) se gâter, dépérir.
decayed carié.
   a decayed tooth une dent cariée.
deceased défunt.
deceit déception f.
deceive tromper.
December décembre m.
decent comme il faut, respectable.
decide décider.
decidedly décidément.
decision décision f.
decisive décisif.
deck pont m.
declare déclarer.
decline décadence, f.; baisse f.
decline (to) décliner; baisser.
declaration déclaration f.
   customs declaration déclaration en douane.
decoration décor m.
decrease réduction f.
decrease (to) diminuer.
decree ordonnance f.; arrêt m.
dedicate consacrer.
deed acte notarié m.; contrat m., exploit m.
deep profond.
deeply profondément.
deer cerf m.
defeat défaite f.
defeat (to) vaincre.
defect défaut m.
defend défendre.

defense défense f.
defiance défi m.
define définir, déterminer.
definite défini.
definitely décidément.
defy défier.
degree degré m., diplôme m. (*university*).
   to get a degree obtenir un diplôme (universitaire).
   Master licence f.
   Doctorate doctorat m.
delay retard m.
delay (to) tarder.
delegate délégué m.
delegate (to) déléguer.
deliberate adj. délibéré.
deliberate (to) délibérer.
deliberately délibérément.
delicacy délicatesse f.
delicate délicat.
delicious délicieux.
delight joie f.
delight (to) ravir.
delighted enchanté.
delightful ravissant.
deliver remettre, livrer.
deliverance délivrance f.
delivery livraison f.
demand demande f.
demand (to) réclamer, exiger.
demonstrate démontrer.
demonstration démonstration f., manifestation f.
denial dénégation f., refus m., démenti m.
denounce dénoncer.
dense dense.
density densité f.; épaisseur f.
dental dentaire.
dentifrice dentifrice noun m. and adj.
dentist dentiste m.
deny nier, démentir.
deodorant déodorant m.
department département m.; rayon m. (*of store*).
   in the dress department au rayon des robes.
department store grand magasin m.
departure départ m.
depend dépendre.
dependence dépendance f.
dependent adj. dépendant (de).
deplore déplorer.
deposit dépôt m.; versement (money) m.
deposit (to) verser (*money*).
depot dépôt m.
depress abattre, déprimer.
depression abattement m. (*mood*).
deprive priver (de).
depth profondeur f., fond m.

deputy adjoint m.
deride tourner en dérision.
derive dériver de; provenir de.
descend descendre.
descendant descendant m.
descent descente f.
describe décrire.
description description f.
desert désert m.
desert (to) abandonner.
deserve mériter.
design dessein m.
design (to) dessiner.
designed (for) destiné à.
desirable désirable.
desire désir m., envie f.
desire (to) désirer.
desirous désireux.
desk bureau m.; guichet m.
desolate solitaire, désolé.
desolation désolation f.
despair désespoir m.
despair (to) désespérer.
desperate désespéré.
despise mépriser.
despite en dépit de.
despondent abattu.
dessert dessert m.
destination destination f.
destiny destin m.
destitute indigent.
destroy détruire.
destruction destruction f.
detach détacher.
detail détail m.
detailed minutieux.
detain retenir.
detect découvrir.
determination détermination f.
determine déterminer.
detest détester.
detour détour m.
detract from déprécier, dénigrer.
detriment détriment m.
develop développer.
development développement m.
device appareil m.; expédient m.
devil diable m.
devise combiner.
devoid of dépourvu de.
devote dévouer.
devour dévorer.
dew rosée f.
dial cadran m. (*clock*).
dial (to) composer (*telephone*).
dial telephone téléphone automatique m.
dial tone bourdonnement m.
dialect dialecte m.
dialogue dialogue m.

diameter diamètre m.
diamond diamant m.
diary journal m.
dictate dicter.
dictionary dictionnaire m.
die mourir.
diet régime m.
differ différer.
difference différence f.
different différent.
difficult difficile.
difficulty difficulté f.
dig creuser, fouiller.
digest digérer.
dignity dignité f.
dim sombre.
dimension dimension f.
diminish diminuer.
dinner dîner m.
dine dîner.
dip (to) plonger, tremper.
diploma diplôme m., baccalauréat m. (*high school*).
diplomacy diplomatie f.
diplomat diplomate m.
direct adj. direct, droit, précis, net.
direct (to) diriger.
direction direction f.; administration f.; sens m.
directions indications f. pl.
director directeur m.
directory annuaire m.; almanach m.
dirt saleté f.
dirty sale.
disability incapacité f.
disable rendre incapable (de).
disabled invalide.
disadvantage désavantage m.
disagree ne pas être d'accord, différer.
disagreeable désagréable.
disagreement désaccord m.
disappear disparaître.
disappearance disparition f.
disappoint décevoir.
disapprove désapprouver.
disaster catastrophe f., désastre m.
disastrous funeste, désastreux.
discharge congé m. (*from a position, etc.*); coup de feu (*of gun*), décharge f.
discharge (to) congédier (*a person*); décharger (*a gun*).
discipline discipline f.
disclaim désavouer, renier.
disclose découvrir, révéler.
disclosure découverte f.; révélation f.
discomfort malaise m.
discontent mécontentement m.
discontented mécontent (de).
discontinue discontinuer.

discord discorde f.

discount escompte m.

discourage décourager.

discouragement découragement m.

discover découvrir.

discovery découverte f.

discreet discret.

discretion discrétion f.

discuss discuter.

discussion discussion f.

disdain dédain m.

disdain (to) dédaigner.

disease maladie f.

disgrace déshonneur m., honte f.

disguise déguisement m.

disgust dégoût m.

disgust (to) dégoûter.

disgusted dégoûté.

disgusting dégoûtant.

dish plat m., vaisselle f.

    dishwasher lave-vaisselle m.

dishonest malhonnête.

disk disque m.

    floppy disk disquette f., disque souple m.

dislike aversion f.

dislike (to) ne pas aimer.

dismay consterner.

dismiss renvoyer, congédier.

dismissal renvoi m.

disobey désobéir.

disorder désordre m.

disown renier, désavouer.

dispense dispenser.

display exposition f., étalage m.

display (to) montrer.

displease déplaire.

displeasure déplaisir m.

disposal disposition f.

dispose disposer.

disprove réfuter.

dispute dispute f.

dispute (to) disputer.

dissolve dissoudre.

distance distance f.

    distance covered parcours m.

    distance in kilometers kilométrage m.

distant lointain.

distinct clair, distinct (de).

distinction distinction f.

distinguish distinguer.

distort déformer.

distract distraire.

distress détresse f.

distress (to) affliger.

distribute distribuer.

distribution distribution f.

district quartier m., arrondissement m. (*Paris*).

distrust défiance f., méfiance f.

distrust (to) se méfier de.

disturb déranger; ennuyer.

disturbance désordre m.; agitation f.

ditch fossé m.

dive (to) plonger.

divide partager, diviser.

divine divin.

division division f.

divorce divorce m.

divorce (to) divorcer.

dizziness vertige m.

dizzy frappé de vertige.

do faire.

dock quai m. (*pier*).

doctor médecin m.

doctrine doctrine f.

document document m.

dog chien m.

dollar dollar m.

dome dôme m.

domestic domestique noun and adj.

dominate dominer.

done fait.

door porte f.; portière f. (*car*).

doorkeeper concierge m. and f.

dose dose f.

dot point m.

double double noun m. and adj.

doubt doute m.

doubt (to) douter.

doubtful douteux, indécis.

doubtless sans doute.

dough pâte f.

down en bas.

downwards en bas.

dozen douzaine f.

draft projet m.; traite f. (*bank*); enrôlement m. (*military*).

draft (to) élaborer (*draw up*); conscrire.

drag traîner.

drain vider, assécher.

drama drame m.

dramatic dramatique.

draw dessiner.

draw back reculer.

drawer tiroir m.

drawing dessin m.

    animated cartoon dessin animé.

    border design dessin du bord.

drawing room salon m.

dread crainte f., terreur f.

dread (to) redouter, craindre.

dreaded redoutable.

dream rêve m.

dream (to) rêver.

dreamer rêveur m.

dress robe f.

dress (to) habiller, s'habiller.

dressmaker couturière f.

drill (to) creuser (*tooth*).

drink boisson f.
drink (to) boire.
drip dégoutter.
drive aller en voiture, conduire (*car*); pousser (*force*).
driver chauffeur m.
drop goutte f.
drop (to) laisser tomber (*allow to fall*); baisser; abandonner.
drought sécheresse f.
drown noyer, se noyer.
drug drogue f.
    drug addiction toxicomanie f.
    drug pusher trafiquant de drogue.
druggist pharmacien m.
drugstore pharmacie f.
drum tambour m.
drunk ivre.
dry sec.
dry (to) sécher.
dry cleaner pressing m.
dry cleaning dégraissage m., nettoyage à sec m.
dryness sécheresse f.
duchess duchesse f.
due dû.
duke duc m.
dull terne (*color*); bête (*stupid*).
dumb muet (*deaf and dumb*); stupide, bête (*stupid*).
during pendant.
dust poussière f.
dust (to) épousseter.
dusty poussiéreux.
duty douane f. (*customs*), impôt m.; devoir m. (*obligation*).
dwell demeurer.
dwelling demeure f.
dye teinture f.
dye (to) teindre.

E

each chaque, chacun.
    each other se, l'un l'autre.
    each time chaque fois.
eager ardent.
eagle aigle m.
ear oreille f.
early de bonne heure, tôt.
earn gagner.
earnest sérieux.
earnestly instamment.
earth terre f.
ease aise f.
ease (to) soulager.
easily facilement.

east est m.
Easter Pâques m. pl.
eastern oriental.
easy facile.
easy chair bergère f.
eat manger.
echo écho m.
economical économe (*person*), économique (*thing*).
economize faire des économies.
economy économie f.
edge bord m.
edition édition f., numéro m. (*publication*).
editor rédacteur m.
editorial article de tête m.
education éducation f.
effect effet m.
effect (to) effectuer.
effective efficace.
efficiency efficacité f.
effort effort m.
egg oeuf m.
egoism égoïsme m.
eight huit.
eighteen dix-huit.
eighteenth dix-huitième.
eighth huitième.
eightieth quatre-vingtième.
eighty quatre-vingts.
either ou.
    either one l'un ou l'autre.
elastic élastique noun m. and adj.
elbow coude m.
elder aîné.
elderly d'un certain âge.
eldest plus âgé.
elect choisir, élire.
election élection f.
elector électeur m.
electric(al) électrique.
electricity électricité f.
elegant élégant.
element élément m.; facteur m.
elementary élémentaire.
elephant éléphant m.
elevator ascenseur m.
eleven onze.
eleventh onzième.
eliminate éliminer.
eloquence éloquence f.
eloquent éloquent.
else autrement, sinon (*otherwise*).
    someone else quelqu'un d'autre.
    somewhere else ailleurs.
elsewhere ailleurs.
elude éluder, éviter.
embankment quai m. (*river*).
embark embarquer, s'embarquer.
embarrass embarrasser.

embarrassing gênant.

embarrassment embarras m.

embassy embassade f.

embody incarner.

embroidery broderie f.

emerge surgir.

emergency circonstance critique f.

eminent éminent.

emotion émotion f.

emperor empereur m.

emphasis emphase f.

emphasize appuyer sur, mettre en relief.

emphatic énergique.

empire empire m.

employee employé m.

employer patron m.

employment emploi m.

empty vide.

empty (to) vider.

enable mettre à même de, donner le moyen de.

enamel émail m.

enclose entourer, joindre.

enclosed ci-inclus, ci-joint.

encourage encourager.

encouragement encouragement m.

end bout m., fin f., but m. (*aim*).

end (to) finir, aboutir (*result*), terminer.

endeavor effort m.

endeavor (to) s'efforcer de.

ending dénouement m. (*play or story*).

endorse endorser, confirmer.

endure supporter.

enemy ennemi m.

energetic énergique.

energy énergie f.

enforce imposer.

engage engager, s'engager à.

engaged couple fiancés m.

engagement engagement m.; fiançailles f. pl.

engine machine f.

engineer ingénieur m.

England Angleterre f.

English anglais noun and adj.

engrave graver.

engraving gravure f.

enjoy s'amuser, jouir.

enjoyment jouissance f.

enlarge élargir.

enlargement agrandissement m.

enlist enrôler, s'enrôler.

enormous énorme.

enormously énormément.

enough assez, suffisament.

enrich enrichir.

enter entrer.

entertain recevoir, amuser.

entertainment amusement m.

enthusiasm enthousiasme m.

enthusiastic enthousiaste.

entire entier.

entitle intituler (*title*), donner droit à (*give one the right to*).

entrance entrée f.

entrust confier à.

enumerate énumérer.

envelope enveloppe f.

envious envieux.

envy envie f., jalousie f.

envy (to) envier.

episode épisode m.

equal égal.

equal (to) égaler.

equality égalité f.

equilibrium équilibre m.

equip équiper, munir de.

equipment équipement m. (*outfit*).

equity équité f.

era ère f.

erase effacer.

eraser gomme f.

erect droit.

erect (to) dresser, ériger, fonder.

err errer, se tromper.

errand course f., commission f.

error erreur f., tort m.

escalator escalier roulant m.

escape fuite f.

escape (to) échapper.

especially spécialement.

essay essai m., composition f. (*school*).

essence essence f.

essential essentiel, indispensable.

establish établir.

establishment établissement m.

estate biens m. pl., propriéte f.

esteem estime f.

esteem (to) estimer.

esthetic esthétique.

estimate appréciation f., évaluation f. (*value*)

estimate (to) évaluer, apprécier.

estimation jugement m.

etching eau-forte m.

eternal éternel.

eternity éternité f.

ether éther m.

euro euro m.

European européen noun and adj.

evade esquiver, éluder.

evasion évasion f.

eve veille f.

on the eve of à la veille de.

even adj. uni, égal, pair (*number*).

even adv. même.

evening soir m.

Good evening! Bonsoir!

yesterday evening hier soir.

tomorrow evening demain soir.

event événement m.
ever jamais, toujours.
every chaque, tous.
   every day tous les jours.
everybody tout le monde.
everything tout.
everywhere partout.
evidence évidence f.
evident évident.
evidently évidemment.
evil adj. mauvais.
evil mal m.
evoke évoquer.
evolve développer.
exact précis, exact.
exactly exactement.
exaggerate exagérer.
exaggeration exagération f.
exalt exalter.
exaltation exaltation f.
examination examen m.
examine examiner.
example exemple m.
exceed dépasser.
excel exceller à.
excellence excellence f.
excellent excellent.
except sauf.
except (to) excepter.
exception exception f.
exceptional exceptionnel.
exceptionally exceptionnellement.
excess excès m.
excessive excessif.
exchange échange m.
   exchange rate le taux de change m.
   exchange window guichet de change m.
exchange (to) échanger.
excite exciter, agiter.
excitement excitation f., agitation f.
exclaim s'écrier.
exclamation exclamation f.
exclamation mark point d'exclamation.
exclude exclure.
exclusive exclusif.
excursion excursion f., tour m.
excuse excuse f.
excuse (to) excuser.
   Excuse me. Excusez-moi.
execute exécuter, effectuer.
execution exécution f.
exempt exempt (de).
exercise exercice m.
exercise (to) exercer.
exert exercer, mettre en oeuvre.
exertion effort m.
exhaust épuiser.
exhaustion épuisement m.
exhibit (to) exhiber, exposer.

exhibition exposition f.
exile proscrit m., exilé m.
exile (to) exiler.
exist exister.
existence existence f.
exit sortie f.
expand amplifier, étendre.
expansion expansion f.
expansive expansif.
expect attendre.
expectation attente f., espérance f.
expedition expédition f.
expel expulser.
expense frais m., dépense f.
expensive coûteux.
experience expérience f.
experience (to) éprouver.
experiment expérience f.
expert expert m.
   to be expert at se connaître en.
expire expirer.
explain expliquer.
explanation explication f.
explanatory explicatif.
explode faire explosion, éclater.
exploit exploit m.
exploit (to) exploiter.
explore explorer.
explosion explosion f.
export exportation f.
export (to) exporter.
expose exposer.
exposed à vif (*nerve*).
exposure pose f. (*photography*).
exposure meter pose-mètre m.
express express (train) noun m. and adj.,
   exprès.
   by express par exprès.
express (to) exprimer.
expression expression f.
expressive expressif.
expulsion expulsion f.
exquisite exquis.
extend étendre.
extensive vaste.
extent étendue f.
   to some extent jusqu'à un certain point.
exterior noun m. and adj. extérieur.
exterminate exterminer.
external extérieur, externe.
extinct éteint.
extinction extinction f.
extinguish éteindre.
extra en plus, supplémentaire.
extract extrait m.
extract (to) extraire.
extraordinary extraordinaire.
extravagance extravagance f.
extravagant extravagant.

extreme noun m. and adj. extrême.
extremely extrêmement.
extremity extrémité f.
eye oeil (pl. yeux) m.
eyebrow sourcil m.
eyeglasses lunettes f. pl.
eyelid paupière f.

F

fable fable f.
fabric étoffe f., tissu m.
face figure f., face, f.
face (to) faire face à.
facilitate faciliter.
facility facilité f., aisance f.
facsimile, fax FAX m.; télécopie f.
   fax machine transmetteur-récepteur de facsimilé *or* de FAX; télécopieur m.
   to fax envoyer par FAX *or* par télécopie.
fact fait m.
   in fact en effet.
factory fabrique f.
faculty faculté f.
fade se faner.
fail faute
   without fail sans faute.
fail (to) manquer (à), faillir.
faint évanouissement m.
faint (to) s'évanouir.
fair droit, juste.
faith foi f.
faithful fidèle adj.
fall chute f.; automne m.
fall (to) tomber.
false faux.
fame réputation f., renommée f.
familiar familier.
family famille f.
famine famine f.
famous fameux, célèbre.
fan éventail m.
   electric fan ventilateur.
   sports fan supporter m., fanatique m.
fanatic adj. fanatique.
fanatic fanatique m.
fancy fantaisie f.; caprice m.
fantastic fantastique.
far loin.
farce farce f.
fare prix de la place m., prix du voyage m., tarif m.
farm ferme f.
farmer fermier m.
farming agriculture f.
farther plus éloigné; plus loin.
farthest le plus éloigné.

fashion mode f.; manière f.
fashionable à la mode, chic.
fast vite, solide.
fasten attacher.
fat adj. gros, gras.
fat graisse f.
fatal fatal.
fate destinée f.
father père m.
father-in-law beau-père m.
faucet robinet m.
fault faute f., défaut m., tort m.
favor service m., faveur f.
   Could (will) you do me a favor? Voulez-vous me rendre un service?
favor (to) favoriser.
favorable favorable.
favorite adj. favori, préféré.
fax *see facsimile.*
fear crainte f., peur f.
fear (to) craindre.
fearless intrépide.
feather plume f.
feature trait m., caractéristique f.
February février m.
federal fédéral.
fee honoraires m. pl., droit m.
feeble faible.
feed nourrir.
feel (to) éprouver, sentir; tâter (*touch*).
feel like (to) avoir envie de.
   I feel like laughing. J'ai envie de rire.
feeling sensibilité f.; sensation f.; sentiment m.
fellow bonhomme m., gars m.
fellowship camaraderie f.; bourse f. (*school*).
fellow worker collègue m. and f., confrère m.
female femelle f.
feminine féminin noun m. and adj.
fence clôture f., barrière f.
fencing escrime f.
ferocious féroce.
ferry bac m.
fertile fertile.
fertilize féconder, fertiliser.
fertilizer engrais m.
fervent ardent.
fervor ferveur f., ardeur f.
festival fête f.
fetch allez chercher, apporter.
fetus foetus m.
fever fièvre f.
few peu.
fiber fibre f.
fiction romans m. pl.
fidelity fidélité f.
   high fidelity haute fidélité.
field champ m.
fierce cruel, violent.
fiery ardent.

fifteen quinze.
  about fifteen une quinzaine.
  two weeks quinze jours.
fifteenth quinzième.
fifth cinquième.
fiftieth cinquantième.
fifty cinquante.
fig figue f.
fight lutte f.; mêlée f.
fight (to) combattre.
figure forme f. (*form*); chiffre m. (*number*).
file lime f. (*tool*); dossier m. (*papers*); archive f. (*computer*).
fill remplir; plomber (*tooth*).
film pellicule f.; film m.; inversibles m. pl. (*for transparencies*).
  color film film en couleurs m.
filthy sale.
final décisif, définitif, final.
finance finance f.
financial financier.
find (to) trouver.
  find oneself se retrouver.
fine adj. beau; fin (*not coarse*).
  Fine! Très bien!
fine amende f.
finger doigt m.
fingernail ongle m.
finish (to) finir; terminer, compléter.
fire feu m.; incendie m.
fireplace cheminée f.; foyer m.
firm adj. ferme; constant (*character*).
firm maison f. (*business*).
first adj. premier.
  for the first time pour la première fois.
first adv. d'abord, tout d'abord.
  at first d'abord, tout d'abord.
fish poisson m.
fish (to) pêcher.
fisherman pêcheur m.
fist poing m.
fit convenable, propre à.
fit (to) convenir, adapter.
fitness à-propos m., aptitude f.
fitting essayage m.
  fitting room salon d'essayage.
five cinq.
fix fixer.
flag drapeau m.
flame flamme f.
flank flanc m.
flank (to) flanquer.
flash of lightning éclair m.
flashbulb lampe-éclair f.
flashcube flashcube m.
flat plat; fade (*taste*).
flat tire pneu crevé m., crevaison f.
flatter flatter.
flattery flatterie f.

flavor goût m., saveur f.; bouquet m.
flea puce f.
Flea Market Marché aux Puces m.
fleet flotte f.
flesh chair f.
flexibility souplesse f.
flexible souple, flexible.
flight vol m. (*in air*), fuite f. (*rout*).
fling (to) jeter.
flint caillou m., pierre à briquet f.
float flotter.
flood inondation f.
flood (to) inonder.
floor plancher m.; étage m. (*story*).
flourish prospérer.
flow affluence f.
flow (to) couler.
flowchart schéma fonctionnel m.
flower fleur f.
fluid fluide.
flute flûte f.
  play the flute jouer de la flûte.
fly mouche f.
fly (to) voler.
foam écume f.
foam (to) écumer.
fog brouillard m.
fold pli m.
fold (to) plier.
foliage feuillage m.
follow suivre.
  follow one another se suivre.
following suivant.
fond (be) aimer.
fondness tendresse f.
food nourriture. f.
fool imbécile noun and adj.
foolish sot.
foot pied m.
football football m.
footstep pas m.
for pour.
  for example par exemple.
  for the first time pour la première fois.
  for the most part pour la plupart.
  for the present pour le moment.
forbid défendre.
force force f.
force (to) obliger.
ford gué m.
foreground premier plan m.
forehead front m.
foreign étranger.
foreigner étranger m.
foresee prévoir.
forest forêt f.
forget oublier.
forgetfulness oubli m.
forgive pardonner.

forgiveness pardon m.
fork fourchette f.
form forme f.; fiche f.; formulaire m. (*printed*).
form (to) former.
formal formel, cérémonieux.
formality formalité f.
format format m.
formation formation f.
former ancien; précédent.
formerly autrefois.
formula formule f.
forsake renoncer à.
fort fort m.
fortunate heureux.
fortunately heureusement.
fortune fortune f.
fortieth quarantième.
forty quarante.
forward en avant.
forward (to) faire suivre.
forwarding agent transitaire m.
foster nourrir.
foul sale, impur.
found trouvé.
found (to) fonder.
foundation fondation f.
founder fondateur m.
fountain fontaine f.
four quatre.
fourteen quatorze.
fourteenth quatorzième.
fourth quatrième.
fowl volaille f. (*poultry*).
fox renard m.
foyer foyer m.
fragment fragment m.
fragrance parfum m.
fragrant parfumé.
frail fragile.
frame cadre m.
frame (to) encadrer.
frank franc.
frankness franchise f.
free libre, gratuit.
free (to) libérer; débarrasser.
freedom liberté f.
freeze glacer, geler.
freight chargement m.
French français noun and adj.
French fried potato frite f.
French Riviera Côte d'Azur f.
frequent fréquent.
frequent (to) fréquenter.
frequently fréquemment.
fresh frais.
friction friction f.
Friday vendredi m.
friend ami m.

friendly amical.
friendship amitié f.
frieze frise f.
frighten effrayer.
frightening effrayant.
fringe frange f.
frivolity frivolité f.
frivolous frivole.
frog grenouille f.
from de; dès, depuis.
front devant, de devant.
frontier frontière f.
fruit fruit m.
fry (to) frire.
frying pan poêle à frire f.
fuel combustible m.
  fossil fuels combustibles fossiles m. pl.
fugitive fugitif noun and adj.
fulfill accomplir.
full plein.
fully abondamment.
fun amusement m.
  have fun s'amuser.
function fonction f.
function (to) fonctionner.
fund fonds m. pl.
fundamental fondamental noun and adj.
funds fonds m. pl.
funny amusant, drôle.
fur fourrure f.
furious furieux.
furnace four m.
furnish garnir, meubler (*a room*).
furniture meubles m. pl., mobilier m.
furrow sillon m.
further ultérieur, plus lointain, supplémentaire.
fury rage f.
future adj. futur.
future avenir m.
  in the future à l'avenir.

G

gadget truc m.
gaiety gaieté f.
gain gain m.
gain (to) gagner.
gallant brave.
gallery galerie f.
gallop galop m.
gamble (to) jouer.
game jeu m., partie f.
garage garage m.
garden jardin m.
gardener jardinier m.

garlic ail m.
garment vêtement m.
gas gaz m.
gasoline essence f. (*for car*).
gate porte f.; barrière f.; portillon m.
    automatic gate portillon automatique
      (*subway*).
gather réunir, cueillir.
gay gai.
gem pierre précieuse f.
gender genre m.
general adj. général.
    in general en général.
general général m.
general delivery poste restante f.
generality généralité f.
generalize généraliser.
generation génération f.
generosity générosité f.
generous généreux.
genius génie m.
gentle doux.
gentleman monsieur m.
    Gentlemen. Messieurs.
    Ladies and gentlemen. Mesdames et
      messieurs.
gentleness douceur f.
gently doucement.
genuine authentique.
geographical géographique.
geography géographie f.
germ germe m.
German allemand noun and adj.
gesture geste m.
get obtenir, recevoir.
    get along se débrouiller.
    get off descendre.
ghastly horrible.
giant colosse m., géant m.
gift don m., cadeau m.
gifted doué.
gilded doré.
girl fille f.
give donner.
    give back rendre, remettre.
    give up abandonner.
glad heureux, content.
gladly volontiers.
glance coup d'oeil m.
glance (to) entrevoir.
glass verre m.
    looking glass glace f., miroir m. (*small*).
    drinking glass verre m.
gleam lueur f.
gleam (to) luire.
glitter éclat m.; scintillation f.
glitter (to) briller, étinceler.
global global.
globe globe m.

gloomy lugubre.
glorious glorieux.
glory gloire f.
glove gant m.
glow chaleur f. (*heat*), lumière f. (*light*).
go (to) aller.
    go away partir, s'en aller.
    go back retourner, rentre, reculer.
    go by again repasser.
    go down descendre.
    go forward avancer.
    go out sortir.
    go to bed se coucher.
    go to meet aller à la rencontre.
    go to sleep s'endormir.
    go up monter.
    go with accompagner.
    take oneself se rendre.
goal-keeper gardien de but m.
goalie gardien de but m.
God Dieu m.
gold or m.
golden d'or, en or.
goldsmith's work orfèvrerie f.
golf golf m.
good bon, bien.
    Good afternoon! Bonjour!
    Good evening! Bonsoir!
    Good morning! Bonjour!
    Good night! Bonsoir! Bonne nuit!
good-bye au revoir, adieu.
goodness bonté f.
goods marchandises f. pl.
goodwill bonne volonté f.
goose oie f.
gorgeous ravissant.
gossip commérage m.; bavard m. (*person*);
    potins m. pl.
gossip (to) potiner, bavarder.
gouache gouache f.
govern gouverner.
grace grâce f.
graceful gracieux.
grade grade m.
grain grain m.
grammar grammaire f.
grand grandiose, majestueux.
    Grand! Magnifique! Epatant!
grandchild petit-fils m.
granddaughter petit-fille f.
grandeur grandeur f.
grandfather grand-père m.
grandmother grand-mère f.
grandson petit-fils m.
grant concession f.
grant (to) accorder.
    Granted! D'accord!
grape raisin m.
grapefruit pamplemousse m.

grasp (to) saisir, comprendre (*understand*).
grass herbe f.
grasshopper sauterelle f.
grateful reconnaissant.
gratis gratuit.
gratitude reconnaissance f.
grave adj. grave, sérieux.
grave tombe f.
gravel gravier m.
gray gris.
grease graisse f.
greasing graissage m.
great grand (*of a person*); énorme (*size*).
greatness grandeur f.
greedy avide, gourmand.
Greek grec.
green vert.
greet saluer, accueillir.
greeting salutation f., accueil m.
grief peine f.
grieve affliger, attrister.
grin (to) ricaner.
grind moudre.
groan gémissement m.
groan (to) gémir.
grocer épicier m.
grocery store épicerie f.
grope tâtonner.
gross grossier, brut.
ground terre f.
group groupe m.
group (to) grouper.
grouping groupement m.
grow croître, grandir; pousser (*vegetation*).
growth croissance f.
grudge rancune f.
   hold a grudge against en vouloir à.
gruff rude, brusque.
guard garde m.
guard (to) garder.
guardian tuteur m., gardien m.
guess conjecture f.
guess (to) deviner, conjecturer.
   guess right deviner juste.
guide guide m.
guide (to) guider, piloter.
guidebook guide m.
guilt faute f.
gum gencive f. (*of the teeth*).
gun fusil m.
gush jet m.

H

habit habitude f.
   to be in the habit of avoir l'habitude de.
habitual habituel.

hail grêle f.
hair cheveu m., cheveux m. pl.
hair (to do someone's) coiffer.
hair clippers tondeuse f.
hairdo coiffure f.
hairdresser coiffeur m.
hair dryer sèche-cheveux m.
half demi, moitié.
   half a dozen demi-douzaine f.
   half-liter of light beer demi de blonde m.
half-hour demi-heure f.
half-time mi-temps f. (*sports*).
hall salle f.
ham jambon m.
hammer marteau m.
hand main f.
hand (to) passer, remettre.
handbag sac à main m.
handful poignée f.
handkerchief mouchoir m.
handle anse f., poignée f.
handle (to) manier, manoeuvrer.
handsome beau, belle.
handy adroit (*person*), commode (*easy to handle*).
hang pendre, suspendre.
   hang up raccrocher (*telephone receiver*).
happen arriver, se passer.
happening événement m.
happiness bonheur m.
happy heureux, content.
harbor port m., asile m. (*refuge*).
hard difficile (*difficult*); dur (*not soft*).
hard drive lecteur de disques m.
harden endurcir.
hardly guère, à peine.
hardness dureté f.
hardship privation f., épreuve f.
hardware quincaillerie f.; matériel, hardware (*computer*) m.
hardware store quincaillerie f.
hardy robuste, vigoureux.
hare lièvre m.
harm mal m.
harm (to) nuire, faire tort à.
harmful nuisible.
harmless inoffensif.
harmonious harmonieux.
harmony harmonie f.
harsh âpre.
harvest récolte f., moisson f.
haste hâte f.
hasten se hâter, se dépêcher.
hat chapeau m.
hate haine f.
hate (to) détester, haïr.
hateful odieux.
hatred haine f.
haughty hautain.

have avoir.
have to devoir.
haven asile m., refuge m.
hay foin m.
he il.
head tête f. (*part of the body*); chef m. (*chief*); chevet m. (*of bed*).
head for se diriger vers.
headache mal de tête m.
heading rubrique f. (*newspaper, magazine*).
headphones casque à écouteurs m.
heal guérir; se guérir; se cicatriser (*wound*).
health santé f.
healthy sain.
heap tas m.; pile f.
heap up entasser.
hear entendre.
   hear about entendre parler de.
   hear that entendre dire que.
hearing ouïe f.
heart coeur m.
heat chaleur f.
heaven ciel m.
   Heavens! Mon Dieu! Ciel!
heavy lourd.
hedge haie f.
heed (to) faire attention à.
heel talon m.
height hauteur f.; comble m.
heir héritier m.
hello allô.
helm gouvernail m.
help aide f., secours m.
help (to) aider.
helper aide noun and adj.
helpful utile.
hem ourlet m.
hen poule f.
henceforth désormais.
her la, lui, son, sa, ses.
herb herbe f.
herd troupeau m.
here ici.
   Here! Tenez! Tiens!
herewith ci-joint.
hero héros m.
heroic héroïque.
heroine héroïne f.
herring hareng m.
herself elle-même.
hesitate hésiter.
hide (to) cacher, dissimuler.
hideous hideux.
high haut.
higher supérieur.
hill colline f.
him le, lui.
himself lui-même.
hind de derrière.

hinder empêcher, gêner.
hinge gond m.
hint allusion f.
hint (to) faire allusion à, insinuer.
hip hanche f.
hire (to) louer, engager.
   for hire à louer.
hiring location f.
his son, sa, ses, à lui, le sien, la sienne, les siens, les siennes.
hiss sifflet m.
hiss (to) siffler.
historian historien m.
historic historique.
history histoire f.
hoarse rauque.
hoe houe f.
hold prise f.
hold (to) tenir.
hole trou m.
holiday jour de fête m.; congé m.; jour férié m., jour de vacances m.
holiness sainteté f.
hollow creux.
holy saint.
homage hommage m.
home maison f.
   home town ville natale f.
homework devoirs m. pl.
homosexual homosexuel (le).
homosexuality homosexualité f.
honest honnête.
honesty honnêteté f.
honey miel m.
honeymoon lune de miel f.
honor honneur m.
honor (to) honorer.
honorable honorable.
hood capuchon m.
hoof sabot m.
hook crochet m.
hope espoir m.
hope (to) espérer.
hopeful plein d'espoir.
hopeless sans espoir, désespéré.
horizon horizon m.
horizontal horizontal.
horn trompe f.; corne f.
horrible horrible.
horror horreur f.
horse cheval m.
horseback (on) à cheval.
hosiery bonneterie f.
hospitable hospitalier.
hospital hôpital m.
host hôte m.
hostess hôtesse f.
hostile hostile.
hot chaud.

hotel hôtel m.
hour heure f.
house maison f.
household ménage m.
housekeeper ménagère f.
how comment.
    How are you? Comment allez-vous?
    How beautiful! Que c'est beau!
    how long combien de temps.
    how many combien de.
    how much combien de.
    how often combien de fois.
however cependant.
howl hurlement m.
howl (to) hurler.
human humain.
humane humain.
humanity humanité f.
humble humble.
humid humide.
humiliate humilier.
humility humilité f.
humming bourdonnement m.
humor humeur f.
hundred cent.
hundredth centième.
hunger faim f.
hungry (be) avoir faim.
hunt chasse f.
hunt (to) chasser.
hunter chasseur m.
hurry hâte f.
    be in a hurry être pressé.
hurry (to) se hâter, se presser, se dépêcher.
hurt (to) faire mal.
husband mari m.
hush (to) calmer, étouffer (*a scandal*).
hyphen trait d'union m.
hypocrisy hypocrisie f.
hypocrite hypocrite m. and f.
hypothesis hypothèse f.

I

I je.
ice glace f.
icy glacial.
idea idée f.
ideal idéal noun m. and adj.
idealism idéalisme m.
idealist idéaliste m. and f.
identical identique.
identification papers pièces d'identité f.
idiot noun m. and adj. imbécile.
idle oisif.
idleness oisiveté f.
if si.

ignition allumage m.
ignoble ignoble.
ignorance ignorance f.
ignorant ignorant.
ignore refuser de connaître, ne tenir aucun compte de.
ill mal; malade.
illness maladie f.
illusion illusion f.
illustrate illustrer.
illustration illustration f.
image image f.
imaginary imaginaire.
imagination imagination f.
imagine s'imaginer, se figurer.
imitate imiter.
imitation imitation f.
immediate immédiat.
immediately tout de suite, aussitôt, immédiatement.
immigration immigration f.
imminent imminent.
immobility immobilité f.
immoral immoral.
immorality immoralité f.
immortal immortel.
immortality immortalité f.
impartial impartiel.
impatience impatience f.
impatient impatient.
imperfect défecteux.
impertinence impertinence f.
impertinent impertinent.
impetuosity impétuosité f.
impetuous impétueux.
impious impie.
import importation f.
import (to) importer.
importance importance f.
important important.
imposing imposant.
impossible impossible.
impress (to) impressionner.
impression impression f., empreinte f.
    be under the impression that avoir l'impression que.
impressionist impressioniste.
impressive impressionnant.
imprison emprisonner.
improve améliorer.
improvement amélioration f., mieux m., progrès m.
improvise improviser.
imprudence imprudence f.
imprudent imprudent.
impulse impulsion f., inspiration f.
impulsive impulsif.
impure impur.
in dans, en.

inadequate insuffisant.
inaugurate inaugurer.
incapable incapable.
incapacity incapacité f.
inch pouce m.
incident incident m.
include renfermer.
included compris.
including y compris.
income rente f., revenu m.
incomparable incomparable.
incompatible incompatible.
incompetent incompétent.
incomplete incomplet.
incomprehensible incompréhensible.
inconvenience inconvénient m.; dérangement m.
inconvenient inconvénient, pas pratique.
incorrect inexact.
increase augmentation f.
increase (to) augmenter.
incredible incroyable.
incur encourir, contracter.
indebted endetté.
indecision indécision f.
indecisive indécis.
indeed en effet, vraiment.
independence indépendance f.
independent indépendant.
index index m.
index finger index m.
indicate indiquer.
indicated inscrit.
indicative indicatif m.
indifference indifférence f.
indifferent indifférent.
indignant indigne.
indignation indignation f.
indirect indirect.
indirectly indirectement.
indiscretion indiscrétion f.
indispensable indispensable.
individual individu m.; individuel adj.
individualist(ic) individualiste.
indivisible indivisible.
indolence indolence f.
indolent indolent.
indoors à la maison.
   go indoors rentrer.
induce persuader, occasionner.
induct installer; initier.
indulge avoir de l'indulgence; s'adonner.
indulgence indulgence f.
indulgent indulgent, complaisant.
industrial industriel.
industrious appliqué, laborieux.
industry industrie f.; application f.
inexhaustible inépuisable.
inexplicable inexplicable.

inexpressible inexprimable.
infallible infaillible.
infamous infâme.
infancy enfance f.
infant petit enfant m.
infantry infanterie f.
infection infection f.
infer conclure.
inference déduction f.
inferior inférieur.
infernal infernal.
infinite infini.
infinity infinité f.
inflate gonfler.
inflict infliger.
influence influence f.
influence (to) influencer.
inform informer, prévenir, faire savoir.
information information f.; renseignements m. pl.
ingenious ingénieux.
ingenuity ingéniosité f.
ingratitude ingratitude f.
inhabit habiter.
inhabitant habitant m.
inherit hériter.
inheritance héritage m.
inhuman inhumain.
initial adj. initial.
initial initiale f.
initiate commencer, initier.
initiation initiation f.
initiative initiative f.
injection piqûre f.
injurious nuisible.
injury blessure f.
injustice injustice f.
ink encre f.
inkwell encrier m.
inland intérieur m.
inn auberge f.
innate inné.
innkeeper aubergiste m.
innocence innocence f.
innocent innocent.
inquire demander, se renseigner.
inquiry recherche f.; enquête f.
inscribed inscrit.
inscription inscription f.
insect insecte m.
insensible insensible.
inseparable inséparable.
inside dedans.
inside intérieur m.
insight pénétration f.
insignificant insignifiant.
insincere peu sincère.
insinuate insinuer.
insist insister.

instantly instamment.
insistence insistance f.
insoluble insoluble.
inspect inspecter.
inspection inspection f.
inspiration inspiration f.
install installer.
installment acompte m., versement m.
instance exemple m.
instant instant m.
instantaneous instantané.
instantly à l'instant.
instead of au lieu de.
instigate provoquer, inciter à.
instinct instinct m.
instinctive instinctif.
institute institut m.
institute (to) instituer.
institution institution f.
instruct instruire.
instruction instruction f.
instructions indications f. pl.
instructor instituteur m., institutrice f.,
    instructeur m.
instrument instrument m.
insufficiency insuffisance f.
insufficient insuffisant.
insult insulte f.
insult (to) insulter, injurier.
insuperable insurmontable.
insurance assurance f.
insure assurer.
integral intégral.
intellect intelligence f.
intellectual intellectuel m.
intelligence intelligence f.
intelligent intelligent.
intelligently intelligement.
intend se proposer de.
intense intense.
intensity intensité f.
intention intention f.
interest intérêt m.
    take an interest in s'intéresser à.
interest (to) intéresser.
interesting intéressant.
interfere intervenir, gêner.
interference intervention f.
interior noun m. and adj. intérieur.
intermediate intermédiaire.
intermission entr'acte m.
international international.
interpose interposer.
interpret interpréter.
interpretation interprétation f.
interpreter interprète m.
interrupt interrompre.
interruption interruption f.
intersection carrefour m.

interurban interurbain (*telephone*).
interval intervalle m.
interview entrevue f., interview f.
interview (to) avoir une entrevue,
    interviewer.
intimacy intimité f.
intimate intime.
intimidate intimider.
into dans, en.
intolerable intolérable.
intolerance intolérance f.
intolerant intolérant.
intonation intonation f.
intrigue intrigue f.
introduce présenter, amener.
introduction introduction f. (*book*);
    initiation f.
intuition intuition f.
invade envahir.
invariable invariable.
invasion invasion f.
invent inventer.
invention invention f.
inventor inventeur m.
invert renverser, intervertir.
invest placer (de l'argent), investir.
investment placement m.
invisible invisible.
invitation invitation f.
invite inviter.
invoice facture f.
invoke invoquer.
involuntary involontaire.
involve impliquer.
iron fer m.
iron (to) repasser.
    have (something) ironed faire repasser.
irony ironie f.
irregular irrégulier.
irreparable irréparable.
irresistible irrésistible.
irritate irriter.
irritation irritation f.
Islamic islamique.
island île f.
isolate isoler.
issue sortie f., résultat m., issue f.
issue (to) émettre, distribuer; sortir, jaillir.
it il.
Italian Italien noun, italien adj.
item détail m.
itinerary intinéraire m.
its son.
it's c'est, il est.
    It's here. C'est ici.
    It's late. Il est tard.
itself lui-même, elle-même, se, même.
ivory ivoire f.
ivy lierre m.

J

jacket veste f.; veston m.
　　business suit complet-veston.
　　two-button jacket veston à deux boutons.
　　woman's jacket jaquette f.
jam confiture f.
jammed enrayé (*mechanism*).
January janvier m.
Japanese japonais.
jar bocal m.
jaw mâchoire f.
jealous jaloux.
jealousy jalousie f.
jelly confiture f., geléc f.
jewel bijou m.
Jewish juif.
job tâche f., travail m., emploi m.
join allier, attacher; rejoindre.
joint joint m., jointure f., articulation f.
joke plaisanterie f.
joke (to) plaisanter, blaguer.
jolly joyeux, gai.
journal journal m.
journalism journalisme m.
journalist journaliste m.
journey voyage m.
joy joie f.
joyous joyeux.
judge juge m.
judge (to) juger.
judgment jugement m.
judicial (*court*) judiciaire.
juice jus m.
July juillet m.
jump saut m.
jump (to) sauter.
June juin m.
junior cadet; plus jeune.
just juste adj.
just (to have) venir de.
　　We have just arrived. Nous venons
　　　　d'arriver.
justice justice f.
justify justifier.

K

keen piquant, aigu.
keep garder.
　　keep back retenir.
　　keep from empêcher (*prevent*); s'abstenir
　　　　(*refrain*).
　　keep in mind tenir compte de quelque
　　　　chose, se souvenir de quelque chose.
　　keep quiet se taire.

　　Keep still! Restez tranquille!
keeper gardien m.
kernel noyau m.
kettle bouilloire f.
key clef, clé f.
keyboard clavier m.
kick coup de pied m.
kick (to) donner un coup de pied.
kid chevreau m. (*goat*); gosse m. or f. (*child*).
　　kidskin la peau de chevreau.
kill tuer.
kilometer kilomètre m.
kin parents m. pl.
kind adj. bon, bienveillant, aimable, gentil.
kind sorte f., genre m.
kindergarten jardin d'enfants m.
kindly aimable.
　　Will you kindly . . . Voulez-vous avoir la
　　　　bonté de . . . Seriez-vous assez aimable
　　　　pour . . .
kindness bonté f., amabilité m.
king roi m.
kingdom royaume m.
kiss baiser m.
kiss (to) embrasser.
kitchen cuisine f.
kite cerf-volant m.
knee genou m.
kneel s'agenouiller.
knickknack bibelot m.
knife couteau m.
knight chevalier m.
knit tricoter.
knock coup m.
knock (to) frapper.
knocking cognement m.
knot noeud m.
know savoir (*have knowledge of*); connaître
　　　　(*be acquainted with*).
　　be expert in se connaître en.
knowledge connaissance f.
known connu.

L

label étiquette f.
labor travail m.
laboratory laboratoire m.
lace dentelle f.
lack manque m.
lack (to) manquer.
lady dame f., madame f.
Ladies. Dames.
Ladies and gentlemen. Mesdames et
　　　　messieurs.
lake lac m.
lamb agneau m.

lame boiteux.
lamp lampe f.
land terre f.
land (to) débarquer (*ship*); atterrir (*airplane*).
landing débarquement m.
landscape paysage m.
language langage m.
languish languir.
languor langueur f.
lantern lanterne f.
lap étape f. (*of race*).
laptop portatif m.
large gros, grand.
laser laser m.
last dernier.
   last night hier soir.
last (to) durer.
lasting durable.
latch loquet m.
late tard, tardif.
lately dernièrement.
lateral latéral.
Latin latin.
latter celui-ci, celle-ci, ceux-ci, celles-ci.
laugh (to) rire.
laughter rire m.
laundering blanchissage m.
laundress blanchisseuse f.
laundry blanchisserie f.
lavish (to) prodiguer.
law loi f.
lawful légal.
lawn pelouse f.
lay (to) poser, déposer; pondre (*hen*).
layer couche f.
lazy paresseux.
lead plomb m. (*metal*).
lead (to) conduire, emmener, mener.
leader chef m.
leadership direction f., conduite f.
leaf feuille f. (*tree*).
leak fuite f.
lean (to) appuyer.
leap saut m.
leap (to) sauter.
learn apprendre.
learned adj. savant.
learning érudition f.
least (le) moins, moindre m.
   at least au moins.
leather cuir m.
leave permission f.; congé m.
leave (to) abandonner (*desert*); laisser (*quit*); léguer (*bequeath*).
lecture conférence f., semonce f. (*reprimand*).
   lecture tour visite-conférence f.
left gauche noun m. and f. and adj.
   to the left à gauche.
leg jambe f.

legal légal.
legend légende f.
legislation législation f.
legislator législateur m.
legislature législature f.
legitimate légitime.
leisure loisir m.
lemon citron m.; rossignol m. (*colloq.*).
   buy a lemon acheter un rossignol.
lemon drink limonade f. (*carbonated*).
lemonade citron pressé m.
lend prêter.
length longueur f., durée f.
lengthen allonger.
lens objectif m. (*camera*).
lesbian lesbienne f.
less moins.
lesson leçon f.
let laisser, permettre (*permit*); louer (*rent*).
   for let à louer.
   to let alone laisser tranquille.
letter lettre f.
   express letter pneu(matique) m. (*Paris*).
level niveau m.
liable responsable, susceptible.
liar menteur m.
liberal libéral.
liberty liberté f.
library bibliothèque f.
license licence f., permission f., permis m.
   driver's license or permit permis de conduire.
lick (to) lécher.
lie mensonge m. (*falsehood*).
lie (to) coucher, être couché; mentir (*tell a falsehood*).
   lie down se coucher.
lieutenant lieutenant m.
life vie f.
life jacket gilet de sauvetage m.
lift (to) lever, soulever; décrocher (*telephone receiver*).
light adj. clair; blond.
light lumière f.
light (to) allumer.
light (up) éclairer.
light meter pose-mètre m.
lighten alléger; éclaircir (*color*).
lighthouse phare m.
lighting éclairage m.
lightning éclair m.
likable sympathique.
like pareil; semblable à, comme.
like (to) aimer; vouloir.
   Would you like to go? Voudriez-vous venir?
likely probable.
liking gré m.
likeness ressemblance f.

likewise pareillement.
liking penchant m.; goût m.
limb membre m.
limit limite f.
limit (to) confiner, borner.
Limoges porcelain Limoges m.
limp (to) boiter.
line ligne f.; queue f.
line up (to) aligner; doubler.
 stand in line faire la queue.
linen toile f., linge m., lin m.
linger s'attarder.
lining doublure f.
link chaînon m. (*chain*).
link (to) lier.
lion lion m.
lip lèvre f.
liquid liquide noun m. and adj.
liquor liqueur f.
list liste f.
listen écouter.
liter litre m.
literary littéraire.
literature littérature f.
little petit; peu de.
live vivant.
live (to) vivre.
lively vivant, gai, animé, vif.
liver foie m.
load charge f. (*cargo*); fardeau m.
load (to) charger.
loan emprunt m., prêt m.
loan (to) prêter.
local local.
locate situer.
location endroit m., site m.
lock serrure f.
lock (to) fermer à clef.
locomotive locomotive f.
log bûche f.
logic logique f.
logical logique.
loneliness solitude f.
lonely solitaire.
long long, longtemps.
 a long time longtemps.
 before long sous peu.
 long ago autrefois, jadis.
long-distance interurbain (*telephone*).
 a long-distance call un appel interurbain.
longing grande envie f.
look regard m., air m., aspect m.
look (to) regarder.
 Look! Tiens!
 Look out! Attention! Prenez garde!
loose lâche.
loosen desserrer.
lord maître m., seigneur m.
lose perdre.

lose one's way s'égarer.
loss perte f.
lost perdu.
lot (a) beaucoup.
 a lot of money beaucoup d'argent.
 a lot of people beaucoup de monde.
lotion lotion f.
 hair lotion lotion pour les cheveux.
loud fort, bruyant.
 Speak louder. Parlez plus fort (haut).
loudspeaker haut-parleur, m.
love amour m.
love (to) aimer.
lovely charmant, délicieux, ravissant.
low bas.
lower (to) baisser, abaisser.
low-necked décolleté.
loyal loyal.
loyalty loyauté f., fidelité f.
lubrication graissage m.
luck chance f.
lucky heureux, qui porte bonheur.
luggage bagages m. pl.
 luggage rack porte-bagage (*car*).
luminous lumineux.
lump morceau m., bloc m., tas m.
lung poumon m.
luxe abondance f.
 de luxe de luxe.
luxurious luxueux.
luxury luxe m.

M

machine machine f.
machine laundry laverie f.
mad fou.
madam madame f.
made fait.
madness folie f.
magazine magazine m., revue périodique f., album m.
magistrate magistrat m.
magnetic magnétique.
magnificent magnifique, formidable.
maid bonne f. (*servant*).
mail courrier m.
 e-mail courrier électronique m.
main principal.
main road grande route f.
main street grand-rue f.
maintain maintenir, soutenir.
maintenance entretien m., maintien m.
majesty majesté f.
majority majorité f.
make (to) faire.
male mâle.

malice méchanceté f.
man homme m.
  men messieurs.
manage gérer, mener, venir à bout de, se
    débrouiller.
management gérance f.
manager gérant m.; directeur m.
manicure manucure m.
mankind humanité f.
manner manière f.
mannered recherché (*painting*).
manners politesse f.; manières f. pl.
manufacture fabrication f., manufacture f.
manufacture (to) fabriquer.
manufacturer industriel m., fabriquant m.
manuscript manuscrit m.
many beaucoup.
map carte f., plan m.
March mars m.
march marche f.
march (to) marcher.
margin marge f.
marine marine f.
mark marque f.
mark (to) marquer.
market marché m.
marketing marketing m.
marriage mariage m.
marry épouser.
marvel merveille f.
marvelous merveilleux.
masculine mâle; masculin.
mask masque m.
mask (to) masquer.
mason maçon m.
mass masse f. (*quantity*); messe f. (*church*).
mast mât m.
master maître m.
master (to) dominer.
masterpiece chef d'oeuvre m., oeuvre
    maîtresse f.
match allumette f.; match m. (*sports*), parti m.
    (*marriage*).
match (to) assortir.
material matière f., étoffe f.
maternal maternel.
mathematics mathématiques f. pl.
matter affaire f., chose f., matière f.,
    propos, m.
matter (to) importer.
mattress matelas m.
mature mûr.
maximum maximum m.
May mai m.
may pouvoir (*to be able*).
mayor maire m.
me me, moi.
meadow prairie f.
meal repas m.

mean moyenne f.
mean (to) vouloir dire.
meaning sens m.
means moyen m., moyens m. pl.
    (*resources*).
meanwhile (in the) en attendant, sur ces
    entrefaites.
measure mesure f.; comble m. (*heaped*).
measure (to) mesurer.
meat viande f.
mechanic mécanicien m.
mechanical mécanique.
mechanically mécaniquement;
    machinalement.
medal médaille f.
meddle se mêler de.
mediate intervenir.
medical médical.
medicine (*science*) médécine f.
mediocre médiocre.
mediocrity médiocrité f.
mediate méditer.
meditation méditation f.
medium adj. moyen.
medium intermédiaire m.; milieu m.
meet (to) rencontrer.
  meet again retrouver.
meeting rencontre f.; réunion f.; meeting m.
    (*political*).
melt fondre.
member membre m.
memorize apprendre par coeur.
memory mémoire f.; souvenir m.
menace (to) menacer.
mend (to) raccommoder, réparer, arranger.
mental mental.
mention mention f.
mention (to) mentionner.
menu carte f. (*food*), archive f. (*computer*).
merchandise marchandise f.
merchant marchand m., négociant m.
merciful clément.
merciless impitoyable.
mercury mercure m.
mercy pitié f., miséricorde f.
merit mérite m.
merry joyeux, gai.
message message m.
messenger messager m.
metal métal m.
metallic métallique.
meter mètre m.
  taxi meter compteur m.
method méthode f.
metropolis métropole f.
microgroove microsillon m.
microphone microphone m.
microwave micro-onde m.
middle adj. moyen.

middle milieu m., moyen m.
  in the middle of au milieu de.
  Middle Ages Moyen Age m.
midnight minuit m.
might force f., puissance f.
mighty fort, puissant.
mild doux.
mildness douceur f.
military militaire.
milk lait m.
milkman laitier m.
mill moulin m.
miller meunier m.
million million m.
millionaire millionnaire noun m. and adj.
mind esprit m.
mind (to) faire attention à, s'inquiéter de.
mine mine f. (*coal or steel*).
mine à moi, le mien, la mienne, les miens, les
  miennes.
miner mineur m.
mineral minéral m.
minimum minimum m.
minister ministre m., pasteur m.
  (*Protestant*).
ministry ministère m.
mink vison m.
minor mineur m. (*age*).
minority minorité f.
minute minute f.
  Any minute now. D'un moment à l'autre.
  Just a minute! Un instant!
  Wait a minute! Attendez un instant!
miracle miracle m.
mirror miroir m.
miscellaneous divers.
mischief espièglerie f.
mischievous espiègle.
misdemeanor délit m.
miser avare m.
miserable misérable.
miserably misérablement.
misery misère f.
misfortune malheur m.
mishap accident m.
misprint faute d'impression f.
Miss mademoiselle f.
miss (to) manquer.
mission mission f.
missionary missionnaire m.
mist brouillard m.
mistake faute f.
mistake (to) se tromper.
  to be mistaken se tromper.
Mister monsieur m.
mistrust méfiance f.
mistrust (to) se méfier.
mistrustful méfiant.
misunderstand comprendre mal.

misunderstanding malentendu m.
misuse abus m.
misuse (to) abuser de.
mix mêler.
mixture mélange m.
mob foule f.
mobile mobile.
mobility mobilité f.
mobilization mobilisation f.
mobilize mobiliser.
mock se moquer de.
mockery moquerie f.
mode mode f.
model modèle noun m. and adj.
model (to) modeler.
moderate modéré.
moderate (to) modérer.
moderation modération f.
modern moderne.
modest modeste.
modesty modestie f.
modification modification f.
modify modifier.
moist moite.
moisten humecter.
molar molaire f.
moment moment m.
  any moment now d'un moment à l'autre.
  Just a moment! Un instant!
monarchy monarchie f.
monastery monastère m.
Monday lundi m.
money argent m., monnaie f.
  small change petite monnaie.
money order mandat m.
  postal money order mandat-poste.
monk moine m.
monkey singe m.
monologue monologue m.
monopoly monopole m.
monorail monorail m.
monotonous monotone.
monotony monotonie f.
monster monstre m.
monstrosity monstruosité f.
monstrous monstrueux.
month mois m.
monthly mensuel.
monument monument m.
monumental monumental.
mood humeur f.
moody de mauvaise humeur.
moon lune f.
moonlight clair de lune m.
mop balai m.
moral moral adj.
morale moral m.
moralist moraliste m.
morality moralité f.

morals morale f.
more (de) plus, davantage.
morning matin m.
morsel morceau m.
mortal mortel m.
mortal adj. mortel, fatal.
mortgage hypothèque f.
mortgage (to) hypothéquer.
mosque mosquée f.
mosquito moustique m.
most la plupart de; le plus de; le plus.
mostly la plupart du temps, pour la plupart.
moth mite f.
mother mère f.
mother-in-law belle-mère f.
motion mouvement m., signe m.
motionless immobile.
motivate motiver.
motive motif m.
motor moteur m.
motor (to) aller en auto.
mount mont m. (*hill*).
mount (to) monter.
mountain montagne f.
mountain climbing alpinisme m.
mountainous montagneux.
mourn se lamenter.
mournful triste, lugubre.
mourning deuil m.
mouse souris f.
mouth bouche f.; embouchure f. (*of a river*).
movable mobile.
move mouvement m.
move (to) remuer, se mouvoir, bouger; déménager (*household*).
movement mouvement m.
movie camera appareil cinématographique m., caméra f.
movies cinéma m.
moving touchant (*emotionally*).
Mr. monsieur, M.
Mrs. madame, Mme.
much beaucoup.
   very much grand-chose.
mud boue f.
muddy boueux.
mule mule f.
multiple multiple noun m. and adj.
multiply multiplier.
multitude multitude f.
mumble marmotter.
municipal municipal.
municipality municipalité f.
munitions munitions f. pl.
murder meurtre m.
murder (to) assassiner.
murmur murmure m.
murmur (to) murmurer.

muscle muscle m.
museum musée m.
mushroom champignon m.
music musique f.
musical musical.
musician musicien m.
must devoir, falloir.
mustard moutarde f.
mute muet noun and adj.
mutter murmure m.
mutter (to) murmurer.
mutton mouton m.
my mon, ma, mes.
myself moi-même.
mysterious mystérieux.
mystery mystère m.

N

nail ongle m. (*finger*); clou m.
nail (to) clouer.
naive naïf.
naked nu.
name nom m.
   first name prénom m.
   last name nom de famille m.
   My name is. Je m'appelle.
   What is your name? Comment vous appelez-vous?
name (to) nommer.
nameless sans nom.
namely c'est-à-dire.
nap somme m.
nape nuque f.
napkin serviette f.
narrow étroit.
narrow (to) restreindre.
nasty désagréable.
nation nation f.
national national.
nationality nationalité f.
nationalization nationalisation f.
nationalize nationaliser.
native indigène m.
natural naturel.
naturally naturellement.
naturalness naturel m.
nature nature f.
   human nature la nature humaine.
   still life nature(s) morte(s).
naughty méchant.
nautical nautique.
   go water-skiing faire du ski nautique.
naval naval.
navy marine f.
near près de, auprès de, prochain, proche.
nearly presque.

neat net.
neatness netteté f.
necessarily de nécessité, forcément, de force.
necessary nécessaire.
necessary (to be) falloir.
necessity nécessité f.
neck cou m.
necklace collier m.
necktie cravate f.
need besoin m.
   be in need of avoir besoin de.
need (to) avoir besoin de.
needle aiguille f.
needless inutile.
needy nécessiteux.
negative adj. négatif.
negative cliché m. (*photography*).
neglect négligence f.
neglect (to) négliger.
negotiate négocier, traiter.
negotiation négociation f.
neighbor voisin m.
neighborhood voisinage m.
neither non plus; ni l'un, ni l'autre; ni.
   neither one ni l'un, ni l'autre.
   neither . . . nor ni . . . ni.
neon néon m.
   neon sign enseigne au néon.
nephew neveu m.
nerve nerf m.
nervous nerveux.
nest nid m.
net filet m.
network réseau m.
neuter neutre noun and adj.
neutral neutre.
never jamais.
nevertheless néanmoins, quand même.
new nouveau, neuf.
news nouvelle f., actualités, f. pl.
   society news mondanités f. pl.
newspaper journal m.
newsstand kiosque m.
next suivant, prochain, ensuite.
nice gentil, agréable.
nickname surnom m.
niece nièce f.
night nuit f., soir m.
nightgown chemise de nuit f.
nightingale rossignol m.
nightmare cauchemar m.
nine neuf.
nineteen dix-neuf.
nineteenth dix-neuvième.
ninetieth quatre-vingt-dixième.
ninety quatre-vingt-dix.
ninth neuvième.
no non.

no longer ne plus.
No Smoking. Défense de fumer.
nobility noblesse f.
noble noble noun and adj.
nobody personne f.
noise bruit m.
noisy bruyant.
nominate nommer, désigner.
nomination nomination f., désignation f.
none ne point, ne . . . aucun.
nonsense bêtise f.
noon midi m.
nor ni, non plus.
   neither . . . nor ni . . . ni.
normal adj. normal.
north nord m.
North America Amérique du Nord f.
northern du nord.
northwest nord-ouest m.
nose nez m.
nostril narine f.
not ne . . . pas.
note note f., billet m.
note (to) noter.
notebook carnet m.
nothing rien.
notice avis m.
   Notice to the public. Avis au public.
notice (to) remarquer.
notify avertir.
notion idée f.
noun nom m.
nourish nourrir.
nourishment nourriture f.
novel adj. nouveau.
novel roman m.
novelty nouveauté f.
November novembre m.
novocaine novocaïne f.
now maintenant.
   now and then de temps en temps.
nowadays de nos jours.
nowhere nulle part.
nuclear nucléaire
   n. arms armes nucléaires f. pl.
   n. energy énergie nucléaire f.
   n. industry industrie nucléaire f.
   n. reactor réacteur nucléaire m.
nude adj. nu.
nude nu m. (*painting*).
nuisance peste f., ennui m.
null nul.
numb engourdi.
number numéro m.
number (to) compter.
numbered numéroté.
numerous nombreux.
nun religieuse f.
nurse bonne d'enfant f., infirmière f.

nursery chambre d'enfants f.
nut noix f.

O

oak chêne m.
oar rame f.
oat avoine f.
oath serment m.
obedience obéissance f.
obedient obéissant.
obey obéir.
object objet m., but m.
object (to) s'opposer à.
objection objection f.
    I see no objection to it. Je n'y vois pas
      d'inconvénient.
objectionable repréhensible.
objective objectif noun m. and adj.
objectively objectivement.
objectivity objectivité f.
obligation obligation f.
obligatory obligatoire.
oblige obliger.
obliging serviable.
oblique oblique.
obscure obscur.
obscurity obscurité f.
observation observation f.
observatory observatoire m.
observe observer.
observer observateur m.
obstacle obstacle m.
obstinacy obstination f.
obstinate obstiné, têtu.
obvious évident.
obviously évidemment.
occasion occasion f.
occasion (to) occasionner.
occasionally de temps en temps.
occupation métier m., occupation f.
occupied occupé.
occupy occuper.
occur arriver, se trouver.
occurrence occurence f.
ocean océan m.
October octobre m.
odd impair (*number*); dépareillé (*not
    matched*); bizarre (*strange*).
odds avantage m.; différence f.
odor odeur f.
of de, en.
off de.
offend offenser.
offense injure f., offense f., délit m.
offensive adj. injurieux.
offensive offensive f.

offer offre f.
offer (to) offrir.
offering offrande f.
office bureau m.; fonction f.
officer officier m.
official adj. officiel.
official fonctionnaire m.
often souvent.
oil huile f.
    oil painting peinture à l'huile.
old vieux.
    my friend, old chap mon vieux.
old age vieillesse f.
old man vieillard m.
olive olive f.
    olive oil huile d'olive.
ominous de mauvais augure.
on sur.
once une fois, autrefois.
    all at once tout à coup.
    at once tout de suite.
    once a year une fois par an.
    once in a while de temps en temps.
one un (*numeral*).
one pron. on, vous, soi, celui, celle, etc.
one's son, sa, ses.
oneself soi-même, se.
onion oignon m.
only seul, simple, unique, seulement.
open adj. ouvert.
open (to) ouvrir, s'ouvrir.
opening ouverture f.
opera opéra m.
opera glasses jumelles f. pl.
operate opérer.
operation opération f.
opinion opinion f.
opponent adversaire m.
opportune opportun.
opportunity occasion f.
oppose s'opposer à, résister.
opposite en face de, opposé.
opposition opposition f.
oppress opprimer.
oppression oppression f.
optimism optimisme m.
optimistic optimiste.
or ou
    either or ou . . . ou.
oral verbal.
orange orange f.
orator orateur m.
oratory art oratoire.
orchard verger m.
orchestra orchestre m.
ordeal épreuve f.
order ordre m.
    in order that afin que, pour que.
    in order to afin de.

   put in order ranger.
order (to) ordonner, commander.
ordinarily d'ordinaire.
ordinary banal, ordinaire.
organ organe m. (*body*); orgue m.
   (*music*).
organization organisation f.
organize organiser.
Orient Orient m.
oriental oriental noun and adj.
origin origine f.
original original.
originality originalité f.
originate créer.
ornament ornement m.
orphan orphelin m.
ostentation ostentation f.
other autre.
ouch! aïe!
ought devoir.
ounce once f.
our(s) notre, nos.
ourselves nous-mêmes.
out dehors, hors de.
outcome conséquence f.; dénouement m.
outdo surpasser.
outer extérieur m.
outlast survivre à.
outlaw proscrit m.
outlaw (to) proscrire.
outlay dépense f.
outlet issue f.; débouché m.
outline contour m., silhouette f.
outline (to) ébaucher, esquisser.
outlook perspective f.
output rendement m., production f.
outrage outrage m.
outrageous atroce; indigne.
outside dehors, hors.
oval ovale noun m. and adj.
oven four m.
over dessus.
overcoat pardessus m.
overcome surmonter, subjuguer.
overflow déborder.
overlook négliger; pardonner.
overpower accabler, subjuguer.
overrule rejeter.
overrun envahir.
overseas outre-mer.
oversight inadvertance f.
overtake rattraper.
overthrow renverser.
overwhelm accabler.
owe devoir.
own adj. propre.
own (to) posséder.
owner propriétaire m.
ox boeuf m.

oxygen oxygène m.
oyster huitre f.

P

pace pas m.
pace (to) arpenter.
   pace up and down arpenter de long en
      large.
pacific pacifique.
pack (to) emballer.
package colis m., emballage m., paquet m.
packed bondé.
page page f.
pain douleur f., peine f.
pain (to) faire mal.
painful douloureux.
paint peinture f.
paint (to) peindre.
painter peintre m.
painting peinture f.
pair paire f.
pale pâle.
pamper gâter.
pamphlet brochure f.
pan poêle f.
pancake crêpe f.
pane vitre f.
panel panneau m.
pang angoisse f.
panic panique f.
panorama panorama m.
panoramic panoramique.
pants pantalon m.
paper papier m.
parachute parachute m.
parade parade f.
paragraph paragraphe m.
parallel parallèle f.
paralysis paralysie f.
paralyze paralyser.
parcel paquet m., colis m., emballage m.
parcel post colis postal.
pardon pardon m.
pardon (to) pardonner.
parent père m., mère f.; parent m.
parenthesis parenthèse f.
Parisian parisien noun and adj.
park parc m.
park (to) stationner (*a car*).
parliament parlement m.
part partie f.; endroit m.
   in hair raie f.
part (to) diviser, se séparer.
partial partiel, partial.
partially avec partialité; en partie.
participate participer (à).

particular particulier.
particularity particularité f.
particularly particulièrement.
partner associé m; partenaire m. and f.
party parti m.
   party (telephone) correspondant m.
pass laisser-passer m.
pass (to) dépasser; passer.
passage passage m., allée f., traversée f.
passenger voyageur m.
passing passager.
passion passion f.
passive passif.
passport passeport m.
past prep. au delà de (*beyond*).
   half-past seven sept heures et demie.
   past ten o'clock dix heures passées.
past adj. passé, dernier.
   the past year l'année dernière, l'an passé.
past passé m.
   in the past dans le passé.
paste pâte f.
paste (to) déplacer (computer)
pastry pâtisserie f.
pastry shop pâtisserie f.
patch pièce f.
patch (to) rapiécer.
patent brevet d'invention m.
paternal paternel.
path allée f., sentier m.
pathetic pathétique.
patience patience f.
patient adj. patient.
patient malade m. and f.
patriot patriote m. and f.
patriotism patriotisme m.
patron patron m.
patronize protéger.
pattern modèle m., dessin m.
pause pause f.
pause (to) faire une pause.
pave paver.
pavement pavé m., trottoir m.
paw patte f.
pay salaire m.
pay (to) payer, régler (*check*).
payable payable.
payment paiement m.
pea pois m.
peace paix f.
peaceful paisible.
peach pêche f.
peak cime f.
pear poire f.
pearl perle f.
peasant paysan m.
pebble caillou m.
peculiar particulier.
pecuniary pécuniaire.

pedal pédale f.
pedant pédant m.
pedestrian piéton m.
peel pelure f.
peel (to) peler.
pen plume f.
penalty peine f., penalty m. (*soccer*).
pencil crayon m.
penetrate pénétrer.
peninsula péninsule f.
penitence pénitence f.
penny sou m.
pension pension f.
people peuple m., gens m. pl.
pepper poivre m.
perceive apercevoir.
percent pour cent.
percentage pourcentage m.
perfect parfait.
Perfect! Parfait! Très bien!
perfect (to) rendre parfait.
perfection perfection f.
perfectly parfaitement.
perform accomplir, exécuter.
performance accomplissement m.;
      représentation f.
perfume parfum m.
perfume (to) parfumer.
perhaps peut-être.
peril péril m.
period période f.; point m. (*punctuation*).
periodical périodique m.
perish périr.
permanent permanent.
permission permission f.
permit permis m.
permit (to) permettre.
perplex embrouiller.
persecute persécuter.
persecution persécution f.
perseverance persévérance f.
persist persister.
person personne f.
personal personnel.
personal computer ordinateur personnel m.
personality personnalité f.
perspective perspective f.
persuade persuader, convaincre.
pertaining appartenant.
petty petit.
pharmacist pharmacien m.
pharmacy pharmacie f.
phenomenon phénomène m.
philosopher philosophe m.
philosophical philosophique.
philosophy philosophie f.
phonograph phonographe m.
photocopier photocopieur m.
photocopy photocopie f.

photograph photographie f.
  take a photograph prendre une
    photographie.
photographer photographe m.
phrase locution f.
physical physique.
physician médecin m.
piano piano m.
pick (to) cueillir, choisir.
pick up ramasser.
pickup reprise f. (*rented car*).
picnic pique-nique m.
picture image f., tableau m.
  take a picture prendre une photographie.
picturesque pittoresque.
pie tarte f.
piece morceau m.; partie f.; pièce f.
pig cochon m.
pigeon pigeon m.
pile tas m.
pile (to) empiler, entasser.
pill pilule f., cachet m., comprimé m.
pillar pilier m.
pillow oreiller m.
pilot pilote m.
pilot (to) piloter.
pin épingle f.
pinch (to) pincer.
pink adj. rose.
pious pieux.
pipe pipe f. (*for smoking*); tuyau m., tube m.
pitiful pitoyable.
pity pitié f., dommage m.
  What a pity! Quel dommage!
place lieu m., endroit m.
  to take place avoir lieu.
place (to) mettre.
placing mise f.
plain adj. simple.
plain plaine f.
plan plan m., projet m.
plan (to) projeter.
plane plan m; avion m. (*airplane*).
plant plante f.
plant (to) planter.
plaster plâtre m.
plate assiette f.
platform estrade f.; plate-forme f.; quai m.
    (*train*).
platter plat m.
play jeu m.; pièce de théâtre f.
play (to) jouer; pratiquer (*sports*).
player comédien m. (*theatre*).
plea requête f.
plead plaider.
pleasant agréable.
please (to) plaire, complaire.
  (if you) please s'il vous plaît.
pleased content.

pleasure plaisir m.
pledge garantie f., gage m.
pledge (to) garantir.
plenty abondance f.
plot complot m., intrigue f.
plot (to) comploter, conspirer.
plow charrue f.
plow (to) labourer.
plum prune f.
plunder (to) piller.
plural pluriel m.
plus plus.
pocket poche f.
  pocket size format de poche.
poem poème m.
poet poète m.
poetic poétique.
poetry poésie f.
point point m.; pointe f.
point (to) indiquer.
pointed pointu.
pointillist pointilliste m. (*painting*).
poise savoir-faire m.
poison poison m.
poison (to) empoisonner.
poisoning empoisonnement m.
polar polaire.
police police f.
police officer agent de police m.
policy politique f.
polish vernis m.; cirage m.
polish (to); polir, cirer.
polite poli.
politely poliment.
politeness politesse f.
political politique.
politics politique f.
pollution pollution f.
  air pollution pollution atmosphérique f.
pond étang m.
poor pauvre.
popular populaire.
population population f.
port port m.
porter porteur m., concierge m. and f.
portrait portrait m.
pose pose f.
position position f.; situation f. (*job*).
positive positif.
possess posséder.
possession possession f.
possibility possibilité f.
possible possible.
post poteau m.; poste f.
postage affranchissement m.
  postage stamp timbre m.
postal postal
  postal service service poste(s) f.
postcard carte postale f.

poster affiche f.

posterity postérité f.

post office poste f.

pot pot m.

potato pomme de terre f., frite f. (*French fried*).

pottery faïence f.

pound livre f.

pour verser.

poverty pauvreté f.

powder poudre f.

power pouvoir m., puissance f.

powerful puissant.

practical pratique.

practice habitude f., pratique f., exercice m.

practice (to) pratiquer.

praise éloge m.

praise (to) louer.

prank espièglerie f.

pray prier.

prayer prière f.

preach prêcher.

precaution précaution f.

precede précéder.

preceding précédent noun m. and adj.

precept précepte m.

precious précieux.

precise précis.

precision précision f.

predecessor prédécesseur m.

preface préface f.

prefer préférer.

preference préférence f.

prejudice préjugé m.

preliminary préliminaire, préalable.

prepare préparer.

prescribe prescrire.

prescription ordonnance f.

presence présence f.

present adj. actuel, présent.

present don m.; présent m.

make a present faire cadeau, faire présent.

present (to) offrir, présenter.

preserve (to) préserver, conserver.

preside présider.

president président m.

press presse f.

press (to) presser, serrer.

press clothes repasser des vêtements.

pressing pressant.

pressure pression f.

prestige prestige m.

presume présumer.

pretend prétendre, faire semblant.

pretext prétexte m.

pretty adj. joli.

pretty adv. assez.

pretty nearly presque.

pretty soon assez tôt.

prevail prévaloir.

prevent empêcher, éviter.

prevention empêchement m.; précautions f. pl.

previous antérieur, précédent.

the previous year l'année précédente.

prey proie f.

price prix m.

pride orgueil m.

priest prêtre m.

principal principal; maîtresse.

principle principe m.

print épreuve f. (*photography*).

print (to) imprimer; tirer.

to have a negative printed faire tirer un cliché.

printed matter imprimés m. pl.

printer imprimante d'ordinateur f. (*computer*).

prison prison f.

prisoner prisonnier m.

private particulier, privé, confidentiel.

privilege privilège m.

prize prix m.

prize (to) attacher beaucoup de prix à.

probable probable.

probably probablement, sans doute.

problem problème m.

procedure procédé m.

proceed avancer, procéder, provenir de.

process procédé m., développement m.

procession cortège m., procession f.

proclaim proclamer.

produce (to) produire.

product produit m.

production production f.

productive productif.

profession profession f.

professional professionnel.

professor professeur m.

profile profil m.

profit profit m.; bénéfice m., bénéfices m. pl.

profit (to) profiter.

profits bénéfices m. pl.

profoundly profondément.

program programme m.

programming programmation f. (*computer*).

progress progrès m.

progress (to) faire des progrès.

prohibit défendre.

prohibition défense f.

project projet m.

project (to) projeter.

promise promesse f.

promise (to) promettre.

prompt prompt.

promptness promptitude f.

pronoun pronom m.

pronounce prononcer.

proof preuve f.

proper comme il faut.
property propriété f.; biens m. pl., terres f. pl.
proportion proportion f.
proposal proposition f.
propose proposer.
prosaic prosaïque.
prose prose f.
prospect prospective.
prosper prospérer.
prosperity prospérité f.
prosperous prospère.
protect protéger.
protection protection f.
protector protecteur m.
protest protestation f.
protest (to) protester.
Protestant protestant.
proud fier.
prove prouver.
proverb proverbe m.
provide pouvoir, fournir.
provided that pourvu que.
province province f.; ressort m. (*sphere of action*).
provision provision f., précaution f.
provoke provoquer, irriter.
proximity proximité f.
prudence prudence f.
prudent prudent.
prudently prudemment.
prune pruneau m.
psychological psychologique.
psychology psychologie f.
public public noun m. and adj.
publication publication f., revue f.
publish publier (*edict, etc.*); éditer (*book, paper*).
publisher éditeur m.
pull (to) tirer.
pulpit chaire f., tribune f.
pulse pouls m.
pump pompe f.
pump up gonfler.
puncture pneu crevé m., crevaison f.
punish punir.
punishment punition f.
pupil élève m.; prunelle f. (*eye*).
purchase achat m.
purchase (to) acheter.
pure pur.
purity pureté f.
purpose but m., propos m.
purse porte-monnaie m. (*change purse*).
pursue poursuivre.
pursuit poursuite f.
push (to) pousser, enforcer (*button*).
put mettre, poser, placer.
    put away mettre de côté.

    put back remettre,
    put off remettre.
    put on mettre.
putting mise f.
    hair setting mise en plis.
putting back remise f.
    put into shape, overhaul (*car*) faire une remise en état.
puzzle perplexité f., énigme f.
puzzle (to) embarrasser.

Q

quaint bizarre.
qualify qualifier.
quality qualité f.
quantity quantité f.
quarrel querelle f.
quarter quart m.; quartier m.
queen reine f.
queer bizarre.
quench étancher, éteindre.
quest quête f.
question question f.
question (to) interroger.
quick rapide, vif.
quickly rapidement.
    Come quickly! Venez vite!
quiet adj. calme, tranquille.
    Keep quiet! Restez tranquille! Taisez-vous!
quiet (to) calmer.
quit quitter.
quite tout à fait, assez.
    quite good assez bon.
quote citer.

R

rabbi rabbin m.
rabbit lapin m.
race course f.; race f. (*ethnic*).
radiation radiation f.
radiator radiateur m.
radio radio f.
radioactive waste déchets radioactifs m. pl.
rag lambeau m. (*tatter*); chiffon m.
rage rage f.
ragged (en) haillons.
rail rail m.
railroad chemin de fer m.
rain pluie f.
rain (to) pleuvoir.
rainbow ar-en-ciel m.
rainy pluvieux.

raise augmentation f.
raise (to) lever, élever.
raisin raisin sec m.
rake râteau m.
rally (to) rallier.
range portée f., étendue f.
range (to) ranger; varier de, à.
rank grade m., rang m.
ransom rançon f.
rapid rapide.
rapidity rapidité f.
rapidly rapidement.
rapture transport m., saisissement m.
rash téméraire (*reckless*).
rat rat m.
rate vitesse f. (*of speech*); taux m. (*of interest*); cours m.
   rate of exchange cours du change m.
rate (to) évaluer.
rates tarif m. (*fare*).
rather plutôt.
   I'd rather go j'aimerais mieux y aller.
   rather good assez bon.
   rather than plutôt que.
ration ration f.
rational raisonnable.
rave délirer.
raw cru.
ray rayon m.
razor rasoir m.
   razor blade lame de rasoir.
reach étendue f.; portée f.
reach (to) arriver à, atteindre; s'étendre.
react réagir.
reaction réaction f.
read lire.
reading lecture f.
ready prêt.
real réel, véritable.
realistic réaliste.
realization réalisation f.
realize réaliser, comprendre.
really en vérité, vraiment, réellement, véritablement.
   Really! Vraiment!
rear (from the) de derrière.
rear (to) élever (*children*).
reason raison f.
reason (to) raisonner.
reasonable raisonnable.
reasoning raisonnement m.
reassure rassurer.
rebel rebelle noun and adj.
rebel (to) se révolter.
rebellion rébellion f.
recall rappel m.
recall (to) rappeler, se rappeler.
receipt recette f.; quittance f., reçu m.
receive recevoir; accueillir.

receiver récepteur m. (*telephone*).
recent récent.
reception réception f., accueil m.
recess trève f. (*time*).
reciprocal réciproque.
recite réciter.
recognize reconnaître.
recoil reculer.
recollect se souvenir.
recollection souvenir m.
recommend recommander.
recommendation recommendation f.
reconcile réconcilier.
reconstitute reconstituer.
record dossier m. (*file*); disque m. (*phonograph*).
record player tourne-disque, m.
recover retrouver; se remettre (*health*); recouvrir.
recruit recrue f.
rectangle rectangle m.
red rouge.
red tape formalité f.
reddish brown roux.
redeem racheter.
redouble redoubler.
reduce réduire.
reduction réduction f.
reed roseau m.
refer référer, se rapporter à.
reference allusion f., référence f.
referring se rapportant à.
refine raffiner, épurer.
refinement raffinement m.
reflect refléter, réfléchir.
reflection reflet m., réflexion f.
reform réforme f.
reform (to) se réformer.
refrain refrain m.
refrain (to) s'abstenir.
refresh rafraîchir.
refreshment rafraîchissement m.
refuge refuge m.
   take refuge prendre refuge, se réfugier.
refund remboursement m.
refund (to) rembourser.
refundable remboursable.
refusal refus m.
refuse (to) refuser.
refute réfuter.
regard égard m., estime f.
   in regard to en ce qui concerne.
regime régime m.
regiment régiment m.
region région f.
register registre m.
register (to) enregistrer, se faire inscrire.
registered immatriculé (*car*); inscrit.
regret regret m.

regret (to) regretter.
regrettable regrettable.
regular régulier, ordinaire.
regulate régler.
regulation règlement m.
rehearsal répétition f.
rehearse répéter.
reign règne m.
reign (to) régner.
reinforce renforcer.
reject rejeter.
rejoice réjouir, se réjouir.
rejoin rejoindre.
relapse rechute f.
relate raconter.
relation parent m. (*relative*).
relationship rapport m.; parenté f.
relative adj. relatif.
relative parent m.
relax se délasser, se relâcher, se détendre.
relaxation détente f.
release délivrance f.
release (to) libérer, décharger.
relent s'attendrir.
relentless impitoyable.
relevant pertinent.
reliable digne de confiance.
reliance confiance f.
relic relique f.
relief soulagement m.; secours m.
relieve soulager; relever (*duty*).
religion religion f., culte m.
religious religieux; divin.
relinquish abandonner.
relish saveur f. (*flavor*).
relish (to) savourer.
reload recharger.
reluctance répugnance f.
reluctant peu disposé à.
rely upon compter sur.
remain rester.
remainder restant m., reste m.
remaining restant.
remake (to) refaire.
remark observation f., remarque f.
remark (to) remarquer, faire remarquer.
remarkable remarquable.
remedy remède m.
remember se rappeler, se souvenir.
remembrance souvenir m.
remind rappeler.
remorse remords m.
remote reculé adj.
remote control télécommande f.
removal enlèvement m. (*taking away*).
remove (to) enlever, supprimer.
remove makeup se démaquiller.
renew renouveler.
rent loyer m.

rent (to) louer.
rental location f.
reopening rentrée f.
repair réparation f.
repair (to) réparer.
repeat répéter.
repent se repentir.
repetition répétition f.
replace remplacer.
replacement rechange m.
reply réponse f.
reply (to) répondre.
report rapport m., compte rendu m. (*of a meeting*).
report (to) rapporter, faire un rapport.
represent représenter.
representation représentation f.
representative représentant m.
repress réprimer.
reprimand réprimande f.
reprimand (to) réprimander.
reprisal représaille f.
reproach reproche m.
reproach (to) reprocher.
reproduce reproduire.
repurchase rachat m.
   retail price prix de rachat.
reputation réputation f.
request demande f., requête f.
request (to) demander, prier, solliciter.
require exiger, avoir besoin de, demander.
rescue (to) délivrer, secourir.
research recherche f.
resemble ressembler (à).
resent être froissé de.
resentment ressentiment m.
reservation réserve f., arrière-pensée f., réservation f.
reserve réserve f.
reserve (to) réserver, retenir (*rooms, seats*).
reside demeurer.
residence lieu de séjour m., résidence f., demeure f.
resign donner sa démission.
   resign oneself se résigner.
resignation démission f., résignation f.
resist résister.
resistance résistance f.
resolute résolu.
resolution résolution f.
resolve décider, résoudre.
resort recours m., ressource f.
resort (to) avoir recours à.
resource ressource f.
   natural resources ressources naturelles f. pl.
respect respect m.
respect (to) respecter.
respectful respectueux.

respective respectif.
respite répit m.
responsibility responsabilité f., charge f.
responsible responsable.
rest repos m.; reste m.
rest (to) se reposer.
restaurant restaurant m.
restless inquiet, agité.
restoration restauration f.
restore rendre, remettre.
restrain contenir, réprimer.
restraint contrainte f.
restrict restreindre.
restriction restriction f.
result résultat m.
result (to) résulter de.
resume reprendre.
retail détail m.
    retail price prix de détail m.
retail (to) vendre au détail (*sell retail*).
retain retenir.
retaliate user de représailles.
retaliation représailles f. pl.
retire se retirer.
retirement retraite f.
retrace rebrousser.
retract rétracter.
retreat retraite f.
retrieve recouvrer.
return retour m., rentrée f.
return (to) revenir, rendre; renvoyer;
    rentrer.
    return home rentrer à la maison.
reveal révéler.
revelation révélation f.
revenge vengeance f., revenge f.
revenue revenu m.
reverence révérence f.
reverend révérend.
reverse contraire noun m. and adj., inverse
    noun m. and adj.
reverse (to) intervertir; annuler (*decision*).
revert revenir.
review revue f.
review (to) revoir, analyser, passer en
    revue.
revise réviser.
revision révision f.
revive faire revivre, ranimer, réveiller
    (*memories*).
revoke révoquer.
revolt révolte f.
revolt (to) se révolter.
revolution révolution f.
revolve tourner.
reward récompense f.
reward (to) récompenser.
rhyme rime f.
rib côte f.

ribbon ruban m.
rice riz m.
rich riche.
richness richesse f.
rid (get) débarrasser.
    get rid of something se débarrasser de
    quelque chose.
riddle énigme f., devinette f.
ride promenade à cheval (horseback) f.;
    promenade à bicyclette (bike ride) f.;
    trajet m. (*length of*).
ride (to) monter (à cheval); se promener (à
    cheval).
ridiculous ridicule.
rifle fusil m.
right adj. droit, exact, vrai, juste.
right droit m.; bien m.
    have a right to avoir le droit de.
    to the right à droite.
right away instantanément, tout de suite.
righteous juste.
righteousness justice f.
rightful légitime.
rigid raide.
rigor rigueur f.
rigorous rigoureux.
ring anneau m., bague f.
ring (to) sonner.
ringing sonnerie f.
rinse (to) rinser.
riot émeute f.
ripe mûr.
ripen mûrir.
rise hausse f.
rise (to) se lever, augmenter.
risk risque m.
risk (to) risquer.
rite rite m.
ritual rituel m.
rival rival noun and adj.
rivalry rivalité f.
river rivière f., fleuve m.
Riviera Côte d'Azur f. (*French*).
road chemin m., route f.
road map carte routière f.
roads (of) routier.
roar rugissement m.
roar (to) rugir; hurler.
roast rôti m.
roast (to) rôtir.
rob voler, piller.
robber bandit m., brigand m.
robbery vol m.
robe robe f.
robust robuste.
rock rocher m., roc m.
rock (to) balancer.
rocky rocheux.
rod baguette f.

roll rouleau m., petit pain m. (*bread*).
roll (to) rouler, enrouler.
roller coaster montagnes russes f. pl.
roller skates patins à roulettes m. pl.
Roman romain.
romantic romantique.
romanticism romantisme m.
roof toit m.
room chambre f.; place f. (*space*).
    make room for faire place à.
    There's no room. Il n'y a pas de place.
root racine f.
rope corde f.
rose rose f.
rot (to) pourrir.
rough rude, grossier.
round adj. rond.
round adv. en rond, tout autour.
round n. tournée f., tour m.
round off arrondir.
rouse réveiller, provoquer.
rousing émouvant.
rout tumulte m.; déroute f.
rout (to) mettre en déroute.
route route f., parcours m.
routine routine f.
rove parcourir, errer.
row rang m., vacarme m. (*tumult*).
row (to) ramer.
rowboat canot m.
royal royal.
royalist royaliste.
rub (to) frotter.
rubber caoutchouc m.
rubbish décombres m. pl; blague f. (*nonsense;
    bunk*).
rude brusque, commun, vulgaire, impoli.
ruffle ride f.
ruffle (to) chiffonner.
rugby rugby m.
ruin ruine f.
ruin (to) ruiner.
rule règle f., domination f., autorité f.
rule (to) gouverner; régler (*lines*).
ruler gouverneur; règle (*for lines*).
rumor rumeur f.
run (to) courir.
    run away fuir.
rural rural.
rush foule f., ruée f.
rush (to) se précipiter.
    rush hour l'heure d'affluence f.
russet roux.
Russian russe.
rust rouille f.
rust (to) rouiller.
rustic rustique.
rusty rouillé.
rye seigle m.

S

sack sac m.
sacrament sacrement m.
sacred sacré.
sacrifice sacrifice m.
sacrifice (to) sacrifier.
sacrilege sacrilège m.
sad triste.
sadden attrister.
saddle selle f.
sadness tristesse f.
safe sain et sauf, sûr, certain.
safe (be) être en sûreté.
safe-deposit box coffre-fort m.
safely sain et sauf.
safety sécurité f., sûreté f.
sail voile f.
sail (to) naviguer.
saint saint m.
sake (for the sake of) pour l'amour de.
salad salade f.
salary appointements m. pl.
sale vente f.
salesman vendeur.
saleswoman vendeuse.
salt sel m.
salt (to) saler.
salute salut m.
salute (to) saluer.
salvation salut m.
same même.
    all the same tout de même.
sample êchantillon m.
sanctuary sanctuaire m.
sand sable m.
sandal sandale f.
sandwich sandwich m.
sandy sablonneux.
sane sain d'esprit.
sanitary sanitaire.
sap sève f.
sarcasm sarcasme m.
sarcastic sarcastique.
sarcophagus sarcophage m.
sardine sardine f.
satellite satellite m.
    satellite dish antenne parabolique f.
satiate rassasier.
satin satin m.
satisfaction satisfaction f.
satisfactory satisfaisant.
satisfy contenter, satisfaire.
saturate saturer.
Saturday samedi m.
sauce sauce f.
saucer soucoupe f.
sausage saucisse f.

savage sauvage, brutal.
save faire des économies (*money*); sauver (*rescue*); enregistrer (*computer*).
    save time gagner du temps.
savings économies f.; épargne f.
savior sauveur m.
saxophone saxophone m.
    play the saxophone jouer de saxophone.
say! tiens!
say (to) dire.
scales balance f.
scalp cuir chevelu m.
scan scruter.
scandal scandale m.
scanty peu abondant.
scar cicatrice f.
scarce rare.
scarcely à peine.
scare (to) effrayer.
scarf écharpe f.
scatter répandre, éparpiller.
scene scène f.
scenery paysage m. (*landscape*), décor m. (*theatre*).
schedule liste f., horaire m.
scheme dessein m., plan m.
scholar savant m.
school école f.
    coed school école mixte f.
    day care école maternelle f.
    elementary school école primaire élémentaire f.
    high school école secondaire f., lycée m.
    junior high school école de cours moyen f.
    private school école privée f.
science science f.
scientific scientifique.
scientist homme de science m.
scissors ciseaux m. pl.
scold gronder.
scope envergure f.
scorn mépris m.
scorn (to) mépriser.
scornful méprisant, dédaigneux.
scrape gratter.
scratch égratignure f.
scratch (to) gratter.
scream cri m.
scream (to) crier.
screen écran m.
screw vis f.
scribble (to) griffonner.
scruple scrupule m.
scrupulous scrupuleux.
scrutinize scruter.
scuba-dive (to) plonger sous-marine.
sculpted sculpté.
sculpture sculpture f.
sea mer f.

seal sceau m., cachet m.
seal (to) sceller, cacheter.
seam couture f.
search recherche f.
search (to) chercher, fouiller.
seashore plage f.
seasickness mal de mer m.
season saison f.
season (to) assaisonner (*flavor*).
seat siège m., place f.
seat (to) faire asseoir.
seated assis.
second adj. deuxième; second (*numeral*).
second seconde f. (*time*).
second (to) appuyer.
secondary secondaire.
secondhand d'occasion.
secret secret noun m. and adj.
secretary secrétaire m. and f.
sect secte f.
section section f.; rubrique f. (*newspaper, magazine*).
    sports section rubrique sportive.
secure adj. en sûreté, sûr.
secure (to) mettre en sûreté; obtenir, fixer.
security garantie f., sûreté f.
see voir.
seed graine f., semence f.
seek chercher, rechercher.
seem sembler, paraître.
seize saisir.
seldom rarement.
select adj. recherché.
select (to) choisir.
selection choix m.
-self -même.
    myself moi-même.
selfish égoïste.
selfishness égoïsme m.
sell vendre.
    sell again revendre.
seller vendeur m., vendeuse f.
semi- demi-.
semicolon point-virgule m.
senate sénat m.
senator sénateur m.
send envoyer, expédier.
    send back renvoyer.
    send for faire venir.
sender expéditeur m.
senior aîné m.
sensation sensation f.
sense sens m.
senseless insensé.
sensibility sensibilité f.
sensible sensé, raisonnable.
sensitive sensible.
sensitiveness sensibilité f.
sentence phrase f. (*grammar*); jugement m.

sentiment sentiment m.
sentimental sentimental.
separate adj. séparé, à part.
separate (to) séparer.
separately séparément.
separation séparation f.
September septembre m.
serene serein.
sergeant sergent m.
series série f.
serious sérieux, sobre.
seriously sérieusement.
sermon sermon m.
servant domestique m. and f.
serve servir.
service service m.; office m.
     religious service office divin.
session séance f.
set adj. fixe, résolu, prescrit.
set assortiment m., service m.
set (to) mettre, placer.
setting décor m. (*stage*).
settle (to) arranger, régler, fixer, s'établir.
settlement accord m., colonie f.
seven sept.
seventeen dix-sept.
seventeenth dix-septième.
seventh septième.
seventieth soixante-dixième.
seventy soixante-dix.
several plusieurs.
     several times à plusieurs reprises.
severe sévère.
severity sévérité f.
sew coudre.
     sew back on recoudre.
sewer égout m.
sewing machine machine à coudre f.
sex sexe m.
shabby usé.
shade ombre f.
shade (to) ombrager.
shadow ombre f.
shady ombragé.
shake (to) secouer, agiter; serrer (*hands*); hocher (*head*).
shallow peu profond.
sham adj. faux.
sham (to) simuler.
shame honte f.
shame (to) faire honte à.
shameful honteux.
shameless éhonté.
shampoo shampooing m.
shape forme f.
shape (to) former.
shapeless informe.
share part f.; action f. (*business*).
share (to) partager.

shareholder actionnaire m.
sharp adj. aigu.
sharp dièse m. (*music*).
sharpen aiguiser.
shatter fracasser.
shave (to) raser.
she elle.
shed hangar m.
shed (to) verser, répandre.
sheep mouton m.
sheer pur.
sheet feuille f. (*paper*); drap m. (*bedsheet*).
shelf rayon m., étagère f.
shell coquille f.
shelter abri m.
shelter (to) abriter.
shepherd berger m.
shield bouclier m.
shield (to) protéger.
shift déplacement m.; équipe f. (*of workmen*).
shift (to) déplacer, changer de place.
shine briller.
ship navire m., vaisseau m.
ship (to) expédier.
shipment expédition f.; envoi m.
shirt chemise f.
shiver frisson m.
shiver (to) frissonner.
shock choc m.
shock (to) choquer, scandaliser.
shoe soulier m., chaussure f.
shoemaker cordonnier m.
shoot tirer.
shooting tir m.
shop boutique f.
shore rive f.
short court.
shorten abréger, raccourcir.
shorthand sténographie f.
shorts slip m. (*men's*).
shot coup m.
shoulder épaule f.
shout cri m.
shout (to) crier.
shove (to) pousser.
shovel pelle f.
show spectacle m.
show (to) montrer.
show around piloter.
shower averse f., douche f.
shown inscrit.
shrill criard.
shrimp crevette f.
shrink rétrécir.
shrub buisson m.
shun éviter.
shut adj. fermé.
shut (to) enfermer, fermer.
shutter release déclencheur m. (*camera*).

shy timide.
sick malade.
sickness maladie f.
side côté m., bord m.
sidewalk trottoir m.
siege siège m.
sigh soupir m.
sigh (to) soupirer.
sight vue f.
sign signe m., enseigne f.
sign (to) signer.
signal signal m.
signature signature f.
significance signification f.
significant significatif.
signify signifier.
silence silence m.
silence (to) faire taire.
silent silencieux.
silent (to be) se taire.
silk soie f.
silken de soie.
silly sot.
silver argent m.
silvery argenté, argentin.
similar semblable.
similarity similitude f.
simple simple.
simplicity simplicité f.
simply simplement.
simulate simuler.
simultaneous simultané.
sin péché m.
sin (to) pécher.
since depuis; puisque.
sincere sincère.
sincerely sincèrement.
    Yours sincerely. Votre tout dévoué.
sincerity sincérité f.
sinew tendon m.
sing chanter.
singer chanteur m., chanteuse f.
single seul; célibataire (*unmarried*).
singular singulier, remarquable.
sinister sinistre.
sink évier m. (*kitchen*).
sink (to) (s') enfoncer, couler, sombrer.
sinner pécheur m.
sip (to) boire à petits coups, siroter.
sir monsieur.
    Thank you, sir. Merci, monsieur.
sister soeur f.
sister-in-law belle-soeur f.
sit s'asseoir, être assis.
site emplacement m.
sitting assis.
situation situation f.
six six.
sixteen seize.

sixteenth seizième.
sixth sixième.
sixtieth soixantième.
sixty soixante.
size taille f., grandeur f., pointure f. (*shoes, stockings, socks, gloves, hats*).
skate (to) patiner.
skates patins m. pl.
skeleton squelette m.
skeptic sceptique m. and f.
sketch croquis m.
ski ski m.
    water-skiing ski nautique.
skid (to) déraper.
skill adresse f.
skillful adroit.
skin peau f.
skirt jupe f.
skull crâne m.
sky ciel m.
sky-blue bleu ciel.
slander calomnie f.
slap soufflet m.
slate ardoise f.
slaughter massacre m.
slave esclave m. and f.
slavery servitude f., esclavage m.
sled luge f., traîneau m.
sleep sommeil m.
sleep (to) dormir.
sleeping bag sac de couchage m.
sleeve manche f.
slender mince, svelte.
slice tranche f.
slide diapositive f. (*photography*).
slide (to) glisser.
slight mince, moindre.
slight (to) dédaigner.
slip combinaison f.; fiche f. (*of paper*).
slip (to) glisser.
slipper pantoufle f.
slippery glissant.
slit fente f.
slope pente f.; piste f. (*ski*).
slot fente f.
slovenly malpropre, négligent.
slow lent.
slowly lentement.
slowness lenteur f., retard m.
    late en retard.
slumber sommeil m.
slumber (to) sommeiller.
sly malin, rusé.
small petit.
smart élégant, habile, chic.
smash (to) briser.
smear tache f.
smear (to) enduire.
smell odeur f., odorat m.

smell (to) sentir, flairer.
smile sourire m.
smile (to) sourire.
smoke fumée f.
smoke (to) fumer.
smooth lisse, uni.
smother étouffer.
smuggle faire passer en contrebande.
smuggler contrebandier m.
snake serpent m.
snapshot instantané m.
snatch arracher, saisir.
sneer (to) ricaner.
sneeze (to) éternuer.
snore (to) ronfler.
snow neige f.
snow (to) neiger.
so (thus) ainsi.
   and so on ainsi de suite.
   so many tant de.
   so much si, tellement, tant.
   so-so comme-ci, comme-ça.
   so that afin que, pour que.
soak tremper.
soap savon m.
soap opera mélo m.
sob sanglot m.
sober sobre.
sociable sociable.
social social.
society société f.
sock chaussette f., socquette f.
socket orbite f.
sofa canapé m.
soft bas, doux, mou.
soften amollir, adoucir.
softly doucement.
software logiciel m., software m.
soil (to) salir, souiller.
solar energy énergie solaire f.
soldier soldat m.
sole semelle f. (*shoe*); plante f. (*foot*).
solemn solennel.
solemnity solennité f.
solicit solliciter.
solid solide, massif.
solitary solitaire.
solitude solitude f.
soluble soluble.
solution solution f.
solve résoudre.
some quelque, quelques.
somebody quelqu'un.
somehow d'une manière ou d'une autre.
someone quelqu'un.
something quelque chose.
sometime un jour.
sometimes parfois, quelquefois.
somewhat quelque peu.

somewhere quelque part.
son fils m.
song chanson f., chant m.
son-in-law gendre m.
soon bientôt, tôt.
soot suie f.
soothe calmer.
sore plaie f.
sorrow douleur f.
sorry triste, fâché.
   be sorry about regretter.
sort sorte f., genre m.
sort (to) trier, classer.
sought-after recherché.
soul âme f.
sound adj. sain.
sound son m.
sound (to) sonner.
soup soupe f., potage m.
sour aigre.
source origine f., source f.
south sud m.
South America Amérique de Sud f.
southern méridional, du sud.
southwest sud-ouest m.
sovereign souverain m.
sow (to) semer.
space espace m., emplacement m.
space (to) espacer.
spacecraft vaisseau spatial m.
spacious vaste, spacieux.
spade bêche f.; pique m. (*cards*).
Spain Espagne m.
Spanish espagnol.
spare adj. disponible.
spare (to) épargner.
spark étincelle f.
sparkle (to) étinceler.
sparrow moineau m.
speak parler.
speaker orateur m.
special spécial, particulier.
specialty spécialité f.
specific spécifique.
specify spécifier.
spectacle spectacle m.
spectator spectateur m.
speculate spéculer.
speech parole f., discours m.
speed vitesse f.
speedy rapide.
spell charme m.
spell (to) épeler.
spelling orthographe f.
spend dépenser.
sphere sphère f.
spice épice f.
spider araignée f.
spill répandre, renverser.

spin filer.
spirit esprit m.
spirited animé.
spiritual spirituel.
spit (to) cracher.
spite dépit m., rancune f.
spiteful rancunier.
splash (to) éclabousser.
splendid splendide.
    Splendid! Epatant!
    That's splendid! A la bonne heure!
splendor splendeur f.
split fendre, partager, se diviser.
spoil gâter.
sponge éponge f.
spontaneous spontané.
spoon cuillère f., cuiller f.
spoonful cuillerée f.
sport sport m.
spot tache f.
sprain entorse f.
sprain (to) fouler.
    se fouler le poignet to sprain one's wrist.
spread (to) étendre, répandre.
spring printemps m. (*season*), saut m. (*leap*),
    ressort m. (*machine*), source f. (*water*).
spring (to) sauter, jaillir, provenir de.
sprinkle asperger, parsemer de.
sprout germer, pousser.
spry alerte.
spur (to) pousser à.
spurn dédaigner.
spy espion m.
spy (to) épier.
squadron escadron m.
squander gaspiller.
square carré noun m. and adj.
squeeze (to) serrer, presser.
squirrel écureuil m.
ssh! chut!
stabilize stabiliser.
stable écurie f.
stable adj. étable.
stack pile f.
stack (to) empiler.
stadium stade m.
staff bâton m. (*stick*); personnel m.
stage scène f., estrade f., étape f.
stain tache f.
stain (to) tacher.
stairs escalier m.
stammer bégayer.
stamp timbre m. (*postage*).
stand position f.
stand (to) être debout, supporter.
star étoile f.
starch amidon m.
starch (to) empeser.
    have (something) starched faire empeser.

starched empesé.
stare (to) regarder fixement.
start (to) commencer, tressaillir.
start over again refaire.
    retrace one's steps refaire le chemin.
starter démarreur m. (*car*).
starve mourir de faim.
state état m., situation f.
state (to) déclarer.
stately plein de dignité.
statement déclaration f.
station gare f. (*railroad*); poste m.
    first-aid station station de secours f.
statistics statistique f.
statue statue f.
statute statut m.
stay séjour m. (*visit*).
stay (to) rester.
steady ferme, stable, sûr.
steak bifteck m.
steal voler.
steam vapeur f.
steamer vapeur m., paquebot m.
steel acier m.
steep adj. raide.
steeple clocher m.
steer (to) diriger.
stem tige f.
stenographer sténo-dactylo f.
stenography sténographie f.
step pas m.; marche f. (*stair*).
step (to) marcher.
stereophonic stéréo(phonique).
sterile stérile.
stern adj. sévère.
stew ragoût m. (*meat*).
stew (to) étuver.
stick bâton m.
stick (to) coller.
stiff raide; empesé.
stiffen raidir.
stiffness raideur f.
stifling écrasant.
still adv. encore, toujours, quand même.
still adj. immobile, calme, tranquille.
    Keep still! Restez tranquille!
still life nature morte f.
stimulate stimuler.
stimulus stimulant m.
sting piqûre f.
sting (to) piquer (*of an insect*).
stinginess mesquinerie f.
stingy mesquin.
stir (to) agiter.
stitch point m. (*sewing*), maille f. (*knitting*).
stock marchandises f. pl. (*goods*); valeurs f.
    pl. (*finance*).
stocking bas m.
stomach estomac m.

stone pierre f.
stool tabouret m.
stop halte f., arrêt m.
stop (to) arrêter, s'arrêter, cesser.
storage battery accumulateur m., boîte d'accus f.
store magasin m., boutique f.
stork cigogne f.
storm orage m.
story histoire f.
stout gros.
stove fourneau m., poêle m.
straight droit.
straighten redresser.
strain tension f., effort m.
strange curieux, étrange.
stranger étranger m., inconnu m.
strap courroie f.
straw paille f.
strawberry fraise f.
straw-colored jaune paille.
stream courant m., ruisseau m. (*small river*).
street rue f.
strength force f.
strengthen fortifier.
strenuous énergique.
stress force f., pression f.
stretch étendue f.
stretch (to) étendre, tendre.
strict strict.
stride enjambée f.
stride (to) marcher, enjamber.
strife lutte f.
strike grève f. (*workmen*).
strike (to) battre, frapper.
string ficelle f.
strip (to) dépouiller.
stripe bande f., galon m.
strive s'efforcer de.
stroke coup m.
stroll tour m., promenade f.
stroll (to) faire un tour.
strong fort, puissant.
structure structure f.
struggle lutte f.
struggle (to) lutter, se débattre.
stubborn opiniâtre.
stuck engagé.
studded with nails clouté.
    pedestrian crossing passage clouté.
student étudiant m., étudiante f.
studious studieux.
study étude f., cabinet de travail m. (*room*).
stuff étoffe f.
stuff (to) bourrer, remplir.
stumble (to) trébucher.
stump souche f.
stun étourdir.
stunt tour m.

stupendous prodigieux.
stupid stupide.
stupidity stupidité f.
stupor stupeur f.
sturdy vigoureux.
stutter (to) bégayer.
style style m., modèle m.
stylish chic.
subdue subjuguer.
subdued sobre.
subject sujet m., propos m.
subject (to) assujettir, exposer à.
subjective subjectif.
subjugate subjuguer.
subjunctive subjonctif.
sublime sublime.
submission soumission f.
submissive soumis.
submit soumettre.
subordinate subordonné.
subordinate (to) subordonner.
subscribe souscrire, s'abonner à.
subscription souscription f., abonnement m.
subside s'apaiser.
subsidy subvention f.
subsist exister, subsister de.
substance substance f.
substantial substantiel.
substantiate prouver.
substantive substantif m.
substitute substitut m.
substitute (to) remplacer, substituer à.
substitution substitution f.
subtle subtil.
subtract soustraire.
subtraction soustraction f.
suburb faubourg m.
subway métro(politain) m. (*Paris*).
succeed réussir, succéder à.
success succès m.
successful heureux.
succession succession f.
successor successeur m.
such tel.
sudden soudain.
suddenly tout à coup.
sue poursuivre (*in law*).
suffer souffrir.
suffering souffrance f.
suffice suffire.
sufficient suffisant.
sufficiently suffisamment.
sugar sucre m.
suggest suggérer, proposer.
suggestion suggestion f.
suicide suicide m.
suit costume m. (*clothes*); complet-veston m.; tailleur m. (*woman's*); procès m. (*law*).
suit (to) convenir à, adapter à.

suitable convenable.
sulk bouder.
sullen maussade.
sum somme f.
summary résumé m.; sommaire m.
summer été m.
summit sommet m., cime f., comble m.
summon sommer, convoquer.
sumptuous somptueux.
sum up résumer.
sun soleil m.
sunbeam rayon de soleil m.
Sunday dimanche m.
sundry divers.
sunny ensoleillé.
sunrise lever du soleil m.
sunset coucher du soleil m.
sunshine soleil m.
superb superbe.
superficial superficiel.
superfluous superflu.
superintendent gérant m.
superior supérieur.
superiority supériorité f.
superstition superstition f.
supervise surveiller.
supper souper m.
supplement supplément m.
supplementary supplémentaire.
supply provision f.
supply (to) fournir.
support appui m.
support (to) appuyer, supporter.
suppose supposer.
suppress supprimer, réprimer.
supreme suprême.
sure sûr.
surety certitude f.
surface surface f.
surgeon chirurgien m.
surgery chirurgie f.
surmount surmonter.
surname nom de famille m.
surpass surpasser.
surplus surplus m.
surprise surprise f.
surprise (to) surprendre.
surrealistic surréaliste.
surrender abandon m., reddition f.
surrender (to) rendre, se rendre, renoncer à.
surround entourer.
surroundings environs m. pl.
survey examen m.
survey (to) examiner, arpenter (*land*).
survive survivre.
susceptibility susceptibilité f.
susceptible susceptible.
suspect suspect m.
suspect (to) soupçonner.

suspense incertitude f.
suspension suspension f.
suspicion soupçon m.
suspicious suspect.
sustain soutenir.
swallow (to) avaler.
swamp marais m.
swan cygne m.
sway (to) balancer.
swear jurer.
sweat sueur f.
sweat (to) suer.
sweep (to) balayer.
sweet doux.
sweetness douceur f.
swell (to) gonfler, enfler.
swift rapide.
swim (to) nager.
swindler escroc m.
swing (to) osciller, se balancer.
Swiss suisse.
switch interrupteur m. (*electricity*).
swollen enflé.
sword épée f.
syllable syllabe f.
symbol symbole m.
symbolic symbolique.
symbolize symboliser.
symmetrical symétrique.
symmetry symétrie f.
sympathetic sympathique, compatissant.
sympathize compatir à.
sympathy sympathie f.
symphonic symphonique.
symptom symptôme m.
synagogue synagogue f.
synthesizer synthétiseur m.
syrup sirop m.
system système m.
systematic systématique.

T

table table f.
   table of contents sommaire m.; table des matières f.
tablecloth nappe f.
tacit tacite.
tacitly tacitement.
taciturn taciturne.
tact tact m.
tactfully avec tact.
tail queue f. (*animal*).
tailor tailleur m.
take (to) prendre.
   take again reprendre.
tale conte m., histoire f.

talent talent m.
talk causerie f.; conversation f.
talk (to) parler.
talkative bavard.
tall grand.
tame soumis, apprivoisé.
tangle (to) enchevêtrer.
tank réservoir m.; char d'assaut m. (*mil.*).
tape bande f., ruban m.
   tape recorder magnétophone m.
tapestry tapisserie f.
tar goudron m.
tardy lent, tardif.
target cible f.
tariff tarif m.
tarnish (to) se ternir.
tarry séjourner; tarder.
task tâche f.
taste goût m., gré m.
taste (to) goûter.
tax impôt m., taxe f.
taxi taxi m.
tea thé m.
teach enseigner.
teacher instituteur m., institutrice f.,
     professeur m.
team équipe f. (*sports*).
tear larme f.
tear (to) déchirer, se déchirer.
tease (to) taquiner.
teaspoon cuillère à café f.
technical technique.
technique technique f.
tedious ennuyeux.
telecommunications télécommunications f.
teleconferencing télé-audio-conférence m.
telegram télégramme m.
telegraph télégraphe m.
telegraph (to) télégraphier.
telegraphic télégraphique.
telephone téléphone m.
   telephone booth cabine téléphonique f.
   telephone call communication f.
telephone operator téléphoniste f.
telephone (to) téléphoner.
television télévision f.
tell dire.
temper colère f.; tempérament m.
temperance tempérance f.
temperate sobre; tempéré (*climate*).
temperature température f.
tempest tempête f.
temple temple m.
temporary provisoire, temporaire.
tempt tenter.
temptation tentation f.
ten dix.
tenacious tenace.
tenacity ténacité f.

tenant locataire m.
tend soigner; tendre à.
tendency tendance f.
tender tendre.
tennis tennis m.
tense adj. tendu.
tense temps m. (*grammar*).
tension tension f.
tent tente f.
tenth dixième.
tepid tiède.
term terme m.
terminate terminer.
terrace terrasse f.
terrible terrible.
terrific épatant, formidable.
terrify épouvanter.
territory territoire m.
terror terreur f.
test épreuve f.
test (to) mettre à l'épreuve.
testify témoigner, attester.
testimony témoignage m.
text texte m.
textbook manuel m.
than que.
thank remercier.
thanks merci m., remerciements m. pl.
that conj. que.
   in order that pour que.
   so that pourvu que.
that (those pl). demons. adj. ce, cet, cette, ces.
   that man cet homme, cet homme-là.
that demons. pron. celui, celle, ceux, celles.
   that is c'est-à-dire.
   That's it. C'est cela.
that relative pron. qui, que.
thaw dégel m.
the le, la, les.
theater théâtre m.
their leur, leurs.
theirs le leur, la leur, les leurs, à eux, à elles.
them les, leur, eux, elles, se.
theme thème m.
themselves se, eux-mêmes m., elles-mêmes f.
then alors, puis, donc.
theoretical théorique.
theoretically théoriquement.
theory théorie f.
there là, voilà; y.
   there is (there are) il y a.
thereafter après cela.
therefore donc.
thereupon là-dessus.
thermometer thermomètre m.
these ces; ceux, celles.
thesis thèse f.
they ils, elles, eux.
thick épais.

thicken épaissir.

thickness épaisseur f.

thief voleur m.

thigh cuisse f.

thimble dé m.

thin mince, maigre.

thing chose f.; objet m.

think penser, croire.

third tiers m.

third adj. troisième.

thirst soif f.

thirteen treize.

thirty trente.

this ce, cet, cette.

    this one celui-ci, celle-ci.

thorn épine f.

thorough (à) fond, complet, achevé, minutieux.

though quoique.

thought pensée f.; idée f.

thoughtful pensif; attentif.

thoughtless étourdi.

thousand mil, mille, millier.

thrash battre.

thread fil m.

thread (to) enfiler (*needle*).

threat menace f.

threaten menacer.

three trois.

threshold seuil m.

thrift économie f.

thrifty économe.

thrill tressaillement m.

thrill (to) faire frémir, émouvoir.

thrilling saisissant.

thrive prospérer, croître.

thriving prospère.

throat gorge f.

throb (to) palpiter.

throne trône m.

throng foule f.

through par, à travers.

throughout d'un bout à l'autre; partout.

throw jeter, lancer.

    throw back rejeter.

thumb pouce m.

thunder tonnerre m.

thunder (to) tonner.

thunderbolt foudre f.

Thursday jeudi m.

thus ainsi.

thwart contrarier.

ticket billet m. (*subway, train, theater*); ticket m. (*bus*); contravention (*traffic*).

    ticket collector receveur m. (*bus*).

    ticket office bureau de location m.

    ticket window guichet m.

tickle chatouiller.

ticklish chatouilleux.

tide marée f.

tidiness ordre m.

tidy propre, rangé.

tie lien m. (*bond*); cravate (*necktie*).

tie (to) lier, attacher (*bind*).

tiger tigre m.

tight serré.

tile carreau m., tuile f.

till jusqu'à; jusqu'à ce que.

    till now jusqu'à présent.

till (to) labourer.

till (to) pencher.

timber bois m.

time temps m.; heure f. (*hour*).

    from time to time de temps en temps.

    in time à temps.

    on time à l'heure.

    to have a good time bien s'amuser.

    What time is it? Quelle heure est-il?

timetable horaire m.

timid timide.

timidity timidité f.

tin étain m.; bidon m.

tinkle tinter.

tint (to) teindre.

    tint one's hair teindre les cheveux.

tiny tout petit.

tip bout m. (*end*); pourboire m. (*money*).

tip (to) donner un pourboire (*give a tip*).

tip over renverser.

tire pneu m. (*car*).

tire (to) fatiguer, se fatiguer.

tired fatigué.

tireless infatigable.

tiresome fâcheux.

tissue tissu m.

title titre m.

to à, en, envers, vers, pour.

toad crapaud m.

toast pain grillé m.; toast m.

tobacco tabac m.

tobacco store débit de tabac m.

today aujourd'hui.

toe doigt de pied m., orteil m.

together ensemble.

toil travail m.

toil (to) travailler.

toilet toilette f.; w.-c. m.

token témoignage m.; jeton m. (*coin*).

tolerable supportable; passable.

tolerance tolérance f.

tolerant tolérant.

tolerate tolérer.

toll (to) tinter, sonner.

tomato tomate f.

tomb tombeau m.

tomorrow demain.

ton tonne f.

tone ton m.

tongs tenailles f. pl.
tongue langue f.
tonight ce soir.
too trop (*too much*); aussi (*also*).
tool outil m., instrument m.
tooth dent f.
   have a toothache avoir mal aux dents.
toothbrush brosse à dents f.
toothpaste pâte dentifrice f.
toothpick cure-dent m.
tooth powder poudre dentifrice f.
top sommet m., dessus m.
topic sujet m.
torch torche f.
torment tourment m.
torture supplice m., torture f.
toss (to) jeter; s'agiter.
total total noun m. and adj.
totally totalement.
touch toucher m.; touche f.
touch (to) toucher.
touching touchant.
touchy susceptible.
tough dur, rude.
tour voyage organisé m., tour m., tournée f.
tour (to) visiter, voyager.
tourist touriste m.
   tourist agency un bureau de tourisme, un bureau de voyage.
tournament tournoi m.
toward vers, envers, pour.
towel essuie-main m., serviette f.
   bath towel serviette de bain.
   face towel serviette de toilette.
   hand towel essuie-main m., serviette de toilette.
   Turkish towel serviette éponge.
tower tour f.
town ville f.
   town hall hôtel de ville m., mairie f.
toy jouet m.
trace trace f.
trace (to) tracer, retrouver.
track traces f. pl.; voie f. (*railroad*); piste f.
trade commerce m.; métier m.
   trade union syndicat m.
tradition tradition f.
traditional traditionnel.
traffic circulation f.
tragedy tragédie f.
tragic tragique.
trail trace f., piste f.
trail (to) traîner.
trailer remorque f.
train train m.
train (to) s'entraîner, élever.
training entraînement m.; éducation f.
traitor traître m.
trample piétiner.

tranquil tranquille.
tranquillity tranquillité f.
transaction transaction f. (*commerce*).
transfer transfert m.
transfer (to) transférer.
transition transition f.
transitory transitoire.
translate traduire.
translation traduction f.
translator traducteur m., traductrice f.
transmission transmission f.
transmit transmettre.
transparency diapositif m. (*photography*).
transparent transparent.
transport transport m.
   transport service messagerie f.
transport (to) transporter.
transportation transport m.
transverse transverse.
trap piège m.
trap (to) prendre au piège.
trash camelote f.
travel voyage m.
travel (to) voyager.
traveler voyageur m.
   traveler's check chèque de voyage m.
tray plateau m.
treacherous traître.
treachery trahison f.
treason trahison f.
treasure trésor m.
treasurer trésorier m.
treasury trésorerie f.
treat fête f.
treat (to) traiter.
treatment traitement m.
treaty traité m.
tree arbre m.
tremble trembler.
trembling tremblement m.
tremendous immense, formidable.
trench tranchée f.
trend tendance f.
trial épreuve f.; procès m.; essai m.
triangle triangle m.
tribe tribu f.
tribulation tribulation f.
tribunal tribunal m.
tribune tribune f.
tribute tribut m.
trick tour m., niche f.
trick (to) tromper.
trifle bagatelle f.
trifling insignifiant.
trim (to) orner, parer.
trimming décor m., garniture f.
trinket bibelot m.
trip voyage m.; parcours m.
   take a trip faire un voyage.

trip (to) trébucher.
triple triple.
triumph triomphe m.
triumph (to) triompher.
triumphant triomphant.
trivial trivial, insignifiant.
troop troupe f.
trophy trophée f.
trot trot m.
trot (to) trotter.
trouble difficulté f., souci m.
trouble (to) déranger, inquiéter.
    Don't trouble yourself! Ne vous dérangez
        pas!
trousers pantalon m.
truck camion m.
true vrai; fidèle; véritable.
truly vraiment; véritablement.
    Yours truly. Agréez, Monsieur (Madame),
        mes meilleures salutations.
trump atout m.
trump (to) couper (avec l'atout).
trumpet trompette f.
trunk malle f.
trunks slip m. (*men's bathing*).
trust confiance f.
trust (to) avoir confiance en; confier à.
trusting confiant.
trustworthy digne de confiance.
truth vérité f.
truthful sincère.
truthfully sincèrement.
truthfulness sincérité f.
try essai m.
try (to) essayer, tâcher.
    Try to be on time. Tâchez d'être à l'heure.
    Try to come. Tâchez de venir.
tube tube m.
tumble (to) tomber, s'effondrer.
tumult tumulte m.
tune air m.
tune (to) accorder.
tunnel tunnel m.
turf gazon m.
turkey dindon m., dinde f.
Turkish turque.
turmoil tumulte m.
turn tour m.
turn (to) tourner.
    retrace one's steps rebrousser chemin.
    turn back rebrousser.
    Turn left. Prenez la première à gauche.
    turn up retrousser.
turned-up retroussé.
    turned-up nose nez retroussé.
turnip navet m.
TV télé f.
TV movie téléfilm m.
tweed tweed m.

twelfth douzième.
twelve douze.
twentieth vingtième.
twenty vingt.
twenty-five vingt-cinq.
twenty-four vingt-quatre.
twenty-six vingt-six.
twice deux fois.
twilight crépuscule m.
twin jumeau m., jumelle f.
twist entorse f.
twist (to) tordre.
two deux.
type type m.
type (to) taper à la machine.
typewriter machine à écrire f.
tyranny tyrannie f.
tyrant tyran m.

U

ugliness laideur f.
ugly laid.
ulterior ultérieur.
ultimate dernier.
ultimately à la fin.
umbrella parapluie m.
umpire arbitre m.
unable to incapable de; être dans
    l'impossibilité de.
unanimity unanimité f.
unanimous unanime.
unanimously à l'unanimité.
unaware (to be) ignorer.
unawares (au) dépourvu, à l'improviste.
unbar débarrer.
unbearable insupportable.
unbelievable incroyable.
unbutton déboutonner.
uncap débarrer (*lens of camera*).
uncertain incertain.
uncertainty incertitude f.
unchangeable immuable.
uncle oncle m.
uncomfortable mal à l'aise (*person*); peu
    confortable (*thing*).
uncommon rare.
unconscious sans connaissance.
unconsciously sans le savoir.
uncouth grossier.
uncover découvrir.
undecided indécis.
undefinable indéfinissable.
undeniable incontestable.
under sous, de dessous, au-dessous de.
undergo subir.
underground souterrain.

underhand adj. clandestin, sournois.
underhandedly adv. en sous-main.
underline souligner.
underneath en dessous.
understand comprendre.
understanding adj. compréhensif.
understanding entente f., chose convenue f.;
    compréhension f.
undertake entreprendre.
undertaker entrepreneur de pompes
    funèbres m.
undertaking entreprise f.
undesirable peu désirable.
undignified peu digne.
undo défaire.
undress se déshabiller (*undress oneself*).
uneasiness malaise m.; gêne f.
uneasy inquiet.
unemployed chômeurs m. pl.; sans travail adj.
unequal inégal.
uneven inégal.
uneventful tranquille, sans événements.
unexpected inattendu, soudain.
unexpectedly à l'improviste.
unfailing infaillible.
unfair injuste, déloyal.
unfaithful infidèle.
unfamiliar peu connu.
unfavorable peu propice, défavorable.
unfit incapable de, peu propre à.
unfold déplier; exposer (*explain*).
unforeseen imprévu.
unforgettable inoubliable.
unfortunate malheureux.
unfortunately malheureusement.
ungrateful ingrat.
unhappily malheureusement.
unhappiness malheur m.
unhappy malheureux.
unharmed sain et sauf.
unhealthy insalubre.
unheard (of) inouï.
unhesitatingly sans hésiter.
unhoped for inespéré.
unhurt sain et sauf.
uniform uniforme noun m. and adj.
uniformity uniformité f.
uniformly uniformément.
unify unifier.
unimportant peu important.
unintentional involontaire.
unintentionally involontairement.
uninviting peu engageant.
union union f.
unique unique.
unison unisson m.
unit unité f.
unite unir.
united uni.

United States Etats-Unis m.
unity unité f.
universal adj. universel.
universe univers m.
university université f.
unjust injuste.
unjustifiable injustifiable.
unkempt inculte.
unkind peu aimable.
unknown inconnu noun and adj.
unknown (to) à l'insu de.
unlawful illégal, illicite.
unless à moins que, à moins de.
unlikely improbable.
unlimited illimité.
unload décharger.
unluckily malheureusement.
unmask démasquer.
unmistakably incontestablement.
unnecessary pas nécessaire, inutile.
unoccupied inoccupé; libre.
unofficial non officiel.
unpack déballer, défaire les bagages.
unpleasant désagréable.
unpublished inédit.
unquestionably incontestablement.
unravel démêler.
unreal irréel.
unreasonable déraisonnable.
unrecognizable méconnaissable.
unreliable douteux (*news*); sur qui on ne peut
    pas compter (*person*).
unrest agitation f.
unrestrained libre.
unrestricted sans restriction.
unroll dérouler.
unsafe dangereux.
unsatisfactory peu satisfaisant.
unsatisfied mécontent.
unscrupulous sans scrupule.
unseemly inconvenant.
unseen adj. inaperçu.
unselfish désintéressé.
unspeakable inexprimable.
unsteady instable.
unsuccessful infructueux.
unsuitable peu propre à.
unthinkable inimaginable.
untidy malpropre (*person*); en désordre
    (*thing*).
untie dénouer.
until jusqu'à, jusqu'à ce que.
    until now jusqu'à présent, jusqu'ici.
untiring infatigable.
untrimmed sans garniture.
untrue faux.
untrustworthy indigne de confiance.
untruth mensonge m.
unusual extraordinaire, rare, peu commun.

unwarranted injustifié.
unwell indisposé.
unwholesome malsain.
unwilling peu disposé à.
unwise imprudent.
unworthy indigne.
unyielding inflexible.
up en haut de.
upheaval soulèvement m.
uphold soutenir, appuyer.
upholstered (with) recouvert de.
upkeep entretien m.
upon sur.
upper supérieur.
upright droit, honnête.
uprising soulèvement m.
uproar vacarme m.
upset bouleversement m.
upset (to) bouleverser.
upside down sens dessus dessous.
upstairs en haut.
upward en haut.
urge (to) prier, faire valoir.
urgency urgence f.
urgent urgent.
urgently instamment.
us nous.
use usage m., emploi m.
use (to) se servir de.
    use up user.
    wear away user.
    wear out user.
used d'occasion.
    used car voiture d'occasion.
used to habitué à.
useful utile.
useless inutile.
usherette ouvreuse f.
usual ordinaire, usuel.
usually habituellement, d'habitude,
        d'ordinaire.
usurp usurper.
utensil ustensile m.
utility utilité f.
utilize utiliser.
utmost le plus.
utter le plus grand; absolu.
utter (to) prononcer.
utterance expression f.
utterly tout à fait.

V

vacant vide.
vacation vacances f. pl.
vague vague.
vain vain, vaniteux.

    in vain en vain.
valiant vaillant.
valid valide, valable.
validity validité f.
valise valise f.
valley vallée f.
valuable de valeur.
value valeur f.
value (to) estimer, évaluer.
valued estimé.
valve soupape f.
van fourgon m.
vanilla vanille f.
vanish disparaître.
vanity vanité f.
vanquish vaincre.
vapor vapeur f.
variable variable.
variance désaccord m.
variation variation f.
varied varié.
variety variété f.
various divers.
varnish (to) vernir.
vary varier, différer sur.
vase vase m.
vast vaste.
vault voûte f.
VCR magnétoscope m., VCR m.
veal veau m.
vegetable légume m.
vehemence véhémence f.
vehement véhément.
vehicle véhicule m.
veil voile m., voilette f.
veil (to) voiler.
vein veine f.
velocity vitesse f.
velvet velours m.
venerable vénérable.
venerate vénérer.
veneration vénération f.
vengeance vengeance f.
venom venin m.
ventilation ventilation f.
ventilator ventilateur m.
venture (to) risquer, se hasarder à.
verb verbe m.
verdict verdict m.
verge bord m.
    on the verge of à deux doigts de.
verge (to) pencher vers.
verification vérification f.
verify vérifier.
versatile aux talents variés.
versatility souplesse d'esprit f.
verse vers m., strophe f.
version version f.
vertical vertical.

very très, même.
very much grand-chose.
vessel vaisseau m.
vest gilet m.
vex ennuyer.
via via.
vibrate retentir, vibrer.
vice vice m.
vice-president vice-président m.
vice versa vice versa.
vicinity voisinage m.
victim victime f.
victor vainqueur m.
victorious victorieux.
victory victoire f.
victuals victuailles f. pl.
videocassette vidéocassette f.
video game jeu-video m.
video-tape bande magnétique f.
view vue f.
view (to) voir, envisager.
vie with rivaliser avec.
vigor vigueur f.
vigorous vigoureux.
vile vil.
village village m.
villain scélérat m.
vindicate défendre.
vindictive vindicatif.
vine vigne f.
vinegar vinaigre m.
violence violence f.
violent violent.
violet violette f.; violet adj.
violin violon m.
virile viril.
virtue vertu f.
virtuous vertueux.
visa visa m.
    entrance visa visa d'entrée.
visibility visibilité f.
visible visible.
visibly visiblement.
vision vision f., vue f.
visit visite f.
    guided tour visite guidée (avec guide).
visit (to) visiter.
visitor visiteur m.
visual visuel.
visualize se représenter.
vital vital.
vitality vitalité f.
vivacious vif.
vivid vif.
vocabulary vocabulaire m.
vocal vocal.
vocation vocation f.
vogue vogue f.
voice voix f.

voice (to) exprimer.
void vide; nul.
volubility volubilité f.
voluble doué de volubilité.
volume volume m.
voluminous volumineux.
voluntary volontaire.
vote voix f.
vote (to) voter.
vouch for répondre de.
vow voeu m.
vow (to) vouer, jurer.
vowel voyelle f.
vulgar vulgaire.
vulnerable vulnérable.

W

wag (to) hocher, agiter.
wager pari m.
wager (to) parier.
wages salaire m.
waist taille f.
wait (to) attendre.
waiter serveur m.
wake (to) éveiller, s'éveiller.
walk démarche (gait) f.; promenade f., marche
    f.; allée f.
    go for a walk se promener, faire une
        promenade.
walk (to) aller à pied, marcher, se promener.
wall mur m.
wallet portefeuille m.
walnut noix f.
wander errer.
want besoin m., manque m.
want (to) avoir envie de; vouloir.
war guerre f.
warble gazouiller.
ward pupille f. (*person*); salle f. (*hospital*);
    arrondissement m. (*Paris*).
wardrobe garde-robe f., armoire f.
ware, wares marchandises f. pl.
warehouse magasin m.
warfare guerre f.
wariness prudence f.
warm chaud.
    be warm avoir chaud.
warm (to) chauffer.
warmth chaleur f.
warn prévenir, avertir.
warning avertissement m.
warrant autorisation f.; mandat m.
warrant (to) garantir; justifier.
warrior guerrier m.
wary prudent.
wash lessive f.

wash (to) laver.
washing machine machine à laver f.
washroom lavabo m., toilette f.
waste gaspillage m., perte f.
waste (to) gaspiller.
watch montre f. (*timepiece*); garde f. (*guard*).
watch (to) observer.
watchful vigilant.
water eau f.
water (to) arroser.
water color aquarelle f.
water skiing ski nautique m.
waterfall chute d'eau f.
waterproof adj. imperméable.
wave vague f. (*sea*); onde f. (*physics*); ondulation f. (*hair*).
wave (to) onduler, agiter.
waver vaciller, balancer.
wax cire f.
way chemin m.; façon f., manière f.; trajet m. (*length of*).
we nous.
weak faible.
weaken affaiblir.
weakly faiblement.
weakness faiblesse f.
wealth richesse f.
wealthy riche.
weapon arme f.
wear porter.
weariness fatigue f.
weary las.
weather temps m.
weave tisser.
wedding noces f. pl.
wedge coin m.
Wednesday mercredi m.
weed mauvaise herbe f.
week semaine f.
weekend week-end m.
weekly hebdomadaire.
weep pleurer.
weigh peser.
weight poids m.
welcome bienvenu.
　　Welcome! Soyez le bienvenu (la bienvenue f.).
　　You're welcome. Je vous en prie (*answer to "Thank you"*).
welcome (to) accueillir.
welfare bien-être m.
well puits m.
well! eh bien! tiens!
west ouest m.
western occidental.
wet mouillé.
whale baleine f.
wharf quai m.

what ce que, ce dont; qu'est-ce qui, qu'est-ce que, quoi.
　　What? Comment? Vous dites?
　　What is it? Qu'est-ce que c'est?
whatever quoi que, quelque, quel que.
wheat blé m.
wheel roue f.; volant m.
　　at the wheel au volant.
when lorsque, quand.
whenever toutes les fois que.
where où.
wherever partout où.
whether si, soit que.
whew! ouf!
which que, quel, qui, dont; lequel, laquelle, ce qui, ce que; quel, quelle.
whiff bouffée f.
while pendant que, tandis que.
　　Wait a while. Attendez une minute.
whim caprice m.
whimper pleurnicher.
whine gémissement m.
whine (to) gémir.
whip fouet m.
whip (to) fouetter.
whirlwind tourbillon m.
whisper chuchotement m.
whisper (to) chuchoter.
whistle sifflet m.
whistle (to) siffler.
white blanc.
who qui, qui est-ce qui.
whoever quiconque.
whole tout, toute, entier.
whole (the) tout m., totalité f.
wholesale en gros.
wholesome sain.
whom que.
whose dont, de qui.
why pourquoi.
　　Why not? Pourquoi pas?
wicked méchant.
wide large.
widen élargir, s'élargir.
widow veuve f.
widower veuf m.
width largeur f.
wife femme f.
wig perruque f.
wild sauvage.
wilderness désert m.
wildness état sauvage m.
wile ruse f.
will volonté f.
will (to) vouloir.
willful volontaire.
willing bien disposé.
willingly volontiers.
win gagner.

wind vent m.

wind (to) enrouler.

windmill moulin m.

window fenêtre f.; guichet m.

windy venteux.

wine vin m.

wing aile f.

wink clin d'oeil m.

winner gagnant m.

winter hiver m.

wipe essuyer.

wire dépêche f., télégramme m.; fil de fer
(*metal*) m.

wire (to) télégraphier.

wisdom sagesse f.

wise sage.

wish désir m.

wish (to) désirer, vouloir; souhaiter.

wit esprit m.

witch sorcière f.

with avec.

withdraw (se) retirer; prélever.

withdrawal retraite f.

wither se flétrir.

within dedans.

without sans.

witness témoin m.

witness (to) être témoin de.

witty spirituel.

woe malheur m.

wolf loup m.

woman femme f.

wonder merveille f.; étonnement m.

wonder (to) se demander, être étonné de.

wonderful merveilleux.

    Wonderful! Merveilleux!

wood bois m.

woods bois m.

woodwork boiserie f.

wool laine f.

woolen de laine.

word mot m.

    word for word mot à mot.

word processing machine de traitement de
texte.

word processor processeur m.

work travail m., devoir m., oeuvre f.

work (to) travailler.

worker ouvrier m.

workman ouvrier m.

work of art objet d'art m.

workshop atelier m.

work yard chantier m.

world monde m.

worldliness mondanité f.

worldly mondain.

worm ver m.

worry ennui m., souci m.

worry (to) se tracasser, s'inquiéter, s'en faire.

Don't worry! Ne vous inquiétez pas! Ne
vous en faites pas! Ne vous tracassez
pas! Ne t'en fais pas!

worse pire m.

worship culte m.

worship (to) adorer.

worst pis.

worth valeur f.

worth (to be) valoir.

worthless sans valeur; indigne.

worthy digne.

wound blessure f.

wound (to) blesser.

wounded blessé.

wrap (to) envelopper; emballer.

wrapping emballage m.

wrath courroux m.

wrathful courroucé.

wreath couronne f.

wreck naufrage m. (*ship*); ruine f.; accident m.
(*train wreck, etc.*)

wreck (to) ruiner, démolir, saboter.

    be wrecked (*of a ship*) faire naufrage.

wrestle lutter.

wrestler lutteur m.

wrestling lutte f.

wretched misérable.

wring tordre.

wrinkle ride f.

wrinkle (to) rider.

wrist poignet m.

write écrire.

writer écrivain m.

writing écriture f.

    in writing par écrit.

written écrit; par écrit.

wrong adj. faux.

wrong mal m., tort m.

    be wrong avoir tort.

    What's wrong? Qu'est-ce qui ne marche
pas?

wrong (to) faire tort à.

X

X-ray picture radio(graphie) f.

X-ray (to) radiographier.

Y

yard yard m., cour f.

yarn fil m.

yawn bâillement m.

yawn (to) bâiller.

year an m., année f.

yearly annuel adj.; annuellement adv.
yearn for soupirer après.
yearning désir m.
yeast levure f.
yell (to) hurler.
yellow jaune.
yes oui, si.
yesterday hier.
yet encore; néanmoins.
yield (to) produire, donner; céder, consentir.
yielding accommodant.
yoke joug m.
yolk jaune m. (*egg*).
you vous.
young jeune.
   young lady demoiselle f., jeune fille f.
your votre, vos; ton, ta, tes (*familiar*).
yours à vous; à toi (*familiar*); le vôtre m., la vôtre f., les vôtres m. and f. pl.; le tien m., la tienne f., les tiens m. pl., les tiennes f. pl. (*familiar*).
yourself vous-même, vous-mêmes pl.; toi-même (*familiar*).
youth jeunesse f.
youthful jeune.
youthfulness jeunesse f.

Z

zeal zèle m.
zealous zélé.
zero zéro m.
zone zone f.
zoo jardin zoologique m.
zoology zoologie f.

GLOSSARY OF PROPER NAMES

Adolph	*Adolphe*
Adrian	*Adrien*
Albert	*Albert*
Alexander	*Alexandre*
Alfred	*Alfred*
Alice	*Alice*
Allan	*Alain*
Andrew	*André*
Anna, Ann(e)	*Anne*
Anthony	*Antoine*
Arnold	*Arnaud*
Arthur	*Arthur*
Beatrice	*Béatrice*
Bernard	*Bernard*
Bertram	*Bertrand*
Blanche	*Blanche*
Carol	*Caroline*
Charles	*Charles*
Charlotte	*Charlotte*
Daniel	*Daniel*
David	*David*
Donald	*Donald*
Edith	*Édith*
Edmund	*Edmond*
Edward	*Édouard*
Eleanor	*Éléonore*
Emily	*Émilie*
Evelyn	*Éveline*
Ferdinand	*Ferdinand*
Frances	*Françoise*
Francis	*François*
Frederick	*Frédéric*
Gabriel	*Gabriel*
George	*Georges*
Gertrude	*Gertrude*
Gilbert	*Gilbert*
Gregory	*Grégoire*
Gustavus	*Gustave*
Guy	*Guy*
Harry	*Henri*
Henry	*Henri*
Hubert	*Hubert*
Hugh	*Hughes*
Irene	*Irène*
Jane	*Jeanne*
Jerome	*Jérôme*
Joan	*Jeanne*
Judith	*Judith*
Julian	*Julien*
Lawrence	*Laurent*
Lewis	*Louis*
Lillian	*Liliane*
Lucy	*Lucie*
Mary	*Marie*
Maurice	*Maurice*
Michael	*Michel*
Miriam	*Miriam*
Paul	*Paul*
Peter	*Pierre*
Ralph	*Ralph*
Richard	*Richard*
Robert	*Robert*
Ruth	*Ruth*
Silvia	*Sylvie*
Theresa	*Thérèse*
Thomas	*Thomas*
Vincent	*Vincent*
Vivian	*Viviane*
William	*Guillaume*

GLOSSARY OF GEOGRAPHICAL NAMES

Africa Afrique f.
Algeria Algérie f.
Algiers Alger m.
Alps Alpes f. pl.
Alsace Alsace f.
America Amérique f.
    North America l'Amérique du Nord.
    Central America l'Amérique Centrale.
    South America l'Amérique du Sud.
Antwerp Anvers m.
Argentina Argentine f.
Asia Asie f.
Atlantic noun and adj. Atlantique
Australia Australie f.
Austria Autriche f.
Bermuda Bermudes f. pl.
Bordeaux Bordeaux m.
Brazil Brésil m.
Brittany Bretagne f.
Brussels Bruxelles f.
Canada Canada m.
Chile Chili m.
China Chine f.
Corsica Corse f.
Czech Republic République Tchèque f.
Denmark Danemark m.
Dover Douvres m.
Dunkirk Dunkerque m.
Egypt Égypte f.
England Angleterre f.
Europe Europe f.
Geneva Genève f.
Genoa Gênes f.
Greece Grèce f.
The Hague (La) Haye.
Hamburg Hambourg m.
(Le) Havre (Le) Havre.
Holland (la) Hollande f.
Hungary (la) Hongrie f.

Iceland Islande f.
India Inde f.
Iran l'Iran m.
Ireland Irlande f.
Israel Israël m.
Italy Italie f.
Japan Japon m.
Lisbon Lisbonne f.
London Londres m.
Lyons Lyon m.
Marseilles Marseille m.
Mexico Mexique m.
Montreal Montréal m.
Moscow Moscou f.
New Zealand Nouvelle-Zélande f.
Normandy Normandie f.
Norway Norvège f.
Pacific adj. and noun Pacifique.
Paris Paris m.

Poland Pologne f.
Pyrenees Pyrénées f. pl.
Rheims Reims m.
Rhine Rhin m.
Rhineland Rhénanie f.
Romania Roumanie f.
Russia Russie f.
Scotland Écosse f.
Siberia Sibérie f.
Sicily Sicile f.
Spain Espagne f.
Sweden Suède f.
Switzerland Suisse f.
Tunisia Tunisie f.
Turkey Turquie f.
United States États-Unis m. pl.
Venice Venise f.
Vienna Vienne f.
Wales Pays de Galles m.

Whether by car, plane or on foot . . .
Living Language has the perfect course for you!

Starting Out in French—An all-audio course great for people on the go. No book needed!

CD Program
978-1-4000-2463-6 • $15.95/$18.95 Can.

In-Flight French—Wondering how to make use of all that spare time on the plane? Between your in-flight meal and in-flight movie, brush up on your French with this great 60-minute program!

CD Program
978-0-609-81066-8 • $13.95/$21.00 Can.

A great way to continue studying with Living Language!

Beyond the Basics: French–For learners who have completed the Living Language Basics series or any other beginner-level language course. Beyond the Basics builds important language skills and natural-sounding conversation. This course features a coursebook, dictionary, and 4 hours of recordings in a compact and portable package!

CD Program • 978-1-4000-2168-0 • $27.95 / $39.95 Can.
Coursebook Only • 978-1-4000-2165-9 • $8.95 / $12.95 Can.

Ultimate French Beginner-Intermediate—Our most comprehensive program for serious language learners, businesspeople, and anyone planning to spend time abroad. This package includes eight 60-minute CDs and a coursebook.

CD Program • 978-1-4000-2105-5 • $79.95 / $110.00 Can.
Coursebook Only • 978-1-4000-2104-8 • $18.00 / $26.00 Can.